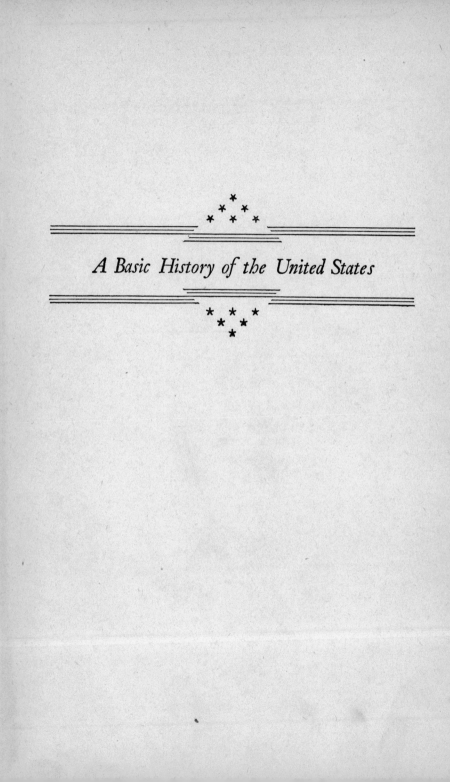

A Basic History of the United States

A BASIC HISTORY

of the

UNITED STATES

BY *Charles A. Beard*
AND *Mary R. Beard*

DOUBLEDAY, DORAN & COMPANY
New York, 1944

An original publication of THE NEW HOME LIBRARY, 1944

THIS ENLARGED AND SPECIALLY ILLUSTRATED EDITION OF A BASIC
HISTORY OF THE UNITED STATES, BY CHARLES A. AND MARY R. BEARD,
IS PUBLISHED BY ARRANGEMENT WITH THE NEW HOME LIBRARY.

DOUBLEDAY, DORAN & COMPANY, INC., 14 West Forty-ninth Street
New York, N. Y.

PRINTED IN THE UNITED STATES OF AMERICA BY
H. WOLFF BOOK MFG. COMPANY, NEW YORK

PREFATORY NOTE

With this book we bring to a close our many years of co-operative efforts in seeking to interpret the long course of American history. As its title indicates, the volume deals with fundamental activities, ideas, and interests which have entered into the development of American society from the colonial period to the contemporary age. Whatever may be added to the record here presented, a consideration of these activities, ideas, and interests is basic, we believe, to any understanding of American history.

Although compact in form and directed to the general public, the book is no mere summary or digest of our previous works. Nor is it a collection of excerpts from any or all of them. On the contrary it is newly designed and newly written to express the historical judgment which we have reached after more than forty years devoted to the study of documents and the observation of life at first hand in all parts of the United States, rural and urban, and in parts of the Old World and the Orient.

CHARLES A. BEARD
MARY R. BEARD

New Milford,
Connecticut.

CONTENTS

MAPS *and* CHARTS

ILLUSTRATIONS

xi

A Basic History of the United States

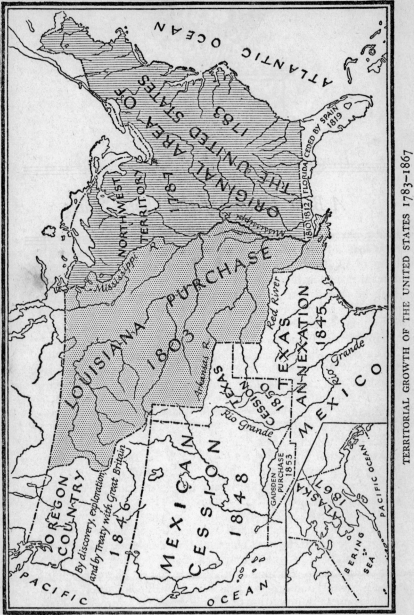

TERRITORIAL GROWTH OF THE UNITED STATES 1783–1867

CHAPTER I

English Territorial Claims and Colonial Beginnings

In far-off times it had been written: "Blessed are the meek for they shall inherit the earth." As if to fulfill the law, Henry VII, King of England, established in 1497 a claim to the continental domain in which the history of the United States was to unfold. Thus he took title to a great portion of the earth for the English people long before anyone, even in England, knew that the voyage of Columbus from Spain across the sea to the West Indies in 1492 had broken the path to a vast new world.

The claim which brought such good fortune to the English nation was based on the voyages of John Cabot, an Italian sea captain. Cabot, with his three sons, was commissioned by Henry VII to seek and find "whatsoever islands, countries, regions or provinces of the heathen and infidels, which before this time have been unknown to Christians." The King and the seamen in his service assumed that heathen and infidels might be found on the way to Cipango [Japan] and China by the coveted but as yet undiscovered all-water route to the trade of the Orient.

Cabot reached Cape Breton Island in 1497 and there planted the standard of the English King, supposing that he had come upon the east coast of Asia. With news of this discovery he went back to England. The next year Cabot was sent out again, on a second voyage, to explore further. This time Cabot sighted the east coast of Greenland but his sailors mutinied against pushing as far north as he wished to go. Turning south, he scouted the shore to a point in the neighborhood of Chesapeake Bay. Unable, however, to find a rich people with goods for profitable trade, he returned to England deeply disappointed.

Nevertheless Henry VII appreciated Cabot's services. Pleased by the result of the first voyage, the King made him a present of ten pounds in cash, entered the item in his account book, and granted Cabot a pension of twenty pounds. For his subjects, the King did more. He claimed a dominion of unknown size that eventually opened for the English the greatest real estate and investment opportunity in the history of Western civilization.

☆

But nearly a century passed before the English began to take full advantage of that opportunity. In the interval numerous and wide voyages by Portuguese, Italian, Spanish, French, and English explorers led to mapping, if roughly, the contours of a large part of the two Americas. And as an outcome Spanish, Portuguese, and French rulers also laid claims to large shares of land in the Western Hemisphere. International rivalry for power over the newly discovered continents lying between the Atlantic and the Pacific oceans was to be a spur to English action in developing the King's claim.

Intrepid explorers under the flag of Spain, by innumerable journeys, were the first to penetrate the mainlands. Spanish conquerors led by Hernando Cortes and Francisco Pizarro invaded Mexico and Peru, robbed them of gold, silver, and precious stones, and excited all Europe by reports of wealth in the New World. Between 1539 and 1542 Hernando de Soto traveled overland from the coast of Florida, with his mounted companions, to the Mississippi River and some distance beyond. During those years Francisco Vásquez de Coronado, with an armed band of horsemen, toiled his way northward from Mexico into the heart of the region lying west of the Mississippi, looking for more treasure in the rumored Indian cities of Cibola. In 1565 the Spanish planted the settlement of St. Augustine in Florida.

By the middle of the sixteenth century the Spaniards seemed about to take possession of the newly discovered world. Though they had not found more gold and silver in regions above Mexico or the elixir of youth sought in Florida by Ponce de Leon, by 1550 the ruler of Spain, Charles V, could claim as his property many islands in the Caribbean; Mexico by right of conquest; all of South America except Brazil, which the Portuguese had seized; and an immense area, if indefinite as to boundaries, north of the Gulf of Mexico and the Rio Grande. To back up his claim he had at his command a big navy, a large merchant marine, and many hardy soldiers. With his conquering hosts were associated dauntless Catholic priests to aid in establishing a New Spain in the New World—a state, church, and feudal aristocracy all resting on the labor of subject peoples.

Before the English government began to develop its territorial rights by occupation the monarchs of France had also become interested in the New World. Francis I laughed at Spain and Portu-

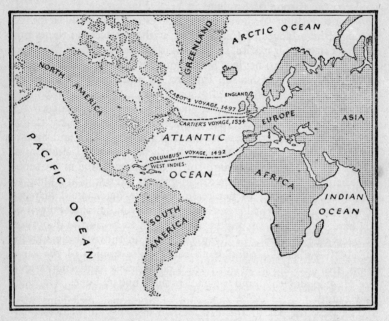

FAMOUS VOYAGES OF COLUMBUS, CABOT, AND CARTIER

gal for pretending to own so much of it, and declared that he wanted to see the will of Father Adam, the first proprietor, bequeathing to them the inheritance they claimed. In 1524, while Henry VIII, who had succeeded his father in 1509, was neglecting the patrimony won by Cabot's voyages, Francis sent an Italian seaman, John Verrazano, across the Atlantic to hunt for a northwest passage to the Orient. Verrazano did not find the passage, but he did sail along the coast of North America and gave Francis good grounds for asserting that he too owned a big share of the new continent. Several years later Francis sent Jacques Cartier forth on two successive voyages. They resulted in explorations of the St.

Lawrence River region, the bestowal of the name Montreal on an Indian village, and a more definite claim to a huge area in that neighborhood.

☆

Such were the rights asserted by England, Spain, and France to enormous masses of land in the New World when Queen Elizabeth came to the throne of England in 1558. Her father, Henry VIII, had done nothing to develop the real estate nominally acquired through the voyages of Cabot. Busy with intrigues on the continent of Europe, his marital troubles, and his quarrels with the Pope, he had continued to neglect his opportunities in the New World. During the reigns of his son Edward VI and his daughter Mary, England had been torn by religious disputes, and the exploitation of land over the sea had been slighted by English statesmen.

With the accession of Queen Elizabeth, however, many things incited English enterprisers to develop the real estate and investment opportunity opened to them by the voyages of Cabot under Henry VII. Elizabeth was high-spirited, well educated in the secular learning of the Renaissance, and greatly interested in adding to the riches and power of her realm. She was determined that her people should be kept Protestant in religion under the Church of England, firmly united, and strong enough to break the dominion of her Catholic rival, the King of Spain, in the Atlantic Ocean. Elizabeth gathered around her Protestant statesmen of the same mind, fostered the growth of the English navy, and encouraged her sea captains to plunder Spanish ships and colonies wherever they could.

The new temper of the Elizabethan age was imperiously displayed in 1577–80 when the English "sea dog," Francis Drake, sailed around the world plundering cities and Spanish ships laden with treasure as he went—down along the east coast of South America, up along the west coast, to the shores of California, and all the way home.

From this exploit English capitalists got an inkling of the investment opportunity before them, on and across the seas. Money for Drake's expedition had been supplied by a corporation in which Elizabeth held shares. The company's original investment was £5000. In return for the stockholders' risk, Drake's treasure ships brought them £600,000 in profits—enough to satisfy the most expectant investor. As a prudent ruler Elizabeth used her portion of the proceeds to pay off the debts owed by the Crown. According to careful estimates, the numerous raids on Spanish ships and colonies during Elizabeth's reign netted the handsome sum of £12,000,000.

With news of splendid returns on investment undertakings at sea ringing in their ears, English merchant capitalists, including investors among fair ladies, began to take a serious interest in the real estate of the English Crown in the New World. Since it was undeveloped real estate—not land occupied by peoples abounding in wealth—its exploitation demanded colonization by the English people themselves and the founding of a "New England" under the Crown of the old England. Having this project in view, Queen Elizabeth gave Sir Walter Raleigh, one of the favorites at her court, a patent to all the territory he might colonize, on condition that he pay to the Crown one fifth of the returns from the mining of precious metals.

Under this patent Raleigh sent out in 1584 an expedition which visited the island of Roanoke off the coast of North Carolina and brought back reports of a favorable climate and country—"the most plentiful, sweet, fruitful, and wholesome of all the world." The next year Raleigh dispatched seven ships and 108 colonists to Roanoke, but the colonial experiment was a failure. Raleigh made another attempt in 1587, only to fail again. The colonists who shared in that venture utterly disappeared from the scene, leaving behind them not even a clue to their fate. The sixteenth century came to a close without the creation of a single permanent English settlement in America.

But the century did not close until the English navy, aided by a terrible storm at sea, had destroyed in 1588 the Spanish Armada, a mighty fleet sent by the King of Spain to crush the rising power of England. This victory for the English helped to clear the way for the development of their real estate when they were ready to go about it again in earnest.

Yet before the English could demonstrate their ability to occupy the territory nominally under the English Crown, other claimants disputed their ownership. In 1609 Henry Hudson, an English navigator in the service of Holland, sailed up the river which now bears his name and thereupon the Dutch government asserted its authority over an immense area in the neighborhood. For a time the Dutch were allowed to develop plantations in their colony of "New Netherland." For a time also the Spaniards were permitted to keep their land in Florida; and the French to hold regions of the St. Lawrence and Great Lakes. It was not until the English had created large and prosperous colonies on the Atlantic seaboard that they were prepared to deal effectively with the three rival claimants to lands on the northern continent.

☆

The establishment of large, permanent, and prosperous colonies was a tremendous task, new in English experience. Beside this complicated undertaking the spectacular dispatch of Drake on a voyage of exploration and the sensational robbery of Spanish vessels were mere theatrical displays of power and daring. To arm a few ships, shoot up Spanish galleons, loot them, and send them to the bottom of the ocean was an operation that required little money —mainly skill in navigation and the fighting spirit. The defeat of the Spanish Armada merely helped to clear the seas for colonizing expeditions.

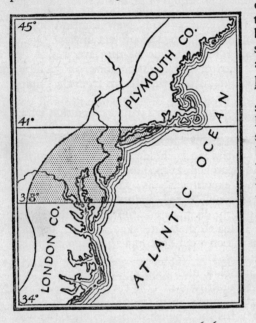

LAND GRANTS BY JAMES I IN 1606

Great pieces of real estate were granted to the London Company and the Plymouth Company. In the shaded portion of the map both Companies could make settlements provided their plantations were at least 100 miles apart.

Qualities and courage of a different sort were necessary to create large and orderly societies in a wilderness. This business demanded huge capital. It was more than men's work: women in great numbers had to be associated with it. All the ideals, arts, and sciences of civilization were involved in it.

Not fully aware of all that colonization implied but eager to exploit the real estate in America, English merchant capitalists sought that privilege from the Crown at the beginning of the seventeenth century. They had already formed trading companies to engage in commerce with Russia, the Levant, and the East Indies. In corporate enterprises of that type they had demonstrated their ingenuity. Besides they had accumulated much capital for investment. This capital they now proposed to use in colonial enterprise, about which they knew so little. Only one aspect of it was clear to them: individual farmers, merchants, artisans, and their families, with small savings or none at all, could not embark unaided on any such undertaking as large-scale colonization.

Under English law all the territory claimed in America belonged to the Crown. The monarch could withhold it from use, keep any part of it as a royal domain, or grant it, by charter or patent, in large or small blocks, to privileged companies or private persons. It was to the Crown, therefore, that English enterprisers bent on colonizing America turned for grants of land and powers of government. And in making such grants by charter or patent, the Crown created two types of legal agencies for colonization: the corporation and the proprietary.

The corporate type of colonizing agency was the company, or group of individuals merged into a single "person" at law by a royal charter. The charter named the original members of the company and gave them the right to elect officers, frame bylaws, raise money, and act as a body. It granted to the company an area of territory and conferred upon it certain powers: to transport emigrants, govern its settlements, dispose of its land and other resources, and carry on commerce, subject to the laws of England. Such a corporation was akin to the modern joint-stock company organized for profit-making purposes.

The proprietary agency for colonizing consisted of one or more persons to whom were given a grant of territory and various powers of government by the Crown. The proprietor or proprietors thus endowed with special privileges had authority to found a particular colony and enjoy property, commercial, governing, and other rights similar in character to those vested in a company by royal charter.

Companies and proprietors did not, however, have a completely free hand in managing their colonial affairs. They were limited by the terms of their charters or patents and were compelled to confer upon free settlers certain liberties and immunities enjoyed by English people at home, including a share in the making of local laws.

Various motives inspired English leaders to form companies or embark on careers as proprietors in America. Among the motives was the desire to extend English power, to make money out of trading privileges and land sales, and to convert the Indians to Christianity. For some companies and proprietors the idea of establishing religious liberty in America for members of persecuted sects was also among the primary considerations in their colonizing activities. Still another purpose entering into the plans of companies or proprietors was that of giving poor and otherwise unfortunate persons in England a chance to work and live better in a new country so open to opportunity. In other words, political, economic, religious, and charitable motives induced English leaders to devote their energies to the business of colonization.

☆

The systematic beginnings of all the American colonies were made by companies or proprietors or under their jurisdiction. By 1733, the year in which the last colony, Georgia, was started at Savannah, there were thirteen colonies under the Crown at London, legally known as the British Crown after the Union of England and Scotland in 1707. These colonies, taken arbitrarily in geographical order, with references to origins, were:

New Hampshire—partly an offshoot of Massachusetts, given a separate status in 1679.

Massachusetts—founded in 1630 by Puritans under the Massachusetts Bay Company; with it became associated in 1691 the colony of Plymouth, established by the Pilgrims in 1620 on land belonging to the Plymouth Company chartered by James I in 1606.

Rhode Island—incorporating two offshoots from Massachusetts, Rhode Island and Providence Plantations, to which, as a single colony, a royal charter was given in 1663.

Connecticut—originating partly in offshoots from Massachusetts planted in the Connecticut River valley in 1635 and partly in settlements on the shore, united under a royal charter in 1662.

New York—founded as New Netherland under the Dutch West India Company in 1624; seized by the English in 1664 and given the name of New York.

New Jersey—founded under Dutch auspices, seized by the English in 1664, and afterward named New Jersey.

Delaware—first settled by the Dutch under the Dutch West India Company and by Swedes under the Swedish South Company; taken by the English in 1664 and placed under the proprietorship of William Penn in 1682.

Pennsylvania—granted to William Penn as proprietary by Charles II in 1681; first settlement at Philadelphia in 1682.

Maryland—granted to Lord Baltimore as proprietary in 1632 and started by settlements on Chesapeake Bay in 1634.

Virginia—founded by settlement at Jamestown in 1607, made under the London Company chartered by James I in 1606.

North Carolina—early settlements made by pioneers from other colonies; passed under an association of proprietors in 1665 by a royal grant covering all the Carolina region, formerly within the jurisdiction of the Virginia Company; given a separate status as the royal province of North Carolina in 1729.

South Carolina—granted to proprietors in 1665; settlements made at Albemarle Point in 1670 and near Charleston in 1672; an independent royal province after 1729.

Georgia—granted to a board of trustees, or company, by George II in 1732; Savannah founded in 1733.

This table, indicating the corporate and proprietary agencies under which English colonization took place, does not give an adequate impression of the amount of free movement by individuals and groups in America, especially after the first settlements had been planted. Nothing less than an encyclopedia could do that.

Take for example North Carolina. Virginians had made a permanent settlement in that region at least five years before it was granted to proprietors in 1665, and other pioneers, mainly Scotch, Scotch-Irish, and Germans from Pennsylvania, went down into North Carolina on their own motion.

Again, take New Hampshire in the far north. An independent settlement was established there as early as 1623 under a royal grant. Other beginnings in New Hampshire had been made before the Puritans came to Massachusetts Bay in 1630. When Puritans pushed over into the New Hampshire region and claimed it as a part of their grant, they encountered stout opposition from the forerunners. Only after many disputes was a final separation from Massachusetts effected by New Hampshire in 1679.

But independent undertakings and individual or group migrations from colony to colony, significant as they were in colonial beginnings, had relatively little influence on the rise of self-governing colonies. It was under companies and proprietors holding grants of land subject to the English Crown that systematic colonization on a large scale was made possible. It was under companies and proprietors that the foundations of all the colonies, except New York, were securely laid, and the old Dutch settlement was developed under the auspices of the English Crown after 1664. Crown, companies, and proprietors—their work in colonization was to have from the outset a profound influence on the course of affairs which eventuated in the formation of the continental United States.

CHAPTER II

Backgrounds of Migration and Settlement

OCCUPATION OF THE TERRITORY claimed by England in America, building "the New England" in the wilderness, required the transfer of thousands upon thousands of men and women from the Old World to the New World. This meant a resettlement on an enormous scale. Trading corporations and proprietors alike confronted that problem. They had titles to great areas of land. They had money. They could buy ships, tools, stock, seeds, and other things necessary to starting agriculture on the virgin continent. But empty lands in America were in themselves worth no more to their nominal owners than lands in the moon. Money in their hands was in itself just so much dead metal. Stock, tools, and implements in storage were equally inert.

Only labor could put the material capital and the vacant lands to use. Only able-bodied men and women possessing many skills and crafts, many arts and sciences, could produce the food, clothing, shelter, and other necessities of a civilized social order, could build prosperous and self-sustaining societies on the territory claimed by England.

But trading corporations and proprietors, even aided by the English government, could not simply commandeer farmers, mechanics, artisans, and managers for colonial adventures. In the nature of things, most of the men and women for the undertaking had to be persons who were willing, even eager, to cross the sea. They had to be volunteers moved by one reason or many reasons to tear up their roots in the Old World and brave the perils and toil of transplanting themselves across the wide ocean into the lonely territory claimed by the English Crown.

The bulk of the white men and women who came to North

11

America between the founding of Jamestown in Virginia in 1607 and the eve of the American revolt against Great Britain came voluntarily. Even those who indentured, or bound, themselves by contract to labor for a term of years as servants, in order to pay their passage, were in the main volunteers.

It is true that many white laborers were kidnaped in England for shipment to the American colonies and that Negroes were dragged out of Africa for that purpose by slave traders. Forced migration of laborers was undoubtedly extensive. Yet the overwhelming majority of immigrants came to America of their own choice.

☆

What lay behind this choice? The whole history of Europe. The long struggle between barbarism and civilization since the beginning of human societies in the Old World. Immediately influential were the convulsions of the age in which the emigrants lived. From the opening of the seventeenth century to the close of the colonial period the Old World was in turmoil—physical, intellectual, moral, religious, military, economic, and political. The feudal order of the Middle Ages was breaking up amid fierce resistance to change.

The years of the great migration from the Old World to the English colonies in the New World were marked by international wars, civil wars, religious controversies and persecutions, political disputes, displays of royal despotism, and social dislocation, accompanied by growing poverty and the enactment of barbaric criminal laws against the poor.

None of these events was sharply separated from others. All were interrelated. For example, wars were connected with national jealousies, ambitions of monarchs, religious hatreds, and rivalries over trade and territory. Religious clashes were associated with the political interests of kings and queens, Catholic and Protestant, with the conflicts of nations over commerce and empire in the Old World and beyond the seas, and with the struggles of classes.

An impression of the almost endless wars waged in Europe between 1618 and 1776 may be derived from the following list of the major wars:

1618–48—The Thirty Years' War, involving Bohemia, Denmark, Sweden, France, German princes, Spain, and other Powers; large parts of Germany were devastated by battles, burnings, and lootings; Protestants and Catholics both engaged in it.

1648–59—France and Spain, two Catholic monarchies, continued the Thirty Years' War, between themselves.

1667–68—The War of Devolution; the King of France, Louis XIV, waged war to wrest neighboring territories from Spain.

1672–78—France waged war on Holland.

1689–97—War of the Palatinate; French, Dutch, and English struggled for power on the Continent; called in America King William's War.

1702–14—War of the Spanish Succession; France, England, Spain, Holland, and other Powers fought over territory on the Continent and over colonial possessions; known in American colonies as Queen Anne's War.

1739–48—War of Jenkins' Ear, between England and France; widened out into the War of the Austrian Succession, involving England, France, Spain, Austria, Prussia, and other Powers; known in the American colonies as King George's War.

1756–63—The Seven Years' War, involving England, France, Spain, Prussia, and other countries; contest between England and France over dominion in Canada, India, and other places; known in America as the French and Indian War.

These major wars, covering in all more than eighty years between 1618 and 1776, to say nothing of many local wars such as short fights between the English and the Dutch, spread ruin in several parts of western Europe. And one reason for the extent of this ruin was a revolution in the "art of war."

In the Middle Ages wars almost endless had been fought largely by a relatively few feudal lords and their retainers—by dukes, earls, barons, knights, and esquires. Into feudal armies workers on the land and merchants in the towns had not been drafted wholesale. With the discovery of gunpowder and the invention of cannon, muskets, and other powerful implements of destruction, however, a new kind of army—the standing army—was organized in Europe.

The standing army could be extended by summoning tens of thousands of men to its ranks, thus far exceeding in size any feudal army. To fill the ranks of the new and bigger armies sturdy young men were caught and dragged to the barracks for training if they could not be got otherwise. Princes drafted their subjects en masse for their own wars and sometimes sold them in large blocks, as mercenaries, to other princes in need of soldiers.

With this transformation in the character of armies, the actual snatching of men for wars and the fear of being snatched made life a genuine terror for innumerable men of military age, their families, and young marriageable women. Moreover the death and destruction spread by wars on a large scale made the "art of war" so practiced more terrible to non-combatants. For all such reasons British and European workers in town and country, as well as yeomen and merchants, could regard the perils and hardships of resettlement in America, in a strange land, as offering trials slight in comparison.

To wars between nations were added conflicts within nations arising from religious and political sources. In the Middle Ages the people of all countries in western Europe were members of one church—the Catholic Church, and belonged to one faith—the Catholic faith. Dissent from that faith, heresy, was forbidden and if it appeared was put down by Church and State.

But during the opening years of the sixteenth century a revolt, known as the Protestant Reformation, broke out against the Pope and the Catholic Church of which he was the head. In southern Germany, Italy, and Spain, the Church and the princes managed to suppress religious uprisings and keep most of the people loyal to the Catholic religion. France, long torn by religious wars, found peace for a time when the King was able to make a truce in 1598 —by granting a limited toleration to the Huguenots, Protestant followers of John Calvin. In Holland, Scandinavia, and the countries of northern Germany, the revolt against the Pope ended in the establishment of independent Protestant churches under the various rulers.

The religious quarrels in England took a peculiar turn. After the power of the Pope was finally cast off under Queen Elizabeth, a state church—the Church of England—was established by act of Parliament and everybody in the realm was ordered to become a member of it under pain of fine or physical punishment. But this official church had scarcely been set up, and Catholics had barely been suppressed, when more religious protests arose among the people.

Some of the new objectors merely wanted to reform, or "purify," the English Church; they were known as Puritans. Others, generally called Dissenters, spurned the English Church entirely and asserted the right of individuals and groups of individuals to form churches of their own and worship God according to their consciences. This was the view taken by Presbyterians, Baptists, and Quakers, for example.

Nowhere in the Old World at the beginning of American colonization was there anything like religious toleration in the modern sense of the term: that is, the right of every person to join any church he or she pleases, or none at all, and to express his or her opinions freely on matters of religion. In the Catholic countries, except France, Protestantism was forbidden and Protestants were persecuted. Even in France the limited toleration of Huguenots was abolished by the King in 1685, and they were subjected to persecution. On the other hand, in Protestant countries Catholicism was forbidden and Catholics were persecuted. In England persecution cut two ways. The government of that country meted out stern punishment to Catholics who clung to their faith and also to Protestants who wanted to "purify" the English Church or to found independent churches. As far as the strict letter of English law was concerned there could be no Catholics at all in England or any Protestants outside the Church of England. Although many religious objectors defied or winked at the law, they were liable at any time to be arrested and fined, imprisoned, mutilated, or put to death.

Religious disputes in England were embittered by a political struggle which broke out between the Parliament and James I, shortly after his accession in 1603. High-tempered and arrogant, James tried to make laws and lay taxes without the consent of Parliament, and Parliament resisted his encroachments on its rights.

Under his successor, Charles I, the quarrel developed into a civil war and a revolution, led by Oliver Cromwell with the general support of the Puritans. The struggle ended temporarily in the execution of Charles, the exile of his son, the flight of many members of the aristocracy, and the establishment of a dictatorship by Cromwell.

In the course of the civil conflict a flood of radical, or "leveling," ideas was let loose in England. It was boldly said that no King or House of Lords was needed at all; that every man should have the right to vote for members of the House of Commons; that all the people had "natural rights" which no government could take away from them.

Shortly after the death of Cromwell the monarchy was restored by the coronation of Charles II, in 1660. But this brought only a few years of internal peace to England. Even then religious and political unrest continued beneath the surface of social peace. It emerged in a revolt soon after Charles II died and his brother, James II, an avowed Catholic, came to the throne. James tried to rule England as autocratically as his grandfather had done, and in 1688 he was driven out in a popular uprising.

The following year, William, the Prince of Orange, and his

wife, Mary, the elder daughter of James II, were called to England. Under an act of Parliament they were crowned king and queen of the realm. In the general settlement which went with the revolution of 1688 the supremacy of Parliament as the lawmaking body of England was acknowledged, a bill of rights for English subjects was proclaimed, and a limited tolerance was granted to Protestant Dissenters—though not to Catholics.

During the many years of this strife in England migration to America was stimulated; and the colonies that had already been founded were deeply affected by rapid changes in the mother country. Resenting the autocratic rule of James I and Charles I, thousands of Puritans and Dissenters fled from the kingdom in search of more political and religious freedom for themselves. While the Puritans under Cromwell's leadership were in power in England, hundreds of their opponents, loosely called "Cavaliers," took refuge in America, especially in Virginia. And all the while news of the disputes in England over the political rights of the people and over religious toleration circulated from one end of the colonial settlements to the other, affecting judgments respecting politics and religion on this side of the Atlantic.

☆

Amid the wars, religious revolts, persecutions, and political upheavals which kept the Old World in convulsions, the feudal order inherited from the Middle Ages was disintegrating. In that order government had been in the hands of kings and princes, supported by the clergy and nobility, as a rule. The land of the various kingdoms and principalities had been held by great landlords, lay and clerical; and most of the earth had been tilled by serfs bound to the soil on which they labored, so that they were unable to leave it even if they desired to do so. The number of merchants was relatively small and they counted for little in the class valuations of early feudal times. Stated in another way, feudal society was a class society in which each class, from serfs at the bottom to princes at the top, had a fixed and permanent place. The mass of the people were not free to move around as they pleased, even in the region in which they lived, or to emigrate to any other country.

But wars, religious upheavals, and the growth of commerce finally shook this rigid class order apart. In England the process of dissolution began early and went forward rapidly, particularly after the Protestant revolt opened in the sixteenth century. Under

Henry VIII great landed estates held by the Catholic Church were seized by the Crown and many of them were parceled out among the King's favorites, thus increasing the number of English landlords. About the same time landlords discovered that they could make more money by raising sheep and exporting wool to the continent of Europe than they could by having the soil tilled for the production of crops. So they turned a vast acreage into sheep pastures and evicted serfs and laborers from the land, forcing them, homeless and forlorn, to search for other work in the towns.

By the beginning of Elizabeth's reign England was swarming with "free" men and women, hunting in the streets and highways for employment or begging for charity. Cruel laws were enacted against them. They were harshly punished for begging, driven into poorhouses, or forced to labor at anything they could find to do at wages fixed by government officials.

In some of the English towns at the opening of the seventeenth century as high as one third of all the inhabitants were paupers dependent for a living on the charity of their neighbors. Although paupers were unequally distributed over England, the number was enormous and their plight was nothing short of horrible.

Everywhere even those fathers and mothers who earned a fair livelihood could see that their children had slight chances of getting along at all or of bettering their condition and that their families might easily fall into the great mass of pauperism. Since most of the English land was monopolized by great landlords it was difficult for anyone to buy a farm; and the oversupply of labor in the cities made competition for jobs an agonizing struggle.

When the cry that cheap land, even free land, was offered to immigrants in America rang through the streets of English towns and cities and through the byways of the English countryside, it awakened in the imagination of multitudes of nameless men and women a dream of liberty, security, and advancement such as had never before come to toiling masses in the Old World. Even the homeless and propertyless were stirred by news from some of the colonies that, if they would bind themselves to service for a term of five years, they would receive at the end of their indenture at least fifty acres of land for their own.

☆

Such were the Old World backgrounds for migration to America. It was in these circumstances, according to estimates from fragmentary records, that about 750,000 people, for one reason or another or for many reasons, journeyed over the ocean between 1600 and 1770 to seek a way of life on this continent. Relatively few of them were from the permanent class of helpless English paupers created by the heartless eviction of peasants from the lands their ancestors had tilled; for paupers did not always have the energy or skills required for successful farming that made them desirable indentured servants. Approximately two thirds of the immigrants belonged to families able to meet the cost of the journey and make a start of some kind in the new country. The other third, composed of indentured servants, although lacking in money or property, had skills and talents which they could apply in making their way in a land of opportunity.

The motives provoking men and women to brave the perils of the sea voyage in slow sailing vessels overcrowded with passengers and to risk their lives and fortunes in a strange continent, far from their native habitats, were no doubt various. But historical records justify such a summary as the following:

A desire to get away from the devastations of the endless wars and conflicts in Europe.

A resolve to flee from the snatching and selling of men for service in the armies of kings and princes constantly engaged in wars.

A longing for an opportunity to find honest and honorable work and create better homes for themselves and their children.

An eagerness to escape religious persecutions and to found communities in which they could worship God in their own ways, free from the domination of church and government officials trying to enforce conformity to other faiths.

In addition to one or more of these motives, immigrants had a quality for which no name can be found. Countless men and women who lived amid the wars, persecutions, and poverty of the Old World and suffered from them as did the emigrants, stayed at home and continued to endure them. If the Old World backgrounds in themselves had supplied the sole motives for migration, then more millions would also have broken away and joined the voyagers bound for the New World. It follows, therefore, that there was something in the spirit of the men and women who voluntarily made the break and migrated, a force of character not simply determined by economic, political, or religious conditions—a force that made them different from their neighbors who remained in the turmoil and poverty of the Old World. That something was a quality of energy, enterprise, daring, or aspiration that was to be a power in the course of American history, immediately and by transmission through coming generations.

☆

The strength of the several motives for migration doubtless varied from immigrant to immigrant, from group to group. The assignment of specific weights to the motives is impossible. But among them a desire to win a larger religious freedom was widely acknowledged as significant and impelling by many immigrants and their descendants. Practically all the immigrants were members of some church or adherents to some religious faith. The overwhelming majority were Protestants—but Protestants who objected, as much as Catholics did, to the faith and government of the Church of England. On this point of objection Quakers, Baptists, Presbyterians, and Lutherans agreed in spite of their differences on other matters. In any event, religious considerations entered into the founding and development of every colony from New Hampshire to Georgia.

The early settlers of Virginia were members of the Church of England and it was the practices of their church which were to be observed in the colony. This church soon became and long remained the Established Church of Virginia, supported by taxation. Nevertheless, in the course of time Protestants of other denominations went into Virginia though, theoretically, they had no legal right to be there. A few Catholics also found their way quietly into the Old Dominion and officers of the law merely winked at their presence. Thus a kind of toleration grew up in practice. But it was far from universal religious liberty and was often marred by persecutions fostered by the Virginia government and Established Church.

The neighboring colony of Maryland, often spoken of as a free refuge for Catholics persecuted in England, was in fact at the outset nothing of the sort. It is true that the first Lord Baltimore, who received the grant of land from King Charles I, was a Catholic in spite of the prohibitory English law, favored and protected by the King. It is true that many Catholics from the British Isles were able to settle in Maryland and enjoy a high degree of religious liberty, although according to English law Catholics were not supposed to exist anywhere under the English Crown. But the second Lord Baltimore, who on the death of his father started the settlements on Chesapeake Bay, was interested in more than a religious refuge. He wanted to develop a prosperous colony by selling his lands to farmers, and he invited Protestants as well as Catholics to migrate to Maryland.

Within a short time the Protestants in Maryland outnumbered the Catholics and prepared to abolish the toleration that had quietly become a custom in the colony. To avoid a disruptive religious conflict, leaders in Maryland arranged for the colonial assembly to pass, in 1649, what is known as the Toleration Act. The term is inexact. It did not establish universal religious liberty in Maryland. It granted freedom of religious worship only to those who professed faith in Jesus Christ, thereby excluding Jews, unbelievers, Deists, and Unitarians from the benefit of this freedom.

In the case of the Massachusetts Bay Colony, religious affairs took a course unlike that in Virginia or Maryland. Although, like Virginians, the Puritans who settled on the bay were members of the Church of England when they arrived, they had wanted to alter some of its practices and soon they separated from it entirely in their new home. After the separation each town set up a church of its own, called Congregational, and taxpayers were required by law to support it. For a long time every voter in Massachusetts had to be a member of a Congregational church.

Strenuous efforts were made to bar immigrants belonging to other religious denominations. Dissenters and critics who appeared among the Puritans were frowned upon and sometimes severely punished, executed, or exiled into the wilderness. In short Puritans came to Massachusetts to develop, among other things, religious liberty for themselves, not to establish an ideal of toleration for all religions—a liberty utterly unknown as practice in the England they had left.

The first English colony in America to grant general religious liberty as a matter of law and principle was an offshoot from Massachusetts, at first called the Rhode Island and Providence Plantations. It was not founded by settlers coming directly from England but by inhabitants of Massachusetts who rebelled against the teachings and practices of Puritan preachers and magistrates. In 1636 Roger Williams, ordered to conform or get out, fled with a few friends into the wilderness and founded the town of Providence at the head of Narragansett Bay. Two years afterward Anne Hutchinson, also outlawed by the Puritan clergy of Boston for her religious and general independence, took refuge with her companions for a while at Portsmouth on Rhode Island.

Both Roger Williams and Anne Hutchinson believed that the government should not force any form of religion by law on anybody; that every person should be free to worship God according to his conscience. This rule of broad tolerance, extended to Quakers and Jews, was retained in the Providence and Rhode Island plantations after all the townships were united in an independent colony—by a charter from Charles II granted in 1663. It made Rhode Island unique among the colonies.

No such general religious liberty was permitted in the second offshoot from Massachusetts, the colony of Connecticut, founded about the same time as Providence. The expedition of Puritans who built the towns of Hartford, Windsor, and Wethersfield in the Connecticut River valley was led by a preacher rightly deemed broad-minded for his time, Thomas Hooker. But neither he nor his companions accepted the liberal toleration proclaimed by Roger Williams and Anne Hutchinson. Likewise strict in their views of religious discipline under government control were the Puritans who made settlements at New Haven and other places on Long Island Sound.

Before and after the two groups of towns were united in a single colony as Connecticut, under a charter granted by Charles II in 1662, the Congregational Church was the established church in each town, and it remained so established by law through the Revolution down to 1818. Catholics, Protestant dissenters of various kinds, especially Quakers, and even members of the Church of England encountered hostility in Connecticut. Immigrants who were not Congregationalists in faith filtered into the colony here and there but full toleration and equality were not accorded to them as a matter of principle and law.

A wide, though not complete, religious toleration was adopted in Pennsylvania under the leadership of the Quaker proprietor, William Penn. By his faith Penn was committed to the principle that religion is a matter for the conscience of the individual and is not to be imposed on anybody by law and government officials. But from the beginning of his settlement at Philadelphia in 1682 Penn opened his colony only to immigrants who professed belief in God. As a proprietor Penn, like Lord Baltimore, was eager to have immigrants settling in his colony, buying farms carved out of the land granted to him by the King, and engaging in lucrative commerce. In his quest for settlers he made special efforts to encourage the migration of Scotch-Irish Presbyterians and German Protestants, as hardy folk with skills and crafts.

Religious considerations entered into the rise and growth of settlements in other parts of America. It was in search of freedom for their form of religious worship as well as a livelihood that the Pilgrims, persecuted in England and for a time exiles in Holland, went to Plymouth in 1620. After the English seized the Dutch holdings in 1664 and renamed them New York, the practice of granting toleration to Protestants of all denominations was followed in New York, although the Anglican Church was established in certain counties of the colony as the official church. Quakers and Presbyterians took part in filling up New Jersey and a similar toleration became the general practice there. Under the Penn proprietorship the inhabitants of Delaware shared the almost unlimited religious freedom established by William Penn for Pennsylvania. While the proprietors of North Carolina and South Carolina were favorable to the Anglican Church, settlers of various Protestant faiths, including French Huguenots, were welcomed and allowed to worship God according to their creeds. In Georgia, founded as an experiment in philanthropy, a rule of religious liberty akin to that in South Carolina soon prevailed generally.

As long as shipping was controlled by companies and proprietors, it was relatively easy to keep people of "undesirable" religious sects out of any colony. But after ports and inland towns were well developed, owners of ships were fairly free to make independent voyages to America. Then colonial barriers crumbled and immigrants of all faiths found easier entrance into all colonies. Ship captains in search of emigrants who could pay their passage were prone to disregard laws on religion or colonial restrictions on the ingress of religious refugees.

Indeed, to promote passenger traffic ship captains offered to carry over to America emigrants who had no money to pay their way, and collected the cost, with a profit, by selling the labor and skills of their passengers to employers for a term of years. Colonists who engaged these laborers were inclined to be more interested in strong bodies and stable characters than in the theological opinions of their servants.

At all events, for one reason or another the religious restrictions that existed in the beginning slowly relaxed, in some places more than in others, but everywhere more or less. And it came about that the English plantations in America were inhabited only in part by men and women who adhered to the Church of England in religious faith. In an overwhelming majority, the colonists were Protestant dissenters from that church—Congregationalists, Presbyterians, Baptists, Quakers, and members of other sects. To these Protestants were added a large number of German Lutherans and a small number of French Protestants, or Huguenots. English and Irish Catholics, no more friendly to the Church of England than Protestant dissenters, found their way into other colonies as well as into the more hospitable Maryland.

In these circumstances no religious denomination was numerically strong enough, had it been so disposed, to force a single form of the Christian religion on all the inhabitants, even though in some colonies people were required to pay taxes to support a colonial church. Accordingly there prevailed in these American societies an amount of religious liberty hitherto unknown in England and in western Europe since the days of ancient Rome. Even Jews, severely oppressed nearly everywhere in the Old World, were able to find shelter from persecution in several seaboard towns and to erect synagogues in which to conduct their religious rites.

Throughout the colonies, therefore, in law or practice or both, a broad religious liberty was accorded to the people. But it was not universal religious freedom. Nor were the American people, by 1776, prepared in spirit to approve that freedom as the law of the land. How do we know this? From the first state constitutions adopted after the break with Great Britain.

With some exceptions those constitutions excluded Catholics, Unitarians, Deists, and Jews from the right to vote and hold office in the new state governments. Individuals, if free to choose their own forms of religious faith and worship, had to remain outside the pale of politics in case they did not conform to the law of privilege. Protestant Christians almost monopolized the powers and offices of government in the states.

Americans had gone a long way toward universal religious toleration by 1776 but they had not completed the journey. In six colonies—Virginia, Maryland, the two Carolinas, Georgia, and New York—the Church of England was an official church under colonial laws. In three other colonies—Massachusetts, Connecticut, and New Hampshire—the Congregational Church, supported in each town by taxation, remained established as the official church. The Old World heritage of religious intolerance and persecution had been severely shattered everywhere in America, even in the nine colonies with established churches, but many vestiges of religious discrimination remained to be cleared away.

CHAPTER III

Laying Foundations in Agriculture

THE WILL OF IMMIGRANTS to separate themselves from the Old World was of course an impetus to resettlement in the New World. But successful resettlement called for a still more positive force of mind and character. For shaping a new and secure life and creating societies in the wildernesses of a continent more was necessary than a feeling of revolt and separatism. This operation required an exercise of intellectual prowess, manual skills, and inventiveness—constructive abilities of a high order.

A few emigrants at the beginning of the seventeenth century, it is true, were lured by the original dream of the London Company that gold and silver for quick riches would be found in its territory. A year before the tiny settlement had been planted on the James River, an actor in the English metropolis had declared on the stage that the Indians' dripping pans were of "pure golde," that their "chaines with which they chained up their streets were of massive golde," that their prisoners were "fettered in golde," and that they "goe forth on holy days to gather rubies and diamonds by the seashore." But neither in Virginia nor anywhere in the colonies were the English to discover, conquer, and loot Indian societies fabulously rich in rare treasures, such as the Spaniards had found in Mexico and Peru. So all the pioneers had to come down to hard earth and create the real wealth which was alone valuable for life—farms, houses, food, clothing, and all the material commodities necessary for the living of civilized people. They had to cherish the values of a working society.

In the new environment the pioneers confronted primitives such as they had never seen before. All along the shores from Maine to

Georgia were scattered tribes of native Indians ranging in degrees of social organization from marauding nomads to more or less settled communities engaged in practicing the economic arts of forest, stream, field, and domesticity. With the Indians the pioneers entered into varied relations: from peace and friendship to treachery and massacre on both sides.

In terms of peace the newcomers sometimes bought lands from the Indians, giving them in exchange such English goods as cloth, beads, hoes, knives, axes, and other implements. For example, when Roger Williams founded his first plantation in Rhode Island in 1636, he displayed good will toward the Indians at once and bought from them the land on which he settled with his companions. Sometimes colonial leaders, occasionally in connection with the purchase of land, made treaties of amity with the Indians. William Penn, for instance, besides protecting the Indians of his colony from the rapacity of white traders, made treaties of friendship with them which they faithfully kept. By the marriage of John Rolfe to Pocahontas, daughter of the warlike chief, Powhatan, in 1614, peace was brought to the settlers of Virginia for eight years. More than once an English settlement was saved from starvation by timely supplies of food furnished by neighboring tribes.

From red Indians "the palefaces" recovered some of the primitive arts of survival which had been lost to the English since their own primitive times. Indian women were farmers, cooks, and practitioners of other domestic arts, and from them English women learned how to handle native foodstuffs, especially Indian corn, and provide nutritious meals. Indian men also had their arts of hunting, fishing, and woodworking, and from them English men acquired various new skills which, combined with their own, enabled them to make rapid progress in every form of economic operation. As hunters adept in the ways of wild animals, Indians knew how to procure fish, game, and furs for their own people. By studying the hunting arts of the Indians and by trading with them, white pioneers were able to get meat more quickly and stocks of furs.

Unhappily, relations with the Indians were not all confined to genial exchanges of arts and commodities. Human nature, red and white, also displayed cruelty and stupidity. From time immemorial Indian tribes had fought among themselves, the warlike nomads preying upon the tribes that tilled the soil, the settled tribes trying to defend themselves, tribes battling against other tribes for other reasons or without rationality. Under the thin veneer of their civilization the barbaric greed and brutality of innumerable whites led them to rob, murder, betray, and try to enslave Indians. White traders sold them whisky and firearms and cheated them in transactions over furs and the purchase of lands. Thus the whites incited retaliations even among Indians formerly disposed to be friendly.

So sporadic brawls, local conflicts, and general wars punctuated the relations of whites and Indians all along the line from North to South and all through the years from the early days in Virginia to the close of the colonial period. After the whites had introduced the Indians to "fire water" and guns the fighting became more desperate and bloody as the years passed and as the frontier advanced upon the Indian hunting grounds. Nothing but stockades, militiamen, and eternal vigilance prevented the Indians from exterminating many of the early settlements and keeping the frontier constantly aflame.

Besides encountering the strange aborigines, the first English settlers found themselves in the presence of new and wide variations of climate. In their old home they had been accustomed to a moderate temperature. Now they had before them a great range of climate from the cold coasts of Maine to the hot savannahs of Georgia, with all the gradations from the far North to the deep South. To the exigencies of these variations, all the immigrants, from the British Isles as well as the Continent, had to adapt their economy and ways of living. Wherever the colonists set to work in clearing land for tillage, building houses, sowing and reaping, and producing the commodities required for living, they had to take into account the conditioning element of climate.

The soil at their feet was likewise a conditioning feature of their life in America. It, too, presented variations, from the small fields in narrow valleys, the rocky ground and steep hillsides of New England, through the broad and fertile valleys of the middle colonies, to the pine barrens, swamps, clay, and shallow loam of the deep South. Yet in every colony settlers could find land on which to produce all the grains, vegetables, and fruits for their staple foodstuffs and grasses for the grazing of livestock. Nothing was needed to furnish a generous and diverse food supply from the cultivation of the earth except implements, skills, good management, and hard labor.

While the soil for the most part was favorable to multiform agricultural production, clay beds and quarries yielded bricks, stones, and marble for building purposes. Primeval forests provided additional means of a livelihood more abundant than that of workers on the land in England or Western Europe. In every section the amazing array of trees offered materials for every kind of shelter from quickly constructed cabins to carefully built great manor houses, for barns and workshops, for the making of furniture and other household equipment, and for the output of staves, barrels, and lumber to be shipped to England in payment of debts partly incurred by the purchase of the finer grades of manufactured goods.

In the forests were also wild animals in a great variety, the furs and skins of which were useful for domestic purposes and profitable for export. In the forests was wild game for food—turkeys, deer, rabbits, and squirrels, for instance—and more meat and more kinds of meat could be procured than the plain peoples had ever enjoyed in the Old World, at first without asking the permission of any lord or gamekeeper or poaching secretly on private preserves. In the forests were nuts, berries, grapes, and other wild fruits available to agile climbers and pickers, aids to a balanced diet and free as the air.

Moreover the rivers, brooks, ponds, and lakes teemed with fish easy even for children to catch, while off the long coast were deep-sea fish accessible to professional fishermen.

☆

Most of the immigrants who came to the colonies, rich and poor alike, knew more about agriculture than about any other practical art; and in turning to the creation of real wealth, by inclination and necessity, they found ways and means of applying this knowledge in old and new forms. At home the English had been accustomed to the production of a few standard commodities—a few grains, fruits, vegetables, and meats. In the colonies, owing to the variations in climate and soil, they were able to produce new and special crops. In many respects this very fact had decisive influences on the branches of agriculture which they developed, on types of commodities entering into the trade with the mother country, on the growth of wealth in America, and on the social characteristics of the several regions from Maine to Georgia.

Besides possessing extraordinary resources for the food, clothing, and shelter required in daily living, the South from Maryland to Georgia had climate and soil especially suitable for the raising of certain staples which supplemented the agricultural economy of England, provided cargoes for English vessels, and business for

English merchants. First among these staples was tobacco. While Virginia was still an infant settlement the raising of tobacco became almost a mania.

Zeal for tobacco production quickly spread all along the Southern coastal plains as new colonies were founded and as supplies of indentured white laborers and servile laborers—Negro slaves—increased. Planters gathered great fortunes from tobacco and the prospect of larger fortunes led them to push into the interior even up into the foothills. News of the prosperity to be won by tobacco growing stimulated the immigration of capitalistic planters and merchants ever ready to handle cargoes. Tobacco planters became land speculators and engrossers of small freehold plots. Until the eve of the American Revolution, Southern riches rested largely on this crop.

A second Southern staple from which flowed new wealth was rice. The settlement near Charleston, South Carolina, founded in 1672, was little more than ten years old when it was discovered that rice could be grown luxuriantly in the swampy lands of the coast and along the rivers. In favorable years planters could make as high as a forty per cent return on their capital invested in rice fields and slave labor. Here, too, was a staple which England and European countries did not produce and hence it furnished a profitable article of export for which there was a large demand. Between 1713 and 1724 exports of rice through Charleston rose from 3000 barrels a year to 124,000 barrels. As the death rate of slaves in the rice swamps was high, rice production fostered the importation of slaves and furnished business for British and New England shippers, adding to their wealth.

Near the middle of the eighteenth century a third staple was added to Southern economy—indigo. This was a precious dyestuff, one of the most important until the rise of modern chemistry, and indispensable to the English textile industry. The successful production of this staple was due to the perseverance of Eliza Lucas, who in her youth took over the management of three plantations owned by her father, then governor of Antigua.

Securing indigo seeds from her father in the West Indies, Miss Lucas tested them on her own land. Previous attempts by others had been failures, but by persistence she demonstrated that crops could be produced successfully in South Carolina. Indigo grown on one of her plantations served as a wedding dower when she married Charles Pinckney, of Charleston, in 1744. Pinckney encouraged his neighbors to go into the business. Four years later the

British Parliament voted a bounty of sixpence per pound to producers. With this aid and a fair price in England, planters could make a profit ranging from thirty to fifty per cent a year. So valuable did indigo become that small cubes of it were used for money during the Revolution when all forms of paper currency became worthless.

Far to the North, in New England, climate and soil confined colonists to the production of agricultural commodities practically identical with those which could be raised in England. Moreover the narrow valleys, rocky hills, and stony yet often fertile land were unfavorable to the establishment of plantations or great landed estates of any type. There were, in truth, many extensive land holdings in parts of New England, especially in early days, but there was available no cheap and adequate supply of labor by which they could be tilled with large profits to owners. Besides, New England was peopled mainly by yeomen used to owning and tilling small farms and by farm laborers eager to get possession of land in their own right.

So in respect of agriculture New England became a region of small holdings on which farming families produced for their own use nearly all the commodities necessary to a comfortable living. Although iron, salt, some tools, and finer cloths, if any were bought, had to come from the towns, practically everything else was grown or made on the farm. Life on such farms was hard—toil from sun to sun. Out of it came no large accumulations of wealth or cargoes of grain, flour, or meat for export. Yet it yielded a high degree of economic well-being and freedom from dependence on the fortunes of British commerce. With it went a spirit of impatience at most forms of official control from above which interfered with the course of farm and community affairs. If New England agriculture produced no great riches for English merchants or investors, it did produce wealth for the support of a large farming population, sturdy, educated, and owing neither rents nor obeisance to overlords.

In the middle colonies between New England and the South, agriculture took other forms. The soil, more level and fertile than that of New England, was adapted to the production of similar crops on a larger scale, but the climate was not favorable to the establishment of plantations for raising tobacco, rice, or indigo in the Southern style. There were many great estates in New York, tilled by tenants under terms akin to feudal bondage. Landlords and speculators—Dutch, English, and American—managed, by investment, chicanery, and corruption, to engross from one half to two thirds of the land in the colony. Enormous holdings, comparable in size to great plantations in the South, were in the hands of a relatively few families, for example, the Van Rensselaers, the Van Cortlandts, the Schuylers, the Phillipses, the Beekmans, the Livingstons, and the Morrises. The estate of the Beekmans embraced 240,000 acres, that of the Van Cortlandts 140,000 acres, and the holdings of the Van Rensselaers about Albany no less than 700,000 acres.

Often the landed families of New York combined agriculture with shipping and merchandising, sometimes by intermarriage. For instance, Frederick Phillipse, a rich Dutch landlord of the Hudson Valley, while traveling at sea on a packet line operated by Margaret Hardenbroeck, a Dutch landowner and merchant, was captivated by her personality and enterprise. Soon afterward, in 1662, they were married, and united in a single household landlordism with zeal for commercial undertakings. While Frederick looked after his estates and later engaged in shipping so irregularly that he was charged with being involved in the piratical activities of Captain Kidd, Margaret attended principally to regular mercantile undertakings and proved to be "a very desirable business partner."

After New Jersey was taken from the Dutch in 1664 and turned over to English proprietors, efforts were made to create large estates there. The proprietors themselves engaged in land speculation, established titles to huge areas in their own names, and in their eagerness to sell land in large blocks carved out many holdings of considerable size. But the inhabitants of New Jersey, especially of the western part, almost rose in arms against this land policy. Even the proprietors came to see, at least dimly, that to increase the population and wealth of the colony provision must be made for selling, even giving, land in small plots to actual settlers prepared to cultivate them.

In Pennsylvania the proprietor had the right, like the proprietor of Maryland, under his charter, to lay out and sell great estates, manors, in his colony and he did in fact lend some encouragement to great landlordism. But most of Pennsylvania was divided into farms that could be tilled by their owners aided only by one or a few extra laborers, if any. Furthermore large numbers of pioneers simply settled on the frontier without asking the permission of Penn or anybody else. Thus farming on a small or moderate scale became the general rule in Pennsylvania agriculture.

With agriculture the population of all the colonies became self-sustaining as regards food products; and by the tens of thousands farmers grew prosperous, as prosperity was rated, in tilling their own soil; not rich in gold coins or paper claims, but secure in real wealth—houses, barns, stock, tools, and all the means of commodious living. The great areas of level land in the middle colonies, free from stones and covered by a fertile topsoil, enabled them to produce a surplus of grains, beef, pork, and bacon for export. Thus they could pay for imported manufactures and enter into competition with British agriculture in respect of its principal staples.

Inasmuch as even the planters of the South usually combined the production of foodstuffs, for their slaves and for their own use, with the raising of special staples for the British market, all the colonies were, therefore, soon independent of the Old World with regard to these primary essentials of living. There were few if any landlords in New England as rich as the largest Southern planters; but from New York to the borders of Virginia there were landlords who could vie in wealth with the greatest Southern planters. Indeed as the soil on the coastal plains of the South was worn down by intensive cultivation and returns from tobacco raising diminished, the relative position of landlords in New York and Pennsylvania improved.

☆

Closely connected with the agricultural pursuits was domestic manufacturing in the strict sense of that phrase—making things by hand at home. This was especially true in the colonies north of Maryland which produced no great staples that were not also produced in Great Britain. Southern planters did raise crops, such as tobacco, rice, and indigo, that did not compete with British agriculture and could therefore be readily exchanged for British manufactured goods, since those crops were desired by British buyers. But from Pennsylvania northward and in all the back-country regions farming families, having no such staples to sell to English merchants, had to make many things themselves or go without them. And countless families refused to be deprived of necessities and comforts of a manufactured kind. Many men and women among them were Jacks-of-all-trades, meaning "artists in living," and they made living an art by their domestic manufacturing. Even great planters in the South established workshops on their estates in which commodities for household use, for supplying slaves, and for other purposes were manufactured out of materials at hand.

The extent to which manufacturing combined with agriculture could go was represented on the estates of Robert Carter, of Virginia, the grandson of a rich planter, colonial officer, land speculator, and businessman in Virginia. Carter's land holding, including his family seat in Westmoreland County, embraced about 70,000 acres (his grandfather had owned some 300,000 acres) and his slaves numbered more than five hundred. Besides raising tobacco and other agricultural produce, he maintained many shops on his properties for making cloth and salt, grinding grain, baking bread, and working iron. Agriculture and manufacturing he supplemented by selling goods as a merchant, lending money at interest like a banker, and sending ships to and fro carrying goods. At his great mansion, so large that it took twenty-eight fireplaces going full blast to warm it in wintertime, Carter whiled away his leisure hours with balls, music, reading, and dinner parties. Yet, with the aid of overseers and superintendents, and his wife's co-operation, he managed to hold all his agricultural, manufacturing, and trading enterprises together and keep them in successful and profitable operation.

On farms and plantations from New Hampshire to Georgia men usually made and repaired farm implements—plows, sleds, wagons, and hoes. Out of furs and skins they made shoes, hats, and caps. Out of wood they fashioned furniture, churns, spinning wheels, and looms. Where wrought iron was available they manufactured nails, shovels, and chains. At the same time women generally turned their skills and wits to making cloth, rugs, soap, candles, bedding, coverlets, tablecloths, and garments. They also operated processing plants, in which bread was baked, meat was packed, fruits and vegetables were dehydrated and preserved, and butter was churned.

As a rule the products of home workshops were used on the farm or plantation but in time women developed an industry which turned out goods for community and colonial markets. With flax for linen at their command and, in the Northern colonies, wool from sheep, they set to work spinning and weaving with such vim that their output soon alarmed British merchants, who wanted the textile markets free for their own manufactures. While most of the cloth produced by women at their homes was coarse in quality and used mainly for "working clothes," the finer linens and woolens compared well with the grades offered by

British merchants. As time went on women so improved the textile art that they made it possible for Americans to clothe themselves well, if not in the finest goods, and to achieve a high degree of economic independence in one primary line of manufacturing.

☆

For the development of agriculture and domestic manufacturing, an abundant and increasing supply of labor, skilled and unskilled, was furnished by the migration of free whites and indentured white laborers and the importation of Negro slaves. On the small farm owned and operated by the freehold family, the husband, wife, and children did all the work in fields, forest, workshops, and the house. At harvest time and on other special occasions, the family might have the co-operative help of neighbors in return for similar labor, but it carried the main burden of its own self-support.

After crossroad settlements and villages arose as centers for stores and craftsmen who made things on order, the farm family could be relieved from certain tasks at home by exchanging farm produce with the smith or woodworker for "odd jobs" or manufactured goods. As colonization proceeded, itinerant artisans —tinkers, smiths, weavers, bakers, tailors, and carpenters—wandered from community to community and worked for their board, lodging, and payments in coin. Yet even in the most populous of the rural regions there was little specialization. The farm family supplied most of the labor for agriculture and domestic manufacturing.

On the larger farms of the North the labor of the owner and his family was often supplemented by the labor of one or more indentured servants. Such a servant was a person bound by contract to work for an employer for a term of years, ranging from four to seven as a rule, in return for board, lodging, and clothing, and some gift or gifts on the expiration of the service. Many men, women, and children kidnaped by gangsters in Great Britain or taken from prisons were shipped over against their will for sale into servitude. But nearly all indentured servants were immigrants who had freely chosen their hard lot in the hope of eventual advantages. They preferred this choice to remaining in the Old World where they could either find no work at all or had to toil all their lives with no prospects of more than subsistence wages.

In all the colonies from early days there were indentured servants, mainly farmers but often household workers and craftsmen. Although the number was small in New England, it was large in Virginia and the middle colonies. Eighteen years after the founding of Jamestown in 1607 more than one third of Virginia's inhabitants were indentured servants. During the closing years of the seventeenth century more than one third of all the immigrants in Pennsylvania were of this class and the proportion did not decrease for a long time.

After they had finished their term of service indentured servants were free to make their way as best they could. Those who were skillful, industrious, and fortunate either acquired farms of their own in the neighborhood or went west to the frontier to settle on new land. Or, if they were especially ingenious in the crafts, they went to the towns and set up shops for themselves or found employment with merchants and master craftsmen. At all events no stigma of servitude rested upon them and, as far as the law was concerned, they could and often did rise to good fortune and even honors in their colony. The fact that they had started near the bottom put no bar against their advancement. Although thousands of servants, on the expiration of their indentures, joined the "poor whites," South and North, the great majority of them merged with the population of farmers and artisans and shared their labors and advantages as free citizens.

In an entirely different position were the Negroes imported from Africa and sold into bondage. As early as 1619 Negroes were brought to Virginia and soon slavery became an established institution under the law. Before many years it spread to all the colonies, and by 1770 about one sixth of the entire population were Negro slaves.

In the North, however, climate, soil, and types of agriculture made slavery on a large scale unprofitable; and, comparatively speaking, the proportion of Negro slaves remained small. In the colony of New York, for example, where it was high, it amounted to about one seventh of the population at the end of the colonial period. On the other hand the climate, soil, staple crops, and plantation system of the South favored the use of slave labor. White bond servants were often intractable, their terms of service made them impermanent laborers, and the most enterprising among them valiantly struggled to get land for themselves as soon as they became free. Negro slaves by contrast had to work for their masters as long as they lived and could be bought in great numbers as the slave traffic increased. Only by slavery, planters insisted, was it possible for them to expand rapidly the cultivation of the soil and make profits in large amounts. At all events, two thirds of the inhabitants of South Carolina were slaves at the close of the colonial period, and along the Southern seaboard the labor of Negroes underlay the wealth and power of masters.

By such means in the great rural resettlement the colonists were able to build up a strong agricultural economy that long continued to be the principal basis of American security. At the end of the colonial age at least nine tenths of the people, from New Hampshire to Georgia, lived on the land and produced for themselves the commodities necessary to a good, if often simple, living. A few thousand great landlords, North and South, grew rich on tenant and slave labor and lived luxuriously. But the overwhelming majority of the white people belonged to families that owned, frequently under mortgage it is true, small farms and worked with their own hands in fields, forests, farmhouses, and little shops.

Their life was toilsome, no doubt, but by their mode of living, their self-supporting economy, and their spirit of independence they made a rural order different from the Old World orders of tenantry, feudalism, and serfdom. In self-sustaining industry, character, and love of their freedom, they formed a body of working people such as had never appeared before in the history of Western civilization.

CHAPTER IV

The Rise of Commerce and Industry

RUNNING ALONG with the development of autonomy in agriculture was the promotion of commerce and industry. Although the population in the colonial age continued to be predominantly agricultural, the character of American life, the evolution of American society, and the total power of American economy, as it gathered force, represented a combination of agriculture, commerce, and industry.

From the beginning of colonization, commerce was integrated with agriculture. It carried over the sea certain raw materials of the colonies and brought back from England tools and other finished commodities that increased the productivity of agriculture and raised the standard of rural life. It speeded up the circulation of commodities within and among the colonies, giving outlets to surplus domestic manufactures and acquainting the people of each section with the people, customs, and economic activities of other sections. Besides pouring commodities into commercial channels, industry evoked the energies of local enterprise, enabled Americans to produce many kinds of things hitherto imported, and demonstrated to discerning persons the immense potentialities of American resources. Together, commerce and industry permitted the accumulation of large capitals in American hands, decreasing dependence on British investors.

The promotion of commerce was an essential element of the mercantilist policy under which the English government operated, and was among the purposes of the companies and proprietors that led in colonization. A provision of the Virginia charter issued in 1606 granted to the London Company special privileges in trade, by laying heavy duties on the commerce of outsiders, English and foreign, and turning the revenue into its treasury for a term of years. To meet the cost of the expedition that brought the Pilgrims to Plymouth in 1620, a large sum was borrowed from English capitalists and the debt could only be paid by gathering in articles of commerce, such as fish and furs, which could be sent back to England. The royal patent of 1681 constituting William Penn proprietor of Pennsylvania also gave him the right to build harbors and docks for commercial purposes and to lay customs duties on goods "to be laded and unladed" at such ports and places. If colonization was to be profitable to English investors, cargoes had to be provided for the return voyages of ships that transported immigrants and their goods to America.

The early newcomers to America were under obligations to look about for objects of commerce almost as soon as they landed. The first ship which deposited settlers in Virginia carried home a cargo of wooden staves prepared for it under the direction of Captain John Smith. Lumber and its by-products became commodities for export from Virginia before settlers in that colony learned to produce, cure, and pack tobacco.

☆

Long before any colonies had been started, English sailors had embarked on large-scale fishing off the coasts of Newfoundland, and the early explorers had excited English interest in this business by glowing reports of haddock, cod, mackerel, and whales in unlimited quantities in the waters of that region. The Pilgrims at Plymouth and the Puritans at Massachusetts Bay, shortly after their arrival, began to build small boats and send out fishing expeditions. In time Boston, Salem, Marblehead, and a few other towns became busy ports for the fishing industry; and all down the coast fishing became a source of lucrative trading.

Besides furnishing supplies to American markets, fishermen cured and packed huge quantities for export. But the English themselves were extensively engaged in this industry, and American fishermen had to seek other than British markets. They found them principally in France, Portugal, Spain, and the West Indies. On the basis of this exchange an immense business was built up. The fish shipped to Spain, for example, were exchanged for citrus fruits and specie, and the specie was used to pay for English manufactures. The fish sent to the West Indies were traded for sugar and specie; a part of the sugar went to the colonies and another part, with the specie, went to England to pay debts and buy manufactures.

With particular doggedness the fishermen of New England turned to whaling. At first they concentrated their efforts largely in the waters off Newfoundland, but in time they pushed their enterprise all over the Atlantic, using the ports of New Bedford and Nantucket as their chief bases of operation.

So extensive were their whaling voyages and so daring were their undertakings that Edmund Burke, when in 1775 he warned the British Parliament against "ill-considered" tampering with the strength and independence of Americans, paused to give a dramatic picture of their whaling industry: "Look at the manner in which the people of New England have of late carried on the whale fishery. Whilst we follow them among the tumbling mountains of ice, and behold them penetrating into the deepest frozen recesses of Hudson's Bay and Davis's Straits, whilst we are looking for them beneath the Arctic circle, we hear that they have pierced into the opposite region of polar cold, that they are at the antipodes, and engaged under the frozen serpent of the South. . . . Nor is the equinoctial heat more discouraging to them, than the accumulated winter of both the poles.

"We know that whilst some of them draw the line and strike the harpoon on the coast of Africa, others run the longitude, and pursue their gigantic game along the coast of Brazil. No sea but what is vexed by their fisheries. No climate that is not witness to their toils. Neither the perseverance of Holland, nor the activity of France, nor the dexterous and firm sagacity of English enterprise, ever carried this most perilous mode of hard industry to the extent to which it has been pushed by this recent people; a people who are still, as it were, but in the gristle, and not yet hardened into the bone of manhood."

Although the British at home caught plenty of fish for themselves and took relatively little from American exporters, they were short of one prime raw material which the colonies had in abundance—timber. They had exhausted many of their forest areas in building houses, shops, and ships, and in supplying charcoal for their iron industries. British shortage of timber was thus an opportunity for the colonists and they made haste to meet it. Almost at the outset of settlement they had to cut down trees in clearing land for cultivation and they saved many choice logs—especially oak, pine, and walnut—for shipment to England.

Within a few years little sawmills were built along the streams and rivers, and enterprising merchants began to produce lumber in various forms for the English market. New England, New York, Pennsylvania, and North Carolina became the main centers of such undertakings.

In time Americans were supplying finished and semifinished timber products for local, intercolonial, and English markets, such as masts and spars for ships, shingles, and staves for barrels and casks. By developing the lumber industry Americans were enabled to discharge debts in England, buy English manufactures, accumulate profits for new investments in colonial lands and business adventures.

Furs and skins furnished another immensely profitable group of articles for commerce. For some time they were readily procured by colonists near their settlements or from Indian hunters who brought them to the very doors of houses, as soon as they learned that they could exchange otter, mink, bear, fox, beaver, and deer furs or skins for beads, metal knives, hoes, hatchets, cloth, and trinkets. Able to buy furs for so little and sell them overseas at enormous prices, white traders reaped golden rewards from this business. Farmers could supplement agriculture by gathering in furs without giving much time to it. Nor did they need capital for the easy traffic. While settlers clung to the shores and forests still stood at the back doors of cabins, dealing in furs was a simpler transaction than the catching and selling of fish or the cutting and shipping of lumber.

But as forests were cleared for farming and settlements pushed inland, the fur business became more restricted for farmers who were not located on the frontier. Now organized enterprise steadily pressed into the collecting and bundling of furs for shipment. Monopolies of the trade in certain regions were sought and sometimes obtained by personal initiative or through government grants. Among the Dutch, who preceded the English as settlers in the Hudson River valley, fur monopolies were rich prizes over which merchants and officials waged many a lusty contest.

Even in favorable circumstances hunters, woodsmen, and trappers who roamed the frontiers freely in search of furs were finally at the mercy of fur merchants who usually fixed the prices at their own pleasure. As the frontier was pushed westward and forests were cleared, the fur business needed ever larger amounts of capital to pay for scouting and the maintenance of trading stations in the far backwoods. So the traffic in furs gradually became highly organized and tended to concentrate in the hands of a few merchants, British and American. By the close of the colonial period competition between them for mastery over this trade often broke out in political quarrels at colonial capitals and in London.

☆

With the expansion of agriculture and commerce, creating and enlarging markets, opportunities widened for the use and sale of ships, iron products, and other commodities that were not supplied by domestic manufacturers. Indeed the colonies were still very young when independent manufacturing industries sprang up in the neighborhood of farms and plantations, especially in the North. Three industries attained first rank: shipbuilding, iron-working, and flour milling.

So abundant in the colonies were ship timber and naval stores, including tar, that shipbuilding soon became an important business. Being British subjects, Americans enjoyed the benefits of British navigation laws; ships built in the colonies and manned by Americans belonged to the merchant marine of the mother country and had the same rights in the shipping business. And special circumstances favored American shipbuilding. It was cheaper to build vessels in the colonies, where materials were abundant, than in England, for the English had to import a large part of their ship timber and naval stores. The rapid growth of the fishing industry also made a local demand for ships.

In response to these opportunities and needs, shipyards sprang up all along the coast, especially north of Maryland; a lucrative industry gave employment to ship carpenters and yielded profits to investors. Before long Americans were building ships as stout and swift as any that sailed the seas.

In its turn shipbuilding spurred other industries, particularly the production of ship timber, tar, chains, rope, anchors, and nails. Now there was a demand for ironworking on a scope larger than that needed for making the few types of agricultural implements then in use.

Here again the state of things in England had to be considered. The English had iron ore in abundance and their iron industry had reached a high stage of development. But they used charcoal for smelting ore and were exhausting their local wood supply. On the other hand, Americans had iron ore in almost every colony and their charcoal sources were practically unlimited.

In these circumstances English interest called for the importation of pig, or rough, iron to be transformed in English foundries into finished products for English usage and for export to the colonies. The Americans could, of course, supply the pig iron to English merchants. But they also had skill for working iron into products necessary to their own agriculture and industry and could approach self-sufficiency in that line.

Iron ore was discovered by the first settlers in Virginia and they sent a large quantity of it to England in 1608. Within a few years they were smelting ore and working iron in the colony and might have gone far with it if tobacco raising had not proved to be a quicker way of making large profits. Puritans also early unearthed iron ore. By 1644 Massachusetts had an ironworks in operation. In the other New England colonies and in the middle colonies the discovery of iron deposits was quickly followed by the building of furnaces for ore smelting and mills for hammering, rolling, and slitting iron.

At the middle of the eighteenth century American ironmasters were making iron products of nearly every kind—chains, anchors, guns, kettles, axes, knives, nails, iron bars, and pipes. For fine iron products, such as the best cutlery, needles, and carpenters' tools, the colonies depended largely on imports from England. But the arts of iron manufacture were being steadily improved; so steadily, in fact, that British merchants grew worried over American competition in the colonial market.

Flour and lumber milling industries rose and flourished as agriculture and shipbuilding advanced. Right at hand was wood for water wheels and mills, and hard stone for millstones. Almost everywhere streams rushing down to the sea could be used for power. With the increase in the production of grain for home consumption, the crude labor of pounding, grinding, and bolting wheat, corn, and rye in domestic shops became so burdensome that farmers welcomed the release from it. As the export of grain from the middle colonies enlarged, merchants saw a chance to add to their profits by substituting flour in barrels for the shipment of grain in the raw state. Very early the demands of shipbuilding outran the supply of lumber which could be sawed slowly by hand, and as prospering colonists prepared to move from log cabins to frame houses local needs for lumber and shingles were multiplied.

So on the streams from New Hampshire to Georgia, mills were built to process grain and saw logs into various types of lumber. Sometimes the two processes were combined at a single mill; often they were separated. In Pennsylvania enterprising flour millers barreled their flour for shipment and even erected shops for baking bread and manufacturing the famous hardtack biscuits served to sailors on naval and merchant vessels.

☆

From the farms and plantations, from the gathering of raw materials, from the ironworks, from mills for grinding grain and sawing timber flowed a swelling stream of various commodities to be marketed in the colonies or abroad and exchanged for colonial or British manufactures. Here were expanding opportunities for specialized merchants and shippers. Often, if not usually, the merchant was a shipowner, and combined the business of buying and selling with the business of transporting. But whatever the form of operation, American commercial enterprise had a spacious theater in which to distribute goods and accumulate gains. At home it could use the coastal waters and navigable streams penetrating interior regions. Before it was the Atlantic Ocean, touching all the ports of Europe and Africa, as well as those of Great Britain.

As the population of America rose—from about 300,000 in 1700 to about 2,500,000 in 1770—trade and shipping were extended. In the beginning most of this business was in the hands of merchants resident in England, who operated personally or through agents in the colonies; but it was not long before Americans entered into a vigorous competition with them. Colonists could build and navigate ships, as well as keep accounts and handle commercial transactions. What was to hinder them from gathering more and more of the business into their own hands? As events proved, nothing could.

Five main avenues of trade were open to American merchants and shippers. One branch of their commerce was with Great Britain. Another was with European ports—French, Spanish, and Portuguese—in certain commodities. A third was with the British West Indies and, often illegally, with the French West Indies. Intercolonial trade also flourished from port to port along the Atlantic coast and from point to point along the navigable rivers reaching into the interior. In prosecuting the slave trade, merchants and shippers, particularly from New England and New York, visited the shores of Africa and carried away cargoes of Negroes for the plantations of the West Indies and the South and to supply the smaller markets of the Northern colonies. When wars were raging—frequently the case in the seventeenth and eighteenth centuries—shipowners could embark on privateering, sometimes akin to piracy, and prey upon French, Dutch, or Spanish commerce.

With the wealth garnered from transporting goods was thus combined the loot of commercial wars. When George III ascended the throne in 1760 American merchants and shippers in the great colonial ports were numerous enough, rich enough, and powerful enough to vie with the stoutest merchants of Bristol and London.

☆

The development of commerce and industry encouraged an increasing immigration of workers who specialized in the several crafts, including shipbuilding; and in the course of time the line between purely domestic artisans and industrial mechanics became sharper in the rural districts and very definite in the towns. At the end of the colonial period the colonies thus had an important, if small, body of industrial workers engaged solely in the manufacture of goods for the markets.

Carpenters, masons, smiths, and woodworkers were among the earliest immigrants in the seventeenth century. Some were freemen. Others were indentured servants. With the rise of shipbuilding, ironworking, flour milling and other industries, the stream of artisans, free and indentured, swelled in size, though it was never large enough in the opinion of business enterprisers in the colonies. Workers from the British Isles, from Germany, Holland, Sweden, Switzerland, and France crowded the incoming ships and played a vital part in the building up of industry, commerce, and the standard of living.

Besides regular workers competent in using wood, stone, and other materials for the construction of simple buildings and the manufacture of articles necessary to a commodious living, there were in all the colonies designers and artisans of special and higher skills. Among them were architects, woodcarvers, silversmiths, wheelwrights, potters, pewterers, and makers of glassware, watches, leatherware, coaches, and cabinets.

After the first years of pioneering were over, architects began to design and erect fine mansions for great landlords and merchants, stately buildings for public purposes, and handsome churches for religious worship. So solid, beautiful, indeed exquisite, was much of their work that it became the pride of discriminating colonists and their descendants. In the designing and making of elegant furniture, objects of glass, panels for walls and doors, mantels, carvings for cornices and porticoes, iron gates and grills, silver ornaments of tableware, masters of such arts could satisfy fastidious taste and at the same time supply markets with goods at prices which enabled even small farmers, storekeepers, and mechanics to incorporate some refinements into their simple ways of living.

☆

Out of the economic activities of numberless men and women, white and black, especially out of the export and import trade in all its branches, developed specialized centers of settlement on the seacoast and at favorable points on inland waters. By 1690 the foundations of flourishing cities had been laid at Boston, Newport, New York, Philadelphia, and Charleston. According to careful estimates, the population of these towns at that time was as follows:

Boston, founded in 1630, 7000.
Newport, founded in 1639, 2600.
New York, founded as New Amsterdam in 1625, 3900.
Philadelphia, founded in 1682, 4000.
Charleston, founded in 1672, 1100.

On the eve of the Revolution in 1774, Philadelphia, serving as a leading port of entry for immigrants and for the shipping of surplus produce from a great hinterland, had forged to the top. With almost 40,000 inhabitants, it stood first in population and was second only to London among the cities of the British Empire. Boston had about 20,000 inhabitants; Newport 12,000; New York between 25,000 and 30,000; and Charleston about 10,000. Except in the case of Boston these were only estimates but, however out of line on one side or the other, they corresponded roughly to the facts.

Among other growing centers of trade on the coast or inland were Salem, Providence, New Haven, Perth Amboy, Baltimore, Richmond, and Savannah. Among the minor towns, as yet little more than overgrown villages but increasing in size, were Albany, Princeton, Trenton, Germantown, Lancaster, Annapolis, Norfolk, and Wilmington in North Carolina. Although the population of all the cities having more than 8000 inhabitants was less than three per cent of the total population of the colonies, their importance in wealth and as centers of economic, social, political, and intellectual activity outweighed the mere number of their inhabitants.

☆

Of the total wealth produced by all the economic activities of men, women, and children in all the colonies from year to year between 1607, the founding of Virginia, and 1774, on the eve of the rift with Great Britain, no official census was ever taken. Nor were any figures recorded from which more than the roughest guesses could be made. The first census taken by the United States, in 1790, gave only the population—3,172,000 whites and 700,000 Negroes. Of this population, according to reckonings by family names, 75.2% were English, Scotch, and Scotch-Irish in origins; 3.7% South Irish; 8.7% Germans, and the rest Dutch, Swedish, French, and miscellaneous.

Although no economic census was taken in colonial times, two well-established facts indicate that the annual output of wealth was immense and on the increase. It was great enough to provide the main support of the rapidly growing population, particularly with regard to the primary staples of living, and a surplus for export. That the output was rising swiftly was disclosed by figures for the trade with Great Britain. In his address to the House of Commons in 1775 *On Conciliation with America*, Edmund Burke presented the following table:

The whole export trade of England, including that to colonies in 1704 .... £6,509,000.
Export to the colonies alone [including Canada and the West Indies] in 1772 .... £6,024,000.

Well could Burke exclaim: "The trade with America alone is now within less than £500,000 of being equal to what this great commercial nation, England, carried on at the beginning of this century with the whole world!"

The exact amount of the English export to the thirteen American colonies was not separated in Burke's figures from the trade with Canada and the British West Indies; but there was no doubt about its magnitude. No longer were the Americans puny colonists almost wholly dependent on Great Britain for capital, primary supplies, and manufactures. They had built up on this continent a great society and provided for it an economic underwriting of unquestionable strength. What was more: they saw extraordinary chances for the expansion of their enterprise and were determined to take advantage of them.

Growth of Social and Intellectual Autonomy

WHATEVER may have been the visions of English kings who chartered companies and granted patents to proprietors for the purpose of founding colonies in America;

Whatever may have been the intentions of the companies and proprietors who planted settlements;

Whatever may have been the dreams of the English leaders who hoped to see a New England established beyond the sea;

Whatever may have been the hopes of immigrants who acquired great estates and became mighty landlords or turned to commerce and became rich merchants able to compete with the most powerful merchants of London;

Whatever may have been the aspirations of the men and women engaged in tilling the soil and building up domestic manufactures, or of the artisans devoted to developing industries and creating the refinements of living;

However much of the Old World heritage the immigrants brought with them to the New World;

There were from the beginning social and intellectual tendencies which reinforced the separatist qualities and energies that had led to migration and worked in the direction of consolidation and autonomy in the colonies.

Giving form and force to these autonomous tendencies were certain elemental facts. In America emigrants from England did not reproduce the whole social order of England—king, lords, established church, and peasantry with no hope of owning land. Nor did they reproduce the whole intellectual outlook of England. Neither did they begin anew, from primitive origins, the history of civilization in the Old World and thus start repeating that history as it had been from the days of savagery. The overwhelming majority of the emigrants to America, from the early years to the close of the colonial period, were dissenters from the Church of England, whether they were English, Scotch, French, or German. No less opposed to that religious establishment were the English and Irish Catholics who found refuge in the colonies. Despite claims to aristocratic origins made by proud descendants, the overwhelming majority of the emigrants to America were from the "middling orders"—agricultural, mercantile, and artisan. And for their activities in America, whatever the ambitions and hopes of any or all the immigrants, there were two conditioning material realities which helped to shape their fortunes—a virgin continent vast in extent and resources, and three thousand miles of water separating them from the world they had left behind.

Helping to sustain autonomous tendencies and strengthen them as they developed were, first, the qualities of the immigrants as such and, second, the knowledge and ideas acquired from the Old World, out of which they came, and modified for their purposes, in the course of colonial evolution. This truth was firmly grasped by Mercy Otis Warren, herself a colonial, born at Barnstable, Massachusetts, in 1728 and long a resident of Plymouth. "The first emigrations to North America," she wrote, "were not composed of a strolling banditti of rude nations, like the first people of most other colonies in the history of the world." On the contrary, she declared, speaking out of direct knowledge: "The early settlers in the newly discovered continent were as far advanced in civilization, policy, and manners; in their ideas of government, the nature of compacts, and the bands of civil union, as any of their neighbors at that period among the most polished nations of Europe." While recognizing that vices of Europe had also come with virtues, Mrs. Warren maintained that "the progress of everything had there [in America] been remarkably rapid from the first settlement of the country. Learning was cultivated, knowledge disseminated, politeness and morals improved, and valor and patriotism cherished, in proportion to the rapidity of her population."

The qualities of mind and character to which Mrs. Warren referred were abundantly illustrated in the little colony of Plymouth, founded in 1620. Two outstanding leaders among the Pilgrims were Elder William Brewster and William Bradford. Brewster was the son of a local bailiff and postmaster in Yorkshire and had spent some time at Cambridge University in his youth.

His library, as a biographer has said, "proves him to have been well read in history, philosophy, and religious poetry and shows that he continued to buy books throughout his life." Bradford, brought up in his youth to follow the plow, was a self-educated man of wide learning who, in his intellectual explorations, read among other books the *Republic* by Jean Bodin, French writer on government and society—a critique of Plato's idealistic and communistic theories. Both Brewster and Bradford displayed qualities of statesmanship, if in a small community, in dealing with lawless and discontented men who made grave troubles for the Pilgrims before and after they landed.

To Massachusetts Bay, during the early years, came more than one hundred graduates of Cambridge and Oxford universities. John Winthrop, the first governor of that colony, was the son of a lawyer and had studied at Cambridge. Roger Williams, who, in rebellion against the government of Massachusetts Bay, founded a freer community at Providence, belonged to a mercantile family of London, had graduated from Cambridge with honors, and was a philosophic thinker of humanist inclinations. Some of the later colonists, notably Charles Carroll, born in Maryland in 1737, were educated at the best Catholic institutions in Europe. Among the leaders in all the colonies were men who had studied law at the Temple in London, or theology, natural philosophy, the classics, medicine, and other branches of learning at the best institutions in Great Britain, on the Continent, or in both places.

From first to last colonial women in large numbers were well educated—though not in universities. Anne Hutchinson, evicted like Roger Williams from Boston for her independence of mind, was the daughter of a Puritan clergyman and wife of a well-to-do merchant, a mother of fourteen children, known for her learning and the vigor of her intellect—the reason for her eviction. Anne Bradstreet—ancestor of Oliver Wendell Holmes and Wendell Phillips—who arrived at Massachusetts Bay in 1630, was the daughter of Thomas Dudley, deputy governor under Winthrop, and the wife of Simon Bradstreet, a graduate of Cambridge. Eight tutors had been employed by her parents in starting her education and the poetry that she composed in America displayed her familiarity with Raleigh's *History of the World*, with Plutarch, Usher, and contemporary French literature. In every colony were numerous women of English, Dutch, Huguenot, and other national origins who had been trained in the classics and modern literature—women of the planting and professional circles, women

Nearly a century followed Cabot's voyage to America in 1497 before international rivalry for power in the New World spurred Queen Elizabeth to commission Sir Walter Raleigh to develop England's claims to a dominion. The destruction of the Spanish Armada in 1588 cleared the way for trading companies and proprietors to found colonies under charters and grants from the English Crown. Thus was opened the greatest real estate and investment opportunity in the history of Western civilization.

Painting by Joseph Boggs Beale. Modern Enterprises, Phila, Pa.

Only able-bodied men and women possessing many skills and crafts, many arts and sciences, could build prosperous and self-sustaining societies on the territory claimed by England. An overwhelming majority came of their own choice; approximately two-thirds were able to meet the cost of the journey and make a start in the new country.

Painting by R. F. Heinrich. Courtesy National Life Insurance Co.

Painting by Gari Melchers. Courtesy Detroit Public Library.

Years marked by wars, religious controversies and persecutions, political disputes, and royal despotism lay behind the decision to leave Europe and migrate to the English colonies. But there was something in the spirit of those who made the break—a force of character not simply determined by economic, political, or religious conditions—that made them different from their neighbors who remained in the turmoil and poverty of the Old World.

Painting by Gari Melchers.
Courtesy Detroit Public Library.

Courtesy National Life Insurance Co.

Shaping a new and secure life in the
wilderness required an exercise of intellectual prowess and constructive
abilities of a high order. Many primitive arts of survival were learned from
the Indians, but the relations between
whites and Indians were punctuated
by sporadic brawls, local conflicts and
general wars.

Variations in soil and climate being favorable to a wide range of agricultural products, thousands of farmers grew prosperous in tilling their own land. In the South, tobacco, rice, and indigo fostered the importation of slaves, provided cargoes for English vessels, and brought wealth to the planters.

Painting by Ezra Winter. Courtesy Bank of the Manhattan Co.

From the beginning of colonization, commerce was integrated with agriculture. When George III ascended the throne in 1760 American merchants and shippers in the great colonial ports were numerous enough, rich enough, and powerful enough to vie with the stoutest English merchants.

Painting by Ezra Winter.
Courtesy Bank of the Manhattan Co.

Painting by R. F. Heinrich.
Courtesy National Life Insurance Co.

The early settlers were as far advanced
in civilization, policy, and manners, in
their ideas of government, the nature
of compacts, and the bands of civil
union, as any among the most polished
nations of Europe. Learning was cultivated, knowledge disseminated, politeness and morals improved, and
valor and patriotism cherished.

Painting by Ezra Winter. Courtesy Bank of the Manhattan Co.

As the widely separated settlements grew into populous and orderly colonies, social and intellectual changes of weighty meaning for the future took place. A leveling of class lines proceeded rapidly as merchant immigrants rose into the class of Southern planters, farmers and artisans embarked on careers as merchants, lawyers or clergymen, and indentured servants became freehold farmers.

Ewing Galloway Photo.

Painting by R. F. Heinrich.
Courtesy National Life Insurance Co.

With the publishing of newspapers
after 1704 Americans could learn
about what was going on in the
colonies as well as overseas. The rise
and growth of a colonial postal system facilitated the spread of knowledge and ideas, news and information. The provincial mind was becoming American in its range of
interest.

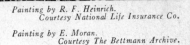

Painting by R. F. Heinrich.
Courtesy National Life Insurance Co.

Painting by E. Moran.
Courtesy The Bettmann Archive.

From the beginning, government played a necessary and formative role in the founding and development of the colonies. By the end of the colonial period thousands of men were acquainted with voting, managing local campaigns, and taking part in elections. This training in the arts of self-government prepared the colonies for asserting their political and economic rights against British authority and for handling their own political affairs.

Painting by Ezra Winter. Courtesy Bank of the Manhattan Co.

The almost universal belief in England that the colonies should be permanently subordinate to the interests of the British governing classes ran counter to American interests. Americans were more concerned with developing the lands and resources at hand—in enlarging their share of international trade and reaping the profits thus accruing to them—than in promoting British commerce.

TAVERN

©1940, Norman Price.
Courtesy Schenley Distillers Corp.

Painting by R. F. Heinrich. Courtesy National Life Insurance Co.

"No taxation without representation." The series of measures adopted by the British government during the period 1763–1767 deeply affected American agriculture, industries, and commerce, freedom of elections, press, and speech. The British were obviously determined to raise revenue by taxation and subordinate the colonies to British interests. The Americans were equally determined to resist—even by actions involving violence, if necessary.

Painting by Joseph Boggs Beale. Modern Enterprises, Phila., Pa.

Although the person who fired the first shot at Lexington, the morning of April 19, 1775, must apparently remain unknown, it is certain that this shot "heard around the world" heralded a war. Congress prepared for the worst, organized a regular army, and appointed George Washington commander of the American forces in Massachusetts.

Painting by R. F. Heinrich. Courtesy National Life Insurance Co.

©1940, Norman Price.
Courtesy Schenley Distillers Corp.

Painting by N. C. Wyeth.
Courtesy Pennsylvania Railroad.

British civil and military officers, instead of relaxing, tightened their efforts to compel obedience to British authority. As prospects for a reconciliation faded, the desire for independence flamed into a fixed resolve. The Continental Congress authorized a committee to draft the Declaration of Independence and upon being approved it was adopted July 4, 1776.

Painting by John Ward Dunsmore. Courtesy Sons of the Revolution in State of New York.

While Washington, almost at the end of his resources, was retiring to Valley Forge for the winter of 1777-78, poorly trained and supplied troops farther north were demonstrating a genius for warfare. Burgoyne's surrender at Saratoga, rightly counted among the decisive battles of history, marked a turning point toward American independence.

Painting by James Bingham. Courtesy Continental Distilling Corp.

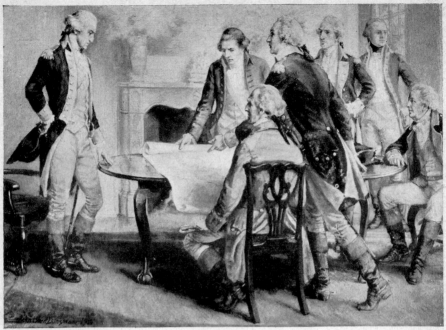

By his action in retiring to Yorktown to await the British fleet, Cornwallis unwittingly prepared for his doom and the end of the war. Stunned by the blow of his surrender to Washington on October 19, 1781, the British government either could not or would not make another gigantic effort to recover its dominion over the colonies. Surrounded by captured British flags Congress rejoiced over the victory.

of the great landed and mercantile families. And a stream of hired tutors in the prosperous families maintained this standard of the proprieties for sons and daughters.

☆

As the sprawling and widely separated settlements grew into populous and orderly colonies, social and intellectual changes of weighty meaning for the future took place. In every colony members of the classes drew together for social and intellectual intercourse and formed permanent ties of customs, manners, and views. In the South the planting and merchant families led in this concentration; generally, in the North, clerical and merchant families took the leadership; in New York and Pennsylvania landlord, merchant, and professional families were preëminent.

In every colony intermarriage strengthened the social ties of the respective communities and intercolonial marriages fortified the enlarging sense of continental solidarity. As generation succeeded generation, memories of family bonds with the Old World grew dimmer and sentiments of attachment to the here and now deepened in their hold upon the minds and hearts of the people. Also, among small farmers and mechanics, increasing density of population was accompanied by multiplying points of contact, and by opportunities for intermarriage and concerted thinking and action relative to common interests. While in many respects these classes were at times in conflict in their communities, in other respects they had common ideas and grew accustomed to think of themselves as Americans.

☆

Among the problems which marked the evolution of the American mind was the question of the permanence of the social system in each colony at each period of its development and the place of that system in the greater British society of which it was a political and economic part. Was this social system impervious to changes under the impacts of changing social facts and ideas? Was it to be defended through thick and thin against encroachments from below and within, and against encroachments from Great Britain—social as well as economic, religious, and political? If its permanence was to be secured, by whom was the feat to be accomplished and under what ideas and declarations?

Arrayed on the side of permanence for the patrician features of the inherited social system was the congenial association between

royal governors and proprietors or their agents and the lords of
land and trade. At imitation royal courts in the capitals of royal
and proprietary colonies social preferment was given to the
colonial upper classes and it deepened their affection for "the
seasoned culture" of the British social order deemed the best and
safest of all social orders. This relationship was dual: it strengthened ties with the mother country and confirmed loyalty to a social
hierarchy in America. At such courts were formed centers of
resistance to the turbulence of popular demands for a break with
the fixations of the class structure in the colonies and the class
domination of British rule.

The fine mansions of royal governors and proprietors or their
agents were matched or surpassed by the mansions of the wealthy
planters and merchants. To dwellers in such mansions mutual
hospitality was extended. The menial services required for lavish
entertainments were performed, alike for the governors and the
governed, by servants, indentured, free, or slave. Similar raiment
of fine woolens, silks, and laces gave distinction to the upper
circles. The same manners, customs, and pretensions tightened the
cords of unity between British and colonial "aristocrats."

If a royal governor or proprietary agent and his retinue of subordinate officials asserted high prerogatives, though flamboyantly,
many of the colonial courtiers accepted the assertion as a part of
British security and their own security within the aristocratic
political and social system. When Governor Thomas Boone,
shortly after his arrival in South Carolina in 1761, installed in his
mansion at Charleston a woman who was not his wife the gentlemen of Charleston accepted his invitations as a necessary recognition of his privilege and their security, though the ladies boycotted
his dinners.

Of the wealthy planting class that sought permanence in the
order of special privilege, yet without servility to a royal governor, William Byrd II, of Virginia, was a pungent example. He
was the grandson of a London goldsmith and the son of an Englishman who had amassed a great fortune in Virginia as a tobacco
planter, merchant, slave trader, and land speculator. Inheriting
that fortune, he established his family at Westover, not far from
Jamestown. He had spent some time in England, studying law at
the Temple and making friends in the ruling circles there. On his
large estate at Westover, Byrd lived the life of a leisured country
gentleman in a magnificent dwelling famous throughout the
colony for its size and elegance, its splendid furnishings, and its

exceptionally large and well-selected library, the largest private library in Virginia if not in all the colonies, containing about four thousand volumes.

For the struggling pioneers on the Carolina border Byrd developed a strong contempt, evident in the diary which he kept and in other writings. If his scorn for the small farmers who labored with their own hands in Virginia was less, he was determined that they should submit to government by gentlemen. For his own rights and property he stood up like a landed warrior. When the royal governor, Alexander Spotswood, tried to establish a high judicial court filled with his own appointees, Byrd went to England and protested with success to the Board of Trade. It was tyranny insufferable, in his opinion, for a governor to choose judges with power "to determine concerning not only the lives and liberties, but also concerning the whole estates" of the Virginia gentlemen.

A similar attitude toward an aristocratic order—permanence and conformity—was illustrated in Massachusetts, before and after it became a royal province in 1691, by a contemporary of Byrd, Samuel Sewall, a rich merchant and public official of that Northern colony. Sewall was the grandson of an English merchant. After graduation from Harvard College he entered upon a mercantile career in which he augmented the family patrimony. Like Byrd he was an omnivorous reader and kept a diary, besides writing on various subjects.

When Massachusetts lost its independence and was compelled to bow before a royal governor, Sewall accepted the new system and wrote in defense of it. He once said that it was "intolerable" for "private persons to print reflections and censures on the highest acts of government." Though he objected to gross corruption in politics, he declared: "I was for upholding Government whether in or out of it." As Vernon Parrington has said of Sewall in his volume, *The Colonial Mind:* "He desired no innovation in church or state; established forms answered his needs and filled the measure of his ideal. The existing system was approved by all the respectable people of the community; there was everything to gain in upholding it."

While the conservatism of Byrd was tempered by a will to resist official interference with his personal interests, and the conservatism of Sewall rejected supine acceptance of corruption in government, that of Jonathan Boucher went to the extreme of advocating servile obedience to duly constituted authorities, British and American. Boucher, the son of a poor English schoolteacher, arrived in Virginia in 1759 and soon afterward was ordained a clergyman in the Anglican Church. For a time he preached in Virginia and then moved with some of his slaves to Annapolis, Maryland, where he served as rector of Saint Anne's.

To restive Americans Boucher taught this doctrine: "Obedience to Government is every man's duty, because it is every man's interest, but it is particularly incumbent on Christians, because it is enjoined by the positive commands of God." If government is mild and free, Boucher argued, the people must be grateful; if it be less liberal than it ought to be in reason, "still it is our duty not to disturb the peace of the community, by becoming refractory and rebellious subjects, and *resisting the ordinances of God.*" In the sermons and writings of Boucher conservatism reached its pinnacle.

☆

Had the order of things which Byrd, Sewall, Boucher, and men of their type defended been unchanging and unchallenged, the conformity which they taught might have been indefinitely accepted. But that order had been and was changing; it was challenged by hard facts and by bold advocates of change. In England the rapid growth of the mercantile class in numbers and wealth was weakening the hold of the old landed gentry and clergy on English government and policy. In the colonies where land was abundant, no class could monopolize all of it as the landlords of Virginia and the Hudson River valley were inclined to engross the land of their regions. On the frontiers freehold farmers who worked with their own hands were increasing in numbers and evolving ideas of their own.

Nowhere were the class lines absolutely rigid. Many, if not most, of the Southern planters had sprung from mercantile or farming families of England and new merchant immigrants were rising into their class. Farmers and artisans in the North were embarking on careers as merchants, lawyers, or clergymen. Indentured servants, as they worked out their terms of service, were becoming freehold farmers and winning elections to colonial legislatures, even in Virginia.

In other words a leveling of individuals and families proceeded rapidly in the colonies soon after the first settlements were planted. According to Voltaire, "History is full of the sound of wooden shoes going upstairs and the patter of silken slippers coming downstairs." In Great Britain and Europe this process—or its reverse—filled the seventeenth and eighteenth centuries with tumult and revolution. In the colonies wooden shoes seemed to be climbing up the stairs steadily as farms and industries multiplied and as commerce expanded.

In no way was the process better illustrated than in the case of indentured white servants. After their term of service expired some of them were able to climb the social stairs by marrying into already prosperous families. Others were able to get land by outright purchase or on mortgage or merely by going to the frontier and settling down upon it as "squatters." Indentured artisans and merchants' clerks, by the hundreds, went into industry or trade for themselves as soon as they were released from their obligations to those who had bought their labor. In the seventeenth century, it is estimated, at least 100,000 servants rose from bondage to freedom. Many, no doubt, continued to be laborers on farms or in towns, but thousands either acquired land or an established position as craftsmen or merchants; and occasionally they became planters or clergymen.

Generally speaking, this leveling up process, which intruded upon the order cherished by landlords and merchants of patrician temper, South and North, went on quietly, but at times it was accompanied by disturbances bordering on revolution. Mutterings appeared early. In the very cabin of the *Mayflower*, as it rode in the harbor of Plymouth, some of the members of the Pilgrim band made "discontented and mutinous speeches" and threatened that they "would use their own liberty" when they landed. Such mutterings had something to do with the decision to draw up the Mayflower Compact binding the Pilgrims to that plan of government.

Nearly everywhere independent pioneers and indentured workers made trouble by running off to the frontier, building homes of their own in the wilderness fringes of the colonies, and demanding from the older communities protection and equal rights in colonial government. In Virginia in 1676 frontier discontent with the policy and actions of the royal governor broke out in a rebellion led by Nathaniel Bacon; it was only suppressed, after a long struggle, by desperate measures on the part of the governor. During the spring and summer of 1766 farmers and tenants of great landlords in the Hudson River valley raised "the great rebellion" against the exactions of landed monopolists and were not put down until troops had been called out against them.

The leveling up process as facts and ideas controverted the system and ideas of government which Byrd, Sewall, and Boucher supported in their conformity to upper-class law and order of the British type. With the steady increase in the number of small farmers the representation of farmers in colonial legislatures grew in strength and the very basis of government was examined by inquiring minds in the colonies. On what did government rest—the prescriptive rights of king, lords, clergy, and merchants?

No, said John Wise, of Ipswich, Massachusetts, in 1717. Wise was the son of an indentured servant, born in 1652, while many founders of the colony were still living. Educated at Harvard College, he entered the Congregational ministry. As a young man he resisted the attempts of the temporary royal governor, Edmund Andros, to impose taxes on the people of his town, was arrested, tried, convicted, and put under bonds to keep the peace. But after Andros was ousted and until his death in 1725 Wise battled for popular rights.

With reference to government, Wise took the ground that "democracy" is "the form of government which the light of nature does highly value, and often directs to as most agreeable to the just and natural prerogatives of human beings. . . . The natural equality amongst men must be duly favored. . . . government was never established by God or nature, to give one man a prerogative to insult over another. . . . The end of all good government is to cultivate humanity, and promote the happiness of all, and the good of every man in his rights, his life, liberty, estate, honor, etc., without injury or abuse to any." In effect, as early as 1717, John Wise rejected the very basis of government by privileged classes then defended in England and the colonies by conformists in State and Church.

A few years after John Wise died a son was born to Joseph and Mary Baker Allen, at Litchfield, Connecticut, in 1738. They named him Ethan. It is said that he was preparing to enter college when the death of his father threw upon him the burden of fending for himself. After serving in the French and Indian War, he went to the frontier of New Hampshire, to the region soon to be known as Vermont, where he engaged in land speculation and farming.

Somehow, somewhere, Allen learned to read and write and acquired the habit of reading books. Writing autobiographically about his reading, he said: "Ever since I arrived at the state of manhood and acquainted myself with the general history of mankind, I have felt a sincere passion for liberty. The history of nations doomed to perpetual slavery, in consequence of yielding up to tyrants their natural-born liberties, I read with a sort of philosophical horror; so that the first systematical and bloody attempt, at Lexington, to enslave America, thoroughly electrified my mind, and fully determined me to take part with my country."

Whether the leveling process went on silently or amid uproar, it was accompanied by "subversive" ideas no less definite and positive than the conventional ideas expressed by Byrd, Sewall, Boucher, and gentlemen of their school—ideas of a different type, based not on theological mandates or the mere legal rights of Englishmen. While yeomen of New Jersey were waging a ten-year conflict between 1745 and 1754 against the claims of great landlords, they uttered provocative doctrines. "No man," they declared, "is naturally entitled to a greater proportion of the earth than another," and land "was made for the equal use of all." By what right then could any person claim the ownership of land? Their answer to this question rested not on existing "law and order" but on what they called "natural justice." A person may appropriate land, they contended, "by the improvement of any part of it lying vacant"; and after a man has thus bestowed his labor upon such a piece of land, it cannot afterward be taken away from him, "without breaking thro' the rule of natural justice; for thereby he would be actually deprived of the fruits of his industry."

☆

In the young colonial societies where the majority of the people belonged to freehold farming families and where class lines, though marked, were so fluid that former indentured servants could and did rise to membership in legislative assemblies, radical sentiments and ideas respecting life and labor, differing from those in England, gained in force. In the mother country, where land was limited in amount and all privately owned, most workers on the soil were tenants or day laborers on the estates of great landlords; and the social lines between the upper classes and the masses of the people were sharply drawn. Essentially true was an old couplet, even if there was something ironical in it:

> God bless the squire [landlord] and his relations,
> And keep us all in our proper stations.

To the majority of American farmers and artisans, who had no fixed "station," such sentiments were not only unreal but offensive.

To American merchants they were equally objectionable. Americans by the hundreds of thousands, amid different circumstances, held tenaciously to other views of themselves, their opportunities, and their duties. And as the colonies grew older—more populous, more self-sustaining in agriculture, commerce, and industry—intellectual leaders formulated American doctrines into a systematic program of thought about American affairs.

In their searching, thinking, speaking, and writing, these intellectual leaders touched upon every major theme that interested reflective colonists and had a bearing on their growth in economic, political, intellectual, and moral power. They raised and answered in their way at least four fundamental questions: What is the origin of human government and by what right does one set of men make laws for, and govern, all the rest of the people? What is the place of the colonists in the British Empire and what rights do they and should they enjoy as British subjects in America and primarily as human beings? What are the sciences, arts, and opportunities of commerce which will promote the economic and social welfare of the American people? What, after all, are the great ends of human life and how may men and women best attain them?

To these questions in one form or another American minds directed their attention and gave answers which in sum made up an American ideology that clashed with the ideology of the British governing class and their allies in the American colonies. The nature of this great American inquiry and the duty of Americans to pursue it were eloquently described by John Adams in 1765:

"Let us dare to read, think, speak and write. Let every order and degree among the people rouse their attention and animate their resolution. Let them all become attentive to the grounds and principles of government, ecclesiastical and civil. Let us study the law of nature; search into the spirit of the British constitution; read the histories of ancient ages; contemplate the great examples of Greece and Rome; set before us the conduct of our own British ancestors, who have defended for us the inherent rights of mankind against foreign and domestic tyrants and usurpers, against arbitrary kings and cruel priests; in short, against the gates of earth and hell.

"Let us read and recollect and impress upon our souls the views and ends of our own more immediate forefathers, in exchanging their native country for a dreary, inhospitable wilderness. Let us examine into the nature of that power, and the cruelty of that oppression, which drove them from their homes. Recollect their amazing fortitude, their bitter sufferings,—the hunger, the nakedness, the cold, which they patiently endured,—the severe labors of clearing their grounds, building their houses, raising their provisions, amidst dangers from wild beasts and savage men, before they had time or money or materials for commerce. Recollect the civil and religious principles and hopes and expectations which constantly supported and carried them through all hardships with patience and resignation. Let us recollect it was liberty, the hope of liberty for themselves and us and ours, which conquered all discouragements, dangers, and trials. . . .

"Let the pulpit resound with the doctrines and sentiments of religious liberty. Let us hear the danger of thralldom to our consciences from ignorance, extreme poverty, and dependence, in short, from civil and political slavery. Let us see delineated before us the true map of man. Let us hear the dignity of his nature, and the noble rank he holds among the works of God,—that consenting to slavery is a sacrilegious breach of trust, as offensive in the sight of God as it is derogatory from our own honor or interest or happiness,—and that God Almighty has promulgated from heaven, liberty, peace, and good will to man!

"Let the bar proclaim, 'the laws, the rights, the generous plan of power' delivered down from remote antiquity—inform the world of the mighty struggles and numberless sacrifices made by our ancestors in defense of freedom. Let it be known that British liberties are not the grants of princes or parliaments but original rights, conditions of original contracts, are coequal with prerogative, and coeval with government; that many of our rights are inherent and essential, agreed on as maxims, and established as preliminaries, even before a parliament existed. Let them search for the foundations of British laws and government in the frame of human nature, in the constitution of the intellectual and moral world. There let us see that truth, liberty, justice, and benevolence, are its everlasting basis; and if these could be removed, the superstructure is overthrown of course.

"Let the colleges join their harmony in the same delightful concert. Let every declamation turn upon the beauty of liberty and virtue, and the deformity, turpitude, and malignity, of slavery and vice. Let the public disputations become researches into the grounds and nature and ends of government, and the means of preserving the good and demolishing the evil. Let the dialogues, and all the exercises, become the instruments of impressing on the tender mind, and of spreading and distributing far and wide, the ideas of right and the sensations of freedom.

"In a word, let every sluice of knowledge be opened and set a-flowing. The encroachments upon liberty in the reigns of the first James and the first Charles, by turning the general attention of learned men to government, are said to have produced the greatest number of consummate statesmen which has ever been seen in any age or nation. The Brookes, Hampdens, Vanes, Seldens, Miltons, Nedhams, Harringtons, Nevilles, Sidneys, Lockes, are all said to have owed their eminence in political knowledge to the tyrannies of those reigns. The prospect now before us in America, ought in the same manner to engage the attention of every man of learning, to matters of power and of right, that we may be neither led nor driven blindfolded to irretrievable destruction."

The business of making these inquiries into fundamentals of intellectual and social life was not monopolized by any small class of persons. It was carried on, as John Adams urged, by "every order and degree among the people"—by multitudes of people in homes, taverns, churchyards, town meetings, and at crossroads stores; by men and women of humble origins and occupations as well as by those who enjoyed the advantages of leisure and higher education. Yet four groups of persons led the great inquest into American rights, duties, and problems: clergymen, lawyers, physicians, and publishers and publicists. And all members of these groups had audiences to hear what they had to say or to read what they wrote in pamphlets, books, and newspaper articles. Furthermore, in homes, in secondary schools, and in colleges, from generation to generation, new leaders were given the rudiments of learning upon which to build in carrying on inquiries and formulating answers.

Primarily charged with the care of souls, clergymen devoted themselves mainly to religious affairs. But then, as ever, no clear line was drawn between the things that belonged to God and the things assigned to Caesar. The Anglican Church, a state church in England and in several colonies, was associated with English policies of state. But the immense majority of the colonists belonged to dissenting and non-conformist denominations. Early in the history of New England, the Puritans became independents in religion and stoutly resisted all encroachments by the English Crown and Church. Presbyterians objected with equal vigor to the doctrines and methods of the Anglican Church and insisted on having liberty for their faith and worship. Besides, many of them had suffered under English legislation directed against their economic interests in their old home in the north of Ireland and had carried to the colonies piercing remembrances of that experience. Baptists and Quakers had undergone persecution in England and strove against any tightening of the English grip on the religious life of the colonies.

Outside the Anglican communion, accordingly, the clergy were concerned with increasing the dissidence of dissent, educating their flocks in dissidence, and fortifying non-conformity. While their sermons and writings were largely theological, many clergymen were interested in all the great questions of human rights, government, and social duty raised in the growth of American economy. They preached on such subjects to congregations from one end of the colonies to the other. They taught their doctrines in the schools over which they presided and wrote pamphlets for general circulation.

The eighteenth century had not advanced far when lawyers began to dispute the intellectual preëminence of the clergy. In the early stages of settlement there was little business for lawyers and dislike for their profession existed in many circles. Throughout the colonial period, in fact, Puritan divines were inclined to look down upon them as a lower order of human beings. When, for instance, the Reverend William Smith learned that his daughter was inclined toward marriage with John Adams, he was distressed; for young Adams was not only the son of a dirt farmer; he was also a lawyer. On principle, the Quakers were opposed to lawyers; they insisted that disputes among members of the meeting should always be settled by private negotiation. It was in Virginia and South Carolina that lawyers were first heartily welcomed and given high standing in the best society.

Yet as the colonies approached maturity, lawyers were prominent everywhere in the cities from Boston to Charleston, and were scattered around in the inland regions. In New England the litigation connected with commerce had become too complicated for field-stump and corner-store justice. In Philadelphia, where Quakers were growing worldly, lawyers flourished and were famous throughout the North for their learning, shrewdness, and boldness. At Williamsburg and Charleston, the Bar was crowded by distinguished attorneys.

Lawyers, if intellectually enterprising, were more than students of law and government. Engaged in litigation for their clients, they were accustomed to preparing briefs—or statements of facts and law—and making oral arguments before judges and juries.

They were acquainted with the art of public speaking and many of them studied the art as represented in the speeches of Cicero and the speeches of statesmen in the British Parliament. Wherever there was a controversy, public or private, lawyers were interested and the best of them could "make a powerful case" for the side on which they were enlisted; that is, marshal facts, lay down ruling principles applicable to the facts, and order facts and principles in a logical form, appealing to sentiments of their supporters and commanding the attention, if not always the respect, of their opponents.

For the practice of law in any case, some intellectual preparation was necessary. There was no law school in any of the colonies and there was no professorship of law at any of the colleges. But leading lawyers usually had some preliminary training at a college and often young men of wealthy families, especially in the South, studied at the Inns of Court in London. Whatever their early education, lawyers had to read one or more legal treatises and the statutes of their colony. The ablest and most intellectual among them read widely in the classics, in works on history, jurisprudence, government, and the relation of the law to the people and the economy of the society in which it was made and enforced.

As the colonial period drew toward a close physicians were also outstanding among intellectual leaders, especially at Philadelphia, the great medical center of the colonies. About 1750, it is estimated, at least eighty-two physicians and surgeons were practicing in that city, many of them trained at the medical school of Edinburgh or on the Continent. While some of them adhered strictly to the professional line, many others took a keen interest in civic affairs and allied themselves with the autonomous tendencies. The latter promoted the arts, music, higher education, the establishment of libraries, and the building of social institutions such as hospitals and homes for the impoverished. Thomas Bond, for example, who had completed his medical education abroad and long practiced with success, joined the Revolutionary Committee of Safety in 1776 and rendered service to the Revolutionary army. Benjamin Rush, distinguished in the medical profession, took an interest in most great public questions from education to the abolition of slavery, was elected to the Continental Congress, signed the Declaration of Independence, and for a time was surgeon general of the Middle Department armies.

Important as were clergy, lawyers, and physicians in shaping American opinion and forming the ideology of American automony, they had able assistants in independent editors and publicists who wrote articles for newspapers and pamphlets for general circulation. Among all the colonists so engaged, Benjamin Franklin, the publisher and businessman, was especially versatile, active, and influential. For the Pennsylvania *Gazette* and for *Poor Richard's Almanack*, which he published, he wrote articles, short and long, on nearly every subject—scientific, moral, and economic—bearing on the affairs of the colonists. These he supplemented by pamphlets on various topics, such as the vital money question. Although his publishing house was in Philadelphia, his writings circulated widely in the North and the South.

☆

Intellectual leaders in America, from those of community or colony prestige to those of intercolonial or international reputation, had at their command, to inform, inspire, and strengthen their minds, a growing literature on American themes. In this literature, by 1750, there were actually thousands of printed titles, running from large volumes to pamphlets, tracts, and broadsides. When intellectual and social autonomy approached its maturity, there was scarcely a nook or cranny of the seaboard region that had not been explored and described by able writers; scarcely a branch of American economy and social life that had not been written up with more or less fullness; scarcely an American institution or custom on which information was lacking to inquiring minds; scarcely an American idea or aspiration unrecorded in print for the instruction of those who searched for enlightenment on that score.

This immense literature included: histories of individual settlements and colonies—such as Robert Beverly, *History of Virginia* (1705), William Smith, *History of the Province of New York* (1757), and Thomas Prince, *A Chronological History of New England* in two volumes (1736–55); books of travel and surveys describing various parts of the colonial dominion—for example, John Archdale, *A New Description . . . of Carolina* (1707), and John Bartram, *Observations on the Inhabitants, Climate, Soil, Rivers, Production, Animals and Other Matters Worthy of Notice* from Pennsylvania to Canada (1751); books on natural philosophy and the practical arts—for instance, Samuel Johnson, *An Introduction to the Study of Philosophy, Exhibiting a General View of All the Arts and Sciences* (1743); books on social morality, including John Woolman, *Considerations on Pure Wisdom, and Human Policy; on Labour* . . . (1768); works on phases of economy and government—as illustrations, Benjamin Franklin, *A Modest Enquiry into the Nature and Necessity of a Paper Currency* (1729) and *An Historical Review of the Constitution and Government of Pennsylvania* (1759). If, as had been said in ancient times, "knowledge is power," American colonials were fortunate in having ample stores of it within their reach.

Intellectual leaders intent on exploring theories of society in general and American relations to the government of Great Britain in particular also had at hand works which they had imported from abroad and kept in their libraries, private and public, for ready use. From these they selected germinal ideas, gave to them meaning in the light of their peculiar experiences in a New World, and applied them, so interpreted, to the accomplishment of their purposes.

Among the imported works generally read in the colonies by assiduous students and thinkers, four were of unquestioned influence on American intellectual leadership:

1628—Edward Coke, *Coke upon Littleton*. Treatise on the legal rights of English subjects, defending them against encroachments by Crown and Church. A textbook on common law for colonial students of law.

1690—John Locke, *Treatise of Government*. Philosophic justification of the Revolution of 1688 in England. Traced the origin of government to a compact among the people made for the protection of their lives and property and asserted the right of revolution to assure such protection against tyranny.

1748—Montesquieu, *Esprit des Lois*. Soon in translations. Dealt with the material and social backgrounds of law and government. An early treatise on "sociological jurisprudence."

1757—Adam Ferguson, *An Essay on the History of Civil Society*. A work on the origins and progress of civil societies (civilization), on social relations, and on human beings as active, creative, and progressive creatures.

Americans of searching intellectual curiosity also had at their command, either imported or from their own presses, books reflecting all the main tendencies of thought in the Old World respecting the nature of mankind's universe. They read, discussed, and wrote about these tendencies so widely that the chief ideas which were shaking Great Britain and Europe became common in all the colonies. And what were these chief ideas?

The rationalism in the work of Sir Isaac Newton that eliminated arbitrary interferences of God in the physical universe, the old basis of astrology and other superstitions.

Deism—rejecting the Hebraic and Miltonic interpretation of the cosmos and substituting, for Jehovah, the universal God of all mankind. As Alexander Pope expressed it:

> *Father of all! in every age,*
> *In every clime adored,*
> *By saint, by savage, and by sage . . .*

The idea of progress—now fortified by the new science and by Voltaire's social history, which rejected the theological view that the earth is a temporary place of misery and maintained that advance in arts, sciences, and social improvement is the supreme destiny of mankind.

The doctrine of natural rights—that all people everywhere, whatever their status, are entitled to the rights of life, liberty, property, and the pursuit of happiness.

The idea of the pursuit of happiness on earth as a legitimate and worthy aspiration of the human spirit. "O happiness! our being's end and aim! Good, pleasure, ease, content! whate'er thy name," wrote Pope in his *Essay on Man*.

The doctrine of utility—that usefulness in well-being is the test of things, institutions, and actions.

As these ideas circulating in Europe presented a revolutionary contradiction to the ideology of kings, lords, clergy, peasants, and serfs, so in America they ran counter to the conservative practices of British overlordship. Not only that. They acquired additional force in America on account of the fact that Americans, as contrasted with Europeans, were in possession of the natural resources that made possible the easier realization of these ideas.

So in America, as in the Old World, the Battle of the Books raged. If William Byrd, in Virginia, could read his *Lucian*, the Greek satirist of the second century, A.D., laugh at the follies of mankind, and learn contempt for everything except his own pleasure and interests, Thomas Jefferson in Virginia could draw from the new writers—Locke, Ferguson, and Pope—a faith in mankind and human progress that prepared him in letter and spirit to write and proclaim the declaration of complete autonomy—independence.

☆

It was not merely to a small, exclusive set of upper-class persons that writers on American matters directed their articles, pamphlets, and books. They wrote for a large audience, for a popular audience, for men and women belonging to farming and artisan classes as well as to the ranks of clergymen, lawyers, professors, physicians, schoolmasters, planters, and merchants.

No census of the number of colonists over ten years of age who could read and write was ever taken, but the number was certainly large. The extensive sale of books, pamphlets, almanacs, magazines, and newspapers was one indication that there was a wide reading public in all parts of America. Foreign travelers in the eighteenth century were deeply impressed by the amount of reading that was done in homes and in taverns "on the house," and they contrasted this mental alertness with the stolidity of the ignorant masses in their own countries. So plainly were American writers taking the people at large into account, as readers, that strangers interested in classes and masses seldom failed to make note of it as a sign of distinction in the intellectual development of the colonies.

How had the large public learned to read? To Protestantism must be attributed the main source of this wide literacy. The colonial population was overwhelmingly Protestant and a tenet of dissenting faith was the right of everyone to read the Bible for himself instead of listening merely to its exposition by priests. Hence the Protestant clergy, especially among Puritans, Baptists, and Presbyterians, made it one of their prime duties to see that children of their sects acquired the ability to read and actually carried reading forward, as they grew up, with a sense of religious obligation.

In extending literacy by means of public schools New England stood apart. Homogeneity in population and religious faith characterized that region. There legislation, beginning with the Massachusetts statute of 1642, required the towns to make some provision for giving the rudiments of learning to those children who did not get them at home. In many places this fiat was more honored in the breach than by observance, but in time all the better New England communities had public primary schools of some type. In other parts of colonial America, dissenting sects—Baptist, Quaker, Presbyterian, Lutheran, and Huguenot—also established town and field schools in which children learned elementary reading, writing, and arithmetic. Such schools were supplemented by private enterprise. Schoolmasters and schoolmistresses conducted private elementary schools, usually in their homes; and itinerant teachers journeyed about "holding school" for short periods of the year wherever a few pupils could be collected and fees obtained.

In thickly populated districts, especially in the larger towns, to elementary schools were added grammar schools and academies at which boys and girls were taught more advanced subjects. Secondary schools founded by private interests often catered to sons and daughters of the upper classes, especially boys on their way to college and girls preparing for the life of "polite society"; their curricula included the classics, mathematics, English literature, and frequently French. But secondary schools were not all of that type. Perhaps more generally, particularly in the middle colonies, they adapted their instruction to the needs of boys and girls who had to look forward early to earning a livelihood by their own efforts. At all events secondary schools gave thousands of Americans a more than elementary training for reading newspapers, pamphlets, and books; for taking part in the discussions of public affairs; and for sharing in the growth of social and intellectual autonomy.

It was mainly to religious motives that colleges, like elementary schools, owed their foundations. Massachusetts was only a few years old when, in 1636, Harvard College was established, primarily to train "learned and godly Ministers." A similar purpose led to the creation of a college at Killingworth in Connecticut in 1701—an institution afterward moved to New Haven and in 1718 given the name of Yale College. William and Mary, organized in Virginia in 1693, and King's College, founded in New York City in 1754, were intended as centers for the advanced education of Anglican men. The College of New Jersey, started in 1747 and removed to Princeton in 1756, relied mainly on Presbyterians for support and guidance. Dartmouth College began to function in 1767 as a Puritan mission to the Indians.

Two colonial colleges were less exclusive in sectarian sponsorship: Brown, founded in Rhode Island in 1764, was interdenominational; a majority of its board of trustees were Baptists, but Congregationalists, Anglicans, and Quakers were included in the membership. The Philadelphia Academy, forerunner of the University of Pennsylvania, formally opened in 1751, also admitted to its board of trustees members of various faiths; and Benjamin Franklin, its arch promoter, would have turned it into secular channels if he could have kept its control in his hands. Franklin, however, was outmaneuvered by the provost, William Smith, an invincible Anglican who gradually managed to dominate this institution.

The instruction offered by colleges included secular learning. The presidents and the professors were generally ministers of religion but, whatever their professions of faith, they opened the gateways to the accumulated knowledge of the ages and colonial writings on every theme. Young men admitted to the colleges all had an opportunity to master classical languages and were given access to the learning of antiquity, for example, to the politics and morals of Aristotle and Plato and the ethics of Seneca and Plutarch as well as the historical writings of Tacitus and the constitutional works of Cicero. Thin as they were, modeled on Oxford and Cambridge patterns, the colonial college curricula contained instruction in the elements of moral or natural philosophy, contemporary science, and a drill in logic that sharpened young men's wits for inquiry and argumentation, in the event that they made use of this drill. Within college walls leaders were trained for all the intellectual activities that marked the growth of the colonies into mature and autonomous societies.

☆

Yet in the acquisition of learning, the development of intellectual powers, and the spread of knowledge and conceptual thought, formal education played a minor role in colonial times. Relatively speaking, only a few men had the benefit of college education and those who did gained from it only a limited body of knowledge. On entering business, professional, or political careers, college graduates often found themselves in intellectual competition with men of little formal training who were their peers, if not their superiors, in mental power. Thomas Jefferson was a graduate of William and Mary College; John Marshall was not a graduate of any college. John Adams attended Harvard; Benjamin Franklin was among the founders of a college, never a student in one. All over the country, in communities large and small, on farms and plantations as well as in towns and cities, men and women who had got the rudiments of an education from their fathers and mothers or hired tutors spent laborious days and nights lifting their education by their own efforts, inspired by their intellectual curiosities and other desires.

Self-education on the higher levels was especially the way of women, to whom the doors of colleges were closed. Eliza Pinckney, of South Carolina, which had no college, went on reading and learning, after her youthful studies in England, as the impulse of her own mind and spirit directed. Abigail Adams and Mercy Otis Warren, of Massachusetts, could not go to Harvard; and Abigail lamented the lack of equal education for women, but how well she could think and write is attested by her letters to her husband and family and friends. Mercy Otis had studied the same subjects under the same tutors as her brother, James Otis, previous to his departure for Harvard. She could not follow him there despite their close intellectual companionship, but she did follow where her mind continued to lead her, learning all the time independently. Anna Maulin Zenger, of New York, who took over the publication of John Peter Zenger's New York *Weekly Journal*, after his death in 1746, must have acquired her education and competence for editing largely by her own efforts, like the numerous other women journalists in the colonies. And even in lonely cabins on the frontiers women as well as men frequently educated themselves and opened for their children the paths leading to the knowledge that enabled them to win high places in the public service. From his mother George Wythe, born on a Virginia plantation in 1726, learned the Latin language and he eventually studied jurisprudence by himself. He was of great influence in the intellectual development of Jefferson.

☆

Books, pamphlets, and tracts that passed from reader to reader, formal instruction in schools, the dissemination of learning by fathers and mothers, training at home by private tutors, formed only a part of the process by which Americans were equipped with knowledge and ideas for dealing with affairs private and public. After the opening of the eighteenth century, newspapers added instruction on current issues to the colonial college curriculum dealing mainly with the past. In April 1704 John Campbell at Boston brought out the first number of the first American newspaper, the Boston *News-Letter*, a periodical so hardy that it lasted till independence was declared. In 1719 Andrew Bradford established in Philadelphia the *American Mercury*. In November 1725 the New York *Gazette* came from the press of William Bradford.

From these beginnings, journalism spread to other colonies in the following order of time:

> 1727—Annapolis, Maryland.
> 1732—Charleston, South Carolina.
> 1732—Newport, Rhode Island.
> 1736—Williamsburg, Virginia.
> 1755—New Haven, Connecticut.
> 1755—New Bern, North Carolina.
> 1762—Wilmington, Delaware.
> 1763—Savannah, Georgia.
> 1777—Burlington, New Jersey.

Among the early newspapers the rate of change and mortality was high as competitors appeared in the leading cities; but this signified a growth and persistence in journalism—signs of new thinking and action for those who could see them.

In the columns of newspapers Americans could learn about many things that were going on in the colonies as well as overseas. The small pages of these papers contained brief notes on British and European "occurrences," reports of happenings in the neighborhood and in other colonies, advertisements of commodities in bewildering varieties for sale at merchants' shops, letters from pleased and irate readers on questions of public interest, and essays on events, manners, morals, customs, and politics. Always under the watchful eyes of royal governors, proprietors, or politicians, colonial editors had to be circumspect in discussing disputes among Americans or between Americans and British officials, but as time passed they became more adroit in their retreating and advancing maneuvers. From the journals of other colonies, local editors in each town clipped notices of general interest and made reports to their communities. Ship captains sailing from port to port and postboys traveling from point to point carried news for editors to use. When, for example, the great agrarian rebellion of 1766 occurred in the Hudson Valley, accounts of it appeared in the newspapers of Boston and Philadelphia as well as in the New York press. Provincial journalism was merging into American journalism.

The dissemination of knowledge and ideas, news, information, and misinformation was facilitated by the rise and growth of a colonial postal system. As early as 1639 the legislature of Massachusetts made provision for a local post office and this example was followed by other colonies as they grew in size and population. Under a royal patent of 1692 an intercolonial postal service was established as a private enterprise. Fifteen years later it was taken over by the English government and developed under successive postmasters general, Benjamin Franklin assuming that office in 1753.

In the course of time post roads were extended, new local offices established, the speed of transmission increased, and packet lines to England and to coastal ports were started. Day and night, through the years, post riders, stages, and coastal ships kept communications throughout the colonies open. Correspondence among citizens, once local and restricted, became general. Newspapers issued for local circulation reached out in influence beyond their communities and broadened the scope of their contents accordingly. The circulation of knowledge and ideas was being enlarged. The provincial mind was becoming American in its range of interest and in the subject matter of its concern.

CHAPTER VI

Practicing the Arts of Self-Government

Accompanying the growth of autonomy in agriculture, industry, commerce, social relations, and intellectual powers, indeed mingled with every phase of it, was a training in the arts of self-government which prepared colonists for asserting their political and economic rights against British authorities and for managing their own political affairs. From the beginning government played a necessary and formative role in the founding and development of the colonies. At the outset, the Crown granted charters and privileges to companies and proprietors, bestowed upon them huge areas of land, and laid down rules as to how they should divide and sell their land and govern the people who settled in their domains. During the entire colonial period the government in London furnished military and naval assistance in protecting the colonies against Spanish and French attacks and at times against Indian raids on the frontier. Without the guardianship of the English government, therefore, individuals and groups would have been unable to cross the seas in safety and to lay on this continent the foundations of the American nation.

"The people," unaided and unprotected by government, did not put out on the sea, land on the shores of America, and establish colonies. At no moment, as the tiny settlements spread into great and prosperous colonies, was government absent from the scene. There was government in the mapping, division, and sale of the lands to be taken up and cultivated by farmers and planters. There was government in protection of the settlements against internal disorders and external foes. There was government protection and encouragement of commerce between the colonies and European countries as well as with the motherland; and without this commerce the colonies in America could not have become prosperous and powerful. However energetic, industrious, and enterprising the people might have been as individuals and groups, it would have been impossible for them to found and build up the colonies by their own efforts. Government was for them indispensable at every step in the starting and progress of the colonies.

This was true, of course, of the Spanish and French colonies but there was one fundamental difference between the policy of the French and Spanish governments and the policy of the English government. French and Spanish colonies were ruled absolutely by royal governors who held office at royal pleasure. In those colonies the inhabitants were not allowed to take an active part in making their own laws, laying taxes, choosing officials, and deciding how public affairs were otherwise to be managed. On the other hand, in all the English colonies a considerable portion of the inhabitants enjoyed a large measure of self-government; in some, from the very beginning and in others after they were securely established. To the development of independence and liberty, exercising the rights of self-government in some measure at least was as essential as the activities in agriculture, industry, business enterprise, and every other phase of autonomous unfolding.

To appreciate the importance of political privileges in the making of the American nation, it is only necessary to imagine what would have happened if every colony had been governed solely by a royal agent from London, endowed with dictatorial powers to make and enforce laws of every kind—laws for dividing and selling the lands; for laying out towns and managing farms and industries; for imposing and collecting taxes as heavy or heavier than the people could bear; for controlling speech, press, and religious worship; for regulating the kinds of work to be done and assigning people to their tasks. If wholly autocratic policies had been pursued by the English government in the colonies, the American people would have felt crushed, and liberty might have been stifled. What is more, the colonists would not have learned the arts of self-government so necessary to the establishment and maintenance of independence, the making of popular constitutions, and the management of local, national, and foreign affairs.

☆

Running through the long period from the founding of Jamestown in 1607 to the declaring of independence in 1776 were two opposing tendencies in colonial government. The first was the development of local legislatures, or lawmaking bodies, consisting in every case of one house elected by the qualified voters and in all colonies, except Pennsylvania and Delaware, of an upper chamber or council or body of assistants. The second tendency was a strengthening of royal power in America by the transformation of eight colonies into royal provinces, each headed by a royal governor appointed by the British Crown.

The Virginia colony was only a few years old when the London Company decreed that the power of its local governor and council should be limited by a local assembly, called the House of Burgesses, to be elected by the voters. In 1619 members of the House of Burgesses were chosen; and the legislature, duly assembled, began to make laws respecting the management of local affairs.

Before the Pilgrims actually set to work at Plymouth in 1620, the men of that little band met in the cabin of the *Mayflower* and drew up a document celebrated in history as the Mayflower Compact. By solemn written agreement they bound themselves together in a "civil body politic," to make "just and equal laws" for the government of the colony, and promised to obey such laws when enacted. The founders of Massachusetts Bay, who followed the Pilgrims to America ten years later, brought their charter with them. After governing themselves directly for a time by meetings of the members, they established in 1634 an assembly composed of representatives from each town.

Even proprietors could not be complete autocrats in the domains granted them by the King. The charter which gave Lord Baltimore the right to found his colony in Maryland required him in due course to seek the consent of the freemen in making laws. Within a short time after the first settlements were made, in 1635, an assembly representing the freemen was set up in Maryland.

In 1639 the men of the towns founded on the Connecticut River by emigrants from Massachusetts drew up for their colony the "Fundamental Orders of Connecticut"—a document called "the first written constitution known to history which created a government." The Orders provided for a general assembly, or "Court," composed of representatives from each of the towns, and for a governor and magistrates to be elected annually. The people of the colony were thus bound together as "one public State or Commonwealth" and they were "to be guided and governed" in their civil affairs by the laws, orders, and decrees properly made by the government so organized.

In contemplation of growth, the Orders provided that new towns were to be given representation in the assembly, reasonably proportioned to the number of their freemen. Four years later, in 1643, the settlements on Long Island Sound united with New Haven in creating a representative legislature. Finally, the royal charter of 1662, which joined the two groups of settlements in Connecticut, made provision for popular government consisting of a governor, assistants, and representatives, all elected by the qualified voters. A similar system was established in Rhode Island.

As popular assemblies came into existence in the other colonies, one after another, they were formed on a common model. Representatives were assigned to each town, city, borough or county, and they were all to be elected by the voters who had the qualifications fixed by law.

The qualifications for the suffrage varied from place to place and from time to time. But on the eve of the Revolution the right to vote was generally restricted to men who owned property of specified amounts. In New York, for instance, voters for members of the assembly had to be freeholders of land or tenements to the value of £40 free from all encumbrances, except in New York City and Albany where all men formally admitted to civic rights as "freemen" could vote. In Pennsylvania the suffrage was restricted to the owners of fifty acres of land "well seated" with twelve acres "cleared," or other property worth at least £50 in lawful money. According to Virginia law the voter had to own at least fifty acres of land if there was no house on it or twenty-five acres with a house at least twelve feet square; or if a dweller in a town, he had to own a plot of ground with a house at least twelve feet square.

As a result of the various limitations on the suffrage a large proportion of the people in each colony were deprived of the vote; and many who were entitled to that privilege failed to exercise it in elections. In the rural districts of Pennsylvania about one person in ten had the right to vote and in Philadelphia only about one in fifty owned enough property to qualify for the exercise of the suffrage. At times in Massachusetts and Connecticut, where approximately sixteen per cent of the population were enfranchised, only two per cent took the trouble to vote. Similar conditions prevailed elsewhere. It was therefore only a small proportion, even of the freemen, who actually participated in the government of their respective colonies.

Nevertheless, there were in America, at the end of the colonial period, thousands of men who were acquainted practically with voting, managing local campaigns, and taking part in elections; and there were hundreds of men who were serving, or had served, as members of legislatures, in the making of laws and the supervision of law enforcement. When important issues were up for action, campaigns were often exciting. Even men and women who could not vote formed opinions about questions under popular consideration and shared in the discussions that went on in country and town.

But as a rule, by the end of the colonial period, the popular assembly was checked by an upper house or council. In seven of the eight royal provinces, members of the council were appointed by the royal governor; in Massachusetts they were elected by the lower house. In Connecticut all high authorities—governor, assistants, and representatives in the legislature—were elected by the voters. Of the proprietary colonies, Maryland alone had a legislative council, a kind of upper chamber, composed of councilors selected by the proprietor or his deputy; the legislature in Pennsylvania and Delaware consisted of a single house based on popular election.

Generally speaking, councilors or assistants were selected from prominent and wealthy families in the colony and exercised large powers in respect of lawmaking and the conduct of executive business. In the royal provinces they were, with some exceptions, warmly attached to the royal governor and the Crown and acted as a conservative force in blocking the desires and demands of the elected representatives in the lower house.

The powers possessed by the colonial legislature in the beginning, or acquired by practice, were extensive. It could make laws respecting the general and local affairs of the colony. It could lay various kinds of taxes for the support of the colonial government. It could appropriate money for public purposes, including the salaries of the governor and other officers. Speaking broadly, it was limited only by the provision that its acts must not be contrary to the laws of England or the terms of the colony's charter. Otherwise the assembly was fairly free to legislate on all matters pertaining to life, liberty, and property, subject to the veto of the governor in the royal and proprietary colonies and ultimately of the Crown in England.

☆

The second important tendency in the history of colonial government—the transformation of company and proprietary colonies into royal provinces, with governors chosen by the King—is traced in the following table showing the steps of this development in the direction of stronger royal control over American affairs:

> 1624—Virginia became a royal province.
> 1679—New Hampshire
> 1685—New York
> 1691—Massachusetts
> 1702—New Jersey, with a separate governor in 1728
> 1729—South Carolina
> 1729—North Carolina
> 1752—Georgia

By 1752, therefore, eight of the thirteen colonies were royal provinces; three were subject to proprietors—Maryland, Pennsylvania,

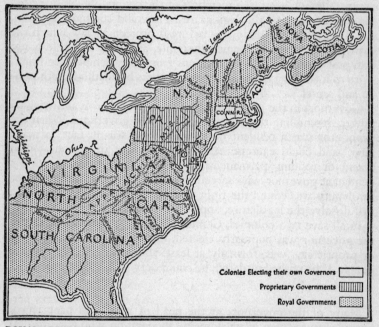

Colonies Electing their own Governors ☐
Proprietary Governments ▥
Royal Governments ▨

ROYAL, PROPRIETARY, AND CHARTER COLONIES ON THE EVE OF THE REVOLUTION

and Delaware; and only two had governors elected by assemblies of voters—Connecticut and Rhode Island.

The powers enjoyed and exercised by the King's governor in the royal province were both extensive and highly effective. He was really the viceroy of the King and exercised in the colony all the civil and military authority vested in him by the Crown. As chief executive he enforced the laws of England applicable to the colony and all the laws passed by the colonial legislature. He appointed, usually with the consent of the council, the important civil officers and directed them in the discharge of their duties. He acted as the head of the highest court in the colony, which tried important cases at first hand and heard appeals from the lower courts. The power of granting pardons and issuing reprieves was entrusted to him. In military affairs he was commander in chief of the colonial forces and appointed officers of high rank.

In relation to the legislature the royal governor also had many prerogatives. Not only did he choose in all the royal provinces, except Massachusetts, the members of the council which served as the upper house of the legislatures. He could summon, adjourn, and dissolve the assembly, lay before it projects of law which the Crown or he himself deemed desirable, and veto bills. He could hear and approve or reject petitions from the assembly, send messages to it, and try to influence its members by methods both public and secret.

Governors in the proprietary colonies had controls and wielded powers resembling those possessed by royal governors. When the proprietor was a resident of his colony he was in fact "a petty king" and could exercise executive authority in person. When absent or residing permanently in England, he acted through a lieutenant governor who served as his agent. In the proprietor or his deputy was vested the right to appoint high officials, summon and dissolve the legislature, approve or veto laws.

In all save two colonies, Connecticut and Rhode Island, where the governor was popularly elected, the colonial executive, royal or proprietary, was, formally at least, above responsibility to the people. If he wished or dared, he could defy public opinion.

☆

Many of the governors at the head of royal and proprietary provinces were men of wisdom and moderation who tried to deal amicably with the colonists. Yet they were all periodically in sharp conflict with the colonial assembly. Whatever their personal merits and views, they were expected to promote, if they could, the interests of the British government or of the proprietors, and to enforce, if they could, British law applicable to the colonies. Placed as they were between two fires—British masters and local assemblies—they were fortunate if a year passed without a quarrel of some kind. If a governor was stiff-necked, the colony over which he presided was likely to be in more or less of an uproar during his entire administration. Examples of such disturbances will illustrate the nature of the difficulties that arose between British governors and the colonists bent on having the substance as well as the form of self-government.

In 1642 Charles II sent over Sir William Berkeley to serve as royal governor of Virginia and for about thirty-five years Berkeley held that post. Along many lines he labored zealously for the welfare of the colony but in other respects he was a martinet. He was almost savage in persecuting Quakers and Puritans who ventured to settle in Virginia. He was opposed to newspapers and free schools and thanked God that Virginia had neither. With an iron hand he tried to keep all branches of the government under his own control. He insulted and cursed Virginians who were brash enough to resist his actions and object to his policies.

As the years passed, things went from bad to worse. When in 1676 he failed to take effective measures against marauding Indians, Berkeley found himself in the midst of an armed rebellion led by Nathaniel Bacon and was driven out of Jamestown. Recovering power for a short time, he put to death so many leaders in the rebellion that even the King of England was disgusted with him and appointed another governor to supersede him. "The old fool," Charles II was quoted as saying, "has killed more people in that naked country than I have done for the murder of my father."

A second illustration of the kind of serious troubles that could arise between a royal governor and colonial leaders occurred in New York under Governor William Cosby, who arrived to take office in 1732. In his dealings with the colonial assembly, Cosby managed to avoid bringing on a revolution, though he was brusque in manner and profane in language. But he quarreled fiercely with some members of his council and with leaders in local politics over jobs and money. He ousted from power the chief justice of New York. The displaced man, aided by rich friends, helped John Peter Zenger, a local printer, to establish a newspaper in New York City and attack the governor's policies in print.

Angered by attacks in Zenger's paper, Cosby took steps to have Zenger arrested and brought to trial for criminal libel. To the defense of Zenger came Andrew Hamilton, of Philadelphia, a lawyer

from that more liberal colony. Appealing eloquently to the jury
in the name of a free press and the right to publish the truth, Hamilton won a verdict of "not guilty" amid cheers from the people
who had crowded into the courtroom. Thus by an effort to curb
a printer, Cosby helped to make freedom of the press a cherished privilege in the American colonies, whether he was right or
wrong on his points of law.

Another type of royal governor and dispute appeared in Massachusetts in 1771 when Thomas Hutchinson was placed at the
head of that province. Hutchinson was born in Boston in 1711,
educated at Harvard, and, as a member of a rich and powerful
family of merchants, quickly rose to an influential position in
colonial politics. Though conservative in temper and loyal to the
King, he opposed many acts of Parliament, such as the Stamp Act,
as bad policy, and sought to pursue a moderate course. Yet he did
not deny the right of Parliament to tax and govern the colonies
according to its own desires; as governor he secretly encouraged
British authorities to adopt strong measures in dealing with colonial agitators. He quarreled with the Massachusetts assembly and
with Samuel Adams, leader in local resistance to British actions. In
an address to the legislature he declared that the supremacy of
Parliament must be admitted and that "the mere exercise of its
authority can be no grievance." Though a man of personal honor
and courage, eager to exert a moderating influence, Hutchinson
added fuel to the fires of discontent in Massachusetts. In 1774,
after the Boston Tea Party, he left for England and was never
able to return to America.

If proprietors had, as a rule, lived in their colonies, they might
have enjoyed greater powers as governors in their own right, but
most of them remained in England and acted through deputies
whom they chose to direct their colonial affairs. Naturally the
proprietary agent in a colony had less of pomp and circumstance
than a royal governor. Yet he had similar legal powers: to appoint members of the council, if there was one; to choose military and civil officers; to grant lands; to veto acts of the legislature; and to supervise the enforcement of the laws. Like the royal
governor, he might be on good terms or bad terms with the colonial legislature. Usually, in the best of conditions, he was more or
less in open conflict with it.

The Penns managed to hold fast to Pennsylvania and Delaware
until the Revolution broke their proprietorship. Although they
and their deputy governors had troubles enough, by twisting and

turning and making concessions to the legislature the Penns were able to keep their property until the rupture with Great Britain.

The career of the Baltimores in Maryland was more stormy. Between 1660 and 1689 they encountered four or five open revolts among their subjects. As a result Maryland was made a royal province. Not until a Protestant heir appeared in the Baltimore family was the colony restored to that family, in 1715, and then Catholics in Maryland were disfranchised.

In South Carolina it was a revolt against the proprietors which ended in the transformation of the colony into a royal province in 1729. Proprietary agents in the North Carolina district were no happier in the executive office. Between 1674 and 1729 six of the deputy governors were ousted by turbulent actions of the colonists, amounting on two occasions to open rebellion.

☆

In contests with royal and proprietary governors and in the ordinary management of legislative business, Americans by the hundreds learned to practice and think about the arts of government. They acquired training in drawing up bills and resolutions expressing their grievances, ideals, or demands. They could stand upon the floors of assemblies, defend the projects they favored, argue with their opponents, and carry on business in accordance with the rules of parliamentary law. They could draft petitions to the governor and appear before him to support their demands upon the executive. They could investigate the measures and deeds of officials in charge of law enforcement, and often compel the governor to remove them, by threats of withholding the money for the payment of their salaries.

No form or function of government in fact escaped their thought or experience. With the theory, practice, and arts of lawmaking and administration they became familiar. There was no work of that type in which they were wholly untrained; there were no mysteries veiled to their understanding. Thus through the years, if not wholly aware of it, Americans were equipping themselves to take over all branches of government, and to direct, as persons adept in the business, the public affairs of America.

As members of legislatures gained in political dexterity and wisdom, they insisted on having, holding, and exercising certain fundamental powers of government. Sometimes, in this respect, they gained ground; at other times they lost it. The lines of the battle with royal and proprietary governors swayed to and fro. But to many rights legislatures clung so stoutly that only a hardheaded and stubborn governor could override them for any long period. Among the claims asserted by the legislatures, nine were regarded by colonists as basic to liberty and self-government:

To introduce and enact bills on all matters of local and general interest in the colony, subject to the terms of the charter and English laws.

To fix the kinds and amounts of taxation to be laid on the people.

To pass upon the governor's actions in the nature of legislation.

To control the voting of money to pay salaries, including the governor's, and audit the disbursement of funds.

To create courts of law and regulate the salaries of judges.

To choose and pay agents charged with lobbying for or against measures pending in the Parliament or before royal officers in London.

To elect the speaker of the lower house.

To decide disputes over contested seats and check any resort to corruption on the part of the governor in elections.

To have periodical elections of members fixed by law at from two to five years.

Although members of the colonial legislature generally agreed on their rights as against the government of Great Britain, its agents, and the deputies of proprietors, they often differed violently respecting the way in which their colonial affairs were to be conducted. Representatives from districts occupied by owners of small farms were frequently at loggerheads with representatives from districts in which great landlords and merchants were numerous and powerful.

In part the roots of this conflict were sectional. From New York to Georgia, along the coastal plain and up to the headwaters of rivers emptying into the Atlantic, big landlords and merchants were usually in the ascendancy, clever enough to keep an upper hand in politics. In the frontier regions back of this coastal strip, small farmers were dominant.

Many and various were the grounds of strife between representatives of the seaboard and representatives of the frontier. As a rule the people of the seaboard had more representatives in the legislature than their numbers warranted and they wanted to run the colony to suit their ideas and interests. On the other hand, farmers from the back regions demanded more representatives in the assembly and more consideration of their ideas and interests. So within each colony, despite agreement on rights as against Great Britain, there were endless controversies over the concrete issues of representation, taxation, the disposition of Western lands, defense against the Indians, and matters of local government. In such controversies also, Americans gained experience in debating, lawmaking, and law enforcement.

☆

In local or community affairs, Americans in each colony were steadily educated and trained in the arts of self-government if on a small scale. Most of the people were engaged in agriculture and duly qualified men in large numbers shared in the local government of rural districts—towns or counties as the case might be.

Throughout New England and parts of the middle colonies the unit of government was the town—a small rural region, usually with a village or crossroads group of houses as a center. Such a town or township was governed by a meeting of the voters who chose its officers, levied taxes, appropriated money, and passed laws pertaining to roads, schools, bridges, and other local matters. There were counties in New England but they were mainly for judicial purposes. At the county seat a court held sessions for trying important civil and criminal cases and hearing appeals from town justices of the peace.

In Pennsylvania and the colonies to the south, the county was the chief unit of local administration. There local business was carried on by sheriffs, justices of the peace, coroners, and other officials, usually chosen by the governor of the colony.

So well entrenched was the system of local government that it was generally retained during and after the Revolution; indeed, it still exists, with some modifications here and there. Thus town and county "schools of government" furnished abundant opportunities for Americans to practice the arts of lawmaking and law enforcement. In the local schools of politics, leaders acquired training for action in the larger realm, colonial or intercolonial.

At many places cities and boroughs grew up in the course of colonial development. In New England they were governed by town meetings modeled on those existing in rural districts. In the middle and southern colonies, it became a custom to incorporate populous centers, such as New York, Albany, Trenton, Philadelphia, and Norfolk; that is, to give them charters and provide a kind of independent municipal government. As a rule the city charter was granted by the colonial governor. By charters qualified voters in a majority of the cities were given the right to elect members of the council and board of aldermen, who in turn chose the mayor and other city officials. In a few places, for example Philadelphia, Annapolis, and Norfolk, members of the city council were named in the original charter and empowered to choose their own successors as vacancies occurred.

Although the suffrage in cities was limited as a rule to the well-to-do classes and in some places there were no popular elections at all, many inhabitants had some share in conducting municipal affairs. Besides, urban residents, if they owned enough property to qualify for the suffrage, took part in electing members to the colonial assembly. So, for one reason or another, townspeople became "politically minded." Nowhere were they just an inert mass ruled by agents of royal governors.

☆

Active as thousands of Americans were in the local and central governments of their respective colonies, they had little to do with the relations of the colonies to one another. Laws regulating intercolonial commerce were made by the British government. Although a large amount of freedom to engage in such commerce was given to all colonists, dominion over it remained in the hands of superior British authorities. In addition, control over the relations of the colonies to foreign countries was a complete monopoly of the British government. As to the management of intercolonial and foreign affairs, therefore, Americans enjoyed little or no power and were relatively inexperienced during the colonial age.

Yet in regard to intercolonial relations, Americans were not wholly ignorant or indifferent. Nor were they totally without experience, or devoid of the desire to foster closer connections. Indeed many things conspired to draw the colonies closer together: the need for defense against Indians; participation in the numerous wars waged by Great Britain against France and Spain, partly on colonial frontiers; the necessity of co-operating in raising troops and supplies for such wars; and the growth of travel, trade, and intercourse along the seaboard.

As early as 1643, Massachusetts Bay, Plymouth, Connecticut, and New Haven formed the New England Confederation. They united in a "firm and perpetual league of friendship and amity for offense and defense, mutual advice and succor, upon all just occasions, both for preserving and propagating the truth and liberties of the Gospel and for their own mutual safety and welfare." For about twenty years the Confederation was active in carrying out the purposes for which it was created. Until 1685 delegates from these united colonies held meetings from time to time and dis-

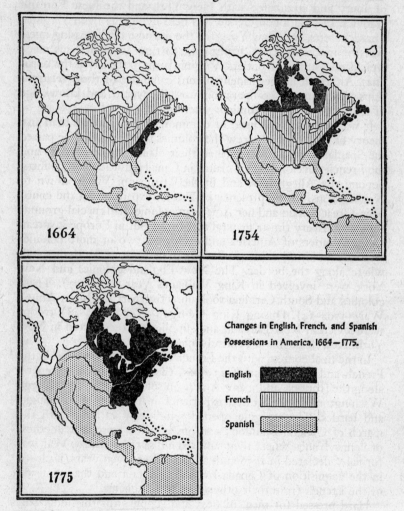

1664

1754

Changes in English, French, and Spanish
Possessions in America, 1664—1775.

English

French

Spanish

1775

cussed common affairs. But as the need for defense against the Indians on their borders declined, the Confederation weakened. By the end of the seventeenth century it had completely broken down. Still it pointed the way to intercolonial action, as a precedent.

Other colonies also discovered the advantages of mutual aid. Near the middle of the seventeenth century Virginia made treaties of amity and commerce with New York and the New England colonies. In 1684 a conference was held by agents from Virginia, Massachusetts, and New York for the purpose of discussing questions of mutual interest. From time to time when Indians made attacks on Southern frontiers, Virginia went to the aid of the Carolinas. Although no permanent unions came out of these relationships, the value of co-operation was discovered and knowledge of it handed down to coming generations.

It was wars and the need of common defense, rather than any theory of union, which drew the colonies together. As time passed the Spaniards tried to strengthen their claims in the Floridas and the French developed their claims in Canada, in the Ohio country beyond the Alleghenies, and in the Mississippi Valley down to New Orleans. In the presence of French expansion on the continent, Great Britain and her American colonies had special grounds for alarm. Every time a general war broke out in Europe it spread to the frontiers of America and each time two or more colonies were drawn into the war—in the North or West or South or somewhere along the border. The New England colonies and New York were involved in King William's War (1689–97). These colonies and South Carolina took an active part in Queen Anne's War (1702–14). During King George's War (1739–48) troops were levied in New England and supplies were collected in New York, New Jersey, and Pennsylvania.

In the final contest with the French and their Indian allies in the French and Indian War of 1756–63, the conflict became general along the frontier; and many American soldiers, including George Washington, then acquired experience in the arts of campaigns and battles. The struggle opened unofficially in 1755 with the march of General Braddock's troops into the western wilderness of Pennsylvania, where they suffered a disastrous defeat. War was formally declared in 1756 and, at the end of seven years, it closed in the acquisition of Canada by Great Britain and the expulsion of the French from their other continental claims.

Hard pressed for men, money, and supplies for this long war, the British government again called on the colonies for help. Most of them were laggard in responding and a few of them did nothing at all. Massachusetts, Connecticut, and New York furnished nearly three fourths of the American troops raised; but out of the experience all the colonies learned something about the bearing of common burdens and responsibilities.

As if in anticipation of the demands to come during the French and Indian War, an ambitious attempt had been made to unite them in a permanent federation. On a suggestion from the British government, an intercolonial conference was held at Albany, New York, in 1754. Among other things its purpose was to bring the colonies under "articles of union and confederation with each other for mutual defense of his majesty's subjects and interests in North America in time of peace as well as war."

Delegates from Maryland, Pennsylvania, New York, and all the New England colonies attended the conference. Without a dissenting vote they quickly resolved that a union of the colonies was "absolutely necessary for their security and defense." A committee, headed by Benjamin Franklin, brought before the delegates a plan to effect this union. The draft was debated, adopted, and sent to the colonies and the British government for approval but, owing to indifference or hostility, it was never put into force.

Whatever the reason for its failure, the Franklin plan demonstrated that some Americans had a deep understanding of intercolonial affairs. It provided for a general council composed of forty-eight members elected by the colonial assemblies. Representation in that body was to be roughly apportioned among the colonies according to wealth and population. Meetings of the council were to be held once a year or oftener if need be. The president was to be appointed by the Crown. He was to choose the military officers with the consent of the council. The selection of civil officers was vested in the council, subject to the president's approval. As to taxation, the new government was to levy such "general duties as appear equal and just" with due regard to the circumstances in the several colonies.

According to Franklin, the Crown disapproved his scheme as "having too much weight in the democratic part of the constitution, and every [colonial] assembly as having allowed too much prerogative." Though it was rejected, the plan of union was extensively discussed at the time and in years soon to follow it served to light the way toward a permanent union.

If no union was effected by this effort or the wars in which they became involved, colonists learned many things from such experiences. They became acquainted with the pull and haul of interests in the different sections of the country and the nature of the compromises that would be necessary to bring about adjustments among the conflicting forces. In raising troops, collecting supplies, and waging wars, they acquired some rudimentary arts of intercolonial co-operation on a large scale and in difficult circumstances. From Braddock's disaster in Pennsylvania, where George Washington was present and displayed bravery under fire, they developed a suspicion that British regular troops were far from invincible, especially in the arts of wilderness warfare adapted to the American terrain. What was more, and no less significant for American autonomy, discerning leaders among the colonists gained insight into the rivalry of governments for power in the Old World as well as for imperial dominion, into their ambitions and hatreds, and into the great game of diplomacy in Europe based on the balance of power. All this, too, was enlightening and useful in developing the arts of self-government in America.

CHAPTER VII

Two Systems and Ideologies in Conflict

OVER AGAINST colonial maturity in matters political, religious, social, and intellectual on this continent stood, across the sea, the British system of politics, economy, and ecclesiasticism. The system was an oligarchy collected around the monarch—an oligarchy composed of lords and the clerical hierarchy. There was in Great Britain, to be sure, a "popular" legislative body, the House of Commons; but, under the restricted suffrage and "rotten borough" scheme of representation, the oligarchy, through personal influence, wealth, and corruption, was generally able to dominate it. In economic terms, the policy of the British system was mercantilism—the permanent subordination of the colonies to the interests of the British governing classes.

The strength of the British oligarchy was fortified by the almost universal belief in England that the colonies were as subordinate socially and intellectually as they were politically and economically. In his *Origins of the American Revolution* (1943), based on microscopic and comprehensive researches in British records, William Miller says, while taking note of exceptions: "One of the convictions most firmly planted in the minds of the eighteenth-century Englishmen was the superiority of true-born Britons to the American colonists. . . . The status of the colonies was fixed for all time: regardless of their strength and population they must remain inferior to the mother country." This inveterate attitude was expressed by Dr. Samuel Johnson in the words: "We do not put a calf into the plow, we wait until he is an ox." In other words the young colonies might play in their youth but they must wear the yoke after they grow up.

87

Though the British oligarchy was often divided over various questions and there were occasional popular outbursts of protest against its harsher measures of government, the ruling classes of Great Britain were fairly united on one thing: they wanted to keep the British Empire intact and to make it contribute to the wealth and power of the mother country. The American colonies furnished many offices and jobs for British lords, their younger sons, and their hangers-on; the American colonies had vast areas of unoccupied land, huge parcels of which royal favorites could obtain for a song if they had the King's approval. British merchants and shippers found American trade highly profitable and naturally sought to get and keep as much of it as they could. British manufacturers looked upon the American markets as their own and as necessary outlets for their woolen cloth, hardware, and other finished commodities. The arable lands and forests of America were the objects of great desire to British enterprisers. British capitalists, whether landlords, merchants, manufacturers, or bankers, ever hunting more advantageous places for the investment of their capital, regarded the American colonies as offering almost unlimited opportunities for money-making.

Associated with British interests in political power and economic advantage were a number of principles—an ideology—which seemed natural, right, and proper to persons who held them. The King and the members of the titled aristocracy, who formed his inner circle, deemed it their right and privilege to hold the colonies tightly and permanently under the British government which they so largely controlled. To British merchants and shippers it was perfectly "reasonable" that they should enjoy ever-enlarging opportunities in the American trade, fix the prices to be paid to American planters and farmers for their produce, and restrain the menacing competition of American merchants and shippers. For British manufacturers it was "natural" to think that Americans should stick at the business of producing grain, lumber, and other raw materials and be compelled, as far as possible, to buy British finished products at good prices. That British capitalists should have special advantages in investing in the lands, fur trade, commerce, and other lucrative enterprises in America was, in their minds, both "right and proper."

These ideas all fitted into the pattern of "mercantilism" which generally prevailed in Western Europe throughout the colonial period. In sum and substance, mercantilism meant that the government should adopt and enforce measures to accomplish the following objects: hold colonies in the status of raw-material provinces supplying the mother country with materials for its manufacturers and foodstuffs for its workers; promote export and import trade in such a way as to bring gold, silver, and other forms of wealth into its coffers; give the mother country the profits that arose from manufacturing; monopolize more or less the commerce of the colonies to the advantage of its merchants. In the theory of mercantilism, the British government in London and its supporters found "good reasons" for believing that their ideas about managing American affairs were "sound" and "patriotic."

For carrying the ideas of mercantilism into effect, certain very definite laws and practices were necessary. The bonds of union between the American colonies and Great Britain must be kept firm and made stronger as the colonies matured in wealth and power. Laws favorable to the interests of British merchants, manufacturers, and investors must be enacted; and the American colonists must be stopped from passing laws and doing other things which interfered with the enforcement of British measures. To carry British legislation into effect, the number of British officers and agents in the colonies must be increased and, if necessary, British soldiers must be stationed there to uphold British governors and agents in the performance of their duties. Given British interests and ideas of values, given the theory of mercantilism as soundly patriotic, British designs for the colonies followed logically.

But in many matters, American interests ran directly counter to British interests. Most Americans were more concerned with developing the lands and resources right at hand than they were in promoting prosperity in Great Britain or upholding the British interests in India and other distant parts of the world. American artisans and manufacturers wanted to develop their own industries and reap the profits accruing from them. American merchants and shippers longed to enlarge their share of international trade. American farmers and planters believed that they could get better prices for their produce if British merchants exercised less control over the export and import trade; if Dutch, French, and other merchants from the continent of Europe could operate more freely in American markets, offering their goods for sale and buying tobacco, grains, and other farm commodities. American capitalists and enterprisers thought they would have larger opportunities for profitable business if all the lands, forests, and minerals at hand were at the disposal of colonial governments. Farmers and planters on the seaboard looked with hungry eyes toward the vacant lands beyond the near frontier and wanted them thrown open to easy settlement or speculation. Moreover, Americans could scarcely help wanting a larger share of the lucrative offices and jobs filled with appointees of the British King and the colonial governors, whose salaries were paid out of American taxes, without colonial representation in Parliament.

To support their counter interests, Americans had a large stock of ideas. One part of the stock consisted of legal ideas, another part of political ideas, and still another of economic ideas. The whole program included the following elements: under the English "constitution" Englishmen everywhere in the realm have certain rights which cannot be taken from them, such as the right to share, through their representatives, in the making of laws and the laying of taxes; the purpose of government is to protect the life, liberty, and property of the people; when tyranny or oppression takes the place of protection, the people have a right to change the government by revolution if necessary; all human beings are equal and have a right to obtain the land necessary to a livelihood. From such legal, political, and economic theories, Americans active in the advancement of their own interests had little difficulty in choosing arguments that fitted their respective cases.

If Americans were to realize their interests and ideas in practice, they believed that two types of measures were necessary. They needed local laws providing more control over the sale of lands, over the issue of currency used in trade, and over their manufacturing and commerce. Defensive measures were also indispensable —measures directed against British regulations and their enforcement in the colonies.

Having a care for such matters, colonial legislatures, from year to year, passed laws designed to serve American interests, despite the fact that acts were often vetoed by the colonial governor, or disallowed and set aside by the British Crown on its own motion or on appeal from objectors. On the defensive side other lines of action were open to Americans who resented British regulations: they could petition the King; they could send a colonial agent to London for the purpose of lobbying on behalf of their demands; they could simply ignore or violate British laws, especially if the royal or proprietary governor was lenient or negligent, as he often was.

☆

In giving effect to mercantilism and British ideology in general, the Parliament in London enacted many laws pertaining to American economic enterprise and political affairs. In general terms such laws fell into three broad classes.

The first class affected shipbuilding and the carriage of freight by water. They were known as Navigation Acts. These acts provided that goods carried both ways between Great Britain and the colonies and between the colonies and European countries must be transported in British-built ships manned mainly by British sailors. Since, in the eyes of the law, Americans were British, the ships the Americans built were "British-built" and the sailors they furnished were also British. In many ways, therefore, the Navigation Acts worked to the advantage of the colonies as well as the mother country. On the whole, the acts stimulated American shipping and promoted American commercial interests.

To the second class of British legislation belonged the Trade Acts. By such laws certain "enumerated" commodities produced in America had to be exported to Great Britain alone. In time the enumerated list included rice, tobacco, iron, lumber, furs, hides, naval stores, and a few other types of goods. Thus many American farmers and planters had to sell their prime produce through British merchants and accept the prices fixed in the British market, subject to no competition by Dutch, French, and other foreign merchants offering better terms.

Under other trade laws, American goods passing to the continent of Europe and European goods imported into the colonies had to go through the hands of merchants in Great Britain who collected their profits on the business. A special trade law, called the Molasses Act, passed by Parliament in 1733, laid taxes on important articles in the trade of the colonists with non-British possessions in America, especially the French West Indies, for the purpose of benefiting British merchants and capitalists engaged in commerce and sugar production in the British West Indies.

But the trade laws as a rule gave Americans many advantages, while restricting their operations in certain directions. To cite an example, for the enumerated articles Americans had a virtual monopoly in the markets of Great Britain as against their foreign competitors.

It was clearly in the interests of British manufacturers, however, to have laws enacted by Parliament for the purpose of restraining colonial industries. These formed a third class of regulatory laws. In 1699 the colonists were forbidden by act of Parliament to export woolen goods anywhere, and even to trade in such goods between towns and between colonies. In 1732 colonists were deprived of the right to export hats, finished or unfinished, to any place in America or abroad. By 1750 British ironmasters were feeling the pinch of their American competitors and in that year Parliament forbade Americans to set up iron mills for working bar or pig iron and for producing finished iron manufactures.

It was not so easy for the British government to enforce laws restricting American manufactures as it was to carry into effect the Navigation and Trade acts. Strict enforcement would have required a British official in every community, for instance, where housewives were spinning and weaving or men were making hats or hardware. As a matter of fact the British government did not attempt to police the colonies in this respect and the American manufacture of the forbidden goods flourished in spite of the laws.

But a turn came in the relatively negligent methods of the British government after the Seven Years' War with France which ended in 1763. In that conflict colonists had taken an active part by supplying soldiers and supplies. A heavy burden, however, had fallen on Great Britain, for the war raged in distant places at sea and at points as far apart as the coasts of India and the frontiers of North America. Although some results of the conflict were fortunate for Britain—the capture of Canada and other territorial gains—the struggle had been expensive and had greatly increased the British debt. As an outcome also, the British government faced other problems; for instance, the administration of the Northwest Territory adjoining the Mississippi and the Ohio rivers, and the regulation of relations with the Indians in that region.

In addition, a highly controversial question arose: Who are to benefit most from the exploitation of Western territories now cleared of the French and opened to development—American or British investors, farmers, land speculators, and fur traders? The British had undoubtedly made prodigious sacrifices in the effort to oust the French from the continent. The war had likewise been costly in men and money to the colonies. Both the British and the Americans therefore had logical and legitimate claims regarding all these matters, but there was no high and impartial court above them to which they could appeal for satisfactory adjudication.

☆

Whatever the merits of the respective claims to the benefits arising from enterprise and speculation in America, the British government eventually embarked upon a program of strengthening, adding to, and enforcing laws and decrees designed to regulate American economic and political affairs. Responsibility for this departure was assumed by the British ministries that succeeded one another after George III came to the throne in 1760, in the midst of the great war between England and France.

George himself, upon whom much of the blame for the trouble was later thrown, had little to do with initiating the program, but in general he approved it. Besides, by bribery and corruption, he helped to support the ministers who formulated it in the Parliament; and he had high notions about his royal prerogatives at home as well as over his "farms," as he referred to the colonies. In no way did the new program run counter to his conceptions of government.

Briefly stated, the program included three principal elements: Americans must be taxed to pay a part of the expense incurred by Great Britain in defending, protecting, and administering her possessions in America; old trade and navigation laws must be more strictly enforced; and new laws regulating British and American commerce and enterprise in the colonies must be enacted.

Within five years after the close of the war with France the following measures had been adopted by the British government:

1763—Royal Order, reserving to the King the disposal of Western lands beyond a certain line.

1764—Sugar Act, taxing certain imports, partly with a view to bringing money into the British treasury for supporting British government in the colonies.

1764—Currency Act, forbidding the colonies to issue paper money.

1765—Stamp Act, taxing numerous articles and transactions in America to help pay the costs of British government in the colonies.

1765—Quartering Act, requiring Americans to help house and feed British regular troops stationed in the colonies.

1766—Declaratory Act, asserting the supremacy of the British Parliament in making laws for the colonies.

1767—Customs Collecting Act, establishing British commissioners in the colonies to collect customs and other duties.

1767—Revenue Act, laying taxes on lead, paint and other articles imported into the colonies.

1767—Tea Act, regulating importation of tea in British dominions in America in favor of the British East India Company.

All these measures deeply affected the American colonists: their agriculture, industries, commerce, and investment opportunities; their habits, practices, and desires respecting self-government; their freedom of elections, press, and speech. The Royal Order of 1763 forbade the colonists to buy any more land from the Indians in the West beyond a certain line, and vested in the Crown the sole power to hold and dispose of such lands. If enforced, this decree would mean that hardy pioneers, land-hungry and bent on acquiring homes for themselves, could no longer go West, take up land, and "squat" on it as their own. It would also mean that American land speculators could not acquire huge blocks of Western land in the hope of making money as land values rose with the advance of Western settlement.

The same order contained another provocative clause. It placed in the hands of royal officers the power of licensing persons engaged in trade with the Indians and thereby deciding who was to enjoy the profits of the lucrative fur traffic. In fact, the proclamation, though designed among other things to introduce order along the frontier, indicated that British officials were henceforward to dispose of large sections of the Western territory and settle the question as to who was to reap the profits of the various operations there, including the fur business. This, in turn, meant that Americans would no longer have the liberty to do very much as they pleased on the frontier—to hunt, trade with the Indians, gather up furs, and roam around at will, looking for adventures or "taking up" land.

The purpose of the Sugar Act was clearly stated in the preamble. It was to promote the business of the British sugar colonies in the West Indies, raise money toward the expenses of "defending, protecting, and securing" British colonies and plantations in America, more strictly enforce the laws against smuggling, and secure and improve the trade between Great Britain and her colonies in the New World. The act, like its predecessor in 1733, laid duties on sugar brought into the American colonies from non-British possessions. It also imposed duties on certain wines, silks, calicoes, and linens imported into the American colonies. With a view to enforcement, the act provided heavy penalties for all shippers, British and American alike, who tried to smuggle goods contrary to the terms of the law.

Explicitly, the Sugar Act taxed Americans for the purpose of raising money to pay the expenses of British officials and soldiers employed in governing the colonies and upholding British dominion over them. In itself, this was enough to rouse American ire. But the act also struck a severe blow at one branch of American commerce. Americans could no longer buy sugar cheaper from the French sugar colonies in the West Indies. They had been buying large quantities there, turning it into rum, and exchanging the rum for African slaves to be brought back to America for sale. This was a highly successful business and a tax on it in favor of British sugar growers and slave traders, if enforced, would hamper an important branch of American commerce.

The Customs Collecting Act of 1767, coupled with many provisions in other new British laws, showed that the British government was determined to stop smuggling and other violations of tax and trade laws on the part of Americans. British revenue collectors, officers of the navy and army, royal governors, and other agents were ordered to be diligent, to see that taxes were collected and regulations observed. Shipmasters engaged in the carrying trade had to be registered in official books and give bond that they would obey the laws. Patrols of British ships guarded the Atlantic coast, with power to halt, search, and hold merchant ships suspected of smuggling. Thus American liberty to trade at will was to be drastically curtailed.

By the Currency Act of 1764, American merchants, farmers, and debtors were adversely affected in numerous ways. No rich mines of gold and silver were discovered in the seaboard regions; so that Americans had no gold and silver of their own coinage with which to pay for domestic goods and meet their debts at home. For the same reason they had difficulty in finding specie to pay for imported British and foreign goods and to discharge the debts they owed British capitalists for money they had borrowed to buy land, stock, tools, and other capital supplies. In their straits, nearly all the colonies had been issuing colonial paper money at one time or another, and had made it lawful in business transactions. Now the Currency Act put a stop to this practice definitely and positively, evoking an early episode in the American battle over the "money question."

None of the British regulatory measures, however, affected large numbers of Americans seriously enough to arouse great popular opposition. It was the Stamp Act of 1765 that first set the colonies aflame. In the preamble of this act also appeared the declaration that its purpose was to provide money for the British treasury, "towards defraying the expenses of defending, protecting and securing the British colonies and plantations in America." That in itself was resented by many colonists. But the clauses of the act intended to raise the money, covering several pages of fine print, prescribed taxes which reached the pocketbooks of Americans from Massachusetts to Georgia.

Americans now had to buy stamps of various kinds, ranging in price from a few pence to several pounds each, to be placed on many classes of papers and articles. Deeds and mortgages relating to property, licenses to practice law, licenses to sell liquor, college diplomas, playing cards, dice, almanacs, and calendars all had to bear British stamps of stated values. More than this: publishers and printers of advertisements, newspapers, and other sheets had to buy stamps for their publications.

If the British Parliament had deliberately searched for taxes that would annoy as many Americans as possible, it could scarcely have improved upon the Stamp Act. The law was especially hard on two classes of Americans who spoke, wrote, and made their opinions heard: the lawyers and the publishers—both given to preaching freedom of speech and press. The very men in the streets were so angry that they instigated boycotts and riots against the act.

In itself the Stamp Act of March 1765 would have made trouble for the British government but it was quickly followed in April of the same year by the Quartering Act which gave the colonists to understand that the laws were to be enforced. Since the British ministry was preparing to send more soldiers than usual to the American colonies, with a view to upholding its authority, it faced the problem of furnishing the soldiers with quarters and supplies.

For this problem the Quartering Act provided what was deemed a solution: Americans were to lodge officers and privates in inns, taverns, uninhabited houses, barns, and other buildings; supply them with numerous articles of consumption; and furnish wagons to haul their goods. American constables, magistrates, and other civil officers in villages, towns, townships, cities, districts, and other places were charged with the duty of seeing that the buildings, candles, liquor, salt, and other articles mentioned in the act were promptly placed at the disposal of the British troops.

Consequently Americans not only had to endure the sight of British troops and the thought of military government; they had to help in housing, feeding, and serving British soldiers. Yet time was required to transport the British soldiers to the colonies and many months passed before American communities were stirred up by the necessity of finding quarters and supplies for them.

It was the Stamp Act which awakened immediate protests and

alarms. Lawyers and merchants were quick to voice their resentment against it. The cry, "No taxation without representation," was taken up in cities, towns, and country regions by artisans, mechanics, farmers, and housewives. Popular societies called the Sons of Liberty and the Daughters of Liberty were organized to resist the sale of stamps. Crowds gathered in the streets of Boston, New York, Philadelphia, and Charleston, and rioted against officers who tried to force people to buy stamps. The offices and houses of royal officials were stoned, in some cases sacked and burned. Going far beyond blocking the sale of stamps, Americans organized groups to boycott British goods of all kinds—to cut down the sale of British manufactures as well as stamps. Indeed there was so much disorder in several colonies that even the protesting merchants and lawyers became frightened and tried to restrain the torrent of popular anger.

Colonial leaders took steps to bring united pressure on Parliament for the repeal of the act. In the Virginia House of Burgesses they forced the adoption of resolutions denouncing the principles of the Stamp Act, asserting that the General Assembly alone could lay taxes on the people of the colony, and branding other methods of taxation as "illegal, unconstitutional, and unjust." It was in supporting this resolution that Patrick Henry delivered the speech which made him famous as a firebrand of the Revolution.

In the spirit of the Virginia Resolutions, the House of Representatives in Massachusetts opposed the Stamp Act and issued a circular letter inviting all the colonies to send delegates to a general congress to be held in New York for the purpose of discussing common problems and taking common action. Nine colonies responded favorably, chose their delegates amid popular excitement, and sent them to New York.

In October 1765 the Stamp Act Congress assembled. Despite some difference of opinion, it agreed on a set of resolutions and the terms of a petition calling upon Parliament to repeal the act. Members of the Congress professed their loyal allegiance to the King and their subordination to the Parliament of Great Britain. But they claimed all the inherent rights and liberties of natural-born British subjects. They declared that no taxes could be laid on the people without their consent, that the colonies were not and could not be represented in Parliament, and that no taxes could be constitutionally imposed upon them without the consent of their legislatures. They also sought to show that various acts of Parliament both burdened the colonies and interfered with trade between them and Great Britain. British merchants were tersely warned that restrictions recently placed on trade would render the people of the colonies unable to purchase British manufactures. While resolutions were respectful and moderate in tone, they were specific and firm.

In consternation over the open resistance in the colonies and under pressure from British merchants hard hit by the American boycott, Parliament in 1766 repealed the Stamp Act. In so doing, however, it did not concede the American claim that it had no right to tax the colonists. In fact, by the Declaratory Act, signed on the same day as the repeal measure, Parliament asserted that the colonies have been, are, and ought to be subordinate to the Crown and Parliament; and that the King and Parliament had, have, and of right ought to have full power and authority to make laws and statutes binding the colonies and people of America "in all cases whatsoever." This language left no loopholes through which Americans could escape admitting their subordination to the British government, but, as they rejoiced over the abolition of the Stamp Tax, they spent little time arguing about the mere legal theory of the Declaratory Act.

Evidently foreseeing the dangers in trying to collect taxes in the colonies directly, the British ministers, still determined to raise revenue in America, took another course. The very next year after the repeal of the Stamp Act, Parliament passed the Revenue Act of 1767, which laid duties on glass, red and white lead, painters' colors, paper, and tea.

At the same time Parliament informed the colonists that these duties were to be collected. It coupled with the Revenue Act a law which had "teeth" in every line. The Customs Commissioners Act of 1767 vested in the hands of British commissioners the duty of supervising the enforcement of the revenue laws. The tax commissioners were to be appointed by the King; they were to reside in the colonies; and they were to be paid from the British treasury, not out of grants of money voted by colonial legislatures. In the Revenue Act itself, Parliament also expressed its resolve to collect the duties: it gave the higher courts in the colonies, made up of British judges, power to issue "Writs of Assistance," authorizing customs officers to search houses, warehouses, shops, cellars, and other places for smuggled goods and to seize them summarily if found.

A third commercial measure passed by Parliament in 1767 was the Tea Act. This act, supplemented by another Tea Act in 1773, among other things relieved the British East India Company of the necessity of paying duties on its tea exported to America. In effect it amounted to giving the company a monopoly of the tea business in America; enforced, it would enable the company to sell tea at lower prices than were asked by other British merchants or, for that matter, even by American merchants who had bought tea from foreign merchants and smuggled it into the colonies. Not without reason did objecting colonists regard the Tea Act as a step toward setting up British monopolies for the control of all American foreign and domestic trade.

☆

Events swiftly following the enactment of the British laws of 1767 revealed to the two parties the sharpness of the conflict. It was now obvious that the British government was determined to raise revenue in the colonies by taxation; to use this revenue toward defraying the expenses of governing the colonies; to enforce its authority through higher officers appointed by the Crown and paid out of the British treasury; to free the royal officers from control by the colonial assemblies; and definitely to subordinate the colonists to British commercial interests. It was made equally plain by events that irate Americans who opposed the British policies would stubbornly resist them by official resolves in colonial assemblies and by popular actions outside the legislative halls—even actions involving violence.

The basic animus of the colonists against British policies became manifest within a year. In 1768 the assembly of Massachusetts, inspired by Samuel Adams, approved the sending of a circular letter to the legislatures of the other colonies, calling upon them to consider their common plight, and declaring the principles of retaliation on which Massachusetts was taking her stand. For this defiance the royal governor at Boston dissolved the assembly.

When assemblies in other colonies approved the doctrines of the Circular Letter, they too were dissolved by their governors. In 1769 the Virginia House of Burgesses proclaimed that it alone had the right to lay taxes in Virginia, and petitioned the King for a redress of grievances. The governor of the colony replied by dissolving that assembly.

Meanwhile a contest especially bitter was going on in New York. In that colony the assembly had refused to make provisions for British soldiers under the Quartering Act of 1765. Parliament answered in 1767 by passing a law suspending the New York Assembly until it was ready to comply with the terms of the Quartering Act. When at length, in 1769, it bowed to British demands, it made no attempt to conceal its indignation; and the necessity of housing and supplying British soldiers stirred up wrath among the residents of the colony.

In 1770 British soldiers, stationed at Boston, jostled and stoned by a crowd of men and boys, fired on their assailants, killing five and wounding several more. News of this "Boston Massacre," as it was described, spread into other colonies, awakening both resentment and anxiety. When in 1772 a British armed vessel engaged in hunting smugglers in Narragansett Bay accidentally ran ashore, it was quickly boarded by men from Providence who seized the crew and set fire to the ship. In 1773 the House of Burgesses in Virginia, meeting in spite of the governor's prohibition, created a standing committee to correspond with leaders in other colonies and bring about combined actions against British policies and measures. Late that year a group of men, disguised as Indians, forced their way upon ships at Boston, which had brought tea for sale to the colonists under the new terms, and dumped their cargoes into the harbor. In 1774 rioters at Annapolis compelled the destruction of a British vessel, the *Peggy Stewart*, and all the tea chests on board. American resistance was taking the form of physical violence when the year 1774 opened.

If members of the Boston Tea Party thought that the British government would yield to their display of anger they were mistaken and soon disillusioned. Early in 1774 Parliament enacted five new laws intended to cure unrest in America. One of the acts closed the port of Boston to all trade by sea. Another revamped the charter of Massachusetts, made the government still more royal in nature, and even subjected town meetings to the control of the governor. A third act empowered royal officials to take to Great Britain or elsewhere in her American colonies all persons in Massachusetts accused of murder in connection with law enforcement. By a fourth act the quartering of British troops in Massachusetts towns was specifically authorized. The fifth act offended Protestants and affected other interests in the colonies: it granted toleration to Catholics in Canada, widened the boundaries of Quebec southward to the Ohio River, and provided for the government of that vast Western territory by a viceroy of the King.

More British soldiers were now sent to Massachusetts and the commander of the British armed forces in the colony, General

Gage, was installed as governor. Such actions on the part of the British government in Massachusetts served as a warning to all the colonists that British authority was not to be denied or defied with impunity. As the spring of 1774 merged into summer, leaders of the opposition to British authority, from Massachusetts to Georgia, had to face that fact and, if still stubborn in their militancy, make further decisions on the basis of it.

CHAPTER VIII

Independence Completed by Revolution

IN THE SPRING of 1774 a cry went up in the colonies for united action and for a general congress to assure such action. The assembly of Virginia, still meeting, if irregularly, in spite of the royal governor's prohibitive orders, expressed sympathy with Massachusetts and favored combined efforts in resistance to British policies and measures. Encouraged by reports from various sources, the assembly of Massachusetts, under the leadership of Samuel Adams, resolved that a continental congress was highly expedient and indeed necessary to deliberate and determine upon wise and proper steps to be taken in recovering the rights of Americans and restoring harmony with Great Britain. As proof of its intransigence it appointed delegates to attend such a congress on the first of the coming September.

In line with the action of Massachusetts, other colonies chose representatives and on September 5 the first Continental Congress met at Philadelphia. Among its members were men soon to be powerful figures in history, such as George Washington and Patrick Henry from Virginia, Samuel Adams and John Adams from Massachusetts. But they differed among themselves as to the best course to pursue. Many favored radical action verging in the direction of independence; others were cautious and conservative; on the whole, moderates held the balance of power. After tempestuous debates, the Congress agreed upon three expedients.

First, it adopted a set of resolutions, in dignified but pointed language, setting forth the rights, liberties, and immunities of the colonists and naming the measures of the British government which, in their view, violated these rights, liberties, and immunities. As to exactly what they claimed and what they were protesting against, members of the Congress left no doubt. By these resolutions they repeated and expanded the claims made by the Stamp Act Congress of 1765.

Second, while promising to support Massachusetts in her struggle against Great Britain, the Continental Congress drew up an address to King George III and another to the people of England and to the inhabitants of British America, in which it respectfully presented American grievances and called for a restoration of American rights. The resolutions and the addresses were words —firm, moderate, positive words; still they were only words.

A third expedient approved by the Continental Congress went beyond words into action. That was a decision to stop the importation of British goods into the colonies until a redress of grievances could be obtained and to vest the enforcement of the boycott in the hands of local "committees of safety and inspection." The boycott was, of course, a violation of British law. It was more than this. It was aggressive. It provided for establishing in every community a boycott committee to prevent the buying of British goods and to discover who was loyal to Great Britain and who was loyal to the American cause, as tested by their acts in buying goods. Words might be debated and hairs split indefinitely but a colonist either upheld the boycott or he was against it and bought British goods in spite of it. He was in short a Patriot or a Loyalist!

Before adjourning in October, the first Continental Congress provided for a second Congress to be held in May of 1775 in case the situation then required such an assembly.

In response to the demands of the first Continental Congress, the British government made one concession: it was willing to relieve any colony of taxation on condition that it would bear its share of imperial defense and provide money for supporting the officers of the Crown within its borders. But with this concession, such as it was, Parliament coupled a set of resolutions pledging full support to the King in the enforcement of British laws in the colonies. These resolutions it supplemented by restraining acts which practically destroyed the commerce of the colonies.

Meanwhile British officers—civil and military—in the colonies tightened, instead of relaxing, their efforts to compel obedience to British authority. It was in the fulfillment of this duty that General Gage, in Boston, dispatched a small force of soldiers toward Lexington and Concord in April 1775 for the purpose, among other things, of seizing some military supplies supposed to be stored in that neighborhood.

Warned by William Dawes and Paul Revere that British soldiers were on the march, a small number of American militiamen gathered on the green at Lexington early in the morning of April 19. With about thirty or forty onlookers the militiamen were standing there when the British forces arrived under the command of Major John Pitcairn. Seeing that armed resistance would be futile, the captain of the militiamen, John Parker, ordered his men to disperse. While they were slowly breaking ranks a shot was fired.

By whom? British who were present at the time laid the blame for the first shot on Americans; and Americans put it on the British. Since that day the question of blame has been repeatedly debated without reaching any generally accepted conclusion. Whoever cares to weigh the evidence of contemporary witnesses who saw the fray with their own eyes may find the testimony admirably summarized in the pages of Allen French's *The Day of Concord and Lexington*.

Although the person who fired the first shot that nineteenth day of April 1775 must apparently remain forever unknown, it is certain that his shot was followed by firing all day, as militiamen poured in from the surrounding country and harassed British troops on their retreat to Boston. It is also certain that this shot, "heard around the world," heralded a war.

☆

If there had been doubts about the need for a second conference of delegates from all the colonies, they were settled by the clash at Lexington and Concord in April 1775. In the next month the second Continental Congress assembled at Philadelphia. Though blood had been shed, most of the delegates were still inclined to be conciliatory toward the British government when sessions of the Congress opened; for they seemed to hope that the American rights previously declared might yet be acknowledged by Great Britain.

But the Congress prepared for the worst—a general war. It provided for organizing the New England militiamen near Boston into a regular army and appointed one of its members, George Washington, as commander of the American forces in Massachusetts. It also resolved to raise money and supplies for an armed conflict if it came; to seek support by opening diplomatic relations with several European countries; and to carry on the struggle until the liberties claimed by Americans could be realized by British concessions or American independence.

These resolves were met in Great Britain by a proclamation from George III denouncing American leaders in the revolt as "rebels" and ordering the British military and civil agents to suppress the insurrection and punish the authors and abettors of "such traitorous designs." The war was now in full course.

In June 1775 American militiamen at Bunker Hill near Boston, though finally driven from their position, proved that they could and would fight as long as they had gunpowder. Taking command of the army at Cambridge the next month, Washington prepared to besiege Boston. In this operation he was so successful that Lord Howe, who had now supplanted General Gage, gave up the city in March 1776 and sailed for Halifax. In his flight Howe carried along, besides his troops, several hundred British officials and Boston residents who were steadfast in their loyalty to King George.

Meanwhile, late in 1775, Vermont militiamen, under Ethan Allen and Benedict Arnold, had seized Ticonderoga and Crown Point, getting possession of strongholds which might block a British drive from Canada. Still later in that year American forces invaded Canada and captured Montreal. But an assault on Quebec failed and they were forced to withdraw, thus losing their hope of bringing Canada to the support of the struggle against Great Britain.

☆

As the war proceeded, prospects for a reconciliation with Great Britain faded and the desire for independence, which only a few Americans had hitherto entertained, flamed into a fixed resolve. On January 10, 1776, while Washington was still besieging the British in Boston, Thomas Paine gave voice to this resolution in a powerful tract called *Common Sense*, published in Philadelphia. Spurning the humble language of loyalty formerly used in petitions to George III, Paine assailed the King in acrimonious words, scorned the once praised British constitution, and demanded immediate and unconditional independence for America. "Now," he exclaimed, "is the seed-time of Continental union, faith, and honor. . . . O! ye that love mankind! Ye that dare oppose not only tyranny, but the tyrant, stand forth."

As edition after edition of *Common Sense*, totaling more than 100,000 copies, came from the press, the call to revolution swept throughout the colonies. The word "independence" had now been spoken and was echoing from New Hampshire to Georgia. The debate with Great Britain over rights claimed as just—rights treasured as the liberties of Englishmen—had become a war of ideas which could not be stopped. Reconciliation, Paine had proclaimed, is "a fallacious dream."

Doubting, wondering, and wavering men in the Continental Congress now began to accept the climax. From all the royal and proprietary colonies, British governors and officials were fleeing as from the wrath to come, accompanied by small bands of American officials and crowds of Americans who still clung to George III. In May the Congress advised every colony to form a government of its own, as if British dominion had actually come to an end. In fact Virginia and other colonies were already taking this fateful step and their example was quickly followed. In short, the colonies were assuming the powers of independent states. South Carolina, having adopted a provisional constitution in March 1776, supplanted it by a definite constitution in 1778.

Strictly speaking, the movement for the break with Great Britain was spreading upward from the colonies to the Continental Congress, rather than downward to the colonies from the Congress. On April 13, 1776, the North Carolina revolutionary assembly gave its delegates in the Congress full power to unite with the other members in boldly declaring independence. Elsewhere the idea was also approved. On May 15 the Virginia delegates at Philadelphia received instructions from a convention of that province to propose independence in the Congress and support it.

Thoroughly aroused by the surge of revolutionary temper from below and incited by daring spirits among its members, the Continental Congress girded itself for final action. On June 7, Richard Henry Lee, speaking for the Virginia delegation, moved that "these united colonies are, and ought to be, free and independent states." But cautious men prevented the immediate adoption of the resolution and the Congress did no more than authorize the appointment of a committee to draw up a declaration of independence. Yielding at length to popular demands, the Congress, by an almost unanimous vote, on July 2 approved a resolution in favor of independence.

Meanwhile the committee appointed in June, composed of five members, including Thomas Jefferson, John Adams, and Benjamin Franklin, was busy framing the document which was to express the ideas and the spirit of independence. A draft of the document was first prepared by Jefferson. It was then reviewed by his colleagues. Adams and Franklin suggested several changes. For example, Jefferson had written: "We hold these truths to be sacred and undeniable." Later it was modified, perhaps by Franklin, to read: "We hold these truths to be self-evident." Finally the draft was completed and laid before the Congress. After making other changes in it, the Congress formally adopted the document on July 4. During a period extending over several months, it was signed by members of the Congress.

The Declaration of Independence set forth in great detail the "causes" that impelled the American people to the revolutionary act of separation from Great Britain. This part of the Declaration was, of course, an American statement of the case against the British government and was directed particularly against King George III as if Parliament bore little or no responsibility for the troubles that had arisen. It put the charges in summary and pointed language which Americans could readily understand, for they had personal knowledge of many a grievance listed in the indictment against the British sovereign.

Unlike the resolutions of the Stamp Act Congress in 1765, which also proclaimed grievances but in a humble tone, the Declaration of Independence was animated by a fixed determination to cast off British dominion and furthermore by a radical theory of government. The theory was not new by any means. It had been known and discussed in the colonies for a long time among students of government and even among people at large. The framer of the Declaration, Thomas Jefferson, was well aware of this fact. Had he invented an entirely novel idea, it would have made less of an appeal to the people. With the aid of Franklin and Adams, he did, however, put all the elements of the theory together effectively and present the whole in a flowing eloquence that electrified American minds and hearts.

In the theory of the American Revolution, as Jefferson formulated it, were three principal features: (1) All men are created equal and endowed by their Creator with certain unalienable rights, among which are life, liberty, and the pursuit of happiness. (2) It is to secure these rights that governments are instituted, and they derive their just powers from the consent of the governed. (3) When any form of government becomes destructive of these ends, it is the right of the people to alter or abolish it, and to institute new government, laying its foundations on such principles and organizing its powers in such form as to them shall seem most likely to effect their safety and happiness.

It was these doctrines, the Declaration asserted, which the British government had violated and the American people were to accept as the basis of their independence and the new governments they were to institute. To all other governments then existing in the world the doctrines offered a revolutionary challenge that was to ring through the centuries. Indeed there were even many Americans who, though they were disposed toward independence, were afraid that "the people" might set up governments destructive of the privileges hitherto enjoyed by particular classes in the colonies.

☆

To incarnate the principles of the Declaration in the life of the nation, it was necessary for the Revolutionists first to overcome the armed forces of Great Britain on land and sea; and for many months the prospects for an ultimate American victory looked gloomy. In August of 1776, less than seven weeks after the fateful July 4, the American troops under General Washington were badly mauled on Long Island by superior British regulars. Instead of capturing New York City as they had expected when they marched southward from New England, they were driven northward to White Plains, then across the Hudson River, and then southward through New Jersey.

Not until near the end of that year did a light appear in the blackness. On Christmas night, while the mercenary Hessian troops under British command were celebrating the season at Trenton, Washington made a surprise attack on them and captured about a thousand prisoners. A few days later, early in January 1777, he struck another hard blow at the British in a battle at Princeton a few miles above Trenton.

But these were merely episodes encouraging to Americans, not great victories. Later in the year Washington was defeated at Brandywine. He lost Philadelphia to the British and narrowly escaped disaster at Germantown. Forced to retire westward with his shattered troops to Valley Forge for the winter of 1777–78, he seemed to be almost at the end of his resources.

Then came news from the north which once more raised the enthusiasm of the Revolutionists to a high pitch—news of a great victory for their side. Under orders from the British war office, General John Burgoyne, at the head of a strong force, had invaded northern New York, expecting to be joined by a band of Loyalists and Indians from the west and to be aided by British troops from Lord Howe's army in lower New York. If successful this invasion would have split the country into two parts and imperiled or ruined the American cause. But it failed miserably for the British. Burgoyne was attacked on all sides, his supplies were cut off, the troops sent by Howe from New York City did not arrive to support him, and on October 17, 1777, he surrendered at Saratoga to General Horatio Gates, the American commander who had replaced General Philip Schuyler just as the American victory was in sight.

Burgoyne's surrender at Saratoga, rightly counted among "the decisive battles" of history, marked a turning point toward American independence. It demonstrated that American troops, though poorly trained and supplied, had a genius for warfare and that they could in certain circumstances cope with British regulars. The victory at Saratoga was also crucial in that news of it tipped the balance in the minds of the French ministers then advising Louis XVI and brought France into the war against Great Britain.

For tedious months Benjamin Franklin, the American minister to France, despite his extraordinary popularity in that country, had sought in vain to bring the French government into the war. Smarting under the numerous defeats and losses suffered in fights with Britain, that government had found pleasure in the prospect of a successful revolt against her in America and had secretly given help to the colonies in the form of money and supplies. It had, however, shrunk from entering into an alliance with the United States and declaring war on Britain. Such a venture might end in another disaster for France. Only after the victory at Saratoga were the French ministers induced to gamble again with fate in an open war on the ancient foe.

In February 1778 the French government made treaties of amity and commerce with the United States. It officially recognized American independence, agreed to an alliance for mutual aid and defense, declared war on Great Britain, and immediately began to take part in the military and naval operations against her. Early the next year Spain joined France in the war, hoping to recover among other things Florida, which the British had annexed in 1763 at the close of the French and Indian War. Later Holland lent support to the American cause by preying upon British commerce.

The alliance with France brought to Americans the kind of assistance they sorely needed: strong naval forces, generous loans of gold, silver, and supplies, and a large body of French officers and soldiers well trained in the arts of warfare. It also encouraged Americans in every way; but it did not immediately turn the tide of war. Nor did it mean that they could escape making more strenuous efforts and assuming burdens heavier than any they had as yet carried.

☆

As a matter of fact Americans suffered many reverses during the three years which followed the signing of the treaty of alliance with France. Anxious about a possible blockade by a French fleet, the British evacuated Philadelphia in June 1778, but they repulsed an American attack soon afterward at the Battle of Monmouth. Late in that year the British captured Savannah and, in many campaigns, planned to conquer the whole South. They overran most of Georgia, South Carolina, and North Carolina, in spite of repeated assaults by local bands of American soldiers.

In May 1780 the British took Charleston. Under the command of Lord Cornwallis they pierced the uplands of South Carolina and defeated the Americans at the Battle of Camden. Flushed by successes, Cornwallis led his troops into the interior of North Carolina though they had been checked by American forces at King's Mountain. After shattering American lines at Guilford Courthouse in March 1781, Cornwallis headed for Virginia.

On arriving in Virginia, Cornwallis tried to capture the American troops led by the Marquis de Lafayette, "the boy," as he called the young Frenchman who had come over to help in the struggle for independence. Failing in this maneuver, Cornwallis retired to Yorktown on the Virginia coast, where he hoped to get reinforcements by sea.

While American armies were meeting misfortunes in the Eastern campaigns, a stroke was accomplished in the West that was to count in the final settlement. Under a commission from Virginia, George Rogers Clark recruited volunteers and in 1778 seized several towns on the east bank of the Mississippi in the Illinois country. The next year he captured the British garrison at Vincennes on the Wabash River. Thus an American grip was fastened on the Northwest.

None of the exploits by the British in the South, discouraging as they were to patriot leaders, proved to be decisive. The British could beat or scatter the Americans in battle but could not round them up wholesale or prevent their gathering again quickly to re-

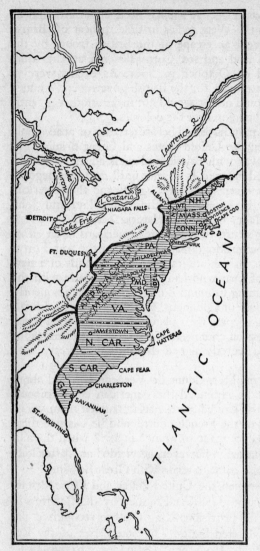

APPROXIMATE FRONTIER LINE OF THE
COLONIES IN 1774

new the struggle. They could make marauding expeditions into the back regions of South Carolina, North Carolina, and Virginia, but they could not occupy those regions and hold them in subjection against bands of American troops skilled in guerrilla warfare. They hit hard and yet they did not conquer. This lesson Cornwallis learned at great cost in men and supplies. It was, in part, for this reason that he drew back upon the coast at Yorktown and waited for the British navy to support him from the sea.

By that action Cornwallis unwittingly prepared for his doom and the end of the war. General Washington and his French allies, then in the North planning an attack on New York, saw what seemed to be a golden opportunity for a conclusive stroke at Yorktown. So American and French troops were rushed South to pen up Cornwallis from the landward side. A French fleet, under Admiral de Grasse, arrived from the West Indies in time to beat off British naval forces and prevent an escape of the British troops by the sea. Under fire from land and sea, Cornwallis ran up the white flag and surrendered on October 19, 1781. As events were to prove, the long war was over; for the British government, stunned by the blow, either could not or would not make another gigantic effort to recover its dominion over the colonies.

Nevertheless many months passed before a treaty of peace could be concluded between the United States and Great Britain. The French were still at war with Britain and their alliance with the United States remained in force. It was not until 1782 that negotiations were opened between the British agents and the American peace commissioners in France—Franklin, John Jay, and John Adams, with whom Henry Laurens was later associated.

Now it was Britain's turn to conciliate Americans in an effort to prevent France from making great gains out of the war. Fortunately for that design, British affairs were in the hands of a new ministry, composed of men who had been sympathetic with the American cause, including Edmund Burke who had so eloquently defended it in the House of Commons. Working quietly with the British agents in Paris, keeping their plans hidden from the French government, the American commissioners won generous terms for the United States and secretly signed the draft of a treaty with Great Britain.

When the French minister, Count de Vergennes, heard about this secret settlement he reminded the American commissioners that the Congress of the United States had instructed them "to be guided by the wishes of the French court," and he charged them with violating the pledges made to France in 1778 when the alliance was formed. Eventually, however, he yielded and, after long negotiations, France also came to terms with Great Britain.

The final treaty between the United States and Great Britain was signed on September 3, 1783, and ratified by the Congress in January 1784. Under its provisions King George recognized the independence of the United States. The boundaries of the Republic were fixed, roughly, from the Atlantic Ocean to the Mississippi River and from the Great Lakes to the Floridas. The navigation of the Mississippi was declared to be open to American citizens and British subjects.

In specific clauses the treaty assured creditors on both sides that there would be no lawful impediments to the collection of just debts. It was also agreed that Congress would recommend to the state legislatures that provision be made for restoring to loyal British subjects all properties and estates that had been confiscated during the Revolution. The right of Americans to fish off the coasts of Newfoundland and in the Gulf of the St. Lawrence in the customary manner was guaranteed by a definite article of the treaty. Even the most zealous patriot in the United States could find little fault with the settlement that brought the war to a conclusion.

☆

The numerous battles and skirmishes waged on land from Massachusetts to Georgia and the exploits of American naval forces at sea, under such officers as John Paul Jones and John Barry, were only a part of the story of the war and the Revolution. During the long contest, men, officers, and supplies had to be provided for the armies, civil government had to be carried on, and many a dispute among Americans over the conduct and aims of the war had to be adjusted or endured.

In itself the war worked havoc in colonial economy and made new economic undertakings necessary to victory. Commerce with Great Britain was practically destroyed and trade with other countries could not fully take its place. Many regions were either occupied or harried by British troops. Loyalists bent on actively aiding the British cause, often with arms, waged a civil war within the war for independence. They in turn were harassed by resentful patriots; many were harshly treated or imprisoned; thousands were driven out of the country, to England or Canada. In important respects, therefore, the revolt against Great Britain involved also a revolution in American affairs—in military power, industry, finance, diplomacy, government, and social arrangements.

In colonial times Americans had relied for their local defense mainly upon militia composed of civilians who gave a limited amount of time to drilling and were officered by men with little more experience than the privates possessed. At the opening of the war militiamen and new volunteers filled the ranks of armies that had to wage battles with trained British regulars.

A large proportion of the recruits were brave men who fought courageously, but they were accustomed to serve for short terms, were undisciplined, not inured to long and grueling campaigns. At the beginning few among them had ever seen a real battle. A majority were farmers who had homes and families and whose minds were filled with their personal cares. After the first burst of enthusiasm died away, especially when they had to go far off from their own communities, hundreds of militiamen insisted on quitting as soon as their terms of service were over, no matter how grave the danger to the American cause and despite the pleas of their officers.

Sorely tried by the conduct of militiamen and volunteers, General Washington again and again begged the Congress to provide for a regular army composed of men enlisted for a long term or the duration of the war. But it was only when failures and defeats threatened utter ruin that the civilians in the Congress, frightened at the mere thought of a standing army as dangerous to civil liberty, yielded to his pleas and offered extra pay to officers and privates pledged to see the war through to the end. At last in the closing years of the conflict Washington had at his command a large body of men so pledged and well disciplined for action in battle.

With regard to officers of all ranks, the colonies were also ill prepared for combat with British regulars. Washington had seen actual, but not extensive, fighting in the French and Indian War. Even he was in fact little equipped by firsthand knowledge for planning and executing great campaigns or coping with the disciplined armies of Britain, enlarged by mercenaries hired from German princes.

None of the high officers on whom he had to rely for help was thoroughly schooled in the arts of war. Henry Knox had been a bookseller in Boston; Nathanael Greene a farmer and blacksmith in Rhode Island; Benedict Arnold, the brave soldier who turned traitor, a merchant in New Haven; Francis Marion a shy South Carolina planter; and John Sullivan a lawyer in New Hampshire. Anthony Wayne was farming in Pennsylvania when he answered the call to arms, raised a regiment, and offered himself to his country. Daniel Morgan, who distinguished himself at Cowpens in South Carolina, had been only a teamster in General Braddock's army during the French and Indian War.

Competent for battle as many American officers proved to be after they had been tried by fire, Washington was fortunate in having the aid of several military men from Europe, who came to help the American cause, for the love of adventure, or in the hope of honors or other rewards: young Lafayette from France; Pulaski and Kosciuszko from Poland; and from Germany, Baron von Steuben, a former officer in the Prussian army, trained in the iron regimen of Frederick the Great and credited with long military service.

It was Steuben who joined Washington during the dark days at Valley Forge, prepared a drill manual for American soldiers, drilled a model company, and laid the basis for discipline throughout the American forces. Steuben's larger manual, later written for general use in giving soldiers the essentials of military instructions, became "the military Bible of the Continental Army." Besides teaching soldiers, Steuben took part in campaigns; he commanded a division under Washington at the siege and capture of Yorktown.

At all stages of the war American troops in the field needed large quantities of arms, ammunition, clothing, food, and other supplies, in addition to the goods furnished by the French and to some extent by the Dutch. Thus the demand for domestic manufactures and farm produce rose rapidly and the home market was widened to include all the states. At once iron, steel, hat, textile, and other industries, which had begun to flourish in colonial times, were expanded; new plants and forges were built; and special privileges were granted to stimulate war production. Women spun and wove more diligently; and spinning clubs were formed in town and country, turning out increasing amounts of woolen, linen, and cotton cloth to meet military and civilian requirements. Workers in iron, wood, and other materials, often from the farms, were drawn into industrial enterprises, especially in New England and the middle states. As a result of the quickened and enlarged activities, now that British restrictions were cast off and British imports materially reduced in volume, American economy advanced rapidly on the way toward emancipation from dependence on the Old World for several prime articles of manufacture.

In the same process, financial independence—of a kind—was achieved. Facing the necessity of providing funds to pay war bills, the Continental Congress and the state governments were forced to wrestle with difficult financial problems. Gold and silver coins of British, French, and Spanish mintage continued in circulation but the supply was wholly inadequate for public and private needs. So the Congress resorted to the issue of paper money—bills of credit—by the millions and, before the end of the war, it had outstanding about $210,000,000 in Continental money—all badly depreciated in value. To this large sum the states added paper notes of their own in an amount almost equal to the total Continental output.

Paper money was supplemented by interest-bearing securities, Continental and state, which were sold to patriotic bond buyers in exchange for specie or paper notes at a fixed rate. More millions were borrowed from France and Holland, yielding the specie desperately needed. Other revenues were derived from the sale of property confiscated from Loyalists who gave aid and comfort to the British. The Congress also called upon the states for quotas of money to meet the common bills, often without getting much in return. In attempts to comply with the demands of the Congress and cover their own requirements, the states laid heavy taxes on their citizens. In this fashion the Congress and the states created a "financial system" of their own or, rather, a financial disorder, for both paper money and bonds dropped rapidly in value—in many cases to a few cents or less on the dollar.

In various phases of war production and financing, as well as in revolutionary pamphleteering, in spying, in making bullets and other munitions, and in direct aid to fighters at the front, patriotic women were active in all the states. While their husbands, fathers, and sons were away under arms, farm women carried double burdens in field and domestic workshops, furnishing food and clothing for the armies. In towns they formed clubs to speed up production. When drives were made to raise money for the war, they organized committees to help, subscribed themselves, and contributed their gold and silver objects to the common treasury.

"Even in their dresses," complained a writer connected with the British army in South Carolina, "the females seem to bid us defiance; the gay toys which are imported here they despise; they wear their own homespun manufactures, and take care to have in their breast knots, and even on their shoes something that resembles their flag of the thirteen stripes. An officer told Lord Cornwallis not long ago, that he believed if he had destroyed all the men in North America, we should have enough to do to conquer the women. I am heartily tired of this country, and wish myself at home."

As colonists, Americans had been subject, in their relations with other countries, to the diplomacy and foreign policies of the government in London. In seeking a place among the independent nations of the earth, the Continental Congress was compelled, on its own responsibility, to make provision for diplomatic representation abroad and evolve the elements of an American foreign policy. As early as 1776 it sent an agent to Paris, Silas Deane, of Connecticut, to open negotiations, if possible, with the government of France. Later Benjamin Franklin and Arthur Lee were instructed to join Deane at the French capital. Other representatives went to Holland, Spain, Vienna, Berlin, and St. Petersburg in quest of recognition and support.

Only in France and Holland did American diplomacy achieve noteworthy results for some time. Spain was cold to American pleas for aid. Russia maintained an attitude of chilly indifference. Frederick the Great of Prussia expressed sympathies but would take no steps likely to involve himself in trouble with Britain. Yet in the end American ministers abroad—whether they procured aid or got no aid—gained a firsthand knowledge of European governments and their foreign policies, of their ambitions, designs, intrigues, and interests in various parts of the world, especially in the Western Hemisphere. Thrown upon their own resources, American diplomats proved ingenious in negotiations and acquired skill in managing foreign relations as they took over this important branch of government, formerly monopolized in America by the British Crown.

Through all the turmoil of war and the activities connected with it, the work of civil government, local and general, was carried on in the United States. While British governors were being driven from power or fleeing for their lives, eleven of the thirteen states set about drawing up plans for full self-government and at the end of the conflict had constitutions of their own. The other two, Connecticut and Rhode Island, made some changes in their old royal charters, under which they had enjoyed a generous liberty, and governed themselves as before. In each state was installed a legislature resting upon popular elections, and in some cases the property qualifications on the right to vote were made lower than they had been in colonial times. In each state provision was made for a governor, elected by the legislature in a majority of cases; in Massachusetts and New York, by popular vote.

Under these written constitutions, in which, except in New York and Massachusetts, the legislature was supreme, elections were held, campaigns conducted, and issues debated by the voters and by citizens who could not vote. Drawing upon colonial experiences, legislatures enacted laws, laid taxes, made provisions for administering state affairs, elected delegates to the Continental Congress, and co-operated, often faithfully, often negligently, with the Congress in the conduct of the war. Now free from British interference, the state legislatures, even during the most trying hours of the Revolution, began to revise and reform radically the laws inherited from England and from the colonial age, and to make American laws conform more closely to the spirit manifest in the Declaration of Independence.

Meanwhile, at the center of things, members of the second Continental Congress—the provisional body hastily assembled in May 1775—gave attention to the strengthening of the union. In June 1776 the Congress appointed a committee to draw up a plan of confederation for the states. The plan, called the Articles of Confederation, was duly reported to the Congress, debated from time to time amid the exigencies of the war business, finally approved late in 1777, and sent to the state legislatures for review and action. By 1779 all the states, except Maryland, had ratified the Articles and Maryland approved them at last, on March 1, 1781. The next day the Congress assembled under the terms of the Articles. Now the states were formally pledged to "a firm league of friendship" and "a perpetual union" created for "their common defense, the security of their liberties," and their "mutual and general welfare." A fateful step had been taken toward a republic, one and indivisible.

☆

As the revolt against Great Britain proceeded to its triumph, a civil revolution began in American society. In the prewar stage of the controversy over British policies Loyalists had warned conservatives in the Patriot party that the destruction of British dominion would lead to popular insurgency and attacks on the privileges of property and class. Their prophecies were more than fulfilled during the course of the Revolution.

Absorbing as the war was, heavy as were the burdens it imposed, most of the American people from 1775 to 1781 were occupied with civilian pursuits and immediately concerned with their economic and social affairs. At the beginning of the war the total population was about 2,500,000 men, women, and children. In 1776 the American army, then at its highest point in numbers, including militiamen and Continentals, had about 90,000 officers and privates—not more than one man in eight of the males able to bear arms. In the latter part of the war, it included only about one man in sixteen of the fighting age.

It would be a conservative estimate, then, to say that at least three fourths of the men, as well as all the women and young people, devoted themselves mainly to civilian affairs, though often engaged in war production. No longer under the dominion of British officials, they insisted on pursuing their interests, discussing public questions as they pleased, exalting their rights, and undermining special privileges. Spurred by the impacts of the war, they began to attack the social order developed during the colonial period.

Thus a landslide toward democracy—a state of affairs dreaded by American conservatives and British Loyalists—was started. During the Revolution a large portion of the upper class collapsed. After the British governors and their horde of officials fled from colonial capitals, thousands of merchants, clergy, landlords, and lawyers who adhered to Britain were forced to leave the country or retire from public life. As a rule Loyalists who remained outside British military lines were silenced. Often they were subjected to physical violence.

Many large estates owned by British subjects, sometimes embracing several hundred thousand acres, were confiscated and then auctioned off in blocks to Americans. Immense areas of unoccupied lands, once at the disposal of the British Crown or its agents, passed under the control of state legislatures and the Continental Congress, to be granted or sold under American laws. The right of American landlords to pass their estates intact to their eldest sons under the rule of "primogeniture" was assailed and either destroyed or materially modified in favor of the division of estates among all heirs, including daughters. Everywhere in the states the English Church was disestablished and religious liberty was generally widened, though not made complete.

Associated with these changes was a rapidly widening interest among the people in social and political issues. The number of newspapers increased despite the handicaps of the war. Thousands of Americans who had hitherto cared little about election campaigns were aroused by the stirring events of the Revolution and began to take part in public discussions and agitations, to vote, if they had the right, and to demand the right to vote, if it was denied to them under the new state laws. In the most crucial years of the war tumult and perils, differences of opinion over politics, government, and reform divided Americans into parties and factions and precipitated conflicts among the patriots themselves, often verging in the direction of physical violence. For an immense number of the American people, the Revolution in all its phases was, therefore, a great social and intellectual awakening.

CHAPTER IX

Constitutional Government for the United States

AFTER THEY HAD WON independence from Great Britain, Americans faced the problem of governing themselves and holding together the union formed during the Revolutionary War. Could they do it? From the three proprietary colonies—Pennsylvania, Delaware, and Maryland—the proprietary officials had been expelled. From the eight royal provinces—New Hampshire, Massachusetts, New York, New Jersey, Virginia, North Carolina, South Carolina, and Georgia—royal governors and their train of subordinates had been driven out. No longer could disputes within and between colonies be carried to London for settlement. No longer did loyalty to the British King or the need for common action in the war against him constitute a unifying principle for Americans. No longer did the British navy and army serve as shields against the warlike Powers of Europe, especially France and Spain, both eager to extend their dominions in the New World.

In colonial times the British government had exercised control over all the colonies in essential matters of public policy and administration. It had conducted foreign affairs and provided common defense against other nations. Foreign commerce, intercolonial commerce, and the monetary system had all been subject to British regulation. The British Crown had served as the chief executive organ for the colonies, and British courts as tribunals of appeal in cases involving the rights of person and property. Now all this central machinery of power had been swept away and each state was set free to do about as it pleased; that is to say, as the majority of the voters represented in the legislature pleased.

During the Revolution, British officials had scoffed at the idea that Americans could successfully carry on the work of government in its higher ranges where great statesmanship was required; and Tories had sneered at them as pettifogging lawyers, riotous mechanics, disorderly farmers, and lawbreaking merchants. Even patriots on the right wing of the Revolution had expressed dislike and contempt for the people and republics. Neither the Declaration of Independence nor the Articles of Confederation nor any of the first state constitutions had mentioned the word "republic." At the time it was like a red flag to conservatives everywhere.

Moreover, educated patriots knew that revolutions in history, democratic and republican, had often resulted in despotism. Again and again in the Greek states of antiquity, democracy had been supplanted by a dictatorship or tyranny. The Roman republic had disappeared in the rule of an absolute emperor. Only about a century before, the Puritan revolution in England had culminated in the military dictatorship of Oliver Cromwell, followed shortly by a restoration of the monarchy.

Reflective Americans who were confronted with the task of governing the country had read about such historic events. Loyalists who had opposed the American Revolution from start to finish expected it to end in a disaster for the patriots and the reestablishment of a monarchy in some form. Indeed a few of them cast about for a suitable prince to be made king of the United States. Many patriots, some in high places, military and civil, abhorring the very idea of popular rule, looked forward with satisfaction to the triumph of a military dictator, supreme throughout the Union.

Even before peace came, Colonel Lewis Nicola wrote to General Washington expressing scorn for republics and calling for a military government, at least in a part of the country. Washington sent him a blistering reply. But other army officers wrote to Washington more or less in the same vein. In fact, he received so many letters hinting at violent action against the government which had been set up that his brooding spirit burst forth with cries of apprehension over the future of his country.

Rumors of a reaction in the shape of a monarchy or military dictatorship were bruited here and there among the people after peace came. In Connecticut Noah Webster heard from some source that military men and merchants in New England were working at plans to overturn popular rule and establish a government of special privileges by force. In Massachusetts Mercy Warren learned from some source that many young men, "particularly students at law and youth of fortune and pleasure," were clamoring for a monarchy and a standing army to support it. She thought there was "a formidable body ready to bow to the sceptre of a king, provided they may be the lordlings who in splendid idleness may riot on the hard earnings of the peasant and mechanic." Governor George Clinton, of New York, confessed publicly in 1788 that in the closing years of the War for Independence a design had been formed in his state to establish a kind of military government.

Rumors and open threats of drastic action against "popular tumults" increased after a band of debt-burdened farmers in Massachusetts, led by Captain Daniel Shays, a soldier of the Revolution, tried to redress their grievances by an uprising in 1786. According to the constitution of that state, drafted by John Adams and put into effect in 1780, the right to vote and hold office had been limited to property owners and taxpayers; and the richer towns were given special weight in the state senate. Under this government, creditors began to sue debtors in the law courts and take property away from farmers who could not pay what they owed.

In protest Shays organized a large body of men in the western part of the state and attempted to shut up the courts by a display of armed force. It was only with difficulty and some bloodshed that the state government put down "Shays' Rebellion." Even then popular sympathies with the uprising remained so strong that the state officials did not dare to execute Shays or any of his followers. Whatever the merits of this popular revolt, it increased the fears of property owners and conservatives in general, inciting them to work harder than ever for a powerful national government.

☆

Amid efforts to substitute for the Confederation a highly centralized government, akin in some respects to the regimen Great Britain had formerly maintained over the colonies, complaints against state governments grew in number and virulence. In all the states except Massachusetts and New York, which both had strong governments, the control of public affairs was in the hands of the legislature elected by the qualified voters, among whom farmers predominated. In short, the states were controlled by popular majorities with little or no restraint from executive or judicial officers, such as British royal governors and the Crown had imposed on colonial legislatures.

In these circumstances states issued their own money in coin or paper or both and, under pressure from farmers, seven states emitted large quantities of paper money. This was done partly for the purpose of raising the prices of farm produce, making it easier for farmers to pay their debts. Before the Revolution Great Britain had stopped the practice; now Americans were at liberty to revive it.

More liberties were asserted by popular legislatures. Urged by special interests, states put tariff duties on imports from foreign countries, modified them, or repealed them, at will. Determined to protect their local interests, some states laid duties on goods coming in from other states; New York, for instance, taxed firewood from Connecticut and vegetables from New Jersey. During the Revolution states had borrowed money for war purposes and several of them were slow in paying off those debts. In short, for a time, the states acted as independent republics ruled by popular majorities represented in the legislatures; and, warmly attached to their own liberties, they went to extremes in their indifference to the fortunes of the Union.

While the states and their legislatures were coming under an increasing fire of criticism from merchants, creditors, and holders of state bonds, a storm of disapproval was gathering against the Articles of Confederation and the Congress of the United States. A part of this censure was directed to the form of that government. The Confederacy, according to the critics, was really a farce; it had no executive to enforce the laws made by the Congress; and the states and the people disregarded the laws with impunity. It also lacked a judiciary empowered to try persons accused of violating the laws of the Union, to hear cases arising under them, or to settle disputes among the states.

The Congress was disparaged as faulty in form and futile in action. In the Congress, states, not the people, were represented; its members were elected by the state legislatures; and in all important matters the states, large and small, were equal, for each had only one vote to cast. Its members were negligent in attendance and public business dragged on from year to year unfinished.

On two special counts critics disparaged the Congress in respect of its powers: the Congress lacked power to make laws necessary to the safety and welfare of the Union; and it had no authority to prevent the states from interfering with matters of common, or general, concern.

The Congress could vote money for the purposes of the Union, but it could lay no taxes directly on anybody; it had to depend upon the willingness of the state legislatures to raise money and pay it into the Confederate treasury. The Congress could provide for an army but it was compelled to rely upon each of the states to supply its quota of men voluntarily. Although the Congress could make treaties with other countries respecting foreign commerce, the states decided for themselves whether or not they would obey such treaties. The Congress could not regulate commerce among the states or establish a single and uniform system of currency for the country. Furthermore, as time passed, the states refused, despite urgent appeals from Congress, to grant it additional financial powers essential to its very existence.

On the score of power the Congress was also assailed because it could not compel the states to quit doing many things which interfered with property and comity. It could not stop their issues of paper money or their interference with interstate and foreign commerce. It had no check on their legislation designed to make it easier for debtors to pay their debts in "cheap money." It could not send troops to help put down insurrections or to enforce the laws of the Union if they encountered popular resistance.

In these circumstances agitations were started in several quarters for changes in the American system of government that had come into being as an emergency government during the Revolution and had been continued under the Articles of Confederation. Former army officers, now organized in the Order of the Cincinnati, and former soldiers of the rank and file found the paper scrip with which they had been paid off at the close of the war so reduced in value as to be almost worthless. Holders of state and Continental securities were disgruntled, for the interest on their bonds was not paid promptly, if at all, and their paper sank in the markets, sometimes to a price as low as ten cents on the dollar. Manufacturers complained that the imports of foreign goods seriously cut down their business. Merchants and shippers grumbled over the lack of protection against foreign merchants and shippers in America and distant ports. Owners of undeveloped lands in the West, including soldiers of the Revolution holding claims to tracts there as part payment for their services and speculators engaged in accumulating great areas with a view to profitable sales to settlers, deplored the lack of a national army capable of suppressing the Indians who hampered the spread of settlements. Creditors fretted over paper-money schemes and other threats to their mortgages on property.

Generally associated with one or more of these economic interests, but often rising above purely personal interests, were critics with national vision who joined the movement for drastic changes in the Articles of Confederation. Familiar with the intrigues and ambitions of European Powers, they feared that the United States might be divided by foreign plotting, might be reconquered perhaps by Great Britain, or fall a victim to France or Spain, both with territorial ambitions in the neighborhood. They were also alarmed by schemes for overturning the republican institutions and establishing a monarchy or military dictatorship. Scarcely less disturbing to them was the possibility of an upheaval from below. Worried by the outlook, these national leaders sought to find a peaceful way of setting up a stronger and yet representative government for the Union.

Among the leaders in the nationalizing movement George Washington was foremost in character and influence. As early as 1783, in a circular letter to the governors of the states, Washington, who had done so much to save the Revolution, warned them of perils ahead and recommended the adoption of a more powerful government, able to "regulate and govern the general concerns of the confederate republic." Meanwhile Alexander Hamilton, who had fought in the Revolution, launched a campaign against the Articles of Confederation and demanded the calling of a new congress or convention to draft a constitution based on different and firmer principles. Other men, well known and less well known, including Pelatiah Webster, put forth plans for amending the Articles or substituting an entirely new form of government.

But all along the line advocates of material changes met vigorous opposition. Although none of the leaders in this resistance had the prestige of Washington, many of them had been eminent in the Revolutionary cause. In the struggle against the powerful grip of the British Crown and Parliament, thousands of Americans had acquired a horror of "strong government." Some among them feared that any strong government might end in a monarchy or that it would mean, in any case, big armies, big navies, heavy taxes, mountainous debts, and interference with personal liberty, in the style of the British government. Especially among farmers, who formed a majority of the people, the idea was rigidly held that the state legislature was the best bulwark for the protection of their interests and rights.

Widespread was the conviction that full autonomy in towns,

counties, and states was the truest and best basis for the life, liberty, and pursuit of happiness proclaimed in the Declaration of Independence. To Americans who had such views nothing seemed more reasonable than the belief that "centralization" was to be dreaded and that the rights of states were to be cherished and preserved.

To change or not to change the form of government—to swing away from more authority or toward it—became by 1786 the burning issue before the American people. At firesides, in taverns, by correspondence, and in the press it was debated with a searching and enlightened intelligence, worthy of the generation that had won independence.

☆

Out of heated discussions came decisive actions. A small group in Virginia induced the state legislature to call a general convention at Annapolis to discuss taxation and commerce. The convention met in 1786 but delegates from only five states appeared on the floor and the prospects were discouraging to its members. One of the delegates, however, Alexander Hamilton, from New York, refused to give up the struggle to realize the aims of the nationalizing movement.

Seizing time by the forelock, Hamilton persuaded the Annapolis convention to adopt a resolution urging the Congress of the United States to take leadership and summon a convention at Philadelphia, for the purpose of proposing amendments to the Articles of Confederation which, when adopted by the states, would make them "adequate to the exigencies of the Union." To this project the Congress agreed. In response, all the states except Rhode Island elected delegates. In May 1787 the new convention assembled in Philadelphia and settled down to the task of devising a stronger government for the United States.

On the roll of the convention, consisting of fifty-five members in all, were many of the most prominent names in America: for example, George Washington, Benjamin Franklin, Alexander Hamilton, James Madison, Robert Morris, Gouverneur Morris, John Dickinson, James Wilson, Roger Sherman, Oliver Ellsworth, Charles Pinckney, and Edmund Randolph. Eight of them had been among the signers of the Declaration of Independence. Nearly all had been active in the Revolution, as military officers, financiers, members of the Continental Congress, and public officials. Among them were men of wealth and influence in their communities—merchants, lawyers, and planters.

On the whole the convention was a conservative body. Thomas Jefferson, then minister to France, a liberal, was not present. Neither was John Hancock, whose name led all the signatures to the Declaration of Independence. That outstanding firebrand of the Revolution, Patrick Henry, though elected a delegate, refused to attend, saying that he "smelt a rat." Even so, great talents, wisdom, and experience in statecraft were represented at Philadelphia in 1787.

The sessions of the convention lasted from May to September 17, 1787, and were marked by many differences of opinion and long debates. Indeed it has been customary for historians to lay stress on the differences of opinion and treat the Constitution which emerged as a mere "bundle of compromises." But this view is far from the whole truth of the matter. Strictly speaking, the agreements of the convention were more numerous and important for the nation than the dissensions and the compromises.

In the course of their proceedings, a large majority easily agreed on the following fundamentals:

The Articles of Confederation must be discarded, not merely amended, and a new constitution substituted.

The new government must have three departments—legislative, executive, and judicial.

The large states must have more power in the new government than the small states, thus giving to it a popular basis.

The new Congress must have the power to legislate on all matters of national concern and all matters with which the states cannot deal competently, including the power to tax, to regulate interstate and foreign commerce, and to spend money for common defense and general welfare.

The debts of the Confederation must be binding on the new government.

Many restraints must be laid on the state governments.

The serious disputes in the convention turned mainly on details and ways and means of realizing the accepted purposes. They involved such questions as these: What shall be the composition of the new Congress? Shall the executive consist of one person or more? How shall the executive be elected? How shall the large states be given their appropriate share of power in the new government and the claims of the small states to equality be recognized? How shall the enlarged power of the new Congress be ex-

pressed in terms of specified powers? How is it possible to create
a strong national legislature and a strong executive and yet prevent
either from becoming all-powerful in the government of the
Union? How shall direct taxes be apportioned among the states in
such a way as not to burden unduly the poorer states? What qualifications shall be fixed for voters in federal elections and for places
of trust in the new government? What provisions shall be made
for amending the new Constitution as times change? How shall the
Constitution be finally adopted and put into force?

Out of the debates that swirled around these and subsidiary
questions for four months was finally evolved, on September 17,
the finished document which thirty-nine delegates, a safe majority,
were willing to sign. By that time several of the members had gone
home, alienated by the spirit and plans of their colleagues. A few
malcontents, who remained to the end, for one reason or another
refused to sign the finished instrument. One of the dissenters,
Luther Martin, of Maryland, was so perturbed by all he had
seen and heard at Philadelphia that he wrote a long letter of denunciation to the legislature of his state and published it widely
in an effort to defeat the ratification of the Constitution. Even
among the signers there were doubts as to particular provisions in
the document, but these were subordinated to the interest of unity
on fundamentals. Washington expressed the general sentiment
of his colleagues when he declared that the Constitution was about
as good as could be expected and the people ought to adopt it,
leaving to the future the making of corrections by amendments.

☆

Running through the text of the Constitution from the Preamble to the last line were evidences of the fundamental propositions
on which the majority of the convention agreed early in its proceedings. Interwoven with them were answers to the questions of
means and details by which the essential purposes of a stronger
Union were to be accomplished. Here and there were signs of the
compromises and adjustments of interests that the framers found
necessary to the settlement of disputes large and small. Only when
so viewed does the Constitution take on the fullness of its meaning for the time and the ages.

First of all, the Preamble made it clear that the framers were
creating no mere league of states. The Articles of Confederation
had declared explicitly that "each state retains its sovereignty,
freedom, and independence"—the high power which state legis-

latures had been exercising. Respecting the sovereignty, freedom, and independence of the states, as such, the Constitution contained not a word, and what it did to the pretensions of the states to full sovereignty stood out boldly in the lines imposing restraints on their powers. The announcement that the Constitution and federal laws were to be supreme over all state actions conflicting with them was unmistakable in its brevity and import.

The Preamble declared that the Constitution was a constitution ordained and established by the people of the United States —not mere articles of agreement between the thirteen states. The Articles of Confederation had called the Union "a firm league of friendship" between the states. The new order contemplated by the Constitution was more than a league of states. The government for which it provided, in the exercise of its powers, was authorized to deal directly with individuals, not states. It was authorized to go over the heads of state officials and legislatures and compel obedience to federal laws by the use of its own agencies of coercion. In fine, the Constitution worked a political revolution—a transformation—in the form of government that had been set up in the violence of the break with Britain. Its critics understood this at the time and history to come validated the fact.

☆

In the structure of the new government this revolution was reflected. The old Congress had been little more than a conference of ambassadors from the states. In one house of the new Congress, it is true, each state, large and small, was to have two senators and the states were thus nominally equal. But each senator was given a term of six years, was to be paid out of the Treasury of the United States, and could not be retired at will or compelled to vote against his conscience by his state legislature. The Senate was given the power to pass upon treaties and nominations to certain high offices proposed by the President.

Sharing the legislative power with the Senate was the House of Representatives, based on population, not on states. Members of this chamber were apportioned among the states according to their respective numbers of free persons, excluding Indians not taxed and including three fifths of "all other persons," that is, slaves. The members of the House were to be elected directly in each state by the persons entitled to vote for members of the most numerous branch of the state legislature. That "the voice of the people" might be heard frequently, provision was made for biennial elections. To prevent state legislatures from interfering too grossly with congressional elections, Congress was given the power to alter and make laws regulating such elections.

In all ordinary legislative matters, the House of Representatives was made equal to the Senate. In one vital matter it was given the supreme weapon of political power—control over the national purse; for the Constitution provided that "all bills for raising revenue shall originate in the House of Representatives." Although in time this provision was allowed to become a dead letter, the intention behind it was indubitable; if it so decided, "the people's house" might exercise supreme power over the purse in the government of the United States.

In another essential respect the weight of the people as against the states counted in the structure of the federal government—in the Executive Department. After careful discussion the convention decided that the Executive should consist of one person, not three or more representing sections of the Union. The President was to be elected, not by Congress as at first decided, nor by popular vote as was proposed, but by electors chosen as the legislatures of the states might decide. In fixing the number of electors assigned to each state, the Constitution recognized both population and the states and so gave the people, as such, a share in the presidency; that is, it prescribed that the number of electors allowed to each state must equal the number of senators and representatives to which it may be entitled. Until a census could be taken in 1790 there were to be sixty-five representatives.

Under the Articles there had been in fact thirteen heads to the confederacy—the thirteen delegations in the Congress, which merely had a presiding officer. Under the Constitution there was to be one head, the President of the United States, endowed with great powers in peace and war. He was to symbolize the unity, not the diversity, of the country. And for strength of support, he was to depend upon numbers of people, not the pleasure of state legislatures.

The unity of the country was also symbolized by the Constitution in the creation of a Supreme Court, the members of which were to be chosen by the President with the consent of the Senate. Congress might at will establish inferior courts, district and circuit, but the Supreme Court was anchored in the Constitution. Its justices might be divided as to cases before it, but its decisions made by a majority of them were to be binding at law throughout the land. Thus in matters of federal concern the will of one high court was to be substituted for the clashing wills of thirteen or more state courts.

The judicial power conferred upon federal courts covered every issue of general interest throughout the Union. It shall extend, ran Section 2 of Article III, "to all cases in law and equity arising under this Constitution, the laws of the United States, and treaties made, or 'which shall be made, under their authority." That was not all. This power was to embrace all cases of admiralty and maritime jurisdiction arising on the high seas and public waters of the Union. It was to include controversies between two or more states; between a state and citizens of another state; between citizens of different states; between a state and citizens thereof and foreign states, citizens, and subjects. Thus special kinds of conflicts between private persons in the several states and between states as such were to be finally resolved by the exercise of federal judicial power, with the Supreme Court as the tribunal of ultimate appeal.

Yet, powerful as was to be the structure of the new government —Congress, Executive, and Judiciary—it was so formed that, in operation, checks could be placed on the accumulation of despotic power in any hands, even in the hands of the people who had the right to vote in elections. How to set up a government strong enough to serve the purposes of the Union and still not too strong for the maintenance of the liberties of the people? That was a prime issue in the convention. It had been in all previous history, and was to be in centuries to come, the central problem in the science and art of government.

This question the framers of the Constitution sought to settle by establishing what is known as the "system of checks and balances." First of all they founded each great branch of the government on a separate basis of political power. They provided that members of the House of Representatives should be elected for a term of two years by persons entitled to vote under certain laws of the respective states; that the senators should be elected for terms of six years by the legislatures of the states; and that the President should be elected for four years by electors chosen as the state legislatures might decide—by the legislatures themselves or by the voters or in any other appropriate manner. Members of the federal judiciary were to be selected by the President and the Senate, both one degree removed from direct popular vote.

Against the possibility of tyranny, therefore, two safeguards were set up in the Constitution. The ultimate source of power, it was recognized, was the people—the enfranchised voters in the states. But under the methods provided for the choice of representatives, senators, President, and federal judges, no political party or faction could get possession of the whole government at a single election. In the long run, through a period of years, the persistent will of the popular majority might prevail. Yet at no moment could the "snap judgment" of a popular majority prevail in all departments of the federal government.

Moreover, within the very structure of the government, power was so distributed that no branch could seize all of it, unless the others deliberately abdicated. The House and Senate were to check each other in legislation. Congress and the President were to put brakes on each other. As against both, members of the federal judiciary were given the independence of tenure for life; and yet the House could impeach them and, by the judgment of the Senate, they could be removed from office. The President was to enjoy a high degree of independent initiative; but he could do nothing unless Congress enacted laws and voted money for carrying his proposals into execution. Besides, he too could be ousted from office by the process of impeachment.

☆

Upon the government so constructed, the Constitution conferred immense powers in terms specific and general. For convenience they may be divided into two classes: powers over domestic affairs and powers over foreign relations. But in fact these powers were so closely interwoven at many points that lines could not be drawn between them. For example, Congress was given the right to tax and appropriate money for defense and the general welfare of the United States.

Among the great powers particularly relevant to domestic affairs the following were vested in Congress in specific terms: to lay and collect taxes, duties, and excises; pay the debts of the United States; borrow money; regulate commerce among the states; establish uniform rules for the naturalization of aliens; enact laws on bankruptcies; coin money and regulate the value thereof; establish post offices and post roads; promote science and the useful arts by giving exclusive rights to authors and inventors—copyrights and patents; establish courts inferior to the Supreme Court; raise and support armed forces; provide for calling out the militia to execute the laws and suppress insurrections; establish penalties for the punishment of persons who counterfeit the coins and securities of the United States.

The powers relative to foreign affairs were not concentrated in the Executive or in Congress but were distributed among the three departments; or, to put it another way, they were vested in the whole government. To Congress was given exclusive power to provide for the common defense; to regulate commerce with foreign nations, including control over the immigration of aliens; to declare war; to raise and support armed forces; to define and punish offenses against the law of nations; and by implication, to establish and appropriate money for ministers, consuls, and other agents of the United States in foreign countries. To the President was granted the power to make treaties with other countries, but only by and with the advice and consent of at least two thirds of the senators. With the consent of the Senate also he was to appoint the consuls, ministers, and other agents to represent the United States abroad.

Since the Constitution was designed to endure for ages in which great changes were bound to come in American affairs, the framers knew that Congress would have to deal with them or be helpless in serving the purposes for which the stronger Union was established. So, besides vesting in Congress powers later called "specific," the Constitution gave it two general powers to make the instrument flexible for adaptation to changes in the needs, ideas, and interests of the American people.

It authorized Congress to raise and appropriate money for "the general welfare of the United States." It also authorized Congress "to make all laws necessary and proper for carrying into effect" its specific powers, "and all other powers vested by this Constitution in the government of the United States or any department or officer thereof." Many a conflict was to rage over these lines but in time they were accepted as giving sanction to types of legislation conceived in the general interest of the nation as distinguished from interests purely local in nature.

☆

While creating a strong government, balanced within itself and endowed with great powers, the framers of the Constitution placed definite limits on the federal government with a view to preserving liberty. They provided, for instance, that Congress shall pass no bill of attainder, that is, no law imposing penalties on any person without a judicial trial. They likewise forbade *ex post facto* laws—measures stigmatizing as crimes actions which had been committed but were not crimes at the time of commission. The trial of all crimes against the United States, except in cases of impeachment, they declared, must be by jury and in the state where committed. "No money shall be drawn from the Treasury," ran another clause, "but in consequence of appropriations made by law; and a regular statement and account of receipts and expenditures of all public moneys shall be published from time to time."

Even a strong and limited government for the Union, the framers decided, was not sufficient to fulfill their national purposes. Hence they laid specific restraints upon the states, forbidding them to meddle with many matters of life, liberty, and property. Some of these restraints pertained to domestic affairs; others, to foreign affairs.

The states were stripped of powers to coin money, emit bills of credit, make anything but gold and silver coin legal tender in the payment of debts, pass bills of attainder and *ex post facto* laws, grant titles of nobility, and enact laws impairing the obligation of contracts. Every state was commanded to give full faith and credit to the public acts, records, and judicial proceedings of all other states; in other words, states were to place no barriers in the way of enforcing legal rights throughout the land. As a guarantee of free migration and commerce throughout the country, the Constitution provided that "the citizens of each state shall be entitled to all the privileges and immunities of citizens of the several states."

No less mandatory were the restraints laid upon the states in respect of foreign affairs. They were forbidden to enter into any treaty, alliance, or confederation. They were ordered to lay no imposts or duties on imports or exports, without the consent of Congress, except such as might be absolutely necessary for the execution of their inspection laws. To use the language of the Constitution: "No state shall, without the consent of Congress, lay any duties of tonnage, keep troops, or ships of war, in time of peace, enter into any agreement or compact with another state, or with a foreign power, or engage in war, unless actually invaded, or in such imminent danger as will not admit of delay."

In return for the many limitations imposed upon the states, the framers of the Constitution offered them pledges of protection. The Constitution provided that "the United States shall guarantee to every state in this union a republican form of government, and shall protect each of them against invasion." As if remembering

Shays' Rebellion of 1786 in Massachusetts, they offered to the states the aid of the United States against "domestic violence."

Having in mind an enduring Union, the framers of the Constitution realized that conferring general powers upon Congress might not make it competent to cope with all the problems of coming times, with formidable changes that might occur in the ideas and interests of the American people. Radical alterations might be necessary in the form and powers of the proposed government.

In recognition of this fact the framers made provision for amending the Constitution; and here, too, they overrode the sovereignty of the states. No alteration could be made in the provisions of the Articles of Confederation without the consent of every state. For this principle was substituted another rule. By Article V the Constitution provided that Congress might, by a two-thirds vote in each house, propose amendments to the Constitution or, on application from the legislatures of two thirds of the states, must call a convention for the purpose of proposing amendments.

Amendments proposed by Congress or by such a convention were to go into effect when ratified by legislatures or conventions in three fourths of the states. Only one exception was made to this plan for binding states against their wills: "No state, without its consent, shall be deprived of its equal suffrage in the Senate."

The Constitution so drawn was strong medicine for advocates of states' rights. Its framers knew this very well. Throughout their proceedings in the convention they were impressed or oppressed by fear that it would not be ratified. How to put it into effect? That was for them a specter. Many state legislatures had refused to permit any increase in the powers of the old Congress. Perhaps that Congress, still functioning under the Articles of Confederation, would reject the new plan of government. Popular opposition to any changes in the existing form of government might be insurmountable. Perhaps state legislatures would refuse to ratify the Constitution. The knot had to be cut and it was cut by the makers of the Constitution with two provisions for ratification.

First, they appealed over the heads of Congress and the state legislatures. They sent their plan to the existing Congress, with two recommendations, namely, that it be referred to the states by the Congress and that the state legislatures call special conventions, elected by the voters, to pass upon the plan. Second, they provided that the Constitution should go into effect when ratified by nine states as between the nine—leaving the other states, if they preferred, out in the cold without a national roof over their heads.

☆

When on September 17, 1787, the secrecy of the convention was broken and the proposed plan was published, a tempest of public debate over its merits began to blow. Critics fell upon it with might and main. It was not a plan for a "federal" union, some said, but a dark plot to establish a centralized despotism and reduce the states to provinces. The President, others insisted, would become a monarch, perhaps worse than George III. It was a device, radicals claimed, by which the rich and powerful would govern the country and oppress the plain people with armies, taxes, and debts. It had no bill of rights, friends of liberty protested. In fact scarcely a line of the Constitution escaped an attack, mild or passionate. On the other hand, able defenders came to its support in pamphlets, articles, and letters. The most comprehensive and cogent defense was made by Alexander Hamilton, John Jay, and James Madison. Between October 1787 and May 1788 they wrote eighty-five long articles, most of which appeared in the press of New York, under the pen name of "Publius." Many of the articles were reprinted in the newspapers of other states. They were all brought out in the spring of 1788 in two volumes entitled *The Federalist*. From that day to this *The Federalist* has been widely regarded as the most profound single treatise on the Constitution ever written and as among the few masterly works on political science produced in all the centuries of history.

While the public debate over the plan was in full course, conventions duly elected in the states assembled to pass upon it. Within three months three states ratified it—Delaware and New Jersey unanimously, and Pennsylvania after a hot contest. Early in 1788 Georgia and Connecticut added their approval. By a close vote Massachusetts accepted it in February. Maryland and South Carolina soon followed. The New Hampshire convention, at first opposed or hesitant, decided favorably before the end of June. Nine states, the number necessary to put the Constitution into effect, had now made the fateful decision.

But two large states wavered. In New York a majority of the convention was against ratification. In Virginia tenacious opponents, including Patrick Henry, kept the result long in doubt, but in the end the supporters of the new plan triumphed there. Then, under the leadership of Alexander Hamilton, the opposition in New York was overcome and a resolution of ratification was adopted. Thus by the autumn of 1788 eleven of the thirteen states had accepted the new Union. The advocates of the revolutionary change in the loose form of government provided by the Articles of Confederation were at last victorious.

Only two states remained aloof. The convention in North Carolina withheld its approval—until November 1789. Rhode Island would have nothing to do with the new Constitution until the spring of 1790, when it added its ratification.

Exulting in their success, victors in the contest celebrated the occasion by organizing spectacular parades in the principal towns. With justification they looked upon the outcome as the triumph of reason over force. Without drawing the sword in a civil war, without shedding a drop of blood, a new plan of government had been proposed, framed, discussed, and adopted. The victors in seven states, it is true, had been forced to appease opponents distressed about dangers to civil liberties by agreeing that a bill of rights, in the form of amendments, should be joined to the Constitution when the new government got under way. But as none of the proposed amendments affected the form of that government, this pledge, fulfilled in 1791, merely confirmed the faith of Americans in the power of the people to govern themselves on a continental scale by peaceful constitutional processes.

CHAPTER X

Establishing the Republican Way of Life

WITH GRATEFUL UNANIMITY presidential electors, chosen after the adoption of the Constitution, cast their ballots for George Washington as the Chief Executive of the United States. Inaugurated on April 30, 1789, amid the plaudits of the people in New York City, the first capital of the new government, he delivered an address emphasizing the solemn nature of the republican experiment that was being launched. "The pre-eminence of free government," he said, should be "exemplified by all the attributes which can win the affections of its citizens and command the respect of the world. . . . The preservation of the sacred fire of liberty and the destiny of the republican model of government are justly considered, perhaps, as *deeply*, as *finally*, staked on the experiment entrusted to the hands of the American people."

In this declaration Washington no doubt expressed the sentiments of all Americans save those intransigent Tories who hoped for the failure of the Republic and a return to the fold of the British monarchy. A new government, republican in form, had been founded. Many Americans living under it, even some who had been ardent in support of the Revolution, feared that it might not endure. One great problem of the opening years, then, was that of making universal—in thought, sentiments, and outward signs—the spirit necessary to sustain it.

The Revolutionary generation, now embarking on the republican way of life, had all grown up under a monarchy. Accustomed to that regime, many of the patriots, some of them high in the political and military circles of the Revolution, believed, even while the fighting was going on, that a monarchical form of government was the only kind that could maintain law and order. According to rumors, private negotiations were carried on with or about possible candidates for the throne in America, including the second son of King George III. Certainly a few officers in the Revolutionary army thought that a military dictatorship of one man should be established over the people. John Adams was of the opinion that the President should be given a title as resounding as that of "His Highness" or "His Majesty" in order to excite great respect or awe among the people for the chief magistrate. Attachment to the aristocratic ideology prevalent among nations across the sea was likewise strong among a large number of Americans who sought to shape the American way of life under its republican forms. If no true aristocracy of blood and lineage could be set up, they thought an "aristocracy of wealth and talents" might be substituted for it.

But the monarchists did not have their way. Nor did an aristocracy based on mere wealth and talents attain supreme power. While members of the upper classes of the United States were proposing to take over the government and direct it according to their ideas and interests, no organized royalist movement, even as a temporary grasp at power, interrupted the transition from monarchy to republic. In the shadows was no dethroned king or queen or ambitious pretender who could form the center of a monarchist reaction. The constitutional way of governing had been widely accepted and, in rallying the people to the Constitution, the planting and mercantile interests, so dominant in the Philadelphia Convention of 1787, had to make concessions to popular, and even leveling, doctrines in efforts to make their policies prevail.

The first President was a military hero—the commander in chief of the Revolutionary army. But he was not to become a Caesar or a Napoleon and put a crown on his own head. He had refused, with wrath at the suggestion, to be a party to any conspiracy for setting up a monarch or a military dictator. Of his own choice he had returned to the old Congress the symbol of his military authority—his commission as commander—the military authority granted him by that body of civilians. Now the unanimous choice of the nation's electors, he was to wear no title superior to that of plain "Mr. President." And he was to go down in the republican tradition, not so much as General Washington as simply George Washington.

There was no impulsion to Caesarism in him. His sense of

dignity prevented hero worship from degenerating into that form
of popular betrayal. Long accustomed to fine horses and equipages,
Washington, as "Mr. President," rode out frequently in the first
capital of the nation in his grand coach drawn by six horses
driven by a slave, accompanied by outriders. But he did not think
of himself as a demigod chosen t ɔ rule the United States. Nor was
he moved to be a lesser divinity and wield power as a demagogue
through a resort to hypnotic oratory. He had no genius for
oratory.

Despite his great wealth and his social position he was essentially
modest in his estimation of his political sagacity. No amount of
public adulation changed his estimation of himself—not even
during the journey from his home in Virginia to New York City.
During that journey he passed through one triumphal arch after
another amid cheering throngs to the capital, where he was welcomed by leading citizens with lavish ceremonies and by huge
crowds that had come from distant places to shout acclaim and
throw flowers at his feet. But nothing fired him with dangerous
vanity.

However intractable the remnants of the monarchical tradition
may have been, George Washington had no desire, and was not
temperamentally fitted, to reinforce it. He was sincere in his profession that he lacked many qualifications for carrying the burden
of presiding over the new government as its highest and most
responsible official. Before he started to New York to assume that
duty, he had written to General Henry Knox that his "feelings
were not unlike those of a culprit going to his execution." In his
diary he had recorded that his mind was "oppressed with more
anxious and painful sensations than he had words to express."

It was with no mere gesture of false pride that he referred, in
his first inaugural address, to his "inferior endowments from nature," his lack of experience in "the duties of civil administration,"
and his other "deficiencies." These were not the ideas of a man
thirsting for power or eager to play the role of a demagogue.
They were rather the confessions of a man prepared to take
counsel with the people, his advisers, and friends, to make compromises with extremists, and rule in the constitutional manner
appropriate to the republican way of life.

Moreover, he soon began to study books which might be helpful, such as Vattel's *Law of Nations* and volumes of the *Debates*
in the House of Commons, making use of the Society Library in
New York City. He had based his scientific plantation manage-

ment on knowledge acquired in part by reading books on agriculture in his own large collection. Now he also looked for such guidance in his public work as books might afford.

Had Washington been inclined to regal or arbitrary habits of rule—and his political associate, James Madison, testified that he never was so inclined—he would have found strong opposition among the people of New York. To be sure, there were still many Tories in the city, reminders of the fact that it had been occupied by the British troops from 1776 to the end of the Revolutionary War. But monarchist loyalties were declining among them. King's College, closed during the British occupancy, had been renamed Columbia College and its learned professors were republicans now, if cautious in their political expressions. Distinguished lawyers, physicians, and surgeons, who had been eminent in the old regime, were adjusting themselves to the new regime.

Furthermore, the city had many influential residents who, while definitely republican in principles, had opposed the adoption of the Constitution. Surrounding Alexander Hamilton, prime exponent of centralization, were unswerving defenders of decentralization. Ratification of the Constitution had been literally wrung from the representatives of the New York voters at the state convention in Poughkeepsie in 1788, less than a year before Washington's inauguration. Members of the state legislature were so avid for power that they could not agree on how presidential electors were to be chosen and so New York had not even voted for Washington in the first election. The governor of the state, George Clinton, enjoying his sixth term in office, had fought ratification and had yielded in his last-ditch battle only after nine states had approved the Constitution. He was a forceful figure in New York society.

So was John Lamb, who had been so fervid in his opposition to the Constitution that he barricaded his residence against a Federalist "mob." He had been a leader of the Sons of Liberty, who had rioted against the Stamp Act in 1765, and a soldier in the Revolution. John Lamb was not inclined to approve centralizing "tyranny" in a new form.

Nor were the "plain people" of New York City likely to uphold an ambitious leader bent on "seizing power." Many of the artisans and tradesmen had supported the adoption of the Constitution in the hope that an improvement in business would follow. But memories of rioting by the Sons of Liberty lingered among them and they certainly did not belong to Alexander Hamilton's set. In meetings of Tammany Hall or in public taverns they continued to argue over public questions; and some of them, going beyond republicanism, began to use openly that more incendiary word "democracy."

Even the plays on the New York stage, which Washington and other members of the government occasionally witnessed with the people of pit and gallery, gave no encouragement to kingly or "high-toned" pretensions. For example, Royall Tyler's play, *The Contrast*, starting on its successful career in 1787, was republican in its argument. Although it dealt humorously with the vanities of small farmers and urbanites alike, it ridiculed British affectations and exalted republican dignity. If it was not agrarian in tone, neither did it lend countenance to royalist designs.

While a "republican court" soon developed among the fashionable circles at the first national capital and was emphatically high-toned in its sympathies, it could not or did not block the tendency toward republican simplicities. Some of its members, according to Jefferson's reports, had doubts whether the constitutional experiment would succeed and even secretly sighed for or expected a return to "kingly rule." Senator William Maclay, one of the earliest outspoken democrats in the country, caustically criticized, in a puritan vein, its balls and dinners, calling them a waste of time and injurious to minds, morals, and the public interest.

But, however skeptically some members of the "republican court" regarded the republican experiment or confidently expected the adoption of a still stronger form of government in case another crisis came, they all rallied to the side of President Washington's administration. They gave to it the support of the "wealth and talents" without which, Hamilton argued, the Constitution could not be successfully launched. Jefferson believed that they were actually royalist in sympathies. But in 1790, when Hamilton told him that the Union was in danger of breaking up, even Jefferson approved a financial measure advantageous to bondholders and speculators on the ground that "the preservation of the Union and concord among the states was more important" than defeating it.

The adoption of New York as the first seat of the new government was in many ways fortunate for what Washington called "the destiny of the republican model of government" on a national scale. The city lay between New England and the South. It cordially received the new government and by generous encouragement helped to make its inauguration an unquestionable success. But, to the regret of merchants, proprietors of taverns, boardinghouse keepers, and hostesses, among other beneficiaries, Congress decided against New York as the permanent capital of the nation.

That decision was the result of a "deal" between Hamilton and Jefferson at a time when Congress was badly split, in 1790, over the issue of assumption of state debts by the federal government. Threats of disunion were thus overcome. Two Southern votes and some Pennsylvania votes were brought over to the support of assumption on condition that Philadelphia was to be the capital for ten years and that the permanent seat of the government was to be located on the banks of the Potomac, as a final concession to the South. Late in 1790 the government of the United States was transferred to Philadelphia. Some New Yorkers found consolation for the loss in the huge profits they had garnered from their speculations in state evidences of indebtedness—speculations made possible by the "deal" between Hamilton and Jefferson.

☆

Philadelphia, the second national capital and the largest city in the Union, also made its peculiar contribution to shaping the spirit and practices of the "republican model." Pennsylvania had never been a royal province. The monarchical tradition was weaker there than in New York. Neither the Penns nor their proprietary agents had imparted to their local administration the glamor that adorned the "court" of a royal governor. Moreover, the population of Philadelphia was more varied in racial stocks than that of New York, and its interests and activities were more diversified. It included some rich landlords and many merchant princes eager to reproduce the "republican court" of New York and prepared to entertain federal officials, members of Congress, and foreign envoys on a scale equally if not more extravagant. At the same time Philadelphia had more small tradesmen and artisans, more schoolmasters, music teachers, lawyers, physicians, surgeons, scientists, and philosophers of a rationalistic and secular bent. Leadership in New York, where the English Church had formerly been established, was still strongly Anglican in religious faith. Philadelphia, on the contrary, had long been the home of religious dissidence, the chief center of scientific inquiry and rationalism.

In Philadelphia there was greater political, social, and intellectual ferment than in the first capital. The state constitution of New York, despite its republican leanings, was, next to that of Massachusetts, the most aristocratic of all the documents drawn up in the early days of independence. The constitution of Pennsylvania, of 1776, on the other hand, was accounted about the most radical of the time—with a legislature composed of a single chamber and a governor subservient to that body—and the new constitution of 1790, though more conservative, was still liberal in spirit. Philadelphia had numerous clubs and societies of tradesmen and artisans addicted to free discussions—political, religious, scientific, and social. The opposition to the adoption of the federal Constitution in Pennsylvania, though not so strong as in New York State, had been bitter; and the memory of it still rankled, particularly in the western regions, which were soon to test President Washington's administrative skill by an open revolt against a federal tax on whisky—the "Whisky Rebellion." If, as the President said, the new government needed, for endurance, the affection of the people, there was ample opportunity to cultivate that attachment in Pennsylvania.

While bestowing its "affection," Philadelphia had many advanced ideas to offer members of the administration and Congress —to Puritans from New England, Anglicans from New York, and planters from the South also usually Anglican in faith. It was the center of the freest thinking in the Union on all matters, human and divine. For a city of those days, it was well laid out and ably governed. Even its wealthy inhabitants displayed a sensitivity to urban poverty and suffering, and maintained institutions of benevolence definitely progressive for the times. In Philadelphia religious toleration was peculiarly broad. Quakers, who made up a large part of the population, were for it on principle and the other denominations, whether on principle or not, accepted it. In scientific inquiries and applications, educational experiments, and civic enterprise, Philadelphia compared favorably with any city in Western civilization.

There the "utilitarian mentor," Benjamin Franklin, had kept the people astir with new adventures in ideas and, though he had died in April 1790, his spirit still enlivened the mood of that city. There the American Philosophical Society which he had promoted was creating intellectual currents that were to spread to all the shores of thought in America. Thomas Jefferson was an officer in this society during the days when he was living in Philadelphia as Vice-President of the United States. Through the port of Philadelphia came travelers, newcomers intending to make America their home, and foreign emissaries, bringing with them, among other intellectual interests, the knowledge and radical philosophy of the French.

Jefferson had become familiar with new French thinking while, from 1785 to 1789, he was minister of the United States at Paris, where he was adjudged a first-rate thinker in his own right. In Philadelphia he encountered congenial minds that fortified his determination to give the government of the United States a firmer bent in the direction of leveling republicanism. His followers in Congress, who had begun to form the nucleus of a political party before the federal government was moved to Philadelphia, were more at ease in the city of Benjamin Franklin than in the metropolis of Alexander Hamilton. In short, Philadelphia aided in smoothing the way for the Jeffersonian "revolution" in politics that attended the next transfer of the capital—to the District of Columbia in 1800.

☆

Under the private agreement and the ensuing act of Congress that fixed the permanent capital of the federal government on the banks of the Potomac, the second President, John Adams, in the summer of 1800, ordered the removal of the administration to the District of Columbia where Congress was to assemble on the first Monday in December. The task of removal was not very burdensome. All told, the federal officers and clerks numbered only one hundred and twenty-six persons. Official papers were boxed and shipped by boat. The officers and clerks made the trip by various routes. President Adams went to see the place in June and later he and his wife Abigail were installed in the "President's House." In a report on the official residence, then unfinished and full of litter, she said that she was using the great "audience room" in the "President's Palace" as "a drying room . . . to hang the clothes in."

In 1801 the District of Columbia was a profusion of forests, hills, and streams interspersed with a few farms, the little village of George Town, some newly laid out streets for the city of Washington, and a few public and private buildings just completed or under construction. Land speculators and real estate promoters swarmed over the place buying and selling lots with little or no respect for community plans of any kind. Good houses dotted the landscape, but the roads between them, in the "city of magnificent distances," were axle deep in summer dust or winter mud. "An awful contrast to the public buildings," exclaimed Oliver Wolcott, Secretary of the Treasury, were the many "small, miserable huts." The inhabitants of the huts, he declared, "are

poor, and as far as I can judge, they live like fishes, by eating one
another." There were no fine churches, no schools, no colleges,
no seasoned residents to extend hospitality at balls and dinners to
members of the incoming government. Laborers' shanties and
brick kilns stood out starkly in the scene—more vividly than the
habitations of the laboring poor in New York or Philadelphia. A
slave market, with its pens and auction block, gave obtrusive
notice that the capital of the Republic had been located in a
region where the "peculiar institution" flourished. The outlook
for republican grandeur did not seem brilliant.

But behind the confusion lay the dream of a splendid city
worthy of the Republic. Major Pierre Charles L'Enfant, a French
engineer and soldier of the American Revolution, whose services
President Washington had enlisted, had drawn a grandiose plan
for the permanent capital, with broad avenues, spacious plazas, and
long vistas, in anticipation of a time when the wealth of the nation
would permit an orderly and full development of his design. Having regard for the republican principles of Thomas Jefferson,
whom he consulted in making his sketches, L'Enfant was careful
to avoid a mere duplication of any European pattern, whatever
might have been his personal preference, and to make room for
the originality of simplicity. It is true that, for the time being,
L'Enfant's plan was largely defeated by real estate speculators and
that he retired from further activity, discouraged and ruined. Late
in the nineteenth century, however, his dream was to be revived
and honor paid to his memory.

Notwithstanding the disputes and divided councils that attended
the laying out of the new city, the architecture of the two outstanding public buildings in process of completion was in keeping
with Jefferson's republican aspirations. For the Congress House,
or Capitol, William Thornton's sketches, with provision for a
great central rotunda, were accepted by President Washington
and, subject to modifications, were used as the basis of construction. The President's House, designed by James Hoban, was
modest in lines and proportions. Both buildings represented a departure from Georgian and other purely colonial architecture and
a tendency toward the severity of classical models set by the
Greek and Roman republics of antiquity.

As if symbolizing this simplicity, the first President to be inaugurated in the new capital of the nation was Thomas Jefferson
himself. His party had wrested the federal administration from the
"aristocrats" and "monocrats" in the party founded by Hamilton

and Washington. Despite his "simplicity," ridiculed as "affected" by his political foes, he was one of the most sophisticated persons of his time in the New World or the Old World. By virtue of

THE UNITED STATES IN THE EARLY DAYS OF THE REPUBLIC

his wide knowledge, his interest in natural science, art, and learning, his geniality, humor, and readiness to listen as well as pronounce, he was exceptionally equipped to assume the leadership of the political community in Washington. Though familiar with cities of Western Europe as with New York and Philadelphia, he loved the country, and Washington was then little more than a village. Though treated as a philosopher among the intellectuals who gathered in the home of Condorcet and his high-minded wife in Paris, he had been snubbed by the socially pretentious landlords and merchants of New York and Philadelphia, and felt happier in the White House at Washington.

According to the custom followed at his Virginia country place, Monticello, Jefferson made the President's House in the permanent capital of the Republic a center of social and intellectual leadership, while he presided as Executive over the young nation. At the dinner table, where conversation among Americans from all sections of the country and foreign diplomats was made easy and informal, he was cordial, skillful, and deeply interested in evoking diversities of opinions and tastes. In this way at the crude capital of the young Republic, he attached all sorts and conditions of people, high and low, to the republican experiment. And fortunately, in this wide-open though experienced hospitality, he was aided by his daughter, Martha Jefferson Randolph, whose education, after the death of his wife, he had carefully and thoughtfully supervised.

It was significant for the future that Thomas Jefferson, with his strong faith in the people, took over in 1801 the administration of the republican system of government which had been framed in deep distrust of the people; that as President he strengthened it before the rising tide of Jacksonian democracy began to beat upon it. The very fact that the seat of the government was then in a mere village, frontier in its physical appearance and isolated as a political community, no doubt was a factor in enlarging Jefferson's influence in Congress and public councils generally.

Distrust of cities had been a cardinal feature of agrarian republicanism. Even John Adams had feared the aggressions of plutocratic merchants and speculators as much as he had feared an uprising of the poor. At all events the presence of Jefferson at the head of the Republic in the village of Washington, though his election had evoked the fury of haughty Federalists, increased "the affections of its citizens" for "the republican model of government," as George Washington had called it, and gave vigor to the republican way of life in the United States.

☆

Influential as was the work of Washington, Adams, and Jefferson in fortifying republican government, their work was only one phase of the transition from monarchy to the republican way of life. To the new order was brought the support of intellectual and artistic talents among the citizens, made manifest in forms of written and oral expression, such as books and dramas, and in visible symbols, such as paintings and engravings. Through the press, the theater, and popular education—formal and informal— the results of these activities became known and appreciated among multitudes of people upon whose thought, aspirations, labors, and character the republican experiment ultimately depended for its success.

By the intellectual and artistic activities of private citizens the doctrine was formulated that the Revolution and the Republic were worthy of the highest esteem in themselves, and admirable in the history of humanity. By the same processes were widened and deepened knowledge and thought respecting the new nation whose fortunes were involved in the republican way of life, with all that it signified in terms of civilization. With increasing interest in society, economy, and the people went inquiries, ever more microscopic, into the physical geography and the natural resources of the continental domain as expansion and settlement proceeded —the material setting in which the republican experiment was being carried on.

During the transition from monarchy to the republican type of life, writers gave expression to the revolution in literally thousands of books on the United States—on its government, people, institutions, and resources. By classes, somewhat arbitrary, these books came under the heads of government, law, economy, geography, travel, public policies, and conditions of the people from the poorest slave at the bottom to the richest merchant or planter at the top. Some of them, however, were so comprehensive that they took in all or nearly all the themes then engaging American interests. Collectively, the books contained knowledge and thought bearing upon almost everything human and material that was germane to the republican experiment, its policies and its possibilities, its ideals and its resources. The scope of this literature is merely indicated, rather than adequately illustrated, by the following selected titles and comments:

1787—Thomas Jefferson, *Notes on Virginia*. A model survey of the government, laws, economy, climate, resources, and people of Virginia—the forerunner of many such treatises on individual states.

1787—John Adams, *Defence of the Constitutions of the United States* (Vols. I–III). A historical study of the science of politics in which the principles of the first state constitutions were defended with great learning.

1788—Jay, Hamilton, and Madison, *The Federalist,* essays written in support of the Constitution, published in book form. Frequently republished. French edition in 1792. A treatise on the sociology, economics, and strategy of republican government which formed the primary textbook for the education of the American people in republican ways of government.

1789—William Gordon, *History of the Rise, Progress and Establishment of the Independence of the United States* (Vols. I–III). Published previously in London. Displeased the English by its American sympathies and was regarded in America as scarcely patriotic enough. Gordon copied wholesale from other writings.

1789—David Ramsay, *History of the American Revolution* (Vols. I, II). More favorable to the American cause than Gordon's work.

1791–92—Thomas Paine, *Rights of Man.* Textbook of republican principles. Sold by the tens of thousands in the two hemispheres.

1805—Mercy Warren, *History of the Rise, Progress and Termination of the American Revolution* (Vols. I–III). Far more original than Gordon or Ramsay. Based extensively on personal knowledge; Northern in emphasis. Discussed the conditions from which the Revolution sprang, leading characters and events of the Revolution. Democratic in sympathies and a warning against monarchical tendencies and the greed for riches that might undermine the Republic and restore tyranny.

1805–07—John Marshall, *Life of George Washington* (Vols. I–V). Based on extensive researches. An eloquent defense and vindication of Washington; Federalist in tone; and did more than any other work to set the tradition of Washington as "the father of his country." Severely criticized by Jefferson and his followers, but remained powerful in influence.

1814—Lewis and Clark, *History of the Expedition . . . to the Pacific Ocean* (Vols. I, II). Summary description of a famous journey and the country through which the explorers passed.

1814—Tench Coxe, *A Statement of the Arts and Manufactures of the United States of America for the year 1810.* Based on a federal census taken in 1810.

1814—John Taylor, *An Inquiry into the Principles and Policy of the Government of the United States.* A philosophical treatise on politics, following the Anti-Federalist or agrarian party line in opposition to the "aristocracy of riches."

1817—William Wirt, *Sketches of the Life and Character of Patrick Henry.* Eulogy on the fiery leader of the Revolution.

1819—David Ramsay, *Universal History Americanized* (Vols. I–IX). Three additional volumes unfinished on the death of the author. A grand design to put the United States in the setting of great history.

How many Americans burned midnight oil studying the histories of Gordon, Ramsay, and Mercy Warren was not entered in the records of the time but there can be no doubt that thousands upon thousands saw, as originals or reproductions, the paintings which celebrated in visible form the Revolution and its leaders. The task of such delineation was deliberately assumed by John Trumbull, who had a vision of the "vast consequences" to flow from the establishment of independence. A former colonel in the Revolution, Trumbull had the spirit of the new age and he gave vivid expression to it on his canvases representing the "Battle of Bunker's Hill," the "Signing of the Declaration of Independence," the "Capture of the Hessians at Trenton," the "Surrender of Cornwallis at Yorktown," and in his portraits of leaders, such as Washington and Hamilton.

Two contemporaries of Trumbull, Gilbert Stuart, of Rhode Island, and Charles Wilson Peale, of Maryland, also painted portraits of the outstanding personalities of the Revolutionary generation. Stuart's portrait of Washington, soon to become the most widely accepted for technical competence, depicted the hero as a polished aristocrat of Virginia. Truer to life, Peale portrayed him in his rugged character as outdoor planter, soldier, and stalwart manager of men. The chief paintings of Trumbull, Stuart, and Peale, reproduced by lithographic processes, soon ornamented public buildings and private homes, great and humble, making lifelike, to all who could see, characters and events connected with the making of the independent Republic.

Moved by a kindred spirit, poets joined in the same celebration. Joel Barlow, of Connecticut, for example, dreamed of a great creative future for America. "The American Republic," he told a friend, "is a fine theater for the display of merit of every kind. If ever virtue is to be rewarded, it is in America." In this mood, Barlow wrote and published in 1787 *The Vision of Columbus*, an epic poem of more than five thousand lines on the real significance of the discovery of America. Recognizing, with his critics, some of the youthful exaggerations of this venture, Barlow later worked over and reworked the theme and republished it in 1807 in two sumptuous volumes as *The Columbiad*. Barlow's object, he declared in his preface, was to demonstrate that Columbus "had opened the way to the most extensive career of civilization and public happiness," to inculcate the spirit of liberty, to discountenance violence and war, and "to show that on the basis of republican principles all good morals, as well as good government and hopes of permanent peace, must be founded."

The convulsive changes which marked the transition to the republican way of life were dramatized by playwrights. Following the success of Tyler's comedy, *The Contrast*, in New York, the play was presented in Baltimore, Philadephia, Charleston, and Boston; and it was published in 1790, with a subscription list at the head of which stood George Washington, the President of the Republic. From year to year in far-scattered places it was reproduced by players both professional and amateur.

Tyler's success encouraged William Dunlap to enter seriously upon a career as a dramatist, dedicating his talents to the service of the Republic, as he believed American artists of every type should do. Knowing that monarchies had been made glamorous by the aid of painters, poets, historians, architects, dramatists, musicians, and novelists, Dunlap felt that the Republic was far more worthy of devotion and should be made attractive to the people by all such forms of art. His father had been a Loyalist during the Revolution and had sent William to Europe to be trained as a painter. But in London William became enamored of the theater; his sympathies with the struggle of the people for liberty were awakened; and on his return home he composed plays and wrote works on the drama and the arts of design.

Dunlap's long career as an important and productive playwright of the Republic opened in 1789 with a drama entitled *The Father; or American Shandy-ism*, in which he presented his view of the "contrast" in the following lines:

> *Now I see in this new world*
> *A resting spot for man, if he can stand*
> *Firm in his place, while Europe howls around him.* . . .
> *Then might, perhaps, one land on earth be found,*
> *Free from the extremes of poverty and riches;*
> *Where ne'er a scepter'd tyrant should be known,*
> *Or tyrant lordling, curses of creation.*

Other forms of literature expressed the ideas, interests, and ideals of the people in the republican era. The novels and tracts of Charles Brockden Brown contained flashes of discussion which illuminated the wrongs of yeomen and the "rights" of women, as well as nearly every other current theme of democratic interest. James Fenimore Cooper, whose first novel came out in 1820, chose to tell stories of the struggle for liberty in the Revolution, and to portray all kinds of Americans from Indians and pioneers to planters and sailors. Poets, such as Philip Freneau, "the poet of the Revolution," tried their lyrical talents on the aspirations of the Republic. Noah Webster wrote to George Washington in 1786: "I am encouraged by the prospect of rendering my country some service, to proceed with my design of refining the language & improving our general system of education." So he went ahead compiling dictionaries on the basis of American usages for scholarly and popular purposes and making plans for giving the children of the people an education that would inspire a devotion to the Republic and prepare them for citizenship in it.

☆

Newspapers for the distribution of knowledge and ideas, true or false, multiplied in the republican era. Forty-three colonial newspapers, it was estimated, lived through the Revolution; in 1810 Isaiah Thomas recorded, in his *History of Printing*, the existence of 366 newspapers scattered all the way from New Hampshire to the Louisiana Territory, with no less than fourteen in Ohio and one on the frontier of Michigan. In this period the daily press entered the journalistic arena, exciting readers every day instead of every week. Philadelphia printers supplied the first daily—in 1784; and by 1809, the end of Jefferson's second administration, there were twenty-seven dailies in the flourishing cities from Boston to New Orleans.

As the party division into Federalists and Republicans deepened, practically all the newspapers, weekly and daily, became ferociously partisan and outdid in the passion of their language anything the colonial age had experienced. But they distributed news, or at all events selections and versions of news, reported on the great public questions and policies of the day, and supplied topics for discussion at dinner tables, in taverns, at corner stores, and by firesides throughout the land.

All the pressures of thought in the new society struggling to establish the republican way of life—insurgent interests and traditional tastes—found outlets in new magazines which burst forth luxuriantly. In their pages, taken collectively, readers were supplied with polite letters, fragments of creative fiction, patriotic boasting, practical philosophies of daily living, scientific information, codes of etiquette, poetic effusions mawkish or brave, essays on humble ambitions and national aspirations, old and new bigotries with their simplicities of dogma, and solid articles on actions and policies directed to the advantages of classes or the progressive attainment of general welfare. Magazine editors seemed to labor hard at meeting every demand, real or imagined, from the supposed needs of gentlewomen eager for "culture" to the requirements, actual or alleged, of popular success in upholding the Republic.

Among the more substantial periodicals was the *Columbian Magazine*, founded by Mathew Carey at Philadelphia in 1786, a miscellany of original and selected articles on government, currency, industries, agriculture, and science. Its pages carried articles by some of the most distinguished writers of the early Republic, for example, Benjamin Rush, physician; David Ramsay, historian; Charles Brockden Brown, novelist; and Joel Barlow, pamphleteer and poet. It started bravely and seemed destined to have a long career, but after four years of struggle it gave up the ghost.

Other magazines tried to fill the void left by its death, only to meet a similar fate. Yet at no time in the early republican era was the country without an ambitious monthly of the general type. At last, in 1815, when the *North American Review* was launched at Boston, a magazine editor received the support necessary to long endurance. Of the flock of magazines founded between 1776 and 1815 that *Review* alone survived the buffets of fortune into the twentieth century.

☆

On no subject were the leaders of the Revolutionary generation more thoroughly united than on the advancement of popular education and science as indispensable to permanence in the republican way of life. The old Congress under the Articles of Confederation had demonstrated its faith by dedicating to public education regular blocks of land in the Northwest Territory. Then President Washington, in his first annual address to Congress, sounded a national note: "Nor am I less persuaded that you will agree with me in opinion that there is nothing which can better deserve your patronage than the promotion of science and literature. Knowledge is in every country the surest basis of public happiness. In one in which the measures of government receive their impressions so immediately from the sense of the community as in ours it is proportionably essential. To the security of a free constitution it contributes in various ways." To Congress at the moment he left the choice of ways for accomplishing this end but later he recommended the establishment of a national university. This recommendation Thomas Jefferson renewed as President.

Although Congress did not adopt the proposal, one state after another made the beginnings of state colleges and universities; and Jefferson, after he retired from the presidency, set an example of fidelity to conviction by taking the lead in founding the University of Virginia at Charlottesville. This university was not projected as merely a college with a classical curriculum. It was designed as a true modern institution of higher learning, dedicated to freedom of thought, inquiry, and teaching, especially in natural science and the humanities.

Lack of interest among the rank and file of politicians—even hostility—did not deter advocates of public education from planning for the future. Some of their programs, notably that of Robert Coram, a brave seaman in the war of the Revolution and an intellectual leader in Delaware, called for the training of all children in the practical arts as means of assuring personal independence and overcoming the poverty which belied civilization. Other plans, especially that of Noah Webster, while pleading for general education, insisted upon the training of women in the philosophy of republicanism, on the ground that women exercise a major influence through their training of the young and must be taught how to bring up the generations in republican ways of living and thinking.

James Sullivan in Massachusetts produced still another plan for a system of republican education. Sullivan was active in public affairs before, during, and after the Revolution—a justice of the Supreme Court in his state, a member of Congress in 1783, a publicist, one of the "richest, ablest, and most powerful" of the Jeffersonians. In his writings on government, politics, and society in America, Sullivan declared that a system of national education was absolutely necessary if the morals of the people were to be shaped according to the genius of republican government and if the people were to realize the ideals of liberty, happiness, and general welfare that had been proclaimed as the objectives of the republican experiment.

In the voluminous literature on education and the advancement of science, stress was placed on the practical aspects of living. Research in the natural sciences was to be promoted and useful inventions encouraged. Yet the moral sciences of community and national living were also to be emphasized to prepare the nation for its opportunities and destiny. The people, Jefferson insisted, must not only be trained in the practical arts; they must be instructed in those branches of learning, especially history, which would enable them to discharge their duties as citizens while maintaining a vigilant watch against the tendencies of government to encroach on human liberty, including the liberty of free inquiry, thought, and speech.

It was, no doubt, this concern with practical and earthly affairs in educational programs that helped to arouse opposition among the clergy, then the chief leaders in such popular education as prevailed, and to arrest the progress of universal and non-sectarian education until the nineteenth century was well advanced. Yet before the Revolutionary generation passed from the scene, its pioneers in thought had worked out and formulated essential principles for the advancement of science and the education of the people—all with a view to making the nation strong and wise in the use of its resources, solicitous for social improvements, and competent in the arts of republican government.

CHAPTER XI

The Revolutionary Generation in Charge of the Federal Government

FOR THIRTY-SIX YEARS after the Constitution went into force—from 1789 to 1825—the new government was headed by Presidents who belonged to the generation of revolutionists: by five men, George Washington, John Adams, Thomas Jefferson, James Madison, and James Monroe.

What a roll of services and honors, what varieties of experiences in war and peace, in domestic and foreign affairs, these five men represented!

Washington had been a member of the Virginia Assembly in colonial times, a soldier in the French and Indian War, a member of the Continental Congress, commander of the Revolutionary armies, a member of the convention that drafted the Constitution, the presiding officer of that body, and was literally "first in war and first in peace."

John Adams had spent laborious years in the Continental Congress during the War for Independence, had led in framing the Massachusetts Constitution of 1780, had represented his country in continental capitals and in London, had written a powerful work, the *Defence of the Constitutions of the United States*, and had been Vice-President under Washington.

Like Adams, Thomas Jefferson belonged to the civilian wing of the Revolutionary generation. He had been a member of the Virginia legislature and the Continental Congress. He had drawn up the Declaration of Independence. He had been governor of Virginia, minister of the United States to France, Secretary of State under Washington, and Vice-President during the administration of President Adams.

Before he became the fourth President, James Madison's lines had also fallen in the field of civilian leadership. He had been an active member of the old Congress. He had been a delegate to the convention of 1787 and, in that assembly, had brought to bear in the framing of the Constitution a profound knowledge of history and statecraft, besides an exceptional talent for negotiation. After the adoption of the Constitution he had been a member of the House of Representatives. For eight years he had served as Secretary of State under President Jefferson.

As in the case of Washington, so in the case of James Monroe the experiences of war and peace were combined. In the war of the Revolution, Monroe had learned the perils of the battlefield. He had represented the United States abroad. Under the presidency of Madison he had been Secretary of State and then Secretary of War. Although neither his talents nor his achievements measured up to those of his predecessors, he had qualities which gave him a place of distinction among the leaders of the Revolutionary generation.

Through all these years American citizens generally agreed that the executive leadership of the nation should be vested in outstanding figures of the Revolution. But they by no means agreed on the policies to be adopted and the measures to be enforced by the government of the United States. Americans had been divided into conservative and radical factions during the Revolution as in the preceding colonial order. This division was still evident during the framing and adoption of the Constitution. For a brief time, however, after the Constitution had been ratified, its opponents, accepting their defeat with good grace, permitted a lull in partisanship. Not until the first Congress under the new Constitution revealed its intentions in a program of legislation and the President began to appoint officials and indicate his domestic and foreign policies did serious dissensions reappear among the people.

☆

To both houses of the first Congress many men were elected who had helped to draft the Constitution or who had worked for its adoption in their several states. In choosing the members of his Cabinet and high officials in his administration, Washington was careful to appoint men known as stanch advocates of the new plan. His Secretary of the Treasury, Alexander Hamilton, his Attorney General, Edmund Randolph, and General Henry Knox, his Secretary of War, belonged to that group.

Perhaps with a view to conciliating an expected opposition,

Washington gave to Thomas Jefferson the important post of Secretary of State. Jefferson had been in France as minister of the United States during the contest over the drafting and ratification of the Constitution. It was known to his intimates that he had at first thought a few amendments to the Articles of Confederation would suffice and had criticized the Constitution in several respects, especially the lack of a bill of rights. But Jefferson had rallied to the Constitution after 1789.

When the first Congress assembled in New York City and Washington was inaugurated as President, in the spring of 1789, the new government of the Republic was in the hands of its friends, experienced leaders, men long outstanding in public life. The cold text of the written Constitution had become flesh and blood. The time for action had arrived. But what actions in domestic affairs and in foreign affairs? That was the question which aroused expectancy among members of Congress and the people of the states.

Soon answers began to come, first in respect of domestic matters. In response to a popular demand for a bill of rights, Congress early proposed a series of amendments to the Constitution; and ten of them, ratified by state legislatures, went into effect in 1791. Still these involved no alteration whatever in the form of government.

Immediately pertinent to the support of the government were the measures, affecting the property and incomes of the people, that began to flow from Washington's administration and Congress. Revenues from taxation were necessary to the very existence of the government. All knew that. But what kind of taxes? On whom and what were they to fall? Taxation had been a sore point with the people since the Stamp Act of 1765. Well aware of it, Congress resorted to indirect taxation at the outset. The first revenue law, in 1789, laid duties on foreign goods imported into the United States. Both Washington and Hamilton thought that such duties should favor American manufacturers, especially of goods required for national defense. So did many members of Congress from the manufacturing states. In subsequent revenue acts "protection" was given to manufacturers of iron and several other commodities. To provide further revenues Congress laid an excise tax on whisky, a liquor distilled in thousands of farmhouses in various parts of the country.

Other measures affecting special interests were passed by Congress, one after the other, during the administrations of Washington and Adams. High on the list were provisions for paying off the big debt owed by the United States to its creditors—in the main to Americans, but in part to bankers in Holland and to the government of France.

This debt had been incurred by the Continental Congress largely for the purpose of carrying on the War for Independence. Interest on it had long remained in arrears. The prices of the bonds and other securities representing the debt had fallen, at times as low as to ten or fifteen cents on the dollar. Discouraged by the prospect of a total loss or needing money, hundreds of Americans had sold their bonds for almost nothing, to speculators who gambled on the chance that the cheap paper would someday be paid off in full by the government.

Should it be paid in full or at a sum below face value? If paid in full, should discrimination be made between the rate paid to persons who had originally bought the bonds from the Continental government and the rate paid to speculators who had bought the bonds from the original subscribers at low prices?

These points became storm centers of public discussion. The Secretary of the Treasury, Hamilton, proposed that the Continental securities be paid, ultimately, dollar for dollar and that no distinction be made between the persons who had bought their bonds directly from the government at the regular price and speculators who had bought theirs from original holders, second or third hand, for mere pittances. After exhaustive debates marked by thoughtfulness as well as passion, Congress adopted Hamilton's proposal. The Continental debt was thus "funded" and all bondholders were given new bonds for their old paper, dollar for dollar.

The states also had big debts incurred in the War for Independence. Some of the states were making payments on interest and principal; other states were delaying. In any case the bonds of the states had fallen in value, many of them to a low price, and speculators had been buying the state bonds too, at various price levels, in the hope of a rise in values.

That the state debts ought to be paid, people generally recognized. But by whom? Hamilton proposed that the federal Treasury assume the burden of paying them all and at face value. He argued that such a course was just, since the debts had been incurred in a common cause, and that it would strengthen the new government by making all bondholders look to its Treasury, instead of state treasuries, for payment of interest and principal. But on that point Hamilton encountered a still hotter opposition than had been raised against funding the Continental debt at face value. Even so, he managed by a close squeeze to win the approval of Congress for this plan, and the state debts were assumed by the federal government. New federal bonds were then exchanged for old state bonds, dollar for dollar, no distinction being made between the original subscribers and the speculators.

Another thing, Hamilton believed, was necessary to strengthen the Union. That was a national currency stable from one end of the country to the other. But the question of money was likewise vexatious. No great mines of gold and silver had been found along the Atlantic seaboard. During the Revolution the states and the Congress had poured out paper money by the bale and the country was full of notes "not worth a Continental," as the saying went. Now the Constitution had forbidden the states to emit bills of credit and had given Congress the power to coin money and regulate the value thereof—not to issue paper money. The only "sound money" in circulation consisted of metallic coins, mostly British, Spanish, and French; and they were being clipped, filed, and shorn by the money-changers.

Soon after Washington's inauguration, Congress made provision for minting new United States coins, but the precious metals available were small in quantity. For the purpose of expanding the amount of money in circulation, Hamilton devised and induced Congress to adopt a plan for a United States Bank. As set up in 1791, the bank was a joint-stock concern, with the United States Government among the holders of shares. The major portion of the stock, however, was subscribed by private investors, partly in specie money and partly in certain new bonds floated under Hamilton's funding and assumption schemes.

Little specie was actually paid in by private investors. So the "capital" of the bank rested principally on the paper bonds of the government. The bank, thus formed, was empowered to receive deposits, issue paper notes of its own, establish branches in various parts of the country, handle government accounts, and lend money at interest. The central office was established in Philadelphia. In time it had a network of branches scattered from Portsmouth, New Hampshire, to Savannah, Georgia. Through the agency of the United States Bank, paper notes of uniform value were put into circulation everywhere in the states; and merchants could now buy, sell, and make exchanges, assured that the bank currency would be both safe and stable.

With a view to promoting other branches of business enterprise,

Congress voted bounties to encourage the growth of American fisheries and granted special favors to American shipping interests. Great Britain and other Old World countries were helping their own shippers and discriminating against American shippers in their ports, according to accepted mercantilist theories. Under a strong government the United States was following suit.

To all such American measures Washington lent the support of his great name. The Constitution, he felt, warranted his doing this. He had been president of the convention which drafted it, had heard the debates, and was familiar with the purposes of the men who framed it. He knew more about those purposes than any of his critics, such as Thomas Jefferson, who had not been members of the convention and were less acquainted with the broad conceptions of government written into the Constitution. Giving expression to them, Washington recommended to Congress the enactment of laws promoting not only commerce and industry, but also agriculture, science, and education, with emphasis on the establishment of a national university for the training of young men for public life under the sway of American principles.

The growing body of federal officers engaged in enforcing the new laws under Washington's executive direction was supplemented by a new federal judiciary. By the Judiciary Act of 1789, Congress established the Supreme Court prescribed by the Constitution and a federal district court in each state, with a set of officials and agents for each court. Washington appointed as Chief Justice John Jay, who had battled for the ratification of the Constitution; and all the other judgeships he filled with men having a similar attitude toward the new order.

As soon as the new courts went into operation, citizens everywhere could look to federal judges for the protection and enforcement of their rights under the Constitution. If they felt that their rights were violated by state legislatures or state courts, they could appeal to federal judges independent of both. For example if a merchant of New York City wished to collect a debt from a citizen in North Carolina, he was no longer at the mercy of a local judge and jury; he could take his case into a United States district court. For interstate commerce and general business transactions, therefore, the federal judicial system was no less important than the United States Bank.

With the rise of party conflicts, the significance of the federal judiciary for the Union increased. Federal judges held office for life and could not be ousted except by impeachment. Presidents and members of Congress could come and go. Federal judges could remain on the bench throughout their lifetimes. Nobody understood this better than John Adams. Just before he left the White House in 1801, Adams made John Marshall, of Virginia, Chief Justice of the United States, and also appointed judges to the new circuit courts which Congress had just created. For about thirty-five years, until after Jefferson, Madison, and Monroe were all dead, Marshall kept at his post. A fervent advocate of a strong national Union from the days when he had fought for independence on the battlefield, Marshall welcomed the opportunity to make his views of the Constitution prevail in law. In case after case he declared acts of state legislatures null and void, as contrary to the Constitution. With the same firmness he upheld the power of Congress to enact laws broadly conceived in the general interest of the United States.

☆

The national program of domestic measures, instituted under Washington and continued under Adams, was thoroughgoing. It was designed to, and did, strike deeply into the life, industry, habits, and sentiments of the American people. It set precedents for ages to come. All this it would have done, if Europe had remained at peace and American foreign relations had been undisturbed. But agitations in the United States over the French Revolution and war in Europe beat against the domestic policies of Washington's first administration. They broke in with such force that he and his successors were compelled to develop, also, a program of actions coming under the head of foreign policy.

A few weeks after Washington was inaugurated in 1789, the once powerful French monarchy began to crumble, revealing its decrepitude as popular demands for liberty and self-government increased in vehemence. At first it made concessions which seemed to promise a peaceful transition to a new political order. The authority of the French aristocracy and clergy was shattered; and the King, Louis XVI, was compelled to grant his subjects a constitution, including a national legislature, elected by the voters, and a bill of rights known as "The Rights of Man."

Soon reform merged into revolutionary violence. The constitution was overturned; a republic was proclaimed. The King was put to death in January 1793. In the autumn of the same year, the Queen, Marie Antoinette, was borne to the scaffold. One group of radicals after another seized power. A "reign of terror," accompanied by executions and a civil war, spread from Paris to the provinces. Before many years had passed the struggle closed in the military dictatorship of the warrior and demagogue, Napoleon Bonaparte, as First Consul, then as Consul for life, and finally as Emperor of the French in 1804.

The turmoil in France would have raised questions for the government of the United States to decide in dealing with the rulers who succeeded one another in that country, even if the revolution had not extended beyond French borders. But it spread far and wide beyond the Rhine; and, terrified by events in Paris, the despotic monarchs of Prussia and Austria started a war on revolutionary France, with the diplomatic support of the British government. In 1793 France declared war on Great Britain.

Then country after country in Europe became involved in the fight. Victorious French armies overran Italy, Belgium, Holland, Scandinavia, the western regions of Germany, and Spain, disseminating doctrines of "liberty" as they marched. For twenty-two years, with a brief intermission (1801–03), the wars of the great European Powers raged in nearly every part of the Continent, on the high seas, in Africa, even creating uproars as far away as India. Since the war between France and Britain on the oceans was a war on commerce, both belligerents preyed upon the ships and trade of American citizens, searching for munitions carriers and blockade runners.

As soon as the war broke out between France and Great Britain in 1793, President Washington faced a question that could not be avoided. In the treaty of 1778, under which France came to the aid of the American cause with money and arms, the United States promised to help France in defending her remaining American possessions if, at some time in the future, she again became involved in a war with the British. Recalling this pledge, the government of France in 1793 asked Washington for aid in its new war.

The dilemma was embarrassing for Washington. The promise had been made. There was no doubt about that, and American sympathies in general were on the side of the French. But getting into another war meant laying heavy taxes, raising armies, building war vessels, and increasing the already large national debt. Furthermore it might, Washington thought, completely disrupt the government just established under the Constitution. After consulting his advisers, including Hamilton and Jefferson, he refused to comply with French demands and proclaimed the neutrality of the United States in the European conflict.

More than this, President Washington decided to get on a better footing with the British government. Several sources of ill-feeling still lingered from the War of Independence. Americans had not paid all the debts they had incurred in dealings with British merchants in colonial times. Loyalists in America whose property had been confiscated still waited for the compensation that had been promised them. The British had not removed their troops from forts in the western part of the United States. And other matters interfered with the development of amicable relations between the two nations.

To promote this development, Washington sent John Jay to London, commissioned to make a treaty with Great Britain that would remove some of the worst irritations. Jay managed to wring very few concessions out of the British government. But Washington approved the treaty Jay had negotiated and persuaded the Senate to ratify it in 1795. The United States, he resolved, was to stay out of the war; to pursue the policy of neutrality toward all the belligerents.

☆

The moment Washington and Hamilton began to frame and put into force domestic and foreign policies, they confronted critics and formidable opponents in Congress and outside. Working as individuals and in groups, some objectors picked at one policy and some at others. But practically all of Hamilton's program encountered protests from members of Congress, pamphleteers, and editors of newspapers. At firesides and in taverns knots of citizens debating his program expressed strong opinions for or against it. Even within Washington's Cabinet the conflict raged. Hamilton and Jefferson engaged in such fierce controversies over the proper course to pursue that Washington could not mollify them, hard though he tried. Within a few years the country was flaming with the polemics of a great dispute.

In a little while two well-knit political parties gave concentration to the scattered fire of the opposing forces. Supporters of Washington's administration, led by Hamilton, called themselves Federalists. Opponents, who at length rallied around Jefferson, were generally known as Anti-Federalists in the beginning—as mere oppositionists. Later they assumed the title of Republicans. In the House of Representatives, in the Senate, in the cities, and in the country districts far and wide, Federalists formed committees or caucuses for the purpose of uniting their forces. The Republicans did likewise. Thus party organizations cutting across state lines spread from New Hampshire to Georgia.

Each of the parties was mixed in membership. But Hamilton appealed particularly to the business interests—to holders of government securities, financiers, manufacturers, shipowners, and speculators in Western lands; and around him gathered advocates of strong and stable government. Since he was sympathetic with Great Britain and hostile to France after the revolution flared up in Paris and the European war opened, former Tories who had remained in America and were now American citizens flocked to his standard. In effect the Federalist party could lay claim to representing "the wealth and talents" of the conservative classes in the United States. "Your people," Hamilton was reported to have said, "is a great beast." In any event, he and Washington resented popular agitations at home, as they abhorred such agitation in France, and they thought that the "democratic societies" springing up in towns and country districts ought to be suppressed before they got out of bounds.

For the agricultural interests, especially for the small farmers who owned and tilled their lands themselves, Jefferson became the prime spokesman—leader of the Republican party. Freehold farmers, he declared, were the best and truest support for republican government. He charged Hamilton and his close friends with being monarchists and British sympathizers. He applauded the rights of man proclaimed by the French reformers and rejoiced in their efforts to erect a republic in France. To his partisans Jefferson, author of the Declaration of Independence, was the American Revolution incarnate—the foe of monarchy and the whole British social system in peace and war. After the French Revolution ended in the Napoleonic dictatorship, Jefferson's ardor for France cooled, but his dislike of British policies and actions long remained intense. He stood like a rock for "the people," against "rich and well-born" aristocrats and "monocrats."

By the time the election of 1796 approached, the Republicans were ready for a campaign to get possession of the government. Distressed by attacks on his policies and pained by assaults on his character despite his long public service, Washington refused to run for a third term as President. Rejecting every plea that he stand again for election, he wrote a farewell message to all his countrymen warning them against party passions at home and against becoming involved in the frequent quarrels, combinations, and collisions of European friendships and enmities.

Unable to persuade Washington to lead them again, the Federalists turned to John Adams, the Vice-President, whose conservatism they approved. Yet Adams was no abject disciple of Hamilton, and the Federalists found it hard to forgive his independence in politics. Though the Revolutionary generation respected his talents, his fidelity to the patriot cause, and his important services, he was not a magnetic figure for a popular campaign.

Yet the Republicans were not strong enough to defeat Adams, although they gave him and his party a fright. When the electoral votes were counted, it was found that Adams had seventy-one and Jefferson had sixty-eight. The narrow victory added nothing to Adams' popularity and his conduct as President reduced it. He did his best to win public favor, but his four years in office were full of troubles and his best was not enough to make him a national hero.

The financial and commercial policies started by Hamilton were continued by President Adams. With regard to Great Britain, he maintained the sympathetic neutrality initiated by Washington. In the case of France, however, affairs were more complicated. The French government in power when Adams became President had denounced President Washington for refusing to aid France in the war against Great Britain and for making terms with the British government in the Jay Treaty. To put it mildly, the relations of France and the United States were strained.

The first efforts of President Adams to ease the strain with France eventuated in an undeclared war between the two nations. In his desire to resolve the difficulties, he sent three envoys to Paris empowered to reach a settlement with the French government. Their reception was frigid. Indeed French agents demanded an apology from the United States, a loan of money, and a bribe to be paid to members of their government.

Exceedingly indignant when he heard about the chilly reception of the American mission and the demand for a bribe, Adams, naming the French agents only as X, Y, Z, reported the affair to Congress and the public. The public response was a cry that ran throughout the United States: "Millions for defense, but not one cent for tribute!" Washington was summoned from his plantation to take charge of the armed forces again. Fighting started at sea. With alacrity Federalists gave their support to Adams while Republicans moderated their criticisms of him. For a moment his leadership seemed to be gaining popularity. Then suddenly in 1799, Bonaparte, who had become dictator in France, proposed a peace with the United States on fair terms and Adams accepted it. Now the war excitement died away and with its disappearance attacks on the Adams administration were renewed.

Bent on suppressing their opponents and keeping power if they could, Federalist leaders rushed through Congress, in 1798, two laws directed to those ends.

The first, the Alien Act, gave the President power for two years to expel from the country any alien whom he might deem "dangerous to the peace and safety of the United States." Although Adams did not deport a single person under the act, the mere passage of the law aroused the ire of many Americans as a violation of liberty. Moreover it frightened unnaturalized Irish and French persons in America, who did not like the foreign policy that favored Great Britain.

The second measure, the Sedition Act, placed heavy penalties on every person, alien or citizen, found guilty of trying to stir up "sedition" or who wrote or published anything "false, scandalous, or malicious" against either house of Congress, the President, or the government. This act, opponents contended, transgressed the first amendment to the Constitution forbidding Congress to make any law abridging freedom of speech or of the press. But the Federalists, in power, brushed aside all objections; and under the Sedition Act several Republican writers and publishers were indicted, fined, or imprisoned for criticizing the President and his administration.

These two acts, instead of fastening the grip of the Federalists on the government, laid them open to attacks in the name of American liberty. Republicans interpreted the conduct of the Federalists as revealing their true colors—their liking for arbitrary government. Back in Washington's second administration that kind of "high-toned" government had been displayed when disorders, described as the "Whisky Rebellion," had occurred during efforts to collect an excise tax on whisky in 1794.

On that occasion Washington and Hamilton had called out 13,-000 militiamen to overcome a few rioters. In his excitement over the riots, Washington had ascribed them to subversive agitations and had privately expressed his belief that the young "Democratic Societies" should be exterminated.

Shocked by the attitude of the government in that affair, Jefferson had helped to turn Washington and his Federalist advisers away from that aggression against civil liberties. Now, four years later, the passage of the Sedition Act confirmed Jefferson's suspicion that Federalists were resolved to destroy critics by fine and imprisonment, after the fashion of Old World despots.

Adopting underground political tactics, Jefferson wrote an indictment of the Alien and Sedition Acts which was sent quietly to a friend in the state of Kentucky, recently admitted to the Union. On the basis of this document the Kentucky legislature formulated and passed, in 1798, a set of resolutions branding the acts as contrary to the Constitution, as null and void. It declared that, when the federal government exceeded its powers, the states had a right to interpose; and it called upon other states to join in demanding a repeal of the laws in question. Receiving little aid and comfort from other states, the Kentucky legislature then passed, in 1799, a second set of resolutions proclaiming the right of states to nullify "unconstitutional" acts of Congress.

Rejecting the doctrine of nullification as likely to endanger the Union, James Madison, now affiliated with the Republican party, induced the legislature of Virginia to pass milder resolutions while joining in the protest against the objectionable acts. In fact Jefferson himself later avowed that he had no intention at the time of encouraging action that might lead to a dissolution of the bonds established by the Constitution. Both he and Madison regarded their tactics as only calculated to fan discontent with the Alien and Sedition Acts and weaken the hold of the sponsors, the Federalists, on the nation.

Just how much effect the arguments over the Alien and Sedition Acts had on the voters cannot be determined precisely. Certainly they contributed little or nothing to the popularity of the Federalist party. Nor did they assure an easy triumph for the Republican party in the ensuing election of 1800. In fact, though the political campaign was bitterly waged, the shift of a few votes in New York, where Aaron Burr was especially strong, would have given John Adams a second term as President. Sixty-five votes were cast for Adams, seventy-three for Jefferson, and seventy-three for Burr.

The tie between Jefferson and Burr threw the election into the House of Representatives as provided by the Constitution in such cases. Only with the aid of Federalists in that House was the deadlock resolved in favor of Jefferson. Although Jefferson called his victory a "revolution," the Federalists were still powerful in Congress and he had to walk warily in exercising his powers as Chief Executive.

On March 4, 1801, when John Adams had left the White House

in a huff over his defeat, Thomas Jefferson took the oath of office as President. In his inaugural address he spoke softly if positively. Federalists had called him an atheist, a Jacobin, the foe of order and property; but from start to finish he refrained from retaliation in abusive epithets and was conciliatory. We are all Republicans, he said at his inauguration; we are all Federalists; the majority has expressed its will at the polls according to the forms of the Constitution and must be obeyed; for resort to the sword, the parent of despotism, is the only alternative to such obedience. But the minority, he proceeded, has its rights and they must be respected. If any citizen would change our form of government, Jefferson pleaded, let him be heard and let truth combat his error. The rights and liberties guaranteed by the Constitution, he insisted, are to be preserved; the Union is to be strong and the states protected in their rightful powers.

Not even Washington had expressed a greater attachment to the nation and its unity under the Constitution than was displayed on that occasion by the author of the Kentucky Resolutions. Despite his talk about his "revolution," Jefferson made no demand for an overthrow of the financial and foreign policies initiated by Washington and Hamilton.

Jefferson had made several pledges, however, in the name of his party, and they were redeemed. The Sedition Act was allowed to expire; men imprisoned under it were released; and the fines collected were repaid. The tax on whisky, which had stirred farmers to revolt, was repealed. Reductions were made in outlays for the Army, the Navy, and federal officers. Judge Samuel Chase, who had denounced Republicans from the bench, was impeached by the House of Representatives and only the Federalists in the higher court, the Senate, saved him from conviction. The formalities and ceremonials observed by Washington and Adams were modified. Like the British king who delivered his speech from the throne to Parliament, they had read their messages to Congress in person. Jefferson quit the practice and sent his message to the two houses in written form.

While he was operating merely as a critic of the Federalists, Jefferson had adhered to the view that the government of the Union was limited to the exercise of specific powers to be literally, or narrowly, construed. Nevertheless, during his eight years as President he did and approved many things not specifically mentioned in the Constitution, thus taking in fact a broad view of the document.

The Constitution, for instance, did not, in exact words, empower the United States to acquire more territory. Yet Jefferson bought from Napoleon in 1803 the vast Louisiana Territory for $15,000,000, and Congress, on his insistence, sanctioned the purchase. By this single stroke, more than doubling the domain of the United States, Jefferson helped to assure the strength and perpetuity of the Union. Perhaps he accomplished as much in that direction as Washington and Hamilton had achieved by the financial and banking measures that he had once opposed.

The Constitution had said nothing about the power of the federal government to build national highways or canals or improve harbors or found a national university. Nevertheless in Jefferson's first administration Congress appropriated part of the money received from the sale of public lands to the construction of highways into the West. In this way it provided for the building of the Cumberland Road, or national highway, extending from the edge of Maryland through Pennsylvania, Ohio, Indiana, and Illinois, into Missouri. With Jefferson's approval, his Secretary of the Treasury, Albert Gallatin, a statesman of broad outlook, made grand plans for a national network of river, harbor, and canal improvements. Following Washington's example, Jefferson recommended to Congress the creation of a national university. He likewise approved the idea of using surplus revenues of the government to promote the interests of commerce, industry, agriculture, and education, even if a constitutional amendment should be needed to accomplish such national purposes.

In foreign affairs Jefferson continued the general policy framed by Washington; and in his efforts to keep the United States out of the European war he interpreted the Constitution liberally. British naval officers were searching and seizing American merchant ships on the high seas at their pleasure and often carrying off sailors alleged to be British subjects. The French navy was likewise preying on American commerce. From year to year British and French actions grew more and more aggressive until at length nearly all American ships bound to and from Europe were liable to be seized by the one belligerent or the other. In vain did Jefferson assert and insist that American rights on the seas must be observed.

Driven into a dilemma by his resolve to avoid getting into war, Jefferson proposed and Congress approved, in 1807, an embargo forbidding all ships to leave American ports except with the President's permission. By this measure, by cutting off all their American supplies, he thought the British or the French or both might be forced to respect American commercial rights. The Constitution empowered Congress to "regulate" foreign commerce; now Congress had prohibited it altogether on the high seas. Yet this measure failed to bring the British and the French to terms, while it infuriated American merchants and shippers. In response to outcries against it, Congress substituted in 1809 a Non-Intercourse Act directed against Great Britain and France alone. It too was more than a mere "regulation" of commerce but Jefferson supported it in his anxiety to uphold American rights and at the same time keep the United States out of the war.

Notwithstanding the dissatisfaction over his handling of foreign relations, Jefferson could have had a third term if he had so desired. In his second campaign, of 1804, he had carried every state in the Union, except Delaware, Maryland, and Connecticut, against his Federalist opponent, Charles C. Pinckney. If his popularity had somewhat diminished by 1808, it was still very great. Instead of playing upon it, however, Jefferson voluntarily promoted the election of his Secretary of State, James Madison, in whom he had implicit confidence. He declared that two terms were enough; that repeated re-elections of a President might lead to election for life. Thus he set a tradition inimical to a third term for anybody.

Madison was victorious in the campaign and then he had to face the preservation of peace which Jefferson had entrusted to him. But the rise in Congress of a war party, called "War Hawks," led by John C. Calhoun, of South Carolina, and Henry Clay, of Kentucky, both young men of the post-Revolutionary generation, took the issue out of his hands. Some members of the war party were for war on Great Britain; others for war on France; and almost a majority for war on both countries.

Nominally the quarrel with Britain was over her preying on American commerce, her seizures of American sailors, and her support of restless Indians on the northwest frontiers of the United States. In large part war actually grew out of a resolve of Southern politicians to conquer Florida and of Western politicians to subdue and annex Canada. At all events, in June 1812 Congress declared war on Great Britain, and Madison set forth the war aims mainly in commercial terms, saying nothing about either Florida or Canada.

For more than two years the war was waged on land and sea. American sailors and soldiers proved their valor by many ex-

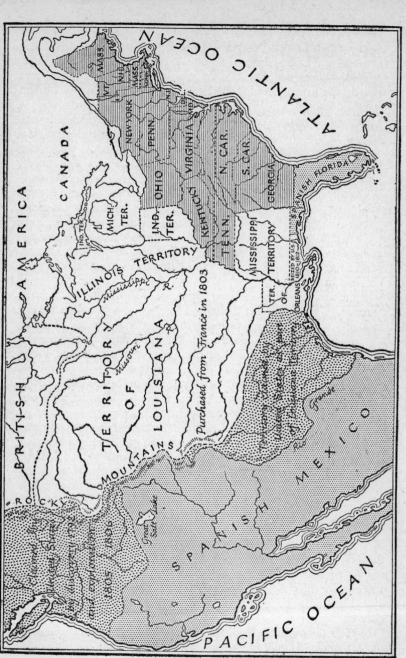

THE UNITED STATES IN 1812

ploits—under Oliver Perry on Lake Erie, under Thomas Macdonough on Lake Champlain, under Andrew Jackson at New Orleans, for example. Even so, the invasion of Canada was a failure; whereas the British invaded the United States and applied the torch to public buildings in Washington.

To make matters worse for Madison, the war was decidedly unpopular in the Northeast where, presumably, a war proclaimed in behalf of free commerce would have been welcomed. In the House of Representatives, Daniel Webster, of Massachusetts, denounced the draft of men as unconstitutional. Federalists decried the conflict as merely "Mr. Madison's war." The governor of Connecticut refused to obey the President's call for troops and the Connecticut assembly declared the state to be "free, sovereign and independent." A convention of delegates from various parts of New England, assembled in Hartford in October 1814, adopted resolutions akin in spirit, if not in letter, to those put forth by Kentucky and Virginia in 1798.

In the meantime negotiations for peace with Great Britain were proceeding at Ghent. On Christmas Eve, 1814, a few days before Jackson's victory at New Orleans, the draft of the treaty of peace was signed in Ghent. It contained not a word about British seizure of American sailors, about British preying on American trade, about British searching of American ships, or British support of Indians on the frontier. But when the news of the peace arrived early in 1815, Americans, passing "from gloom to glory," shouted with joy, rang bells, and held holiday parades.

None of the war aims was realized, neither those publicly announced by President Madison nor those unofficially cherished by the "War Hawks." Moreover Madison and his fellow Republicans were in "a sea of troubles" over domestic problems in the aftermath of war. The war had cost a huge sum of money and business was badly deranged. Hamilton's big national debt had been condemned by Republicans; now they confronted a bigger debt. Even the currency was in disorder, the dollar fluctuating violently in value. Manufacturers who had built up industries to furnish the armies with munitions and other supplies clamored for protection against the inrush of cheap British goods. Soon veterans by the thousands were demanding pensions for their services. From day to day the perplexities of the Republicans increased.

In their dilemma the Republicans resorted to the very measures of Alexander Hamilton, which they had so long assailed. His

United States Bank had perished when its charter expired in 1811; they established a second United States Bank on the principles of the old one. They funded the scattered government debts into a consolidated debt, larger than the debt they had once condemned. Hamilton had fostered a tariff designed to protect American manufacturers. In 1816 the Republicans passed a tariff measure outstripping in its high protectionism the tariff projects of Washington and Hamilton. Even Jefferson, the champion of agricultural interests, endorsed protectionism, thus joining hands with Calhoun and Clay. In 1819 the first great business panic in the history of modern industrialism burst upon the country, and the Republicans did not know what to do about that.

☆

President Madison closed his second term in 1817 with relief at the thought of turning the office of Chief Executive over to someone else. He proposed James Monroe as his successor and his choice was approved by his party. In the election of 1816 the Republicans had a landslide, the Federalists carrying only three states. Some Federalists had lost ground on account of their opposition to the war. Other Federalists refrained from activity in the campaign in view of the fact that the Republican party had put their program and their principles into effect. For a time the two-party system appeared to be at an end—in the "era of good feeling." Yet a new party was really coming into existence. Monroe was re-elected in 1820 but that was the last act in the short-lived, one-party play.

Three great measures of Monroe's administrations added to the strength of the Union and the feeling of attachment to it. In adopting them Monroe went counter to his former views. He had opposed the ratification of the Constitution in 1788 and had sided with Jefferson in his strict interpretation of that document. But on these three measures Monroe took a broad view of the Constitution—as Jefferson had done on many occasions during his tenure as President. Although he did not renew Jefferson's proposal for a national university, he abandoned his strict constructionism when he had to deal with issues involving the fortunes of the nation.

Among the first problems before President Monroe was that of the Floridas, East and West, which Great Britain had given back to Spain in 1783. Owing to the uncertainties of the Florida boundaries, the United States had some claims to West Florida. Moreover, the swamps of the Floridas were the hiding places of Indian marauders who emerged from time to time to harass American settlements. Ordered by Monroe, after one of these attacks, to pursue a band of Indian raiders to their retreat, General Andrew Jackson marched after them into East Florida, where he did more than fight them; he took possession of the region. Now the Spanish King, who claimed the ownership of this coveted territory, faced what is called in diplomacy a *fait accompli*—a dead certain fact; namely, occupation by Americans.

Caught in a jam, the King ceded his Florida land to the United States in 1819, in exchange for not more than $5,000,000, to be paid to American citizens who had damage claims against his government. As Jefferson had done on the constitutional issue, President Monroe simply overlooked the question as to whether the government of the United States had any express power under the Constitution to buy more territory. In this instance "strict construction" was not allowed to interfere with the transaction.

The second outstanding measure of Monroe's administration also involved an interpretation of the Constitution. Under its power to make "all needful rules and regulations" respecting territory belonging to the United States, could Congress lawfully exclude slavery from such territory? That subject was not mentioned in the document, but it was squarely raised in 1818–20 during a dispute over the admission of Missouri to the Union as a slave state. By that time Northern states had abolished slavery within their borders, or had provided for gradual abolition, and anti-slavery sentiment was growing insistent in the country.

Opposition to the admission of another slave state was outspoken in Congress and a deadlock occurred on the issue. After many angry words had been uttered, the standstill was broken by a compromise: Missouri was to be admitted with slavery, and the balance of political power maintained by the admission of Maine as a free state. In addition, as a part of the compromise, slavery was to be prohibited in the rest of the Louisiana Territory north of the line 36° 30′.

On the one side it was claimed that Congress had no authority to prohibit slavery in this territory. On the other, attention was called to the fact that the Northwest Ordinance, adopted in 1787 and ratified by Congress in 1789, had excluded slavery from the Northwest Territory; so it was argued that Congress could lawfully do this under the Constitution.

While the constitutional point was being argued, President

Painting by Albert Herter. Ewing Galloway photo.

A convention assembled at Philadelphia in May 1787, for the purpose of amending the Articles of Confederation. Out of the debate over the burning issue whether to change the form of government—to swing away from more authority or toward it—marked by many differences of opinion, finally emerged the Constitution four months later. A storm of criticism followed and delayed its ratification by all thirteen states, but the faith of Americans in the power of the people to govern themselves on a continental scale by peaceful processes, was confirmed.

Painting by Norman Price (not copyrighted). Courtesy Metropolitan Life Insurance Co.

Painting by Ezra Winter. Juley photo.

With grateful unanimity presidential electors, chosen after the adoption of the Constitution, cast their ballots for George Washington as the Chief Executive of the United States. Leaving Mount Vernon upon receiving notice of his election, he journeyed by coach to New York City, the first capital of the new government. Here he was inaugurated on April 30, 1789, amid the plaudits of the people.

Painting by John Ward Dunsmore. Courtesy Sons of the Revolution in State of New York.

Painting by N. C. Wyeth. Courtesy Pennsylvania Railroad.

Congress deciding against New York City as the permanent capital of the nation, the federal government was transferred to Philadelphia in 1790, on the condition that after ten years the permanent seat of government was to be located on the banks of the Potomac. In 1800 the administration was moved to the newly laid out city of Washington and John Adams installed in the unfinished "President's House."

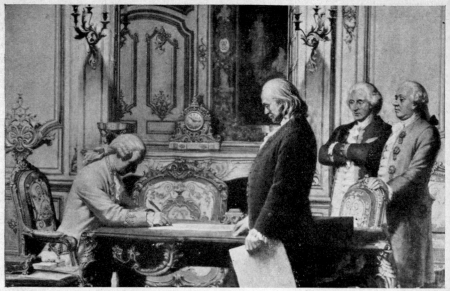

Painting by C. E. Mills. Brown Brothers photo.

During his lifetime Benjamin Franklin kept the people astir with new adventures in ideas and created intellectual currents that were to spread to all the shores of thought in America. Before the Revolutionary generation passed from the scene, its pioneers of thought had worked out and formulated essential theories and proposals for the advancement of science and the education of the people.

Painting by R. F. Heinrich. Courtesy National Life Insurance Co.

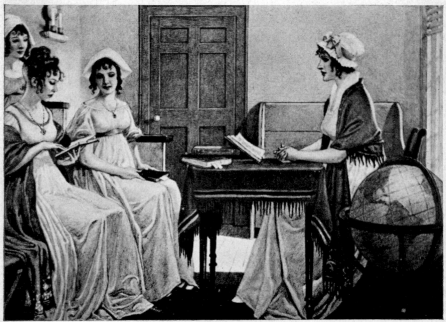

With the signing of the Louisiana Purchase Treaty in 1803 Thomas Jefferson, by a single stroke, more than doubled the domain of the United States and helped to assure the strength and perpetuity of the Union. To collect data on the new territory, find an overland route to the Pacific Ocean, and to report on its resources, he sponsored an exploration under Lewis and Clark.

Nominally the quarrel with Britain, which led to the declaration of war in June 1812, was over her preying on American commerce, her seizure of sailors, and her support of restless Indians on the frontier. In large part the war actually grew out of the resolve of politicians to conquer Florida and annex Canada. The frigate Constitution, launched in 1797, achieved ever memorable fame during the War of 1812.

Painting by W. C. Grauer. Ewing Galloway photo.

Under the generous provisions of the Northwest Ordinance, pioneers crossed the Alleghenies and poured into the territory north of the Ohio River. With the west-ward-moving Americans were mingled newcomers from the Old World—British, Germans, Swiss, and immigrants of other nationalities.

Painting by C. Y. Turner. Juley photo.

Painting by Maynard Dixon. Acme photo.

The expansion of the West followed closely on the heels of such intrepid explorers as Zebulon Pike and John C. Frémont. Pike had explored the headwaters of the Mississippi in 1804 and later led an expedition as far west as the mountain now known as Pike's Peak in the Rockies. Frémont crossed the mountains into the Sacramento Valley in 1844. In half the time it took American colonists to achieve independence, California was admitted to the Union.

Painting by Tom Lea. Courtesy Section of Fine Arts Public Buildings Administration.

Painting by Joseph Boggs Beale. Modern Enterprises, Phila., Pa.

After granting large blocks of land to encourage settlement in the Southwest territory, Mexico became frightened by the deluge of settlers, abandoned the policy, and sought to check immigration. The ensuing conflicts culminated in a revolt, the defeat of the Mexican army sent to quell the uprising of Texans serving under General Sam Houston; and Texas gained its independence in 1836. Disputes arising over boundaries precipitated a war with Mexico and in 1848 New Mexico, Arizona, and California were ceded to the United States. A year later gold was discovered at Sutter's Mill and the gold rush to California was on.

Painting by Oscar Berninghaus. Courtesy Treasury Department Art Projects.

Painting by William H. Jackson. Courtesy Clarence S. Jackson.

By 1830 the Santa Fé Trail was opened from Independence, Kansas, to Los Angeles. Several years later the Oregon Trail, which ran northwest across Kansas and Nebraska to Fort Laramie, Wyoming, and thence through the mountains to the valley of the Columbia River, had become the accepted overland wagon route to Oregon. Even when traveling in large wagon trains the pioneers were faced with the constant threat of Indian attacks and the ever-present dangers of starvation, exhaustion, and sickness.

Painting by Joseph Boggs Beale. Modern Enterprises, Phila., Pa.

Synchronized with the great events in westward expansion was the Industrial Revolution wrought in manufacturing and economy by the invention and use of steam engines and power-driven machines. In 1787 John Fitch made a successful demonstration with his steamboat, Oliver Evans completed a high-pressure steam engine in 1802 of greater efficiency than James Watt's engine, and in 1807 Robert Fulton's *Clermont* steamed up the Hudson to Albany and back.

The Bettmann Archive photo.

Painting by Joseph Boggs Beale. Modern Enterprises, Phila., Pa.

The thousands of inventions made between 1790 and 1850 utterly transformed methods that had been employed unchanged for centuries in manufacture, mining, communication, and agriculture. Eli Whitney patented his cotton gin in 1793, the Erie Canal was opened in 1825, and in 1833 Cyrus McCormick patented his automatic reaper.

From an old lithograph. Brown Brothers photo.

Painting by Joseph Boggs Beale. Modern Enterprises, Phila., Pa.

From one great Post Road in 1774, a large network of post roads spread westward to the Mississippi River by 1834. By this time the railroad era had dawned and steam trains were running on the Hudson and Mohawk Railroad and between Charlestown and Hamburg in South Carolina. With the releasing of the production and transport of goods from the limits of human hands, the possibility of abundant production loomed on the horizon for the first time in history.

Painting by R. F. Heinrich. Courtesy National Life Insurance Co.

Although many men in the South saw the immense potentialities of machine industry, their efforts to introduce manufacturing met with only slight success. In 1850 the annual value of manufactures produced in the free states was more than four times the output of the slave states. Iron products and leather goods alone equaled in annual value all the cotton grown in Southern fields.

From paintings by Howard Pyle.
The Bettmann Archive photos.

Attending the expansion of the nation to the Pacific Ocean and the transformation wrought in economy by steam and machinery was the rise of national democracy. Many men who helped frame the Constitution had expressed an aversion to democracy. Jefferson had taken a radical step when he called his party Republican, and Jackson did not officially proclaim himself a Democrat. Not until 1844 did the name Democratic Party appear. After voting in New Jersey from 1797 to 1807, women lost that right. During the Jacksonian age thousands of women banded together to demand equal civil liberties with men in all States and in 1848 the woman suffrage movement was launched with the adoption of a Declaration of Sentiments at Seneca Falls, New York.

Painting by George Caleb Bingham. Brown Brothers photo.

With the spread of democracy the restriction of offices to men of wealth or specific religious denominations was destroyed. By 1840 the national party convention had become an established political institution and the practice of framing and publishing a platform adopted. The "spoils system" had become general throughout the Union and after each election crowds of public officials were removed to make room for men belonging to the victorious party.

Monroe laid it before members of his Cabinet. They agreed that Congress could prohibit slavery in the territories; and, with their approval, he signed the bill on March 6, 1820, dedicating the major part of the Louisiana Territory to freedom.

Following Washington's example, President Monroe, in 1823, formulated a momentous declaration of foreign policy for the United States—the third notable measure of his administrations. Recently Spain's colonies in the New World had nearly all declared their independence, and President Monroe, like other Americans, was troubled in mind lest European monarchs help the Spanish King in his efforts to recover control over them. From such schemes Great Britain, however, held aloof. British merchants, winning a profitable trade in Latin America, were reluctant to see Spain's commercial monopoly restored. Fully appreciating their situation, the British government proposed to the minister of the United States in London that the two countries join in upholding the independence of the Latin American republics.

On receipt of the news President Monroe turned to Jefferson, Madison, and John Quincy Adams, the Secretary of State, for advice. They all agreed on the desirability of backing up the freedom of the Latin American republics. Jefferson welcomed the assistance of Great Britain in such a project—one so clearly advantageous for the security of the United States in the Western Hemisphere. With the aid of Adams, Monroe framed a message on the question and sent it to Congress in December 1823.

In this message, which was to bear his name in coming times as the Monroe Doctrine, the President made four clear-cut assertions. First, the United States did not propose to interfere with any colonies still owned by European Powers in the New World. Second, any effort on the part of monarchs in Europe "to extend their system to any portion of this hemisphere" would be regarded as "dangerous to our peace and safety." Third, the attempt of a European government to oppress or control colonies that had declared their independence would be viewed as showing "an unfriendly disposition toward the United States."

With reference to a claim to a part of the Pacific coast which the Czar of Russia had lately put forward, Monroe made the fourth assertion: "The American continents . . . are henceforth not to be considered as subjects for future colonization by any European powers." While proclaiming freedom for the Western Hemisphere, however, he informed European governments that in turn the United States would not interfere in European affairs.

Coupled with Washington's Farewell Address to the nation, the Monroe Doctrine was long a main "cornerstone" of American foreign policy. Thus the last, as well as the first, of the Presidents belonging to the Revolutionary generation fortified the independence of the United States and the security of the Republic.

CHAPTER XII

Expansion to the Pacific

It took American people one hundred and seventy-five years to build up and achieve independence for thirteen colonies with about three million inhabitants. In less than one third that span of years seven new states were established in the region immediately westward and occupied by a population larger than that of the whole United States when the census of 1790 was taken. In less than half that number of years five additional states were formed in the Louisiana Territory still further west, Texas was brought into the Union, a vast area to the southwest wrested from Mexico, and California admitted to statehood.

Events in this westward expansion followed one another in no regular order. For example, when the Louisiana Territory was acquired in 1803, Indiana and Illinois, to the east of the Mississippi, had only a few inhabitants. Louisiana and Missouri, in the Louisiana Territory, reached statehood before Michigan. Texas was admitted to the Union three years before Wisconsin; and Wisconsin had been a state only two years when California, on the Pacific coast, became a full-fledged member of the federation. But for the sake of convenience, the expansion to the West may be treated in three stages: settlement of the region between the old seaboard states and the Mississippi River; exploration and settlement in the Louisiana Territory; and occupation of the far Southwest.

☆

When independence was won several Eastern states had claims to territory in the region stretching westward to the Mississippi —claims based on royal charters and colonial grants. But by 1786

179

they had all surrendered to the Union their rights in the territory north of the Ohio. In a short time the territories south of the Ohio were separated from the seaboard claimants—Virginia, North Carolina, South Carolina, and Georgia. Thus the Western lands were cut loose from the overlordship of individual states, put into a national pool, and thrown open for settlement to emigrants from all parts of the seaboard region and also from the Old World.

More than this, it was decided that settlers on the Western lands were not to be held permanently under the dominance of the United States Government. They were to be allowed, subject to certain rules, to form governments in their respective territories, draw up constitutions of their own, and at length, as states, join the Union as partners in every respect equal to the thirteen original states. Thus a promise of self-government preceded the great westward migration.

Both in character of settlement and in form of government, therefore, the occupation and management of the region westward to the Mississippi diverged fundamentally from that process in colonial times on the seaboard. The authority in general charge of the operations was at first the old Congress under the Articles of Confederation and then the new government established under the Constitution of 1787. It was an American and a republican government, not a British monarchy located in distant London. No companies chartered by the British Crown, such as the Virginia Company, no great proprietors holding patents from the Crown, such as Lord Baltimore or William Penn, got permanent possession of immense areas in this Western region. Huge blocks of land, it is true, were granted to companies of American citizens; but no company had the right to govern as well as own the district assigned to it, or to hold the district indefinitely as a semi-feudal principality. A few American companies which acquired large holdings did assist in outfitting and transporting emigrants to the West; but in the main the work of occupation was effected by individuals, families, and small groups of pioneers, on their own initiative.

The spirit of the new enterprise in land settlement appeared in the Northwest Ordinance, adopted in 1787 by the old Congress under the Articles of Confederation and continued in force by the first Congress under the Constitution. This ordinance applied to the territory north of the Ohio River. Other congressional acts provided for official surveys of the Northwest Territory. By such surveys the region was laid out into townships each six miles square, and each township was subdivided into sections, each containing 640 acres, readily divisible into half sections, quarter sections, and even a smaller acreage. The surveys furnished definite maps and facilitated the location and purchase of lands. At first the price of land was fixed at two dollars an acre, but this was cut in 1820 to one dollar and a quarter.

The Northwest Ordinance itself made provision for temporary territorial government under governors chosen first by the Congress and later by the President of the United States. As soon as there were 5000 free male adults in a particular territory they could establish a local legislature under the supervision of the federal governor. A territorial government so formed consisted of the federal governor, federal judges, a legislative council, and a house of representatives. When a territory acquired 60,000 free residents its people were entitled to a constitution of their own making and to be admitted to the Union "on an equal footing with the original states, in all respects whatever."

The Northwest Ordinance contained more than a plan of government. It stipulated that religious freedom should prevail throughout the region, that the inhabitants should enjoy the right of trial by jury, and that other forms of liberty should be observed. It declared that "schools and the means of education shall forever be encouraged." And this declaration was more than a verbal pledge. Land laws, already passed in connection with the surveys, set aside a section of land in every township to be devoted to the support of schools. A crowning provision of the ordinance, so vital to the growth of liberty, was the article which read: "There shall be neither slavery nor involuntary servitude in the said [Northwest] territory, otherwise than in the punishment of crimes, whereof the party shall have been duly convicted."

Under the generous provisions of the ordinance, pioneers poured into the Northwest Territory. One stream sprang from the South, especially from Virginia, North Carolina, and Kentucky, and flowed into the southern counties of Ohio, Indiana, and Illinois. Other streams sprang from Pennsylvania, New York, and New England. With the westward-moving Americans were mingled newcomers from the Old World—British, Germans, Swiss, and immigrants of other nationalities. Nearly all the families quickly settled down to tilling lands which they had bought either outright or on installments. They built log cabins and cottages, cleared the forests, and prepared fields for crops.

Clues to the swiftness of this movement and the scale of the settlement can be gleaned from the following table showing the dates on which states were admitted to the Union, and the population in the year 1820:

Admission to Union	Population 1820
1803—Ohio	581,400
1816—Indiana	147,100
1818—Illinois	55,200
1837—Michigan	8,800
1848—Wisconsin	

The occupation of the Western territory south of the Ohio River differed in several respects from that of the Northwest. Long before the close of the eighteenth century the Kentucky region of western Virginia was dotted with settlements. By 1792 it had more inhabitants than either Delaware or Rhode Island. Separating itself from Virginia in that year, Kentucky entered the Union as an equal state, with the full consent of Virginia. The Tennessee region, to which North Carolina had claims lasting from the colonial era, was ceded to the Union by the parent state; and for a little while was governed as a territory of the United States. But in 1795, when a census showed that Tennessee had more than 60,000 inhabitants, a local constitution was drafted and the following year, in 1796, Tennessee became a state in the Union.

In regions surrendered by South Carolina and Georgia the remainder of the Southern land was organized under the acts of Congress as a territory of the United States. In 1817 this territory was divided. The western part was admitted to the Union as the state of Mississippi. The eastern part, after two years of territorial status, was given statehood as Alabama.

By 1819 all the divisions of the territory between the original seaboard states and the Mississippi River, except the districts of Michigan and Wisconsin in the north central part, had become equal partners in the Union, as states with their own constitutions. To the list was added, in 1845, the state of Florida in territory acquired from Spain in 1819.

☆

In the meantime expansion beyond the Mississippi was under way. Shortly after Jefferson was inaugurated President in 1801 news reached him that Spain had ceded to France the huge Louisiana Territory extending from the Mississippi River to the Far West. American pioneers over the Appalachians now feared that

Napoleon, the head of the French government, would close New Orleans to their shipment of grain and other farm produce by water to the Eastern seaboard and to the Old World. So they urged Jefferson to prevent that misfortune, and he sent a special agent to France with a commission to buy New Orleans and West Florida if possible.

Before the agent arrived Napoleon had concluded that he might lose his American possessions in a war with Great Britain, and had informed the American minister at Paris that he would sell the whole territory to the United States for $15,000,000, from which certain American claims against France could be deducted. Surprised at the size of the territory offered so cheaply, Jefferson at first hesitated. But at length the purchase was completed in 1803, despite laments from Federalists on the Atlantic coast. Thus at one stroke and without warfare the territory of the United States was more than doubled, though the boundaries of the Louisiana Purchase were vague.

To collect information on the new territory, Jefferson sponsored an expedition headed by Meriwether Lewis and William Clark to explore it, find an overland route to the Pacific, and report on its resources. Under their leadership a party of hardy adventurers was formed near St. Louis. Special boats were built and a traveling outfit was assembled. On May 14, 1804, they set out on the Missouri River for the Northwest. A year later they reached the great falls of the Missouri in Montana. From that point they made their hazardous way across the mountains, with the guidance in part of an Indian woman named Sacawajea. Over the mountains they arrived at the headwaters of the Columbia River, where they built new boats, embarked on the river, and floated swiftly to the Pacific Ocean, reaching their goal in November 1805.

Having blazed the way, the explorers were able to make the return trip more quickly, and in less than a year they were safely back at St. Louis, having completed a long and dangerous journey of about eight thousand miles in two years and four months. From the records kept by Lewis and Clark a report was soon compiled and published. As a result Americans who felt cramped in the East had at their command considerable knowledge of the newest West and could make plans for going where there was more elbow room.

In the same year that Lewis and Clark started from St. Louis on their journey, Zebulon Pike, leading another party, explored the headwaters of the Mississippi. When Pike had finished that

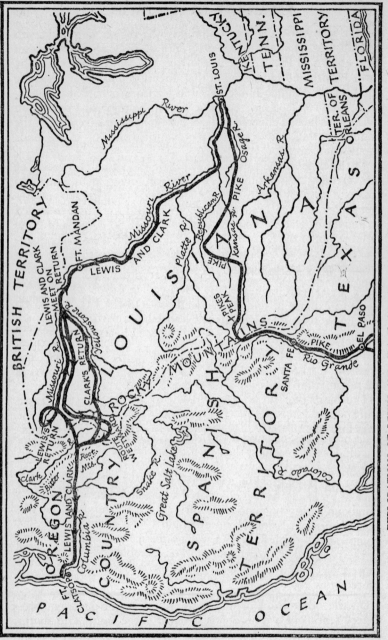

EXPLORATIONS OF LEWIS AND CLARK AND ZEBULON PIKE IN THE FAR WEST

task he was sent on an expedition into the region west and south of St. Louis. He kept on his way until he came to the mountain now known as Pike's Peak in the Rockies. Shortly afterward he turned south and journeyed in that direction until he reached the Rio Grande. Finding himself then in territory occupied by Spaniards, Pike retraced his steps. But in 1810 he published reports on the regions he had covered and persons inclined to adventure in the Southwest thus had access to more information of many kinds about that frontier.

At the time of the Louisiana Purchase the white population of the territory was estimated at figures running from 50,000 to 80,000. The great majority of the inhabitants were French—mainly descendants of the French pioneers who had long before settled at important trading centers, particularly at St. Louis and New Orleans, under the King of France. Among them were many Spanish residents, who had moved up from Spanish territories or from Spain itself, after Louisiana had been turned over to the Spanish King in 1763, at the close of the Seven Years' War. Here and there were also Americans who had crossed the Mississippi even while the west bank was under a foreign flag.

To all the inhabitants of the Louisiana Territory, however, were guaranteed by the treaty of cession "all the rights, advantages, and immunities of citizens of the United States." By act of Congress the territory was divided into two districts later known as the territory of Louisiana and the territory of Missouri.

The more thickly populated region to the south was granted statehood as Louisiana in 1812. As Americans poured across the river into the Missouri district to the north, they began to seek admission to the Union. But a national agitation over slavery delayed admission. In 1819 there were twenty-two states in the Union— half of them slave states and half committed to freedom. If Missouri came in with slavery the balance of power in the Senate of the United States would be upset.

In the North, anti-slavery sentiment was growing. Slavery had been abolished or was rapidly on the way to extinction in all the original states north of Delaware. Ohio, Indiana, and Illinois were free states as required by the Northwest Ordinance. In the House of Representatives, based on population, counting three fifths of the slaves, the strength of the free states was rapidly increasing.

On the other hand, with the spread of cotton planting, pro-slavery sentiment was becoming stronger in the South. Old Southern statesmen, such as Washington, Jefferson, and George Mason, had looked upon slavery as an evil and hoped that in time it could be uprooted. But a new generation of Southerners was beginning to regard slavery as good for both whites and blacks, and to speak of it as a permanent institution to be extended wherever climate and soil were suitable. In these circumstances the admission of Missouri as a slave state was hotly opposed in Congress by Northern men and championed with no less heat by Southern men.

As we have seen, a compromise was reached. Under a congressional act of 1820 Missouri was admitted with slavery; but it was balanced by the admission of Maine, a free state, formerly a part of Massachusetts, now given a separate status by mutual consent. Accompanying this settlement was another compromise destined to be the subject of political agitation in years to come. Slavery was prohibited "forever" in all the territory ceded by France to the United States, under the name of Louisiana, lying north of 36° 30' north latitude, except Missouri. As to slavery in the rest of that territory, nothing was said in the law; silence merely gave consent to its existence in that region.

Another balancing act was performed in 1836. The territory of Arkansas, definitely laid out at the time of the Missouri Compromise, had been filling up with pioneers, many of them planters with their slaves, and others working farmers. By 1836 the Arkansas settlers numbered more than 47,000 and, in the customary way of Americans from the early days of colonization on the seaboard, they demanded self-government. Acceding to their demand, Congress admitted Arkansas to the Union as a slave state, with the provision that the sixteenth section of land in every township be set aside for the support of schools. Far to the northeast, the people of Michigan, with equal zeal, were putting forth their claims to greater autonomy; and the following year, 1837, they entered the Union as a free state. The voting power of slave-owning planters in the Louisiana Territory was thus offset by the voting power of free farmers in the Northwest Territory.

Long before Arkansas and Michigan were "balanced" in the Union, farmers from New England, New York, Ohio, and other Eastern states were moving in long wagon trains into the region known as Iowa. There they staked out for themselves freehold farms in every direction. Three prosperous trading centers sprang up on the Mississippi: Dubuque, Davenport, and Burlington. Academies and colleges were established. In 1846 Iowa won self-government as the fourth state to be erected in the Louisiana Territory, balancing Florida (1845). The fifth state to be carved out of Jefferson's great land purchase was Minnesota, admitted in 1858, without slavery.

☆

Meanwhile, at the extreme western end of the Louisiana Purchase—in the Oregon country—fur traders, missionaries, and farmers from the East were building a new free colony, in the American style. In 1843 Oregon settlers, feeling the need of mutual aid, held a meeting at Champoeg and, after listening to a Fourth of July oration, drew up a compact for governing themselves "until such time as the United States of America extend their jurisdiction over us."

As a matter of fact the United States Government had been in trouble over Oregon and was still in trouble. The northern boundary of the country was vague. Under the obscure terms of the Louisiana Purchase and rights of exploration, the United States claimed all the territory up to the line of 54° 40' north latitude—to the borders of the Russian territory of Alaska. But that claim was stoutly contested by the government of Great Britain, and in 1818 the two governments made a kind of truce providing for temporary joint occupation. This agreement was renewed in 1827 for an indefinite period. Yet it was unsatisfactory to British as well as American fur traders; and settlers insisted that an end be put to joint occupation by drawing a definite boundary line between the British and the American parts.

For years neither side would surrender to this demand. In the presidential campaign of 1844 the Democrats declared for "Fifty-four Forty or Fight"; that is, announced that they would, if necessary, wage war rather than give up the old claim. No fighting ensued, however. The victorious candidate of the Democrats, James K. Polk, had not been long in the office of President when he made, in 1846, a treaty with Great Britain fixing the Oregon boundary at the forty-ninth parallel, not the fifty-fourth. In 1859 the southern part of the Oregon country, the most thickly settled, was admitted to the Union as the sixth state in the Western territory. Many other sections in that territory were also filling up with settlers, and meanwhile the United States had entered upon the third phase of its westward expansion—into the far Southwest.

☆

Under the terms of the purchase from France the boundaries of the Louisiana Territory in the Southwest were also indefinite. At first the United States, on good grounds as later evidence proved, claimed that the boundary ran from near the mouth of the Rio Grande on the Gulf of Mexico in a northerly direction along the course of that river to about the forty-second parallel of north latitude, and thence west to the Pacific Ocean. Spain rejected this claim as encroaching upon her territory, and after long negotiations the boundary was fixed, in 1819, in such a way as to cut off a part of the Louisiana Territory in the Southwest.

The line as then defined started on the gulf at the western border of the state of Louisiana, ran northward along that border, and thence northwesterly and westerly in such a fashion as to leave the Texas country and adjoining regions in the hands of Spain. It was in connection with this settlement of 1819 that the Spanish King ceded to the United States all his claims to the territory east of the Mississippi, known as East and West Florida.

For years before the signing of the treaty of 1819 that established the new boundary for the Louisiana Territory, Spain had been involved in struggles with revolutionists in Mexico; and two years later, in 1821, the last Spanish viceroy to Mexico was forced to recognize the independence of that country. Consequently it was the republic of Mexico, now in the disorders of revolution, with which the United States had to deal in the Southwest.

From the border of Louisiana to the Pacific, especially in the region later known as New Mexico and California, Spanish settlements and missions had been established. But the Southwest as a whole was sparsely settled. In 1821 it was estimated that, excluding the Indians, there were about 4000 Mexicans or Spanish in the Texas country, not more than 3000 or 4000 in Upper California, and perhaps 15,000 or 20,000 in the vast intervening area. The size of the Indian population was unknown, but, unlike that of Mexico proper, it was small and thinly dispersed. In other words, the great Southwest was mostly unoccupied and there were no signs that colonists from Mexico, owner of the territory, would soon, if ever, people that region.

To encourage the settlement of this territory by Americans and other alien immigrants, the government of Mexico granted large blocks of land to contractors who would bring in colonists. In 1820, for example, it arranged with Moses Austin, of Connecticut, to found an American settlement near Bexar, in Texas, and the undertaking was carried out by his son, Stephen F. Austin. By 1830 at least 20,000 American farmers, planters, and traders had established themselves in Texas and more were on the way.

Then, frightened by the deluge, Mexico abandoned the policy of granting land to aliens, declared invalid many grants already in effect, abolished slavery, and otherwise sought to check immigration.

Besides being futile, these actions irritated the Americans already in Texas and ensuing conflicts culminated in an American revolt in 1836. The Mexican army sent to quell the rebels was defeated by American forces under General Sam Houston; and Santa Ana, the Mexican general, was taken prisoner. Texas was now in effect an independent country.

Having achieved their independence, Texans organized a government of their own and sought admission to the United States as a slave state. Owing to the strength of the anti-slavery opinion in the North and in the House of Representatives, admission was long postponed. Andrew Jackson was sympathetic with the Texan appeal but he did not push the matter. Nor did his successor, Martin Van Buren, who was at heart opposed to slavery.

But when John Tyler became President on the death of William H. Harrison in 1841 the outlook for the Texans improved. Yet even Tyler, a pro-slavery man from Virginia, moved slowly in the affair. At last in 1844, near the end of his term, a treaty of annexation was concluded with Texas, only to be rejected in the Senate where the two-thirds vote for ratification could not be mustered.

In their political campaign of that year the Democrats joined with the Oregon slogan, "Fifty-four Forty or Fight," another slogan, "The Reannexation of Texas." Under these battle cries they were successful in the election. Tyler and his supporters now took a new course. Before the new President, James K. Polk, was inaugurated, they gave up the idea of a treaty and in February 1845 Congress adopted, by a simple majority vote, a resolution admitting Texas to the Union.

Texas was in the Union but what was its southwestern boundary? Texans claimed that it was the Rio Grande. Mexicans insisted that it was the Nueces River. President Polk ordered American troops under General Zachary Taylor to cross the Nueces and hold the disputed territory. Soon they were attacked by Mexican forces and President Polk responded by declaring that war had begun "by act of Mexico." With the support of Congress he carried it forward. While General Taylor drove southward into Mexico an expedition, sent by sea and overland under General Winfield Scott, captured Mexico City; and Americans on the

Pacific coast, with aid from American naval commanders, raised the Stars and Stripes in California.

In February 1848, Mexico gave up the unequal fight. New Mexico, Arizona, California, and other districts were ceded to the victor. To this huge domain the United States, by treaty with Mexico five years later, added a small strip known as the Gadsden Purchase in the Gila Valley along the southern border of Arizona. The enormous region between Texas and California, bounded on the north by the Oregon country, was soon divided into two organized territories, Utah and New Mexico, clearing the way for occupation.

Long before war broke out between the United States and Mexico in 1846, a migration of Americans to California had started. For many years shipmasters and merchants from the Atlantic seaboard had been sailing around Cape Horn, visiting California, and trading pots, pans, shoes, and other manufactures with Spanish owners of great estates and with trappers for hides, furs, and other raw materials. News of the mild climate, the fertile soil, and the resources of the region attracted other fortune hunters. By 1830 a trail was opened to Los Angeles from Independence, Kansas, by way of Santa Fé. In 1844 John C. Frémont, intrepid Western explorer, went over the mountains into Sacramento Valley. By 1846 at least one fifth of the people in the little town of San Francisco were citizens of the United States; and Americans were taking part in the quarrels between the Mexican governor of the province and his distant superiors in Mexico City. Trouble was already brewing and had there been no war with Mexico the American colonization of California would have become ominous to its Mexican owners.

In fact the government of the United States already had an eye on the rich prize of California. As early as 1845 the Secretary of State in Washington secretly informed an American agent in Monterey that he could count on help in case difficulties occurred. The Secretary told him that the United States would not foment a revolution there, but it would protect Californians if they revolted against Mexico. The next year some Americans in upper California flung out a flag on which was painted a bear, and began to shout for independence. The Bear Flag movement was quickly submerged when the war with Mexico opened; but Frémont, with the aid of Commodore John Sloat, Commodore Robert Stockton, and General Stephen Kearny, clinched American possession of the whole region. On July 7, 1846, Commodore Sloat raised the American flag over Monterey and proclaimed the annexation of California to the United States.

The war with Mexico had just closed in 1848 when gold was discovered at Sutter's Mill in the Sacramento Valley, and the gold rush to California began—along the overland trails, around Cape Horn, and by way of the Isthmus of Panama. Within two years, it was estimated, about 100,000 immigrants from all parts of the United States and the world had crowded into the gold regions and neighboring towns. With prospective miners were associated merchants, farmers, doctors, teachers, mechanics, lawyers, and laborers, all seeking good luck in the latest Eldorado.

For the future of California the character of the immigrants was decisive. Planters with droves of slaves were not to occupy the territory and add another slave state to the Union. Without waiting for action by Congress, Californians held a convention in 1849, drafted a constitution, put a prohibition on slavery, and demanded statehood. That was a shock to the pro-slavery politicians in the South and the East, but as a part of a general compromise reached by Congress in 1850 California was admitted to the Union as a free state.

The territorial settlement at the close of the Mexican War and the rapid progress of California in population and wealth affected the career of one of the strangest communities in the whole story of American pioneering. This was the Mormon colony in Utah. The Mormon sect had started on its course under the leadership of Joseph Smith, of New York, in 1830, and had been pushed from place to place by hostile neighbors before it settled finally in Utah. Its members had tried living in Missouri. From Missouri they moved to Illinois. Having now adopted the practice of polygamy, or "plural marriage," and given it an elaborate religious sanction, the Mormons seemed to multiply their enemies on every hand. When Brigham Young became their second leader, they decided to go to some remote region where they might live and work in their own fashion with no interference from outsiders. After inquiring about the distant West, Young selected a spot so far away and so arid, he supposed, as to invite few if any intruders; and in 1847 he led his flock to the Salt Lake Valley.

By hard labor and efficient management, the Mormons in Utah made that desert blossom like a rose, as Young had said they would, and built up a prosperous society. Their freedom in the wilds of the West was, nevertheless, soon curtailed. In organizing the territory of Utah the government of the United States brought them under its control; and the gold rush to California over the trail running through Salt Lake City introduced "foreigners" and the lure of gold into their midst. Moreover, many Gentiles insisted on settling down in Utah. Thus the Mormons' longed-for escape from the difficulties of relations with other people proved to be no escape at all. They were destined to be merged in the great Union as the tide of immigration rolled westward toward the Pacific.

CHAPTER XIII

The Industrial Revolution

THE WESTERN SETTLEMENT—from the Appalachians to the Mississippi, beyond the Mississippi, and to the Far West—had great repercussions in the politics and economy of the original thirteen states based on the British colonies. The West broke the Eastern monopoly over the choice of candidates for the presidency of the United States and assumed the right to have its share in making party platforms. The West also affected the economy of the East in both its commercial and planting aspects. It opened more domestic markets for seaboard merchants, enlarged their export business, augmented the demand for capital to invest in lands and industries, and created new demands for manufactured goods. Its spreading plantations in the Southwest brought severe competition to the planters in Virginia, the Carolinas, and Georgia as producers of cotton and other staples.

On the other hand an economic revolution in the East had immense repercussions in the West. This was the Industrial Revolution wrought in manufacturing and social life by the invention and use of steam engines and power-driven machines.

☆

All through the years from the enactment of the Northwest Ordinance in 1787 to the admission of California to the Union in 1850, announcements of inventions and mechanical experiments synchronized with great events in westward expansion.

The following table of events in the history of inventions and applications is merely illustrative in selection but gives an impres-

sion of parallels in time between steps in the Industrial Revolution
and the westward expansion:

1787—John Fitch's steamboat made a successful demonstration on the
Delaware River.
The Northwest Ordinance was enacted.

1791—Samuel Slater put a spinning mill in operation in Rhode Island.
Congress authorized Kentucky to form a new state.

1793—Eli Whitney's cotton gin was patented.
General Anthony Wayne was placed in command of troops in
Ohio to protect settlements against Indians.

1797—A solid cast-iron moldboard for plows was introduced.
Andrew Jackson took his seat in Congress as senator from
Tennessee.

1798—David Wilkinson patented a machine, with slide rule, for making machines.
Kentucky protested against the Alien and Sedition Acts.

1802—Oliver Evans completed a high-pressure steam engine of greater
efficiency than James Watt's engine.
Ohio drafted a constitution for self-government.

1807—Robert Fulton's steamboat, the *Clermont*, made its successful
trip from New York City to Albany and back.
Meriwether Lewis reported to President Jefferson on his exploration of the Louisiana Territory to the Pacific Ocean.

1825—Erie Canal connected New York City with the Great Lakes.
The Mexican legislature of Texas-Coahuila opened the door of
Texas to American colonists.

1831—Steam trains began to run from Charleston to Hamburg, South
Carolina.
Steamboat *Yellowstone* made its first trip on the upper Missouri
River.

1833—Patents were taken out for automatic reapers by Obed Hussey
and Cyrus McCormick.
Abraham Lincoln began to read Blackstone's *Commentaries* at
Salem, Illinois.

1844—Samuel Morse's electric telegraph line opened between Washington and Baltimore.
John C. Frémont's expedition reached Sacramento Valley, California.

1847—Richard Hoe's printing press was printing 8000 copies of the
Philadelphia *Public Ledger* per hour.
American army occupied Mexico City.

1849—McCormick reaper works were established in Chicago.
Great exodus to California gold mines began.

1851—William Kelly started developing "air-boiling" process of making steel, anticipating the discoveries of Bessemer.

The territorial legislature of Oregon created the county of Umpqua.

1852—First railway train ran from Philadelphia to Pittsburgh.
Leland Stanford settled in California.

1853—Baltimore and Ohio Railway entered Ohio.
Chicago and St. Louis Railway line opened.

☆

In application the thousands of inventions, major and minor, made between 1790 and 1850, utterly transformed methods that had been employed almost unchanged for hundreds of years in manufacture, transportation, mining, communications, and agriculture. Considered in its largest terms, this revolution meant releasing the production and transport of goods from the limitations of human hands and strength, supplemented by animal, wind, and water power. No longer was the amount of goods produced to be determined by the number of human beings employed in the process. Henceforward production could be expanded indefinitely by the substitution of mechanical fingers for human fingers and mechanical power for human power. For the first time in the history of the human race the possibility of an abundant production, freed from the leash of mere human energy, loomed on the horizon of peoples capable of developing the Industrial Revolution toward the goal set by the potentials of technology.

Slowly in the beginning but steadily gaining momentum, machinery, driven first by water power and after about 1810 by steam engines, was used to produce commodities in great factories, swiftly and on a large scale. In 1807 only fifteen cotton mills existed in the United States and they were operating only 8000 spindles. Four years later the number of mills had increased to eighty-seven and the number of spindles to 80,000. Within four years, more than 500,000 spindles were whirring under the watchful eyes of 76,000 tenders, becoming known as "industrial workers."

When the eighth census was taken in 1860, the leading commodities used for food, clothing, and shelter had been caught up in the Industrial Revolution with astounding results in output. For the year ending June 1, 1860, the total value of machine and hand manufactures, including fisheries and mining, and excluding very small shops, was placed at $1,900,000,000, nearly twice the output of 1850 and more than four times the total national wealth in 1787.

In order of respective values of output the following commodities were highest on the list: flour and meal, cotton goods, lumber, boots and shoes, leather, clothing, woolen goods, machinery, steam engines, etc., books, newspapers, sugar, spiritous liquors, cabinet furniture, bar and other rolled iron, malt liquors, agricultural implements, paper, soap, and candles. The very list of articles and amounts of each exhibited the advance Americans had made on the road to the manufacturing independence foreshadowed in colonial times.

America was ceasing to be a mere raw-material country for manufacturing nations in the Old World. Census takers of 1860 reported that 1,385,000 persons were employed in American manufacturing establishments and enterprises; they estimated that, counting the dependents of these persons, about one sixth of the whole population was directly supported by manufactures. Adding to this number all the persons engaged in the production of raw materials for manufacturing and in the distribution of manufactured goods—capitalists, transportation workers, merchants, and clerks, for instance—the census reporters declared: "It is safe to assume, then, that one third of the whole population is supported, directly or indirectly, by manufacturing industry. . . . The nation seemed speedily approaching a period of complete independence in respect to the products of skilled labor."

A mechanical revolution in the carriage of goods and passengers by water and land went along with the swift advance of manufacturing. In 1807, sixteen years after Samuel Slater put his spinning mill in operation, Robert Fulton's steamboat made a successful trip from New York City to Albany and back. In 1819 an American ship driven by steam and sail crossed the Atlantic Ocean. By that time steamships were plying the coastal waters of the Eastern seaboard, the navigable streams of the Mississippi River system, and the Great Lakes. Between 1840 and 1850 the tonnage on lakes, rivers, and coastal waters more than doubled. Already steam navigation to California by way of Cape Horn and the Isthmus of Panama had been opened. In 1829 the number of steamboats on the Mississippi system was 200; in 1836 it was 240.

The Erie Canal, establishing water connections between New York City and the Great Lakes in 1825, and the Pennsylvania Canal to the West, completed in 1834, had scarcely started the promotion of rapid and long-distance transportation when they were challenged by the railway, which completely emancipated the carriage of passengers and freight from bondage to watercourses. Before the Pennsylvania Canal was finished, steam trains were running between Charleston and Hamburg, South Carolina, and the railway era had dawned.

Soon there were railway connections between the chief cities of the Northern seaboard. By 1860 trains were running regularly between Baltimore, Philadelphia, New York, and Boston; those cities were linked by rail with Cleveland, Cincinnati, Chicago, and St. Louis. Meanwhile the chief cities of the South were joined by railways, and connections were established between them and the Northern network. The time of travel for passengers had been cut from weeks to days and the cost of carrying freight from dollars to cents per ton-mile.

☆

In the train of the mechanical revolution followed a rapid growth of population in old cities and the appearance of new cities, even in the Western wildernesses. In 1790 only five towns —Boston, New York, Philadelphia, Baltimore, and Charleston—had more than 8000 inhabitants each and their combined population was under 135,000, a little above three per cent of the total population of the United States. Thirty years later there were thirteen communities having 8000 inhabitants or more, with a combined population of almost 500,000. New York alone in 1830 had as many people as all the five towns of 1790 put together; and in 1860 the population of New York, including surrounding districts later drawn under its jurisdiction, had passed the 1,000,000 mark.

In the eight industrial states of the seaboard—from Massachusetts to Maryland, inclusive—there were in 1840 eleven cities with over 20,000 inhabitants; by 1860 the number of cities in that class had increased to twenty-four; and the twenty-four had more than twenty-seven per cent of the total population of the eight states. In 1840 nine towns to the west of the mountains had a combined population of about 150,000—Pittsburgh, Cincinnati, Louisville, Chicago, St. Louis, Milwaukee, Detroit, Cleveland, and Buffalo; within twenty years their aggregate population had risen to about 800,000.

To the factories and shops in the cities moved a steady procession of young people from American farms and small towns. In New England it was led by the daughters of farmers in the neighborhood of the spinning mills, who had been taught that it was their

moral and patriotic duty to be as useful as possible in such industries. Indeed to a large extent young women "manned" the first
textile mills of that section. Wherever machine industries appeared
men and women from the rural regions flocked to them in search
of work; and the number of "mill hands" was swelled by child
laborers—socially an uprooting phase of the new production
methods.

In the growth of manufacturing centers, as in the settlement of
the West, immigrants from the Old World became factors of increasing importance. The Industrial Revolution was in reality a
new spur to immigration and its effects in this relation were soon
manifest in the shipping records. Between 1820 and 1860 more
than 5,000,000 alien passengers arrived at the ports of the United
States on ships from foreign countries. In 1820 they numbered
8385; in 1850, 310,004; in 1854, 427,833. This inflow of labor forces
was stimulated by steamship companies, by employers of labor
seeking a plentiful supply to keep wages as low as possible, as well
as by other influences within the United States and in the lands
of the emigrants.

Reckoning the immigrants of the period by economic classes,
the most numerous were as follows:

Laborers	872,000
Farmers	764,000
Mechanics	407,000
Merchants	231,800
Miners	39,900
Textile workers	11,500

In the list of callings and occupations that classified other immigrants who entered the country between 1820 and 1860, the census reported: mariners, shoemakers, tailors, milliners, actors, clergymen, lawyers, clerks, physicians, engineers, artists, teachers,
musicians, printers, painters, masons, hatters, millers, butchers,
bakers, and servants.

More than twenty countries were recorded as supplying quotas
of immigrants during those forty-one years of American expansion. The United Kingdom furnished the largest of all, 2,750,000,
of whom 967,000 came from Ireland. Germany stood next with
1,486,000; France third with 208,000; British America fourth, with
117,000. Among the other countries represented were Spain, Prussia, Norway, Sweden, Poland, Italy, China, Mexico and other
Latin American nations. To the population of the United States—

in 1790 about three-fourths British in origin—were thus added national strains more diverse in origins, languages, and customs.

Although thousands of aliens moved into the West seeking farms to own and till, other thousands stayed in the rising industrial towns on the seaboard and furnished skill, enterprise, and labor for manufacturing, transportation, and commerce. If George Washington could have journeyed again from Virginia northward in 1860, as he had done in 1789 by carriage and on horse, he would scarcely have known the land to whose independence he had dedicated his talents.

☆

Apart from the farmers and great landed proprietors in 1790, the chief economic class among the owners of property had been the merchants who handled exports and imports and interstate commerce. After the Industrial Revolution got under way the role of manufacturers was magnified in American society. Often, if not generally, at first, the manufacturer who assembled machinery and workers for industries came from the old class of mechanics and craftsmen. Frequently he developed his little hand-labor shop into a factory, using machines and steam power. Sometimes, like Samuel Slater in Rhode Island, he began anew by building a great mill, frequently with the financial aid of merchants who had capital to invest.

As opportunities for manufacturing multiplied, individual enterprisers, finding their own resources inadequate, banded together in corporations to raise larger capital. These concerns sold stock to the public and borrowed money from banks. Long before 1850 corporations had become numerous and powerful in every branch of industry, transportation, and commerce.

As industries expanded in size and number, manufacturers became more closely associated with inventors engaged in devising new machines and processes and with capitalists seeking opportunities for profitable investment. In the early days of the factory system manufacturers usually managed their own plants, aided by foremen; but with the rise of corporations they often turned this responsibility over to deputies. Out of the varied development of machine economy six groups of enterprisers emerged; manufacturers, specialized inventors, industrial bankers, capitalists pure and simple, corporation lawyers, and industrial managers.

For building and operating machine industries large bodies of skilled and unskilled workers were necessary. They were procured from two principal sources: first, from the mechanics of the towns and the men, women, and children of the farms, that is, Americans of the old stock; and then from the new immigrants. From whatever source they came industrial workers were generally dislocated in respect of their historic status and their historic opportunities.

In the handicraft economy of earlier times, manufacturing was carried on extensively in connection with agriculture, in the households and in small outside shops; and the workers were not solely dependent upon the sale of sheer labor power for a livelihood. Furthermore, as owners of their tools and their time, they had direct control over their hours of labor and working conditions, onerous as those might be. Even master mechanics who lived in towns, and worked apart from the land, were likewise owners of their tools and shops; and their employees were often apprentices who expected in due time to be their own masters.

Under the new machine economy, on the other hand, few workers personally owned their tools and implements of production; nor, in the nature of things, could any large proportion of them look forward confidently to becoming mill owners. Their wages, hours of labor per day, and even employment on any terms were largely or wholly beyond their control—in the hands of employers, subject to the invisible but imperious conditions of the market for the manufactures produced by capital and labor.

From the point of view of labor and its prospects, therefore, a striking feature of the Industrial Revolution was the immense increase in the proportion of workers dependent wholly upon wages for their subsistence and upon the fluctuations in the market for employment. In former days, on account of the abundance of land open for settlement on easy terms, industrious farm workers including indentured servants had good prospects of acquiring farms of their own. Labor was arduous on the land but families that tilled it could usually count on having some food, clothing, and shelter in the worst of times.

In a different situation were workers connected with machine industries. Thousands of them rose, it is true, into the employing and professional classes, owing to economic opportunities and the fluidity of American society. But the vast majority of them were destined to remain wage workers throughout their lives, and to be subject to the vicissitudes of the panics and depressions which afflicted machine industries. Not only did this destiny present a strange problem to individual men and women in the disruption of the old family economy. It brought to the nation unprecedented problems in class relations and in public policies.

☆

As a result of the Industrial Revolution, a new conflict over the balance of power took form. From the early days of colonization freehold farmers had clashed with seaboard landlords, merchants, and money-lenders. They had struggled to get power, first in the colonial and then in the state legislatures. They had constituted a substantial part of the opposition to the adoption of the Constitution and had rallied in politics to the support of the Republican party under the leadership of Jefferson. Now wage workers in machine industries by the thousands surged into the political arena and began to form organizations for the promotion of their interests.

In large numbers they flocked to the party of Jacksonian democracy, although it was largely a farmers' party. But their interests did not exactly coincide with agrarian interests. They had needs, demands, and methods of their own. Crowded together, as they were, in cities, they could easily create associations of their own to voice their interests and bring pressure to bear on employers, politicians, and on society in general, for the redress of their grievances real or alleged.

The associations organized by or for industrial workers after the rise of machine industries were numerous and varied in nature and purposes. But the most persistent type was the trade union. Between the end of the eighteenth century and the middle of the nineteenth century the trade-union movement went through four rather definite stages, as to forms of organization.

The first stage was the creation of local unions in single crafts or trades, for the purpose of influencing wages and the length of the working day. As early as 1792 the shoemakers of Philadelphia formed a union. Two years later the printers of New York and Philadelphia organized typographical societies. By the end of Jackson's second administration in 1837 workers in the leading trades of Boston, New York, Philadelphia, Baltimore, and several other towns had established local unions. Among them were unions of bookbinders, machinists, ironworkers, hatmakers, jewelers, type founders, glassmakers, millwrights, ship joiners, furriers, leather dressers, shoemakers, printers, boilermakers, loom weavers, and plumbers.

As local unions in single trades multiplied they showed a tendency to draw together in their respective cities, and this marked the second phase of their evolution. New York led off with the establishment of a central or city trades union, a union of trades, in 1833. Within five years there were similar city organizations in Baltimore, Philadelphia, Boston, Newark, Albany, Troy, and Pittsburgh, and also in the Western towns of Cincinnati and Louisville.

During these very years trade unionism entered the third stage in its development: the federation of local craft unions in a national association representing a single trade, an industry, or a craft. For this movement the journeymen cordwainers, or shoe and leather workers, were pathbreakers. In March 1836 they held a convention in New York City, composed of delegates from cordwainers' unions in New York, New Haven, Brooklyn, Newark, Paterson, Philadelphia, Washington, and several other places. Then and there they formed a constitution for the National Cooperative Association of Journeymen Cordwainers and framed a platform pledging mutual assistance. In the same year unionist printers, after many exchanges of letters, sent delegates to a general convention in Washington and entered into a loose national federation. Other trades followed these examples, with ups and downs in fortune, until within twenty years each of the principal crafts had a national organization of some kind.

The fourth step in the organization of labor—the union of all unions in a national federation—was the most difficult of all and was not permanently effected until more than fifty years after the cordwainers had formed their national craft federation in 1836. But the project had been planned in the early stages of trade-union development and efforts had been made to realize it as soon as local unionism had gained its first strength.

An experiment in general organization was attempted in New England in 1831, with the formation of the New England Association of Farmers, Mechanics, and Other Working Men. Although some unionists were represented in its meetings, the association was as much concerned with politics and social reforms as with hours, wages, and working conditions. Within three years it went to pieces.

A stronger effort at national federation on a unionist basis in respect of membership was made in 1834 at a convention of delegates from trades unions held in New York City. After extended debates the National Trades Union was formed under a constitution which declared its purposes to be moral, intellectual, and pecuniary. This national union held conventions in 1835 and 1836 and then collapsed in the panic of 1837. The foundations for such a national union of unions had not yet been securely laid and nearly thirty years were to pass before another undertaking of the kind was even attempted.

☆

Amid the uprush of factories and cities, the multiplication of wage workers, the relative decline of handicraft production, and the growth of trade unions, a thoroughly dislocating force broke into the economy of the nation. That was the periodical panic followed by a widespread industrial collapse. Such crises had often occurred in the past but as long as the overwhelming majority of the people tilled the soil for a livelihood depressions did not create destitution for the masses. Now, however, hundreds of thousands of people were concentrated in great industrial centers and divorced from the soil with its food-giving crops, its raw materials for clothing and shelter, and its enduring opportunities for productive employment. Now a breakdown in industry and business enterprise meant, for such urbanized workers, unemployment, no wages, actual lack of the vital necessities—food, clothing, and shelter.

The first terrific smash in the machine-production age occurred in 1819; another in 1829; the third and most severe in the history of the United States up to that date opened in 1837 and lasted for about five years. A brief recovery was only a prelude to a fourth collapse in 1847. Ten years later, in 1857, another depression settled over the nation and almost crushed the labor movement entirely.

Even in the intervals called prosperous, poverty and distress haunted the working-class districts of the great cities. Famines and misery had marked the course of all history in the Old World and the Orient, but slaves and serfs had usually had some shelter and some bread even in hard times. There had been poverty in colonial times in America and in the early days of the Republic, but it had been widely dispersed and its evils mitigated in considerable measure by charity and poor relief.

Whether the Industrial Revolution increased the relative amount of poverty or not, it made the position of mere wage workers more precarious than that of the serf or the farmer; and it concentrated poverty-stricken persons in urban masses so large that only the blind could fail to see their plight. Such poverty, on a scale so enormous and so obtruding, so contrasted in the cities with flaunting riches, was a new thing; and it aroused consternation among American citizens who had social sympathies and cared about the security of the Republic. Their interest was heightened by the agitations and protests of labor leaders, charity workers, and political reformers.

In a land where the objectives of society and government were declared to be life, liberty, equality, the pursuit of happiness, and the general welfare, what was to be done about such poverty? Were the institutions and ideas derived from the great Revolutionary age of the Republic sufficient to meet the new problems? Fifty years after the Declaration of Independence Americans were impelled to thinking more comprehensively than their forebears had done in the days of the Revolution itself.

Before the industrial upheaval had gone far the American stock of ideas on society and government, on industry and agriculture, on the rights of men and women, was reviewed, reinterpreted, modified, and augmented. Reforms bewildering in number were proposed. They were forced upon the attention of political parties. They were written up in books, pamphlets, and newspaper articles, and made subjects of discussion in circles high and low, from one end of the country to the other. During the advance of the Western frontier, the contests of politicians, the westward sweep into the Louisiana Territory and the Southwest, the upsurge of cities and industries, the building of canals and railways, the celebration of a growing population and mounting wealth—amid all this—plans for recasting the heritage received from the founders of the Republic were forced into the thought of reflective people concerned with the future of the United States. In nature these ideas and plans ranged from specific reforms to an overhauling of the entire social order.

Reformers who spoke from the ranks of labor or in the name of labor presented a long bill of specific demands: equal suffrage for all white men and, sometimes, for women; free and equal public education; the abolition of imprisonment for debt, which especially oppressed the poor; an independent labor press; the dissolution of monopolies; full right of labor to organize, strike, and bargain collectively with employers; a ten-hour day, with hints of an eight-hour day; payment of wages in cash instead of "store goods"; restriction of immigration; sound money for wages, instead of fluctuating bank paper; regulation of factories and mines in the interests of safety and health; and the division of the public domain into small homesteads to be given, not sold, to persons willing to occupy and develop them.

Other reformers, including many men and women distinguished for their idealistic leadership, declared that such schemes were not enough to cure the ills of poverty or release the full productive force of machine economy; and they offered a variety of panaceas. One of the earliest of such reforming groups advocated a peaceful reconstruction of American society, especially that type expounded by the French idealist, Charles Fourier, under a theory of utopian socialism. The utopists of this school were generally called "associationists." They proposed to abandon the capitalist factory system, found colonies of associated workers on the land, and combine farming with manufacturing. In colonies of the kind, they believed, workers could be self-sufficing, share their wealth on equal terms, and acquire economic stability and independence.

One school of American associationists, in their thinking, used extensively the ideals propagated by the British utopian socialist, Robert Owen, who made lecture tours in the United States and, with his son, Robert Dale Owen, founded a socialist colony at New Harmony in Indiana. They were especially impressed by Robert Owen's three revolutionary propositions: the enormously increased productive powers which man in modern times has acquired involve, and in a measure necessitate, great changes in the social and industrial structure of society; the world has reached a point of progress at which co-operative industry should replace competitive labor; society, discarding large cities and solitary homes, should resolve itself into associations—communities uniting agriculture and manufacturing. If in theory Owen's propositions were revolutionary, in practice his program was intended to be pacific, for the independent communities were to be established by the voluntary co-operation of capital and labor.

Convinced that they were on the right line, American associationists made experimental tests of their doctrines. They established several colonies in different parts of the country; but only those motivated by religious fervor and sacrifice managed to survive for more than a few years.

Also revolutionary but at an opposite pole of thought from utopian socialism, and violent rather than peaceful in its implications, was the interpretation of recent industrial events proclaimed by disciples of Karl Marx, whose *Communist Manifesto* was issued in Europe in 1848. Three years later a German apostle of Marx, Joseph Weydemeyer, landed in America and founded a newspaper to spread the doctrine that the historical role of the working class was to overthrow the whole capitalist system and usher in a "co-operative commonwealth." But Weydemeyer did not make much headway with his propaganda in the American labor movement. When the Civil War started he enlisted as a captain in the Union army and by valiant service rose to the rank of general. Though his call for a revolutionary labor party gained no material support in the American labor movement, Marxism was thrust into the ferment of the new industrial age in the United States.

☆

The influence of the mechanical revolution was not confined to urban centers. Indeed one great machine industry, railway transportation, coupled with the electric telegraph, ran out in every direction until at length it spanned the continent. Railways cut channels from the seaboard to the West, through which manufactures flowed to farmers and planters and farm produce flowed back in exchange. One striking feature of the trunk lines was the close economic union effected between the Northeast and the old Northwest Territory before the sixth decade of the nineteenth century closed.

By that time enterprisers of the North and the South were projecting trunk lines to the Pacific. Had it not been for a dispute over the route—whether it was to go through the Southwest or the Central West—and the political struggle over slavery, beginnings of construction would have been made before 1860.

Rapid transportation between the manufacturing regions of the East and the farming regions of the West did not prevent Westerners, however, from developing industries of their own. Cleveland, Chicago, Cincinnati, Milwaukee, St. Louis, and Louisville early became manufacturing as well as merchandising centers. A survey of American economy published in 1854 reported: "Cincinnati, Ohio, appears to be a great central depot of ready-made clothing, and its manufacture for the Western markets may be said to be one of the great trades of that city. . . . Latterly sewing machines, of varied construction, have been largely employed. . . . At Louisville, Kentucky, and St. Louis, Missouri, the manufacture of clothing is extensively carried on; but Cincinnati may be considered as the great mart of ready-made clothing for the Western states, and, in a measure, for those of the South also. In 1851 there were in the latter city 108 establishments, employing 950 hands in their own workshops, and upwards of 9000 females either at their own homes or under 'bosses.' The proprietors are chiefly German Jews, and most of the operatives are Germans."

A petty village with a few inhabitants when Cook County, Illinois, was organized in 1831, Chicago soon became a focus for shipping on the Great Lakes and for distributing Eastern manufactures brought by water and rail. Then its enterprisers turned to manufacturing. After the establishment of the McCormick reaper works in 1849, Chicago rose to be the leading center for the manufacture of plows, reapers, threshers, and other machinery needed for the expansion of farm production as vast areas of level Western land were opened up for cultivation, especially enormous corn- and wheat-growing regions.

Although many men in the South saw the immense potentialities of machine industry for economic welfare and sought to balance the agriculture of that region by the introduction of manufacturing, their efforts, for one reason or another, met with only slight success. It is true that by 1840 Virginia, North Carolina, Georgia, Tennessee, and Kentucky had many cotton mills in operation, but these factories were small in size and in their growth fell far behind Northern competitors. In 1850 the annual value of manufactures produced in the free states was more than four times the output of manufactures in the slave states. Omitting Maryland, Kentucky, and Missouri from the list of slave states, it was more than eight times the Southern output. In 1857 the free states had 17,800 miles of railway lines; the slave states only 6800 miles.

By the middle of the century four portentous facts stood out in the economy of the United States. First, the capital value of industrial and urban property overtopped the capital value of all the farms and plantations from the Atlantic to the Pacific. Second, the Northeast and the Northwest, linked together by common interests, greatly surpassed in manufacturing wealth and production all the Southern states, especially the slave belt below Maryland, Kentucky, and Missouri. Third, the iron products and leather goods, including boots and shoes, alone equaled in value of annual output all the cotton grown in Southern fields. Fourth, by similarity of freehold agricultural practices, the people of a vast section between the Southern seaboard and the Mississippi—in western Virginia and North Carolina, and in eastern Kentucky and Tennessee—were affiliated by economic habits and kindred sentiments with Northern farmers, rather than with the planters of the coastal plain who used chattel slaves to till their soil.

Over continuously larger areas of the continental domain the interests and ideologies of the early Republic were undergoing changes and transformations fundamental in character. Inherited productive methods of agriculture and manufacturing were being outmoded. The American population was becoming increasingly urban. The family system of economic and cultural unity was giving way to the factory system which drew even young children into its fold. An organized movement was beginning to assert the claims of labor to a larger share of the profits of capitalistic enterprise; and revolutionary social theories were competing with loyalty to capitalism in the ranks of labor. Localism was yielding ground before the invasion of new laws, customs, institutions, and social problems national in scope. The trend of thought and interest was toward a more consolidated national Union and a fuller realization of the opportunities for the life commodious and abundant on this continent.

CHAPTER XIV

Rise of National Democracy

ATTENDING the expansion of the American nation to the Pacific Ocean and the transformation wrought in economy by steam and machinery was the decimation of the governing elite, in the name of democracy. Previously the very word "democracy" had been terrifying to ruling classes throughout the world. In America only a few groups of persons belonging to the Revolutionary generation of the eighteenth century had used the word "democracy" as a symbol for their political and social ideals and programs. Such groups had been regarded with horror by those men and women of the times who believed with Chief Justice Oliver Ellsworth that Jeffersonians were the "apostles of anarchy, bloodshed, and atheism"; or with Elbridge Gerry that "the evils we experience flow from the excess of democracy. The people do not want virtue, but are the dupes of pretended patriots."

This fright at the thought of democracy was illustrated in the systems of government set up in the states by the leaders of the Revolution. Those systems in a majority of cases limited the right to vote to men who owned property or paid taxes, and put high property qualifications on the right to serve in legislatures and important offices. In this way they excluded from government a substantial proportion of white males. But since the number of white male property owners and taxpayers was large, the suffrage was widely extended. And in fact, with the abolition of British control, legislatures became very powerful in all the states, representing a positive tendency in the direction of democracy.

On the eve of the revolt against Great Britain the Americans, possibly with some exceptions, were wholehearted monarchists.

During the Revolution the word "democracy" was little used. It did not appear in any of the great public documents of the age— neither in the Declaration of Independence, nor in any of the first state constitutions, nor in the Constitution of the United States. In the convention which framed the Constitution powerful statesmen expressed aversion to democracy and sought to put checks on majority rule by the people. Thomas Jefferson did not publicly call himself a democrat or use the term in any of his public addresses and messages. He was convinced that government by a simple majority—even of farmers—could be as despotic as a one-man tyranny and he especially distrusted "the mobs of the great cities."

Indeed even the word "republic" frightened timid souls. None of the first state constitutions mentioned the word. The Constitution of the United States did not officially declare the new nation to be a republic. Only gradually did that term come into official use. Jefferson was really promoting the idea when he called his party Republican.

During the Revolution, however, multitudes of disfranchised people thought and acted in the domain of public affairs. Throngs who were excluded from the privilege of voting and holding office took part in boycotting British goods. Many men who could not vote fought in the War of Independence. After the new governments were established local, state, and national elections were held periodically and struggles over public questions and for political power quickened the minds of thousands who had no actual share in the government. Elections and campaigns also stimulated political interest among men entitled to vote but hitherto indifferent to their rights and duties as citizens. Political newspapers multiplied. Books, pamphlets, leaflets, and broadsides on politics and government rolled from presses in swelling streams, helping to make citizens more alert to the importance of public questions for themselves and their country.

In this political awakening the advocacy of democracy spread rapidly, especially after the opening of the French Revolution in 1789. Democratic agitations accompanied the outburst of American sympathy for the French Republic when it became involved in war with Great Britain in 1793. During those years of excitement local societies were organized in nearly every state in the Union for the purpose of carrying on political education and propaganda—from Addison County in Vermont to Charleston, South Carolina; from Philadelphia to Lexington in Kentucky.

Forty-two such societies are reported by E. P. Link in his *Democratic-Republican Societies, 1790–1800*, published in 1942. Of this number at least fifteen called themselves "Democratic" societies; others chose the more conservative word "Republican" as their title; two adopted the hyphenated title, "Democratic-Republican."

So active were the societies that conservatives, such as Hamilton and Washington, saw the specter of a revolution from below and considered ways and means of suppressing it. In fact the Alien and Sedition Acts, pushed through Congress by the Federalists in 1798, were aimed at such agitations fomented by the popular societies. Nevertheless, respectable leaders in local affairs, apparently in ever larger numbers, were boldly speaking of their political aspirations as "democratic."

The outcome of the French Revolution in the dictatorship of Napoleon Bonaparte cooled the ardors of the democratic and republican societies and most of them as distinct organizations seem to have disappeared by the opening of the nineteenth century. But their places were taken by local party machines which had been growing up in every state and populous community. For the fateful election of 1800 both the Federalists and the Anti-Federalists, or Republicans, were well organized.

Each of the two parties in Congress formed a separate group, or caucus, to promote its political interests. In cities, towns, and counties, from New Hampshire to Georgia, from Pennsylvania to Tennessee, members of the opposition to the Federalists held local conventions and established local committees, each free to choose its name. Most of them adopted the name "Republican"; some preferred the title "Democratic-Republican"; a few candidly called themselves "Democrats."

As the decades of the nineteenth century passed, more and more members of the Republican party appropriated the Democratic label. But national leaders of that party continued to insist they were simply Republicans. State and local committees of the party used the one or the other title, according to their degree of sympathy with popular demands. Since no national party convention was held until 1831, there was no official body empowered to fix the party name.

Madison, Monroe, and even Andrew Jackson clung to the name "Republican." In no state paper or official address did Jackson proclaim himself a Democrat or refer to the United States as a democracy, although in private letters he occasionally used the words with approval. Nor did the early national conventions of the party desert the name given to it by Jefferson. The national convention of 1840 spoke of "cardinal principles in the Democratic faith"; but not until 1844 was its national convention ready to discard officially all references to the "Republican" brethren and declare the party to be "the American Democracy"—"the Democratic party of this Union."

☆

Intimately related to the spread of the democratic ideal were changes in political and social arrangements which registered the growth of democratic practices. All the states admitted to the original Union between 1789 and 1840—New Hampshire, Kentucky, Tennessee, Ohio, Indiana, Illinois, Louisiana, Mississippi, Alabama, Florida, Missouri, Maine, Michigan, and Arkansas—differed in several features of their social structure from the old seaboard states with their colonial backgrounds. In none of them was there an upper class of wealth and political power comparable to that represented by the great landlords or the rich merchants of the original thirteen states. In short, there was more equality in wealth and social condition in the new agricultural states than in the old.

Furthermore the constitutions of the new states were more democratic in many respects than the constitutions of some older states. The new states all adopted white manhood suffrage or at most slight qualifications on the right to vote. They also opened places in legislatures and public administrations to adult males in general. As the number of senators and representatives from new states increased in Congress, as Western states acquired more voting power in presidential elections, even seaboard politicians who had no natural liking for democracy were forced to accept some of it as a hard fact or retire from public life.

At the same time the old East was undergoing a transformation which favored the growth of democracy there. The number of freehold farmers was increasing in the regions behind the seaboard, from Maine to Georgia. Popular agitations were making more farmers politically conscious, and changing them from negligent into active voters. New industrial cities were springing up. The population of the older cities was rising rapidly. Immigrants were flooding in from the Old World and acquiring American citizenship. Industrial workers were forming trade unions and labor parties.

These events helped to erode the prevailing class structures of the Eastern states and promote the growth of political democracy —a vote for every white man at least and the opening of all public places to white men of every rank in society. Far and wide, people of democratic inclinations were recalling that the Declaration of Independence had declared all men born equal and pointing the logic that all men ought to have the right to vote and hold office.

So the democratic changes did not all occur in the Western states. As a matter of fact low suffrage qualifications were adopted in several Eastern states before many Western states had come into existence. This was in line with the principles of 1776, reinforced by agrarian and labor agitations in the East since the establishment of the Republic. It had little or nothing to do with the so-called "frontier."

Step by step, seaboard states altered their constitutions, in various parts, in such a way as to abolish or qualify the rule that only owners of property could vote and to confer the suffrage on nearly all adult white males. The property requirement for voting was removed among the original thirteen states in the following order of time:

1778—South Carolina	1821—Massachusetts, New York
1784—New Hampshire	1842—Rhode Island
1789—Georgia	1844—New Jersey
1792—Delaware	1850—Virginia
1810—Maryland	1856—North Carolina
1818—Connecticut	

In several cases, when the property-ownership qualification on the right to vote was abandoned, the payment of a small tax, on the Pennsylvania model of 1776, was substituted or continued; but in time that tax was also generally abolished. By the middle of the nineteenth century practically all white male citizens in the original states could vote. Thus two movements between 1776 and 1850 —one in the East and the other in the West—converged to make white manhood suffrage prevail generally in the country.

In the same span of years property qualifications on the right to hold office were removed, along with various religious qualifications. Under many of the first state constitutions public officials and members of the legislatures had to be the owners of property in fixed amounts. For example, according to the Massachusetts constitution of 1780, the governor had to own freehold property worth at least £1000; under the South Carolina constitution of 1778 the governor's property qualification was at least £10,000 freehold.

Many of the first state constitutions also contained provisions which limited the suffrage or office-holding or both to Christians or to Protestants alone. But with the spread of democracy the restriction of offices to men of wealth and members of specific religious denominations was destroyed.

Coupled with the extension of the suffrage and the removal of property and religious qualifications on office-holding were two other practices also called democratic. The first was the custom of giving short terms to public officers, known as "rotation in office"; the second was the rule that the victors in an election should take over the political jobs held by their predecessors—"to the victors belong the spoils of office."

Democrats early resented the tendency to keep men of old and rich families in office from generation to generation. They maintained, moreover, that long service in places of power was likely to make men arbitrary and aristocratic in the management of public business. A change of officers every few years, they insisted, was necessary in a democracy and conducive to the right conduct of administration. Short terms, frequent elections, and rotation in office, therefore, became popular watchwords.

To them was added one less theoretical: "Turn the rascals out and give the jobs to our 'boys.'" By 1840 "the spoils system" had become general throughout the Union, even in the federal government at Washington. After every election crowds of public officials, including clerks, accountants, and doorkeepers, were removed to make room for men belonging to the victorious party or faction.

Another feature of the democratic tendency was the adoption of the rule that presidential electors must be chosen by popular vote. The original Constitution provided that each state shall appoint in such manner as the legislature thereof may direct the number of electors to which it may be entitled—that is, the number equal to its whole number of senators and representatives. This method of election had been adopted by the convention of 1787 instead of other plans presented, such as election by Congress or by direct popular vote. It was intended to remove the selection of the President from the heats of political campaigns. Presidential electors so chosen, it was thought, would be free to review all the candidates, pass careful judgments on the merits of the men available for the office, and cast their votes according to their best opinions.

In the beginning presidential electors were chosen by the state legislatures themselves in several states, but five states established popular election at the very outset. By 1824, when twenty-four states participated in the election, eighteen had provided that the presidential electors must be chosen by the voters; in only six states were they selected by the legislatures. In the next election, 1828, electors were popularly chosen in all states except Delaware and South Carolina. Meanwhile presidential electors had lost their freedom of choice; they had become "dummies," bound to vote for the candidate for the presidency duly nominated by their political party. Thus popular election had been substituted for the deliberative electoral process contemplated by the framers of the Constitution.

In another respect the election of the President was made still more popular—by the rise of the national party convention as a machine for selecting candidates prior to the election. After the retirement of Washington, whose election had been unanimous, Federalist members of Congress organized a caucus or unofficial committee to select their candidate. The Republicans soon followed their example. Until 1828, one or more candidates were regularly nominated by congressional caucuses. But in that year "King Caucus met his death." Jackson's supporters had outlawed the practice as aristocratic and contrary to the Constitution besides. For a short time there was no national party assembly for nominating purposes.

In 1831, however, a new machine was created—the national nominating convention. In that year the Anti-Masons and the National Republicans, or Whigs, held conventions to choose their candidates for the coming election. The following year the Jacksonian Republicans also summoned a convention, at which Martin Van Buren was nominated to run for Vice-President with Jackson their presidential nominee. By 1840 the national party convention had become an established political institution in the United States.

Delegates to the national convention of each party were chosen by party committees or conventions, state or local or both, in each state. They were, Jacksonians alleged, "fresh from the people." Yet in reality every national convention was dominated by office-holders and professional politicians, including senators and representatives from the Congress of the United States. Nevertheless it was not as secret and autocratic as the congressional nominating caucus which had met and carried on its negotiations behind closed doors. Moreover it was a national assembly which drew together partisans from all sections of the country. It was both more democratic and more national than the caucus.

Besides serving as an assembly for the selection of candidates, the national convention, soon after its appearance, adopted the practice of framing and publishing a platform, or declaration of the party principles, that helped to define and fix the issues of the campaign for public discussion. Hitherto in presidential elections there had been no party statement giving the public any official information respecting the policies for which the candidate stood and which he might carry into effect if given his chance by voters at the polls.

After the election of 1840 the voters had for use in every campaign the national platforms of the rival parties; and the speeches of the campaign could be focused on the doctrines and planks of the platforms. As a wag once said, the platform was often "a thing to get on by and not a thing to ride on." But, vague and elusive as it frequently was, it was usually more definite than the rumors, private letters, and newspaper stories which had formed the chief basis for popular information and judgment in the campaigns held prior to the appearance of the national nominating convention. Henceforward the people had before them in campaigns, besides the personalities of the candidates, statements of party purposes which they could criticize, approve, or reject. Whatever its shortcomings, the practice of issuing platforms was an advance in the democratic process and political education.

☆

During this democratic development women asserted claims to rights and privileges denied them in law and custom. From early colonial times women had been active in public as well as private affairs. They had not only carried on domestic industries that fostered national independence; they had edited and published newspapers, written and printed pamphlets, tracts, poems, and plays in support of the Revolution; they had organized boycotts against British goods and participated in essential work throughout the war against Britain. They had expressed their opinions respecting the course of events at the conclusion of that war; and forceful women had objected to the way in which men proposed to monopolize voting and lawmaking in the nation whose interests women were promoting and defending. Now in the Jacksonian age women were banding together to demand equal rights with men as fellow citizens of the United States. They were applying the principles proclaimed in the Declaration of Independence to their own legal and social status.

Following their excursions into reforming fields, leaders among women came to feel the need of an organized and directed movement for overcoming discriminations against women in law and practice. With the sympathy and aid of several prominent men that movement was formally launched by the holding of a convention at Seneca Falls, New York, in 1848. Lucretia Mott, of Philadelphia, and Elizabeth Cady Stanton, of Seneca Falls, were the prime instigators of this undertaking. After a long debate the convention drafted and adopted a Declaration of Sentiments, or principles, on which to base appeals for united and nationwide action.

Almost in the language of the Declaration of Independence, the women's declaration opened: "When, in the course of human events, it becomes necessary for one portion of the family of man to assume among the people of the earth a position different from that which they have hitherto occupied, but one to which the laws of nature and of nature's God entitle them, a decent respect to the opinions of mankind requires that they should declare the causes that impel them to such a course. We hold these truths to be self-evident: that all men and women are created equal . . ."

Then, after the style of that earlier declaration which had asserted the natural equality and rights of man, there followed a long list of "repeated injuries and usurpations on the part of man toward woman": among other things, man has denied to her the right to vote, compelled her to submit to laws in the making of which she has no voice, taken from her rights in property and the wages she earns, denied to her the facilities for obtaining a thorough education, and monopolized "nearly all the profitable employments."

Having set forth the grounds of women's revolt in the clear terms of the Declaration of Independence and cited the grievances to be remedied, the Seneca Falls convention demanded that women "have immediate admission to all the rights and privileges which belong to them as citizens of the United States." To the Declaration of Sentiments the convention added a set of resolutions dealing with these rights and privileges, and affirming specifically that "it is the duty of the women of this country to secure to themselves their sacred right to the elective franchise."

In demanding equal civil and political rights and in carrying on discussions of public questions women now had a broad program for inspiration and guidance. It was greeted with abuse and derision in many quarters; but, despite rebuffs and setbacks, women pressed forward with their agitation for "the rights and privileges" which they claimed as citizens of the United States.

Equal suffragists were rapidly gaining adherents when the excitement of the slavery crisis broke over the land. Then leaders in the woman movement concentrated largely on the cause of freedom for slaves and the preservation of the Union. But after those causes had triumphed in 1865 they renewed their agitation and started with invincible resolve on the course that led, first, to gains in communities and states and, finally, to national triumph in the Nineteenth Amendment of 1920 which provided that the right to vote shall not be denied or abridged on account of sex.

☆

With the forward surge of democracy the idea took firmer root that free public schools supported by taxation should be established for the education of the children of the people, not otherwise educated. In this school movement many purposes and forms of advocacy were commingled. Large numbers of radicals regarded education as a cure for many social ills and as a means of preparing the people to win more privileges by reducing the power of the educated minority to dictate the terms on which the masses were to work and live. Only an educated people, reformers avowed, can govern themselves, supply competent officials all over the huge continent, and assure the safety of the Republic. On the other hand conservatives thought that public education would be useful in preventing the spread of "wild ideas" among the people and make them less responsive to appeals for their support from "agitators" and "demagogues."

Immigration was likewise brought into the pleas for free and universal education. Swarming thousands of men, women, and children were arriving in America from foreign lands. Many of them were unacquainted with the English language and with the arts of self-government. Among them was a large proportion of Catholics; and Protestants feared that the Catholics would gain too much power in politics and public affairs generally if they were not "Americanized." In this situation it was argued by educational reformers that free schools were needed to start the children of immigrants on the way to citizenship in the Republic and offset the feudal heritage brought from Europe.

Under the impulse of varied motives the movement for free public schools made headway against opposition and indifference. But by no single master stroke throughout the land was universal education established. On the contrary, progress in popular education took the form of local gains slowly accumulated in towns, cities, and states.

Horace Mann was active in formulating the comprehensive program of education finally adopted in Massachusetts; it encompassed, with elementary public schools, training schools for teachers, and free libraries in towns. Henry Barnard was the prime leader of a similar development in Connecticut. Besides working in their own communities, Mann and Barnard labored in other parts of the country for the establishment of free schools. Able men and women by the thousands in many communities and states, including governors, legislators, town councilors, and other officials, gave time and strength to this cause, by speaking and writing, by framing plans and drafting laws.

Grudgingly, stone by stone, amid the grumblings of taxpayers, the foundations of the system of free public education were laid in all the Northern states and in several Southern states by 1860. According to official estimates for that year every white inhabitant of the country received, in public or private schools, on the average, more than five times as many days of schooling as such inhabitants received in 1800.

In this attack on ignorance the following phases were salient:

Grants of public funds to aid charity, church, and private schools, all free from public control.

Laws permitting cities, counties, towns, and other districts to lay taxes for schools if the voters so decided.

Laws making special provisions for the education of the indigent poor.

Laws *requiring* communities to make provision of some kind for education, occasionally with grants from the state treasury, supplemented by small tuition fees.

The abolition of all tuition fees, thus making instruction free.

Equalization of education by abolition of pauper schools and of grants to schools maintained by churches.

Creation of normal schools for the training of teachers.

Organization of regular boards of education, state and local, for the establishment and management of schools.

Mandatory and statewide laws requiring the establishment of elementary, free, and compulsory education in every district.

Limited measures providing for the creation of public high schools to furnish advanced education.

Establishment of state colleges and universities, crowning the system of lower schools.

Yet the phases did not follow one another exactly in order of time. For example, the University of Virginia, designed by Thomas Jefferson, was organized in 1819, but not until 1846 did the Virginia legislature enact a comprehensive law providing for school districts, regular taxation for the support of elementary schools, and county school commissioners. By 1860 only Massachusetts, Connecticut, New Jersey, New York, Pennsylvania, Michigan, Rhode Island, Illinois, and Minnesota had normal schools for the training of teachers.

☆

Tendencies toward continental unity coursed under and through the ferment of the democratic interests and ideas expressed in the widening of the suffrage and provisions for popular education, in the erection of new states in the West with liberal constitutions, and in the entry of women's organizations into agitations for egalitarian laws and practices. Emphasis on the rights of individuals to their own personalities and political privileges by no means dissolved the nation into anarchy. On the contrary bonds were forged among the people by visible and invisible relations tending to weld the democracy into a national unity.

Better methods of communication speeded the process of nationalization. The development of post roads was almost unbelievable in its rapidity. In 1774 there was only one great post line—the shore road from Portsmouth, New Hampshire, to Savannah, Georgia; except for the road from New York City to Albany there were practically no regular post connections with the interior. Sixty years later, in 1834, there was a large network of post roads from the Atlantic Ocean to the Mississippi River, from the Great Lakes to the Gulf of Mexico, with three lines running beyond the Mississippi to forts on the far frontier. The great Cumberland Road, or national highway, started in 1811 under a congressional act of 1806, had penetrated the heart of Ohio and regular stagecoaches were running over it to and from the seaboard. The Erie Canal linked the regions of the Great Lakes with New York City and intervening points. The Pennsylvania Canal joined Philadelphia to the headwaters of the Ohio and the whole Mississippi basin. Steamboats plying along the Atlantic shore quickened communications between seaboard cities; they were running from seaboard towns to New Orleans and to all settled centers on the Mississippi and its navigable tributaries.

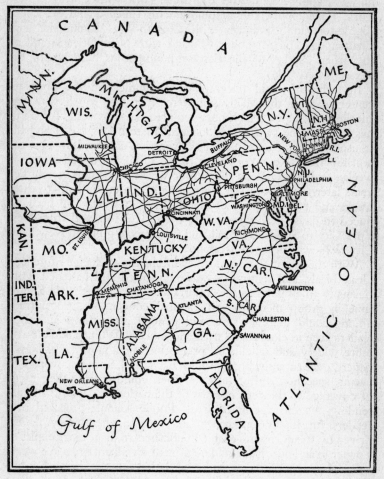

RAILROADS OF THE UNITED STATES IN 1860

Before Andrew Jackson left the White House in 1837 the building of railways had begun and a few years later the first message by electric telegraph was flashed between Washington and Baltimore. By the close of the sixth decade all the main regions between the Atlantic and the Mississippi were bound together by telegraph wires, over which news as well as private messages could be transmitted in a few minutes. In 1860 telegraph lines as well as railways connected Boston and New York with Chicago; New York, Philadelphia, and Baltimore with Chicago and St. Louis; Charleston and Savannah with Chattanooga; Richmond with Chattanooga and Memphis; Chicago with New Orleans; and all the urban centers of the East with numerous branches of the Western network.

In terms of rapid telegraphic communication the populous centers east of the Mississippi were in instant touch with one another; and news, which once required days or weeks for transmission, became swiftly nationalized. In terms of travel and the transport of goods, a similar nationalization occurred. In 1800 the journey from New York City to St. Louis consumed about six weeks; to New Orleans about four weeks by sailing vessel. Ten years later the time of the journey had been cut in half—to three weeks and two weeks respectively. In 1857 weeks had been reduced to days: it now took only three days to travel from New York City to St. Louis by rail, and five days to go from New York City to New Orleans by steamboat.

With the aid of these and other means the exchange of general ideas, ideals, and sentiments was augmented and hastened. Politicians from all parts of the country could get together in a short time in group meetings and national conventions. Local trade unions could unite in state and general associations and their leaders keep in close touch with one another. Women could travel more widely and quickly in promoting their movement. Newspapers, once intensively provincial, even local, in their coverage of events, speeches, and literary activities, could enlarge their range of coverage to the very borders of the nation, expediting and extending the circulation of ideas. Public schools prepared new readers for books, magazines, and newspapers. Rotary presses driven by steam engines enabled publishers to print more copies of a paper in an hour than could be printed on a hand press in a week.

So the multiplication and circulation of the printed word reached immense proportions. In 1839 a report of the Post Office placed the number of newspapers and periodicals in the United States at 1555. Eleven years later a special census fixed the number of dailies, weeklies, and other periodicals at 2800 and the number of copies printed annually at 422,600,000. Into this outpouring flooded books, pamphlets, leaflets, and broadsides.

The web of unity, while becoming more complex, was growing tighter. Regions, sections, and states remained, but sentiments and loyalties were becoming more uniform. Democratic customs and a public opinion accepting them were spreading without regard to physical boundaries.

In this transfusion of thought and interests the press played an active role. An intimation of its strength may be gathered from the following table for the year 1839, showing the number and the distribution of newspapers and periodicals over selected settled regions of the continent:

Massachusetts	124
New York	274
Pennsylvania	253
Ohio	164
Indiana	69
Illinois	33
Missouri	25
Michigan	31
Virginia	52
South Carolina	20
Georgia	33
Louisiana	26

It is evident from this table that in 1839 New York had twice as many newspapers and periodicals as Virginia, South Carolina, Georgia, and Louisiana combined; a single new state in the West, Ohio, had more than all of the four Southern states combined. Indiana had more than Virginia; and the frontier state of Illinois, in which Abraham Lincoln was growing up, had more than South Carolina, the home of John C. Calhoun. Even so, there were now more newspapers in Virginia in 1839 than there had been in all the states when their independence was declared in 1776.

☆

As an outcome of the stirring and converging forces at work in the United States the little Union formed by the original thirteen states on the seaboard—the Union now continental in extent—was becoming national in its ideas and feelings, even in the South as pro-slavery secessionists learned from the number and vigor of their opponents in their very midst. It is true that nowhere in the Constitution of the United States did the word "nation" or the word "national" appear. In their secret convention at Philadelphia in 1787 the framers of the Constitution at first resolved that they were seeking to establish a government "national" in all departments; but they struck out the word "national" from their resolutions, thinking, no doubt, that it would disturb advocates of states' rights. Nevertheless Madison, Jay, and Hamilton used the fateful and prophetic words in *The Federalist*. Washington, Jefferson, and Jackson repeatedly referred to the United States as a "nation" and to its great interests as "national." Although as late as 1850 it was still customary in popular usage and in prayers for divine blessing to speak of "these" United States, events were outrunning the language. In the travail of the democratic insurgency these states were fusing into an American nation—one and indivisible.

CHAPTER XV

A Broadening and Deepening
Sense of Civilization

BLENDED WITH the insurgency of democratic thought and action as expressions of individual rights was concern with American society as a whole and on the continental scale. This concern involved a search for the bonds of social, economic, intellectual, and spiritual loyalty cutting across the variations of states, regions, and classes. It raised such fundamental questions for exploration and treatment as these:

What is the social mission of this nation in its continental home?

What duties and virtues are necessary to the fulfilment of its historic mission?

What opportunities for action lie open to the people?

What knowledge is necessary for the accomplishment of their highest purposes?

What principles, inherited or newly devised, should be applied for progress toward the goal called American?

This interest in American society as a whole, more comprehensive than interest in republican or democratic politics, was affirmed with growing frequency under the covering word "civilization."

The word was new in all the history of thought and represented a new idea or ideal. It first appeared in French and English writings, it seems, about the middle of the eighteenth century and was first used in America, apparently, by writers of the Revolutionary age; by Thomas Jefferson, Thomas Paine, Mercy Warren, John Adams, and Joel Barlow, for example. Amid the upheavals of the democratic age it came into wider usage among orators, writers, and publicists, who employed it to distinguish the ways of rational, ethical, and progressively more refined human relations from the ways of barbarism. "The exact measure of the progress of civilization," said the historian, George Bancroft, in an address before the New York Historical Society in 1854, "is the degree in which the intelligence of the common mind has prevailed over wealth and brute force; in other words, the measure of the progress of civilization is the progress of the people."

Thought about popular progress had entered into the daily work of men and women who by labors of mind and hand had brought American society into being and given it a stable government, wealth, and strength. In the democratic era special circumstances favored the rise of thinkers dedicated to the business of speaking and writing, and more or less freed from the tasks associated directly with domestic, agricultural, or industrial enterprises. With the reading public enlarged by popular and secular education, publishers of newspapers, books, and magazines reached out for its patronage. The opportunities to earn a living by studying and writing expanded correspondingly. In other words, there was now a widening market for essays, articles, and books written in a popular style and dealing with every theme of human interest —economic, scientific, political, historical, social, religious, and philosophical.

Avenues opened to abilities in writing for a democratic public by the invention of machines for cheaper printing were paralleled by avenues opened to public speakers by the rise of the platform. In this democratic age auditoriums of many kinds for general assemblies were constructed in the leading cities and many smaller platforms were made available for smaller meetings. A Lyceum Lecture Bureau was organized to furnish speakers on various subjects to clubs and societies on a circuit reaching from the seaboard to the frontier. In Lyceum lecture rooms thousands of Americans heard letters, art, science, and the issues of the time discussed by "the best minds" of the nation. Mass meetings came into vogue, organized by men and women who wished to put before the people at large their proposals for innovations and to ask for popular support.

Though liberty of speech, as well as of press, was guaranteed by federal and state constitutions, free speech from public platforms had not been a general practice before the advent of democracy; and when first attempted it encountered sore trials and tribulations. Unruly elements hissed, booed, and often stoned orators engaged in analyzing traditional theories and practices, pleading for new rights, and demanding reforms, mild or radical, in customary ways of thinking and acting. Yet against opposition and disorder the platform grew in influence as audiences were disciplined by eloquence or were moved to reason by the power of argument. Public speaking became a practice of increasing importance in agitation and the formation of public opinion. In time hundreds of women from the middle class, self-educated by intensive or wide reading and activated by experiences in public life, were addressing audiences with pleas for social improvement.

As platform facilities multiplied and public speaking became an accepted way of distributing knowledge or disseminating ideas, innumerable organizations for education and propaganda sprang up like mushrooms, in communities large and small. Scarcely a proposal, from the amelioration of prison conditions to temperance reform, from the revision of marital relations and family life to easier divorce and woman suffrage, from modifications in the wage system to the abolition of slavery, was without a society devoted to promoting it by concerted efforts.

When Alexis de Tocqueville traveled in the United States during Jackson's administration, studying American habits and customs, he was astounded by the number of civic societies; and in his *Democracy in America* he wrote: "In no country in the world has the principle of association been more successfully used, or applied to a greater multitude of objects, than in America. . . . In the United States, associations are established to promote the public safety, commerce, industry, morality, and religion. There is no end which the human will despairs of attaining through the combined power of individuals combined in a society."

☆

As the idea of civilization in the United States broadened and deepened in the consciousness of the people it became more generally recognized that the destiny and opportunity of the American people lay first of all in their own development. Political independence had signalized that fact. As industries flourished an increasing economic independence corroborated it. Multiplying presses for the publication of books and other writings invited consideration of it. Thought confirmed it, sometimes in boastful arrogance and at other times in calm, rational admission of intellectual and moral obligations.

In an essay published in 1837, Ralph Waldo Emerson acclaimed the growth of national consciousness: "Our day of independence, our long apprenticeship to the learning of other lands, draws to a close. The millions, that around us are rushing into life, cannot always be fed on the sere remains of foreign harvests. Events, actions arise, that must be sung, that will sing themselves. . . . There are creative manners, there are creative actions and creative words. . . . That is, indicative of no custom or authority but springing spontaneous from the mind's own sense of the good and fair."

Was political democracy, into which millions were rushing in America, among the things which Emerson called "good and fair" and a sure promise of advance in civilization? Followers of Andrew Jackson and politicians who were beneficiaries of popular suffrage thought that it was. Walt Whitman agreed that it was with the ardor of a poet, while finding in democracy more than votes to be counted on election days and the spoils of office to be captured. He accepted joyfully as brothers and sisters all sorts, conditions, and classes of people from the sidewalks of New York to California's shores. He rejoiced in their "companionship as thick as trees," and gave his pledge to it: "For you these, from me, O Democracy, to serve you. . . . For you! for you, I am trilling these songs."

Here on this continent Whitman envisaged the making of "the most splendid race the sun has yet shone upon; . . . with the love of comrades"—America linked to humanity by mystic bonds and yet emancipated from many ties to Europe. "Nothing," he declared, "merely copied from and following out the feudal world will do. . . . The entire stock in trade of rhyme-talking heroes and heroines" must be discarded and the songs of a free people sung. Here, in Whitman's vistas, democracy was to build a civilization of greater freedom, equality, and fellowship than the world had ever known.

But the Federalists surviving from Hamilton's era, still clinging to Hamilton's social outlook, and new Federalists bearing the name of Whig were openly skeptical. Josiah Quincy, of Massachusetts, who had been an "insurgent" among the Federalists in the election of 1820, concluded, after he had witnessed the Jacksonian upheaval, that this democracy would fall into anarchy, try revolution, and end in despotism, unless the children of the people could be educated to respect the law, defy demagogues, and play a better role as citizens. And as to that he was by no means optimistic.

Among the Whigs of the South similar views of democracy were stoutly defended. Alexander Stephens, of Georgia, publicly said that the equalitarian ideas espoused by Jefferson and other early leaders of the Republic were simply wrong—"fundamentally wrong" as applied to slavery. Indeed the wealth and talents of the Southern planters were largely enlisted in the opposition to Jacksonian democracy. Whether applied to white men or to slaves, the free and equal doctrines of the Declaration of Independence were regarded by most of their spokesmen as dangerous—to property and prestige.

Writing in a philosophic vein, Emerson took a middle course with respect to the issue of democracy. Many reforms championed by democracy he approved. "The philosopher, the poet, or the religious man," he said, "will, of course, wish to cast his vote with the democrat." The spirit of equality, the spread of popular education, the refinement and elevation of society in all its parts, the opening of opportunities to all the people—these he praised as desirable features of democracy. Such progress was in many ways inevitable in the United States, he thought, and worthy of universal support.

But Emerson refused to admit that the Democratic party was synonymous with democracy. He insisted that it was "the party of the Poor marshalled against the Rich" and was directed by "a few self-seeking deserters from the Rich or Whig party," who misled the people by seeming to be their spokesmen while loving to dine and wine with the wealthy and privileged. In saying this, however, he disclaimed any intention of endorsing Whig denunciations of democracy. "From neither party, when in power," he lamented, "has the world any benefit to expect in science, art, or humanity, at all commensurate with the resources of the nation." In other words political democracy, in Emerson's opinion, was one necessary phase of civilization in the United States and yet not without its gloomy prospects.

☆

For the advancement of civilization, speakers and writers argued, innumerable reforms must be undertaken in order to bring practice more closely into harmony with the humane ideals professed by and for the American people. High among the needed reforms, perhaps the most generally advocated, they listed the revision of laws inherited from colonial times and reproduced to some extent in the new states admitted to the Union. The inherited laws had been heavily freighted with feudal customs, with cruel and barbaric punishments, and with English class doctrines respecting property, crimes, and punishments. When, for example, the

leader of the agrarian uprising against the Hudson Valley landlords in 1766 was caught and tried, he was condemned to be
hanged, disemboweled, and otherwise mutilated; and nothing but
the mercy of the King of England saved him from this horrible
fate. At the opening of the nineteenth century the laws of England
still prescribed the death penalty for about two hundred and fifty
offences, ranging from petty stealing to such high crimes as
murder and treason.

Under the statutory and common law of England, from which
the colonists had derived many legal principles applicable to property and domestic relations, innumerable rules upheld personal and
class discriminations. The English law governing the inheritance
of landed property tended to concentrate it in the hands of a few
families through transmission to the eldest sons, leaving younger
sons and the daughters to fare as best they could. In the absence of
prenuptial contracts and other private arrangements the personal
property of a married woman, even her wages, according to common law, became the possession of her husband and her landed
property passed under his management.

According to this old law children were almost the property
of their parents, particularly the father. Savage treatment could
be and was at times meted out to them.

By no means all of those harsh English legal principles had been
adopted in the colonies. Colonial legislatures had abolished or
amended many of them. A further renovation took place during
the Revolutionary period and, amid the upswing of democracy, reformers began even to advocate a revolt against the whole English
legal heritage, including the common law. After all, it was asked,
what is the intellectual and moral foundation of the law in
America?

Speaking to this point, a judge in Connecticut in 1819 declared
that it was the purpose of "our ancestors" to found a pure government in church and commonwealth, "bottomed on the word of
God," and that they "brought with them no more affection for
the common law than the canon law, the court of star chamber,
and high commission, from which they fled with horror and de-
testation."

This was an extreme view, not universally entertained. But
twenty years before it was expressed, the legislature of New Jersey
had by law forbidden lawyers to cite in the courts of that state
any treatise, decision, or opinion made or written in Great Britain
since July 1776. With some modifications this principle had been

incorporated in the laws of Kentucky and Pennsylvania. Such extremes were in many ways unworkable. Nevertheless the concept of founding American law, criminal and civil, on the humanizing ideals of the Republic exerted a powerful influence on popular thinking about law and on legislation in the United States.

Reforms in law, proposed and in part realized in practice, followed specific lines of the new thinking. The law of landed property, it was contended, should assure equality of inheritance rights to all children, daughters as well as sons. Equality of legal privileges for women, respecting their personal liberty, their property and wages, their children, and control of their own affairs, was deemed in accord with the principles of the Republic and a progressive civilization. Children, it was argued, are not property to be used or abused at pleasure by their parents but should be protected by the government in the interests of their development and community welfare. Imprisonment for debt, so burdensome to the poor, was stigmatized as a relic of barbarism. The horrible punishments meted out under old laws were condemned as brutal; and a call was made for further reduction in the number of capital crimes—to a very few, such as treason and murder. In this general overhauling of the law the idea of punishment as a mere retribution for evil action—an eye for an eye—was steadily modified by the introduction of practices shaped by the thesis that the true purpose of punishment is to protect society and reform the criminal if possible.

The reforming zeal of the age struck at the slave codes in the name of civilization and at the institution of slavery itself. The codes Lydia Maria Child analyzed acutely with a historical retrospect, in her *Appeal in Favor of That Class of Americans Called Africans,* published in 1833 while Andrew Jackson, a slave owner, resided in the White House. And her carefully formulated attack on slavery became a veritable textbook for those political leaders in the North who adopted the anti-slavery cause.

In other works by succeeding writers slavery was assailed in the name of civilization—as violating all the rights of persons upon which liberty and democracy rested for justification, as the very antithesis of civilization. Defenders of slavery, it is true, also appealed to the idea of civilization and maintained that Negroes as a race were devoid of the capacities and character necessary to help carry civilization forward. But within a few years after William Lloyd Garrison founded his anti-slavery paper, the *Liberator,* in 1831, the intellectual and moral crusade against slavery had gained such momentum that it ripped into the discussion of almost every national question.

So wide-ranging was the reforming thought of the time that it reached all phases of human misery which challenged pretensions to civilization in the United States. "I come to present the strong claims of suffering humanity," wrote Dorothea Lynde Dix in a memorial to the legislature of Massachusetts in 1843, ". . . I proceed, Gentlemen, briefly to call your attention to the state of Insane persons confined within this Commonwealth, in *cages, closets, cellars, stalls, pens: Chained, naked, beaten with rods* and lashed into obedience!" At last the mentally ill, long treated cruelly even in the most enlightened communities, were to be brought within the circle of humanity.

In three years Dorothea Dix, with tireless spirit, traveled more than ten thousand miles, studying prisons, poorhouses, county jails, and houses of refuge. For long years afterward she journeyed, spoke, and wrote in behalf of the unfortunates who had done no wrong and yet suffered so grievously at the hands of people called civilized. Though President Franklin Pierce vetoed a bill granting federal aid for the care of the mentally ill which she had finally persuaded a reluctant Congress to pass, Miss Dix toiled on and on in aid of her wards. Before her death in 1887 she had wrought an irrevocable change in American thought and practice relative to these helpless and burdensome members of society, and paved the way for much prevention of mental illness through the study and promotion of mental hygiene.

☆

Of the many contradictions to civilization in the United States which troubled humanitarians and enlisted reforming efforts, none was more obtrusive and persistent than the misery of poverty— the poverty of strong and active men and women who sought work and bread without finding them.

Scattered poverty Americans had always known, and sensitive persons from colonial times had tried to deal with it by private charity and public relief. Social derelicts, often sodden by drink, had evoked the solicitude of temperance workers. But as the Industrial Revolution swept forward in the great cities of the North, another kind of poverty assumed congested and more morbid forms. During the economic crashes which periodically reverberated throughout the country, from the great thundercrack of 1819 to the milder storm of 1857, the poverty of the strong and unemployed was aggravated beyond the silent endurance of the victims or of the comfortable citizens who cared about the making of civilization in the United States.

Nor was the "perfect civilization" of the South, as planter apologists called it, immune from the scourge. If Horace Greeley, in the terrible winter of 1837–38, found unbearable the "filth, squalor, rags, dissipation, want, and misery" of the sixth ward in New York City, William Gregg, of Charleston, South Carolina, was scarcely less distressed by the perennial squalor and misery of the "poor whites" of the Southern uplands.

The problem of poverty in its manifold forms, this contradiction to civilization, was viewed from various angles. Theologians might regard it as a mysterious ordinance of God—an opportunity for the faithful to display the virtue of charity and make the best of two worlds. But numerous intellectual leaders of the democratic age refused to accept it with complacency. They inquired into the nature of private property, the industrial system, and social as well as individual responsibilities. For some inquirers education seemed to be the remedy, especially vocational training. Others looked to collective bargaining between employers and employees for an escape from poverty due to low wages even in times of business prosperity. Many offered as a solution free lands in the West. Defenders of industrialism relied on an expansion of capitalist enterprise to extirpate poverty in a triumphant and universal prosperity; utopists on voluntary co-operation, productive and consumer; and radicals on a thoroughgoing reconstruction of society with reference to the potentials of the new technology.

In his *Recollections of a Busy Life*, Horace Greeley, the great New York editor, gave his explanation of the existence of poverty in the midst of plenty:

"I. I believe that there need be, and should be, no paupers who are not infantile, idiotic, or disabled; and that civilized society pays more for the support of able-bodied pauperism than the necessary cost of its extirpation.

"II. I believe that they babble idly and libel Providence who talk of surplus Labor, or the inadequacy of Capital to supply employment to all who need it. . . . Where Labor stands idle, save in the presence of some great public calamity, there is demonstrated deficiency, not of Capital, but of brains.

"III. I believe that the efficiency of human effort is enormously, ruinously diminished by what I term Social Anarchy. . . . It is quite within the truth to estimate the annual product of our National Industry at less than half what it might be if better applied and directed.

"IV. Inefficiency in production is paralleled by waste in consumption. . . .

"V. Youth should be a season of Instruction in Industry and the Useful Arts, as well as in Letters and the Sciences mastered by their aid. . . .

"VI. Isolation [of workers] is at war with efficiency and with progress. . . ."

Writing from Europe as a correspondent of Horace Greeley's *Tribune*, Charles A. Dana expressed the conviction that radical changes in the social order were necessary to progress in civilization. "The antique civilization . . . reached its climax and then perished," Dana recalled. "It is for us to take a lesson from its fate. It perished because it was based on slavery. . . . The basis of the social structure is industry. If there is wrong in the relations of industry—that is, of property and labor—the time will arrive when they must be reformed, or the whole structure will go to pieces. . . . Under the existing system of labor, modern society has reached the utmost development which that system will allow. New methods of industry must be established, as much superior to the wages system as that is superior to slavery, or else the doom will be pronounced and executed."

Having offered his clue to the crisis in civilization, Dana then addressed himself to the question whether that doom could be avoided and arrived at an optimistic conclusion: "It should not be forgotten that the civilization of modern times is fortified against an overthrow as that of the antique world was not; the railroads, the steamships, the manufactories, the wealth more abundant and more generally divided, which exists now, are so many substantial guarantees that society is to go forward to higher forms without the sad necessity of beginning the circle anew with barbarism and ignorance for its elements. . . . The principle of co-operation is surely, I believe, supplanting that of competition."

On methods of eliminating poverty and waste, of assuring employment and plenty, writers and speakers of the time ran the gamut of reforming speculations. At one extreme Greeley and Dana held that the answer to the riddle lay in the establishment of co-operative communities owning land, machines, and tools in common and practicing communal industry and agriculture. At the other extreme George Fitzhugh, of Virginia, in his volume

Cannibals All! or, Slaves without Masters, advocated the creation of a fixed class system in which each owner of property would be compelled to act as a guardian of a number of paupers proportioned to his wealth. As their guardian, the owner could command their labor, while assuring them a livelihood. But, argued Fitzhugh, they "would work no harder than they do now . . . would be relieved of most of the cares of life. . . . What would they lose in liberty and equality? Just nothing!"

Most reformers, though aware of the immense potentialities in technology, thrust aside as visionary the formation of co-operative colonies proposed by associationists, especially after so many experiments of that kind ended in failure. Fitzhugh's plan for establishing the class servitude of a new feudalism they dismissed as simply fantastic. Nor did they esteem more highly the Marxian scheme for a spring into freedom by means of a sudden proletarian revolution.

Threats of a mass revolt against special privilege had flared up in American history from time to time since Bacon's Rebellion in colonial Virginia; and slogans of revolutionary defiance ran through the speeches and writings of many labor champions in the age of the Jacksonian uprising against "the money power." But the great majority of American reformers and most labor leaders preferred pragmatic programs, embracing many lines of attack on poverty—through the organization of labor and political action in support of specific measures directed to the redress of specific grievances. The freedom of speech and press enjoyed under the American constitutional system permitted them to express their discontents openly and obtain a hearing for their indictment of poverty and their proposals to overcome it. The privilege of the vote, won in state after state for white males, enabled agricultural and industrial workers to engage frankly and above ground in political action for a redress of grievances—a uniquely American liberty and form of power in that time.

☆

Sensitive to the agitations of democracy and the demands for reform in every direction, many clergymen of various denominations inquired into the relation of the Christian religion to the unrest around them. From time immemorial Christian leaders had taught the worth of every human being and the spiritual equality of all persons in the sight of God. They had advocated charity and care for the needy and suffering. What was the bearing of such doctrines on the new tendencies of democracy and reform, both of which rested their justification on moral grounds?

To Protestant clergymen especially this question was immediately challenging. They were the most numerous of the clergy and they gave it the most attention. Catholics, of course, were not indifferent to it; but, despite the rich store of ethical writings in Catholic literature, including the emphasis on the "just price" and the "just wage," no Pope had as yet issued an encyclical on labor and reform. Moreover the Catholic priests who had accompanied the new immigrants to the United States had come principally from agricultural countries in which feudal traditions and practices were still strong and the problems of the Industrial Revolution had not yet become so acute as in the United States. At all events, for various reasons opinion among the Catholic clergy did not endorse reforms as drastic as those proposed in American democracy. On the whole, as Charles A. Dana said at the time, Catholics did not seem to sympathize with "a radical improvement in the social relations of mankind."

To Protestants and Catholics alike, it was one thing to write into constitutions, state and federal, provisions for religious freedom and seek to remove all signs of the intolerance which had been so cruelly manifested through the centuries. It was another thing to make the ethical teachings of religion real in the life and industry of every community and the nation. Yet to this effort at the realization of Christian ethics in human relations—in social theory and practice—numerous religious leaders devoted abilities and energies. Some stopped short at mild measures of legislation and gentle admonitions to the rich. Others went as far as Horace Greeley and Charles A. Dana in demanding a thorough renovation of American society and made acceptance of this program a duty for Christians.

The age, exclaimed William E. Channing, distinguished Boston preacher, "requires an enlightened ministry. . . . A new spirit of improvement is abroad." In a sermon delivered at Philadelphia in 1841, Channing amplified his meaning: "The multitude is rising from the dust. Once we heard of the few, now we hear of the many; once of the prerogatives of a part, now of the rights of all. . . . Even the most abject portions of society are visited by some dreams of a better condition for which they were designed. The grand doctrine, that every human being should have the means of self-culture, of progress in knowledge and virtue, of health, comfort, and happiness, of exercising the powers and affections of a man, this is slowly taking place as the highest social truth. . . . That the great end of government is to spread a shield over the rights of all—these propositions are growing into axioms, and the spirit of them is coming forth in all departments of life."

While the struggle for the public schools went forward, slowly but steadily, against protests of taxpayers and religious sectarians, an educational philosophy befitting the spirit of the democratic age was formulated by leaders in the battle for free schools. They generally agreed upon several propositions. The vote had been given to nearly all white men, and women were demanding it in the name of the equality and human rights proclaimed in the Declaration of Independence. Multiplying factories using technology were demanding greater knowledge and skill on the part of workers in industry. Poverty was a blight on American civilization. People were commonly lacking in knowledge of the simplest rules for health and healthful living. Illiteracy barred the way to that knowledge as well as to the treasures of the world's best thought.

Therefore, said the philosophers of educational progress, public education must prepare pupils for citizenship in the Republic. It must train them in the elements of the arts and sciences used in industry and agriculture, and necessary for earning a livelihood. It must inculcate the habits and manners of civility as values in themselves conducive to happiness and as indispensable to the practice of self-government in the community and the nation. Education, in sum, is to advance civilization in all its phases.

"Its general purpose," said Horace Mann, indefatigable leader in the public-school movement, speaking of education, "is to preserve the good and to repudiate the evil which now exists, and to give scope to the sublime law of progression." Training for citizenship Mann placed high among the specific aims of education: "Since the achievement of American independence, the universal and ever-repeated argument in favor of free schools has been that the general intelligence which they are capable of diffusing, and which can be imparted by no other human instrumentality, is indispensable to the continuance of a republican government."

While Mann thought that children should be taught respect for property, law, and order, he did not regard everything in this relation settled for all time. "Our advanced state of civilization," he admonished his readers, "has evolved many complicated questions respecting social duties. . . . We want no more of those patriots who exhaust their patriotism in lauding the past; but we want patriots who will do for the future what the past has done for us." By this he meant, bring wisdom, knowledge, and virtue to bear upon the improvements of the conditions of the people. "To diffuse a knowledge of improvements" he made a primary function of education.

To the grand end of a happy and virtuous life for the individual and the progress of civilization in American society Horace Mann subordinated all other aims of education. He advocated strict training in the arts and sciences of industry, in civil habits, and in care of the physical body, but no American, he insisted, can claim the elevated rank of a statesman, "unless he speaks, plans, labors, at all times and in all places, for the culture and edification of the whole people."

☆

The debates over the merits of democracy and innumerable reforms in laws and customs were accompanied by efforts to work out a system of political economy corresponding to the peculiar conditions of the United States. A primary issue was raised by these efforts: Are the conditions of the United States really peculiar or does the British system of economic theory apply precisely to this country as well as all others? A large number of American writers and teachers who dealt with economic theory seemed to think that the "laws" of the British economy were universal and thus reigned in the United States as well as in Great Britain.

In the British theory, especially as it had been worked out by David Ricardo and Thomas Malthus, two principles were firmly fixed: (1) each country, in the division of labor among nations, should produce the things which its natural circumstances enable it to produce the cheapest and all nations should adopt a policy of free trade; (2) large-scale poverty is due to overpopulation, the improvidence of the poor, and the decline in the amount of fertile land available for cultivation.

As applied to the United States by economists, these principles required this country to concentrate on agriculture and continue to be, as in colonial times, mainly a raw-material province for nations far advanced in mechanical industries. They also decreed that large-scale poverty is inevitable and that little or nothing can be done to reduce its area or its miseries.

In various respects British economic theory fitted very well into some beliefs already current in the United States. Many Americans still clung to the doctrine, once asserted by Thomas Jefferson, that popular government must depend for its success on a population composed chiefly of freehold farming families. Farmers alone, ran the dogma, possess the independence and virtue necessary to liberty and self-government. Jefferson had in fact given up the doctrine later, and had endorsed the introduction of manufacturing in order that the United States could become economically independent of Europe, especially in the production of arms and other things imperative for the national defense, necessary to assure political independence.

But representatives of planters and farmers held fast on practical grounds to Jefferson's emphasis on agriculture as the surest basis for a republic. They argued that producers of agricultural commodities would be more prosperous if they could sell their produce abroad, and import manufactures freely from Great Britain where labor was cheap and machine industries were further developed than in the United States at that time. As to poverty, they were often disposed to make that evil the inevitable outcome of manufacturing by the machine process.

Though the British theory of America as a raw-material producing country had been challenged on this side of the water from colonial times, first by manufacturers and then by political leaders such as Washington and Hamilton, it was not until near the middle of the nineteenth century that writers developed a countervailing theory better fitted to the peculiar conditions and potentialities of the United States. The outstanding personality associated with this trend of thought was Henry C. Carey, the son of Mathew C. Carey, a Catholic refugee from Ireland who had taken part in the intellectual battles of the early Republic.

In numerous writings, including his *Harmony of Interests* published in 1851, Henry Carey broke completely away from several fundamentals of British theory. The abundance of land and natural resources in the United States, he maintained, made possible the most prosperous society mankind had ever created. The way to advance civilization here, in his opinion, was to diversify the economy of every region by building factories and workshops in the very midst of the farms. This would reduce the cost of hauling goods long distances, open up various employments to workers of all kinds in their own communities, spread science, art, education, and literature everywhere, and enrich the life of every community throughout the land. If such a policy were adopted, Carey contended, American talents would be encouraged and rewarded and poverty would be materially reduced if not entirely eliminated. In his plans for implementing his industrial program he incorporated a proposal for a government-managed currency, as distinct from Hamilton's system of bank currency managed by capitalists.

Although American economic theorists generally repudiated Carey's doctrines as unsound, several of his proposals were followed in practice by American governments, state and federal. And they were destined to have a great influence on the economic thinking of coming years.

Writings which might be classified as "political science," as distinguished from the more comprehensive political economy, were mainly legalistic in form and spirit. That is, they were primarily concerned with the mere forms and powers of government, particularly the nature of the federal Union and the interpretation of the functions of the federal government. But writings on political science sometimes bore the stamp of the great constitutional controversy then rife among politicians and the people. Is the Union perpetual and are the powers of the federal government to be construed broadly in the interest of general welfare or narrowly in the interest of states' rights?

The answer of Joseph Story, justice of the Supreme Court, in his *Commentaries on the Constitution*, three volumes published in 1833, was unmistakable. The Union, he claimed, cannot be lawfully dissolved by state action; Congress may provide for the common defense and for the general welfare. On the other hand, Nathaniel Beverley Tucker, professor of law at William and Mary College in Virginia, enemy of Jacksonian democracy and friend of aristocratic government, argued with great learning in favor of the right of secession and a strict interpretation of the Constitution. This theme he elaborated in *A Discourse on the Importance of the Study of Political Science as a Branch of Academic Education in the United States* (1840) and other writings, including novels of which *The Partisan Leader* was the most argumentative.

Two treatises dealing with political questions, however, went beyond legalistic theorizing to the substance of politics, as *The Federalist* had done. According to that ever-memorable work, which continued in circulation, political science encompassed geography, economic interests, common customs, laws, and practices, and great functions of government, domestic and foreign. To these subjects Story and Tucker gave little heed.

But John C. Calhoun, in his *Disquisition on Government*, published after his death in 1850, after examining the theory of majority rule under equal suffrage, drew an unglossed picture of the clash of economic interests in the operation of government and sought ways and means of defeating the logic of democracy in the interest of economic privilege. Eager to protect the planting interests founded on slavery against the growing population of the North, Calhoun's treatise bore the stamp of political controversy. Nevertheless it dealt with enduring fundamentals in politics.

So, too, did another volume, on the other side of the slavery debate, Hinton Rowan Helper's *The Impending Crisis*, a prophetic attack on slavery published in 1857. Although by no means academic in tone, it took into account, even more than *The Federalist* had done, all important branches of economy, the arts, sciences, letters, education, manners, customs, and habits of the people, as presenting vivid contrasts between the South and the North. Though greeted as fiercely partisan, Helper's volume went deeper than law and theory, to the sources of the social conflicts amid which government was carried on, and took the whole range of civilization within its compass.

Into the ferment of opinions and judgments pertinent to the direction of American aims and activities, historians injected their interpretations of American life. The publication of new works on the history of the whole United States, not merely histories of colonies and separate states, signified an enlarging consciousness of the time process in which the American Union was developing into a consolidated society. George Bancroft, of Massachusetts, trained in scholarship at Harvard and in European universities, especially in Germany, author of a many-volume work, the *History of the United States*, frankly ranged himself and God on the side of the people. He made the march of the people heroic, from oppression to independence; identified civilization with the progress of the people in all civilian modes of refinement; and, to the horror of New England conservatives, declared himself a Democrat and accepted offices under Democratic presidents. The spirit of his conviction gleamed through the pages of his writings. The first three volumes of his *History* were issued between 1834 and 1840, right in the middle of the Jacksonian upheaval. Originally he had intended to bring it to "the present time," but his last volumes, not published until 1882, ended with the formation of the Constitution.

While Bancroft was developing his interpretation of American history, Richard Hildreth, also of Massachusetts and a graduate of Harvard, published between 1849 and 1852 a six-volume history of the United States covering the period from 1497, the year in which King Henry VII established his claim on this continent, to 1820, the year of the Missouri Compromise. Hildreth was a Whig and had no deep affection for democracy itself or the Democratic party as he observed its practical operations in defense of slavery and machine politics. And his pages, cold and dry in style, contrasting starkly with the purple flourishes of Bancroft, disclosed not the jubilant march of democracy but the struggles and clashes of economic interests that had entered into the making of the American nation.

Neither Bancroft nor Hildreth, however, departed far from political, military, and diplomatic history—not even Bancroft with all his professed interest in democracy. As one of their contemporaries, George Perkins Marsh, said: "History has been written for the ruler, not for the people." On this ground Marsh made an eloquent plea at Union College in 1847 for a new kind of history —a history of the people, adapted to civilization in the United States and to "a commonwealth where government is recognized as being both for and from the people." This was in the temper of Nathaniel Chipman, of Connecticut, a philosopher of the American Revolution and a soldier in it who, in his *Principles of Government*, published first in 1793, had declared that the civil and political institutions of the United States "differ in principles and construction very essentially from all that have preceded them."

A history faithful to the realities of American life, Marsh pleaded, should deal with the condition of the people at different periods; in a word, should be social history broadly conceived. It should cover, besides traditional subjects, the work of city governments, the course and character of commerce, the methods and purposes of education, arts, sciences, industries, ceremonies, festivities, family life, "the sanitary and economic condition of the people, the position of the learned professions, the correspondence of families and confidential friends, the character and tendency of public amusements, the ephemeral popular literature of different periods, and the private biographies of the humble as well as the great." History of this kind, Marsh thought, would furnish guidance to citizens and to statesmen in the conduct of private and public affairs. Still, he did not attempt to write that social history. The task he left to others and no one in his time undertook it.

☆

To the broadening of the American outlook natural scientists brought the force of free inquiries and supplied factual knowledge for industrialists and workers in the practical arts and for reformers concerned with programs for the welfare and happiness of the people. Natural science was the monopoly of no section or class. In that respect it was completely democratic. It could escape domination by any special interest in American society and elude the ill-tempers of political conflicts. As a person, a scientist could be partisan. As a scientist, if a genuine scientist, he was above and beyond partisanship in his researches and reports on his findings.

Reformers could of course use the results of scientific inquiries for their own purposes. Indeed they knew that if there was to be progress in national well-being, increasing study of the physical world was one of the imperatives. Yet the scientific spirit in itself was concerned with a search for exact knowledge and not with a quest for reform. Scientists might long to conquer such ills as chronic diseases and epidemics, for instance, but only by gaining precise knowledge could they realize their longing, and they had to start on that basis.

So fruitful and varied was progress in knowledge of the natural sciences in the democratic era that it opened up visions of human welfare never before imagined. In every domain inquiries were pursued and discoveries were reported. Writers of history took little note of the scientists and their achievements. Books on history seldom if ever mentioned so much as their names. Nevertheless, scientists made history—great history as revelation and aspiration.

Among their numbers were John James Audubon in ornithology; Benjamin Silliman, Sr., at Yale College, in chemistry, geology, and mineralogy, and as founder of the *American Journal of Science and Arts* in 1818; Matthew Maury, in the physical geography of the sea; Joseph Henry in physics, meteorology, electricity, and electrical transmission by wire; Constantine Rafinesque in botany and general natural science; Asa Gray in botany; Richard Harlan in zoology and vertebrate paleontology; Josiah Willard Gibbs, one of the world's greatest scientists, in mathematics, physics, and chemistry; Parker Cleaveland in mineralogy and geography; Benjamin Silliman, Jr., in chemistry, with notable achievements in the chemistry of petroleum.

Besides working as individuals, scientists formed organizations to pool their knowledge and promote research in particular fields. Special societies were supplemented in this work of promotion by the establishment in 1847 of a general society—the American Association for the Advancement of Science. National support was also given to scientific inquiries by the founding of the Smithsonian Institution in Washington in 1846 on the basis of a gift by James Smithson, a British chemist who bequeathed a large fortune to the United States for the encouragement of science.

Scientists made advances no less striking and useful in medicine and surgery than those achieved in the physical sciences strictly defined. In general terms the medical advances included more careful and accurate descriptions of human diseases, especially those epidemic in nature; demonstrations in daring surgical operations not hitherto attempted; more precise knowledge of the composition of chemicals in relation to their curative and other properties as applied to disease and suffering; the founding of new medical schools, for example, at Yale in 1810, at Transylvania in Kentucky in 1817, and at Chicago in 1837; scientific writings on surgery, materia medica, dentistry, obstetrics, insanity, diseases of the eye, and medical jurisprudence; and the beginning of popular education in human physiology and anatomy.

In many branches of medical and surgical research hundreds of scientific inquiries were pressed and marvelous results came out of the labor. With the early use of anesthetics, to deaden pain and permit otherwise impossible operations in surgery, were associated Crawford Long, Charles T. Jackson, John Warren, Horace Wells, and W. T. Morton. William Beaumont, of Michigan, did original research in gastric digestion; his book describing his experiments, published in 1833, has been called "the greatest contribution ever made to the knowledge of gastric digestion." Daniel Drake, of Kentucky, was a pioneer in raising the standards of medical education, and wrote a path-breaking work on the *Diseases of the Interior Valley of North America* (1850–54). William Gerhard, of Philadelphia, specialized in the identification and diagnosis of diseases, and differentiated between typhus and typhoid fever, both age-old destroyers of humanity. In South Carolina, James M. Sims made bold experiments in the surgery of gynecology and founded a school of disciples in that field. At Boston, Oliver Wendell Holmes, Sr., employed his fine mind in studying the infectious nature of puerperal fever and discovered ways and means of reducing the death rate of mothers in childbirth.

Appalled by the amount of ignorance among women respecting their own bodies—an ignorance so serious for personal and maternal health—Paulina Kellogg Wright Davis studied anatomy and physiology with a view to helping them overcome their ignorance. Medical men were lecturing to selected audiences on those subjects. She lectured in a more popular way to groups of women, using a manikin in her demonstrations, much to the disgust and alarm of prudists but no doubt with much value to women. She further shocked even male doctors by demanding that medical schools be opened to the training of women in the profession of medicine. Women had been doctors and surgeons since the dawn of human history, but licenses were now being required for the practice of the healing arts. Hence formal training, preliminary to the obtaining of a license, had to be won if women were to continue in their historic relation to these arts and carry them on with the aid of the most modern learning and skills. By demanding medical training for women Mrs. Davis and other forceful women helped to cleave the stolidity of minds reluctant to recognize the role and function of women in the arts of healing and living.

All in all the epoch of "Jacksonian democracy," the "era of the common man," the "fabulous forties" and the fermenting fifties, was a time of dramatic mental activity and creative thinking in respect of everything human.

CHAPTER XVI

Party Strife over Control of the Federal Government

THE RISE of democracy in a nation continent-wide, undergoing a transformation by steam and machinery and charged with the turbulence of old and new kinds of thinking about society in the United States, was accompanied by the struggles of political parties, under old and new names, for the possession of the government of the country. The "era of good feeling," associated with the one-party system of the "Virginia dynasty," began to fade in the second term of Monroe—the last member of the Revolutionary generation to occupy the White House. A new era of fierce party battling burst forth. New personalities, of the younger generation, strode upstage as leaders of political cohorts, and employed novel methods of reaching popular audiences and arousing devotion to factional and party interests.

As the party strife grew in intensity, as travel and communication became easier and swifter, candidates for public office started the practice of making direct personal appeals to the people. In the early days of the Republic, Washington, John Adams, and Jefferson made no open bid for popular support. They conducted their campaigns quietly by writing letters or negotiating with friends. But after the democratic march got into full swing, especially after the campaign of 1840, candidates "went to the people." They made public speeches from platforms; they "took to the stump"; they toured whole regions delivering addresses; and sometimes rival candidates for the Senate of the United States joined in debating publicly the issues that divided them and their parties.

This was the era of monster political parades, torchlight processions, popular campaign songs, and huge barbecues, or picnics, attended by thousands of men, women, and youths who swarmed to "camp grounds" in wagons, buggies, and carts to see and hear the candidates. To aged Federalists all this uproar seemed to be the full and natural outcome of sheer demagogy gone insane; but to members of the younger generation it was an appropriate way of organizing parties, conducting campaigns, and letting the people share actively in the determination of public affairs.

☆

In the campaign for a successor to Monroe four candidates were offered to the voters: two from the new West, one from the Northeast, and one from the deep South. The candidates from the West were General Andrew Jackson, of Tennessee, a popular military hero, victor in the Battle of New Orleans; and Henry Clay, of Kentucky, one of the "War Hawks" who had helped to bring on the second armed struggle against Great Britain in 1812 in which Jackson won the accolade for heroism. W. H. Crawford, an upland planter of Georgia with a frontier outlook, who had held high offices in the federal administration, was the presidential aspirant from the South. John Quincy Adams, of Massachusetts, son of the second President, was the candidate from the Northeast.

The strong figures in the campaign were Jackson and Adams, about as unlike as two men could be, but neither won a majority of the votes. So the election of the President was thrown again into the House of Representatives, as it had been in the case of Aaron Burr and Thomas Jefferson in 1800. After a long contest in the House, in which Clay was especially active, John Quincy Adams was chosen as the Chief Executive. When Adams' appointed Clay as his Secretary of State, the angry followers of Jackson, who had polled the largest popular vote, shouted that a "corrupt bargain" had brought about the victory of Adams.

Though John Quincy Adams was the son of John Adams, he had moved further in his thinking, amid the social changes of his time. Yet his personality, like that of his father, did not appeal to the people at large and he was no more popular than his father had been during his term of office. A Federalist by birth, John Quincy Adams had pained elder Federalists by joining the Republican party, largely from sympathy with Jefferson's foreign policy—a heresy in their ranks. He had served Madison faithfully as minister to Russia. He had supported Monroe with equal fidelity as his

Secretary of State. He had been pleased over the adoption of Hamilton's major financial policies by the Republicans in 1816. But he was not a mere disciple in any school of politics.

His view of the Constitution was a broad view, broad enough to take account of the revolution being wrought by science and invention in industry and agriculture. He felt a deep admiration for Washington as a public character and statesman; and he wished to work in the tradition of great nation-making. Indeed his conception of that task took in the whole range of civilization in America and the long future before it.

With a frankness and a fullness rare in politics, Adams laid his national policies before the country in his inaugural address and in messages to Congress. He insisted that Congress had ample powers under the Constitution to enact laws for the general welfare of the country. Above all he believed that the heritage of land, forests, and minerals should be held by the government in trust for the nation and used for the common good—to employ labor, build highways and canals, support education, and advance science.

To administer this heritage honestly and efficiently, Adams maintained, the nation needed a permanent body of trained and competent public servants, enjoying tenure of office during good behavior. In short, he looked upon the national government as an agency for economic, intellectual, and moral improvement. In his political philosophy government was not a mere police force to keep order while politicians scrambled for the "spoils of office," while businessmen intrigued for special favors, while speculators snatched at and gambled in public lands, while everybody sought to feather his own nest.

But in holding that the great object of government was to improve the condition of the people by well-considered and positive measures, John Quincy Adams was out of harmony with current political and economic avarice. Thousands of politicians were merely hungry for offices and jobs. Land grabbers, including many members of Congress, wanted to seize the public lands, as he said, "with the thirst of a tiger for blood."

And Adams was not the man to educate the country into accepting his policies. He had no genius for drawing multitudes to the support of his ideals. He was cold in manner, suspicious of his foes and critics, and hot in temper. At the end of four years in the White House he was, if anything, less popular than in the beginning. The one important measure that came from Congress during his administration was an act of 1828 raising the protective tariff on manufactures, and his approval of it offended agrarians.

Against everything that Adams stood for, the tide of a new "people's party" was setting in. In membership and doctrines this new party stemmed from the left wing of the revolutionary movement that had won independence for America.

Though merged for a while with conservatives in Jefferson's party, several of the leaders in the faction out of which it sprang had even criticized his policies as too "high-toned." After a Republican Congress had re-enacted Hamilton's chief measures into law in 1816, dissidents in the Republican camp declared that the Republican party managers had swallowed Federalism whole and by so doing had betrayed the people. An increasing number of the objectors began to call themselves "Democrats" publicly or "Democratic-Republicans."

With the crowding into Washington of farmers, planters, and lawyers elected to Congress from the new states of the West and South, the dissidents grew in strength; and attacks on the Republicanism which had absorbed Federalism became irrepressible. Then the new people's party arose. It found its leader in "Andy Jackson"—in a "son of the soil," a "man of the people," also a war hero. Born on a small farm somewhere near the border between North Carolina and South Carolina, he had gone into Tennessee in his youth and there had made his way to a fortune by old Southern methods—as a planter, merchant, and slaveowner.

Daring by nature and intrepid in action when quarrels were involved, Jackson had won distinction in the Tennessee militia and as a general in the Army of the United States. His education was meager but by the exercise of his wits he had risen to prominence in local politics and served in the national Congress. His attachment to the Union was emphatic and steadfast; his followers could be sure of that. But his attitude toward such issues as the tariff, the United States Bank, the management of public lands, and public improvements was obscure. He had never publicly proclaimed himself a "democrat," or a "Democrat." Yet through the shimmer of hero worship he was represented as a champion of the people.

With Jackson as their banner bearer his admirers swept him into office in 1828 and again in 1832. This party, later adopting officially the name "Democratic party," carried every presidential election between 1828 and 1856 inclusive, with two exceptions in 1840 and 1848. Thus the party now commonly described as the party of Jacksonian democracy held the presidency from 1829 to

1861 save for two interludes of four years each. After two terms in office Jackson passed his mantle to Martin Van Buren, of New York, elected as his successor in 1836. Though Van Buren had held high offices in his state and in the federal government, he had

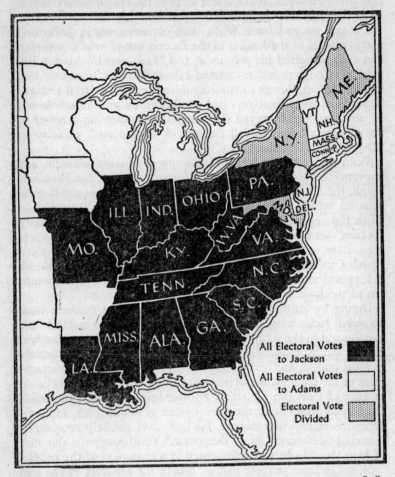

All Electoral Votes to Jackson

All Electoral Votes to Adams

Electoral Vote Divided

SWEEP OF THE NATIONAL DEMOCRACY. THE ELECTORAL VOTE IN 1828.

also sprung from the people—the "plain people." He had learned the art of popular politics as a taproom boy in a tavern at Kinderhook, New York, before he began to steer his own course in the world; and it was said of him that as a politician he rowed toward every objective with muffled oars.

The interludes in the Democratic sway over the federal government were brief enjoyments of power by another new party calling itself the Whig party. The title, borrowed from the Whig party in England, celebrated for its resistance to high royal prerogatives, fitted very well the American opposition to the autocratic operations of Jackson. Before Jackson's first term expired men adhering to Federalist principles and discontented Republicans, spurred by Henry Clay, of Kentucky, and Daniel Webster, of Massachusetts, had formed a combination against his re-election.

They did not call themselves Whigs immediately. In the beginning they were generally known as National Republicans, as if to deny any taint of states' rights and yet capture Republican voters. They gave no hint of the exact policies they would pursue if installed in power, any more than Jackson had done in his first campaign; but it was understood that both Northern and Southern members of this new party were, as a rule, disciples of Hamilton and incensed at the people's party for which Jackson spoke. Although Clay and Webster veiled none of the political views they personally held, the Whig party was largely a negative party—against Jacksonism rather than for anything definite as a substitute.

The Whigs came into the campaign of 1840 with a military hero of their own as their candidate—William Henry Harrison, of Ohio, who, like Jackson, had fought in the War of 1812 and had been victorious over Indians at Tippecanoe in Indiana. They boasted that Harrison had a wing to his house made of logs. They sang campaign songs in praise of log cabins, coonskins, and hard cider, to demonstrate that Harrison was as close to the people as Jackson. They accused Van Buren of putting cologne on his whiskers and taking his meals in the White House from massive gold and silver plate. In their propaganda the Whigs promised the voters "two dollars a day and roast beef," instead of Van Buren's "policy, fifty cents a day and French soup." On such flimsy pledges the Whigs carried the election and William Henry Harrison served as President for one brief month. Then death ended his career and the Vice-President, John Tyler, of Virginia, succeeded him.

In the next election, of 1844, the Whigs were defeated and the Democrats made their way back to power under the leadership of James K. Polk, a kind of heir to Jackson in that he also lived in

Tennessee and was a son of the soil. Whigs tried their luck again in 1848 and found it with another military hero, General Zachary Taylor of Mexican War fame, a Louisiana planter whose political ideas were as nebulous as those of Harrison. That success was their last presidential triumph. Though often strong in Congress after 1840, the Whigs, as an organized party, finally disappeared from presidential campaigns like the Federalists before them. In 1860 they adopted the name "Constitutional Unionists" but the name did not save them from defeat in that last grasp at power.

☆

Amid the clashes, personalities, and rhetorical flourishes of the political campaigns waged by Democrats and Whigs, five primary issues remained fairly constant as sources of their differences. All these issues had arisen in the early days of the Republic, but changing circumstances led to varying degrees of emphasis:

Low tariffs in the interests of planters and farmers vs. high tariffs for the protection of American "infant industries."

State banks and state paper money vs. a national bank and national currency.

Federal aid to internal improvements—highways, canals, and railways vs. state aid, or none at all, to such enterprises.

Free land vs. sale for revenue purposes.

Freedom vs. slavery in the territories.

The division between Democrats and Whigs over these issues was by no means clear-cut. On some of them both parties were split. On none of them was the Northeast, the Northwest, or the South actually "solid." Neither of the great political parties was purely sectional. Whigs and Democrats throve in every state. The South furnished great Whig leaders, such as Alexander H. Stephens and Henry Clay, who ranked in learning and eloquence with Northern men, such as Daniel Webster and Edward Everett. The same was true of the Democrats. Yet in time these parties showed a marked tendency to line up on one side or the other of these paramount questions of the age.

☆

Not long after Southern Republicans had agreed to the tariff of 1816, they began to change their minds and oppose the very idea of protection for American industries. Within a few years they formulated a well-rounded argument against it and began to de-

nounce it as a form of robbery under government auspices. Special
duties on imported manufactures, they claimed, are contrary to
the interests of all agricultural states, North and South; such protection raises the prices of goods which planters and farmers must
buy; it is, in effect, a tax on them for the benefit of manufacturers;
planters and farmers can prosper best by selling their produce
abroad and buying their manufactures from the industrial nations
of the Old World with their cheaper labor. On such grounds
Southern politicians sought to make an alliance with politicians in
the farming regions of the North, especially the Northwest.

It took nearly forty years, however, for advocates of low
tariffs, "for revenue only," to win a substantial victory, and it was
transient when it came. While Jeffersonian Republicans were still
nominally in power, Congress raised the duties on imports twice—
in 1824 and in 1828. The second act, decried as "the tariff of
abominations," though modified later in details, produced a revolt
in South Carolina. In 1832 the state legislature called a convention,
and that assembly, duly elected, condemned the protective tariff
as contrary to the Constitution of the United States and hence null
and void. The delegates further resolved that, if the federal
government tried to coerce the people of the state into obeying the
law, they would withdraw from the Union and establish an independent state. This was the doctrine of nullification in an extreme
form.

Infuriated by the threat of South Carolina, President Jackson
issued a proclamation denouncing its action from start to finish.
He branded nullification as a violation of the letter and spirit of
the Constitution. He exalted the Union as supreme and perpetual
and spurned the thesis that it was a mere league of sovereign states
from which they could withdraw at will. He informed South
Carolina that he would enforce federal laws with all the agencies
of power at his disposal and that, if any blood was shed in opposition to the national laws, he would hang the first guilty persons he
could catch in the act. To back up his words, he prepared to
mobilize the necessary military forces.

Yet Jackson also strove for peace. He advised Congress to alter
the tariff that had made the trouble and lay protective duties only
on manufactures required for national defense. Then he asked
Congress to pass a "force bill," a measure giving him more power
in executing federal laws.

Under the leadership of Henry Clay a compromise was reached
in 1833. Congress provided that the tariff should be gradually

reduced until by 1842 it would be about on a level with the rates set in 1816. It also enacted the force bill into law. Thus both sides could make a show of claiming the laurels. South Carolina repealed her nullification ordinance and a truce reigned for a time.

It was only a truce. Fired by their victory in 1840, the Whigs broke the compromise of 1833 and raised the protective duties on imported manufactures. They made it clear that Clay's "American system" of protection for manufacturing industries was to be a fixed part of their domestic policy. The battle line was thus firmly drawn and Democrats accepted the challenge. In their platform of 1856 they endorsed the idea of progressive free trade throughout the world. Their triumph at the polls they followed up by enacting the law of 1857 which, though far from a free-trade act, made substantial cuts in many protective duties.

☆

The second primary issue of politics—banking and currency—also had sectional aspects. Planters in the new Southwest, often heavily in debt for the purchase of land, slaves, and implements, had a partiality for inflation—an abundance of paper money—to raise the prices of their produce. Farmers in the new Northwest, likewise often in debt for their lands and equipment, were inclined to concur. It was mainly, though not entirely, in the seaboard regions of the East that the United States Bank, re-established in 1816 by the Republicans, and the currency it issued were considered "good for the country."

Appealing especially to farmers and mechanics, President Jackson, the pride of the West, opened a war on the United States Bank soon after he entered the White House. He declared that it was contrary to the Constitution, gave special privileges to the rich, and was against the interests of the plain people. Congress answered in 1832 by passing a bill to renew the bank on the expiration of its charter in 1836. Jackson vetoed the bill. By executive order he removed federal deposits from the vaults of the bank. And as the number of his supporters increased in the Senate and House of Representatives he had the pleasure of seeing the bank utterly destroyed before he retired to his beloved Hermitage in Tennessee in 1837.

Then with no national bank to interfere, state banks, chartered under state laws, burgeoned everywhere more luxuriantly than ever. In the Mississippi Valley such banks, sometimes owned entirely by state governments, sprang up like weeds and issued torrents of paper money based on little or no gold and silver coins. The notes of the worst of these institutions, derided as "wildcat banks," usually fell rapidly in value and often became worthless as the issuing banks blew up in bankruptcy.

Once more in its history, as in Revolutionary times, the United States had fluctuating paper currencies—dollars worth one hundred cents in coin in conservative states and anywhere from ninety-nine cents to almost nothing in the wildcat-banking states. Once more commerce among the states was impeded by paper notes of varying values. But in spite of determined and unremitting efforts, the Whigs were unable to carry through Congress any kind of a bill for establishing another United States Bank.

☆

Over internal improvements—the third leading question of the time—the ranks of both parties were badly broken. Yet, in general, Democratic presidents were inclined to the view that Congress had no constitutional power to build great national roads and should not engage in the business anyway. In taking this position they reversed precedents set under President Jefferson, their political godfather; but consistency had never been a law with politicians. So for a brief period zeal for internal improvements by federal action cooled off.

Not until the success of railways was fully demonstrated did it flare up again. Then Southern Democrats and Northern Whigs agreed that a continental railway should unite the Atlantic coast with the Pacific coast and that federal aid should be provided for the construction of the line. They disagreed, however, over the route to be chosen. Should it be through the Southern or the Northern part of the country? That question was still in dispute when the fateful campaign of 1860 opened.

☆

As railroads were extended from the East into the Mississippi Valley and gave easier access to the Western territories, the fourth political issue became more acute—the disposition of the unoccupied land in the national domain. For a long time after the adoption of the Constitution, Congress had followed the policy of selling this land, either in small plots to settlers or in large blocks to speculators. The price fixed for the land—at first two dollars an acre and later a dollar and a quarter—though low was largely designed to bring revenue into the federal Treasury.

Low as it was, the figure made it hard for poor farmers and city workers in the East to "take up" lands in the West and establish homesteads there. Having to pay for public land at all was deemed contrary to the spirit of democracy and a hindrance to the abolition of poverty in industrial centers. Hence a clamor went up for a sharp reduction in the price of government land, and finally for a law giving it away to settlers in lots of one hundred and sixty acres.

For leaders in both parties this proposal made trouble. Whig manufacturers in the North were inclined to believe that free land in the West would entice workers away from their mills, or at least force the payment of higher wages to employees as an inducement for them to stay in the factories. Whig planters in the South could reason that free land would mean a more rapid growth of the Northwest, more free states, and the supremacy of free states over slave states in Congress and the Union. Yet the Whigs of neither section were in complete harmony on the point. Nor were the Democrats.

The division among Democrats over federal land policies deepened as the agitation over the slavery question grew more intense and reached a climax in 1859. Free land for the poor was eloquently and steadfastly championed in Congress by a Democrat from the farming regions of Tennessee, Andrew Johnson, an outspoken friend of farmers and workingmen; and around his standard many Democratic senators and representatives collected.

On the other hand, under the inspiration of Horace Greeley, a Whig, but also a friend of farmers and urban workers, many Whigs flocked to the free-land cause.

At length a combination of Democrats and Whigs was formed; a bill granting free homesteads to settlers was pushed through Congress and sent to President Buchanan for his signature in 1860. Buchanan was on a ticklish spot. The bill was unquestionably popular, but a host of pro-slavery Democrats were against it. After making his political calculations, Buchanan vetoed the bill, thus leaving the free-land issue to be settled at some indefinite time in the future.

☆

Entangled with the free homestead problem was the question of slavery or freedom in the territories. Twice before the advent of Jacksonian democracy answers had been made in the form of compromises. By acts of Congress slavery had been excluded from the Northwest Territory and permitted in the territories below the Ohio River. Again, by act of Congress, at the time of the Missouri Compromise in 1820, the major portion of the Louisiana Territory had been dedicated to freedom and the smaller portion tacitly left open for slavery. After a great region had been wrested from Mexico by war the issue was revived and brought on a spirited contest in Congress and outside.

Once more an adjustment resulted—the Compromise of 1850—in which both sides sought peace, the Whigs under the leadership of Henry Clay and Daniel Webster, now old men on the verge of the grave. The slave trade, not slavery itself, was abolished in the District of Columbia. That was a concession to freedom if a slight one. It was more than offset, however, by a new and drastic law making it easier for masters to secure the return of slaves who had run away to the North. Under its terms a master merely had to claim a Negro as his slave before the proper federal agent; the Negro so claimed had no right to have a jury trial, to call witnesses, or be heard in his own behalf in open court. If the agent ruled that the claimant was the master, the slave was handed over to him. As to the new territories, the Compromise of 1850 provided that they could come into the Union in the future with or without slavery as their constitutions might provide at the time of their admission.

One-sided as the Compromise of 1850 was in fact, the voters seemed to approve it, for they gave an emphatic majority to the Democratic candidate, Franklin Pierce, in the presidential election of 1852. Had Democrats been content, the issue of slavery in the new territories might have been allowed to languish. But under the leadership of a restless and ambitious Democrat from Illinois, Stephen A. Douglas, the old Missouri Compromise on slavery was abrogated in 1854 by an act of Congress for the organization of the Kansas and Nebraska territories.

These districts were in that part of the Louisiana Purchase where slavery had been abolished by the agreement of 1820. Nevertheless, the new law of 1854 provided that the people of the two territories, or territories formed out of them, might come into the Union with or without slavery as their constitutions prescribed at the time—in short might have slavery if they wanted it. To ring the death knell of the Missouri Compromise on slavery the law expressly repealed it. Settlers, or "squatters," who went into these territories were thus to decide for themselves by popular vote whether they would have slavery or not. In this way the vast interior of the continent, dedicated to freedom in 1820, was thrown open to slavery under the doctrine of what was called "squatter sovereignty." A question long regarded as closed became again the subject of a nation-wide clash.

According to outward signs the repeal of the Missouri Compromise and the opening of all territories to slavery seemed to mean that the Democrats would command the power of the United States Government indefinitely. The tempest of protest that flashed out against the repeal was apparently without avail, for two years later, in 1856, the Democratic candidate for President, James Buchanan, was triumphantly elected. A Virginia editor had once exclaimed that the South nominated candidates and the Northern Democracy elected them. Judging by the election returns, it was still true. A great barrier to the spread of slavery in Western territories had been removed—the Missouri Compromise prohibiting it—and the people at the polls had apparently approved that concession to slave-owners.

Two days after the inauguration of Buchanan on March 4, 1857, the Supreme Court of the United States seemed to clinch the Democratic grip on the government forever. In the Dred Scott case it declared, in effect, that the Missouri Compromise had been null and void from the beginning and that Congress had no power under the Constitution to exclude slavery from the territories.

A majority of the justices in the court were loyal Democrats and in their decision they followed the party line. They had done this with some hesitation but the upshot was clear. Now slavery could be banned from the territories only by an amendment to the Constitution; and, given the number of slave states, the three-fourths majority of the states necessary to ratify it could not be secured. Besides being successful at the polls, pro-slavery Democrats seemed to be permanently entrenched under the Constitution by Supreme Court sanction.

☆

As a matter of fact all the five primary issues, over which Whigs and Democrats struggled for possession of the United States Government, were debated in the form of constitutional interpretations. Whatever the Whigs demanded, some Democratic orator was almost certain to declare unconstitutional. At length, in the Democratic view, a protective tariff was unconstitutional. So was a national bank and a sound bank currency. So were internal improvements and subsidies for shipping, as well as the exclusion of slavery from the territories. John C. Calhoun was so extreme as to maintain that Congress could not constitutionally accept a gift of money to establish the Smithsonian Institution in Washington for the advancement and diffusion of knowledge.

On the other hand, to Whig orators, everything they wanted the government to do was thoroughly constitutional. Daniel Webster took the position that, in letter and spirit, the Constitution empowered Congress to promote commerce, industry, and "sound practices" in banking. Henry Clay supported him with an eloquence scarcely less impressive. As arguments, they cited precedents set by George Washington and Alexander Hamilton, who, as members of the convention of 1787, presumably knew the primary purposes of the Constitution.

In the course of the constitutional debates over the details of the five specific issues two well-rounded theories as to the very nature of the Constitution were formulated. These theories were given definite shape during a great debate in the Senate in 1830 between Robert Y. Hayne, of South Carolina, and Daniel Webster, of Massachusetts. The Union established by the Constitution, Hayne asserted, is merely a compact between sovereign states; it is simply a league of independent states; and states may at their pleasure lawfully withdraw from the Union. On the other side, Webster protested that the Constitution is ordained and established by the people of the United States; the Union is perpetual; its laws are binding on the states; and states cannot lawfully leave the Union.

Enmeshed with these theories respecting the nature of the Constitution were two theories bearing on the powers of the federal government under the Constitution. By 1850 Democratic leaders in general had committed themselves to the proposition that the powers were confined within narrow bounds: to what they themselves called the explicit, specific, and enumerated purposes set forth in the Constitution. To this fixation Whig leaders opposed the doctrine that the powers conferred on the federal government were, in the very language of the Constitution, broad enough to cover all matters of "general welfare"; that Congress, as the Constitution declared, could make laws on many matters not mentioned at all in the Constitution because Congress was authorized to make all laws necessary and proper for carrying all its powers into effect.

When the dispute over the nature of the Constitution and the powers of the federal government was culminating in a deadlock of interpretations, all the men who had taken part in the framing of the Constitution were dead. James Madison lived long enough to protest against the South Carolina doctrine of nullification, but even his long life had been closed in 1836. Moreover, the debates in the secret sessions of the convention of 1787, as Madison had recorded them, were still sealed in his private papers, utterly unknown to the public. While airing their theories in 1830, neither Hayne nor Webster knew the purposes and intentions of the framers of the Constitution as written down in Madison's notes taken in the Philadelphia convention of 1787. Even after Madison's notes were published in 1840 Calhoun and his disciples went on arguing as before in defense of their narrow interpretation of the Constitution. Nor did the public pay much attention to the revelations contained in Madison's papers. Democrats in power at the national capital continued to claim the sanction of the Constitution for their political program, no matter what their opponents said to the contrary.

☆

At the height of their power, in 1857, the Democrats had a majority in the Senate and House of Representatives. The presidency was in their hands. And a majority of the Supreme Court had come from their ranks. On such good grounds they could exult.

Yet over the bright horizon a tornado was brewing. Dissensions were rising even among the Democrats. Critics were assailing their program and the institution of human slavery associated with it. Public protest was mounting, and an opposition party was preparing to drive slavery out of the territories, despite the repeal of the Missouri Compromise and the decision of the Supreme Court.

In many ways, apart from its merits or demerits, slavery was involved in Democratic measures, actions, and successes. Slaves furnished the labor for the plantations of the agricultural South; and planters were powerful in the councils of the Democratic party. If as planters they took issue with Whigs over protective tariffs, banking, or the currency, Whigs could reply by attacking them as slaveowners. If slavery was to be preserved and the planting interests promoted by federal laws, it was necessary for Southern planters to have more slave states to maintain a balance of power in the Senate against the growing number of free states in the North. Giving free homesteads to free farmers forecast the destruction of that balance. For various reasons, therefore, slavery entered naturally or was deliberately drawn into the debates over all the major political issues of the age.

Meanwhile slavery, the source of economic and political power for planters, was being attacked increasingly and more emotionally as a moral evil, as a violation of the human rights proclaimed in the Declaration of Independence. In 1776 slavery had been lawful in the North, as well as in the South. But it was neither popular nor profitable there. One after another Northern states either abolished slavery or made provisions for gradual emancipation. Massachusetts outlawed it in 1780. New York eradicated in 1827 the last vestiges of slavery within its borders. In Southern states strong sentiments against it were expressed. Great Virginian slave-owners themselves, such as Washington, Jefferson, and George Mason, had condemned it as injurious to both slaves and masters, and had voiced the hope that in coming years it might be abolished. Washington's will provided for freeing his slaves after the death of his wife. Slavery was not mentioned in the Constitution; but Congress, given power to stop the importation of slaves in or after 1808, had exercised that authority at the earliest opportunity. Relatively few leaders of the Revolutionary generation ever undertook to defend slavery through thick and thin.

It was an easy thing, however, to dislike slavery and to hope that in some manner it might pass away. It was possible to give up one's own human chattels and feel more comfortable in conscience. It was really revolutionary to demand the instant and wholesale extirpation of slavery, root and branch. That was what William Lloyd Garrison did when, in 1831, he started publishing at Boston his anti-slavery paper, the *Liberator*. Garrison scorned "gradual emancipation," and called for immediate and unconditional abolition. In vitriolic language he denounced slavery and slaveowners alike, declaring that he would be harsh as truth and would be heard. Stoned and otherwise assaulted by mobs in the streets of Boston, he kept up his agitation with unwavering fervor, powerfully aided by Theodore Weld, a Christian evangelist, pamphleteer, and organizer.

In many parts of the North, from the seaboard to the Mississippi Valley, abolitionists formed groups to work with Garrison or to carry on the crusade against slavery in their own ways. Sarah and Angelina Grimké, of South Carolina, did more than give up their slaves, as many other Southerners did; they also dedicated themselves to the cause of general abolition by going North to join in the agitation against slavery. Their example of conviction and action was an inspiration in the abolition movement.

Negroes who had escaped from bondage told of their tragic experiences and gave firsthand knowledge of slavery to audiences far and wide in the North, helping to inflame antagonism to that system—especially Frederick Douglass, Sojourner Truth, and Harriet Tubman, "the Moses of her people," who led some three hundred Negroes out of the South by hazardous exploits, one after the other. Dramatizing the worst features of slavery in a novel, *Uncle Tom's Cabin*, Harriet Beecher Stowe startled at least a million readers with her selected pictures of its sorrows and cruelties, making slavery odious to an immense number of persons in the North who had thought little about that labor system below the Mason and Dixon border.

In 1859, John Brown, with a few backers, invaded Virginia and at the risk of his life tried to start a general slave insurrection. Like uprisings previously made by slaves, it did not succeed, but it threw fuel into the fire. Higher and higher rose the flame of resentment as political struggles for power over the possession of the federal government engaged the voters in successive campaigns.

Criticisms of slavery, in the North, at length found political expression in the creation of the Free Soil party. Yet this party, which put forward a candidate first in 1844, did not demand immediate abolition. The central point of its program was the exclusion of slavery from the territories. On that program alone, however, the Free Soilers made little progress. In their first campaign in 1844 they polled only about 62,000 votes out of over 2,500,000. Free Soilers made gains in 1848 but in 1852 their vote fell off more than one third. The mere exclusion of slavery from the territories did not then seem to be the issue on which a candidate could ever carry the country.

Nevertheless the repeal of the Missouri Compromise by Congress in 1854 and the opening of all the territories to slavery changed the temper of many voters with respect to the issue. By this action Congress dispelled the hope that slavery would die out gradually or could be confined to the states where it existed. It indicated the possibility that slavery might become dominant in vast regions of the West and in fact spread throughout the nation.

Unwilling to accept such prospects, many citizens in the North demanded a new party squarely committed to shutting slavery out of the territories; that is, to preventing its expansion. At a public meeting in Wisconsin, called shortly after Congress repealed the Missouri Compromise, a committee composed of Whigs, Democrats, and Free Soilers was appointed to start the organization of this party.

In selecting a name for it, the managers were shrewd. The Federalist party had long been dead. The Whig party was dying. Some other and more attractive title was necessary to capture public interest. Recalling their party memories, the leaders in the new movement at last chose the name "Republican party"—the old but still appealing title that had been adopted by Jefferson for the popular party that overwhelmed the "monocrats" and "aristocrats" of Hamilton's following in 1800. Under the long shadow cast by Jefferson's fame, the new Republicans nominated as their candidate for President in 1856 John C. Frémont, famous as an explorer of California, and adopted as their campaign motto, "Free labor, free speech, free men, free Kansas, and Frémont!" They were defeated in the election but the size of their vote, 1,340,000, encouraged them to expect victory in the next presidential contest.

☆

Watching the tides of public opinion flowing and ebbing through these turbulent years was a Whig of Illinois who had long been active in the politics of that state—Abraham Lincoln. Born in a log cabin in Kentucky in 1809, brought up in log cabins in Indiana and Illinois, Lincoln was certainly "a man of the people." He was poor enough and humble enough to suit any "democrat" in all the land. But, given only the barest rudiments of learning in his boyhood, Lincoln, like Franklin and Washington of the Revolution, educated himself, and well, by reading, besides a few law books, many classics in the English tongue, including the Bible, Shakespeare, and Aesop's Fables.

After a tough struggle against poverty Lincoln won some local renown as a lawyer and as a Whig member of the Illinois legislature. For a brief period, 1847–49, he served as a member of the House of Representatives in Washington. Still, as he approached the age of fifty, Lincoln was little known except as a local politician in Illinois.

With regard to the slavery issue, Lincoln was no abolitionist. Yet he believed slavery was an evil and was opposed to its extension in the territories. To abolitionists he was thus "a trimmer"; while to pro-slavery Whigs and Democrats he was "unsafe," if not "dangerous."

Lincoln's faith in the people was as stanch as that of any Democrat. Indeed Lincoln confessed that he had learned the first principles of popular government from Jefferson. Even so, he was cautious. He did not leave the Whig party until 1854. Four years later he was nominated by the Republicans as a candidate for the United States Senate.

He was defeated at the senatorial election but during the campaign he became a national figure. In a series of debates with Stephen A. Douglas, the opposing Democratic candidate, Lincoln manifested qualities of greatness—an exceptional knowledge of American history and government, genius as an orator, barbed analytical skill, and a clear conviction on a paramount issue of the times—the exclusion of slavery from the territories.

From the debates with Douglas, Lincoln emerged as a thoughtful leader commanding the confidence and admiration of throngs of citizens. To the discussions men and women had flocked on horseback, in farm wagons, in carriages, and on foot. Amid a fanfare of banner waving, band playing, and parading, however, they had demonstrated that they had serious purposes. They followed the arguments of the debaters and weighed the clashing opinions, soberly, with due recognition of their significance. At the same time newspapers had carried far and wide full reports of the debates; and citizens all the way from Maine to California could make up their minds on the merits of the arguments and the plans for meeting the impending crisis. So cutting and lasting was the impression which Lincoln made on the country by his speeches against Douglas and others delivered subsequently that the new Republican party nominated him for the presidency in 1860. In Southern eyes he was radical on the slavery question, but he was not too radical for the public in the North.

In choosing Lincoln the Republicans elbowed aside William H. Seward, of New York, who had long been prominent in public affairs. Seward was in some respects more radical than Lincoln and in other respects more conservative. He had gone beyond Lincoln by condemning the system of slavery itself. He had also spoken the ominous words: "the irrepressible conflict." Yet Seward had been associated with the "money power" centralized in the East and hence was no favorite in the Democratic strongholds of the West.

Remembering that they had been beaten at the last election when they had adopted the exclusion of slavery from the territories as the main plank in their platform, the Republicans in 1860 drafted a platform that made a wider appeal to voters. They renewed their pledge to shut slavery out of the territories but they inserted two new planks. One of these endorsed the device of a protective tariff to encourage the development of "the industrial interests of the whole country." That was gratifying to Whigs in the North. Another new plank advocated a homestead law giving a farm of moderate size to anybody who was inclined to go out and till it. That pleased thousands of Democrats, especially in the Middle West, who had supported the homestead bill which the Democratic President, James Buchanan, had vetoed. In other words, Republicans in 1860 "had three strings to their bow"— opposition to slavery in the territories, protection for American industries, and free homesteads for people discontented with their lot in the East.

Over these issues the Democratic party split asunder. One wing, dominated by Southern leaders, nominated for President John C. Breckinridge, of Kentucky, and declared that slavery must be permitted in the territories and protected there by the government of the United States. A second wing held a separate convention and nominated Stephen A. Douglas on a platform of "squatter sovereignty," that is, letting the voters of the territories decide whether they wanted slavery or not. A number of Whigs, clinging to the Clay-Webster program of compromise, took a fresh title, Constitutional Unionists, and selected as candidates for President and Vice-President John Bell, of Tennessee, and Edward Everett, of Massachusetts. In their platform, as if no slavery question tormented the land, they called upon the voters to support the Constitution, the Union, and the enforcement of the laws.

Consequently four parties were in the field for the campaign of 1860. In these circumstances Lincoln carried all the free states except New Jersey. But the number of popular ballots cast for him was smaller by about a million than the number received by his three opponents. In fact, the candidates of the two relatively conservative parties, Bell and Douglas, together received more votes than were polled by the Republicans. Still Lincoln's popular vote was so distributed among the states that he won a majority of all the electoral votes and under the Constitution was lawfully elected to the presidency. Aware that he represented only a minority of the people, though duly chosen for the office of Chief Executive, he looked forward with anxiety to the day of his inauguration.

CHAPTER XVII

National Unity Sealed in an Armed Contest

NEWS OF LINCOLN'S ELECTION in November 1860 was taken as a signal for secession in South Carolina. The state legislature called upon the voters to elect delegates to a convention endowed with full powers of action on that issue. In December the convention assembled and by unanimous resolution it withdrew South Carolina from the Union. Early the next year other Southern states followed this example: Florida, Georgia, Alabama, Mississippi, Louisiana, and Texas.

In February delegates from six of the states met at Montgomery, Alabama, formed a new union called the Confederate States of America, drew up a provisional constitution, and chose as provisional President Jefferson Davis, a Mississippi planter who had formerly served the national Union with distinction in war and peace. A few weeks later a permanent constitution was framed for the Confederacy. It was ratified by the seceded states; members of the Confederate Senate and House were chosen; and Davis was elected as regular President of the Confederacy.

In taking this action secessionists based their expectations on one or both of two theories. The first was that the North would permit the Confederate States to secede in peace and establish friendly relations with their government. The second was that, if permission was denied and war came, the South could maintain its independence by arms.

Though the Southern states were outnumbered by the Northern states in population, wealth, and all the great industries necessary to provide the sinews of war, there were at the time several reasons for Southern confidence in victory. It was assumed that Great

Britain would need cotton to keep her mill wheels turning and would intervene in support of the Confederacy; and that Napoleon III, Emperor of the French, would sympathize with the planting aristocracy and co-operate with Britain in aiding the Confederate government. It was widely believed in the South that Northern farmers and mechanics would not fight; or, if they did, that they would be outmatched by Southern valor. Another source of Confederate optimism was the faith that all the other slave states, except Delaware, would join in secession; and that blocking the mouth of the Mississippi River to the commerce of the Northwest would make states in that region eager to come to terms with the Confederacy. In the opening months of 1861 few if any Confederates could foresee how vain such expectations would turn out to be.

When Lincoln was inaugurated on March 4, 1861, he faced a hard dilemma: the Union seemed to be dissolving; the Confederacy must be allowed to go in peace; a compromise must be reached; or the Union must be maintained by arms. Between his election and his inauguration, Lincoln had refrained from the use of inflammatory language in speaking of the South. By letters and in other ways he let Southern leaders know that he had no intention or power to interfere with slavery in their states. Before his inauguration Congress passed a resolution for amending the Constitution in such a manner as to guarantee that the federal government could never attack slavery in the states where it existed. To this position Lincoln gave his personal approval.

On behalf of the South a proposal was made that the old Missouri Compromise line be drawn through the Western territories—with slavery on one side and freedom on the other. But Lincoln had been elected on a platform promising that slavery would be abolished in the territories. On that point he was adamant and he rejected the proposal.

Lincoln's inaugural address was an appeal for solving the problem within the limits of the Constitution. He declared that the Union was older than the states and that no state could lawfully secede. Under the Constitution slavery was legal in the states where it was established. This fact he recognized and again assured the South that he had neither the right nor the intention to disturb slavery there. The law providing for the return of fugitive slaves to their masters was on the statute books and Lincoln promised to enforce it. To this attitude respecting the Fugitive Slave Act the stoutest slaveowner in the Confederacy could scarcely object.

Lincoln also said clearly, however, that to him was entrusted the power to hold, occupy, and possess the property and places belonging to the government and to collect the duties and imposts; and he added that he was under a solemn oath to "preserve, protect, and defend" the government of the United States. Still he closed on a note of hope—that "the better angels of our nature" would in the end keep the bonds of Union unbroken.

As yet neither side had committed an act of violence. Only words had been spoken, papers written, and pacific measures employed. For more than a month uncertainty as to the outcome of secession prevailed, while representatives of the Union and of the Confederacy feverishly sought, more or less unofficially, to reach a compromise or a settlement of some kind. But a straight-out test of power was in the offing.

On a little island in the harbor before the city of Charleston stood Fort Sumter—a spot of land which belonged by law to the government of the United States and was garrisoned by a small Federal force in command of Major Robert Anderson. Without fresh supplies this garrison could not long hold out. The Confederate government demanded a surrender of the fort but refrained at the moment from any overt act. Its officials merely stopped the flow of provisions to Major Anderson, reckoning that he would soon be compelled to yield.

For Lincoln the plight of Fort Sumter created a delicate situation but after many delays he decided to send supplies to Major Anderson by sea. Having received news of this decision, President Davis, thinking that the garrison would quickly be starved out, issued only vague orders to General P. G. T. Beauregard, in command of troops at Charleston, instructing him to continue negotiations.

Beauregard dispatched agents to consult with Major Anderson and they received from him a pledge to surrender on April 15, if no contrary orders came to him from the national capital in the meantime. Deeming this reply unsatisfactory, the agents, without consulting Beauregard or any superior authority, reported their views on the next procedure to a Confederate artillery commander; and at half-past four on the morning of April 12 the bombardment of Fort Sumter began. After a spirited defense Major Anderson surrendered about sunset on the evening of the next day and formally evacuated the fort on Sunday, April 14.

Among many uncertainties one thing was now certain: the first act of violence had been committed by Confederates—the flag of the United States flying above Federal troops had been fired upon. The effect was electric. Millions of people in the North who had been lukewarm or hesitant now declared their unequivocal readiness to defend the Union. On April 15, Lincoln issued a call for 75,000 soldiers—not to wage a general war on the Confederacy but first of all "probably" to repossess the forts, places, and property which had been taken away from the Union—a purpose to be accomplished with the least possible disturbance to peaceful citizens in any part of the country. In the same proclamation he summoned both houses of Congress in special session for July 4, "then and there to consider and determine such measures as, in their wisdom, the public safety and interest may seem to demand."

In the South the firing on Fort Sumter and Lincoln's call for troops were also followed by swift and drastic measures. On April 17, Virginia seceded from the Union. Soon Arkansas, Tennessee, and North Carolina likewise went over to the Confederate side. Then prompt military intervention on the part of Lincoln stifled attempts to withdraw Maryland, Kentucky, and Missouri from the Union.

But the South was far from "solid" in the desire to leave the Union. As a matter of fact in Georgia, Alabama, Mississippi, and Louisiana a strong opposition to secession had appeared in a large minority vote against it. In Virginia western counties were so opposed to it that they withdrew from the Old Dominion and later entered the Union as the state of West Virginia. In the western part of North Carolina, Unionist loyalty widely prevailed. In the eastern parts of Kentucky and Tennessee, Unionists were undoubtedly in a majority and thousands of them joined the Federal army. Although opinion in Maryland and Kentucky was sharply divided, little force was needed to keep those states in the Union. Secessionists in Missouri were numerous enough to create a civil war in that state but at length they were driven out or suppressed, after several pitched battles. Less than a year after the firing on Fort Sumter the hope of Confederates that the border states would come to their aid in the struggle for independence had been dispelled.

☆

When war began in full force the Confederacy had only eleven states on its side as against twenty-three states in the North. Nine million people in the South, more than one third of them slaves, were aligned against 22,000,000 people in the North, nearly all

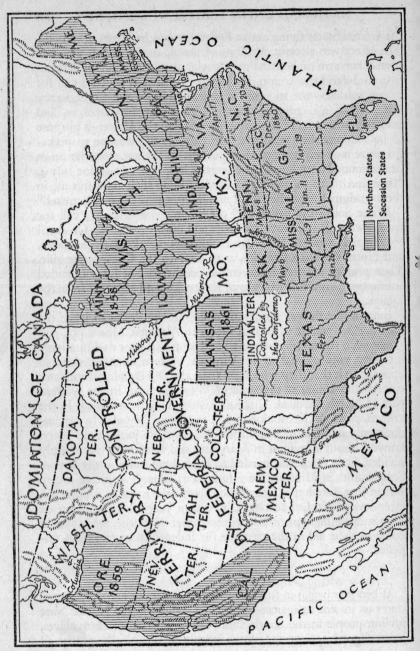

free. States predominantly agricultural were arrayed in mortal combat with states rich in manufacturing as well as agricultural resources, reinforced by gold and silver from Western mines. Considered merely in terms of men and metal, Southern strength was inferior; but the South soon demonstrated ingenuity and enterprise in mobilizing materials and high competence in the art of warfare.

As the war got under way the Federal government at Washington and the Confederate government installed at Richmond, Virginia, confronted immense tasks for which neither was well prepared. Armies had to be raised and organized, munitions and other supplies furnished in staggering amounts, and commanding officers chosen to direct military and naval operations. The treasuries of both governments were almost empty and funds had to be provided to pay bills which aggregated before the close of the war far more than all the money the United States Government had spent since the establishment of the Republic. Relations with European governments had to be conducted with a view to securing support and warding off unfriendly acts. Problems of domestic economy and civilian affairs, numerous and perplexing, had to be considered and handled in a manner to preserve internal harmony and promote unison in arms. Finally it was necessary, among all these trials, for both governments to plan campaigns and direct fighting over immense areas of land and water. To these tasks, on their respective sides, Lincoln and Davis, aided by their advisers and legislatures, devoted their minds and energies from the spring of ·861 to the spring of 1865—for four terrible years of civil war.

During the early months of the armed conflict both governments relied for soldiers upon volunteers who at first rushed to enlist. Soon, however, enthusiasm waned. By special acts passed in April and September 1862, the Confederate Congress authorized President Davis to draft soldiers from among able-bodied males between eighteen and forty-five years of age, with many exemptions including owners or overseers of large plantations. In the last days of the war the Confederacy even made provisions for enrolling slaves; and plans for emancipating slaves in a general conscription were under its serious consideration. In August 1861, Lincoln ordered a draft of militiamen, which turned out to be disappointing as to numbers. In March of the next year the Congress of the United States enacted a law making all able-bodied males, with some exceptions, liable to military duty; and the practice of drafting men continued till the fighting ceased.

On both sides conscription encountered bitter animosity, and desertions from the armies were so numerous as to be serious in effects. When drawings began in New York City on July 13, 1863, a general riot broke out and was not subdued until many people had been killed and a large amount of property burned or otherwise destroyed. The troubles of Davis were equally great if not greater. His recruiting officers met resistance in many places. Governors in some Confederate states, especially Georgia and North Carolina, refused to aid in the strict enforcement of the draft laws. A cry, "rich man's war and poor man's fight," reverberated through the South and men deserted the Confederate ranks in shoals. Nevertheless great and powerful armies were raised by both parties to the conflict and fought valiantly in battles that never seemed to end.

Respecting munitions and other war supplies, the North had a clear superiority of productive power in the beginning and increased its facilities as the war went forward. Able to keep the seas open for Northern shipping, the Union could supplement its domestic output with heavy importations from Great Britain and the Continent. Though the South started with more limited resources, it displayed remarkable energy in building new mills and turning out quantities of war materials. Its achievements were all the more extraordinary by reason of the fact that the Federal blockade of its harbors almost cut off imports of iron, steel, munitions, and other goods. But as the blockade grew tighter, Confederate armies and the civilian population in the South sank into dire distress from the want of adequate supplies.

With regard to financial resources the two governments locked in war were decidedly unequal. At the outset the Union had a Treasury Department and a monetary system; the South had neither and was compelled to create both. The North could command enormous outputs of gold and silver; the South had little hard money and early exported a large portion of what it had to buy military supplies. For raising money both governments resorted to the ancient devices of public finance: taxes, bond sales, and issues of paper notes.

On the Federal side repeated increases were made in customs duties on imports and in excises on tobacco, liquor, other commodities, and occupations; and to these were added taxes on inheritances and incomes. By the sale of bonds and notes the Union Treasury collected a total of $2,600,000,000 during the war. It adopted the third expedient, paper currency, in 1862; and before the conflict closed it issued $450,000,000 in "greenbacks," supplemented by $50,000,000 worth of fractional currency, with notes as low as three cents in face value.

Similar measures were put into force in the Confederacy, coupled with calls upon its states for quotas of money to be raised by direct taxes on property. Confederate bonds were exchanged for specie, produce, and state and Confederate notes. Altogether, about $1,000,000,000 worth of paper currency was emitted, in addition to notes floated by the states, banks, and business concerns.

While Federal bonds dropped in value during the darker days of the war and greenbacks once fell as low as thirty-nine cents on the dollar, Federal financing was, comparatively speaking, sound and stable. In the Confederacy, on the other hand, the course of bonds and notes was on the whole steadily downward as new issues poured out and consumers' goods became scarcer. In the summer of 1862 tea sold in the South at five dollars a pound and boots at twenty-five dollars a pair. In 1862 one dollar in gold was worth twenty-two dollars in Confederate currency; shoes were selling at a hundred and fifty dollars a pair and flour at three hundred dollars a barrel. Early in 1865 beef was six dollars a pound, flour a thousand dollars a barrel, and firewood five dollars a stick. After the surrender at Appomattox in the spring of 1865 Confederate bonds and paper currency dropped dead in the hands of the possessors. According to a current saying of the people, a Confederate dollar was "not worth a Continental," in memory of the paper money issued by the Continental Congress during the Revolution, which hit bottom long before the War for Independence was over.

Especially with reference to foreign relations, the problems of the two governments differed. The government at Washington was already recognized by foreign countries as the lawful government of the United States. Its prime cares were to keep this status unimpaired, to prevent the recognition of the Confederacy as independent, to ward off intervention in the war by Great Britain and France, and to hold the channels of commerce open. On its part the Confederacy struggled to achieve recognition as an independent government, to win financial assistance, to break the blockade on its commerce, and if possible to gain direct intervention on its behalf by Great Britain and France. In this situation Northern measures were essentially protective—against radical changes in foreign relations. Those of the South were essentially exploratory—directed to securing a position as an independent nation among the nations of the earth.

During the first year of the war the Confederacy was recognized as a belligerent by Great Britain and France, though not as an independent state; and it sent two agents abroad, James Mason and John Slidell, to represent it at London and Paris respectively. When the two men were taken from a British steamer by Captain Wilkes, in command of a Union vessel, Great Britain protested against this act of search and seizure. To avoid worse perils, perhaps a foreign war on top of the civil war, Lincoln ordered the Confederate agents released and they went on to Europe to appeal for a recognition of Southern independence and for aid to the Confederacy.

Confederate bonds to the face value of about $15,000,000 were sold in Britain and France. British shipyards, defying an old rule of international law, built war vessels for the Confederacy and the British government allowed them to escape to sea, where they preyed on the commerce of the United States. The sympathies of the British aristocracy and government, of the ruling classes in France, and of Napoleon III, Emperor of the French, were overwhelmingly on the side of the South. In both countries aristocrats hoped that "the upstart Yankee Republic" would be destroyed in the war and many British and French newspapers rejoiced in the prospect. But working people in English cities held mass meetings in protest against giving assistance to slaveowners; and Queen Victoria counseled her Cabinet to be cautious.

Napoleon III attempted to form a European coalition for intervention in the war. In 1861 he suggested to the Czar of Russia that certain great Powers take joint action respecting America, but he met a firm if polite refusal. Meanwhile the British government was toying with the idea. Yet when Napoleon proposed intervention to the British in 1862 he was told that the time was not ripe. One member of the British Cabinet openly declared that the Confederacy was in effect a success; but the Prime Minister, who was watching closely the course of the war in America, was unwilling to take the plunge in aid of the South.

Unable to restrain his meddlesome spirit, Napoleon sent a message to Lincoln offering his services as a mediator between the North and the South. Lincoln responded courteously, declining the offer. In language less urbane Congress replied by passing a resolution telling the French Emperor, in effect, that he should keep his nose out of American affairs.

If it had not been for the decisive Northern victories at Gettysburg and Vicksburg in the summer of 1863, British and French intervention might have come. Those triumphs in arms, however, seemed to assure the future of "the upstart Yankee Republic" and serve as a warning to impertinent foreign Powers. At all events Great Britain and France never recognized the independence of the Confederacy. Nor did they officially intervene in the war.

☆

While raising and supplying armies, providing financial support for the war, and conducting foreign relations, both governments in America framed and tried to enforce complicated measures in direct aid of their respective battle fronts. Acting under war powers conferred upon him as commander in chief by the Constitution, Lincoln struck out vigorously in the spring of 1861. He declared a blockade of Southern ports and ordered the Union navy to halt all vessels, Confederate and foreign, endeavoring to enter or leave those waters. In effect this blockade almost destroyed all Southern commerce. Although some blockade runners escaped the net, the number was not large enough to prevent a growing paralysis of the Confederate export and import business. The trade in cotton, the prime reliance of the South, was for practical purposes completely ruined.

To check Northern citizens who wanted to help the Confederacy and critics who might weaken Federal war efforts, Lincoln resorted to two forms of stringent action. He suspended the writ of habeas corpus and empowered military authorities to arrest, hold, and try persons accused of giving assistance to the South or of interfering with the movements of Federal troops. In the name of military necessity he authorized the arrest and imprisonment of many newspaper publishers, orators, and agitators who printed or uttered severe criticisms of the Federal government and its war activities. The exact number of arrests under those orders is not known, but it was large.

The most celebrated of all Lincoln's war measures was the Proclamation of Emancipation on January 1, 1863. His resolve to effect this historic stroke of state had matured slowly. At the outbreak of the war idealistic men and women in the North urged him to do it and continued their insistence from month to month, rolling monster petitions into the national capital to reinforce their pressure. But for various reasons Lincoln long hesitated. Weighty among them, no doubt, was his fear of losing the support of the slave states which remained in the Union, and his knowledge that the North was seriously divided over abolitionism in every form. He was aware also that a declaration of emancipation would be futile unless confirmed by victory at arms.

It was not until the summer of 1862 that Lincoln decided to act. In July of that year he read to his Cabinet the draft of a proclamation of emancipation which he had written and might issue when occasion seemed to make it feasible. Encouraged by the Federal victory at the battle of Antietam in September, he announced his resolve to the world. He gave notice that unless the states in arms against the Union returned to their allegiance he would, on January 1, 1863, deliver a blow directly at slavery. When the New Year arrived he fulfilled the promise.

In the Proclamation of Emancipation, issued under his war powers, Lincoln declared thenceforward and forever free all the slaves in all the districts of the United States then in arms against the Union. From one point of view this was an empty threat. It freed no slaves in fact. In the loyal districts of the Union slaves remained slaves and, in the districts still controlled by Confederate arms, slaves also remained slaves. But the Proclamation electrified the imagination of all who loved liberty and was indeed a move toward the abolition of slavery throughout the United States.

Even in the South, supposed to be solid, rigorous means were adopted in efforts to stamp out criticisms and crush overt actions interfering with its war program. Early in 1862 the Confederate Congress authorized President Davis to suspend for a term of months the writ of habeas corpus and proclaim martial law in regions where open resistance occurred. Under this act, from time to time, martial law was declared in Richmond, the very capital of the Confederacy, in several Virginia counties, in parts of South Carolina, including Charleston, the hotbed of the secession movement, and in other places in the South.

When this law expired it was not immediately renewed, partly on account of the outcries against it. But in 1864 another temporary act of the kind was passed by the Confederate Congress, in response to a message from President Davis asserting that "disloyalty and hostility to our cause" existed in certain localities and that deserters were being protected by the civil courts.

Actions under such Confederate statutes were numerous and often stern, but apparently fewer and less drastic than similar actions by the Union government in the North. If President Davis had found ample support in the Confederate Congress he might have used martial law mercilessly in trying to prevent the dissolution of the Confederacy during the closing months of the war, but such support was never granted to him.

For Jefferson Davis, as well as Abraham Lincoln, emancipation became a practical issue before the close of the conflict. In desperate straits for soldiers to fight its battles, the Confederate Congress, near the end of the war, passed an act for the employment of slaves in military services. That law had the approval of General Robert E. Lee, as well as of President Davis, and he aided in recruiting Negroes as soldiers. While the language of the statute and of the orders issued under it was vague, it was interpreted to mean that a slave acquired freedom by joining the Confederate army.

Even plans for complete emancipation were discussed at the Confederate capital. In 1864, Duncan Kenner, a member of the Confederate Congress, proposed to President Davis that an agent be sent abroad with power to offer to the British and French governments the emancipation of slaves in exchange for their official recognition of the Confederacy. Davis acceded to the plan. He appointed Kenner as minister plenipotentiary to carry out the project; and Kenner was abroad working at the scheme early in 1865—too late. Had the war continued, real emancipation might have been a Southern act of war.

☆

Armies, supplies, finances, foreign policies, and specific measures in support of war were auxiliaries in the contest at arms. In final analysis the appeal had been made to the ultimate arbiter, force, and the decision had to be rendered on battlefields. After Fort Sumter had fallen and war had become a fact, what war plans, what systems of strategy were to be devised and followed? That was a major problem for both President Lincoln and President Davis. Having withdrawn from the Union and fired the first gun, the Confederacy confronted the task of making real by arms the independence it had asserted. If the Union was to be saved, Lincoln and his advisers had to prepare for an invasion of the South and make decisions respecting the routes to be chosen and the strategy of each movement.

At the start the Confederacy had about 400,000 men and large stores at its command and was better prepared for war than the Union in respect of those details. Some of its military officers advocated immediate offensive action against the North, especially an assault on Washington and the seizure of the capital. Such tactics, it was argued, would quickly bring the government of the United States to its knees.

Other Confederates were more wary. The idea of a possible compromise and a peaceful separation lingered among them even after blood had been shed. A blend of caution and hopes finally fixed for them the nature of their strategy. The invasion of the North was not given up; attempts at it were made, too late and with too little strength. So the South was irrevocably committed to fighting a defensive war, on the theory that the Northern armies might thus be beaten or worn down and forced to accept the independence of the Confederacy.

For the military strategists of the Union geography was of course an element to be reckoned with in planning warfare. The Appalachian Mountains separated the South into two great areas—the East, with Virginia as the bulwark; and the West, divided by the Mississippi River. Victory in either area would be more than a local success. If achieved in the West, it would split the Confederacy to the Gulf of Mexico. If it occurred in Virginia and was crowned by the capture of Richmond, it would weaken the prestige of the Confederacy at home and abroad.

Spurred to immediate decision by armchair strategists, shouting "On to Richmond!" in July 1861 an attack was made by a Union army under General McDowell on Confederate forces under General Beauregard near Centreville, Virginia, close to a little stream called Bull Run. The battle ended in a disaster for the Northern troops, and from this awful lesson President Lincoln learned that the conquest of Virginia would not be a simple affair.

It was in the Western region that military events of decisive significance for a Union victory first occurred. During the summer and autumn of 1861 small engagements in Missouri clinched the grip of the Union on that state. Early the next year Federal forces under Ulysses S. Grant started a drive into Tennessee, by way of the Tennessee River from its outlet in the Ohio. By gunboats on the river and by infantry on the landward side, Grant attacked the Confederates at Fort McHenry in upper Tennessee and forced them to surrender, on February 6.

Dispatching some of his men by gunboats around to Fort Donelson on the Cumberland River, Grant marched eastward with the rest of his soldiers. On February 16 that fortress fell before the assaults of his troops. At many subsequent battles in western Tennessee the Confederates were defeated or seriously crippled and pushed aside; by the opening of 1863 Federal forces had penetrated upper Mississippi and Alabama.

Leaving other officers to cope with the Confederate forces still intact in Tennessee, Grant began to move on Vicksburg, the great stronghold on the Mississippi River. With the aid of gunboats and transports on the river, he besieged the city and starved General John B. Pemberton, the Confederate general, into surrender on July 4. A few days later Port Hudson on the banks of the Mississippi, over the border in Louisiana, was taken by General Banks, one of Grant's aides.

As a naval detachment under Captain David Farragut had opened up the lower Mississippi River and seized New Orleans in the spring of the previous year, the "Father of Waters," as Lincoln said, now flowed "unvexed to the sea." On July 16, 1863, a steamer from St. Louis arrived with a cargo of goods at the docks in New Orleans. More serious battles were yet to be fought in Tennessee and Georgia, but the Confederacy was cut in twain by the summer of 1863 and never reunited.

Federal forces in the Eastern theater of war had accomplished nothing decisive when news of the capture of Vicksburg reached Lincoln in July 1863. Battle after battle, often long, desperate, and costly in lives, had been fought in the East: at Antietam, Fredericksburg, and Chancellorsville, for example. Lincoln had tried general after general in a vain search for a man who could win battles there—McClellan, Hooker, and Burnside, among them.

Meanwhile the army of Virginia under General Robert E. Lee, though repelled at Antietam in September 1862, remained powerful and confident. Indeed Lee felt so sure of his strength that he invaded Pennsylvania, by way of the Shenandoah Valley, in 1863. At Gettysburg, in the early days of July, his advance was stopped, but after receiving a terrible punishment he managed to retire successfully into Virginia. When the year 1864 opened, Lee's army, apparently invincible in defense, barred the roads along which Union armies would have to march if they tried to plunge into the eastern stronghold of the Confederacy.

Two master feats for the Union cause were put through, however, in 1864. In May, General Grant, in command of all the Federal armies, took personal charge of the Virginia campaign and started a relentless drive on Richmond, sparing neither men nor resources in his determination to capture it. That same month Grant's trusted companion in arms, General William T. Sherman, began his march from Chattanooga to Atlanta.

While Grant slashed his way southward, undeterred by heavy losses, crossed the James River, and laid siege to Petersburg, near Richmond, Sherman advanced on Atlanta. In September Sherman took the city. After a delay of a few weeks he led his army off on a march across Georgia, foraging, burning, destroying as he went. On December 20, Savannah crumpled up. From that scene of victory Sherman's army turned northward and pursued its course across Georgia and South Carolina, leaving ruins in its wake, into North Carolina and onward toward Virginia.

The last phase of the war was drawing to a finish. On April 2, 1865, Grant took Petersburg. The next day the Union flag floated over the Confederate capital at Richmond, abandoned by President Davis in a hurried flight. At the head of a shaken if as yet unbeaten army, Lee moved rapidly westward in the direction of Lynchburg, with Grant racing at his heels and General Philip Sheridan on his flank.

For a time Lee seemed to think that he might escape into North Carolina, join forces there with General Joseph E. Johnston, and continue the war. But on April 9, finding that hope forlorn, he gave up, and at Appomattox handed his sword to General Grant. About two weeks later General Johnston laid down his arms. Far away in the West, General Kirby Smith, commanding Confederate troops beyond the Mississippi River, surrendered; and the last fragment of the Confederate army was dissolved during the first days of June. The war, launched with the bombardment of Fort Sumter in 1861, had at last run its course.

Soon it was possible to reckon some of the cost. A careful estimate placed the number of enlistments in the Federal army at 2,898,304 and in the Confederate army at about 1,300,000. The total number of deaths from all causes in the Federal forces was placed at 359,528 and in the Confederate army at approximately 258,000. This was exclusive of the hundreds of thousands of men wounded or made invalids for the remainder of their lives. Estimates of the cost in terms of the money spent on war by the two parties depended on the time fixed—whether up to April 1, 1865, or some later date to cover pensions paid to veterans on both sides. As of April 1, 1865, calculations reported the cost to the Union at about $3,250,000,000 and to the Confederacy at approximately $1,500,000,000; or $4,750,000,000 in all. After pensions, interest on the Federal debt, and the value of property destroyed were added, a conservative computation established the total cost of preserving the Union and abolishing slavery at above $10,000,000,000.

For less than half this amount freedom could have been bought for all the 3,953,857 slaves recorded in the census of 1860—the compensated emancipation which Congress and President Lincoln had proposed in 1862.

☆

Consuming as were the events of the war and the measures of public policy immediately connected with it, the thought and activity of the people on both sides of the struggle were by no means wholly monopolized by it. The life and work of millions in both sections continued to be civilian in nature and emphasis.

The South was disturbed by complaints that civilians gave too much attention and energy to their own interests and too little to the prosecution of the war. Governors of Southern states, members of state legislatures, and members of the Confederate Congress concerned themselves continually with the protection of local and civil rights against the encroachments of military power under the leadership of President Davis. All departments of the Confederate government, amid the distractions of war, considered plans and took actions with reference to economic interests, and with a view to the reordering of affairs after independence was secured. But with the collapse of the Confederate system, legal and financial, and the occupation of the South by Federal armies, such plans and actions in respect of Southern economy and social policy came to naught or at least to little if anything.

On the other hand, in the North, untrampled by invading armies and free from the devastation of battles, the civilian way of life was less upset. There debates over political issues that had shaken the country before the war went on; and significant laws bearing on these issues were enacted by Congress. In response to the increasing demands created by government buying for war purposes, industry and agriculture flourished and the Industrial Revolution drove forward. Out of war profits prodigious masses of capital were accumulated in private hands for new investments in business. Additional millions of acres were brought under the plow by freehold farmers in the West. During the war years the supremacy of manufacturing and commercial interests over the planting interests, in wealth and the number of workers employed, became indisputable.

With senators and representatives accustomed to speak for the planting interests absent from the national capital, the Federal Congress was of course freer to enact laws long demanded by industrialists, financiers, farmers, and reformers. In providing revenues for war purposes it increased again and again the duties levied on imports and raised the discriminative protection accorded to American manufacturers to the highest point yet attained in American history. For example, the tariff on pig iron, which stood at six dollars a ton in 1861, was pushed to nine dollars a ton in 1864, and the tariff of twelve cents a pound on general woolen manufactures was doubled by the act of 1864. Neither the old Federalists nor the Whigs had ever dreamed of favors to industry so generous. Nor were the farmers overlooked in the tariff bills. The duty of three cents per pound for imported raw wool of the lower grade, imposed by the law of 1861, was lifted to six cents a pound in 1864. At the close of the war the free trade which Democrats had once advocated in their national platform seemed as dead as a doornail.

The second great issue over which politicians and statesmen had argued since the days of Hamilton and Jefferson—a national banking system—was likewise settled for a time in connection with efforts to raise money for military expenditures. Hamilton's United States Bank had lapsed in 1811. The second United States Bank established in 1816 had been abolished by Jacksonian Democrats. From 1836 to the outbreak of the war state banks had dominated banking and inundated the country with their paper notes, some sound, some unsound, others fluctuating wildly in value. To cope with financial disorders and help the sale of bonds, Congress in 1863 established a new banking system. It centered the system in the Treasury Department of the Federal government, rather than in a banking corporation such as had been set up in 1791 and 1816, only to be repudiated.

The new law authorized the formation of local banking associations or companies. It empowered them to engage in the general banking business and to issue paper money based on the Federal bonds they bought and deposited with the Treasurer of the United States. The next year, in 1864, Congress made provision for forcing all state banks entirely out of the currency business by laying a prohibitive annual tax of ten per cent on state bank notes, beginning July 1, 1866. Even after they returned to power in Washington, the Democrats, hitherto sworn foes of national banking, did not dare to overthrow it and restore state bank currency. Hamilton had truly triumphed over Jefferson.

During this distribution of national largess by legislative acts, the agrarians got a portion, in the form of free homesteads on the public domain. In their platform of 1860 the Republicans promised free land as well as protection for manufactures. This pledge Congress redeemed two years later by passing the Homestead Act, which President Lincoln gladly signed.

Under the act any person, man or woman, head of a family or twenty-one years old, either a citizen or an alien who had declared his intention of becoming a citizen, could enter a claim to 160 acres on the public domain; and by occupying it for five years, besides making certain improvements on it, the entrant was to have full possession of the property. One vital exception was made, however: excluded from this right to free land were all persons who had borne arms against the United States or given aid and comfort to the enemy. The free land was to go to loyal Unionists including soldiers in the Union army and immigrants from foreign countries.

LANDS GRANTED BY THE GOVERNMENT TO RAILWAYS COMPANIES
BETWEEN 1850 AND 1871

Other momentous measures passed by Congress during the war years included laws chartering companies to build railway lines to the Pacific coast. By acts of 1862 and 1864 provision was made for a line in the central region, serving Federal interests. The

Union Pacific Company was to start from a point in Nebraska, later fixed at Omaha, and build westward. The Central Pacific Company was to begin at San Francisco or a place on the navigable waters of the Sacramento River and build eastward. At some spot, to be determined by speed of construction, the two lines were to meet, thus completing the overland route. In 1864 the Northern Pacific Company was authorized to construct a railway from Lake Superior to Puget Sound by a northern route.

To speed up the work of the Union and Central Pacific Companies, Congress granted them an enormous acreage of land in the form of free rights of way and alternate sections on each side of their lines. In addition it lent them a large sum of money for every mile of track laid—a sum varying according to the difficulties of construction.

At last the continent was to be spanned by railways. Manufacturers, merchants, and capitalists were delighted at the prospect: their markets and investment opportunities were to be widened. Land-hungry men and women were delighted also: the railways would make it easier for them to go West with their movable property and occupy the now free land; railways would provide transportation for agricultural produce to Eastern markets and would increase the value of farm homesteads. And, what was more, the North would be made stronger in wealth and in ties of communication.

While debating and passing bills relative to the conduct of the war, taxes, tariffs, banking, homesteads, and railways, Congress dealt with the question of slavery. In April 1862 it abolished slavery in the District of Columbia. About two months later it prohibited slavery in all the existing territories of the United States and any that might be acquired at any time in the future. In June 1864 it repealed the Fugitive Slave Act passed in 1793 and amended in the Compromise of 1850. In January 1864 a resolution for an amendment to the Constitution abolishing slavery throughout the United States was introduced in Congress; and about a year later, after prolonged discussion, it received the requisite two-thirds vote in both houses. It was sent to the states for consideration, ratified, and put into effect in December 1865. Thus the verbal emancipation which Lincoln had proclaimed in 1863 under his war power was extended to include all slaves and implemented by the Thirteenth Amendment.

☆

Although amid the drastic actions taken by President Lincoln and Congress the North presented a firm war front to the Confederacy, the government in Washington and the people of the North were far from united over the merits of the conflict and the measures adopted during the war years. No more than the South was the North actually "solid." From his first inauguration in 1861 until his death in April 1865, Lincoln was involved in controversies with members of his Cabinet, members of Congress, and leaders in his own party. Congress was dissatisfied with his management of the war and created a committee to investigate and supervise it. Senators and representatives bent on destroying slavery at the earliest possible moment protested against his cautious and hesitating methods.

As soon as any former Confederate state was occupied by Union troops advancing into the South, members of Congress began to take issue with Lincoln over the treatment to be meted out to that state—its relation to the Union and the kind of government it was to have. Abolitionists fumed impatiently at his delays in dealing with slavery. Nor were they all content with the elusive emancipation in his Proclamation. "Radical Republicans" in Congress and even members of Lincoln's Cabinet intrigued against him, belittled his character, and attacked many of his measures.

Behind the armed front of the Union, Northern civilians were also engaged in political struggles with one another during the war years. In the congressional elections of 1862 the Democrats gained so many seats in Congress that it looked as if Lincoln and his party might be thrown out of power at the next election. In fact the Republicans were so perturbed in 1864 that they generally dropped their name and called themselves the Union party. And for the purpose of conciliating Democrats, they nominated, as their candidate for Vice-President, Andrew Johnson, a stanch Democrat from Tennessee who had courageously demonstrated his fidelity to the Union from the beginning of the war.

During the presidential campaign of 1864 Lincoln foresaw probable defeat and for a time the outlook for his re-election was indeed dark. In their platform of that year Northern Democrats denounced the war as a failure and called for a conference to restore the old Union under the Constitution. But this defiance alienated voters in their party. The very candidate whom they nominated, General George B. McClellan, insisted in his speech, accepting the nomination, that the war was not a failure, thereby confounding the confusion. At the polls the Democrats carried only three states: New Jersey, Delaware, and Kentucky.

With gratitude to the people for their confidence in him, expressed by re-electing him, Lincoln pushed the war to a conclusion. He was preparing for a peace of reconciliation when, on April 15, 1865, he died at the hands of an assassin—John Wilkes Booth—a martyr to the cause he had served so singleheartedly.

The executive burden passed to the Vice-President, Andrew Johnson. With the office went much of the ferocious criticism that had been directed against Lincoln on account of his conciliatory attitude toward the defeated Confederates and his liberal proposals for restoring the Confederate states to the Union. With Johnson's assumption of his high office the heat of criticism rose and was intensified in many quarters on other scores. Early in 1868 animosity reached such a pitch that the House of Representatives impeached President Johnson before the Senate and he escaped conviction with removal from the presidency only by the margin of a single vote in the Senate.

CHAPTER XVIII

Reconstruction and Economic Expansion

WITH THE SHIELD of the Union assured and the issue of chattel slavery finally settled, the people of the United States turned in the spring of 1865 to peacetime tasks. The tasks were, as usual, in the main political, economic, and moral. The setting for actions was now the unbroken continental domain. But grave problems lay before the people: the rights of the Southern states in the Union, the economic advancement of the South, civil liberties for Negroes, the payment of the huge national debt, the formulation of public policies for general economic expansion, the disposition of natural resources, the development of territories into states.

☆

In respect of these problems the government of the United States played a leading role in the framing of policies and the determination of actions. Imperative among its first obligations was Southern rehabilitation—economic and legal—amid the lingering passions of the war and in circumstances painful to both sides. Southern farms, plantations, and cities had been the scenes of battles. Over large areas buildings and fences had been destroyed, cattle driven off, and implements of production smashed. Miles of Southern railways had been torn up; rolling stock had been wrecked; railway stations and offices had been burned. Families that had led in business and agricultural development were impoverished. The financial system lay in ruins. Confederate bonds were worthless and all thought of reviving them was blasted by the Fourteenth Amendment to the Constitution of the United States adopted in 1868. Confederate paper money was valueless and specie had almost disappeared from circulation. From the ashes of war a new start had to be made in the South.

To complicate the situation, a revolution had been wrought in Southern society by the abolition of slavery. Millions of Negroes, hitherto held in bondage, generally illiterate, little experienced in management if often skilled in the arts of industry, without property, were now "free." Most of them in the Confederate states had been loyal and helpful to their masters and mistresses during the war and had not deliberately sought their freedom.

There were exceptions, to be sure, thousands of exceptions. At least 100,000 Negroes had served in the Union armies as soldiers and laborers. As the Union armies advanced in the South, other thousands of Negroes gave them aid and support in the hope of forwarding their own liberation. In the South as well as the North, hundreds of Negroes, intelligent and educated, furnished some leadership for their bewildered people.

But from the economic point of view, emancipation in general deprived Negroes of their assured livelihood on plantations and set them adrift in the world, homeless, toolless, and penniless, like the evicted peasants of England in the seventeenth century, ill equipped to enter the fierce competition for existence about them, still wearing the color badge of servitude. At the same time slaveowners, besides losing property valued at about $4,000,000,000, lost their supremacy over the labor supply for their farms and plantations. Old laws pertaining to labor relations had expired on the statute books. Old practices of slave days were forbidden. What new laws and practices were to be devised? How much power of self-determination remained in the South?

Now the old ruling class was subject to the military power of the Union and deprived of representation in the Congress of the United States. In this plight that class could do little except wait for the end of the armed occupation and political action by the President and Congress of the United States. Meanwhile small white farmers of the South were jostling it in the contest for power. Upland farmers had long struggled with the seaboard planters in attempts to secure representations in the state legislatures proportioned to their superior numbers; and in the aftermath of the war among the states they were seeking, with more confidence of success, the power hitherto denied them. But neither former slaveowners nor freehold farmers could make any basic decisions in matters of government until their states were restored to the Union in one form or another.

The position to be accorded to the Southern states had become a major question for the government at Washington as soon as its armies had permanently occupied a large area of the South; and it continued to be a primary problem for the President and Congress for many years after the war. Plans proposed in Washington for the treatment of the South, almost endless in number, fell into a few broad patterns. Utopians who had wanted to make the whole war a war for liberty yearned to hold the Southern states down, utterly destroy the great landlord class by the confiscation of its estates, divide the land among Negroes and poor white farmers who had been loyal to the Union, give the suffrage and full civil rights to the hitherto dispossessed, and force upon the defeated Confederacy the principles of liberty that Thomas Jefferson had celebrated as the perfect good.

Astute Republican politicians, knowing that their party represented a minority in the nation, had a care for measures that would keep themselves in power. Some of them encouraged and made use of the utopians; but all along they fixed their minds on the instant need of things and made plans adapted to their interests.

All the plans, whatever their source, rested on theories about the nature of the Union, the Confederate revolt, and the power of the President and Congress of the United States.

If Lincoln's theory was right—namely, that the states could not lawfully withdraw from the Union—then none of them was ever out of the Union, even during the height of Southern military strength. If this theory was sound, as the Confederate states came under Federal authority with the progress of Federal arms the loyal citizens in each were entitled to restore loyal state governments. But against Lincoln's theory it was argued that the Confederate states, by armed rebellion, had actually left the Union, were bound to come back as "conquered provinces," and in instituting governments must submit to the decrees of the conquerors.

Who was to make decisions about the restoration of the Southern states? The President or Congress? And what plans were to be followed in the process of restoration? As events developed the process was divided into two stages: "presidential" reconstruction, as it was called, and "congressional" reconstruction. Lincoln's proposals were, relatively speaking, moderate and generous; those of Congress were severe and punitive.

Under his war power Lincoln claimed the right to prescribe the terms on which military government was to be withdrawn from the states of the Confederacy as, one after another, they came under Federal authority again. When the Union forces drove southward in the Mississippi Valley, in 1862–63, he appointed military governors—in Tennessee, Arkansas, and Louisiana—and instructed them to take charge while loyal governments were being formed in those states.

Late in 1863, Lincoln issued a proclamation of amnesty memorable for its conciliatory tone. The decree offered, in the first place, to restore the suffrage to all voters who would take the prescribed oath of loyalty to the United States, with exceptions excluding practically all leaders in the Confederacy. It then provided that, as soon as ten per cent of the voters in any state had taken the oath of loyalty, they could form their own government and, having done so, would be entitled to the recognition of their state by the President of the United States. This plan, which Lincoln amplified in some respects in 1864, was, in its general outlines, followed by his successor Andrew Johnson.

Under the presidential plan of reconstruction, which did not force Negro suffrage on Southern states, new state governments were established as the Confederacy crumbled. By 1866 all of the Southern states had conformed to the terms of the plan and were ready to take their places in the Union again. But in the course of their operations the new Southern legislatures undertook to deal with the "Negro problem," and many of them enacted laws imposing severe restrictions on the rights of freedmen. These laws, known as new "black codes," excited great opposition in the North and were attacked there as attempts to restore slavery under another name.

In these circumstances reconstruction passed into its second, or congressional, stage. The war had ended and the war power of the President had been curtailed. Whatever the President might do about governments in the states that had seceded, the Senate and the House of Representatives claimed the right, by constitutional provisions, each for itself, to admit or exclude men from the South who, duly elected, were ready to take their seats.

With this weapon in their hands, radical Republicans in Congress took charge of reconstruction. In June 1866, Congress adopted a resolution to alter the federal Constitution by adding a fourteenth amendment. This proposal was intended to confer citizenship on all Negroes, establish the right of all persons to life, liberty, and property, and reduce the representation in Congress of any state which deprived adult male citizens of the right to vote in major elections. On April 9, 1866, Congress passed the first Civil Rights Act, a measure designed to assure to Negroes the full civil equality before the law enjoyed by other American citizens. In July of the same year Congress extended the life of the Freedmen's Bureau, established the previous year for the purpose of giving material relief to the emancipated slaves, and enlarged the power of the Bureau to cover protection of civil rights.

While the Fourteenth Amendment was pending before state legislatures for ratification, Congress overrode the presidential plan for reconstruction and enacted a series of bills based on different principles. These laws, the first passed on March 2, 1867, constituted a plan that was almost, if not entirely, arbitrary in nature. All the former Confederate states, except Tennessee, were divided into five military districts and each was put under the control of a Northern army officer invested with full power to keep order and supervise the process of reconstruction.

In each state a large class of former Confederate leaders was temporarily deprived of the suffrage; and the vote was given to other white men and to Negro men on equal terms. The voters so enfranchised in each state were to hold an election for the purpose of choosing delegates to a state convention authorized to frame a new constitution, including a provision for Negro manhood suffrage. On completion this constitution was to be submitted to the voters for approval or rejection. As soon as a new constitution was established by this process, the state legislature held under it was to ratify the Fourteenth Amendment. After all these steps had been taken and the Fourteenth Amendment had been proclaimed a part of the Constitution of the United States, the state thus reorganized was to be restored to the Union and its people entitled to representation in the national Congress.

The congressional plan of reconstruction was indeed a bitter pill for the former Confederates. It outlawed their recent efforts at recovering a place in the Union on other terms. But, supported by Northern arms, it was carried out. One after another Southern states yielded to its dictates. In 1868, Arkansas, Louisiana, Alabama, Georgia, Florida, South Carolina, and North Carolina complied with the terms of the plan and were restored to the Union. Texas, Mississippi, and Virginia completed the return journey in 1870. Except for Federal troops stationed in a few localities, and subject to the new conditions imposed upon all states by the Thirteenth and the Fourteenth amendments, the South had been "reconstructed."

As if not yet sure that its designs would finally prevail, Congress in 1869 submitted to the states for ratification the Fifteenth Amendment, which provided that the right of citizens of the United States to vote shall not be denied or abridged by the United States or any state on account of race, color, or previous condition of servitude. Just as the last of the states were returning to the Union in 1870 the Fifteenth Amendment was proclaimed in force.

For a brief period the governments of Southern states were in the hands of Negro men and the white men who had not been disfranchised for supporting the Confederacy. That is, in the main, voters who owned small farms or had no property at all held the reins of government. With delight, of course, they accepted the power entrusted to them and began to make laws and distribute offices with a view to their own interests. Many of their laws, for example those providing for free public education, measured up to enlightened conceptions of the age. Others fell far beneath that standard. Corruption and waste of public funds were common in the legislatures, sometimes in the grossest forms. Disgust spread among the disfranchised whites, to crown their resentment at being deprived of their former power.

Whatever the merits or demerits of the new Southern governments, disfranchised white men and white voters otherwise indignant at the new regime quickly set about overthrowing it by methods open and covert. They employed arguments and threats to keep Negroes away from the polls. Secret societies, such as the Ku Klux Klan, terrorized Negroes and their white sympathizers. In state after state "white supremacy" was re-established: in Tennessee in 1869; in Virginia and North Carolina in 1870; in Georgia the next year; in Arkansas, Alabama, and Texas in 1874; in Mississippi in 1875; and in Louisiana, Florida, and South Carolina in 1877—the year in which the withdrawal of the last Federal soldiers of occupation took place.

☆

While Southern people were groping among social and economic ruins for economic security and reorganizing state governments, Northern economy was expanding with unprecedented speed. In the decade after the war nearly 7,000,000 persons were added to the population of the country, counting new immigrants; but the increase in the North and the West was far greater than in the South. By 1870 the population in the United States had risen to 38,500,000; by 1880, to 50,100,000; by 1900, to 76,100,000. Augmented by immigration from foreign countries, the nation now had more energies, stout hearts, and willing hands to subdue the rest of the continental domain and raise the production of wealth to heights undreamed of in the fancies of the Republic's founders.

With millions of dollars at their command for investment, captains of industry leaped forward to build more factories and railways, open up and develop additional resources, and enlarge the output of machine industries in every direction. At their disposal inventors and searchers, besides improving old machines, placed new machines, materials, and processes, on which new industries of gigantic proportions were constructed. Among the discoveries and mechanical inventions of the period the following were so important as to herald the coming of a second industrial revolution:

1859—Great "strike" of petroleum in western Pennsylvania.
1868—C. L. Sholes's typewriter ready for production.
1875—G. F. Swift's refrigerator freight car in use.
1876—Alexander G. Bell sends first telephone message.
1877—Thomas Edison has a phonograph playing.
1879—George Selden's patent for a "gasoline carriage."
1882—Edison's electric power plant starts operation in New York City.
1896—Langley's airplane makes experimental flight.
1901—The Wright brothers finish an airplane glider.

Two of the machines put into use in this period meant an industrial transformation all along the line. The first was the "gas engine," the internal-combustion engine, which emancipated manufacturing and farming from the limitations of the cumbersome steam engine, and furnished an immense market for petroleum products. The second was the electric dynamo and the transmission of power by wire for use in running machines as well as lighting houses, factories, and city streets.

The extension of facilities for the transport of passengers, farm produce, and manufactures kept pace with rising industries. Between 1860 and 1890 the railway mileage increased from 30,000 miles to 166,000 miles. At the opening of the century it stood at 240,000 miles. In 1869 the last spike was driven on the central line to the Pacific and rail communications were opened from the Atlantic to the Pacific, with way stations. Within twenty years three other transcontinental lines were completed, to the north and the south of the central line. Meanwhile new railways were built in the East and the South, short lines were combined into systems, and countless little towns and villages in far-scattered rural regions were linked to the great cities and with one another. On navigable rivers, on the Great Lakes, and in coastal waters, steamships supplemented railway transportation, increasing in some waters and declining in others according to the nature of rail competition.

To the westward rush of pioneers, which had continued even during the Civil War, a powerful new impetus was now given. Northern soldiers and citizens released from the strain of war crowded to the frontier by the thousands. They were joined by thousands of aliens—German, British, Irish, and Scandinavian—fresh from the Old World. Railways facilitated the rush.

Between the tier of states on the west bank of the Mississippi River and Oregon and California on the Pacific coast, only two states had been admitted to the Union during the war period—Kansas in 1861 and Nevada in 1864. All the rest of that vast region was still sparsely settled and under territorial government when the army of Virginia laid down its arms in 1865. But the Homestead Act of 1862, the grants of land to railway companies, and laws providing for the quick sale of timber and mineral lands prepared the way for rapid settlement and for the upswing of mining, lumber, and other industries.

Never before in the history of mankind had agricultural and industrial enterprise, so well equipped with capital and machines, enjoyed such a bounteous opportunity for exploitation. Before the close of the nineteenth century practically all the arable land in the Western regions of rainfall and nearly all the grazing lands in dry or semiarid regions had passed into the hands of farmers, railway companies, stock raisers, purchasers of Spanish grants sometimes embracing hundreds of thousands of acres, land speculators, and engrossers native and foreign. The public domain, especially in Alaska, was still large. It embraced 730,000,000 acres in 1909 and included valuable forest and mineral lands.

But by 1893 it could be officially announced that the frontier hardly existed any longer; that the best of the farming lands had all been given away or sold. The America of cheap or free land had vanished forever. An epoch of nearly three hundred years had closed. The "escape valve" through which millions from the old East and from Europe had moved from poverty and unemployment to home-owning and independence on the frontier was shut. One sensational phase of economic enterprise in America was at an end.

In the lavish parceling out of the national domain, a large acreage went directly to men and women who entered lands under the Homestead Act. Relatively speaking, however, it was small in size. By 1923 approximately 213,860,000 acres had been given away to settlers real and pretended since 1868. The word "pretended" is important, for homestead entries were honeycombed with frauds; individual entrants had often acted as dummies for land and mining companies. In the course of the years at least 620,000,000 acres had been sold directly to companies and individuals, granted for the purpose of making internal improvements and building railways, or turned over to states in aid of education and other public functions.

Millions of acres of valuable timber, mineral, and grazing lands were literally stolen under the eyes of dishonest or negligent officials in the federal land office; and other millions were wrested from the government by chicanery of one kind or another. In the history of political corruption, seldom, if ever, had there been transactions on a scale so prodigious or conducted with more brazen effrontery. Thousands of great fortunes in the East as well as in the West were built out of resources wrung from the government for a pittance or for a bribe to its officials, if not actually stolen.

Nevertheless, in the process of dividing the national domain millions of new farms were staked out in the West; grazing lands fabulous in extent were brought into use and overuse by cattlemen and ranchers; and other resources were exploited by mining and manufacturing concerns. Between 1865 and 1900 billions of new wealth were added annually to the national output.

As farmers, miners, prospectors, cattlemen, and lumbermen, with or without families, poured into the Western territories, demands for statehood went up from every region. In 1867 the territory of Nebraska, reduced in size, was admitted to the Union. By 1875, Colorado claimed a population of about 100,000, largely composed of miners, farmers, cattle raisers, and prospectors. The following year it was granted statehood by Congress.

By this time the territories along the northern border of the United States were filling up and boasting of their progress. Within ten years their political leaders were knocking at the doors of Congress. In 1889 the pleas of North Dakota, South Dakota, Washington, and Montana were favorably heard and they were admitted to the Union. The next year Idaho and Wyoming took their places among the states. Having prohibited polygamy and forced the Mormons to adopt a constitution incorporating that prohibition, Congress finally conferred statehood on Utah in 1896.

This left only three regions, besides Alaska, under a territorial form of government, and they were soon given statehood. Oklahoma came into the Union in 1907 and Arizona and New Mexico in 1912.

At last the continental domain was fully organized, in forty-eight states, all presumed to be "free and equal" under the Constitution of the United States. Each now had a constitution of its own making and a government resting upon popular, if not universal, suffrage.

☆

The swift industrial development and westward expansion were made possible, in a large measure, by the stream of immigrants that flooded into the United States, subject to no retarding legal restrictions of any moment until the Chinese Exclusion Act was passed in 1882. Although the number coming into the country rose or fell from year to year, the general tendency was upward. In 1864 it was 193,000; in 1874, 313,000; in 1884, 518,000; in 1891, 560,000; in 1907, 1,285,000.

During these years striking shifts appeared in the national origins of immigrants. For a short time after 1865 the flow was still mainly from Great Britain, Ireland, Germany, and Scandinavia. Then the number of immigrants from northern Europe diminished relatively, and immigration from Italy, Russia, and Austria-Hungary increased. At the opening of the twentieth century these three countries furnished more than three fourths of all the immigrants. Polish, Hungarian, Czech, Slovak, Croat, Russian, and Jewish immigrants then far exceeded in number all the British, Irish, and Germans making their way into the United States. To give exact figures, between 1871 and 1880 the total number of immigrants from western Europe was 2,000,000, and that from eastern and southern Europe was 181,000. Between 1901 and 1910 the numbers from the two European regions were 2,000,000 and 6,100,000 respectively.

The striking shifts in the national origins of immigrants corresponded roughly to the disappearance of free land in the West and the diverting of immigrants to industries in the cities. In the urban centers immigrants of each nationality formed large colonies, or quarters, of their own, with separate languages, newspapers, and customs. Similar conditions prevailed to some extent among immigrants who settled on farms in the West; but the rise of "foreign cities" within American cities was an extraordinary characteristic of the period that followed the Civil War.

From decade to decade, as the following table shows, the number of foreign-born inhabitants in the United States rose rapidly:

1860, total, 31,400,000; foreign-born, 4,100,000
1880, total, 50,100,000; foreign-born, 6,600,000
1900, total, 76,100,000; foreign-born, 10,300,000

At the end of the century, according to these figures, about fourteen per cent of the total population was foreign-born. But the cities showed different proportions. In the cities of more than

PER CENT OF POPULATION IN CITIES HAVING OVER 30,000 INHABITANTS AND OUTSIDE SUCH CITIES FOR SPECIFIED YEARS: 1790–1916.

25,000 inhabitants in 1900, approximately twenty-six per cent, were foreign-born. For cities of over 100,000 inhabitants the proportion of foreign-born was about thirty-five per cent, and in a few of the largest cities it was fifty per cent or more. At that time the rapid inflow of immigrants indicated that the percentage of foreign-born in the cities at the next census would be still larger.

As Americans from farming regions and immigrants from abroad turned increasingly to industries and commerce for employment, the growth of urbanism destroyed the almost undisputed supremacy of the rural regions that had characterized the American past. In 1789 only about three per cent of the inhabitants were city dwellers and there were only five cities of more than 8000 inhabitants. By 1890 about one third of the people lived in towns of 4000 inhabitants or more.

Even more remarkable was the growth of great cities. In 1890 New York and Brooklyn combined had 2,300,000 inhabitants; Philadelphia and Chicago had crossed the 1,000,000 line; and Boston, Baltimore, and Washington each laid claim to 500,000. In Massachusetts, Rhode Island, and Connecticut the urban concentration of population was highest. Four fifths of the Massachusetts population lived in urban towns of 4000 or more; and in Rhode Island, nine tenths.

On every hand boasters exulted in the thought that the United States would soon outstrip, in respect of urbanism, England, where about four fifths of the people were living in towns of more than 10,000 inhabitants, as if urbanization was the crowning glory of national achievement. In fact for many years the fulfillment of the prophecy seemed a possibility.

☆

Deeply engaged, as Southerners were, in the struggle for existence among the wreckage of the war and for emancipation from the rule of Northern officials supported by arms, many of them forged ahead energetically with activities which entered into the productive expansion that covered the continent. At first planters faced the burden of getting their fields into production again. Though deprived of their chattel labor supply, they still held their lands; all the radical proposals for breaking up their estates and dividing them among freedmen and landless whites failed of realization.

Dismayed by the prospects of defeat under the new labor system, numerous planting families fled to the cities, South and North, where they went into the professions or business pursuits. Those who remained on their estates usually resorted to one or all of three devices for carrying on production: allowing the former slaves to live in their old cabins and work as before, but for wages or payment in goods; "letting" small blocks of land to freedmen or whites in return for a cash rental or a share of the crops; and selling plots outright while continuing to operate the remainder on a wage or rental basis.

The dilemma of the planters afforded opportunities to many poor whites and freedmen for acquiring land. Since colonial times small farmers had been pressed back into the uplands by the apparently relentless advance of large plantation economy from the seaboard. Now, as many great plantations dissolved, small farmers were often able to buy better land and raise their standard of living. Generally the white farmer and his family supplied all or most of the labor on his freehold; if his acreage was large he hired a few workers at wages. The more thrifty or fortunate Negroes, likewise sharing in this opportunity, were frequently able to buy land and establish homesteads.

Two figures indicate the tendency. In 1860 the average land holding in the Southern states was 335.4 acres; in 1880 it was 153.4; and in 1900 it was 138.2. Yet the tendency to dissolution was checked by the end of the century, leaving many large estates intact. Furthermore, especially in times of depression, urban bankers, lawyers, merchants, investors, and corporations acquired extensive holdings of Southern land and frequently demonstrated the efficiency of large-scale farming as against small-farming, for which skill or capital was lacking.

It was in relation to the system of land economy that emancipated Negro men and women had to find footholds for themselves. If planters had been able to furnish adequate capital and pay wages regularly, many more Negroes would have become permanent wage workers on the land. But the planters after the war were usually handicapped by lack of money. Often they obtained credit for supplies from merchants and furnished the Negroes who worked for them with food, clothing, and shelter as they had done in the slave system; but at the end of the year, in the settlement, the Negroes were likely to have no balance coming to them as wages. They were apt to be in debt to the planter, even when the books were honestly kept by their employers.

Under the wage system Negroes grew discouraged and restless. Thousands left the land for neighboring or distant towns and sought employment as domestic or casual laborers. The more determined among those who remained in the country struggled hard to procure land to be worked on other than wage terms—to achieve an economic underwriting. Many became renters of small farms, paying their rent in a share of the crops—the "sharecroppers." Others by dint of exacting labor and thrift became owners of land, either outright or on mortgage. In 1874, nine years after emancipation, Negroes owned 338,769 acres of land in Georgia alone, either outright or subject to mortgage. By the end of the century, it was estimated, about one fourth of the Negro workers on the land had become freeholders of the one type or the other.

On the whole, particularly as to the production of cotton, none of these schemes for land use proved to be highly efficient. It was not until 1880 that the Southern cotton crop, measured in bales, rose again to the figure of 1860. It is true that twenty years later, in 1900, the output of cotton was about three fourths larger than it had been in 1860, but that was in part due to the extension of the cotton belt in Texas where white labor and management predominated.

If Southern economy had been compelled to depend as largely on cotton production as in the ante-bellum days, its prospects would have been dismal. But diversification in agriculture offered other sources of wealth. To the old staples—cotton, tobacco, rice, and sugar—new products were added: apples, peaches, oranges, lemons, pineapples, peanuts, watermelons, and vegetables in a large variety. As the mileage of railways increased and rapid transportation by refrigerator cars developed, Southern agriculture found large home markets for these commodities in neighboring cities and in the distant North. Thus the subordination of the South as a raw-material province utterly dependent on the world cotton market at Liverpool was mitigated by diversification and by the creation of special ties with the national market.

The stresses and strains of the struggle for existence on the land were also relieved by the growth of manufacturing in the South —an economic enterprise which contributed materially to the expansion of the national productive activities so typical of the period between 1865 and 1900. Leadership in Southern manufacturing enterprise, as Arthur M. Schlesinger has pointed out in *The Rise of the City*, was taken by industrialists who came, in overwhelming proportions, from Southern families outside the former slave-owning groups. During the early stages of its development both capital and management also sprang principally from Southern sources. Thus history seemed to vindicate Southern writers who had claimed before 1860 that the slave system hampered the direction of Southern energies to the industrial use of rich natural resources right at hand.

Scarcely had the brazen clangor of the fratricidal war subsided when Southern promoters exclaimed: "Bring the mills to the cotton!" By 1880 Southern cotton mills were turning out a volume of goods equal to almost one fourth the output of New England's mills. Between 1860 and 1900 the number of Southern spindles increased from 298,000 to 4,300,000. The rise of tobacco manufactures was hardly less spectacular, especially in Virginia, North Carolina, and Kentucky.

In the expansion of capitalist enterprise great coal beds were opened and worked in the Appalachian regions from Maryland to northern Alabama. All the way from Virginia through Alabama to Arkansas and Texas immense deposits of iron ore were unearthed and forced to yield supplies for iron mills; in a few years Birmingham, Alabama, took pride in being "the Pittsburgh of the South." In Kentucky, Tennessee, Louisiana, Arkansas, and Texas petroleum was discovered and the products of the oil industry were added to Southern wealth. Cotton, tobacco, coal, iron, and oil industries were supplemented by the lumber and cottonseed industries. At the opening of the new century the output of Southern lumber mills more than equaled that of the mills in the huge forests of the Great Lakes region.

In the train of the Southern industrial revolution followed the manifold consequences of such an economic upheaval. Around mines, factories, mills, and other scenes of operation congregated armies of industrial workers. Since immigrants from foreign countries generally preferred to settle in the North and West, Southern enterprise had to draw mainly on local sources for its labor supply. Into its industries were lured men, women, and children from rural communities—thousands of "poor whites" from the pine barrens, the uplands, and the mountains, where they had lived on the very margin of subsistence. Now they were to have some cash and be drawn into the social movements of the nation.

As in the North long before, new factory towns shot up in Southern rural scenes, and old towns grew rapidly in population. Richmond, Atlanta, Birmingham, Dallas, Houston, and San Antonio became thriving centers of manufacturing and commerce. To cope with the demands for transportation additional railway lines were built, old lines improved, and consolidations made among short lines. Between 1865 and 1880 the mileage was more than doubled. By 1900 it had been more than doubled again.

Before Hinton Rowan Helper, author of the prophetic *Impending Crisis*, died in 1909 the planters and merchants who had led the South in the days of slavery had been challenged and undermined by white farmers, by great industrialists, by high-powered merchants, and by industrial workers—with their persistent and special interests. Although in national elections the South as a rule seemed "solid," it was in fact divided into strong factions over the problems that went with the swift transformation of its economy—as it was drawn tighter and tighter into the expanding economy of other sections, North and West.

CHAPTER XIX

Centralization of Economy

BEFORE THE PROCESS of economic expansion had reached the continental borders, economic centralization was setting in; that is, the self-sufficiency and independence of families and communities were diminishing, and their insufficiency and interdependence were increasing. If, as Brooks Adams declared in *The Law of Civilization and Decay*, published in 1895, the movement of energies in society is inexorably toward centralization, the course of economic and political affairs in the United States certainly provided illustrations. Indeed the swiftness of the economic expansion had been made possible in a large measure by centralizing activities of private enterprise and the federal government.

Without the lavish aids from the federal Treasury the continental railways, facilitating the westward expansion, could not have been built so rapidly. Without the protection against the Indians afforded by the United States Army the frontier settlements could not have been pushed to the Pacific within such a short time. Without the investment and speculative activities of Eastern capitalists and corporations, often aided by foreign loans, the resources of the West would have lain dormant for many years to come if not permanently.

In turn the very nature of the dispersion of economic activities over the continental domain in itself worked for centralization. Above all it was marked by intense specialization. Colonization between the Mississippi Valley and the Pacific Ocean, unlike that in the old Northwest Territory, was not principally colonization by farming families whose homesteads were at first made largely self-sufficing by domestic manufacturing as well as by food production. By climate, soil, and resources each region in the Far West was fitted for one or more particular lines of production—wheat, corn, cattle, lumber, or minerals. For a long time Western industries were limited to a few specialties, such as the milling of grains and minerals or the manufacture of timber products. It was only by specialization that settlers could make the highest profits.

If these special interests in agriculture and industry had not been furnished outlets by railway lines into the national markets, they would have proceeded at a slow pace, comparable perhaps to the languid ways of Spanish landlords in the early history of the Southwest. It was the rapid communication with the larger markets that enabled special agricultural interests to flourish so luxuriantly and in such a short time. Similar conditions made possible the rapid advance of the South in agriculture and industry after the war at the middle of the nineteenth century.

Specialization and integration, of course, were indispensable features of the mechanical revolution in industry. Their rise and growth rested on the extension of markets and the protection of the government that assured the unity of the American markets. In short, as the Industrial Revolution spread, as farming pioneers between 1865 and 1890 pushed into the regions of the Far West, where climate, soil, and resources were peculiar, a higher degree of centralization became necessary to the lucrative expansion of production.

Indeed the settlement itself on a large scale was associated with the building and operation of railway lines—the arteries of commerce which made local specialties profitable. Amounts of capital relatively monumental were required to construct and operate even short lines of fifty or a hundred miles. Only companies or corporations of limited liability were likely to take the original risk or could have raised the money required to make the venture a reality, as had been the case in early English colonization. The longer the lines, the greater the capital needed, the more certain the reliance on corporate enterprise. To cross and encompass the continental domain called for sums of money which made the outlays of the New England factory builders look trifling.

After the principal long and short lines were completed, consolidations among them into systems and trunk lines, advantageous to the rapid and efficient movement of freight and passengers, were effected. They were engineered by actual mergers and physical connections, or by agreements for pooling and routing trains. This process was marred by frauds, gambling ventures, and

The Bettmann Archive.

Brown Brothers photo.

Amid the upheavals of the democratic age the idea of civilization broadened and deepened in the consciousness of the people. The invention of cheaper printing methods and the rise of the public platform favored an increase in the number of thinkers dedicated to the business of speaking and writing. Thousands of Americans attended lectures and heard letters, art, science, and issues of the times discussed by the "best minds" of the nation. This was the era of Emerson, Bryant, Hawthorne, Irving, Whitman, and many other notable writers.

Painting by R. C. Woodville. Juley photo.

Painting by R. F. Heinrich.
Courtesy National Life Insurance Co.

With the reading public enlarged by popular and secular education, publishers of newspapers, books, and magazines reached out for its patronage and the market widened for essays articles, and books dealing with every theme of human interest. Writers and speakers argued for innumerable reforms and the reforming zeal of the age struck at the slave codes and at the institution of slavery itself.

Painting by Henry Alexander.
Brown Brothers photos.

So fruitful and varied was progress in knowledge of the natural sciences in the democratic era that it opened up visions of human welfare never before imagined. Advances no less striking were made in medicine and surgery. All in all the "era of the common man," the "fabulous forties," and the fermenting fifties was a time of dramatic mental activity and creative thinking.

Brown Brothers photo.

Painting by Joseph Boggs Beale.
Modern Enterprises, Phila., Pa.

AUCTION
SALE
OF
SLAVES

1831

The Missouri Compromise of 1820
definitely divided the Union into
North and South—free states and slave
states. During the struggle over the
Compromise of 1850, with both sides
seeking peace, the Whigs were under
the leadership of Henry Clay and
Daniel Webster. Had the Democrats
been content, the issue of slavery in
the new territories might have been
allowed to languish but under the
leadership of Stephen A. Douglas
Congress abrogated the old Missouri
Compromise and a subject long regarded as closed became the subject
of a nation-wide clash.

Painting by Thomas Hovenden. Ewing Galloway photo.

Over the bright horizon of Democratic prospects in 1854, a tornado was brewing. After the repeal of the Missouri Compromise an opposition party, to be known as the Republican Party, began preparations to exclude slavery from the territories. Far and wide abolitionists in the North inflamed antagonism against slavery. Harriet Beecher Stowe's *Uncle Tom's Cabin* excited a million readers, and John Brown's ill-fated attempt to start a general slave insurrection threw fuel on the fire.

Painting by Joseph Boggs Beale. Modern Enterprises, Phila., Pa.

Watching the tides of public opinion through these turbulent years was a Whig of Illinois—Abraham Lincoln. Nominated by the Republicans as a candidate for the United States Senate he opposed Stephen A. Douglas, the Democratic candidate, in a series of debates. Here he manifested qualities of greatness—an exceptional knowledge of American history and government, barbed analytical skill, and genius as an orator. Although defeated in the election he emerged a national figure and a leader commanding confidence and admiration.

News of Lincoln's election as President in November 1860 was taken as a signal for secession in South Carolina. Before his inauguration the following March seven more Southern states had followed this example and Jefferson Davis had been inaugurated President of the Confederate States of America. The Union seemed to be dissolving. Having withdrawn from the Union and fired the first gun at Fort Sumter, the Confederacy was confronted with the task of making real by arms the independence it had asserted. If the Union was to be saved Lincoln and his advisors had to prepare for an invasion of the South.

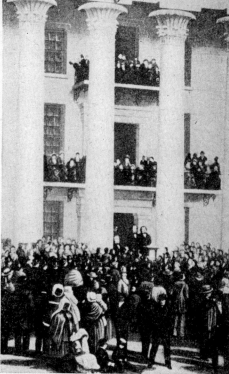

In the Proclamation of Emancipation, issued January 1, 1863, Lincoln declared all slaves free thenceforward and forever in the parts of the South then under arms against the Union. In that year Lee invaded Pennsylvania, was stopped at Gettysburg, and retired to Virginia. In November 1863 Lincoln delivered his Gettysburg Address. The year 1864 opened with Lee's army apparently invincible in defense. At its close Sherman had taken Atlanta and Savannah and Grant was laying siege to Petersburg. The last phase of the war was drawing to an end.

Brown Brothers photo.
Painting by Rico Tomaso.
Courtesy New York Life Insurance Co.

Petersburg fell to Grant April 2, 1865, and the next day the Union flag floated over the Confederate capital at Richmond. On April 9, finding hope forlorn, Lee surrendered to Grant at Appomattox and at long last the war had run its course. For less than half its cost, freedom of all the slaves could have been bought under the compensated emancipation proposed by President Lincoln and Congress in 1862.

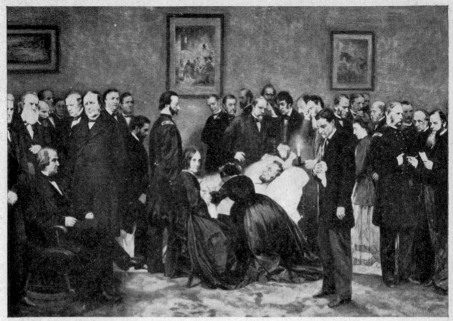

Painting by John D. Bachelder. Brown Brothers photos.

In the campaign of 1864 the outlook for Lincoln's re-election was dark. With gratitude to the people for re-electing him, he was preparing for a peace of conciliation when, on April 15, 1865, he died at the hands of an assassin—John Wilkes Booth. The Vice-President, Andrew Johnson, took up the burden and with the office came much of the criticism directed against Lincoln's conciliatory attitude toward the Confederates. Animosity reached such a pitch that he was impeached and he escaped conviction only by the margin of a single vote in the Senate.

Radical Republicans in Congress took
charge of reconstruction and a Reconstruction Committee was appointed. A
series of acts placed the South under military rule and outlawed former Confederates. For a brief period government in
the Southern states was mainly in the
hands of Negro men and white men who
had not loyally supported the Confederacy, and corruption and waste of public funds were common in the legislatures. Indignant disfranchised white men
quickly set about the overthrow of the
new regime, and by 1877 "white supremacy" was re-established.

Samuel Morse flashed the first message by electric telegraph between Washington and Baltimore in 1844. By the close of the sixth decade all the main regions between the Atlantic and Mississippi were bound together by telegraph wires and in 1866 Cyrus Field completed the laying of the Atlantic cable and messages were passing between America and the Old World.

Painting by Hull. Keystone View Co. photo.   *The Bettmann Archive.*

In 1869 the last spike was driven on the central line to the Pacific and rail communications were opened from the Atlantic to the Pacific. Within twenty years three other transcontinental lines were completed. Meanwhile new railways were built in the East and South, short lines were combined into systems and countless little towns and villages in far-scattered rural regions were linked to the great cities and with one another.

Painting by Oscar Berninghaus. Courtesy Treasury Department Art Project. The Bettmann Archive.

Northern soldiers and citizens released from the strain of war crowded to the frontier. The Homestead Act of 1862, the grants of land to railway companies, and laws providing for the quick sale of timber and mineral lands prepared the way for rapid settlement and for the upswing of mining, lumbering, and other industries. Millions of acres of valuable land were literally stolen under the eyes of federal land office officials and thousands of great fortunes were built out of the resources wrung from the government. By 1893 the frontier hardly existed and the America of cheap or free land had vanished forever.

Paintings by W. R. Leigh. Courtesy Woolaroc Museum, Frank Phillips Ranch, Bartlesville, Okla. Acme (below).

Without the lavish aids from the federal Treasury to the continental railways and the protection against Indians afforded by the United States Army, the westward expansion could not have proceeded so rapidly. The last serious stand against white encroachment on their lands was made in 1876 by the Indians at the Battle of the Big Horn where General Custer and his entire command were destroyed.

Paintings by Tom Lea, William E. L. Bunn, and Oscar Berninghaus. Courtesy Section of Fine Arts, Public Buildings Administration.

Climate, soil, and resources fitted each region in the Far West for one or more particular lines of production—wheat, corn, cattle, lumber, or minerals. As farmers, miners, prospectors, cattlemen, and lumbermen poured into the Western territories, demands for statehood went up from every region. With the admission of Arizona to statehood in 1912 the continental domain was at last organized in forty-eight "free and equal" states under the Constitution of the United States.

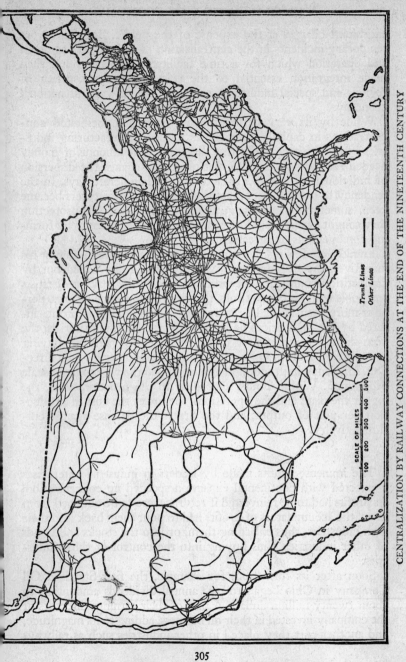

SCALE OF MILES
0 100 200 300 400 500

Trunk Lines
Other Lines

CENTRALIZATION BY RAILWAY CONNECTIONS AT THE END OF THE NINETEENTH CENTURY

exorbitant charges at the expense of the public. But these were temporary incidents in the centralization of railway management and operation which for a time facilitated dispersion and then made integration essential to the existence and prosperity of regions and special industries—to the whole network of national economy.

While by its very nature railway expansion facilitated concentrations in capital, other forces pushed manufacturing industries in the same co-ordinative direction. The amount of money needed for the building of great plants ran against the dispersion of individual ownership characteristic of handicraft days. In the tendency to overbuild, competition among manufacturers became keen, sometimes sanguinary; and often in sheer self-protection they sought escape from low returns or even bankruptcy by forming combinations or agreements.

Frankly confessing that the profit motive was high among his incentives, the manufacturer who saw his profits wiped out by competition could turn the profit motive to the making of trusts and pools with his competitors, thereby reaping some returns, perhaps more than he had been reaping. Or, finding his profits injured by the high prices he had to pay for his raw materials, the keen-sighted manufacturer could increase his gains by buying raw-material sources and concentrating them under his own direction. Efficiency in production also smoothed the way to large-scale production. Within limits, according to the processes used, the bigger the plant and the operations, the lower the cost of production per unit of output, and the firmer the defense against cut-throat rivalry.

☆

The immense profits made by leaders in industrial enterprises connected with continental expansion speeded up concentration. As profits had to be reinvested if returns were to be obtained from them, the accumulators of profits had to pour them back into their own industries, thus enlarging them, or into the stocks and bonds of other industries, thus buying into the control of those industries.

Soon after its formation, for example, the first Standard Oil Company in Ohio began to pay annual dividends amounting to about twenty million dollars. A part of their earnings directors of the company invested in their oil business, adding to its magnitude, and another part they placed in other industries such as railways and iron mining. By 1887, William Rockefeller had become a director of the Chicago, Milwaukee, and St. Paul Railroad, and John D. Rockefeller had bought his way into a number of railways and into a great company engaged in opening up the iron resources of Minnesota. About the same time Andrew Carnegie was extending the area of his control by investing profits from iron manufactures in railways, mining, and Great Lakes shipping. In the course of time, as concentration proceeded, the same industrialist might be serving as a director in ten or fifteen highly diversified manufacturing concerns.

A similar expansion and concentration occurred in nearly all the great staple manufacturing industries as the Industrial Revolution advanced after 1865. In 1873 a group of capitalists headed by Andrew Carnegie, who had accumulated the necessary means in iron, coal, railways, oil, and bridgemaking, started a monster steel mill on the banks of the Monongahela near Pittsburgh. A few years later this group acquired the Homestead Works in the same neighborhood. In the next decade the Carnegie interests became affiliated with the coal and coke business of H. C. Frick and Company; and several other works were united in the huge Carnegie Steel Corporation.

Now firmly established, the Carnegie concern branched out by buying beds of iron ore in the Lake Superior region. To cut freight charges it opened a railway line from Pittsburgh to Lake Erie and, putting a fleet of ore carriers on the Great Lakes, it established direct and cheaper connections between mines and mills. Then, to the dismay of competitors, it proposed, partly as a threat to the J. P. Morgan interests, to diversify its operations by manufacturing many other iron products, such as wire, hitherto beyond its scope of activities.

At this point in the development of the Carnegie interests, iron and steel men and their bankers began to fear that the competition of the new facilities would end in overproduction and the ruin of many companies. Manufacturers of raw iron were invading the field of finished products already occupied by independent producers. They were closing in on the coal, ore mining, and transport business. It looked as if a battle of the giants might end in disaster for the weaker men.

Put on guard by these tendencies and seeing a chance to make more money, the J. P. Morgan banking company in New York City took the lead in forming the first billion-dollar corporation in the history of the country. Under its direction in 1901 a consolidation of many concerns was effected in the United States Steel Company, and $1,400,000,000 in stocks and bonds was issued to the parties in the transaction. To the Morgan underwriting syndicate, stock having the cash value of $62,500,000 was given in the form of a commission for its services.

Later the Federal Bureau of Corporations estimated that the tangible value of the property of the corporation in 1901, the year of its establishment, was $682,000,000, against which $1,400,000,000 in stocks and bonds had been issued. How correct was this estimate became a matter of dispute, but at all events the common stock of the concern soon fell with a crash, and many outsiders who had risked their money in the venture lost heavily.

While Andrew Carnegie was operating in iron and coal resources which, as he afterward said, he got for little outlay of money, John D. Rockefeller was working in the new petroleum industry, first at Cleveland, Ohio. Having hoarded his earnings as a clerk and small merchant, he began to invest in the construction of oil refineries. Soon he found competition keen and, for self-protection as well as for the sake of gain, he set about forming a combination to "stabilize" if not control the local oil business.

After experimenting with small undertakings of this kind, Rockefeller united, in 1870, a group of capitalists in the Standard Oil Company of Ohio and embarked on oil refining on a mammoth scale. With a view to increasing its power, the Rockefeller group took over the South Improvement Company two years later and used it as a means of securing from railway companies rebates or special rates on its shipments of oil, and other favors profitable to the oil company. By extending its operations to the production of oil in the fields, and the transport of oil by pipe lines to the Atlantic coast, the Standard Oil Company of Ohio and its subsidiaries got control over about nine tenths of the refining business within ten years after its formation.

In 1882 the Rockefeller group centralized its many concerns in the form of a trust; that is, the stocks of its concerns were placed in the hands of a few trustees, including John D. Rockefeller, in exchange for "trust certificates of ownership." A few years later the Standard Oil Company of New Jersey, one of its concerns already doing business in New Jersey, was enlarged and in effect assumed responsibility for the management of the trust.

This step was taken under a New Jersey law empowering companies duly incorporated to buy, hold, and vote stock in any other corporation or corporations in New Jersey or any other state—in other words, permitting it to form a "holding company" for the purpose of centralizing control in one industry or many industries. Under this device the Standard Oil Company of New Jersey was able, within a year, to dominate from two thirds to three fourths of the national business in oil and oil products; and to pay its stockholders annually, for several years, from thirty to forty-eight per cent in dividends.

With perhaps even more speed concentration was brought about in the new electrical industry. To secure capital and aid in developing his patents for electric motors, dynamos, lamps, and other products, Thomas Edison, with the help of J. P. Morgan and other financiers, established the Edison Electric Light Company in 1878. After several competing concerns had appeared in the industry, a combination of the Edison and other interests was brought about by the formation of the General Electric Company in 1892. About the same time another consolidation of electrical interests was made by George Westinghouse and his friends, with the incorporation of the Westinghouse Electric and Manufacturing Company. Soon the two companies reached working agreements as to the joint use of patents and divided between them the major portion of the manufacturing business in the chief lines, despite the rise, especially in subsidiary lines, of many independent manufacturers.

Efforts equally determined, if often less successful, were made during this age of industrial expansion to get control over the production of other staple articles of manufacture and mining—sugar, copper, linseed oil, cottonseed oil, whisky, plate glass, and coal, for instance. In 1884 a combination appeared in cottonseed oil; in 1885 in linseed oil; in 1887 in sugar, lead, whisky, cordage, plate glass, and wire nails; in 1899 smelters and coal producers drew together; in 1900 the sugar "trust" was established.

Some of these companies were short-lived and their careers were marked by dubious if not corrupt practices. Others suffered from bad luck and were merged in larger organizations. But by the end of the century the major portion of manufacturing in each of several great lines was concentrated in the hands of corporations—in some lines, a few corporations.

Although not many of these gigantic concerns had complete monopolies in their fields of business, they had a power so great that they could often exercise a decisive influence over the cost of raw materials, the prices of finished products, and the fortunes of independent competitors. Besides wielding the control over their particular areas of the national economy such as oil or steel, corporation promoters built up a wider dominion over economy in general, over politics, and over public opinion by creating interlocking directorates among corporations and other forms of affiliation with business interests.

Concentration in industrial enterprise was facilitated by concentration in the banking business. A vast amount of money was needed for the construction of plants and for current operations. Special agencies were necessary to sell stocks and bonds to investors in large blocks. Here strong banks proved to be valuable adjuncts, and bankers found opportunities to harvest mounting profits. They made loans to corporations, aided in forming combinations among them, and took part in the sale of their securities.

For carrying on the more extensive operations several banks often joined to form an "underwriting syndicate." In the division of financial business certain banks became associated with particular enterprises; for example, the J. P. Morgan Company with the New York Central Railroad Company and the United States Steel Company. In many cases, even early in the process of centralization, bankers took the initiative or actively participated in the creation of trusts, corporations, and combinations.

Since bankers usually acquired vital interests in the companies they financed, it became a common practice to put bank presidents and directors on the boards of trustees in charge of railway and manufacturing companies. By way of reciprocity, heads of industrial corporations were also installed among the directors of banks. Through various banking activities a substantial part of the control over industry passed from the original magnates of manufacturing to magnates of finance. So industrial capitalism was transformed into what was called "finance capitalism."

Inasmuch as the greatest banks, the headquarters of numerous corporations, and the chief stock exchange for dealing in corporation securities were in New York City, that metropolis became the principal center of consolidation in the United States. There bankers and corporation presidents mingled freely with one another. Often they engaged in spectacular battles over power and wealth. Often they united in the exercise of control over finance and industry, adding personal union to legal and economic union.

In his book, *The Truth about the Trusts* (1904), a contemporary expert in financial affairs, John Moody, described the situation in the following language: "Around these two groups [the Morgan-Rockefeller interests], or what must ultimately become one greater group, all other smaller groups of capitalists congregate. They are all allied and intertwined by their various mutual interests. For instance, the Pennsylvania Railroad interests are on the one hand allied with the Vanderbilts and on the other hand with the Rockefellers. The Vanderbilts are closely allied with the Morgan group, and both the Pennsylvania and the Vanderbilt interests have recently become the dominating factors in the Reading system, a former Morgan road and the most important part of the anthracite coal combine which had always been dominated by the Morgan people. . . . Viewed as a whole, we find the dominating influences in the trusts to be made up of an intricate network of large and small capitalists, many allied to another by ties of more or less importance, but all being appendages to or parts of the greater groups which are themselves dependent on and allied with the two mammoth, or Rockefeller and Morgan groups. These two mammoth groups jointly . . . constitute the heart of the business and commercial life of the nation." At this state had American economy arrived thirty years after the death of Abraham Lincoln, whose life had been sacrificed to the preservation of the Union and the emancipation of slaves.

☆

Paralleling in time, though not in power, the expansion, diversification, and concentration in manufacturing, transportation, and finance were efforts to effect a consolidation among dispersed industrial workers. Unlike capitalists who throve on profits from war industries during the civil conflict, industrial workers found it difficult, if not impossible in that wartime, to force an upturn in wages equal to the rise in the cost of living. Yet they sought to make advances in that direction by increasing the number of trade unions; and they came out of the war with many gains in organization.

At its close the number of local unions existing in 1860 had about trebled and to the national craft unions already formed had been added at least ten new national unions of that type. But the membership of all the unions, local and national, was small; under 250,000, it is reckoned. Even so, in 1865 nearly every large industrial city had, besides its local craft unions, a city trades assembly representing the crafts. Certain labor leaders considered the time ripe to renew the attempt, made back in 1834, to effect a permanent consolidation of unions on a national scale.

Leadership in this undertaking was assumed by W. H. Sylvis, a veteran idealist in the labor movement. In 1864, largely at his instigation, a convention called the Industrial Assembly of North America was held at Louisville, Kentucky, and a plan was framed for establishing a continent-wide association of labor organizations. At a following convention, in Baltimore in 1866, the plan was carried out by the formation of the National Labor Union.

Based mainly on the representation of local unions and city trades assemblies, not directly on national craft unions, the new organization was one degree removed from strictly craft interests. It strove, it is true, to secure the recognition of unions by employers, to raise wages, to reduce hours, and to establish the practice of adjusting labor relations by agreements between employers and employees. Yet the National Labor Union also tried to promote various political and social reforms, including the establishment of workshops owned and managed co-operatively by the workers.

Some of its demands, such as an eight-hour day for certain federal employees, were granted, but its main projects for social reform fell by the wayside. Gradually "pure and simple" trade unionists, interested primarily in wages and hours of work, began to desert the organization. After a troubled existence of six years the National Labor Union perished for lack of support.

Meanwhile another project for uniting industrial workers in a single national organization was taking shape on broader organizational lines. The germ of this movement was the Noble Order of the Knights of Labor, a local union formed among garment workers at Philadelphia by Uriah Stephens in 1869. By much agitation several unions of the kind were established in that city and in other industrial cities of the East.

Believing that the hour had struck for a concentration of forces, leaders in these unions called, in 1875, a national convention to which they invited representatives of other associations as well as their own. Out of this assembly the Knights of Labor expanded into a national organization capable of exerting for more than ten years a powerful influence in the industrial world and in labor debate and opinion.

In form and policy the Knights of Labor made departures from the attempts to federate the craft unions composed of skilled workers. It is true that the Knights sought the co-operation of local and national craft unions as fellow members of its order; but its aspiration was broader than theirs in that it tried to unite all laborers, skilled and unskilled, men and women, white and colored, with the castes of trades and crafts, in one big union. While it campaigned for higher standards of labor conditions and rewards within industrial plants and carried on many strikes, local and general, in efforts to gain these ends it did more. Like the National Labor Union, it sponsored co-operative workshops among industrial workers. Still more: it cherished a dream of transforming the capitalist system into a socialist commonwealth. As a step in that direction it advocated the public ownership of utilities such as railways and waterworks.

By its effective battles for higher wages and extensive social reforms, the Order of Knights of Labor for some time drew into its ranks thousands of actual industrial workers and thousands of sympathizers belonging to the middle class not gainfully employed in industry. At the height of its vigor, about 1880, when Terence V. Powderly was at its head as "Master Workman," it claimed an enrollment of approximately 700,000 men and women; and employers then felt themselves in the presence of an ominous challenge to capitalism. But rather suddenly a rapid decline of the Order and its power set in, due in part to the failure of mass strikes, to the strong desire of workers for immediate advances in wages and a reduction of hours, and to the disdain of craft unionists for the methods and ideals of the Knights.

Strong as it proved to be for about ten years, the Knights of Labor movement did not submerge the local craft unions, the city trades assemblies, or the national organization of crafts, from many of which it received aid. On the contrary, such unions were growing in numbers and power while the Knights were still apparently dominant. From year to year new federal unions of crafts were formed: for example cigar makers in 1864; railroad conductors in 1868; locomotive firemen in 1873; iron and steel workers in 1876; and cotton spinners in 1878.

By 1884 the national craft unions, claiming 300,000 members in good standing, showed signs of permanence despite their vicissitudes. Several of the national craft unions were led by capable men and had money in their treasuries. This was especially true of the cigar makers, with whom were associated Adolph Strasser and Samuel Gompers, both hardheaded and skillful in the work of organization and administration. In their national organization the central officers had full authority over local unions, and a part of the dues were set aside to build up benefit funds for members in distress for various reasons or unemployed. Here in firmly knit national craft unions were solid materials for the next and more successful step in concentration—a federation of all unions in one national association, with strong treasuries for tiding the members over the hazards of strikes, competently managed by directors loyal to the interests of the members.

Labor leaders of the "practical" type, quick to appreciate the opportunity before them, now urged the creation of a national organization more limited in structure and purpose than the Order of the Knights of Labor with its miscellaneous membership and its broad program of social reconstruction. At Pittsburgh in 1881 the new labor leaders took action by forming the Federation of Organized Trades and Labor Unions at a convention representing national unions, local unions, and Knights of Labor assemblies in the United States and Canada. Yet even the newest federation did not prosper at once.

Unbeaten, however, its sponsors summoned another conference of delegates, at Columbus, Ohio, in 1886; and after searching debates they merged their organizations in an association called the American Federation of Labor. This federation they grounded squarely on strong national unions of crafts already in existence, state federations of unions, and city assemblies. Representation of mere local craft unions they allowed only in cases where such unions were not federated into national craft organizations.

Under the leadership of Samuel Gompers, who served as president until his death in 1924, except for one year, the American Federation of Labor pursued a utilitarian policy—trade unionism "pure and simple." Gompers had been associated with socialism but now he avoided radical theories, defeating efforts of socialists to capture the federation. The organization clung steadfastly to a simple program: standard hours and wages; fair conditions of labor; collective bargaining with employers; and the accumulation of benefit funds for meeting emergencies. It accepted the capitalistic system of production and ownership and sought to improve the position of labor, especially skilled labor, within that framework. Refraining from declarations of unmitigated class warfare, the federation co-operated where it could with associations of employers and citizens interested in securing to labor bargaining privileges in the industrial world; with the National Civic Federation, for instance.

The success of the American Federation of Labor soon gave wide currency to three rather obvious interpretations of history: first, the Industrial Revolution had brought into being a numerous and permanent body of working men and women, despite the fluidity of class lines; second, the individual worker, with little or no savings between himself and want, was not "equal" in a wage negotiation—under "freedom of contract"—to a million-dollar corporation ruled by industrial magnates; and, third, only by unions of workers could a "fair balance" in wage negotiations be attained.

It was hard for Americans, who were still thinking in terms of handicrafts and freehold farming, to accept facts so "foreign" to old American experience. But in time many citizens acknowledged the changed situation and began to be active in bringing about fundamental modifications in the laws respecting the right of labor to organize, deal collectively with employers, procure better working conditions, and have recognition as one of the great interests of the nation. In the program, tactics, and gains of American organized labor and its middle-class sympathizers the thesis of the unmitigated class war, evolved on the continent of feudal Europe, was completely disavowed.

Though stoutly opposed to the formation of a separate labor party with a blanket program of radical reforms, the American Federation of Labor did, nonetheless, put forward at its annual conventions specific demands for new laws to be won by political action. It called for legislation to provide safety in industries and mines, compensation for workers injured in the course of their duties, the abolition of child labor, equal pay for men and women engaged in equal work, the regulation of the use of injunctions in labor disputes, and indeed a long list of definite proposals. At elections leaders of the federation resorted to the political tactics of "rewarding our friends and punishing our enemies." In presidential elections they often tried to throw the labor vote to the Democrats in return for concessions of one kind or another.

Starting with a membership of about 150,000 in 1886, the American Federation of Labor soon doubled it and by 1904 reported that 1,670,000 workers were on its union rolls. Outside its jurisdiction, but usually co-operative, were other powerful national unions. Among the independent unions the four railway brotherhoods—engineers, firemen, conductors, and maintenance men—had first rank.

Fifty years after the close of the Civil War approximately 3,000,000 industrial workers had been organized on a national scale, centralized through federation, and bound together on a program that presaged not only permanence but growth in numbers and power, economic and political. Although they demanded no overthrow of capitalism, likewise in the process of centralization, they were determined to dictate some of the terms on which capitalism was to function. Whether or not by their actions they increased the proportion of the total annual output that went to labor as a whole, they had certainly wrung favorable laws from legislatures and raised wages for the highly organized craft unionists. Though they spurned independent labor party action, they were active in politics and made labor increasingly conscious of its political strength, actual and potential.

☆

Accompanying and promoting centralization in the sphere of industrial ownership and operation was a centralization of legal power provided mainly by the federal judiciary. Under the Constitution of the United States as it stood in 1860, the ownership of property and the conduct of industrial enterprises were wholly within the authority of the several states, except insofar as interstate and foreign commerce were involved. Each state by law defined property for itself and determined what should be the limits imposed on the use of property. The power to charter corporations and control their management also belonged to the states. Therefore capitalists, corporations, and other industrial concerns that had grounds, real or imaginary, for complaining against state laws and the actions of state officials had to resort, as a rule, to state legislatures and state courts for relief. Only in a narrow range of cases could the federal courts accept appeals, intervene on their behalf, and afford them protection. But in 1868 the Fourteenth Amendment became a part of the federal Constitution. Henceforward the ultimate protection of life, liberty, property, privileges, and immunities was to be a function of the federal judiciary, with the United States Supreme Court as the final tribunal of appeal.

Although many advocates of the Fourteenth Amendment insisted that it "nationalized civil liberty"—put everything affecting liberty and property under national authority—the Supreme Court of the United States refused to accept that view for several years after the adoption of this amendment. It held that the amendment was mainly, though not exclusively, designed to sustain the civil rights of the newly emancipated slaves, and not to reduce the historic power of the states over personal and property rights.

At that stage in its interpretation of the amendment, the Court ruled that each state could regulate, for example, the rates of railways within its borders; and when railway companies complained that they were deprived of their property by such regulations the Court told them that they must look to the state legislatures for help, not to the federal courts. Judicial decisions of this type thus continued the dispersion of legal power over property, corporations, and industry among the states, that had prevailed in the days of agricultural supremacy in 1787 when about ninety per cent of the people were engaged in farming.

Under such judicial rulings business corporations operating throughout the country were subject to the varied and often conflicting regulations of as many legislatures as there were states in the Union. Efficient centralization in corporate management became difficult if not impossible. Endless lawsuits over regulations and taxation in states and endless conflicts with state politicians harassed and impeded the formation and operations of corporations, trusts, and combines, as concentration proceeded in industry and transportation. Not without reason did lawyers for dissatisfied capitalists insist that such "anarchy," such a dispersion of legal authority to regulate and control the use of property, if appropriate for earlier times, was unfitted to the prosecution of industrial enterprise on a national scale. Well paid for their advice, lawyers for corporations kept appealing to the Supreme Court of the United States for protection against state legislation adversely affecting the property interests of their clients.

Eventually they were successful in getting a reinterpretation of the Fourteenth Amendment. Under that amendment corporations were "persons" at law and no "person" could be deprived of life, liberty, or property without due process of law. As justices of the Supreme Court died or resigned and new justices were appointed, judicial opinions respecting the rights of corporate persons changed.

In 1889 the Supreme Court decided that, while state authorities could regulate the rates of railway companies, they could not fix rates so low as to deprive the companies of their property without due process. "If the company," said the Court, "is deprived of the power of charging reasonable rates for the use of its property, and such deprivation takes place in the absence of investigation by judicial machinery, it is deprived of the lawful use of its property, and thus, in substance and effect, of the property itself without due process of law and in violation of the Constitution of the United States." Under ruling of this type state regulations of property had to be of such a nature as to allow for a "reasonable" profit to the owners; and the question of reasonableness was a matter to be finally determined by the Supreme Court of the United States in cases duly brought before it.

By this and many other cases decided before the end of the nineteenth century the once almost sovereign powers of the states over property and business within their borders were reduced to mere shadows of their former greatness. Now all laws and actions by state authorities that seriously affected the property rights of corporations and industrial concerns throughout the country were subject to review and possible annulment by a single authority— the Supreme Court at Washington. This was a centralization of legal power practically ultimate in nature; for beyond that tribunal lay no formal appeal, save to the latent power of the people to amend the Constitution by an extraordinary majority in Congress and of the states.

Under the Fourteenth Amendment, so interpreted, innumerable laws and decrees by state, municipal, and county legislatures and officials were declared void. Everywhere state authorities were notified in effect that they could no longer pursue "populistic" or "communistic" policies in dealing with business enterprises; that they must observe the fundamental rights of property as taught in capitalistic economics. According to the letter of the Constitution, the power to make civil and criminal laws yet remained with the states, but that power was in fact strictly limited by the new jurisprudence created by the Supreme Court.

Another practice sanctioned by the Supreme Court gave additional impetus to economic centralization. According to the Constitution, actions at law between citizens of different states could be taken, on certain conditions, into the federal courts. Corporations, besides being persons, were "citizens" within the meaning of the word so used. They were often engaged in interstate commerce which was also subject to federal authority.

As the labor movement grew in strength, and strikes became more frequent, often tying up the trunk lines of railway companies, lawyers adopted the practice of appealing to federal judges for aid against strikers. One form of relief for which they asked was a writ of injunction, forbidding strikers to picket the property of their former employers and otherwise interfere with the operation of their employers' business.

Recourse to the injunction by employers became increasingly frequent during and after the great railway strikes which broke out in the depression of 1873–78. A climax in this development was reached in 1894 on the occasion of a strike ordered by the

American Railway Union in Chicago in sympathetic support of strikers against the Pullman Company. In the midst of that labor contest the federal district court in the city issued a blanket injunction forbidding all persons engaged in the strike to interfere with the movement of trains. The president of the American Railway Union, Eugene V. Debs, manager of the strike, was accused of violating the injunction, arrested, and imprisoned for contempt by the federal court from which the injunction issued. On appeal the Supreme Court of the United States upheld the lower tribunal at Chicago and declared that summary imprisonment, without jury trial, for contempt of court in such cases did not violate the federal Constitution.

Having the full sanction of the highest court in the land for the free use of injunctions in labor disputes, lawyers for industrial concerns availed themselves of this legal weapon in every direction to crush strikes and block the efforts of trade unions to force their terms on employers. Thus a new instrument of control was added to the decisions of the Supreme Court, subjecting all state authorities to its dominion in respect of their actions seriously affecting the rights of property. Now the practice of issuing injunctions freely in labor disputes gave to centralizing industry a powerful weapon against coercive measures of the centralizing labor movement.

Therefore, in contests between capital and state governments and between capital and labor, while economic concentration advanced, the balance of legal power was weighted on the side of capital. Insofar as government was involved in its operations, industrial enterprise could now turn with confidence to the federal judiciary for negative relief and for positive assistance in gaining all the profits that, as one lawyer put it, "the traffic will bear." It was after observing such history in the making that Henry Adams was led to wonder in 1895 whether the country was "on the edge of a new and last great centralization, or of a first great movement of disintegration."

CHAPTER XX

Centralization as Involved in the Political Struggle

THE LAST HALF of the nineteenth century was crowded with events that shook from center to circumference the economic system handed down from the age of Andrew Jackson. The chief events were a civil war and the abolition of slavery—the very basis of the Southern plantation system; an upheaval in the race and class relations of the South; occupation of the great West; the disappearance of free land for farming families and the transference of natural resources to private persons or corporations; expansion and concentration in industry and transportation; increase in immigration and in the number and size of cities; the creation of a plutocracy, or money aristocracy, flaunting its wealth in the brazen display of new riches; a powerful labor movement; and judicial backing for business enterprise.

This age was also characterized by panics and depressions, nationwide in scope, unprecedented in extent, unemployment, poverty, violence, and the destruction of property. Of the span between 1870 and 1910 about two thirds of the years were years of depressions, long or short in duration: for example, 1873–78; 1884–87; 1893–98. Certainly during half the time farmers, industrialists, and industrial workers were outside the range of what was boastfully called "prosperity."

Every depression season was punctuated by strikes, local and general. The great railway strike of 1877 was accompanied by so many disorders and so much bloodshed as to make Daniel Shays' rebellion in 1786 appear like a mere argument at a garden party. Before it was over the Pennsylvania railway station in Pittsburgh had been seized by rioters and burned. Shortly afterward a railway strike in the Southwest, led by Martin Irons for the Knights of Labor, tied up more than 5000 miles of lines in Missouri, Arkansas, Kansas, Indian Territory, and Nebraska. It too was attended by the seizure of railway property and the sabotage of engines. So disturbing was the railway strike of 1894, in connection with the labor dispute at the Pullman Works in Chicago, that President Cleveland used the troops of the United States to suppress it.

If disruptive strikes could be set down to "the evil spirit" or "ignorance" of American working people, "misled by foreign agitators," the numerous politico-economic scandals which exploded in rapid succession during these eventful years could not all be laid at their doors. In New York City, William Marcy Tweed and a gang of Tammany politicians were exposed to public scorn in 1871 as robbers and bribers who had looted the city treasury and corrupted judges in the highest courts of the state. The next year the New York *Sun* "scooped" the news of a still greater scandal—the Crédit Mobilier peculations in the recent construction of the Union Pacific Railroad. Before this sensation was over the people learned that members of Congress had accepted "favors" which were in effect bribes, and that no less a person than the Vice-President of the United States, if not guilty of gross misconduct in connection with the "deal," was at least by no means impeccable.

While the Crédit Mobilier affair was on the public stage, another inquiry showed that the "Whisky Ring" had been cheating the government of taxes. The trail of that scandal led to the very doors of the White House—to President Grant's private secretary. Another ring, the Star Route gang, including federal officials and members of Congress, was caught defrauding the government in connection with the carriage of mails. It was indeed a rare year that did not produce a fresh exposure in high places.

Among the revelations of the period was the disclosure of monstrous poverty in urban quarters. As foreign immigrants by the millions and native workers from the least prosperous rural districts rolled into the centers of industry and commerce, areas of congestion, the "slums," swelled into huge proportions. Every city had its large districts of poverty, overcrowding, misery, and crime.

Americans had read in their histories about the proletariat of ancient Rome. Now they could actually see a proletariat in every urban region of their own Republic. "It is the city," exclaimed the

Congregationalist home missionary, Josiah Strong, in *Our Country*, published in 1891, "where . . . the Sway of Mammon is the widest, and his worship the most constant and eager. Here luxuries are gathered . . . here is the most extravagant expenditure. Here also is the *congestion* of wealth the severest. Dives and Lazarus are brought face to face; here, in sharp contrast, are the *ennui* of surfeit and the desperation of starvation. . . . As a rule, the greater the city, the greater are the riches of the rich and the poverty of the poor. . . . Is it strange that such conditions arouse a blind and bitter hatred of our social system?"

No longer did an abundance of free land offer an escape from this poverty. No longer could politicians delude the poor by proclaiming that "free land" was the solution for the problem of poverty. Nor were all farmers actually on the land becoming stalwart freeholders. When the census takers of 1880 had collected the figures of farm ownership, they reported that twenty-five per cent of all farmers were already tenants. Twenty years later the proportion had increased to thirty-five per cent and was on an upward climb.

☆

To many American observers of these social earthquakes, including such prominent figures as James Russell Lowell, Walt Whitman, and E. L. Godkin, the situation was appalling. Yet throughout most of the period neither of the two major political parties, which contended for power and in one season or another governed the nation, took much account of the volcanic upheavals in American life and labor or made any substantial alterations in the form, methods, or concepts of their obligations. Nominating conventions, "fresh from the people," were held as in the good old days of Andrew Jackson. Amid open convention uproars or back-room negotiations among politicians, candidates were chosen for approval by the voters. On the morning after a triumph at the polls the spoils of office were distributed among the victors, in the style consecrated by long custom. "What are we here for?" a convention delegate once exclaimed when a reformer asked his party colleagues to endorse a civil-service proposal for removing a few hundred jobs from the grip of politicians. At party conventions political experts drafted platforms in the customary manner, praising themselves, damning their opponents, and making vague promises savoring of the millennium.

As in the past, professional politicians controlled conventions and committees, were nominated to high offices, directed party affairs, and, if elected, administered the machinery of government, local and national, with an eye to party advantage. After the overthrow of the planters in the Southern revolution, the monopoly of the professional politicians, mostly lawyers, became more complete. Businessmen, farmers, and industrial workers left to this "elite" the ostensible function of ruling the nation.

In the struggle of the two major parties for power the Republicans gained strength for some time. They had been a minority in 1860 but they emerged from the civil conflict augmented in numbers and influence. During the period of reconstruction in the South they were able to count on the support of the new Negro voters grateful for emancipation and for the civil rights accorded to their race by the party of Abraham Lincoln. To that party bankers and investors in United States bonds looked for the payment of interest and principal and for security against the inflation menace of paper currency. Railway promoters, mining prospectors, cattle kings, timber hunters, and land speculators, already enriched by government bounties, preferred to see the national government in Republican hands. To the Republicans the beneficiaries of the higher tariffs turned with eager expectancy for continued protection. Industrial workers were told that only under such protection could they enjoy higher wages than the "pauper labor of Europe" received. Farmers who were getting free homesteads in the West and Union veterans of the war entitled to land and pensions had reasons for allegiance to Republican leadership. As possessors of the Executive Department in Washington, Republicans dispensed the spoils of office among the faithful.

With these material considerations were united moral advantages in aid of the Republicans. It was under their auspices that the Union had been saved, that the perpetuity of the Republic had been assured. Theirs was the party of Lincoln, which had struck the shackles from four million bondmen—the greatest act of liberation in the tragic history of chattel slavery. The "twin relics of barbarism—slavery and polygamy," orators could say, had been abolished throughout the land by courageous and enlightened Republicans. To whom except Republicans, it was asked, can the liberty of the people and the fortunes of the Republic be safely entrusted?

On the other hand the Democrats long lay under a cloud. They were deprived of the able and powerful leadership once afforded by Southern planters and their lawyers and they were now vilified by Republicans as the abettors of slavery and disunion. They had been split into two factions in 1860. They had officially proclaimed the war a failure in the platform of 1864. What glittering program could they now offer to the voters? Their old pledges of lower tariffs with hints of free trade ahead and their doctrine of states' rights had less popular appeal during the distractions that followed the collapse of the Confederacy.

Besides, their ranks were wavering. They had lost to the Republicans many farmers in the West who had once rallied around their flag, and they were further weakened by the subjection of their fellow Democrats in the South. Thus badly crippled, they seemed to have poor prospects of ever recovering the proud dominion over national affairs previously exercised. Even South Carolina, where secession had started, went Republican in 1868! The main prospect of the Democrats for a reconquest of power, even temporarily, appeared to lie in the mistakes or corruption of the Republicans or in taking advantage of business panics and depressions to urge stricken and distressed farmers and industrial workers to turn away from Republican leadership.

Of the nine presidential elections between 1868 and 1900 inclusive, the Republicans carried all but two and in every instance with a military hero, large or small, as a candidate. General Ulysses S. Grant had exhibited little interest in politics and had voted only once in his life—the Democratic ticket in 1856; but he was perhaps the outstanding figure in national life after the death of Lincoln in 1865. Capitalizing on Grant's popular strength, the Republicans chose him as their candidate for President in 1868, elected him, and then renewed his term in 1872. During the depression which cast gloom over Grant's last years, they picked for the presidency Rutherford B. Hayes, of Ohio, a former general in the Union army, to pit against the Democratic nominee, Samuel J. Tilden, an able lawyer and politician from New York. The contest was close and the returns were disputed, but a special commission, in which the Republicans had a majority, awarded the palm to Hayes. Although Hayes had qualities, character, and intelligence, the Republicans turned from him in 1880, nominated another general, James A. Garfield, also of Ohio, and won that election. When Garfield was cut down in his first year by an assassin's bullet, the presidency passed to the Vice-President, Chester A. Arthur, a colorless man, unable to provoke national enthusiasm.

Republican fortunes were ebbing. War passions were cooling. The services of the party in saving the Union and freeing the slaves were being forgotten in the fleeting years, amid the sensational scandals of the Republican administrations at Washington. Yet Republican leaders were still so confident about their position that they thought they could elect a civilian at last. Instead of gathering around a military hero in 1884, they nominated James G. Blaine, of Maine, who had served in Congress, not on battlefields, during the war. But Blaine had been singed if not scorched by the Crédit Mobilier scandal.

Taking his selection as an "affront," disgruntled Republicans, called "Mugwumps," deserted their party in large numbers and cast in their lot with the Democrats, who had pinned their faith in victory on Grover Cleveland, governor of New York, as their candidate. Cleveland was no war hero either. Indeed, he had hired a substitute to fight for him in the war. But though intellectually complacent and incapable of emulating a fiery Andrew Jackson in his popular appeals, Cleveland had been an efficient public administrator at Albany and had the reputation of being an honest man and a trustworthy official. Despite unparalleled vituperation in the campaign, Cleveland slipped through—by a narrow margin. The switch of a few hundred votes in New York City, or perhaps an accurate count of the votes cast there, would have sent his competitor, Blaine, to the White House in his stead.

Having read their lesson in that outcome, the Republicans then returned to the practice of going to the voters with a military hero. In 1888 they chose as their candidate Benjamin Harrison, of Indiana, who, like Grant, Hayes, and Garfield, had been an officer in the Union army during the war. A cold personality and a rather drab figure in every way, Harrison nevertheless managed to whip up enough support on his military record and other grounds to carry the day against President Cleveland, renominated for a second term by the Democrats.

If there was anything heroic in the stature of Harrison after he became the Chief Executive, the people failed to appreciate it. After four years' experience with him, they retired him to private life in 1892 and restored to the presidency Grover Cleveland, the civilian, nominated again by the Democrats. Once more, and for the last time, in 1896, the Republicans staked their chance of winning an election on a former soldier of the Union army, Major William McKinley, of Ohio. Under his leadership, promoted by a shrewd political financier, Marcus A. Hanna, they recovered their control over the national administration. When the new century opened they thought themselves firmly buttressed in power—though signs of a revolt against historic methods in party politics loomed on the horizon.

While the presidential elections in those years revealed a numerical weakness in the Democratic party, they were not the sole tests of its vitality. In the congressional elections, where the great funds and pressures of the national campaign were less available, the story was different. Except for two bienniums, the Democrats had possession of the House of Representatives during all the years from 1875–95; for four of those years they had a majority in the Senate as well as in the House. During Cleveland's first administration, 1885–89, they controlled the House, while the Republicans held the Senate. For two years in Cleveland's second administration the Democrats marshaled a majority in both Houses of Congress. At no time did they despair of capturing the presidency.

Their anticipation of final triumph was energized by the fact that after the restoration of white dominion the South was really "solid." Before the civil conflict it had been politically divided and indeed it was badly split in the election of 1860. Hundreds of the richest and most powerful planters had feared, if not despised, the democracy of Thomas Jefferson, for they saw in its gospel of human equality a peril to their labor system. But after the emancipation of slaves and the rise of the Republican mastery, all the South below the border states became firmly Democratic. Furthermore, its strength in the House of Representatives was actually increased by emancipation. Before that event a slave had been treated as only three fifths of a person in the apportionment of representatives under the Constitution; after it, all Negroes were counted in fixing the number of representatives accorded to the Southern states. The Negroes now counted in representation; the whites chose the representatives and had more in Congress.

☆

At every presidential election between 1868 and 1892 each of the two major parties put forth an official platform—a declaration of its views respecting the national needs and a statement of its program for reform or conservatism if victorious at the polls. In these successive documents were mirrored the intelligence and thought of the governing elite and its popular supporters.

In the main the platforms dealt with issues that had been uppermost since 1789: tariffs, banking, currency, taxation, internal improvements, and the disposal of the public domain. The hatred of monopolies, the great animus of Jacksonian Democrats, now and then still blazed out in platform attacks on railway corporations, "trusts," and "combines." But on the whole both parties passed over with slight recognition the basic changes that were taking place in American economy under their very eyes. For several years, it is true, Republicans laid stress on promises to uphold the civil rights of Negroes in the South but as time passed that issue relaxed its hold on public interest and on theirs.

From season to season, while pointing fingers of scorn at Democrats, Republicans stood on their record, claiming it as sufficient proof that they merited an indefinite tenure of power. In assailing that record Democrats emphasized Republican corruption and mismanagement and made much of the popular slogan: "Turn the rascals out!" Of course the charges were occasionally reversed. When the Democrats were in power briefly, they too gloated on their "achievements," and the Republicans took their turn at urging the voters to eject the rascals. Thus praise of their own virtues and abuse of their opponents furnished a major part of the stock in trade drawn upon for campaigns by the leaders of both parties.

"We charge the Democratic party," proclaimed the Republicans in their platform of 1876, "with being the same in character and spirit as when it sympathized with treason . . . With reasserting and applauding in the national Capitol the sentiments of unrepentant rebellion; with sending Union soldiers to the rear, and promoting Confederate soldiers to the front; with deliberately proposing to repudiate the plighted faith of the government; with being equally false and imbecile upon the overshadowing financial questions. . . . With proving itself, through the period of its ascendancy in the lower House of Congress, utterly incompetent to administer the government; and we warn the country against trusting a party thus alike unworthy, recreant, and incapable." Treason, imbecility, incompetence, unworthiness, and incapacity! These were Republican words supposed to describe the qualities of the Democratic party.

The Democrats retaliated in kind. In their platform of 1884 they paid their respects to their opponents in similar terms: "The Republican party, so far as principle is concerned, is a reminiscence. In practice it is an organization for enriching those who control its machinery. . . . The Republican party, during its legal, its stolen, and its bought tenures of power, has steadily decayed in moral character and political capacity. . . . Honeycombed with corruption, outbreaking exposures no longer shock its moral sense. Its honest members, its independent journals, no longer maintain a successful contest for authority in its canvasses or a veto upon bad nominations. . . . We denounce the Republican party for having failed to relieve the people from crushing war taxes, which have paralyzed business, crippled industry, and deprived labor of employment and its just reward." Thievery, moral decay, corruption, incapacity! These were Democratic words supposed to describe the qualities of the Republican party.

☆

Performances—as distinguished from professions and denunciations—registered, on the statute books of the United States, the measures which the two parties deemed appropriate and necessary in the age of economic transformation. Five times between 1868 and 1900 the tariff rates on imports were altered, generally in the form of more protection for manufacturers. In 1872 and 1883 minor modifications were made. In 1890 the Republicans, by the McKinley Act, ventured upon a substantial increase in protectionism. In 1894, Democrats, for the moment in control of the presidency and both houses of Congress, juggled the rates again and passed a bill also so protectionist in nature that President Cleveland, unwilling to approve it, allowed it to become a law without his signature.

On the currency question Republicans and Democrats blew hot and cold. In 1875, Congress passed the Resumption Act providing for the redemption of the paper currency, or "greenbacks," in gold, beginning in 1879. But to please the paper-money factions in both parties, Congress in 1878 and in 1890 passed silver-purchase laws authorizing the Treasury to buy annually certain quantities of silver for coinage. Mindful of outbursts against the spoils system in both parties, it enacted in 1883 a civil-service law under which appointments to a few federal offices were removed from the system and made subject to an examination of candidates for efficiency, held under a civil-service commission. At the discretion of the President other offices could be placed, according to this law, under the new "merit system." Judged by such performances, the two major parties were becoming as much alike in their interests and sentiments as two bottles of the same size and shape, differing only in their labels.

During the entire period from 1868 to 1900 only three notable measures passed by Congress were designed to cope with complicated problems raised by industrial concentration and the spoliation of natural resources. The first of these, the Interstate Commerce Act of 1887, forbade interstate railway companies to engage in such practices as pooling freight and giving rebates to shippers "on the inside." It also provided for the Interstate Commerce Commission, empowered to regulate and supervise railways in limited respects. The act had imposing features but no teeth. For many years it was little more than a dead letter.

The second major law bearing on recent developments in American economy was directed against concentration in industry. It was the Sherman Antitrust Act of 1890 which prohibited trusts and combinations "in restraint of trade" and imposed penalties for violations. This act was neither imposing nor effective. For a long time presidents allowed it to sleep in the statute book.

The third law, far from imposing but foreshadowing crucial actions relative to natural resources, was a mere amendment attached to another bill in 1891—a few lines authorizing the President to set aside and hold as national forests certain areas of the public domain. The process of despoiling the national heritage was not stopped by this act but a change in policy was implied.

To the list of the three measures might have been added the provision for a federal income tax incorporated in the tariff bill enacted by Democrats in 1894. This was supposed to make the rich bear their share of taxation. But most of it was declared unconstitutional by the Supreme Court of the United States the very next year.

Such, according to the official platforms and the major pieces of legislation, was the insight of the political elite of the two major parties into the meaning of the catastrophic events in American economy between 1868 and the end of the century. Such were the ideas and actions which they deemed sufficient to meet the challenge of basic changes and to assure what they were fond of calling the prosperity, liberty, and perpetuity of the Republic. Such was their vision of the future, their appreciation of the "shape of things to come," the Americanism they thought adequate for transmission to rising generations, to be maintained forever.

☆

While Republicans and Democrats, each party pleased with itself and displeased with its opponent, thus conducted politics according to their conceptions of fitness or their power, they were all along bothered by critics in their own ranks and by minor political parties that appeared from time to time. If a disturbance was small within their own coteries or among the people in general, they could ignore it. If it was large, as indicated by the number of protests made at the ballot box, they sought to conciliate it by promises of mild reforms and political jobs. For nearly thirty years they were able to prevent revolts started by discontented people from seriously upsetting party calculations—party use and wont.

Not until 1896 did one of the major parties fall a victim to an uprising from below. Then it was the Democrats whose national machine, captured by agrarians under William Jennings Bryan, of the young generation, ceased for a time to function as of old. More years passed. Then the Republican machine was disrupted by Theodore Roosevelt, also of the young generation. But the storms which made these wrecks were slow in gathering. Their beginnings were small and for many years could be lightly disregarded by men occupied with "large and practical" affairs.

Judged by their programs and the economic interests to which they appealed, the critics who protested against the offerings of the major parties and demanded a different order of things belonged mainly to two groups: labor reformers and agrarians. The first group was concerned primarily with industrial workers and their claims; the second with farmers and tenants on the land who had not received all the blessings of prosperity to which they thought themselves entitled. Yet no deep gulf separated these two groups and their ideas about public policies. Their demands often coincided, and members of both groups looked upon the political struggle as involving farmers and industrial workers alike as in Jackson's day. Sometimes they were able to unite. At others they pursued separate courses and no effort at co-operation brought about a permanent union.

The first break with regular political affiliations after 1865 was made in the name of industrial labor. In 1872 a convention of delegates from seventeen states, calling themselves Labor Reformers, met at Columbus, Ohio, and adopted a platform on issues which the major parties had ignored. As to doctrines, they declared, in the American tradition, that all political power is inherent in the people and that government is established for their benefit; that all citizens are entitled to the use and enjoyment of the fruits of their labor and skills; that no man or set of men is entitled to special privileges from government except in consideration of public services rendered.

As to practical proposals, the Labor Reformers demanded a national currency issued to the people without the intervention of banking corporations; restriction of the sale of public lands to bona fide homeseekers; exclusion of Chinese laborers; an eight-hour day in all government employment; abolition of contract labor in prisons; government regulation of railway and telegraph corporations to assure equitable rates; civil-service reform; modification of patent laws in the interests of inventors; and the subordination of military power to the civil power. The Reformers' candidate for President, Charles O'Connor, of New York, polled a vote of less than 30,000—more in Texas than in New York, and more in Georgia than in Illinois.

Discouraged by the outcome, Labor Reformers gave up the political battle or merged temporarily with the agrarians. But in 1888 another labor party sprang up—the Union Labor party. It held a convention in Cincinnati and adopted the chief principles put forth by the Labor Reformers, adding an endorsement of woman suffrage and the popular election of United States senators. In the same city at the same time another convention of delegates assembled, the United Labor party, and displayed more radical propensities. These Laborites denounced both Republicans and Democrats as "hopelessly and shamelessly corrupt," and among other things approved an increased taxation of land values and government ownership and control of railway and telegraph lines. But the new Laborites also polled a small vote.

Then in 1892, after local beginnings, the Socialist Labor party launched an independent national campaign, appealing especially to industrial workers for support. Its platform in this campaign was reformist. It advocated government ownership of public utilities, progressive inheritance and income taxes, universal and equal suffrage, free education, municipal home rule, abolition of child labor, employers' liability legislation, and the secret ballot. It also proposed to reconstruct the federal government by abolishing the presidency and the Senate, and setting up an executive board to be elected and subject to recall by the House of Representatives.

At the end of the century, in 1900, a second socialist party, the Social Democratic party, entered the lists with a complete program for nationalizing all the major instruments of production. As an evidence of its militancy, the new party placed at the head of its ticket Eugene V. Debs, who had been imprisoned for his labor activities during the Pullman strike of 1894. In the election Debs received only 94,800 votes.

None of the labor or socialist parties made heavy inroads upon the monopoly of politics possessed by the Republicans and Democrats. But agrarian agitations, persistent since early colonial times, threatened in the closing years of the nineteenth century to. fracture that monopoly. In 1876 farmers entered the national campaign with their own organization, the Independent National party, advocating the historic remedy of farmers for their distresses, namely paper money. The "Greenbackers" now proposed to suppress all bank currency and have the federal government issue notes directly to the people on the basis of its own credit and obligations. This demand for national inflation, instead of the state inflation adopted in Jacksonian times, was a striking note in the long effort of American farmers to defend themselves against deflation and get control over the national medium of exchange. Yet agrarians made little progress with a party of their own until 1892 when they invited industrial workers to unite with them and, at a national convention in Omaha that year, formally launched a farmer-labor party named the People's party, shortened by the public to the "Populists."

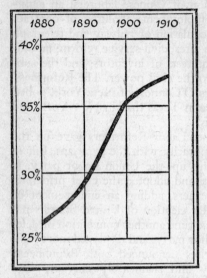

RAPID RISE OF TENANCY IN THE UNITED STATES, 1880–1900

Increasing percentage of farmers who were tenants between 1880, when the first census of tenancy was taken, and 1910. From report of President Franklin D. Roosevelt's Committee on Tenancy, 1937.

Before 1892 labor reformers and agrarians had spoken contemptuously of the two major parties, but the Populists at Omaha in 1892 blew against Republicans and Democrats such a blast as had never before come from a political convention. "Corruption," they declared, "dominates the ballot box, the legislature, the Congress, and touches even the ermine of the bench. The people are demoralized. . . . The newspapers are largely subsidized or muzzled; public opinion silenced; business prostrated; our homes covered with mortgages; labor impoverished; and the land concentrating in the hands of capitalists. The urban workmen are denied the right of organization for self-protection; imported pauperized labor beats down their wages; a hireling standing army, unrecognized by our laws, is established to shoot them down, and they are rapidly degenerating into European conditions. The fruits of the toil of millions are boldly stolen to build up colossal fortunes for a few, unprecedented in the history of mankind. . . . We have witnessed for more than a quarter of a century the struggle of the two great political parties for power and plunder, while grievous wrongs have been inflicted upon the suffering people. . . . They propose to drown the outcries of a plundered people with the uproar of a sham battle over the tariff. . . . The interests of rural and civic labor are the same; their enemies are identical." Then followed a long list of demands for radical changes in the law, the currency, the government, and the economy of the United States. On that platform, with General James B. Weaver, a veteran of the Civil War, a former Democrat who had become a Republican in 1860, as their candidate, the Populists polled more than 1,000,000 votes. Signs of an upheaval in party politics were visible.

Despite their appeal to industrial workers in 1892 and notwithstanding the large national vote they received, the Populists polled, relatively speaking, only a handful of votes in the great industrial regions of the country. For example, out of nearly 1,000,000 votes cast in Pennsylvania, only 8700 went to their candidate; out of about 400,000 in Massachusetts, only 3200 bore the Populist mark. Thus the Populist party proved to be mainly agrarian in character and its power lay principally, though not entirely, in Democratic strongholds.

Capitalizing on the panic, depression, strikes, unemployment, and increasing economic distress of the next four years, the Populists and their sympathizers captured the Democratic convention at Chicago in 1896. There the Democratic President in the White House, Grover Cleveland, was unequivocally spurned, conservatives in the party were treated with derision, a radical platform was adopted, and the young politician from Nebraska,

William Jennings Bryan, was nominated as the Democratic candidate for President.

From beginning to end the Democratic convention of 1896 vibrated with revolutionary fervor. Bryan lifted the delegates to their feet with a cry that the toiling masses were not to be crowned with thorns and crucified upon a cross of gold! The platform adopted at Chicago denounced the Supreme Court for invalidating the income tax law of the previous year and demanded a reconstruction of the Court so that the burden of taxation could be equally apportioned and wealth forced to bear its due share. The use of injunctions in labor disputes was condemned as highly dangerous to the rights of the people; and the employment of federal troops in the recent strike at Chicago was branded as an unconstitutional and violent interference with the rights of states. "As labor creates the wealth of the country," ran one plank, "we demand the passage of such laws as may be necessary to protect it in all its rights." To farmers in particular, this Democratic platform promised the free coinage of gold and silver at the ratio of sixteen to one. This was a demand for an inflation of the currency in favor of debtors, that vociferous historic class of rebellious Americans, as against the contraction in favor of creditors—a contraction brought about, it was charged, by using as the monetary standard of the United States the gold controlled by private bankers.

Warned that a crisis impended, the Republicans, led by an astute manager, Marcus A. Hanna, an industrial magnate of Cleveland, Ohio, had prepared to meet it at their convention, held previously at St. Louis. Having picked as his candidate William McKinley, of Ohio, Hanna at first hoped to make protection for industries the main issue, thus playing down the fact that McKinley himself had once been an advocate of free silver.

But conservatives at the convention met the issue head on, even at the price of losing the support of the free-silver faction in Republican ranks. They committed the party unreservedly to "sound money" and opposed the free coinage of silver except by international agreement with the leading commercial nations of the world —"which we pledge ourselves to promote."

Speaking on the floor of the convention, Henry Cabot Lodge arrayed his party against "not only that organized failure, the Democratic party, but all the wandering forces of political chaos and social disorder . . . in these bitter times when the forces of disorder are loose and the wreckers with their false lights gather at the shore to lure the ship of state upon the rocks." With Mc-Kinley as their candidate, the Republicans raised a great fund and launched their campaign on an extraordinary scale.

The battle between Bryan and McKinley, accompanied by censorious charges and terroristic threats, aroused the country from coast to coast, as it had not been moved since 1860. Bryan defended his cause and his followers against what he called "English toadies and the pampered minions of corporate rapacity." His party, he declared, represented "the masses of the people, the great industrial and producing masses of the people . . . the men who plow and plant, who fatten herds, who toil in shops, who fell forests, and delve in mines . . . who produce the wealth of the republic, who bear the heaviest burdens in time of peace; who are ready always to give their lifeblood for their country's flag."

The Democratic program and movement McKinley countered by declaring that Republicans would squarely face this "sudden, dangerous, and revolutionary assault upon law and order and upon those to whom is confided by the Constitution and the laws the authority to uphold and maintain them." Bryanism, the editor of the New York *Tribune* assured his readers, had sprung from "the assiduous culture of the basest passions of the least worthy members of the community." Bryan himself the editor portrayed as the willing puppet "in the blood-imbued hands of Altgeld, the anarchist, and Debs, the revolutionist, and other desperadoes of that stripe."

On the side of Bryan was aligned nearly all the discontent with the course of national affairs that had been made manifest by Labor Reformers, Greenbackers, Single Taxers, and Socialists in recent years—all the inveterate hostility to concentrated wealth. No doubt millions of Democrats voted for him out of party habit, as unreflecting partisans, but in so doing they gave sanction to his attack and program. At the election Bryan polled about 1,000,000 more votes than Cleveland had received in 1892—a larger vote than the party was to muster when it elected Woodrow Wilson in 1912. Nevertheless, Bryan was defeated by the new or hitherto lethargic voters who flocked to McKinley's banners—2,000,000 more than had voted the Republican ticket four years previously.

Though victorious in the contest for power, Republicans confronted the fact that 6,500,000 Americans had planted themselves on the side of Bryanism against the 7,100,000 committed to "Mc-Kinleyism," as Henry Adams called it. If the Republicans' victory was "glorious," as orators were wont to say, it was narrow enough to make them realize that their avenue to power was not to be the same in time to come as it had been since the election of Grant in 1868. It was precarious enough to set them wondering how the ghost of Bryanism could be laid—by frontal assault, concession, or diversion?

CHAPTER XXI

The Breach with Historic Continentalism

NEARLY THREE CENTURIES lay between the founding of the English colony of Jamestown in Virginia and the inauguration of McKinley in 1897. Through this long procession of years the energies of the people, of many national origins, called Americans, had been concentrated on expansion and development in this continental theater. Here their labor, interests, and affections centered, as under a sense of great history, often embodied in the somewhat mystical concept of "manifest destiny," as they advanced to the shore of the Pacific. By 1897 the continental domain had been rounded out. All the territories, save three, had been admitted to the Union as equal states possessing self-government under the federal Constitution.

This is not to say that no Americans—in thought, ambition, and enterprise—had gone beyond the continental borders. Keels of American ships had plowed the waters of all seas bearing masters and merchants in search of foreign markets and opportunities to garner in large profits from foreign trade. American warships had bombarded many ports in distant foreign lands in retaliation for native interference with the operations of American traders. Ambitious naval officers, such as Commodore Matthew C. Perry, who opened to American commerce the barred gates of Japan, had dreamed of and proposed the seizure of islands and territories in far-off lands; and indeed a hold was established in the Samoan Islands by 1889.

In the days of slavery, politicians among the planters had contemplated the seizure of Cuba and advances far into Mexico with a view to adding more territory for planters and their slaves. A few Northern politicians had also imagined further expansion. For example, William Seward, Lincoln's Secretary of State, had proclaimed a different type of "manifest destiny" to include all of North America and war with Russia, on the plains of Manchuria, over dominion in the Far East. In 1867, Seward bought Alaska from Russia and, by methods none too nice, forced Congress to approve his action. General Grant, as President, had tried to annex Santo Domingo in the Caribbean and would have done it if the Senate had not stood foursquare against it. But most of these plans and activities, even when fostered by the United States Government, did little to divert the interests, treasure, and affections of the people from the task of developing their continental home.

Indeed the foreign policy of the United States, prescribed in Washington's Farewell Address, in Jefferson's messages, and in the Monroe Doctrine, rested on the proposition that the fundamental interest of the American people was, and should be, concentrated on their continental opportunities—for many reasons, political, economic, and moral. According to that definite policy this hemisphere, the seat of American power, was to be kept independent and protected against further colonization and conquest by European Powers; the United States was not to intervene in the eternal vicissitudes of European power politics; territories outside the easy reach of effective defense were not to be acquired; and the protection and advance of American civilization in this continental arena was to be the primary and indefeasible objective of the United States Government in all its relations with foreign Powers, near or distant. Not until about 1890 did American politicians begin seriously to plan and publicly to advocate a reversal of this positive policy, propose active intervention in the affairs of Asia and Europe, and urge the transformation of the United States into a "great world Power"—the goal to which European imperialists had been vaingloriously leading their countries.

☆

Like every scheme in politics, the scheme of world power for the United States had its formulators and plans for application. High in the ranks of the men who made the new world image for Americans to live and die by was an American naval officer, Alfred Thayer Mahan, author of large books on sea power. Openly and covertly Mahan labored to steer American politicians out into the new course—of building a big navy, pushing commerce everywhere in the world, and seeking positive power, physical and moral, in the ancient and perpetual controversies of Europe and Asia.

Nominally a naval officer dedicated to the defense of his country, Mahan was actually an amateur historian and a vigorous politician, publicist, and negotiator. He realized in the beginning that his self-appointed task of converting the nation to world-power politics would be difficult; there was, he said, "no aggressive action in our pious souls." Though he confessed that American citizens did not understand what was going on in his line, he told them that they would soon be deeply involved in European and Asiatic politics whether they liked it or not.

A second agitator for the plunge into world-power politics was Josiah Strong, a militant Protestant missionary who lectured and wrote unctuously on the subject. In his book, *Our Country*, published first in 1886 and in an enlarged form in 1891, Strong declared that the United States was in peril of socialism and social upheavals; that the Anglo-Saxon race was chosen by God to civilize the world; and that the major responsibility for running this crusade belonged to the people of the United States.

Associated with the school of aggressive adventurers were two young members of the Republican party then seeking political careers. One was Theodore Roosevelt, of New York, a man of moderate wealth, leisure, and ambition, full of egotism and bluster. To him Mahan's wine of imperialism was little short of a godsend as he cast about for a big role in politics. The other was Henry Cabot Lodge, son of a Boston merchant made wealthy in the China trade, who had battled his way from Massachusetts into the United States Senate in 1893. Bosom friend of Roosevelt and Mahan, Lodge spared no time or strength in preaching the new gospel of world-power politics and in striving to force it upon balky Republicans of the older generation.

In many respects the times were auspicious for the young agitators' designs on America and the world. European Powers, with Great Britain at the head, were then going into imperialism on a vaster scale than ever. They were building bigger navies, raising bigger armies, seizing territories in Asia, Africa, and the islands of the seas, forming secret alliances, carrying on undercover diplomatic maneuvers, and preparing for the climax—the World War which opened in 1914. The sight of this "grand strategy" in Europe filled the American world-power politicians with envy and a burning desire to get into it. Besides, they well knew as expert politicians that a diversion of the people's thought from domestic discontent over plutocracy and poverty, such as embroiled the land in the campaign of 1896, to world politics and wars would damp if not extinguish radicalism at home. It would smother, they trusted, those other agitators: Bryan, Debs, John P. Altgeld, and all such "incendiaries," as they were described in conservative circles.

Another consideration entered into the world-power design of young Theodore Roosevelt. For about thirty years the American people had been at peace. The bloodshed, sufferings, and destruction of the Civil War had almost been forgotten—in the North at least. The country, he said, was growing "soft," martial virtue was on a decline, and another war would be "a good thing" to tone up the people. In 1895, while President Cleveland was engaged in a vehement quarrel with Great Britain over her alleged encroachment on the territory of Venezuela, Roosevelt wrote to Lodge: "Personally I rather hope the fight will come soon. The clamor of the peace faction has convinced me that the country needs a war." The efforts of fellow citizens, particularly at Harvard University, to encourage a pacific settlement with Great Britain filled him with disgust. He asked Lodge whether he should not write to the Harvard magazine, the *Crimson*, "a smashing letter . . . giving my views and saying a word for Patriotism and Americanism."

Within a short time the agitators' program for America's thrust into world-power politics was well formulated and contained the following propositions. The United States, long an infant nation, had "grown up," had become "adult," must cast off the provincialism of its youth and, as a grown man, press into the grand game of power politics played by the grown men—the "big men"—of Europe and Asia. To continue in the old ways at home would be childish. All the free land and natural resources in the United States had passed into private hands and been developed; there was no more living room for Americans on this continent. Hence Americans must look far away for room in which to expand.

Americans, said an Indiana recruit to world-power politics, Albert J. Beveridge, produced more agricultural commodities and manufactures than they could consume; they must have new markets and colonies to exploit or American economy would be paralyzed with surplus wealth. Nations, argued Mahan in the language of Darwinism, must struggle with one another for existence and unless the United States was strong in the struggle it would perish. Millions of brown, yellow, and black men, lamented Josiah Strong, sat in the shadows, outside the blessings of Christianity, and by conquering those benighted multitudes, the United States would spread the helpful gospel of Jesus. Therefore, ran the "practical" side of the argument, the United States must build a big navy, seize new naval bases and colonies, force distant markets open, and enter full-panoplied into the competition of the great nations for the possession and domination of the earth.

In summation, the prophecy of the imperialists embraced the features deemed good politics and likely to allay domestic outbreaks against special privileges. The two great expedients of the preceding fifty years had failed to obliterate popular unrest and the will to self-expression. Free homesteads had been bestowed bountifully on settlers in the West; now those very settlers were filling the country with the uproar of a populist revolt against conditions objectionable to them in respect of government. The protective tariff had been tried as a device to assure full employment at good wages for industrial workers, but the McKinley tariff of 1890, the highest yet in American history, had been followed by the devastating panic of 1893–98, with its riots, hunger marches, and threats of revolution.

If politicians were to hold power or to get it if out of office, some new instrument was necessary and they found it in imperialist prophecy. The economic tenets of that prophecy boiled down to two mass appeals: imperial expansion would provide better markets for farmers, outlets for their "surpluses" of produce at prices profitable to them; and it would create jobs for industrial workers, fill their dinner pails.

No less important in imperialist calculations was a realization among the shrewder politicians that a foreign war and a "strong" foreign policy would in themselves divert the attention of the people from their domestic tribulations and programs of reform. In 1895, when a war with Great Britain seemed impending, Thomas Pascal, a Democratic politician of Texas, wrote privately to President Cleveland's Secretary of State that such a war would knock more pus out of the "anarchistic, socialistic, and populistic boil" than "would suffice to inoculate and corrupt our people for the next two centuries."

To the politicians of imperialism this outlook was charming; with no disturbance whatever to vested interests at home a panacea for their troubles could be offered to dissatisfied farmers and industrial workers and public attention distracted from politics on the home front.

☆

An occasion to put the plan for world-power politics into effect was afforded by a dispute with Spain about her island of Cuba, rampant when McKinley was inaugurated in 1897. For years Cuba had been torn periodically by revolts against Spanish dominion, and in 1895 a new rebellion had flamed up. Opposed to imperialism on principle, President Cleveland had studiously sought to pursue a policy of neutrality in the war between Spain and the Cubans. Personally pacific in spirit, President McKinley at first seemed inclined to follow that precedent.

But the American people were deeply moved by the stories of cruelties practiced by the Spanish generals in Cuba especially as narrated by William Randolph Hearst and Joseph Pulitzer in their "yellow journals." To the stories of atrocities were joined pleas for American aid to the "brave Cubans fighting for liberty and independence" and demands for help from American capitalists whose plantations and sugar mills in Cuba were being destroyed in the civil war.

In the midst of the excitement early in 1898 an American battleship, the *Maine*, which had been sent to the harbor of Havana "to safeguard American interests," was blown up by an explosion. Two officers and 258 members of the crew lost their lives in the disaster. Spanish officials were accused of committing the deed, but they denied it and the mystery of its origin was never solved.

For seeming to rely on pacific measures in respect of Cuba and the *Maine* affair, President McKinley was accused by impatient Americans of being weak-kneed. Theodore Roosevelt declared that he had the backbone of a chocolate éclair. Still McKinley persisted in his negotiations with Spain and was able to wring from the government in Madrid a promise to restore peace in Cuba and grant Cubans a form of self-government amounting to autonomy, if not independence. Then suddenly, on April 11, 1898, without fully revealing to the public the Spanish promise, the President sent a message to Congress calling for a resolution authorizing him to expel Spanish forces from the island of Cuba.

Although an overwhelming majority of the representatives and a safe majority of the senators were hot for war on Spain, the form of the resolution recognizing the independence of Cuba, then under consideration, became the subject of analytical debate. Among the senators especially a dread was voiced that the war would lead to unknown adventures; that the McKinley party would take advantage of it to annex Cuba and accomplish other designs than the expulsion of Spanish authorities from that island.

A leading question, therefore, was raised: What was to be the status of Cuba after Spanish dominion was destroyed? Some Americans believed that the Cubans were not fit for self-government and that the island should be annexed or in some way put under American hegemony. But Congress declared in the war resolution that the people of Cuba were, and of right ought to be, free and independent.

For the most cautious senators, suspecting ulterior purposes, that was not enough. On motion of Senator Henry M. Teller, who had bolted the Republicans in 1896 as a free-silver reformer, another provision, more precise, was added to the resolution: "The United States hereby disclaims any disposition or intention to exercise sovereignty, jurisdiction, or control over said island except for the pacification thereof, and asserts its determination, when that is accomplished, to leave the government and control of the island to its people." This prescription seemed to leave no loophole for imperialists and annexationists of the Mahan school.

With the Teller Amendment added, Congress passed on April 19 the resolution for Cuban independence, empowering the President to use the armed forces of the United States, if necessary, to expel the Spanish government from the island. That was in effect a declaration of war, and under it war began. It was supplemented, however, on April 25, by another resolution declaring war to exist in fact and directing the President to employ the land and naval forces in waging it. War had begun, without any official reference to Spain's island of Puerto Rico or her possessions in the Far East —the Philippines. To all appearances it was a war for the liberation of Cuba from Spanish dominion—an altruistic, moral war.

The hour had come for the planners of world-power politics to steer the country out on the course of imperialism. In a few weeks the naval and land forces of the United States disposed of the Spanish navy and troops in and about Cuba. Then American forces occupied Puerto Rico without having to fight a battle. Meanwhile, as American naval authorities had planned it, the American fleet in the Far East, under Admiral George Dewey, destroyed the Spanish war vessels in the harbor of Manila on May 1, and in effect ended Spanish rule in the Philippines. In August when Spain made overtures for peace, Cuba was freed from her dominion and Puerto Rico and the Philippines were at the command of the United States. Although most Americans had not thought of the war as a war for imperial expansion according to the Mahan-Lodge-Roosevelt formula, they now faced the issue of turning the war for the liberation of Cubans into a triumph for imperialism.

They had a foretaste of what was coming, moreover, in the annexation of the Hawaiian Islands on July 7, 1898, by a joint resolution of Congress. The Hawaiian Islands had long been coveted by several European Powers and by Japan. American missionaries had gone there early in the nineteenth century and Americans had taken part in the development of Hawaiian sugar interests. Before the close of the century Americans in the islands had grown restless under the government by native rulers. In 1893 they had revolted against Queen Liliuokalani, compelled her to abdicate, and established a republic. Under the administration of President Benjamin Harrison they had negotiated a treaty with the United States providing for annexation; but not long after he was inaugurated President on March 4, 1893, Grover Cleveland deliberately blocked the project.

The Republicans simply bided their time. In June 1897 the McKinley administration made a second treaty of annexation with the government of Hawaii controlled by Americans, and its ratification by the United States Senate was pending when the war with Spain broke out. Fearing endless delay, if not defeat, sponsors of annexation then substituted for the treaty a joint resolution of Congress, which required only a majority vote in each house for passage. The resolution was carried. On August 12 the islands were formally annexed and in 1900 they were given a territorial form of government.

In the preliminary peace settlement with Spain in August 1898 it was agreed that Cuba should be free, that Puerto Rico should be ceded to the United States, and that Manila should be occupied by American troops until the terms of the formal peace were determined.

For weeks McKinley withheld his decision on the fate of the Philippines. Meanwhile advocates of annexation, on the platform and in the press, worked hard to convince the American people that it was their opportunity and duty to annex the distant islands and spread American civilization among the natives.

At length McKinley made up his mind in favor of annexation and Spain was compelled to yield. In the final treaty drawn up at Paris, independence was granted to Cuba; Puerto Rico and Guam were ceded to the United States; and the Philippines were transferred to the United States in exchange for a payment of $20,-000,000.

When the treaty of peace, including provisions for the annexation of the Philippines, was placed before the Senate for ratification, senators of the anti-imperialist school felt that their worst forebodings were to be justified. In war resolutions of April 1898 they had barred all plans for the annexation of Cuba and repudiated in stern and specific language every imperialist ambition in that connection. Now they realized that, by the treaty, the United States was to be thrust into the eternal wars of the Orient and into the endless intrigues of the great Powers of Europe.

As they understood the departure from the traditional foreign policy, America was henceforth to be one of the imperialist empires of the world, following the course of Spain and Great Britain in conquering and ruling subject peoples, forever warring for more territory, commerce, and dominion over other races. Immediately there was formed in the Senate an opposition so determined that the McKinley administration, backed by Theodore Roosevelt, Lodge, Mahan, and their followers, was greatly worried lest ambitions for world power be thwarted.

Soon the politicians of the McKinley school discovered that they might not be able to secure even a bare majority of the senators for the approval of the annexationist treaty, to say nothing of the two-thirds majority required by the Constitution. Exasperated by the prospect of losing their prize, they denounced the proposal to reject or recast the treaty as shameless effrontery, a reckless repudiation of national honor. In their perplexity and quest for backing they even welcomed William J. Bryan, so recently described by Republicans as an addlepated criminal, when he came to Washington and urged his followers in the Senate to vote for ratification on grounds of national honor; for without the support of Democrats and Populists defeat was certain. By strenuous efforts enough senators personally antagonistic to imperialism were at last rounded up by party whips, and the treaty was ratified with a declaration to the effect that the question of the future of the Philippines was to be left indeterminate. The fateful commitment had been made. Two years later Cuba was forced to accept the so-called Platt Amendment establishing an American protectorate over the island.

Before the conflict over the treaty with Spain was settled in 1899, news arrived that a rebellion had started in the Philippines. For years these islands had seethed with resentment against Spanish rule. The leader of the opposition, Emilio Aguinaldo, was in open revolt when the United States declared war on Spain and his aid had been sought by American army officers in defeating Spanish forces in the Philippines. When this object had been achieved he and his supporters hoped or assumed that at last independence was to be established for the Philippines, as it had been promised to Cuba.

Their expectation of freedom was soon dispelled. On February 4, 1899, a slight collision occurred between Aguinaldo's men and American soldiers and several lives were lost. Ignoring his efforts to arrange an amicable settlement, American authorities pressed the war against the "insurrectionists," who regarded themselves as "patriots." This war went on for more than three years. Early in 1901, with the assistance of Filipinos who had been loyal to the Spanish regime, Aguinaldo was captured and forced to take an oath of allegiance to the United States. But guerrilla fighting continued until July 1902, when President Theodore Roosevelt officially declared it to be at an end.

While the Philippine war was in full blast during the summer of 1900, members of a secret society in China, called the "Boxers," started an organized rout of foreigners. They murdered missionaries in the provinces, killed the German minister in the streets of Peking, and besieged the British quarters in Peking to which hundreds of aliens of various nationalities had fled for safety. At once the United States joined Japan, Russia, Great Britain, France, and Germany—the great imperialist Powers—in sending troops to the Chinese capital, where they broke the siege of the British quarters and put down the Chinese "insurrection" against foreigners.

In connection with the settlement at the close of this conflict, John Hay, the American Secretary of State, adhered to a policy for the Far East, now known as the "Open Door." He proposed that the rights already guaranteed to foreign Powers in China by treaty and international law be protected; but he urged that "Chinese territorial and administrative entity" be preserved and that "the principle of equal and impartial trade with all parts of the Chinese Empire" be safeguarded for the world. For the damage to foreign lives and property, done by the Boxers, heavy indemnities were imposed on the Chinese government, and Hay's doctrine was conveniently ignored by the great Powers engaged in seizing and dividing the spoils of China.

☆

Against the background of these war events the presidential campaign of 1900 was carried on. The Republicans renominated McKinley and associated with him Theodore Roosevelt, now ac-

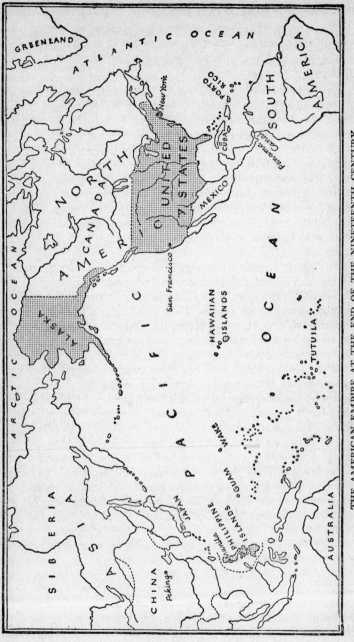

THE AMERICAN EMPIRE AT THE END OF THE NINETEENTH CENTURY

claimed a hero of the Spanish War in which he had done a little fighting, as candidate for Vice-President. In their platform they took a firm position in support of the gold standard, celebrated the "splendid triumphs" of business and commerce under the McKinley administration, and stood fast against everything that smacked of Bryanism in 1896. Concerning foreign affairs, they declared that the war with Spain had been "unsought and patiently resisted," but had been "triumphantly waged" when it came. As a result of the war, "to ten millions of the human race there was given a new birth of freedom," and to the American people "a new and noble responsibility." With respect to the Philippine insurrection against this birth of freedom, the Republicans proposed to put it down and "to confer the blessings of liberty and civilization upon all the rescued peoples." In other words, they advanced confidently in defense of their domestic program and their foreign policies.

In response to this challenge on domestic and foreign policies, the Democrats renominated Bryan and, besides reaffirming their faith in their principles of 1896, declared their belief that imperialism was a curse to the nation. They lashed it as a new and dangerous threat to the American Republic. They asserted that the Filipinos could not be made citizens without undermining our civilization or subjects without imperiling our form of government. Since the United States now had these wards, however, the Democrats promised them a stable form of government, independence, and then protection against outside interference. They condemned "the greedy commercialism" which dictated the Philippine policy of the Republican administration and impugned the war against the Filipinos as a war of "criminal aggression." "Militarism" they decried as meaning "conquest abroad and intimidation and oppression at home." They were not willing, they declared, "to surrender our civilization or to convert the Republic into an empire." While assailing imperialism, Bryan insisted on upholding his program for the home front that had been formulated for the campaign of 1896.

In justifying their new course Republican orators bore down hard on two types of argument. The first was that of "our responsibility." Their policy, they insisted, was not imperialism; it was the fulfillment of duty to the peoples that had been brought under American jurisdiction as if by an "accident" of history. The Philippines had come to the United States unexpectedly, amid the fortunes of a war fought to free Cuba, and it was our moral obligation to protect these helpless peoples, to civilize them, to educate them, to raise their standard of life, and to confer on them the blessing of liberty.

The second argument of the Republicans pertained to the insurrection in the Philippines, and they shaped it into a question of American patriotism. "Don't haul down the flag!" Theodore Roosevelt shouted as he toured the country in the campaign. It had been raised in the Philippines, enemies had fired on it, every patriot must defend it, and only "copperheads" and traitors sympathized with Filipinos who wanted to pull it down and substitute their banner of independence.

Against imperialism, from the very inception of the war with Spain, a strong opposition was presented by publicists; and in the campaign Democratic politicians contributed their denunciations. William Graham Sumner at Yale University, in an article entitled "The Conquest of the United States by Spain," portrayed the United States as adopting the very course that had led to the downfall of Spain. Imperialism and its works, he contended, would result in bigger armies and navies, bigger debts, a contempt for the Constitution, and more wars whenever the politicians decided that the country needed them. Mark Twain ridiculed the program "for giving civilization to the man who sits in darkness," and condemned the whole imperialist business as a pious fraud devised to conceal commercial greed and lust for power. Andrew Carnegie inveighed against imperialism so fervently that John Hay declared the ironmaster to be "off his head." Bryan crowned it all by proposing to stop the bloodshed in the Philippines at once and make immediate arrangements to prepare the Filipinos for independence.

By the popular decision at the polls in November, McKinley remained President of the United States. He received 100,000 more votes than in 1896; while Bryan, with his program for concentration on the domestic front, dropped below his record of 1896 by nearly 130,000. Imperialists interpreted McKinley's re-election as a final approval of their quest for world power. As in other elections, however, it was impossible wholly to separate the influence of foreign policies in the campaign from the influence of domestic policies.

In any event McKinley's victory, substantial though it was, did not obscure the existence of a powerful opposition. The balloting by counties revealed a pronounced shift of party loyalties, especially in the West where agricultural prices had improved materially after 1896. That signified a return of many farmers to the Republican fold but not necessarily an endorsement of imperialism. Still committed to measures which Republicans attacked as radical and dangerous, the Democratic party was far from death's door and there were many signs that the apparent endorsement of imperialism might not be real, especially in the farming regions of the West and South.

☆

Nevertheless the Republicans were preparing for a rapid advance along their line of world-power politics when President McKinley was assassinated in September 1901. Although his successor, Vice-President Theodore Roosevelt, promised to uphold McKinley's policies unbroken, he had ideas and purposes of his own. McKinley had been timid about foreign adventures, in spite of all that had happened in recent years. He had belonged to the old generation brought up in the belief that the foreign policy of Washington, Jefferson, and Monroe was the correct policy for the Republic. The plans of Lodge, Mahan, and Roosevelt for world imperialism had been alien to his outlook upon national destiny.

Theodore Roosevelt, on the other hand, was of the new generation and, besides loving power for its own sake, he insisted that the nation should pursue a course of power politics in dealing with foreign governments. At the same time he was far less conservative in declaring new domestic policies than were the older leaders of his party. With his imperialism, he coupled pledges of reform on the home front almost in the spirit of Bryanism. He assailed trusts, combines, concentrated wealth, and plutocrats as fiercely as Bryan and the Populists had done. He spoke openly of a more equitable distribution of wealth, of the poverty in great cities, and of social perils within the United States, due to inequalities of wealth.

In fact as President, Theodore Roosevelt, by uniting world-power politics and domestic social reform—pomp and prestige in world affairs with the conciliation of discontented farmers and industrial workers at home—formed a combination of policies that made a strong appeal to the American electorate. He "took the wind out of Bryan's sails," as the saying went, by his operations on the home front, by his "square deal," and provided the people simultaneously with almost daily excitement in his handling of foreign relations. His versatility in this type of statesmanship, or "demagogy" as his opponents defined it, was conclusively demonstrated in the presidential election of 1904.

For that test the Democrats shoved Brvan aside at last, nominated Alton B. Parker, a conservative New York judge, and jettisoned most of the Populist program of reform. Nominated by the Republicans to succeed himself, President Roosevelt came back to the White House in a whirlwind. His popular vote was larger by about 400,000 than McKinley's poll in 1900; Parker fell below Bryan's last vote by more than 1,000,000 and below Roosevelt's by more than 2,000,000. About half a million voters went over to the Socialists and the Populists, but in the Republican avalanche of November 1904 their protests against imperialism and capitalism could be ignored by the Republicans.

Under the leadership of President Roosevelt for nearly eight years a "vigorous" foreign policy was pursued. The insurrection in the Philippines was crushed. An organic law, modeled on that enacted for Puerto Rico in 1900, was put into force in the Philippines in 1902, with provisions for giving the Filipinos self-government piece by piece. The policy of the "Open Door," which was presumed to give American capitalists equal trading rights in China with the British and other capitalists, was upheld and highly praised as indicating something permanent. When Russia and Japan approached a deadlock in a frightful war in 1905, President Roosevelt offered his services in bringing the belligerents together, opened their peace conference at Portsmouth, New Hampshire, and filled the newspapers with blazing headlines about that conference for several days. He negotiated the "Gentlemen's Agreement" with Japan, which forbade the immigration of Japanese laborers to compete with American laborers. With the idea of exhibiting the naval strength of the United States, he sent a fleet around the world in 1907–09. By this action, in defiance of opposition in Congress, he sought to demonstrate to Americans and the rest of mankind that the Navy of the United States was ready for what the diplomats of world-power politics called "eventualities."

In the sphere of action nearer home President Roosevelt pressed for the construction of a canal across the Isthmus of Panama which, in addition to promoting water-borne commerce, would make possible the movement of American naval forces between the two oceans. When he came to the presidency a treaty had been negotiated with Great Britain, permitting the United States to go ahead with the canal. That arrangement set aside an old treaty of 1850 providing for joint construction and authorized the United

States to proceed alone, on condition that there was to be no discrimination among nations in rates fixed for the use of the canal.

Two routes for the canal were then being discussed: one through Nicaragua and the other through Panama. After a heated argument the second was chosen and Roosevelt set about making terms for its construction with the government of Colombia, of which Panama was a part. A draft of the treaty was framed but the Senate of Colombia rejected it. Annoyed by the delay, a few men in Panama, feeling certain that the government of the United States would support them, provoked a revolt against Colombia in 1903. Within a few days President Roosevelt recognized their independence and made a treaty with the new Panama government that granted the United States the right to build the canal through its territory.

Soon "the dirt began to fly," as Roosevelt expressed it, and in 1913 the waters of the Atlantic and the Pacific were joined; the voyage between New York and San Francisco was shortened by nearly 8000 miles. Roosevelt was criticized for his "highhanded action" in dealing with Colombia and he later confessed that he simply "took" Panama to stop endless talk and get the work done.

Just as the building of the canal began Roosevelt resorted to another action in the Caribbean region, also deplored by his critics as autocratic. Santo Domingo had long been heavily in debt to European investors, and their respective governments were considering the use of naval forces to collect the debts. Interpreting it as an omen of possible occupation of the island, President Roosevelt intervened and made a treaty with Santo Domingo authorizing the United States to supervise its finances and the payment of its debts.

When this treaty was rejected by the United States Senate, Roosevelt went forward with his plans anyway. He had an American put in charge of the customs-house in Santo Domingo and sent warships there as a sign that he had force at his command. Senators accused him of violating the Constitution and acting arrogantly, besides ignoring Congress and the rights of the people in Santo Domingo. No doubt some of the European claims against that little country were more than tinged with fraud, but Roosevelt insisted that he was conducting the foreign affairs of the United States and would not be hampered by opponents.

During the conflict over Santo Domingo, Theodore Roosevelt gave to the world a new interpretation of the Monroe Doctrine thoroughly imperialistic in letter and spirit. Was the United States, under that doctrine, to prevent European Powers from using battleships to collect debts in the Latin American countries? If so, what was to prevent them from seizing territory in defiance of the doctrine? Or was the United States to see that such debts were paid? Or should these matters be submitted to arbitration by an international tribunal?

On the issues Roosevelt took a positive stand. Foreign Powers, he declared, are not to seize any more territory in this hemisphere, as the old Monroe Doctrine affirmed; moreover controversies of the kind are not to be submitted to any international tribunal. Then he also proclaimed a new doctrine all his own: if governments in Latin America cannot keep order and pay their debts the United States, having prevented other Powers from acting, must intervene, stop disorders, and make sure that just debts are paid. This pronouncement by the President of the United States was immediately characterized in Latin America as crass "Yankee imperialism." Nevertheless, on this theory, presidential actions in the Caribbean region were multiplied.

Under Roosevelt's successor, William Howard Taft, who had beaten William Jennings Bryan in the election of 1908, imperialistic activity by the President received another name. Republicans now simply called it "dollar diplomacy." The rose under a new name meant that it was the duty and right of the United States Government to seek out and protect opportunities that would allow American businessmen to operate freely in foreign countries and American bankers to make profitable loans abroad. "The diplomacy of the present administration," President Taft explained in 1912, "has sought to respond to modern ideas of commercial intercourse. This policy has been characterized as substituting dollars for bullets. . . . It is an effort frankly directed to the increase of American trade upon the axiomatic principle that the government of the United States shall extend all proper support to every legitimate and beneficial American enterprise abroad."

In conformity with this axiom foreign policy was conducted during Taft's administration. He intervened personally, for example, in China, and tried to secure for American bankers a share of a loan that was being floated in Peking under the auspices of European financiers. Under his leadership advantages were taken of a disturbance in Nicaragua to land American marines in that country and establish there an American "protectorate."

When Woodrow Wilson, after defeating President Taft in the election of 1912, assumed the presidency in Washington, he officially renounced imperialism as theory, but as practice it was by no means entirely discarded. Although President Wilson refused to support Taft's plans for American bankers in China, he adopted strong measures in the Caribbean. The protectorate in Nicaragua was continued. In 1914, Wilson landed marines in Santo Domingo. Two years later he ordered a full military occupation of that country, suppressed its government, set up American military authority, and had a new constitution for Santo Domingo drawn up in Washington.

In 1915, during a revolution in Haiti, American marines were dispatched to the scene, order was restored at a heavy cost of lives, and Haiti put under the control of American military authorities. On this occasion the Secretary of State explained the action in sanctimonious language reminiscent of McKinley: "The United States Government has no purpose of aggression and is entirely disinterested in promoting this protectorate." As a part of the program for strengthening American power in the Caribbean, President Wilson negotiated a treaty with Denmark by which, in 1917, the Danish West Indies, not far from Puerto Rico, were transferred to the United States. Not without reason it could be boasted that the Caribbean had become an "American lake." The phrase was not exactly pleasing to Latin Americans but it rather closely fitted the facts in the case.

Meanwhile troubles had been seething in Mexico and the pot was boiling over when Wilson was inaugurated President. In 1911 its President, Porfirio Diaz, who had long ruled his country with an iron rod, was confronted by a threat of revolution. Too old to fight back as he had hitherto done on such occasions, Diaz resigned and fled to Europe. His flight was followed by one uprising after another. President Taft, then near the end of his administration, was urged to intervene, and "restore order." He refused, however, and left the thorny problem to President Wilson.

For a time Wilson pursued a policy described as "watchful waiting." But in fact he did intervene in Mexico. He declined to recognize the government of a new military dictator, Huerta, who rose to power in the confusion. In so doing Wilson took the position, revolutionary in the history of America's foreign policy, that it was his duty and right to withhold recognition from any government which did not measure up to the moral, political, and commercial standards of the United States. This made the American government a kind of censor over all governments established in foreign countries and seeking recognition in Washington.

Acting on events in Mexico, President Wilson ordered the landing of American marines in Vera Cruz and the seizure of that city in 1914. After Huerta gave up his office a settlement was made and the marines were withdrawn. Again, in 1916, after a Mexican bandit had raided a neighboring town in New Mexico, President Wilson sent American troops under General John Pershing on an expedition into Mexico in search of the marauder. Such was the state of American-Mexican relations when the energies of the United States became engaged in the war on Germany in 1917.

By this time imperialism everywhere was in a crisis. Indeed the United States had scarcely embarked on the new course of seeking world power when even leaders of imperialism in the Old World began to profess anxiety over the growing armaments and darkening perils of universal war. For various reasons, some hidden from public view, the Czar of Russia called upon other governments to hold a general conference on peace. The assembly, including delegates from the United States, met at The Hague in 1899, but did little or nothing to reduce the dangers of war. It adopted a rule that any neutral country could rightfully offer its services as a mediator between nations at war; and it established at The Hague a court for hearing international disputes voluntarily submitted to it.

After two more wars had intervened—the Russo-Japanese War and the war between the British and the Boers in South Africa— the Czar called a second "peace conference" at The Hague, in 1907. Like the first, it did nothing to reduce the growing armaments of the world and was, if anything, a more obvious failure. As later revelations respecting the proceedings of the two conferences disclosed, both were dominated by men holding imperialist doctrines, all bent on gaining advantages for their respective countries. Certainly it could be said with truth that the adventure of the United States in world-power politics had not brightened the outlook for world peace.

CHAPTER XXII

Widening Knowledge and Thought

WITH more or less relation to the ambitions and energies that rounded out the continent and directed political strife, yet not wholly swayed by them, a quest was carried on for more exact knowledge and a better understanding of the physical universe, biology, human history, and the society made by human beings in the United States. Knowledge and thought, of course, had been mingled with the life and labor of men and women from colonial times; and through the years, as American society afforded increasing opportunities and leisure, individuals had devoted themselves, partly or entirely, to searches for more knowledge and to inquiries into the meaning of knowledge and the use of it.

Until near the end of the nineteenth century the American people had depended for the advancement of knowledge and thought, beyond the necessities of working routines, on the sporadic inquiries of curious persons who studied particular subjects and wrote about or taught them. Governments, it is true, often looked into such topics as population, wealth, natural resources, and the output of farms and factories, and issued bulky reports; but knowledge of other matters and theories respecting them were mainly provided by private persons who hunted for facts and figures, made observations, thought about their findings, and published articles, pamphlets, and books.

As the nineteenth century drew to a close and the twentieth century advanced toward its meridian, individuals, as hitherto, continued to enlarge knowledge and bring thought to bear on its meaning and uses. Seekers after precise information and its significance for American society still worked alone, at their own

expense and on their own initiative, and their findings were often
so important for the advancement of American civilization as to be
epoch-making. But to the explorations of self-directed individuals
were now added the explorations of individuals and groups of
workers, financed by mammoth sums of money dedicated to research, who made inquiries in every domain of knowledge,
physical and human. They labored under the auspices of governments, federal, state, and local; of civic societies concerned with
the humanities and civilization; and of special interests desiring
information useful to their designs. In other words, to a considerable and an increasing extent, searching and thinking became more
specialized, more organized, and more heavily financed.

☆

For the simple economy of farms, handicrafts, and small towns
the old method of acquiring and extending knowledge by individual and haphazard research met fairly well the needs of the
people. At all events it was the method generally employed. But
after the Civil War new and vast industries rose in all parts of the
country from ocean to ocean; markets widened from communities
to the national borders and beyond them to the outer world; trade
unions, local and national, were organized; conflicts of capital and
labor upset social peace; and the business of government, state and
federal, became more and more complicated. For a long time
government had been confined mainly to keeping order, building
roads, collecting taxes, and administering poor relief. Now its
officials encountered new and more intricate responsibilities, such
as the regulation of railways and utilities, the adjustment of relations between capitalists and industrial workers, and other problems not to be "solved" by rule of thumb.

On the impacts and problems of this crucial transformation in
economy and politics individual inquirers, as in previous times,
concentrated intellectual energies. The huge collection of American books, articles, and pamphlets dealing with the physical and
human universe, accumulated during the eighteenth century and
enlarged in the age of Jacksonian democracy, was now expanded
by literally millions of publications, general and special, covering
the physical resources of the continent, every branch of economy
to its minutest details, every tendency in action, thought, and
aspiration.

The findings and reports ranged so far and wide that nothing
short of the great rooms of the Congressional Library filled with

card catalogues could indicate their sweep. Any selection of titles minimizes their magnitude. Was it the matter of a better understanding of social beginnings in prehistoric ages won by a long and intensive study of the American Indians? Lewis Henry Morgan, in his *Ancient Society*, published in 1877, illuminated the history of all civilization. The labor movement? John R. Commons and his associates gave a portrayal of it in their *History of Labour in the United States* (1918). The woman movement? A three-volume *History of Woman Suffrage* (1881–87) unfolded that story. A more comprehensive history of the nation? John B. McMaster began to make an answer with his *History of the American People*, the first volume of which came out in 1883. Was it the nature of American intellectual interests? Vernon Parrington dealt with that in his *Main Currents of American Thought*, published in 1927–30. Did citizens seek knowledge of anything else? Vast libraries managed by technical competence furnished bibliographies of specialized writings on a moment's notice.

But mingled with the work of individuals and enlarging it in every direction were the researches of persons and groups set apart for that purpose and financed from public and private funds. Systematic research for knowledge was fostered by the founding and expansion of universities, public and private. State institutions created in earlier times were granted more money by legislatures with which to build laboratories, assemble great libraries, and conduct graduate schools for advanced studies in the sciences, letters, and arts. Old private colleges, such as Harvard and Columbia, were transformed into universities, with research and publication as a primary aim. New universities were established on the basis of gifts by men who had accumulated wealth mainly in the manipulation of natural resources or the expansion of industrial enterprise.

The Johns Hopkins University at Baltimore, endowed by a leading capitalist of that city and named for him, opened its doors in 1876—one hundred years after the Declaration of Independence. About ten years later Stanford University was founded in California by Leland Stanford, a pioneer capitalist on the Pacific coast. In 1892 the University of Chicago, endowed with funds from the oil magnate, John D. Rockefeller, also began the promotion of research and instruction in almost everything under the sun.

By the opening of the twentieth century there were few colleges in the country, new or old, which were still content to teach routine subjects from books in the traditional style. The smallest and poorest of such institutions made efforts to extend the boundaries of knowledge and to teach the new learning that was coming from private inquiries and the graduate schools of the universities.

Systematic research for scientific knowledge and discovery was also carried on by many other agencies. Large industrial corporations built their own laboratories and engaged experts in physics, chemistry, and mechanics to invent new machines and devise new commodities for manufacture. During the opening decades of the twentieth century it became a practice for rich men and women to establish foundations for the promotion of research in the sciences and the humanities directed toward the welfare of mankind, the Carnegie Corporation, the Rockefeller Foundation, and the Russell Sage Foundation being conspicuous examples. In endowed institutions able minds concentrated on medical research that might lead to the conquest of pain and disease or on pure science from which might flow practical results in the physical and moral universe.

In 1916 the National Industrial Conference Board was organized by industrialists and supplied with funds for making studies of industrial and economic questions. Independent institutes of special types, such as the Brookings Institution in Washington, D.C., and the Bureau of Economic Research in New York were created to conduct research in the fundamental problems of economy and government. Trade unions, discovering that matters of collective bargaining were complicated, adopted the practice of employing experts in law, economics, and finance to furnish them information for guidance in policy making and action.

Governments, federal and local, more and more realized the need for organized continuous research. Earlier they had relied mainly upon the knowledge of persons who happened to be in office or upon hasty inquiries by legislative committees in emergencies. Now, confronting new and perplexing problems in administration, they established one after another, often as a result of popular or special demands, bureaus or other agencies of research, frequently in connection with the matter of expenditures and the laying of taxes—that is, in budgetary operations. By the second decade of the twentieth century research and planning agencies, associated with governments, had been set up in all parts of the United States. By that time it had also become a practice for Congress and state legislatures to appoint special committees authorized to employ experts and carry on extensive investigations, before undertaking the business of lawmaking relative to such intricate matters as the regulation of railways, conservation of natural resources, and the provision of social security.

As a result of such inquiries and reports the American people had available an increasing amount of knowledge for use in their private pursuits and callings, in the shaping of their own character and purposes, and in reaching decisions respecting policies of government and social improvement. They could either buy, or read at the swiftly multiplying libraries, books on every subject of historical or current interest; for example, business, industry, agriculture, labor organization, wealth, taxation, politics, natural science, religion, psychology, sociology, anthropology, archaeology, technology, the arts, health, home ownership, crime, poverty, the family, the relation of the individual to society, foreign commerce, international affairs, and the changes which were taking place in national affairs.

Though American life was not so complicated in his day, the first President of the United States had been conscious of the role that knowledge must play in a progressive society. In his first annual address to Congress, President Washington had said: "There is nothing which can better deserve your patronage than the promotion of science and literature. Knowledge is in every country the surest basis of public happiness. In one in which the measures of government receive their impressions so immediately from the sense of the community as in ours it is proportionately essential. To the security of a free constitution it contributes in various ways." When the two-hundredth anniversary of his birth was celebrated in 1932 his desire was being realized in part: the people of the United States had at their disposal a wealth of knowledge of things physical and human—science and literature— to use for the purposes of civilization if they could.

☆

More or less affected by the new knowledge ran currents of thought about its implications, as the continent was rounded out and the inherited society of farms and small towns was transformed into a continental nation of closely integrated parts. In these trends of thought two theories or interpretations competed for supremacy. One placed the individual at the center of interest and made individual enterprise the primary source of invention, progress, wealth, and national greatness. The other emphasized society and general welfare as the controlling concern and insisted that the individual, however enlightened and powerful, owed his existence, his language, most of his knowledge, and his opportunities to the society in which he lived and worked. Both were used by powerful interests in American society.

To the first line of thought the name "individualism" was given. This was a new word that first came into play in the nineteenth century. It was used by Tocqueville in his book, *Democracy in America*, published in an English translation in 1835. As he employed the word, it meant a kind of individual anarchy—the conduct of any person who arbitrarily cut himself off from his family, friends, and society. Near the middle of the nineteenth century economists took up the new idea, individualism, and built a whole system of thought around it.

About the same time reinforcement of the idea came from natural science. In 1859 the English scientist, Charles Darwin, published the *Origin of Species*, mainly emphasizing biology and the struggle of the individual animal for existence—a kind of biological war of each against all. In his later work, *The Descent of Man*, published in 1871, Darwin definitely connected man with the kingdom of lower animals and again laid stress on the struggle for individual existence.

Darwin himself was cautious in his statements respecting the role of the individual in evolution, but the "Darwinians" in the United States and other countries made dogmas of his speculations, maintaining that they were truths beyond argument. Consequently when Americans, released from the strain of their Civil War, rushed to the conquest of the continent and impetuously went into the business of trying to get rich quickly, they had ready for use a theory, an ideology, that justified the strong in accumulating all the wealth they could in any way not too outrageous and in doing what they liked with their possessions.

Between 1865 and 1900 this theory of individualism was worked out by many American writers of marked intellectual power, who published articles and big books on the subject. Soon after he became a professor of political and social science at Yale University in 1872, William Graham Sumner sought to show that all civilization had come from free individual initiative; that all hope of progress and improvement lay in giving the fullest liberty to individuals; and that government interference with this liberty was injurious to mankind. As a sociologist, Sumner gave the support of his branch of learning to the individualist argument.

A contemporary at Columbia University, John William Burgess, a professor of political science, wrote brief articles and large treatises on government and liberty in which he made political science serve the cause of individualism. In the department of economics at Columbia, one of Burgess' colleagues, John Bates Clark, building on the work of other writers, American and European, constructed a whole system of economics out of individualism. At the University of Chicago another economist, J. Laurence Laughlin, taught a version of the theory about as extreme as imagination could make it, short of sheer anarchy.

Meanwhile Charles A. Dana, who had been a kind of utopian socialist in the days of Jacksonian democracy but was now a conservative editor of the New York *Sun*, daily preached individualism with withering scorn for all doubters; and as editor of the *Nation*, E. L. Godkin gave weekly versions of the same doctrine to his readers. In 1893 Frederick Jackson Turner, a professor of history in the University of Wisconsin, published a paper on "The Frontier in American History," which made individualism an interpretation of American history, by ignoring families and communities—that is, mutual aid—and tracing the secret of American uniqueness to the stoutest of all alleged individualists— the man of the frontier, as if there had been no women or families or communities or books or schools or churches there.

When the twentieth century opened, the doctrine of individualism had become a potent influence in American thought. Thousands of men and women, who knew little or nothing of its origins or were indifferent to its one-sided nature, had accepted it as a law of nature in private affairs and public policy. In fact the history of the preceding twenty-five years—the rapid opening up of the West, the swift rise of industries, and the increase of national wealth—seemed to them proof that the theory was in accord with reality.

To coming generations it was transmitted by instruction in universities, colleges, and lower schools as if it had never been analyzed and controverted by minds as able as those by which it had been formulated. So thoroughly intrenched was it in places high and low that President Hoover won rounds of popular applause when he prefixed an adjective to it and spoke of "rugged" individualism. Judging by the fervor of that applause, rugged individualism was the supreme characteristic of the American life, character, and purposes.

The thesis that human beings are actuated merely by a competitive struggle for existence and that society is a product of such individualism was countered by a thesis directing attention to the co-operative nature of human beings and the power of mutual aid in the origin and evolution of society. The sponsors of the associative principle in human life insisted that the creed of individualism, pushed to the extreme of dogmatism, was false to the facts of history, including the history of the United States; or at least so false as to be a gross distortion of reality. They pointed out, with copious illustrations, the heavy debt of all the individuals in the United States to American society for all the tools they worked with, for education, for opportunity, for the protection and benefits bestowed by the government as the representative of society. To ruthless individualism they traced much of the poverty and misery, ugliness and waste, which had marked the years of the uprushing business enterprise. To social action by groups and agencies of government they looked for the measures necessary to master these evils and bring about a greater equality of condition— a higher standard of life for all the people. The ideal of these "humanitarians" was best expressed by their own term "social meliorism"—gradual but effective improvement by social action.

If William Graham Sumner was the sociologist of individualism, Lester Ward was the sociologist of social meliorism. For leadership of this kind Ward was prepared by varied experiences and studies. After serving during the Civil War in the Union army, from which he was honorably discharged on account of wounds, Ward entered the employment of the United States Government and achieved distinction in scientific inquiry and reporting. While pursuing his work in natural science he took up the study of social evolution and in 1883 published the first volume of his *Dynamic Sociology*.

In this and other works Ward dwelt on the co-operative nature of human societies from the earliest times and on the opportunities, devices, and services provided by society for individual happiness and advancement. He marshaled a mass of countervailing knowledge against the individualist, or laissez faire, doctrine of Sumner and his school, and contended that co-operation among individuals, rather than a merciless and unfeeling competition for wealth and power, is the secret of human progress toward welfare for each and all. From his intensive study of the past Ward moved to the conclusion that government, representing society, should be positive not negative in policy and should adopt measures deliberately directed to social improvement. On the constructive side, therefore, Ward chose a middle way between individualism and socialism. By writing and lecturing in this median line of thought until his death in 1913, he helped to give social meliorism a firmer hold on American minds.

Building upon the work of the sociologists and independent inquiries, Anna Garlin Spencer, in *Woman's Share in Social Culture* (1913), dealt systematically with the role of women in social evolution from primitive times to the modern age. In this book she described the important part played by women in the original invention of the domestic, or civilian, arts; in the long development of the productive activities by which the family and society are sustained; and in the formation of the social sentiments necessary for the harmony and welfare of society.

Taking up the conditions of her own times, Dr. Spencer examined the varieties of activities carried on by women in all branches of national life, from industry to education. She demonstrated that women had been energetic in every kind of social improvement and argued cogently that, since in the modern age government was assuming positive duties in raising the standards of welfare, it was a logical and necessary step to grant equal suffrage to women—an equal share in the government. In this contribution to knowledge and thought Anna Garlin Spencer furnished a broader social philosophy for the woman movement then rapidly gaining in force and influence. She also vitalized the whole case for social meliorism by teaching and lecturing on the subject from the pulpit and in leading universities and public halls.

In the domain of economic thought the doctrine of individualism was likewise questioned, especially after about 1880, by several university economists, including Richard T. Ely, Simon Patten, and Edmund J. James. These critics attacked the doctrine on many grounds. They declared that it did not correspond to innumerable facts of human experience. They said it was simply an armchair theory and advised students of economics to go out into the real world, make observations, examine the ways in which industry and labor actually operated, and adjust theories to the facts of economy.

By setting everyone against his neighbor individualism, these critical economists declared, was contrary, moreover, to good morals, especially Christian morals. Poverty, they maintained, was due in part to legislation; not solely to individual idleness, improvidence, and incompetence. Great riches heaped up by individuals they ascribed in part to favors conferred by society, and in part to special privileges bestowed by government. According to their views it was therefore the duty of government to change unjust laws, bring about a more equitable distribution of wealth, and take an active part in improving the lot of the people.

Among the economists who refused to take individualism as the ultimate word was Thorstein Veblen, for a time a teacher at the University of Chicago. He did not concern himself, however, with meliorist reforms. What he did especially was to compare the actual conduct of American capitalists with the theories about their conduct promulgated in the works of the orthodox economists and taken by capitalists at face value. After studying court records and legislative reports on the methods of trusts, combinations, and financiers, so often ignored by theorists, Veblen presented a conclusion startling to defenders of apologetic economics.

In summary, he pointed out that modern business was carried on largely by corporations, not by individuals; that great fortunes had accrued to individuals by the formation of trusts and combines which closed many competitive plants and raised prices; that other great fortunes had been accumulated by selling pieces of paper, called stocks and bonds, to investors at prices far above their true value; that instead of increasing the production of wealth, in innumerable cases big business operations actually reduced the production of wealth.

In a way this was what populists had been saying for years but Veblen expounded the criticism, in his treatise, *The Theory of Business Enterprise*, in 1904, in an ingenious form of learning that made it more palatable to economists in universities and to other persons interested in public behavior and general welfare. This book made no case for social meliorism but it helped to blunt the edge of individualism conceived as guaranteeing the utmost production of wealth and a distribution of wealth according to "merits."

The theory of individualism as applied to political science by John W. Burgess and his school was also countered by other political scientists. According to the individualist thesis recently built up in American books on political science, government represented "the people" and its primary duty was to keep order, defend life and property, and refrain from interfering with economic enterprise. By numerous writers this thesis was attacked as in part contrary to historical facts and in part contrary to the professed ideals of the Republic. They asserted that the government of the United States from the beginning had in fact represented powerful economic classes—manufacturers, financiers, bankers, and planters—actually opposed to the interests of the people at large, and that it had constantly interfered with agriculture and small economic enterprises in order to benefit the holders of special privileges. Even justices of the Supreme Court in Washington, publicists charged, did not merely enforce the Constitution, as some theorists declared, but read into it opinions favorable to "big business."

The meliorist revolt conducted against individualism by political scientists was concisely described by J. Allen Smith at the University of Washington, in *The Spirit of American Government,* published in 1907. In a few words Smith characterized the Constitution as a "scheme of government . . . planned and set up to perpetuate the ascendancy of the property-holding class leavened with democratic ideas." The major political parties he represented as dominated by corporations and men of great wealth. The sources of many evils, such as corruption, he found "not in the slums . . . but in the selfishness and greed of those who are the recognized leaders in commercial and industrial affairs."

Individualism as "no government interference with business," Smith described as merely "the selfish view" of a "relatively small class which, though it controls the industrial system, feels the rein of political control slipping out of its hands." By way of remedies for the situation so described, he proposed the breaking up of big trusts, government ownership of many public utilities, progressive taxes on incomes and inheritances, and other measures included in the program of social meliorism.

By the ferment of critical thought respecting the nature of society historians were the least affected. Busy as a rule with writing stories of political and military events narrowly construed, they paid little attention to social and economic events or to the general ideas entertained by the people. John Bach McMaster's *History of the People of the United States,* the first volume of which came out in 1883, was a notable exception, but it was more of a catalogue or chronicle than a social history as its name implied. History, it was often said, provides the lamp of experience for guidance in the present, but the histories written merely as professional exercises or for the edification of the public dealt with only a small part of the human experience and even with that in a very limited fashion. It was even declared that scholarship must narrate events or meticulously analyze documents and avoid interpretation.

Not until 1895, when Brooks Adams' *The Law of Civilization and Decay* appeared, was much recognition given to the fact that written history in every form had a bearing on what was taking place in the United States and on what would probably come to pass in the future of the nation.

Although Brooks Adams' volume dealt with history in Europe, it set forth a theory covering history in general. His theory was that all human societies pass from a stage of wide dispersion on the land to a stage of high concentration; that they fall under the sway of capitalistic usurers; and that they then enter a period of decay and dissolution.

The theory, whether true or false, was applicable to the United States as well as to ancient Rome and modern Europe. While apparently remote from American politics in 1895, it crashed into the free and easy optimism of many editors, including Charles A. Dana of the New York *Sun*, and of many politicians, especially young Theodore Roosevelt, then at the beginning of his public career, who commented on it in a long review.

At any rate Adams' book was an evidence that some Americans of intellectual attainments were not convinced by the rosy exposition of individualism or of social meliorism either. They did not believe that all was well in the United States and were expecting serious troubles in the years ahead. Indeed, Henry Adams, a brother of Brooks, who had read the manuscript of *The Law of Civilization and Decay* two years before it was published, said in an open letter to the American Historical Association that the big social explosion would come in about fifty years—that is, about 1944.

☆

The changing conditions of American life and the new knowledge and thought were also mirrored in imaginative letters. Authors of novels dealing with the eternal triangle—one man and two women or one woman and two men—even when "historical" in pretensions, were more or less influenced by their times. Imaginative letters after 1865 carried descriptions and interpretations of the swift changes—continental and regional—which had occurred as the national domain was rounded out, industries were expanded, and concentration set in.

Nearly everything human and material seemed to be noted in the myriad pages of "fiction," turned out from year to year: reconstruction in the South; westward pioneering and settlement;

regional customs and practices; conflicts between capital and labor; strikes, riots, and disorders in industry; struggles of immigrants for footholds and social places; the grievances that flared up in populistic and socialistic revolts; every shade of opinion from Puritan distress over the poverty and grime of factory towns to communistic resentments at the whole course of capitalism; variations and clashes of opinion from decade to decade; all phases of the strife for social improvement in every direction; efforts to apply Christian teachings to the perils within the Republic.

Support for the broad statement that imaginative letters were sensitive to all phases of American history is supplied by at least two comprehensive works on American literature: the third volume of Vernon L. Parrington's *Main Currents in American Thought*, published in unfinished form in 1930 shortly after the death of the author, and Alfred Kazin's *On Native Grounds*, published in 1942. Literary critics took account of the fact in current reviews. They generally agreed, of course, that the quality of a novel depended upon the genius, skill, and discipline of the author rather than on the mere quantity or nature of the facts in his pages. But they also held that accuracy of portrayal, whether of regions or characters, and accuracy in representing ideas, whether conservative or radical, were necessary to the creation of "great" literature.

The volume, continuity, and variety of the imaginative literature which depicted the many phases of American life in all parts of the country is illustrated by the following list of twenty-two works selected from two or three hundred novels of recognized quality written between 1870 and 1940:

1871—Elizabeth Stuart Phelps, *The Silent Partner*. A Puritan protest against factory conditions in New England and a plea for better treatment of labor.

1873—Mark Twain and Charles Dudley Warner, *The Gilded Age*. Political corruption and greedy citizens in the age of President Grant.

1880—Henry Adams, *Democracy*. A defense of democracy against the indifference, contempt, and pessimism of the rich.

1881—Helen Hunt Jackson, *A Century of Dishonor*. Cruel treatment of the Indians by the United States Government.

1884—John Hay, *The Bread-Winners*. An attack on labor leaders in the spirit of individualistic capitalism.

1888—Edward Bellamy, *Looking Backward*. Utopian picture of abundance and a good life under a socialistic regime in the year 2000.

1890–98—Hamlin Garland, *Main-Travelled Roads*. Hard-bitten and impoverished farming families of the Middle West struggling for a livelihood.

1894—W. D. Howells, *A Traveler from Altruria*. Conflict between classes and masses in the light of a democratic and socialistic ideal.

1900—Theodore Dreiser, *Sister Carrie*. Cruel fate of the poor and humble in the land of great riches and prosperity.

1901—Frank Norris, *The Octopus*. An epic of great wheat production in California.

1905—David Graham Phillips, *The Deluge*. For democracy against corruption and oppression by the privileged few—financial manipulators.

1905—Edith Wharton, *The House of Mirth*. The new plutocracy against a background of seasoned riches.

1906—Upton Sinclair, *The Jungle*. Poverty, filth, and suffering in a great industrial center.

1910—Jack London, *Revolution*. Industrial strife at a high pitch and in a revolutionary temper.

1911—Edith Wharton, *Ethan Frome*. Cold fate of the poor in New England farming community.

1920—Sinclair Lewis, *Main Street*. Drab, small-town culture in the West—and almost anywhere else in the United States.

1925—Ellen Glasgow, *Barren Ground*. Struggles against poverty and defeat in a rural community of the South.

1933—Jessie Fauset, *Comedy American Style*. Follies of Negroes and whites.

1934—Stark Young, *So Red the Rose*. The South of romance.

1935—Sinclair Lewis, *It Can't Happen Here*. Fascist tendencies in conflict with American ideals of liberty.

1936—James Farrell, *A World I Never Made*. Irish working-class family in a harsh struggle for existence in the urban world of industry and business.

1938—John Dos Passos, *U.S.A.* Graphic pictures of suffering and struggling among victims of misfortune during the great depression, contrasted with the pomp and pretensions of politicians and the rich.

☆

While knowledge in every field, much of it microscopic in detail, was being accumulated, and thought about American society was finding expression in various media, facilities for distributing facts and ideas among the people were multiplying or enlarging. A major facility was the system of education. The principle of free and compulsory education in primary subjects for all children, widely accepted by 1860, was applied in every part of the country, with variations according to the wealth of states and communities and their social composition. By 1910 it was a poor district indeed which had made no provision whatever for primary education.

As the extension and improvement of primary schools proceeded, American people were being induced to accept the idea that even higher education should be opened more freely to the youth of the land and were voting fabulous sums of money for realizing it. Evidence of the advance in higher education is afforded by the following table showing the growth in the number of high schools between 1880 and 1910:

In 1880 800
   1890 2,526
   1900 6,005
   1910 10,213

After the high school had achieved a secure position came a demand to bring college education nearer to the people. In part this demand was met by university extension work and in part by the creation of "junior colleges" in communities able to pay for them through taxation. In 1917 there were 39 such colleges in the United States; by 1932 the number had risen to 181.

With the growth of educational facilities illiteracy declined, despite the mounting immigration of persons who could not read. In 1880 17% of the people ten years of age or more were reported as illiterate; thirty years later, in 1910, the percentage of such illiterates had fallen to 7.7; and, among the white population, to 4.9. At the same time the proportion of boys and girls pursuing higher learning rose. In 1930 one half of all the children of secondary school age were attending a secondary school of some kind, and one person in every seven of college age was enrolled in a college. Nevertheless in 1940 3,000,000 Americans twenty years of age or more had never completed as much as one year of formal schooling.

Popular interest in education was partly measurable in terms of the money spent for it. In 1925 the total annual outlay for all public and private schools, colleges, and various institutions of higher learning amounted to more than $2,000,000,000.

The distribution of knowledge and ideas was widened and

accelerated by the increase in the number and kinds of newspapers, magazines, and books, ranging from the solid volumes of individuals and learned societies to a growing flood of simple comics and "salacious literature" appealing to the lowest common denominators of interest: sex and crime. Improvements in the technology of printing made possible the publication of books, even the classics, at figures ranging from five cents to fifty and sixty-odd cents a copy and such books at low cost were turned out and sold by the millions. A rapid growth in rural free delivery under the United States Post Office, coupled with highway improvement and the automobile, brought the metropolitan daily to the doors of farmers who had hitherto relied mainly upon rural weeklies for news of the country and the world.

Given such opportunities for public education and self-education, only the most unfortunate or the most indifferent and shiftless in the American population remained outside the circle of widening knowledge and thought. If as an outcome of this development there was to be a degradation of American democracy in the coming years, as Brooks Adams prophesied, a share of responsibility would have to be laid at the door of those who sought financial profits in the literature of degradation as well as those who chose to buy it in the market place.

As progress in facilities for distributing knowledge and ideas gathered momentum, the radio appeared, producing an upheaval in education, the results of which were immeasurable. As early as 1916 the electrical transmission of sounds by wireless methods had reached such a stage that Lee de Forest could begin experiments with the broadcasting of music. A few years later, in 1921, the KDKA broadcasting station was opened in Pittsburgh. By 1925 so many stations were in operation that they interfered with one another and the federal government had to intervene and apportion among them "time and space on the air." In 1941 there were 915 licensed broadcasting stations in the United States and the number of receiving sets was at least 56,000,000.

The country had become a vast radio auditorium. In that auditorium the people, literate and illiterate alike, who had ears could hear, amid the confusion of advertising, music, and other "entertainment," speeches by the men and women who thought they had anything to say, on every conceivable subject from canning fruits and vegetables to ways and means of running the whole world.

As to the effects of all this broadcasting, there were acute discrepancies of opinion. Optimists called it progress. Doubting

Thomases suspected that it would lead to a demoralization in both knowledge and thought, with consequences disastrous to the Republic. But at all events, for good or ill, the radio was distributing information and misinformation, ideas useful or pernicious, to millions of people who did not have the brains or the energy or the competence or access to facilities necessary to educate themselves in the old and hard way, or who preferred the new form of instruction.

Into this "educational" tumult the motion picture likewise thrust its power with incalculable effects. What has been claimed to be the "first motion-picture feature" was shown publicly at Richmond, Indiana, in 1894, by the inventor of the machine, C. F. Jenkins. His contrivance was built on the basis of experiments by other inventors extending back in time more than fifty years and was soon improved beyond recognition. In 1905 the first motion-picture theater was opened at Pittsburgh. In 1927 sound-reproduction devices made possible the "talking picture."

By 1942 every town of any size from Maine to California had its film theater—and the combined capacity of the "palaces" was 10,000,000 lookers and hearers. In that year the estimated weekly attendance was approximately 85,000,000. Quickly adopted by colleges, universities, and lower schools, the motion and talking picture was used to supplement and enliven by visual education the customary methods of education.

All the forms of noise that the radio diffused could be utilized by motion pictures, and more too. Now the people, high and low, everywhere, could not only listen to the speeches, lectures, and addresses of talkative men and women on every kind of subject, hear music in all its ranges from symphonies to the syncopations of Tin Pan Alley, and catch the roar and clatter of mass assemblies; they could see animated pictures of persons directing "messages" to them and asking them to support every sort of program, panacea, or scheme of full salvation.

In short, the American people now had at their command agencies almost illimitable in range and speed for the distribution of knowledge and the circulation of ideas true, false, or simply nonsensical. What the consequences of this revolution in communication would be was a theme of emotional debate and sober examination throughout the nation. Would intelligence be stimulated or arrested or destroyed? Certainly mere facilities afforded no guarantee that the information distributed so swiftly and widely was founded on accurate knowledge or that the general ideas put before the people were valid in themselves or good for practical applications. Reports formulated by psychologists who explored the new types of human behavior seemed to indicate that neither mere knowledge nor general ideas nor instruments for their diffusion could add anything to that elusive quality of the human spirit known as intelligence. Opinions respecting the probable outcome, near and distant, of the new agencies and the uses to which they were put varied as widely as the ideas themselves which were shot forth through the air or on paper or on the silver screen to the public at large.

CHAPTER XXIII

Revolts against Plutocracy Grow in Political Power

IF THE glittering prophecy of benefits offered by proponents of imperialism had been fulfilled to the pecuniary advantage of everybody, if capitalists, farmers, and industrial workers had been satisfied with what they received, complaints of populists, trust busters, socialists, muckrakers, and systematic critics of American economy might have fallen on deaf ears. It was not realized. Like all wars, the war with Spain and in the Philippines furnished an immediate boom; but that boom was far from full and permanent prosperity. Dazzling strokes in war and diplomacy gave diversion to many people, especially Republican editors and propagandists. But the public was either fickle or the diversion was incomplete. Protests against the imperialist excursion, during the war with Spain and in the Philippines, grew in volume and intensity as the years passed, especially as the mirage of universal prosperity vanished and public interest converged again on fundamental domestic issues.

In the nature of things there were limits to imperialist ambitions. Territorial expansion could not go on indefinitely without incurring awful war hazards for which the American people were in no mood. By 1900 the world had nearly all been parceled out among the imperialist Powers of Europe and Asia and only petty fragments of territory remained for Americans to acquire if they could. Gone were the huge unexploited spaces around the globe, such as had existed in 1800 and could be easily wrested from defenseless natives. There were no more spoils to be seized by Americans without fights with Great Britain, France, Germany, Japan, or Russia.

In view of the opposition at home to expansion in the Philippines, even the most forthright imperialist scarcely dared to propose more war of that kind, at least candidly, as a policy likely to awaken great popular enthusiasm. John Hay made plans for seizing some territory in China but they were official secrets, and he drew back when Japan suggested that they did not comport with the noble professions of the "Open Door." Besides, the official thesis of the Republicans held that they had intended no imperialism in 1898 and that the Philippines had come to the United States inadvertently during the discharge of a duty imposed upon the country, by an accident or an act of God. Though the Republicans were successful in the elections of 1900, 1904, and 1908, they encountered a formidable antipathy even to that version of their purposes. A similar animosity was displayed by the Democrats against imperialism in the Caribbean region—until their own leader, President Woodrow Wilson, embarked upon it in Haiti and Santo Domingo.

Moreover, from the "empire" acquired in 1899 no streams of riches flowed into the United States, such as Great Britain had drawn from India. No endlessly expanding markets for the "surpluses" of American factories and farms were found. Instead of garnering wealth from their empire, American taxpayers had to face increasing levies by the government of the United States for military and naval outlays and for subduing the guerrilla warfare in the Philippines.

A cold balance sheet of the imperialist undertaking showed a large net loss to the nation as a whole. Filipinos and Puerto Ricans, most of them in wretched poverty, could not buy American goods in billion-dollar lots. Furthermore the agricultural products imported from the "empire" soon entered into competition with the surpluses of American farms. As for increasing the relative export of American goods, that proved to be another delusion—a political romance confuted by experience. There was no relative increase in fact. The export of goods in 1900 amounted to about 10% of the exportable goods produced in the United States. In 1914 the percentage was 9.7; in 1929, 9.8.

Soon after the first flush of war excitement passed it was discovered even by philosophers of the Mahan school that the current naval expenditures, though many times larger than ever, would not provide adequate defense for the Philippines if powerful aggressors chose to operate against them from land bases in the neighborhood. Before he died in 1919, Theodore Roosevelt himself realized this and exclaimed that the Philippines were the Achilles' heel of the American Republic. Only swivel-chair strategists in the Navy Department continued to imagine that American dreadnaughts with superior fire power could easily destroy the Japanese navy and effect American supremacy in the Far East. By no form of economic or military calculation could the imperialism of 1898 be called a blessing to the American nation; or, indeed, from any point of view, an unqualified success. Moreover it failed to divert Americans from their primary interests at home or to quell completely the political uprising against centralized capitalism that had grown to ominous proportions in 1896.

For a time after 1898, it is true, newspaper headlines daily shrieked sensational news of the war with Spain and then sensational news of the war for suppression of the native revolt in the Philippines. Magazines carried solemn articles on "our new obligations" in the dependencies and descriptions of the lands occupied by "our" new subjects. Professors wrote bragging books on America as a "world Power," on colonial administration, and on foreign affairs. Protestant ministers preached sermons on "our new opportunities to save souls." The same newspapers, magazines, professors, and preachers, as a rule, paid slight regard to populist complaints at home about either domestic or foreign affairs, except to curse them as the fruits of evil minds. Judging by such literary appearances, the American people were absorbed in "great" world politics and blind and deaf to the agitations of men and women, now called "mollycoddles," "calamity howlers," and "ignoramuses," who insisted on going forward with Bryan's "battle," or with other kinds of reforms on the home front.

☆

Yet in time the throbs of the war drums were silenced, veterans of the Cuban and the Philippine wars were granted pensions, and the furor over "our new wards" faded out. After all the American people could not live on newspaper headlines, books, magazine articles, or sermons about Christianizing people in remote places. Nor, as events indicated, did many Americans take more than a transient interest in the emotional diversions created by and in the name of imperialism. If millions seemed to approve it in the elections of 1900, 1904, and 1908, with varying intensity of conviction, other millions voted with the Democrats, who denounced every feature of it.

As a matter of fact, in June 1898, while the war with Spain was at its height, Congress, though dominated by Republicans, created an Industrial Commission, composed of senators, representatives, and eminent private citizens, and charged it with studying the disturbing problems of capital and labor. In 1900, while the Philippine war was still in progress, the commission made a report that filled many large volumes and carried recommendations for reforms in capitalist methods.

Indeed, at no stage in the development of political insurgency against centralized capitalism had Republicans been wholly untouched by it. In its origin the very Republican party was itself an expression of insurgency against the supremacy of what it called the "slave power" in the government and politics of the United States. Its hero, Abraham Lincoln, had confessed that he owed the first principles of his policy to Thomas Jefferson, who in 1776 had announced the philosophy of revolutionary equalitarianism, and by destroying slavery Lincoln had dared to commit a revolutionary act himself. Not without justification could Theodore Roosevelt, in an hour of concern with domestic politics, claim that the Republican party "in the days of Abraham Lincoln was founded as the radical progressive party of the Nation."

During the agitations of the subsequent years, that party was harassed by a left wing and supplied recruits to the Greenbackers and Populists. It was a former Republican, Senator Teller, who had tried to strike a blow at incipient imperialism by imposing a self-denying ordinance on the resolution that led to war against Spain. It was a Republican, Senator Hoar, who believed that, had it not been for the intervention of Bryan on McKinley's side, he could have stopped the imperialist adventure in 1900. It was in Republican states and under Republican auspices that the most enlightened labor and social legislation had been inaugurated as the great industrial expansion proceeded.

Insurgency in Republican ranks was accelerated soon after Theodore Roosevelt had settled down in the White House as the successor of McKinley. The high Republican manager, Marcus A. Hanna, sensitive to trends of popular opinion, had insisted on the nomination of Roosevelt as Vice-President in 1900 partly with a view to capturing votes in the West, so deeply infected by agrarianism, and at a time when Republican bosses in New York wanted to get him out of the state on the ground that he was a political "troublemaker." Now this young man of impulses deemed "radical" by his party colleagues had possession of the greatest citadel of political power in the country.

By training, experience, and private reading Theodore Roosevelt was a variant from his predecessors who had come up to power through the pull and haul of politics and had given little thought to the great historical process in which they pulled and hauled. Although, as he said, he learned nothing but orthodox laissez-faire economics at Harvard College, young Roosevelt had studied some history and had early formed some decided views on social conflicts in history and the ways of plutocracy.

In 1897 Roosevelt had published, in the *Forum* magazine, a long review of Brooks Adams' *The Law of Civilization and Decay*—a prophecy of the death of civilization under the heel of capitalistic usury. While he distinctly repudiated Adams' gloomy verdict, Roosevelt confessed that "there is in it a very ugly element of truth. . . . That there is grave reason for some of Mr. Adams' melancholy forebodings, no serious student of the times, no sociologist or reformer, and no practical politician who is interested in more than momentary success, will deny. . . . The rich have undoubtedly grown richer; . . . there has been a large absolute, though not relative, increase in poverty and . . . the very poor tend to huddle in immense masses in the cities. Even though these masses are, relatively to the rest of the population, smaller than they formerly were, they constitute a standing menace, not merely to our prosperity but to our existence." Cautious and qualified as this statement was, it referred to matters which Republican party managers had not noticed, officially at least. They were the matters over which farmer and labor insurgency was highly articulate.

As President, Theodore Roosevelt abated none of his zest for his "big stick" policy in "extraterritorial," that is, extracontinental, affairs. He indulged in feverish exchanges with European diplomats, supported the Open Door in China, and almost daily provided "hot news" for the press by "strokes of state" in foreign policy. In this sphere his constant activities fretted many old Republicans of the Hanna school as well as social actionists who wanted to concentrate on political and economic reforms at home. Those old Republicans felt that they had been hustled into the imperialist adventure by the young "war hawks" of the twentieth century and they were deeply troubled over the possibility that Theodore Roosevelt might involve the nation in a foreign war really perilous to taxpayers, domestic finances and economy, and the management of business in the customary manner.

While Theodore Roosevelt worried conservative Republicans by his lunges into foreign affairs, he won enthusiastic support among liberals and radicals by his domestic policies. When business as usual was threatened by a big coal strike in 1902, President Roosevelt manifested sympathies with the miners. Instead of sending Federal troops to suppress strikers, as the Republican President Hayes had done in the railway strike of 1877, and the Democratic President Cleveland had done in the Pullman strike of 1894, he prepared to use the troops to keep the mines open and productive. He forced the mine owners to accept the arbitration which they had rejected; and he was instrumental in bringing about a settlement advantageous to labor. He also sought to stop the spoliation of natural resources by adopting a policy of conservation—withholding timber and other lands from the grasp of private interests and speculators. Moreover he introduced "righteousness" into politics. While praising "good trusts" and "sound labor leaders," he denounced the "bad" trusts, "malefactors of great wealth," and "anarchistic labor leaders." He also publicly censured many a conservative representative and senator in Congress, while he was careful not to alienate the most powerful men of his party in that body.

Meanwhile reinforcements for progressive insurgency, political and economic, came from many directions in articles, books, and magazines. For example:

Henry George's *Progress and Poverty*, issued first in 1879, grew in influence, spreading the doctrine that many millionaires owed their wealth to the "unearned increment" arising merely from increases in land values.

In 1889, Andrew Carnegie began to publish articles on wealth and labor in which he demonstrated that, while in part great fortunes had grown out of inventions and management, also in large part they had sprung from mere land ownership and speculation, from the markets developed by the social growth of the country, and from easy opportunities afforded manufacturers to acquire immense natural resources at nominal prices, or for nothing.

In 1894, H. D. Lloyd issued his *Wealth against Commonwealth*, assailing the Standard Oil Company, challenging the whole system of individualistic acquisition, and calling for a new order of cooperation.

In 1902, Ida Tarbell began the serialization of her critical articles in *McClure's* magazine, "The History of the Standard Oil Company."

In 1902, W. J. Ghent's *Our Benevolent Feudalism* portrayed

American society as a hierarchy of classes dominated by men of wealth at the top.

In 1901, W. J. Bryan started publishing the *Commoner*, a weekly journal, which soon attained a large national circulation.

In 1906, David Graham Phillips commenced a series, entitled "The Treason of the Senate," in the *Cosmopolitan* magazine, attacking it as a body of rich men who legislated for the rich and defeated the aspirations of the people.

☆

A large school of reformers from right to left attributed most if not all the evils of the Republic to the control of party machinery and all branches of government by Theodore Roosevelt's "malefactors of great wealth," operating through political bosses, local and national. Their proposal for breaking this control was to "restore the government to the people"; and one of the first points of their attack was the Senate of the United States elected not by the people but by the state legislatures—in fact by party caucuses and bosses behind the scenes.

Back in the age of Andrew Jackson, when the Senate of the United States was under fire from popular strongholds, it had been proposed that senators should thereafter be elected directly by the voters of the state—no longer indirectly. In 1893 the House of Representatives mustered a two-thirds majority for a resolution authorizing this change by an amendment to the Constitution. Satisfied with things as they were, the Senate, however, refused to concur and so repelled this attack on its position. Beaten in Washington, advocates of direct election turned to the states and sought to circumvent the Constitution by ingenious devices for having candidates for the Senate nominated at popular primaries.

To make the popular choice at the polls binding on the state legislature, Oregon in 1901 established a system by which the voters could name the United States senator at a regular election and the candidates for the state legislature could pledge themselves to vote for the "people's choice," no matter to what party he belonged. Soon Oregon witnessed the extraordinary spectacle of a Republican legislature electing a Democrat to represent the state in the national Senate.

By 1910 at least twenty-eight states, mainly in the West and South, had in force one scheme or another compelling state legislatures to elect senators actually chosen, previously, at a primary or popular election. Thus the personnel of the national Senate and its temper were gradually altered between 1893 and 1910. In this period also the legislatures of two thirds of the states passed resolutions calling upon Congress to submit to the people an amendment providing for popular election of senators in a regular and constitutional manner.

At length, "softened up" by the arrival of new senators "fresh from the people," the Senate yielded to the House in 1912 and approved a resolution of amendment. It was sent to the states for action. With alacrity the states replied by ratifying the Seventeenth Amendment and the very next year it went into effect. As if derisively timed, the amendment was proclaimed in force by William Jennings Bryan, then Secretary of State. Only sixteen years previously he had been cursed as an anarchist for proposing to lay his rude hands on this bulwark of conservatism, placed in the Constitution by the fathers of the Republic. So swiftly had insurgency advanced in the intervening years that Bryan himself, arch-critic of the plutocracy, had become the chief cabinet officer in the Democratic administration of Woodrow Wilson.

Running along with the movement to expel "plutocrats" from the Senate was an agitation for taking the nomination of all major candidates—local, state, and federal—out of the hands of conventions ruled by professional politicians and entrusting it to the people at the polls. This action was also undertaken by states, one after another.

The instrument chosen for it was known as the direct primary. Laws applying it varied in form from state to state, but their purpose was to force all seekers after nomination for important places in government—local, state, and federal—to offer themselves to the voters of their respective parties in a party election called the primary. By 1910 at least twenty-one states, chiefly in the West and South, had direct primary laws stringent in nature.

These laws by no means eliminated the power of professional politicians over the nomination of candidates, but they disconcerted the "old-line bosses" for a time; they made it possible for many energetic young leaders to appeal immediately to the voters and ride to high places of power in government, in spite of the bosses. For years insurgents had inveighed against the "corrupt machines" of both major parties. Now they had a strong weapon in their hands if they could use it.

Another protest against the machines operated by professional politicians had represented the ballot system in vogue as permitting them to buy votes and watch the voters deliver the "stolen goods" at the polls. This system had been created by politicians themselves. Under it each party printed its own ticket or list of candidates for each election and on paper of a distinctive color. At the polls on election day the agents of each party handed out its ballots—red, white or blue, as the case might be—and kept their eyes on each voter until he dropped his colored ticket into the ballot box.

In many places a practice of "straight-arm voting" had been adopted; that is, party voters were lined up, a party ticket was put into the hand of each, and they were then marched to the polls in formation, keeping ranks until their ballots were deposited. Not only was it easy for party managers thus to lead their henchmen to the polls: they could see who was voting the opposite ticket and, if strong enough, could intimidate men who refused to vote "right." It was an almost perfect system for exposing workingmen and insurgents to surveillance, oppression, and even violence if they refused to follow the party line.

The device adopted for breaking this tyranny over voters was the Australian ballot, containing the names of all the candidates of all the parties, printed at public expense, and distributed only at the polls by public officers. Where it was used the voter indicated his own choice by marking the column of his party himself or the names of persons for whom he wished to cast his ballot. A closed booth was provided so that ballots could be marked secretly and ballots were folded so that no one could discover for whom citizens voted.

This reform was introduced first in Massachusetts, and in Kentucky in a limited fashion, in the year 1888. Within eight years thirty-six other states had adopted it. Additional legislation improved the system, and by the opening of the century such secret balloting had become a general rule in the United States. Thus intimidation at the polls was reduced and the political independence of voters increased. Money provided by the campaign funds of the parties and threats of retaliation, or even physical injury, could no longer be as effective as in the "good old days of open voting."

While the revolt against established political methods was drawing the governing power closer to voting men, the demand of women for the right to vote was renewed and gained strength. A national suffrage organization was formed. A proposed amendment enfranchising women throughout the nation was introduced in Congress in 1869. Three years later women pressed their claims on the Republicans and in doing so reminded them of the services rendered by women in the recent war for the preservation of the Union. Republican leaders still wanted the aid of women, especially help from the magnetic orator, Anna Dickinson—the "American Joan of Arc"—in the campaign of 1872, and the Republican party declared that it welcomed women to spheres of wider usefulness; that their demand for additional rights deserved "respectful consideration."

But women soon learned that they were to have no automatic victory in the national capital and they took the hard road to their goal by winning the suffrage, step by step, in the states, under the nationwide leadership of such indomitable citizens as Elizabeth Cady Stanton, Lillie Devereux Blake, Mathilda Joslyn Gage, and Susan B. Anthony. These women and others traveled up and down the land and appealed for the enfranchisement of women to voting men in the cities, villages, distant rural districts, and on outlying farms. They argued their case before members of state legislatures and constitutional conventions, published journals of agitation, wrote articles and letters to the newspapers, issued books on the subject, and spared no labor in their efforts to persuade the hostile or indifferent that their cause was just and vital to the advancement of democracy.

For some years their gains in the states were discouragingly small. Wyoming, which had established equal suffrage while still a territory, continued the practice after admission to the Union in 1889, despite strenuous objections in Congress. Four years later women won the ballot in Colorado. In 1896 they were victorious in Utah and Idaho. During the furor over imperialism and conferring the blessings of liberty on "our brown brothers" in distant dependencies, no advances were made, though women carried on their agitation with unremitting tenacity. After that militant outburst had lost its glamor women began to win victories rapidly: in Washington, 1910; California, 1911; Oregon, Kansas, and Arizona, 1912; Nevada and Montana, 1914. At length the ice was broken on the middle border: Illinois in 1913 conferred on women the right to vote for presidential electors and so gave them a greater leverage in national elections.

After older leaders had procured the ballot in several states, younger women, mostly college graduates, turned to the weapon of political power to shorten the struggle for full national enfranchisement. They built a backfire against obstinate members of Congress and Eastern politicians who aspired to the presidency. Led by Alice Paul and Lucy Burns, women organized, in the states

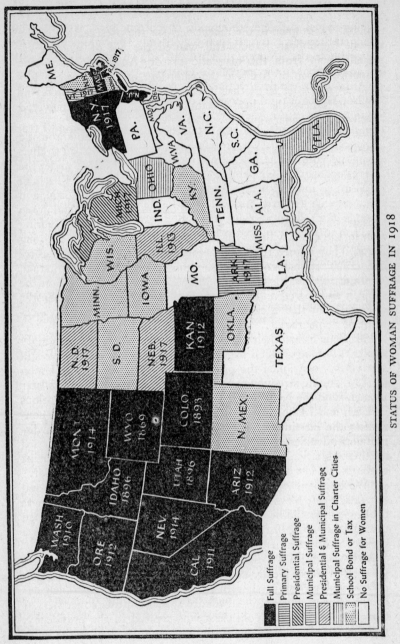

STATUS OF WOMAN SUFFRAGE IN 1918

Full Suffrage
Primary Suffrage
Presidential Suffrage
Municipal Suffrage
Presidential & Municipal Suffrage
Municipal Suffrage in Charter Cities
School Bond or Tax
No Suffrage for Women

having equal suffrage, thousands of enfranchised women who pledged themselves to cast their ballots only for candidates openly favorable to the adoption of equal suffrage on a national scale—by an amendment to the federal Constitution.

Although these new tacticians were unable to move Woodrow Wilson from his rigid opposition to such an amendment during the campaign of 1916, they secured the endorsement of the Republican candidate, Charles E. Hughes, and a helpful support from Theodore Roosevelt. On a referendum the next year, 1917, women won the vote in the great state of New York, and in 1918 they were successful in Oklahoma, South Dakota, and Michigan.

With so much power already in the hands of women voters it was difficult for any politician in Washington to treat their demands with historic ridicule or indifference. Indeed President Wilson was finally moved to call upon Congress in September 1918 to pass the suffrage amendment to the Constitution. With the aid of Republicans, who secured possession of both houses in the elections of the following November, the requisite two-thirds majority was won for the Nineteenth Amendment—in the following June. Quickly ratified by three fourths of the state legislatures, it went into effect in time for the presidential election of 1920. Equal suffrage had been made the law of the land.

☆

As insurgency flourished in the form of verbal criticism and new methods for making it effective by direct elections were brought into use, conservative managers in both the major parties were finding it harder to keep a tight rein on candidates, legislatures, executives, and courts in the former style. In seeking to escape the perils of defeat they had to make concessions to this growing independence. King Canute had to move his throne.

Aware in 1908 that the Republicans would have to meet again the resolute Bryan running on a platform of revolt in the spirit of 1896, President Theodore Roosevelt planned to take at least some of the wind out of the "Great Commoner's" sails. Having decided not to run for a "second election," he fixed upon his Secretary of War, William Howard Taft, as his successor and presented him to the country as a progressive, as a man who would follow "my policies." Roosevelt then threw the weight of executive influence and patronage on the side of Taft and had the pleasure of seeing the Republican convention bow to his will. Conservatives in the convention did it with a wry face, but they yielded as gracefully as they could.

Yet the Republican platform of 1908 gave little recognition to the unrest abroad in the land. The platform was "safe" enough to please even the followers of the late Marcus A. Hanna. After consultations with President Roosevelt, however, the candidate, Taft, made several gestures to the left in his campaign speeches. He declared himself in favor of the popular election of United States senators, which stalwarts in his party had long opposed as an assault upon the Constitution. The taxation of incomes, execrated in 1895 by Joseph Choate as communistic and populistic, Taft endorsed in 1912 mildly, not enthusiastically. Labor, he said, had a legal right to organize, strike, and bargain collectively; and in some cases, he admitted, the courts had oppressed labor by the use of injunctions.

The methods of modern business, Taft thought, were generally sound, but since there had been too much speculation, stock watering, and fraud, reforms were needed in this relation also. The currency system, assailed by Bryan, was, in Taft's opinion, defective in various respects and should be made more flexible. As for socialism, he spoke gently of its "very humane and kindly theories," while dismissing it as wholly impracticable. In other words, from the Republican view of 1896, Taft was tainted with insurgency, but with the aid of the doughty Roosevelt and his followers he defeated Bryan, who stood fast on his populistic principles and made another vehement campaign that terrified conservatives.

Reflecting changes of the intervening years, President Taft translated some progressive policies into action. He supported the adoption of the resolution by Congress which provided for the income-tax amendment to the Constitution. He pressed for a revision of the tariff, a thorny question carefully avoided by Roosevelt. He urged upon Congress, in defiance of express companies, a bill for the establishment of a parcels post and Congress complied with his recommendation.

Many bankers had long opposed a plan for creating a postal savings system in the Post Office Department. Under Taft's leadership the plan was enacted into law by Congress. Since the passage of the Sherman Antitrust Act in 1890 the prosecution of trusts and combinations in restraint of trade had been neglected. President Taft launched an active campaign against them and the Supreme Court responded by ordering the Standard Oil Company and the American Tobacco Company to dissolve. Compared measure by measure with Theodore Roosevelt's regime, President Taft's administration, though less spectacular, could be correctly characterized as on the whole more "progressive."

Nevertheless soon after Taft's term opened a rebellion broke out against him within his own party. Several Republican senators and representatives, including Senator Robert M. La Follette, of Wisconsin, and Senator Albert J. Beveridge, of Indiana, were enraged by the high rates in the tariff bill of 1909, voted against it, and took the stump against it. On his return home from a hunting trip to Africa and a visit to Europe, Theodore Roosevelt expressed irritation over Taft's policies and measures, accused him of taking a reactionary tack on the tariff, conservation, and other issues, and launched an opposition in the Republican camp in 1910.

Hints of a general insurrection were received when the voters in the congressional election of that autumn sent a Democratic majority to the House of Representatives. In 1910, also, insurgent Republicans and Democrats in the House overthrew the system by which the Speaker, Joseph Cannon, and a few chairmen of committees were permitted to determine whether any bill was to be debated or passed. Populists had condemned this system, in season and out, and now a Republican House had annihilated it. The next year a group of Republicans, up in arms against Taft's policies, met at the home of Senator La Follette in Washington and formed a Progressive Republican League to unite all the forces of insurgency within the party.

As the campaign of 1912 drew near, Democratic managers were all agog with excitement. In Republican dissensions they saw at last a chance to carry the election—the first since 1892 when Cleveland had won his second term and then, by his conservative policies, had split his own party asunder. The only question among the Democrats was whether they were to turn right or left in this golden opportunity. Three times they had failed with Bryan as their leader and radicalism as their inspiration. But they had failed far more miserably in 1904 when they veered over to the gold standard and conservatism.

Even with the Republicans divided, the prospects were clouded. Would Bryan run again—for the fourth time? If so, could he be elected? If he withdrew or could be pushed aside, what man and what policies were most likely to bring the triumph at the polls for which Democratic hearts panted? It took a shrewd calculation to discover the person and the appeal that would carry the Democratic banner to victory in a time when the historic patterns of both parties were being badly shaken along a broad front.

For years an influential journalist in the East, George Harvey, long closely associated with powerful men in the "plutocratic" wing of the Democratic party, had been thinking that Woodrow Wilson, president of Princeton University, had the right character and the right ideas for a successful career as a Democratic politician. As a professor Wilson had taught politics and government, and from his youth he had nursed political ambitions. While professor and president at Princeton he had always taken a conservative position on public questions. He had despised Bryan and everything connected with Bryanism. He had angrily opposed Bryan in 1896, had even refused to sit on a platform with him, had attacked his theories as "foolish and dangerous," and in a private letter had expressed the hope that Bryan might be "knocked into a cocked hat."

For the policies of Theodore Roosevelt, Wilson had a dislike almost as intense. He had denounced government regulation of railways and assailed federal regulation of corporations. As late as 1909 he had upbraided trade unions for interfering with individual liberty. In fact there was scarcely an item in the populist or progressive program which Wilson had not frowned upon in public addresses and in private letters. From the standpoint of Harvey and his Wall Street friends, therefore, Woodrow Wilson seemed to be the ideal candidate to swing the Democratic party back to the conservatism of Grover Cleveland, and capture control over the government of the United States.

After some astute negotiations Harvey induced the Democratic boss of New Jersey, James Smith, to nominate Wilson as the party candidate for governor of the state in 1910. Weakened by the factional fights in their ranks, the New Jersey Republicans were ill prepared for the fray; and Wilson, without going beyond generalities in his campaign speeches, won the election with little difficulty. The first step in Harvey's plan to make Woodrow Wilson President of the United States had been achieved, and now the President-maker turned to the final act of his play. At the masthead of *Harper's Weekly*, which he edited, he flung out a sign reading: "For President, Woodrow Wilson."

But it was known that the J. P. Morgan Company had once come to the financial aid of the Harper publishing firm and, besides, Woodrow Wilson had plans of his own. With keen discernment he decided that Harvey's conservative designs did not comport with the progressive temper of the country and would bring disaster in the election. So he brusquely told Harvey that his open support was no longer desired. Wilson's name was taken from the masthead of *Harper's Weekly* and he assumed direction of his own campaign for nomination and election.

Having severed ties with "reactionaries" in his party, Wilson set about securing the Democratic prize. He toured the country, even to the Far West, and made numerous speeches in the progressive vein. He repudiated conservative doctrines he once had espoused; he approved nearly all the items that had long been listed in the populist program. He sought the friendship of Bryan whom, a few years before, he had wanted to see knocked into a cocked hat, and declared in his presence at a great public dinner: "There has been an interesting fixed point in the history of the Democratic party, and the fixed point has been the character, and the devotion, and the preachings of William Jennings Bryan." To the horror of incredulous Democrats he endorsed direct democracy—the initiative and referendum—although he did not press that issue. With the support of Bryan at last secured, Wilson won the nomination for President at the Democratic convention in Baltimore after a hard tug of war among the politicians.

Aware that progressive interests were laying hold of the country, Theodore Roosevelt threw his hat into the ring for the Republican nomination. But he was rejected in favor of President Taft at the party convention in Chicago. Declaring that the nomination had been "stolen" from him, Roosevelt and his followers then formed an independent party and adopted for it the name "Progressive." At a separate convention he was nominated as the Progressive party candidate for President.

The platform of the new party endorsed practically all the insurgent political reforms, such as direct primaries, popular election of senators, the initiative, referendum, and recall, woman suffrage, and recall of judicial decisions annulling social legislation. It approved the regulation of corporations, conservation of natural resources, income and inheritance taxes, and limitations on the use of injunctions in labor disputes. In fact William Jennings Bryan was delighted with the doctrines enunciated by Roosevelt and the Progressives. He declared, ironically, if wistfully, that they were a long time coming around to the propositions for which he had battled for the last twenty years.

In his campaign Wilson expounded many views of economic and political affairs that squared with the assertions made by laborites, populists, and socialists during the previous thirty or forty years. While rejecting their remedies he agreed with their contention that the Industrial Revolution had fundamentally altered the economic scene, that old political theories did not fit the new order, and that the government of the United States had long been run by concentrated business interests in their own behalf.

"Our life has broken away from the past," Wilson exclaimed. "We have changed our economic conditions, absolutely, from top to bottom; and, with our economic society, the organization of our life. The old political formulas do not fit present problems; they read now like documents taken out of a forgotten age. . . . The government of the United States at present is a foster child of the special interests. It is not allowed to have a will of its own. . . . The government of the United States in recent years has not been administered by the common people." Continuing in the spirit of the revolt against the plutocracy, Wilson maintained that "the masters of the government of the United States are the combined capitalists and manufacturers of the United States"—"the big bankers, the big manufacturers, the big masters of commerce, the heads of railroad corporations and of steamship corporations."

Theodore Roosevelt's speeches vibrated with similar denunciations of the "big interests" and similar promises to restore the government to the people. Caught between the fire of Roosevelt and the fire of Wilson, President Taft, in a sober and dignified manner, defended his administration against their charges and sought to show that in fact it was both progressive and enlightened. Having again nominated Eugene V. Debs as their candidate, the Socialists contended that if big capitalists did rule the country, as the politicians were now agreeing, it was time to break their dominion by nationalizing the means of production from which they derived their money and their power.

The votes in the election of 1912 revealed unmistakably the growing revolt within the two major parties and outside. They also disclosed sharp differences of opinion as to what must be done about the problems brought to the front by American thought respecting the Industrial Revolution, especially the accusation that the country was dominated by plutocratic interests. Wilson was elected but his popular vote was smaller than that given to Bryan in either 1896 or 1908. Indeed it fell short by nearly 2,500,000 of the total vote cast against him. Roosevelt polled about 700,000 more votes than Taft but the combined Progressive and Republican vote was below that polled by Roosevelt in 1904 and even below that received by Taft in 1908.

There was no better evidence of the strength of the political revolt than the number of ballots cast for the Socialist candidate, Eugene V. Debs. Notwithstanding the radical talk of Wilson and Roosevelt against "big business," the vote for Debs was more than double the Socialist vote of 1908. It approached the million mark —that point which hitherto in American history had indicated an impending explosion.

Despite the clashes of opinion over what was to be done about the problems of domestic economy, one thing seemed verified: the glittering promises of prosperity to be won by imperialism and the expansion of foreign trade made little appeal to the voters. Indeed Republicans did not make much of their "dollar diplomacy" in the campaign; and Democrats spurned imperialism as they had in previous years. The glories of empire and aggressive foreign policies had not, as prophesied by populists, extinguished progressive insurgency on the home front. Nor had they eased the clashes of interests on the home front.

As if in recognition of a national uprising against imperialism and all its works, Theodore Roosevelt veered back to domestic issues. Not long before, he had declared that the country needed a war and that everybody who opposed it was a "mollycoddle"; but he was compelled at the Progressive convention in Chicago to come to terms with Jane Addams, an invincible pacifist and anti-imperialist. There he joined in castigating the "barbaric system of warfare among nations, with its enormous waste of resources even in time of peace and the consequent impoverishment of the life of the toiling masses"; and in advocating an international agreement to limit naval forces, with the proviso that two battleships should be built a year until such agreement was reached. There at Chicago he gave up the gospel of imperialism and united with the Progressives in a declaration proclaiming the responsibilities of the Americans at home: "Unhampered by tradition, uncorrupted by power, undismayed by the magnitude of the task, the new party offers itself as the instrument of the people to sweep away old abuses, to build a new and nobler commonwealth."

Confident that he had a popular mandate to act forcefully, Wilson as President assumed the leadership of his party; and during his first term in office, with the aid of progressives and dissidents from both parties in Congress, the following program of legislation was enacted:

The tariff was reduced, not to free trade or a revenue basis, but to a lower level than the country had seen for years.

A new banking law set up the Federal Reserve System, in which old Federalist ideas of centralized banking were combined with more flexibility for the currency and more government control over banking administration.

Laws against trusts and combinations were strengthened and efforts were made by administrative action to tear apart interlocking relations of banks, corporations, and business concerns in the interest of free enterprise—if with little effect.

To organized labor three offerings were made: provisions presumed to liberate trade unions from prosecution as combinations in restraint of trade and to limit the use of injunction in labor disputes; a law fixing eight hours as the standard day for trainmen employed on interstate railways; and the La Follette Seamen's Act assuring better treatment to sailors on board American merchant ships.

Farmers, who had complained about the extortions of Eastern bankers, were conciliated by the establishment of federal land banks empowered to lend them money at a lower rate of interest.

With a view to formulating and enforcing "fair" trade practices for commerce and industry, the Federal Trade Commission was created and endowed with powers to inquire into "unfair" actions in business and make recommendations for legislation to stop them. Though vague in its phrasing, the Federal Trade Commission Act of 1914 departed from the old faith that sharp competition would of itself bring prosperity, and indicated a trend toward a new faith—in government regulation of business enterprises for the public interest.

CHAPTER XXIV

Realizations in Social Improvement

OLDER than the political insurgency that went by the name of Progressive, related to it, and yet in many respects fundamentally independent of political partisanship, were efforts of humanitarians to realize ideals social in nature that transcended personal desires for self-perfection, wealth, prestige, and power. The humanitarians worked in the spirit of civilization which had found expression in colonial times, the Revolution, the early Republic, the democratic awakening, the Civil War, and the preceding age of the rising plutocracy. Now they took advantage of the new knowledge and thought evolved at the turn of the nineteenth century. They sought to apply the theories of social meliorism developed by the economists, sociologists, and political scientists who analyzed and pointed out inadequacies in the doctrines of individualism. The humanitarians were more than students, theorists, and writers, though some of them were all those persons; they were primarily activists anxious to get reforms established. They made minute surveys of blighted areas in national life and searched for ways and means of integrating social theory and social practice.

Literally millions of men and women participated in this wider movement of thought, program making, and implementation. The sources of the movement were broken into special activities by groups of citizens, such as the Association for Labor Legislation, the National Consumers' League, the National Housing Association, and the Association for the Improvement of the Condition of the Colored People, which worked for the realization of special programs. But the movement as a whole was inspired by the common purpose of raising the standards of living, promoting physical and mental health, enlarging the concept of social justice and its applications—in short, advancing civilization in the United States. In social origins and continuous support this movement was mainly, though by no means entirely, instigated by the middle class. It gave effect to aesthetic, ethical, and humane impulses in the democratic way—by proposal, discussion, adoption—within the limits of a reforming, socializing capitalism.

Few of the men and women who carried this movement forward received during their lives the newspaper publicity accorded to warriors, politicians, plutocrats, and criminals. Nor in their death were many of them given revealing obituaries or places in the twenty volumes entitled Dictionary of American Biography. Nevertheless their force of character, intellectual powers, steadfastness in research, in educating the public, in drafting legislation and advocating it before committees of government, municipal, state, and federal, so influenced the thought of the nation that ideas once "dangerous" became commonplaces, accepted by persons who had formerly fought to the last ditch the new proposals put up to the country. The humanitarians not only broke down the resistance of private interests and legislatures. They also compelled a reconstruction or re-education of the United States Supreme Court which for more than forty years had been reading into the federal Constitution, as Justice Oliver Wendell Holmes remarked, the laissez-faire doctrines of Mr. Herbert Spencer, English individualist.

Chief among the labors of the humanitarians were attempts to overcome, by public and private collective actions, the poverty, diseases, misery, and hazards of ill-fortune which millions of Americans suffered. It was their thesis that such adversities mocked the liberty, equality, pursuit of happiness, and general welfare professed as American ideals at the establishment of national independence.

In the struggle over social improvement advocates and opponents were aligned as groups and organizations. The alignment was not as wholesale or always as sharp as in the strife of political parties, but conservatism and insurgency appeared within it as in political struggles for power.

In the run-of-the-mill opinion social conservatism signified the support of measures and practices which protected concentrated wealth, and the methods of acquiring wealth, against interference on the part of government. "We have among us," wrote the economist, Richard T. Ely, in 1894, "a class of mammon worshippers, whose one test of conservatism, or radicalism, is the attitude one takes with respect to accumulated wealth. Whatever tends to preserve the wealth of the wealthy is called conservatism, and whatever favors anything else, no matter what, they call socialism." A person may love old ways and draw his ideals from a past which he deems saner in its views of wealth, Ely went on; yet if he would, "by social action," endeavor to change certain tendencies and conserve the treasures of the past, "he is still a radical in the eyes of those men whose one and sole test is money."

This was not, however, the whole creed of social conservatism. Many elements entered into it—some of them inherited from the days when America was a country of free land and immense natural resources open to energetic individuals capable of improving their condition by initiative and persistent labor. Other features were newly formulated under the head of individualism—a theory which, as we have said but repeat for remembrance, enclosed four main propositions as follows. It is individuals struggling to make a living and acquire property who set productive activities in motion and create the wealth which makes the country great and prosperous. In this struggle each individual is rewarded according to his personal contribution to the stock of wealth; his wages or profits are the measure of his contribution. Poverty is the "natural" outcome of individual idleness, lack of enterprise, imprudence, improvidence, and in many cases drunkenness. Although Christian charity may relieve poverty here and there, nothing vital can be done to prevent or remove its mass. Efforts to overcome it by government action—that is, by collective action—will merely hurt the capable portion of the population and pauperize the poor.

The theories advanced by the activist humanitarians against the thesis of conservatism were not closely knit into a single argument or philosophy, as a rule. Yet, however formulated, the theories of the activist humanitarians denied the truth of the conservative assertion that gross inequalities of wealth, signifying poverty, are decreed by any iron law of nature; that the riches of the rich are merely the rewards of their thrift and enterprise; that the poverty of the poor is solely due to indolence and improvidence. They accepted the contention of the sociologists such as Lester Ward and Anna Garlin Spencer to the effect that the individual, no matter how enterprising, derives the knowledge, the inventions he makes and uses, and the security he enjoys from the common life of society and the government that holds it together.

The active meliorists insisted that ills in society have various origins—such as accidents in industry, insanitary and congested conditions of labor and living, contagious diseases, and other adverse factors which can be removed or prevented or diminished by special measures. These changes, they argued, can be brought about peacefully, by group and public action, and this dire poverty can be abolished, misfortunes mitigated, special privileges inimical to the interests of society destroyed, and the quality of the common life improved.

☆

A summary of the concrete proposals for social improvement conceived in the meliorist spirit was presented to the country in two works issued near the turn of the nineteenth century. The first was *Socialism, Its Nature, Strength and Weakness*, published in 1894 by Richard T. Ely, a teacher of economics who combined studying, observation, and theorizing with the formulation of programs for social action. The second was *Poverty*, published in 1904 by Robert Hunter, a student of economics who turned to social work in the slums of New York City and witnessed the making of poverty at first hand. Taken collectively, the proposals for action offered by Ely and Hunter included these:

Taxation of incomes and inheritances, and application of the revenues to social purposes.

Making all factories and tenements sanitary and safe.

Stamping out contagious diseases by public-health measures.

Shortening hours of work, especially in dangerous and laborious industries and for women and young people.

Public care of defectives and dependents, separating them from the body of employable and industrious workers.

Insurance against sickness, unemployment, and accidents in industry.

Compensation to workers injured in industries through no fault of their own—a great source of poverty and family distress.

Old-age pensions.

Establishment of minimum hours and wages in "sweated" industries and enforcement of sanitary standards by public authority.

Regulation of tenements, planning and improvement of cities with provision for parks, playgrounds, and other recreational facilities.

Conservation and wise use of natural resources.

Raising standards of physical well-being by compulsory public-health measures.

Extension and improvement of public education for all the children of all the people.

Long before the nineteenth century came to a close practically all the ideas of social improvement which Americans of later generations were to debate, modify, amplify, and apply had been formulated and thoroughly discussed by reflective persons from one end of the country to the other. Moreover for the first time serious studies had been made of the actual distribution of wealth in the United States. For a hundred years or more that subject had been talked about but few facts had been available as a basis for informed talk. Social reformers made guesses respecting the amount of wealth and poverty that existed. Conservatives admitted that there was some poverty in the United States but they declared that it did not amount to much or was deserved; that in any case America was the most prosperous nation in the world and good enough for anybody. At length statisticians tried to reduce the loose talk about concentrated wealth and poverty to something like a statement of facts.

In 1893 George K. Holmes, of the United States Census Office, formulated the following estimate: "Twenty per cent of the wealth of the United States is owned by three-one-hundredths of one per cent of the population; seventy-one per cent is owned by nine per cent of the families, and twenty-nine per cent of the wealth is all that falls to ninety-one per cent of the population." Holmes' generalization was immediately attacked as inaccurate. Richard T. Ely, in using it, admitted that, owing to the backward state of the American census, calculations respecting the distribution of wealth in the United States were "extremely uncertain." But he added: "All estimates agree in one respect, and that is in attributing a greater concentration of wealth to the United States than to any other modern country." This did not mean that a larger proportion of the people in the United States than in European countries were in poverty. Such was not a fact, Ely conceded. Yet there was no doubt in his mind that America was cursed by widespread poverty in spite of all that could be truly said about prosperity.

Determined to find out with as high a degree of exactness as possible just how much poverty there was in the United States, Robert Hunter made an extensive study of the subject, using the various kinds of available figures. In 1904 he reported the results of his work in his book bearing the plain title, *Poverty*. This was his summary: "There are probably in fairly prosperous years no less than 10,000,000 persons in poverty; that is to say, underfed, underclothed, and poorly housed. Of these about 4,000,000 persons are public paupers. Over 2,000,000 working men are unemployed from four to six months in the year. . . . Probably no less than 1,000,000 workers are injured or killed each year while doing their

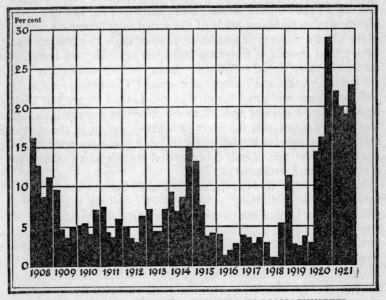

PERCENTAGE OF ORGANIZED WORKERS IN MASSACHUSETTS
UNEMPLOYED, 1908–1921

work . . . We know that many workmen are overworked and underpaid. We know in a general way that unnecessary disease is far too prevalent. We know some of the insanitary evils of tenements and factories."

If Hunter had examined conditions in rural regions as carefully as in the cities, he could have noted that a special census of 1900 reported more than thirty-five per cent of American farmers as tenants—an increase over 1880 and 1890. He did state, however, that over fifty per cent of the farmers were either tenants or held their land under mortgages—propertyless or only partial owners of their homes.

Hunter's estimates were in turn attacked and shown to be in some respects lacking in accuracy if not exaggerated. Owing to the indifference or hostility of certain officials nothing approaching precise and comprehensive figures on poverty was accessible to the people of the "greatest nation on earth." Though precision as to the total picture was impossible in these circumstances, it was certain that there were millions of persons on some form of relief and that millions of self-respecting workers were from time to time unemployed or received wages which were too small or too irregular to keep them from the uncertainty of livelihood and the pinching want known as poverty. At all events, while statisticians disputed, Americans who observed poverty at first hand or suffered from it personally protested against it and demanded amelioration by concerted efforts, private and public; and leaders in the labor movement, who had direct contact with social conditions in industrial cities, promoted what was frequently called the "war on poverty."

Since one of the first needs in the quest for social improvement was the facts in the case of wages, hours, employment, unemployment, industrial accidents, and similar matters pertaining to the actual condition of the people, a demand went up for two immediate actions for meeting this need: the creation of labor bureaus to collect such figures; and the addition of questions to those already used in the decennial census taken by the government of the United States. Massachusetts replied to the first demand in 1869 by establishing the first bureau of labor statistics in America. Between 1869 and 1885 similar bureaus were set up in several other states. In the latter year provision was made for a federal Bureau of Labor in the Department of the Interior. Subsequently the bureau was transferred to the Department of Commerce and Labor and in 1913 it became a separate Department of Labor in the federal administration. Among its duties the Department of Labor was to "foster, promote, and develop the welfare of wage earners, to improve their working conditions, and to advance their opportunities for profitable employment."

The year before the separate department was established, Congress created the Children's Bureau "to investigate and report upon all matters pertaining to the welfare of children and child life." In 1920 the Women's Bureau was set up in the Department and charged with "formulating standards and policies for promoting the welfare of wage-earning women, improving their working

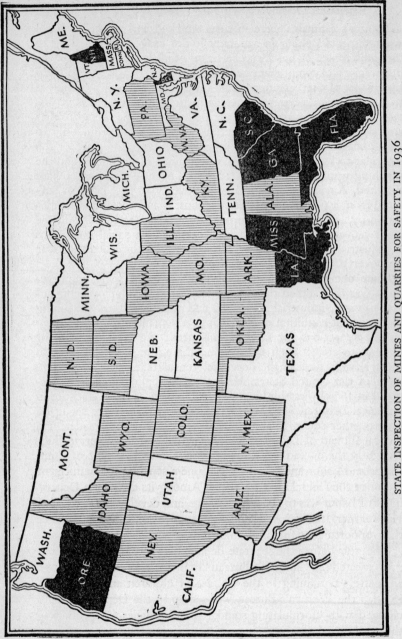

STATE INSPECTION OF MINES AND QUARRIES FOR SAFETY IN 1936

Twenty-three states (white) empower state labor departments to inspect mines and quarries to enforce safety and sanitation laws. Seventeen states, (vertical lines) assign this duty to independent state mine departments. Eight states, (black) do not provide for state inspection of mines and quarries, but some of these have little or no mining or quarrying.

conditions, increasing their efficiency, and advancing their opportunities for profitable employment."

Meanwhile the census takers of the United States were ordered to ask more questions of the people; various departments and bureaus of the federal government collected additional figures relative to all great branches of American economy; and state governments increased their annual output of figures and descriptions bearing on the health, employment, wages, home-ownership, and welfare of the people under their jurisdictions. These reports were supplemented by special studies of all the major phases of American life, from overcrowding in city tenements to tenancy and poverty in the most backward country districts. Eventually Americans, who cared and wanted to know realities, could acquire solid information on the conditions of the people everywhere in the United States.

☆

In practice social improvement advanced along many lines as men and women, individually and in organizations, moved against what they conceived to be specific evils in the general situation of substandard living. The march toward these objectives was uneven and the gains varied from place to place.

Massachusetts, for example, led the attack on factory conditions harmful to industrial workers. Building upon a law of 1842 which fixed a ten-hour day in industries for children under twelve years of age—itself eloquent of the "good old times"—Massachusetts established a system of factory inspection in 1867; a state labor department in 1869; an effective ten-hour law for women in 1874; and a general law respecting industrial safety in 1877.

Soon statutes of this type began to flow in a large volume from the legislatures of the most highly industrialized states. In special occupations and industries the working hours of men were curtailed by legislation. By 1910 nearly a third of the states had fixed an eight-hour day for labor on public works. In the single year of 1907 twenty-three states enacted laws reducing the hours of toil for men in mines, smelters, and underground work generally, on trains and in other occupations where the strains and dangers of industry were peculiarly severe. Although the courts were early inclined to hold that men would have to look after themselves, the principle was finally established that the hours of labor for men, as well as women, could be regulated by law; the old idea that endless drudgery was the unavoidable lot of all workers had been widely abandoned and the doctrine of shorter hours both to relieve fatigue and enable workers to have the benefits of some leisure, in which to develop their other powers, was fairly well established.

A second type of labor legislation pertained to sanitation and safety in factories and mines. The Massachusetts general law on this subject, enacted in 1877, was followed by amendments in that state which steadily elaborated the details of public control over the building and operating of factories once regarded as a purely private matter for owners and managers. Other states soon framed laws based on the Massachusetts model and within twenty-five years such regulations were in force in nearly all great industrial regions.

Henceforward in progressive communities it was necessary for factories to be built with more regard to safety and ventilation; for dangerous machinery to be guarded by protective devices; for heat to be supplied in cold weather; for boilers to be maintained in good order and regularly inspected; for certain standards of cleanliness to be observed; and for sanitary appliances to be installed. Henceforward it was necessary for mine owners to provide their mines with arrangements for ventilation, safety, and the escape of workers in cases of explosions and other accidents if such escape was at all possible. Henceforward manufacturing in tenements was restricted and in the case of many commodities wholly forbidden for reasons of sanitation and general welfare. From year to year the early laws were supplemented by amendments and new statutes which made tighter and tighter the public control over the material surroundings in which industrial workers labored—a control of vital importance for the safety, health, comfort, and well-being of millions engaged in industry and mining.

Lagging far behind legislation respecting sanitation, safety, and hours was the extension of aid to working people injured in the course of duty. Here the traditions of the common law were used by lawyers and employers to throw the burden of accidents mainly on the workers. Under those traditions the employer was not liable for damages unless he was personally responsible for an accident; he was not liable at all for accidents due to "unpreventable causes" or to the negligence of the injured employee or a fellow employee. And any person injured in an industry could secure damages only by a lawsuit which might be long, expensive, and futile. Thus employers were under no economic compulsion to take every possible care against accidents by providing safety appliances; and the poverty of the poor was increased by the necessity of meeting the costs of most injuries incurred in mills, factories, mines, and transportation industries.

Proposals to shift the burden of accidents to industry itself were made early in the rise of the factory system but they were fiercely and effectively combatted by employers. This reform, it was said, would take money unjustly from employers and give it to workmen guilty of carelessness or malicious negligence. Judges and lawyers usually adopted this view respecting life, liberty, and property.

As machine industries multiplied, accidents increased. "Fourth of July orators," declared H. R. Seager, the social economist, in 1910, "delight to point out the various fields in which we excel, but there is one field of which they say very little, and that is that we kill and injure more workingmen in proportion to the number employed on our railroads, in our mines, and factories than any other country in the world." Statistics of accidents, like those of poverty, were far from complete, but there were enough to show that in the number of accidents America certainly led the whole world.

To extirpate this source of pain and poverty men and women from coast to coast held meetings of protest, drafted remedial laws, and besieged the halls of Congress and the state legislatures. Two schemes were proposed, one mild, the other thoroughgoing. The first modified the old common-law rule and compelled the employer to pay compensation for injuries whenever accidents were due to his negligence, that of his employees, or to the necessary risks of the industry. The second was a system of accident insurance. It required employers to insure their employees against accidents just as they insured their buildings against fires, cyclones, and explosions; it provided for easy and inexpensive methods of compensating injured persons, or their families in case of death, without requiring them to engage in tedious and costly lawsuits.

In 1913 the state of New York, by constitutional amendment, authorized legislation of both types and the backbone of the resistance to industrial insurance was broken. Some men and women who had begun the struggle for this social improvement, amid the din of "great party battles" in the eighties and nineties, lived to see the principle of accident insurance well established in every enlightened state in the Union.

Even more devastating than dangerous machinery as a source of poverty and misery was chronic disease or intermittent sickness.

Through the long centuries bad health had been looked upon as a necessary evil or an act of God or as a private matter between the individual and his doctor, if he could afford a doctor. But with the advance of medical knowledge mankind discovered that, while many diseases seemed to be hereditary or due to personal faults, others were social in origin—sprang from contagion and from methods of working and living in society. Indeed a large number of them were new "occupational diseases," arising from the use of chemicals and materials in certain processes, such as the making of matches and pottery, or from sheer fatigue.

Slowly it also dawned in the public mind that even those diseases due to heredity or personal faults constituted a costly burden for industry and society. They reduced the efficiency of workers and the number of working days in industry. They increased the heavy public expenditures to maintain hospitals and institutions for the sick, injured, and defective. In short, besides direct cost for care running into millions of dollars each year, diseases reduced the productive power of the people to a degree calculated in terms of money at billions of dollars annually.

Here then was another recognized problem, partly individual and yet involved in factory management beyond the control of individual workers. Operating as single investigators and in groups, men and women concerned with raising the standards and values of life in the United States studied this problem. They made careful surveys and devised remedial plans to be enacted into law and enforced by public agents.

Near the middle of the nineteenth century their activities were accelerated as epidemics of smallpox and cholera aroused national interest in a new subject, "public health," or social health. Amid the terror over epidemics Massachusetts created in 1849 a commission to investigate the sanitary conditions in the state and the report of that body served as the basis for extensive legislation directed against the social sources of disease. In 1853, shortly after cholera had spread death and fright in the city of New Orleans, the State of Louisiana, at the insistence of public-spirited men and women, organized a department of public health and began a public attack on the roots of disease with a view to prevention. As research enlarged medical knowledge during the closing years of the nineteenth century, a public-health movement, led by enlightened citizens and many special societies, professional and lay, carried on agitations in favor of "social medicine." They forced city councils and state legislatures to act in the interest of public health and gained victory after victory over indifference, ignorance, and often virulent opposition.

Before the twentieth century had advanced far the death rate in the country beginning with infant mortality had been materially reduced; great codes of law incorporating the latest discoveries of preventive medicine had been enacted; every state and every city had a department or office of public health charged with carrying the laws into effect. The war on disease, and on the poverty and misery accompanying disease, had won impressive victories. Not only this. The strategy of new public-health campaigns had been laid out and ideas for achievements hitherto beyond the sweep of imagination had been formulated. Moreover a young generation of doctors and health workers was being trained to carry on through the years of the twentieth century. In summarizing her years' labors in the movement for public health, Dr. S. Josephine Baker, head of the Bureau of Child Hygiene in New York City, symbolized those labors in the title of her autobiography, *Fighting for Life.*

Related to the attacks on conditions partly responsible for disease, but also connected with concern for comfort, beauty, mental hygiene, and social stability, was a collateral drive on the evils of ill-housing, the congestion of people in tenements, the spreading slums, hideous and crime-breeding. As the right of the individual to look after his own diseases had once been deemed sacred, so the right of property owners to herd tenants like cattle into buildings, and yet wrench exorbitant rents from them as human beings, had been regarded as a vested privilege, never to be invaded by government—to be protected in fact to the last penny.

Out of the exercise of this privilege came housing conditions "indescribable in print," as a New York tenement-house report of 1903 put the case: "vile privies and vile sinks; foul cellars full of rubbish; . . . dilapidated and dangerous stairs; plumbing pipes containing large holes emitting sewer gas throughout the houses; rooms so dark that one cannot see the people in them; cellars occupied as sleeping places; . . . pigs, goats, horses, and other animals kept in cellars; dangerous old fire traps without fire escapes; . . . buildings without adequate water supply—the list might be added to almost indefinitely."

In such places lived thousands of industrial workers in the United States; into them crowded new immigrants from Europe. What was to be done about them? They furnished millions of dollars annually to owners in rents and increased land values. One of the most opulent and fashionable religious bodies in New York City had large investments in such property. Thus powerful private interests were arrayed against change and denounced change as subversive and revolutionary.

But men and women of the age lightly called "gilded" declared war on American "rack-renting" and slums, and advanced inch by inch against the vested "rights" of landlords. Campaigns were made and laws drafted to cut away first this evil and then that evil. Windowless rooms were forbidden here; the installation of toilets instead of block privies was ordered there; dangerous firetraps were condemned to repair or destruction. While McKinley and Bryan were arguing about the currency and imperialism, the complaint that reformers would be next demanding bathtubs for the people rose in the land. In 1902 the state of New York enacted a comprehensive and detailed housing law applicable to the tenements of its great cities. Resistance, though by no means broken, was wavering, and the idea of decent housing for the people was competing in the market place of opinion for recognition as a necessity of civilization in America.

From exercising public control over houses and buildings in the interest of public safety, health, and welfare, it was a logical step to the concept of planning whole cities in the general interest. American cities, with a few exceptions, had grown up rapidly and in a haphazard fashion under the stimulus of free enterprise, including the acquisitive instinct. Landowners and real estate speculators had encouraged urban anarchy, with the barest reference if any to the convenience of industry and commerce, to comfort for the residents, to recreation, beauty, and wholesome living. Only here and there, and largely by accident, parks and breathing spaces had been reserved among square miles of brick and mortar and wooden buildings.

But many men and women were thinking about this outcome of greed and carelessness and ignorance. They realized that every social improvement—in factory legislation, health protection, and tenement-house control—was in some way connected with city life as a whole. In response to a growing interest in municipal affairs, a city planning movement came into being. All reflective persons admitted that some city planning seemed necessary. The question was: how much? Engineers and economists studied the subject and wrote on it. In 1907 the city of Hartford, Connecticut, created a city planning commission empowered to make, though not enforce, general plans for the control of building in the community. The example was soon followed in other municipalities. In 1909 the National City Planning Association was founded and began to hold annual conferences. Another field of social improvement was to be occupied.

In the general uprising against poverty, misery, and the inequality of wealth and opportunity, another proposal for curtailing exploitation and effecting a more equitable distribution of wealth gained headway. Corporations holding franchises for operating public utilities in cities had long insisted that they were entitled to earn "all the traffic will bear," and to determine the kind of services they were to render within the usually loose terms of their charters. Next to the large landholders in cities they had profited most from urban development. They had garnered for their stockholders and managers millions of dollars more than a "reasonable return" on prudent investment would have yielded. But efforts were made in cities and states, as well as at the national capital, to reduce and hold within reasonable limits the rates charged by public utilities for supplying water, transportation, electricity, and other services to the public.

By hundreds of state statutes and municipal ordinances enacted during the early years of the twentieth century, the granting of loose and perpetual franchises to utility corporations was definitely ended in American practice; the rates and services of such corporations were subjected to minute regulations in the public interest; and exploitation by corruption and manipulation was curtailed. Even the directors of utilities themselves were so affected by the movement of thought and action that they began to style their companies "public-service corporations." By that time the principle was being firmly established that such corporations were entitled to charge rates no higher than those yielding a fair return on prudent investment.

A primary foundation of the enormous wealth accumulated in the hands of a few thousand families in the United States had been the natural resources of the states and the national domain, bought at low prices and in many cases acquired by fraud and manipulation. As natural resources were diminished through almost unrestrained exploitation, and the glaring waste committed by the exploiters was exposed by investigations, a movement was launched for the conservation of the national heritage in forests, lands, minerals, water power, and other natural riches. Here too a contest was waged against resolute vested interests determined to get possession of the remaining resources still in public ownership, while handling as they pleased the property they already had. In this crusade progress was slow and halting. Yet progress was made.

While General Grant was still occupying the White House a committee of the Association for the Advancement of Science recommended, in cautious language, a change of national policy in disposing of the national forests. Scientists, engineers, economists, and other citizens concerned with the conservation of resources gave thought to the problem, wrote about it, and delivered speeches on it. Gradually they built up a body of exact knowledge and a strong public opinion in favor of protecting and making a wise use of the nation's physical heritage.

Governments in states, such as New York, that still held public lands, began to safeguard them and even to legislate respecting the use of resources in private hands. In 1891 the Congress of the United States, at last affected by the growing demand from conservationists, empowered the President to withdraw forest lands on the national domain from sale. President Harrison and President Cleveland took action under the law, though in no spectacular spirit, and established enormous forest reserves. In 1882, under the inspiration of Bernhard Fernow, the American Forestry Congress was organized to promote the study of forestry and the conservation of forests.

Four years later Fernow was appointed head of the forestry division in the federal Department of Agriculture and inaugurated a systematic study and administration of the national forests. Gifford Pinchot, an associate of Fernow in the movement, became head of the division. From him Theodore Roosevelt caught an enthusiasm for conservation and, as President, by innumerable addresses, conferences, and actions, he dramatized it as a great national obligation.

Hard-driven by the pressure of public opinion, Congress grudgingly enacted new laws for withdrawing resources from sale and making better use of the lands in public ownership. In 1910 it provided for the separation of the subsurface from the surface of coal-bearing lands and for the retention of coal deposits in public hands, while disposing of the surface for agricultural uses. The same year it authorized the President to reserve lands "for water-power sites, irrigation . . . or other public purposes." In 1911, Congress made a radical departure by beginning the policy of buying great areas of forest land in Eastern states where there was no national domain and placing them under federal authorities. Meanwhile other acts made provision for the more efficient control and administration of forests, minerals, grazing lands, and other resources under the jurisdiction of the federal government. Before President Taft retired in 1913 the foundations for the development of national conservation had been securely laid.

☆

All these measures of social improvement merely affected the distribution of wealth more or less indirectly, despite the fact that they were continuously assailed as undermining the vested rights of property owners. But at length they were supplemented by a direct attack on concentrated wealth through the use of income and inheritance taxes. Neither tax was exactly new to American fiscal policy. The income tax and inheritance tax had been employed by Congress in its desperate search for additional revenues during the Civil War. A light inheritance tax, also for revenue purposes, had been adopted by the Republicans in connection with financing the war on Spain. When, however, the Democrats in 1894 attempted to renew the income tax, for the avowed object of making the rich bear their share of national burdens, the Supreme Court declared nearly every feature of the tax unconstitutional.

Defeat only spurred its advocates to more determined efforts; and so impressive was the agitation that a Republican Congress in 1909 submitted to the states an income-tax amendment to the Constitution. Duly ratified in 1913, the Sixteenth Amendment allowed the Democrats, under the presidency of Woodrow Wilson, to make the taxing of incomes a regular part of federal financing. By this time a large number of states had also begun to lay progressive taxes on incomes and inheritances.

Against protests of conservatives that it was communistic, populistic, or socialistic, the principle of apportioning taxes according to riches—ability to pay—was now generally accepted as just. What was more, the use of other forms of taxation for social as well as revenue purposes was securely established in the law of the land.

To utopians—those eternal dreamers and prodders of mankind, always testing practice by purely ideal concepts of life, labor, and government—the achievements of the humanitarians seemed excessively prolonged; meager in proportion to the magnitude of the problems thrown up by the Industrial Revolution; painfully limited in view of the potentials for the production of all the goods deemed necessary to an ideal standard of living; and complacent respecting a possible abundance for the people in the forms of leisure and meditation and work in the creative arts. Notwithstanding such strictures, however, the achievements of the humanitarians, by contrast with the state of things in 1865, certainly represented substantial progress—*Ethical Gains through Legislation*, as Florence Kelley conceived their movement, in which she was herself a national leader. Moreover these accomplishments, in the face of the venomous opposition from individualists, kept alive the spirit of civilization, augmented its force, and prepared the way for grappling with still greater social problems.

CHAPTER XXV

Gates of Old Opportunities Closing

"A FEW GENERATIONS AGO," wrote Theodore Roosevelt with reference to the great coal strike of 1902, "an American workman could have saved money, gone West, and taken up a homestead. Now the free lands were gone. In earlier days a man who began with pick and shovel might have come to own a mine. That outlet too was now closed, as regards the immense majority, and few, if any, of the one hundred and fifty thousand mine workers could ever aspire to enter the small circle of men who held in their grasp the great anthracite industry. The majority of the men who earned wages in the coal industry, if they wished to progress at all, were compelled to progress not by ceasing to be wage earners, but by improving the conditions under which all the wage earners in all the industries of the country lived and worked, as well, of course, as improving their own individual efficiency."

In an autobiography, the story of his long struggle as a labor leader to uphold and improve American standards of life and work, Samuel Gompers dealt with changed conditions of national economy near the end of the nineteenth century and gave his reasons for believing that the unlimited flood of immigrants was threatening to "submerge standards of life and work that we had established." "The majority of immigrants," he explained, "no longer came from western Europe where language, customs, and industrial organization were similar to those of the United States but from the countries of eastern Europe where lower standards of life and work prevailed. As these immigrants flooded basic industries, they threatened to destroy our standards. . . . In the early days, boundless and undeveloped resources made possible and expedient a policy of stimulating immigration. It was not until

411

industrialism developed and there were evidences that the newer immigration was not being assimilated that as a nation we began to consider policies of regulation. The labor movement was among the first organizations to urge such policies. . . . Although I realized that the American people in their generosity wished to maintain the United States as an open, free asylum to the oppressed of the whole world, yet we realized also that the United States could not solve all the problems of the world and that the struggle for human freedom and advancement would largely have to be worked out by each country for itself."

Whatever faults could be found with these pronouncements by Theodore Roosevelt and Samuel Gompers, both statements pointed to an indubitable fact: an epoch in the history of the United States—and the Old World—had come to an end. For four hundred years European adventurers, conquerors, capitalists, and emigrants had been operating in huge regions of the earth's surface, always with open spaces before them—in North America, South America, Australia, the vastness of the African continent below the northern shoulder, and in islands of the seas. There they had enjoyed elbowroom and opportunities for acquiring a living or riches by crude labor processes or exploitation. Into those spaces European countries could dump their surplus population and their "surplus manufactures." As the nineteenth century drew to a close practically all the "waste spaces" had been seized, carved out, and divided up among old and new nations.

After the founding of the English colonies in America, especially after the launching of the American Republic and the opening of the West, venturesome men and women by the millions had crowded into the United States in search of more liberty and wider opportunities for earning a livelihood, for trade, for acquiring land, and for working natural resources. For a full century this immigration had been practically unimpeded by legal restrictions. On the contrary, it had been actively encouraged, by federal laws, state laws, shipping concerns, land speculators, industries in search of abundant, cheap, and docile labor, and by sympathizers with refugees from European tyranny.

With sturdy, able-bodied, industrious, skilled, intelligent, and talented men and women had come criminals, paupers, paralytics, prostitutes, persons suffering from loathsome and contagious diseases, imbeciles utterly unable to take care of themselves, and cripples—all without let or hindrance. European governments had swept up paupers from their poorhouses and paid their way to

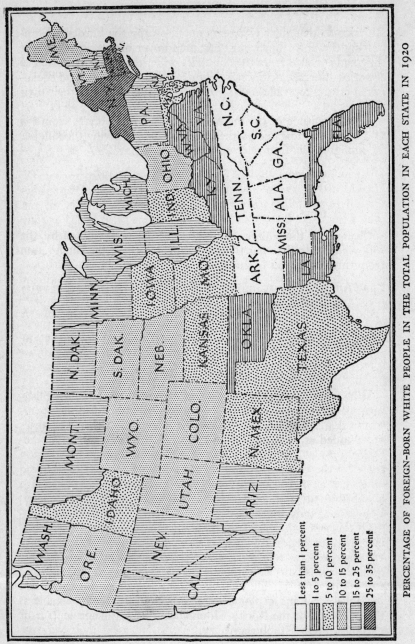

PERCENTAGE OF FOREIGN-BORN WHITE PEOPLE IN THE TOTAL POPULATION IN EACH STATE IN 1920

Less than I percent
I to 5 percent
5 to 10 percent
10 to 15 percent
15 to 25 percent
25 to 35 percent

America so that their taxpayers could escape the burden of supporting the unfortunates of their own lower orders. Furthermore they had expelled from the countries under their control—often to America—liberals, democrats, labor leaders, reformers, and socialists in efforts to evade social problems and agitations in their own societies.

The magnitude of the migration to the United States from the Old World is indicated by the following tables, giving the number of immigrants in four selected decades:

1821–30	106,508
1851–60	2,452,660
1881–90	4,737,046
1901–10	8,136,016

Changes in the sources of this migration are revealed by the following table showing the percentage of the total immigration from three countries in successive periods:

From Austria-Hungary, in 1861–70, percentage of total, 0.33; in 1901–10, 24.4 of the total.

From Italy, in 1861–70, percentage of the total, 0.51; in 1901–10, 23.3 of the total.

From Russia, in 1861–70, percentage of total, 0.10; in 1901–10, 18.0 of the total.

☆

When the trickle of immigration expanded after the establishment of independence, the United States had at its disposal an immense domain of Western lands and resources. Other territories were added at each stage of the westward movement. In all, between 1781 and 1853, the year of the last continental extension made by the Gadsden Purchase, the public domain of the United States had amounted to approximately 1,400,000,000 acres—an area about five times as large as the combined areas of Germany, France, and Italy.

Of this vast public domain all except a mere fragment had passed into private hands by 1900. Of the 1,400,000,000 acres only 186,000,000 acres remained in public possession in 1924; and that domain consisted mainly of mountains, deserts, arid regions, and forest lands not suitable for cultivation. The dearth of more land for cultivation and exploitation was now a fact as indisputable as the existence of the Rocky Mountains. The shrinkage of free or cheap land was a stubborn reality.

It was also portentous for the economy of the United States and the rest of the world. Every informed and thoughtful citizen of the Republic became aware of its implication in terms of diminished opportunity for economic anarchy. No longer was it possible for industrious, prudent, and determined persons of any nationality to make a living or a fortune by exploiting free or cheap natural resources in the crude manner long followed in agriculture, cattle raising, mining, and industry. Newcomers would now have to compete for a livelihood with the industrial, business, and professional classes in America—classes that were becoming "overcrowded." Even Alaska, which had been added in 1867, was nearly all staked out within fifty years and offered little escape from the occupied continental domain.

Not only had the bulk of the arable, grazing, forest, and mineral lands passed into private hands, shutting off such easy acquisition to individuals and corporations. In exploitation the land and mineral resources in private hands were being denuded and depleted in the most extraordinary carnival of waste yet recorded in all history. Arable land by the millions of acres was stripped of topsoil and eroded into ruins by greedy and ignorant cultivators. Grasslands were plowed up and turned into dust storms or overgrazed into deserts. Forests were slashed without regard to future growth, and magnificent trees by the millions were lost in forest fires. Oil, iron, and other mineral resources were exploited so recklessly and swiftly that by 1940 experts in this field of "economics" were justified in announcing that the "richest nation on earth" would be deprived within an appreciable time of the prime raw materials essential to its welfare and defense. It was with the support of confirming facts and figures that young Henry Cabot Lodge could declare on the floor of the Senate in 1943 that the United States was now in some essential aspects to be included among the "have not" nations of the earth.

Equally meaningful was the closing of the American gates against manufactures from the Old World. When the overwhelming majority of the people of the United States had been engaged in agriculture, practically all their exports to the Old World consisted of foodstuffs and other raw materials. With the opening of the Far West, the very soil of America was literally "mined" and sent to Europe in the form of wheat, corn, and other products, at prices actually below the cost of production, counting in the cost the value of the wasted soil. American exports supplied food for millions of industrial workers in Great Britain and on the continent of Europe and raw materials for innumerable industries there. In those days Americans took in exchange an immense volume of manufactured products annually, thereby contributing to the unprecedented prosperity of the Old World.

As the final decades of the nineteenth century passed, however, the percentage of raw materials and foodstuffs included in the total export of the United States declined, while the percentage of manufactured goods in that export increased. Either on account of or despite the protective tariff, the United States as a manufacturing nation was becoming a stiffer competitor of Great Britain and Europe in all the world markets. For the years 1926–30 crude materials, crude foodstuffs, and manufactured foodstuffs amounted in dollar values to only 40.5% of the total export of the United States; while semimanufactures and finished manufactures amounted to 59.4% of the total. That too was a stubborn fact: the gates of the United States were closing on the once wide-open American market for Old World manufactures, and the gates for the outflow of American agricultural commodities were drawing closer together.

Nor did even the Democrats at any time venture to destroy the protective tariffs under which the relative export of foodstuffs and raw materials was falling and the relative export of manufactures was rising. In 1856 they had announced in their platform that "the time has come for the people of the United States to declare themselves in favor of free seas, and progressive free trade throughout the world." But never thereafter did they officially repeat that declaration or even attempt to make a slashing reduction of the protective rates to a mere revenue basis.

Their President, Cleveland, in 1887 severely criticized the existing rates of duty and called for modifications. But he was careful to declare: "In a readjustment of our tariff, the interests of American labor engaged in manufacture should be carefully considered, as well as the preservation of our manufactures. . . . The question of free trade is absolutely irrelevant."

From time to time Democratic platforms condemned the tariff as the "mother of the trusts" or as the cause of various economic distresses. Yet they contained no planks demanding free trade. When in 1913 the Democrats, led by President Wilson, got possession of both houses of Congress and had the legal power to cut tariff rates to a low point, they enacted a tariff bill that was strongly protective, despite many substantial reductions in rates.

Though they returned to power again in 1933, with Franklin

D. Roosevelt as President and a still larger majority, the Democrats refrained from a frontal attack on the tariff duties raised in the meantime by the Republicans to the highest point in American history. In fact President Roosevelt rather brusquely broke up the London Conference of 1933 at which experts had hoped to reduce tariff barriers and reach an agreement on a monetary standard of international trade. He slammed the door on all such undertakings, cut loose from the countries which still clung to the gold standard, and adopted a managed currency for the United States.

Although the Democrats in Congress later authorized President Roosevelt to make "reciprocal" trade treaties with other nations and modify tariff rates, they set limits to the modifications and to the term of his powers under the Reciprocal Trade Act. The act shifted the making of specific rates from Congress to the State Department, over which presided a free-trader, Cordell Hull. But the treaties made under the law, while favoring certain American productive interests as against others, were by no means free-trade treaties.

With endless reiteration the slogan of "lower trade barriers" was repeated, and professors of economics continued to recite the free-trade formulas of their "science," borrowed largely from Mid-Victorian England. Nevertheless the force of stubborn fact was working against projects for wide-open free trade throughout the world. Indeed all the other great nations went over to some form of managed economy, some in the direction of socialism— managed economy in full form.

☆

While agriculture was rapidly expanding as virgin soil was brought under cultivation, while industries were multiplying as resources were exploited by crude methods, protests against the swelling torrent of immigration were ineffective. George Washington, Thomas Jefferson, and John Adams had warned their countrymen against free migration from countries whose people were wholly inexperienced in self-government; but the second generation of Americans mostly ignored their warnings.

It is true that by 1840 immigration had become so extensive that loud objections were raised against it. Protestants were alarmed by the great influx of Catholics. Old-stock Americans were incensed at seeing recently naturalized foreigners flocking to the polls "under bosses" in the cities, and taking possession of municipal governments. In fact opposition to the foreign vote took an aggressive form in the organization of the Native American party in 1848; and later, of the United American, or Know-Nothing, party.

Such protests were largely confined to the East, however, and leaders of the major political parties were skittish about listening to them. Often a presidential election turned on a few thousand votes and candidates quailed at the thought of offending any minority of voters that might have political influence.

At no time before the end of the nineteenth century did either of the major political parties officially call for closing the gates to any immigrants, except oriental coolies. On the contrary, the Republicans in 1864, for the moment styling themselves the Union party, actually endorsed the encouragement of immigration and enacted a law providing for the importation of immigrants bound to labor by contract in such a way as to ensure the payment of their passage.

Although sporadic criticism of untrammeled immigration continued, it was not until organized labor in the United States began a national struggle to maintain and improve standards of work and wages—standards of living—that effective pressure for restrictions on immigration appeared in Congress. Then candidates for the House and the Senate in many districts or states had to calculate whether they had better chances in appealing to the "labor vote" or to the "foreign vote." Other interests were enlisted on the side of restriction, but the labor interest was the best organized and the most persistent. In time its demands were heeded.

Excepting an act of Congress passed in 1875, forbidding the importation of prostitutes and alien convicts, and an act of 1882 excluding idiots, convicts, and persons obviously unable to take care of themselves, the first material restriction imposed on immigration by federal legislation was the Chinese Exclusion Act of 1882. States, to be sure, had attempted to bar paupers. Massachusetts in 1820, New York in 1824, and Maryland in 1833 had enacted laws directed to this end. But such efforts did not cut down immigration, for shipmasters who brought over human derelicts could land them at ports in other states.

It was only at the worst of pauper immigration that Congress struck in 1875 and 1882. The very nature of the two statutes indicated the reckless practices that had prevailed for nearly a hundred years. Prostitutes, criminals, persons likely to become public charges in poorhouses soon after their arrival, and other defectives had been entering the country freely. Now at last the gates were to be closed against such persons from foreign lands. Americans were feeling that they had all the burden they could bear in caring for defectives and delinquents.

The Chinese Exclusion Act of 1882 was the outcome of a long agitation against cheap Chinese labor, in the East as well as on the Pacific coast. In connection with early efforts of the United States to force open the ports of China to American merchants and adventurers, the ports of the United States had been opened to Chinese immigrants by treaty provisions. Americans apparently could not, with a straight face, declare to the Chinese government that they had full freedom to enter China at their pleasure, without granting the Chinese similar rights in the United States. At all events in the treaty of 1868 between the United States and China, the high contracting parties "cordially" recognized "the mutual advantage of the free migration and emigration of their citizens and subjects . . . for purposes of curiosity, of trade or as permanent residents." Taking the cordiality of the American invitation as genuine, and stimulated by appeals of American employers for cheap labor, especially in railway construction, Chinese immigrants soon began to press into the states of the Pacific coast, and many found their way as far east as the factories of Massachusetts.

Very soon conflicts arose between American workers and their Chinese competitors, on many grounds, and as early as 1879 Congress passed a bill virtually providing for the exclusion of Chinese immigrants, in defiance of the treaty with China. President Hayes vetoed the bill. As an act of courtesy a commission was sent to China for the purpose of revising treaty relations. A new treaty was negotiated in 1880 and finally under its terms Congress in 1882 suspended the admission of Chinese laborers for a term of years—later making exclusion permanent.

The enforcement of this law led to constant friction with the Chinese government but efforts to weaken its categorical terms were in vain. The treaty of 1868 had definitely stated that nothing in its provisions should be held to confer the right of naturalization on the Chinese in the United States or on Americans in China. That provision for "reciprocity" could be kept by both parties; and it came about that there was no large "Chinese vote" to worry American politicians.

Responding also to demands from organized labor, Congress passed in 1885 the Contract Labor law—a blow at the importation of any cheap labor by employers seeking to break strikes or cut wages. The act forbade persons, companies, partnerships, and corporations to prepay the passage of aliens or in any way to encourage their immigration under a contract—written, oral, or implied—to perform services or service of any kind in the United States.

Employers soon found a vulnerable spot in the law. They evaded the act by issuing notices that laborers entering the country could find employment at specific places on their arrival. Steamship companies, nearly all of them owned in foreign countries, aided American employers by distributing such notices in Europe and bringing over shiploads of laborers who had full knowledge that they were to work at certain shops, factories, or mines. On renewed petition from organized labor, Congress made the alien Contract Labor law stricter by amendments passed in 1887 and 1888.

It was in connection with efforts to check the practice of drumming up and importing strike-breaking and wage-cutting laborers that Congress, in the act of 1888, introduced a new principle into immigration legislation. As early as 1850 demands had arisen in Eastern cities for the deportation of alien paupers who, soon after their arrival, had to be put into American poorhouses and supported at public expense. Against such demands the government of Württemberg in Germany had protested. It had been sending paupers to the United States to get rid of them and avoid its own responsibility; and it now objected to the idea that the United States could send them back. But at that time American politicians were so intimidated by the foreign vote that they enacted no laws to prevent even such flagrant abuses by foreign interests.

Not until 1888 did Congress provide for the deportation of aliens who had unlawfully entered the United States. In that year it served notice on employers, steamship companies, and foreign governments that the United States had the right and intended to deport aliens at will; that steamship companies or employers guilty of abetting the unlawful entry of aliens would have to pay the expense of carrying them back to their native countries.

Agitation over the exclusion of the Chinese, who unlike Europeans were few in numbers in the United States and so without political power, was accompanied by growing objections to free immigration from all quarters. By 1888, Chinese laborers, contract laborers, insane persons, idiots, and persons likely to become public charges had been denied entrance to the United States. The laws were loosely enforced, but they were at least written in the books. Then, in 1891, Congress grew sterner.

To the list of classes excluded it now added paupers specifically, polygamists, persons suffering from loathsome or dangerous contagious diseases, and, subject to qualifications, persons whose passage had been paid in whole or in part by others. The law also stiffened the enforcement of restrictions imposed by prior acts, especially the prohibition forbidding employers, steamship companies, and their agents to recruit immigrants abroad by advertisements, inducements, and promises of any kind.

In a careful revision of immigration restrictions, in 1903, after the assassination of President McKinley by Leon Czolgosz, a German Pole, Congress increased the list of persons excluded. It proscribed, among others, anarchists and persons believing in and advocating the overthrow of all governments by violence and the assassination of public officials. Again, in 1907, Congress added to the roll of persons excluded. By this time it was bold enough to shut out consumptives, unmistakable imbeciles, and feeble-minded persons in general.

☆

As the gates against free and easy immigration were pushed together inch by inch, opposition to additional restrictions and to the full enforcement of existing laws became consolidated; and it was strengthened by the support of the vested interests. Many American citizens insisted that the old doctrine of the United States as an asylum for the oppressed of all lands was still valid and should never be infringed. They could point, in confirmation of their view, to the inscription on the Statue of Liberty, unveiled in 1886, four years after the passage of the Chinese Exclusion Act:

> Give me your tired, your poor,
> Your huddled masses yearning to breathe free,
> The wretched refuse of your teeming shore.
> Send those, the homeless, tempest-tost to me,
> I lift my lamp beside the golden door!

They argued that sturdy sons and daughters of toil from other lands helped to promote the rapid development of the nation's resources, added to its wealth, enriched its culture, and fortified the love of liberty.

Other opponents of restriction were neither so tenderhearted nor so disinterested as the advocates of liberty in the abstract. At the turn of the century when a new immigration bill was up in Washington, the general agent of the North German Lloyd Steamship Company, then engaged in carrying immigrants from various European ports, wrote to his local agents all over the United States: "Immigration bill comes up in the House Wednesday. Wire your congressman, our expense, protesting against proposed exclusion and requesting bill be defeated, informing him that vote in favor means defeat in next election." Editors of newspapers in which the steamship company carried advertising were also informed by wire that they were expected to oppose the bill.

To such vested interests in the opposition were joined others: American railway interests which transported trainloads of immigrants to the West; employers ever struggling to keep wages low; and a horde of "labor bosses" who profited by supplying laborers of their national origins to big industries, often in the process robbing and cheating their own people in the United States.

The situation was complicated for advocates of additional restrictions and for immigrants themselves, by immigration agents operating alone or in connection with steamship companies and American employers of cheap labor. In Europe these agents gave to prospective emigrants a rosy view of the money they could quickly make in the United States, aided them in evading the immigration laws, and offered them all kinds of inducements for the adventure. In the United States they herded immigrants into blocs according to their national origins, found employment for them, supplied strikebreakers on occasion, and despoiled them of their earnings.

Deluded by the promises and frequently finding their new conditions harsher than those they had suffered at home, many immigrants turned upon the country of adoption in a natural wrath, aggravating the discontent and radical agitations among Americans themselves and evoking more resentment against the influx of foreigners. Extreme radicals joined the hue and cry against restrictions, on a Marxian theory that the worse the plight of workers became, in the United States as well as everywhere else, the sooner would be the revolutionary spring into their kingdom of heaven. On such grounds they harried the American Federation of Labor in its efforts to maintain and raise the standards of life for industrial workers by limiting immigration. Thus, while seeking to keep the gates open, they played into the hands of the very interests which exploited immigrants.

The United States Immigration Commission, appointed to make extensive inquiries into various aspects of immigration, reported in 1911 that economic interests deliberately organized were mainly responsible for the tremendous inflow of Europeans: "The present emigration from Europe to the United States is in the largest measure due to economic causes." Immigrants already here, it conceded, incited immigration by writing enthusiastic letters home to relatives and friends and by sending money to bring them over; but a considerable portion of it was artificially stimulated by "quasi labor agents" and by the "many thousands of steamship ticket agents and subagents operating in the emigrant-furnishing districts of southern and eastern Europe." In other words, the commission found that, apart from the actions of former immigrants settled in the United States, the promotion of immigration had become a money-making game highly profitable to those engaged in it.

☆

Now an old cry, which had been little heeded in the political din of the Jacksonian era, was revived and reinforced: "Immigration is a peril to the Republic, to the institutions of self-government and liberty." Henry Cabot Lodge the elder, senator from Massachusetts, took it up, despite his affiliation with Republican industrialists in search of workers at low wages. Though opposed by many members of his party, especially by Joseph Cannon, Speaker of the House of Representatives, Senator Lodge organized a new drive against immigration. The only question with him was the formula under which it was to be effected. What new and large class of immigrants was to be excluded?

An answer was provided by a proposed literacy test. So far Congress had excluded the Chinese coolies, contract laborers, paupers, idiots, polygamists, anarchists, and other special classes, but no barrier had been erected against persons totally illiterate, such as were now coming from southern and eastern Europe in enormous numbers. A literacy test would push the gates closer together. And on this proposal both Senator Lodge and Samuel Gompers agreed. "So far as I remember," wrote Gompers, "this is the only issue upon which I have ever found myself in accord with Senator Lodge."

Late in 1912, Congress passed a bill designed to shut the gates on illiterates from Europe. Early the next year President Taft vetoed it, and its supporters in Congress could not muster enough votes to carry it over executive disapproval. The succeeding Congress passed another bill similar in principle. President Wilson vetoed it, regarding it as a serious departure from traditional policies. Again Congress failed to muster the two-thirds majority necessary to make it a law in spite of the presidential opposition.

In the following session Congress renewed the battle by passing another bill embodying the literacy test. When President Wilson also vetoed this one Congress defied him by rolling up a huge majority and making it a law without his signature, on February 5, 1917. At this time a great war was raging in Europe, immigration was curtailed anyhow, and there was no opportunity to measure its results in "normal" conditions; but the intentions of the act were clearly and firmly expressed in its provisions.

With certain exceptions, especially affecting persons fleeing from religious persecution, the law of 1917 excluded "all [European] aliens over sixteen years of age, physically capable of reading, who cannot read the English language, or some other language or dialect, including Hebrew and Yiddish." Besides this barrier raised particularly against immigration from southern and eastern Europe, the law of 1917 added to the number of classes of persons already excluded under previous legislation and plugged up many crannies through which evasions had been effected. Moreover, it supplemented the Chinese Exclusion Act by placing an absolute bar against practically all immigration from Asia, except from Japan. Immigration from that country, however, had been cut down since 1907 under the Gentlemen's Agreement between President Theodore Roosevelt and the Japanese government.

Designed to curtail immigration from southern and eastern Europe, two great areas of illiteracy, the law of 1917 by no means guaranteed a reduction in the total number of immigrants admitted annually to the United States. Like other "qualitative" laws, it merely defined the character or quality of persons to be deemed admissible. In legal terms the gates were still wide open to any number of qualified immigrants.

At the close of the first World War all signs pointed to an enormous increase in the annual migration from Europe to America. Then Congress struck at it decisively by putting numerical limits on immigration. By an emergency act in 1921 it fixed the number of aliens of any nationality, to be admitted annually, at three per cent of the number of the foreign-born persons of such nationality actually resident in the United States in 1910 as determined by the census of that year. This cut the total immigration from Europe to 309,556 for the fiscal year 1921–22, to about one fourth the number of immigrants admitted in 1913. As a positive quantitative cut in immigration, the act showed a determination on the part of Congress to put an end to free and easy immigration for all time.

Having made this provision, in the face of an outburst of objections, Congress elaborated it in 1924. In the act of that year it placed a maximum limit on the total annual immigration from Europe—temporarily at 150,000. This number it apportioned among various European countries on the basis of two per cent of the number of foreign-born persons of the respective nationalities, as determined by the census of 1890, with a maximum quota of 100. The return to the census of 1890, which meant a clear discrimination against the countries of southern and eastern Europe, raised a storm of protest from people affected by it. But Congress refused to bow to the tempest. It insisted on making the drastic cut, with its discrimination against southern and eastern Europe. And, responding to labor and other demands from the Pacific coast, Congress in the act of 1924 also placed an absolute bar on the immigration of laborers from Japan; it overthrew the Gentlemen's Agreement of 1907 and assigned to Japan the same position as other oriental countries, in respect of immigration.

Subsequently, as provided in the act of 1924 and later amendments, the total number of quota immigrants for each year was fixed at 154,000 and the quota to be allowed to each foreign country coming under the law was established by a complicated process of calculation. The census of 1920 was taken as the basis. The number of persons in the United States belonging to each nationality in that year was estimated. The ratio of such number to the total number of inhabitants in the United States was then ascertained—as amounting to a certain percentage of the whole. Finally, to each nation entitled to send emigrants under the act was given a number—a quota equal to this percentage of the total number, 154,000, to be annually admitted. That is, for example, if the number of persons of a given national origin in the United States was two per cent of the American population in 1920, the immigrant quota of their country in Europe was two per cent of 154,000, or 3080.

The spirit of the national resolve against free immigration was expressed in the House of Representatives by Knud Wefall, of Minnesota, when, referring to the bill of 1924, he said: "The question [of immigration] is our own to solve in the manner we see fit to solve it. . . . We do not intend to close the door because we were here first but because it is our door. We are now under a reaction of the effects of the first World War. . . . We now want to close the door more tightly while we take stock of ourselves."

The die was cast. The proportion of foreign-born Americans was to decline swiftly. The continent had been rounded out. No more free land beckoned pioneers to the West. Crude exploitation of the continental domain by crude labor and crude capitalism had come to an end. Science might raise visions of wider opportunities for the production of wealth by other methods. But whether such visions were to be realized or not depended upon the competence of the people in the United States to order their economy and govern themselves. There could be no return to the state of things existing in 1900 or 1880 or 1870. And as threats were made in Congress from time to time to reduce immigration to a bare trickle or stop it entirely, prospects of removing the restrictions faded. Only immigrants from Canada, Newfoundland, Mexico, Cuba, Haiti, the Dominican Republic, and the independent countries of Central and South America were exempted from the quota restrictions; even they were subject to numerous restrictions. The gates of the once wide-open "asylum for the oppressed of all lands" had been brought together with a bang that awakened repercussions throughout Europe and Asia. Not even the war gesture to China in 1943, repealing total exclusion and allotting her a quota of 105 immigrants a year, altered this situation.

CHAPTER XXVI

World War and Aftermath

IN THE SUMMER of 1914 the interests of the American people were especially directed to pressing domestic problems. The presidency and Congress were under the control of the Democrats, committed to the reforms of the "New Freedom"—and to the emancipation of the country from its "masters . . . the combined capitalists and manufacturers of the United States," as the Chief Executive of the nation phrased the issue. Since 1899 the Democrats had fumed against imperialism and the entanglements in world politics which imperialism of necessity involves. Now the Department of State was headed by William Jennings Bryan, who had so intransigently combined advocacy of world peace, through treaties renouncing war, with opposition to imperialism.

Despite this concern with urgent domestic affairs, the rivalry of imperialist Powers in Europe and Asia was widely known in the United States. For years the news from Europe and Asia had carried stories respecting the alliance of Germany, Austria, and Italy on the one side; and working agreements between Britain, Japan, France, and Russia on the other side. News reports, books, articles, and essays in increasing volume had made it clear in America that all those Powers were engaged in a frantic race to build up their armaments for war, piling taxes and debts upon peoples already groaning under heavy financial burdens. Observers of world operations along such lines, including President Wilson, suspected that this rivalry among the foreign Powers, if it continued unabated, would end in a holocaust of war, the most destructive that mankind had ever experienced. And yet all that distant quarreling among great nations had not diverted the

American people from concern with their domestic problems.

☆

It was upon a people largely intent upon their own purposes that the calamity of European war burst during the first days of August 1914. When the news of the war came, shocking though it was, the general sentiment of Americans was undoubtedly opposed to participation in the conflict. On August 4 President Wilson issued a proclamation declaring the neutrality of the United States and the following day he supplemented it by another in the same vein. Two weeks later he made a special appeal to the American people to observe the letter and spirit of neutrality: "The effect of the war upon the United States will depend upon what American citizens say or do. Every man who really loves America will act and speak in the true spirit of neutrality."

Despite the President's admonition, the American public was soon deeply agitated by the war and the course of its events, especially as propagandists from both parties to the conflict in Europe descended in hordes upon the country to elicit American support. Many Americans of English descent frankly sympathized with the Entente Allies. On the other hand many Americans of German descent publicly professed their attachment to the Fatherland. Irish, remembering their own history, could scarcely conceal their satisfaction over the thought of a British defeat in the war. Jews, recalling the terrible persecutions which had recently befallen their people in Russia, as a rule deemed the Germans more civilized and more worthy of victory. On the whole, however, the sympathy of a popular majority was on the side of the Allies. Even so, that did not mean that the Americans wanted or expected to become actual fighters in the war.

But as neutrals Americans had certain historic rights under international law and were carrying on activities that were seriously affected by the war in Europe on land and on the high seas. Among the long-established rights of neutrals were the following:

1. Neutrals may sell goods to, and trade with, belligerents in a war—both munitions and goods of peace, or non-contraband goods.

2. Belligerents may lawfully suppress this trade by imposing a blockade on each other to stop the passage of ships carrying such goods; but a blockade to be lawful must be effective, that is, carried out by a sufficient number of patrolling war vessels.

3. If a peaceful merchant ship, whether belonging to a neutral

or an enemy, is caught by a belligerent, it may be seized and confiscated in certain circumstances, but it must not be sunk or destroyed without provision for the safety of the crew and passengers.

Under international law and the laws and policies of the United States, it was the duty of President Wilson to see that these rights of Americans to engage in commerce as citizens of a neutral Power were enforced against both the belligerents in Europe. Thus he was compelled, as the Chief Executive of the nation, to consider American complaints against violations of neutral rights and to act on violations by the parties to the war.

At the outset of the conflict, the government of Great Britain made two decisions affecting the rights of Americans as neutrals. It proclaimed an iron blockade on the ports of the Central Powers and the ports of neighboring neutrals through which goods might pass to those Powers. The perils from German submarines made it impossible for Great Britain to sustain an effective blockade by keeping rings of ships near the blockaded ports; yet in spite of this fact, she declared her blockade effective. The second British decision reduced the number of non-contraband goods which neutrals had a right to sell to belligerents and other neutrals, if they could get them through the blockade. In time the British government included in the list of forbidden goods nearly every important article of commerce, including grain, other foodstuffs, and cotton, hitherto regarded as non-contraband.

Numerous British actions invaded the rights of Americans as neutrals to trade and travel. Great Britain insisted on stopping and seizing American ships bound for neutral countries bordering on Germany, such as Holland, Denmark, Norway, and Sweden. This she did on the ground that the goods they carried would eventually go to Germany or release goods in those neutral countries for sale to Germany. In November 1914 the British government declared that Germans were sowing mines in the open seas and proclaimed the whole North Sea a war zone closed to neutral shippers, subject to British orders.

Against these decisions by the British government, the State Department at Washington made strong objections. It asserted that they were unlawful, violated American rights, and were not necessary to British self-preservation.

Meanwhile the German government was also defying international law and endangering American lives as well as property on the high seas. In 1915, Germany proclaimed all the waters around

Great Britain a war zone and announced that German ships, meaning her submarines now in use, would sink every enemy vessel found within that zone. Under the established international law Americans had the right to travel all the seas on their own merchant ships, on British ships, or on the ships of other countries. If such a merchant ship was caught by an enemy war vessel, the safety and lives of passengers were to be protected by the captor. But a submarine ordinarily could not take on board the passengers and crew of a captured ship about to be sunk. Hence a new instrument of war entered into the extension of the war and helped to destroy the code of international law built up by agreements among the nations.

Against the German threat to merchant shipping in the zone marked out, President Wilson lodged a protest in February 1915. In very clear language he informed the German government that it would be held accountable for American lives destroyed in its submarine campaign. Nevertheless, on May 7, a great British ship, the *Lusitania*, with American passengers and some munitions on board, was torpedoed by a German submarine near the coast of Ireland and 114 American men, women, and children went down to death on the sinking vessel.

To this deed President Wilson objected vehemently and declared that the government of the United States would not "omit any word or act necessary to the performance of its sacred duty of maintaining the rights of the United States and its citizens and of safeguarding their free exercise and enjoyment." The German government replied evasively. In two additional notes to it, President Wilson repeated his objections and warnings. At length in September 1915 the German government replied: "Liners will not be sunk by our submarines without warning and without safety of the lives of non-combatants, provided the liners do not try to escape or offer resistance." It looked as if President Wilson had won a great diplomatic victory.

Although war agitations continued to fan excitement in the United States, as the presidential campaign of 1916 drew near, the majority of the people still seemed in a mood to keep out of the European conflict. At least such appeared to be the judgment of political leaders. With the Progressive party now dying, the Republicans, counting on their recovered unity for success at the polls, nominated Charles E. Hughes as their candidate and in their platform declared that they would maintain American rights "at home and abroad." At the same time they announced: "We desire peace, the peace of justice and right, and believe in maintaining a straight and honest neutrality between the belligerents in the great war in Europe." Renominating President Wilson unanimously, the Democrats praised "the splendid diplomatic victories of our great President, who has preserved the vital interests of our government and its citizens and kept us out of war." The campaign was boisterous and the election was close. At first it was reported that Hughes had carried the country but belated returns from California shifted the balance and gave the presidency to Wilson for a second term by an electoral vote of 277 to 254.

☆

Hoping, perhaps, that he might be helpful in bringing the war to an end, President Wilson, soon after his triumph at the polls, addressed "peace" notes to the belligerents in Europe. His appeal for a peace conference was fruitless. Growing firmer in his resolve to intervene in the diplomacy of the war, he declared to the Senate, in January 1917, that the United States ought to take part in the establishment of peace on certain principles: "peace without victory"; the right of nations to have liberty and self-government; independence of Poland; freedom of the seas; reduction of armaments; and the abandonment of entangling alliances. A few days later the German government announced that it would renew its unlimited submarine warfare. Then without reviving the verbal argument with Berlin, President Wilson dismissed the German ambassador in Washington, Count von Bernstorff, and severed relations with his government.

Within two months six American ships were torpedoed and sunk. By April it was plain that this time Germany would not be stayed or turned in pursuing her peculiar methods of warfare. On April 2, 1917, President Wilson called upon Congress to "declare the present course of Germany to be in fact nothing less than war against the government of the United States." Four days later the war resolution was passed by Congress with a few dissenting votes—fifty in the House of Representatives and six in the Senate.

Having adopted the war resolution, Congress began to frame and pass measures for winning the war, which slashed deeply into the ways of American life. It quickly decided that a volunteer army would not be sufficient for the task ahead or indeed founded on correct principles, and that a great armed force must be raised by a draft of able-bodied males. At first it fixed the age limits at twenty-one to thirty-one inclusive and later at eighteen to forty-five inclusive. To support the armed forces, Congress provided for the floating of loans running into the billions. It increased taxes in every direction, devised new taxes, and raised the rates of income taxes to the incredible figure of sixty-three per cent in the highest brackets—a figure that must have made the eyes of radicals and conservatives surviving from 1896 start from their sockets. Heavier taxes were laid on inheritances. A high excess profits tax was imposed on corporations and partnerships.

Upon the President, Congress conferred broad power to control, regulate, and commandeer natural resources, industries, labor, the sale and distribution of food supplies—in fact to regiment men and women, all callings and occupations, and all activities, in the interest of winning the war. At the same time freedom of press and speech was put under the government ban by Espionage and Sedition Acts, the most severe yet passed in the history of the country. Never before had life and property in the United States been subjected to restrictions so numerous, so onerous, and so deep-thrusting.

A disciplined master of the English language, skilled in the art of clothing noble sentiments in lofty and telling phrases, President Wilson employed his talents in framing war aims and delivering addresses on the subject to Congress, the American people, and the world. In his earlier diplomatic notes to Great Britain and Germany he had dwelt upon American rights of commerce and travel. In his war message of April 2, 1917, he sought to lift the war above such practical considerations. "The World," he said, "must be made safe for democracy. Its peace must be planted upon the tested foundations of political liberty. We have no selfish ends to serve. We desire no conquest, no dominion. We seek no indemnities for ourselves, no material compensation for the sacrifices we shall freely make. We are but one of the champions of the rights of mankind."

Later the President expounded the "war for democracy" as also a "war to end war," to establish permanent peace throughout the world, to make certain territorial changes in the interest of oppressed nationalities, and to force the adoption of new measures for the conduct of international relations. His specific objectives he summarized in fourteen points in a message to Congress on January 8, 1918. Chief among his points of political significance were these: open treaties of peace, openly arrived at, to supplant secret treaties, intrigues, and alliances; freedom of navigation on the seas; the removal of trade barriers among nations, "so far as possible"; reduction of armaments; more liberty for the nationalities in Austria-Hungary; and an association of nations to afford guarantees of rights and peace for all nations, large and small.

Respecting territorial matters, President Wilson favored the re-

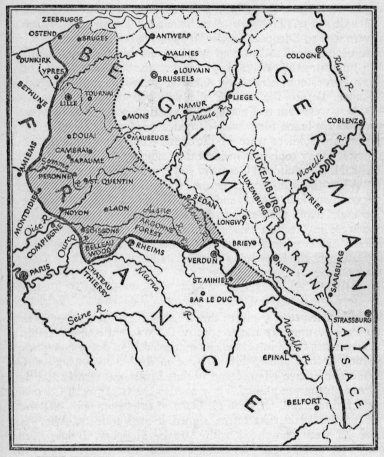

CHIEF THEATER OF AMERICAN ACTION IN THE WORLD WAR

storation of Belgium, which Germany had invaded and overrun during the war; righting the wrong done to France in Alsace-

Lorraine; changes in Italian frontiers for transferring Italians to the homeland; restoration of Serbia and Rumania; alterations in the Turkish Empire; the independence of Poland; and fair treatment for Russia, then in the throes of revolution. What about subject peoples of European empires? Colonial claims, President Wilson maintained, should be adjusted in the interest of the subject peoples.

In the prosecution of the war—widened in December 1917 to include Austria-Hungary—detachments of American naval forces were sent to European waters to co-operate in the hunt for German submarines and to convoy merchant ships carrying supplies. In June 1917 the vanguard of the army, the American Expeditionary Force, commanded by General John J. Pershing, reached France. Before the end of the war over 2,000,000 American soldiers were sent to France; while nearly 2,000,000 more were in training at home for service abroad if needed. By October 1917, American soldiers were in European trenches. From that time forward they took part in increasing numbers in the great battles which finally subdued Germany and Austria-Hungary.

When the armistice came on November 11, 1918, more than 75,000 American soldiers and sailors had sacrificed their lives in the struggle. More than 200,000 had been wounded or were missing or were in German prison camps. In the meantime the United States had furnished to the Allies enormous financial credits and great quantities of supplies for civil and military uses.

☆

In January 1919 agents of the Allied and Associated Powers met at Paris to draw up the treaties of the war settlement. President Wilson was there in person, accompanied by a peace commission which he had chosen himself. For months the delegates at the Paris conference labored and disputed over the terms to be imposed on the vanquished. Early in May the treaty with Germany was finished and, on June 28, German delegates, with bitterness of protest against its terms, signed it at Versailles. Afterward treaties were completed with Austria, Hungary, Bulgaria, and Turkey. In all these proceedings, Russia, still in the toils of the revolution that began in 1917, took no part.

By the various treaties the map of Europe and a part of Asia was refashioned. Alsace-Lorraine was handed over to France. Other parts of Germany were joined to neighboring countries. Poland won independence. Russia was reduced in size by the creation of small states on her western borders. Czechoslovakia and Yugoslavia were brought into existence. The German colonies in Africa were transferred to Great Britain and France, to be held as mandates under the League of Nations. The province of Shantung, which Germany had seized in China, was given to Japan for temporary administration. The German navy was surrendered and the German military power diminished to a mere shadow of its former strength.

In several respects the terms imposed on defeated Germany did not conform to the war aims which President Wilson had so eloquently proclaimed to the world. But compared with the terms which Germany had imposed on conquered Russia at Brest Litovsk the preceding year, the provisions of the Versailles Treaty were mild. Indeed if it had not been for President Wilson's moderating influence, they would have been harsher, and the government of France would have taken immediate steps to occupy and hold Germany down by military force for an indefinite period. President Wilson himself thought that the Versailles Treaty had many faults but he expressed the hope that its injustices would be corrected in peaceful councils of the Powers under the association of nations for which a section of the treaty provided, largely on his insistence.

According to the provisions of this section, known as the Covenant, a League of Nations was to be established. Within the League were to be included the Allied and Associated Powers, countries that had been neutral in the war, and in time the countries defeated in the war. The League was to be governed by an assembly consisting of one delegate from each country and a council composed of representatives from the great Powers, to be elected by the assembly.

The nations in the League were bound by the Covenant to keep the peace themselves and to join in protecting one another against external aggression. They were to submit their disputes to the council for arbitration and inquiry. If a member violated its pledge to follow peaceful methods, measures to coerce it might be taken by the League. Provisions were to be made for disarmament. Thus if the United States joined the League it would be under obligations to observe the rules of the Covenant and to take part regularly and continuously in the adjustment of controversies arising among the nations of the earth. Only by becoming a member of the League and sharing its responsibilities, President Wilson averred, could a lasting peace be achieved for the United States and all other countries.

In the summer of 1919 the Versailles Treaty, including the Covenant of the League of Nations, was laid before the Senate and people of the United States for discussion and action. Hitherto many plans for permanent world peace had been proposed and debated in the United States. Now large and loose theories were reduced to a very definite scheme for a League of Nations which, its sponsors claimed, would guarantee permanent peace. Instead of many nebulous projects, the people now had before them a blueprint for a world association and parliament.

By the very nature of politics, the debate over the League became entangled with debates over foreign and domestic affairs in general and particular. The Covenant of the League was tied into the treaty, which prescribed severe terms for the Germans. Americans of German origin made all they could of that fact. Americans of Irish origin disliked the provision giving Australia, Canada, New Zealand, and South Africa, as well as Great Britain and Ireland, each a delegate in the League Assembly, thus strengthening British power in the League. Other critics assailed the transfer of Shantung to Japan instead of to China, its former owner. The war had been unpopular in many sections of the United States among Americans of old and new stocks and, now that freedom of discussion was partially restored, opponents of the war could voice their dissatisfaction with the treaty which came out of the war.

A large number of liberals and radicals, who might have favored the idea of a league of nations in the abstract, were loath to do so on account of revelations respecting some sordid origins of the war that made them question the possible efficacy of the proposed League and its setup. In January 1919, for instance, a New York newspaper published a number of secret treaties by which Russia, Great Britain, France, and Italy, either before or during the war, had agreed to divide the spoils at the end of the conflict. These startling documents disclosed deep-seated imperialistic ambitions as among the real war aims of the Entente Allies. Moreover, while peace negotiations were pending, American troops, without a declaration of war by Congress, were waging war on Russia, a former associate of the United States, at Archangel and in Siberia —solely under orders of President Wilson.

Into the confused situation was injected the question: Who is now to govern the United States—League of Nations or no League? Dissatisfaction with the Democratic party, for various reasons, was intensifying. In the congressional campaign of 1918, while the war was still raging, President Wilson appealed to the voters to elect a Democratic Congress for the support of his policies. On November 5, 1918, the people had their first opportunity since the outbreak of the war to pass judgment on the Democratic administration, and their verdict was emphatic against it. The Republicans won a majority in both houses of Congress. This outcome, Theodore Roosevelt declared, was tantamount to a national repudiation of President Wilson's leadership and doctrines. No doubt some Republican enmity for the Democratic party and its President was transferred to the League of Nations, just as some Democratic enmity was enlisted in its behalf.

Reflecting the popular divisions of opinion, the Senate was in turbulence. At one extreme in positions was a large group of senators prepared to ratify the treaty as drafted and to approve the League of Nations as incorporated in the treaty. At the other extreme was a small number of irreconcilables, among whom Senator Borah was prominent, determined to keep the United States out of further European entanglements by defeating American participation in the League. Between the extremes stood Republican and Democratic senators ready to vote for the League if some modifications or reservations were made in its plan. Caught between opposing tempers, President Wilson refused to make any significant compromises as the debate went on for weeks and months. At length on March 19, 1920, both the treaty and the League definitely failed, by eight votes, to receive the two-thirds majority of senatorial votes required by the Constitution for adoption.

In the national election of that autumn a "solemn referendum" was taken on the League of Nations. Nominating James Cox, of Ohio, for President and Franklin D. Roosevelt for Vice-President, the Democrats championed the League before the country. Choosing as their standard-bearer Warren G. Harding, of Ohio, and Calvin Coolidge as candidate for Vice-President, the Republicans assailed the Democratic administration from top to bottom. Harding condemned the proposed League but vaguely approved an indefinite kind of international association in the interest of peace. Some of his supporters endorsed the League outright and asserted that the election of Harding would mean participation in it. Other supporters, with equal assurance, told the voters that a Republican triumph would keep the United States out of the League and all such foreign entanglements.

Whatever the election returns of 1920 actually did imply, as a verdict for or against the League, there was no question about the party outcome: the Democrats were blown from power in a tornado of ballots. Harding carried every Northern state and even Tennessee in the South. His popular vote was 16,150,000 as against 9,140,000 cast for Cox. Nearly 1,000,000 votes, the heaviest Socialist vote ever polled, were cast for the Socialist candidate, Eugene V. Debs, then in prison for having denounced the war as an imperialist and capitalist conflict. So the repudiation of President Wilson's policies which had been foreshadowed in the congressional elections of 1918 seemed to be confirmed and the Republicans came back to power—for what proved to be a twelve-year period.

☆

Irrespective of the New Freedom's merits as a political slogan and as exemplified between March 4, 1913, and August 1, 1914, the accomplishments of Wilson's administration had not closed the long struggle over domestic policies, including those affecting the distribution of wealth in the United States. Nor had it brought about a high degree of economic felicity by the summer of 1914. Business had in reality entered a slump during the preceding winter.

An expert in labor conditions, John B. Andrews, reported: "From the point of view of the wage earner seeking work, the year 1914 was the worst since the year following the financial panic of 1907." According to an authority on industrial tendencies, they too were moving downward, "in most instances reaching such an alarming state as to place the year on a par with the severe depression of 1907–08." If agriculture was in a better state than business, farmers were far from satisfied with the prices of their produce in the dull markets.

And as the Democrats, in their customary style, had promised prosperity through "lowering trade barriers," so the Republicans in their customary style laid the slump to the reduction of the protective tariff by the Democrats. Whatever the reason for it, an implacable discontent with the New Freedom was abroad in the land—a revulsion which materially reduced the Democratic majority in the House of Representatives in the congressional elections of 1914 and destroyed it in the congressional elections of 1916 when Wilson was re-elected President.

About this time the economic slump disappeared temporarily. The war in Europe had scarcely started in the summer of 1914 when Great Britain and France began to buy enormous quantities of farm produce, manufactures, and semifinished raw materials in the United States. From month to month their purchases increased in volume, as they poured their own money into this country and began to borrow huge sums from American banks and investors. By the end of 1916 most branches of manufacturing and agriculture were booming; unemployment had almost disappeared; wages were higher; businessmen and farmers were gathering in large profits.

Although this spurt of prosperity before the United States entered the war was largely due to the purchases made by the Entente Allies, Wilson's partisans attributed it in some measure to the New Freedom. But leading Democrats, including the President himself, knew that it was mainly artificial and that the defeat of the Allies or the ending of the war would bring in its train an economic crash in the United States. In fact, to some members of the administration this was an argument for enlarging the borrowing facilities of the Allies and, finally, for entering the war directly. At all events, after the United States did enter the war, the business and agricultural boom grew to huge dimensions.

Yet even during the war and economic boom the domestic struggle over matters of capital and labor, over conservation of resources, over problems of taxation, and all the other issues relative to American living standards continued among the people and on the floors of Congress. Indeed, in some respects, the war magnified the problems and sharpened the issues.

Opposition to the war, such as it was, and to various measures adopted in carrying on the war, prevailed largely among the farmers and industrial workers who had fostered populistic or socialistic movements during preceding years. The arrest, prosecution, and imprisonment of war dissenters and labor agitators, notably Debs, revealed that the war for liberty and democracy abroad could be accompanied by stern measures of repression at home, under the very administration of President Wilson, world spokesman for those exalted war aims.

The social order was disturbed by strikes, numerous and widespread. Progressive and radical Democrats and Republicans in Congress tried to "make the rich pay for the war," to impose heavy taxes on profits, and to "restore the government to the plain people." During the war they also developed postwar plans for government ownership of the railways and for other features of "social reconstruction" in the United States.

It was generally understood that the domestic struggle would go on after the war and that provisions would have to be made for dealing with the economic crisis bound to follow the peace. But President Wilson proposed remedies couched primarily in international terms. The United States, he said, would have to join the League of Nations and promote world trade in order to find market outlets for the enlarged productive capacity of American industry and agriculture. Americans must do this, he insisted, "or you have ruined the United States." Even the settlement of controversies between capital and labor within America, he contended, cannot be effected unless we have "frank discussion" and "friendly discussion" and "those are the very things that are offered to us among the nations of the world by the Covenant of the League of Nations."

Years before, Republican leaders had promised manufacturers and farmers ever-expanding markets and prosperity, if they would support imperialism. Now President Wilson proposed to resolve pressing domestic difficulties in industry and agriculture by having the United States join the League of Nations and by promoting the reduction of protective tariffs, by opening American ports more freely to commodities from foreign lands.

By their actions, however, a large majority of the American people—Democrats as well as Republicans, Progressives, and Socialists—took issue with President Wilson on this point. They eventually made it evident that, in their opinion, joining the League of Nations or trying to drum up more foreign trade would not settle any of the major domestic disputes respecting national economy, poverty, or labor relations; or, for that matter, advance the brotherhood of mankind very far. Indeed in February 1917, while the entrance of the United States into the "war for democracy" was imminent, Congress passed, over President Wilson's veto, an act restricting immigration, and put it into effect May 1, 1917. Again, under pressure from President Wilson himself, Congress passed, in 1918, the Webb Act, which eased up the Sherman Anti-Trust law and permitted American businessmen to form combinations, loose cartels, in the export trade, for the purpose of combatting foreign concerns more vigorously in the international competition for world markets. As a matter of fact the conviction was generally held that, whatever might be done about the League of Nations, the Americans would still have immense tasks to perform at home and that the struggle among domestic interests was not likely to be stopped or materially modified by even the most fortunate posture of international affairs.

☆

The period of Republican rule from 1921–33, commonly described as the age of "normalcy," was marked by a foreign policy that practically ignored the League of Nations, though "observers" were sent to its headquarters at Geneva from time to time. Imperialist activities conceived as in the interest of trade were pushed everywhere. Former associates in the war were urged to pay the war debts they owed to the United States. The tariffs on imported manufactures were twice raised. Peace was made with Germany, reserving to the United States all the rights against that nation, established by the Treaty of Versailles, which the Senate had rejected.

American investors were encouraged to lend billions of dollars to Germany, thereby helping to restore her economic power and enabling her to make payments on the reparations to the victors in the war, especially on the heavy damages levied by Great Britain and France. Wilson's policy of refusing to recognize revolutionary Russia, on the ground that he did not approve its government, was continued. In this way Russia was treated as a pariah among nations; while the State Department encouraged American capitalists to make money out of Russian trade if they could. The floating of loans to foreign countries and capitalists was promoted; the export trade of the United States was pushed by federal agents; imperialist policy was revived in the Philippines; and efforts were made to keep ajar the so-called Open Door in China for American business enterprise.

Nevertheless under Republican auspices regard was paid to ideals of peace prevalent in the United States. At an arms-reduction conference held in Washington in 1921–22, Great Britain, Japan, and the United States agreed to stop their naval race for a specified time and limit the size of their battleship fleets. In 1928 the United States joined France in promoting the Kellogg-Briand Pact, an arrangement by which all the great nations of the earth bound themselves to outlaw war as an instrument of national policy and to settle their disputes henceforth by peaceful methods. Ardent advocates of internationalism hailed this act as putting an end to war and guaranteeing world order.

The age of normalcy also became in many ways an age of

disillusionment in respect of foreign affairs. As the strife among the governments of Europe and Asia for world power, economic privileges, and other advantages went forward within the League of Nations and outside its councils, indifference to its fate widened in the United States. For this spectacle Americans who had opposed the entry of the United States into the League had only derision; and idealists who had sought to carry America into the League got cold comfort from it. The treatment accorded to revolutionary Russia by European governments contributed little to the comity of nations. Imperialist rivalries flourished as before—in Africa, Asia, and the islands of the seas.

At the same time secret agreements, made long before 1914, between Russia, France, and Great Britain, were unearthed by historians working in the archives of Russia, Germany, and Austria thrown open to researchers by revolutions in all those countries. On the basis of clear documentary evidence scholars dissected the myth, propagated by those Powers, that Germany was wholly responsible for inaugurating the war; that on Germany must be placed all the war guilt; that the governments of Great Britain, France, and Russia united by the secret agreements were administered by innocent civilians suddenly and unexpectedly attacked by a bloodthirsty villain.

By reading copies of these diplomatic documents, scholarly works in European history founded on them or the publicity given to the findings, literate Americans in large numbers learned something of the innumerable lies, deceptions, and frauds perpetrated by the governments of Czarist Russia, Great Britain, and France, as well as of the Central Powers, at the expense of their own peoples and other nations. The gleaming mirage that pictured the World War as purely or even mainly a war for democracy and civilization dissolved beyond recognition. Countless Americans who in 1914–18 had yearned for a "brave new world" at the conclusion of the war were disheartened by the proofs of sinister purposes running against their dreams.

☆

Although the Republicans could claim, with some justification in the election returns of 1920, that the country had turned its back on President Wilson's internationalism, they were not able, in domestic affairs, to stamp out the spirit of progressive or radical insurgency, old in American tradition and yet ever new in its application to changing conditions. In fact in 1924 they encountered a progressive revolt. Progressive Republicans and Democrats, disgusted with both the old parties, put into the field a third ticket, headed by Senator Robert M. La Follette, of Wisconsin, and Senator Burton K. Wheeler, of Montana. But the regular Democrats nominated for President John W. Davis, nominally of West Virginia, in reality a New York lawyer for the firm of J. P. Morgan and Company in Wall Street. In the election the Republican candidate, Calvin Coolidge, who had succeeded to the presidency on the death of Harding in 1923, received more than half the total vote cast. Yet the 4,800,000 votes polled by the Progressives indicated that the country was far from converted to Republican "normalcy."

Nor in truth did the election of 1928, in which the Republicans received a longer lease on power, indicate an exact return to any previous state of affairs. The Republican candidate, Herbert C. Hoover, who had been Secretary of Commerce since 1921, was not a mere replica of a McKinley, a Taft, or a Harding. In that office he had convinced many businessmen that he was a financial wizard. He had promoted the export of manufactures by the lavish use of public funds. He had encouraged American investors to "prime the pump" abroad for American industries by lending billions to foreign governments and corporations, thus enabling foreigners to "buy" American goods. Though Hoover praised "rugged individualism" and was commended as a "great business leader," he was widely known also as a philanthropist and a man of avowed social sympathies. He had headed American relief in Belgium during the World War and later disbursed American money abroad by the millions in relieving famine-stricken regions.

Never before in their history had the Republicans nominated for the presidency a man who had spoken with such anxiety about the depressing aspects of American society against which the spirit of progressive insurgency had been continuously directed. Nor had any Republican candidate advocated so repeatedly the removal of these afflictions by private co-operation and governmental action.

In 1923, for example, Hoover had urged insurance companies to attack the problem of unemployment by adding that evil to the list of casualties against which they provided underwriting: "There is one field of insurance not yet covered. You have covered the great range of accidents and disaster, but one great disaster that comes to our workfolk has yet been unguarded. . . . It is less than eighteen months ago when we had five millions of unemployed men in our streets, of men who wished to work but for whom no work could be found. There is nothing that leads to such despair and such decay of self-respect as the man who wants a job and wants to work, the support of whose family is in jeopardy."

Hoover had also opposed child labor and endorsed a constitutional amendment authorizing Congress to abolish it. He had commended and aided the work of associations for the improvement of housing conditions, public health, the care of children, and other substandard features of American society.

Gross inequalities in the distribution of wealth, long the subject of populistic, progressive, and socialistic criticism, Hoover had frankly faced, to the alarm of conservatives; and he proposed to attack them by the use of the inheritance tax. The inheritance tax, he declared in 1919, "does redistribute overswollen fortunes. It does make for equality of opportunity by freeing from the dead hand control of our tools of production. It reduces extravagance in the next generation and sends them to constructive service." To Republicans who had assailed the income tax of 1894 as communistic that must have sounded like treason to the Grand Old Party; and to scholastic economists, a foolish flouting of "natural law."

Nor did the Democrats in 1928 nominate a Cleveland Democrat. They selected a liberal, of progressive social sympathies, Alfred E. Smith, of New York. While legislator and governor in that state, Smith had consistently promoted social legislation in line with progressive aspirations. He had defended freedom of speech amid the hysteria of the World War and with a proclamation of liberty had pardoned a communist imprisoned on account of his opinions. With Smith's social and political doctrines, liberals and progressives were generally in agreement. But he was handicapped by two disqualifications for a popular appeal at the time: he was a Roman Catholic in a country loyal to its Protestant heritage; and he had consistently opposed prohibition since the adoption of the Eighteenth Amendment in 1919, in defiance of the powerful anti-saloon organizations behind it. If the votes cast in 1928 proclaimed another extension of Republican power, they did not in any case mean that the processes of American history were reaching a standstill.

☆

In spite of their three successive victories in presidential elections and many pledges of a return to the "good old days" of free enterprise—no government interference with business—Republicans did not wipe out the measures of reform that had been accumulated since 1900. They did not reverse history and go back to the policies and legislation of the McKinley regime. The efforts which some of them exerted to effect such a reaction were defeated in Congress even when they had indisputable majorities in both houses. Retreats toward the age of McKinley by the wholesale repeal of laws, if desired by Republican die-hards, did not take place.

On the contrary, reformist measures, once condemned by conservatives of every type, were retained on the statute books, if occasionally with changes; and new laws conceived in the reform spirit were added. Moreover, the struggle to level down the special privileges of the plutocracy and raise the living standards of the masses went on within both great political parties, while the agitations of minor parties on the left wing gave the public no rest. The nature of constructive persistence even in the face of "normalcy" was illustrated in respect of every issue still before the nation—issues which had been before it for more than fifty years.

Hopes of abolishing or reducing to nominal rates the federal taxes on income and inheritances, entertained in some quarters, came to naught after the return of the Republicans to power in 1921. Twenty years previously nearly all the revenues of the federal government were derived from indirect taxes—customs duties and excises on consumption. At that time conservatives had decried income and inheritance taxes as socialistic or communistic. And advocates of such taxes had admitted publicly that they were framed to shift a part of the burden of taxation from the poor to the rich; while intransigents among them had declared that these taxes were steps toward the destruction of the plutocracy and greater equality in the distribution of national income.

On this question President Coolidge took a traditional position: "I do not believe that the government should seek social legislation in the guise of taxation. If we are to adopt socialism it should be presented to the people of this country as socialism and not under the guise of a law to collect revenue."

Yet of the $4,100,000,000, collected by the federal government in revenues in the fiscal year ended June 30, 1927, more than half came from income taxes on individuals and corporations. And President Coolidge's Secretary of Commerce, Herbert Hoover, publicly expressed the belief that "the present inheritance, income, and excess-profits tax tend to a better distribution of wealth." No clearer proofs could have been adduced to show that normalcy, in its effort to retreat, did not in fact go all the way back to the beginning of the twentieth century. Indeed, it advanced beyond the timid income-tax measure of 1913, enacted during the New Freedom.

Another phase of the domestic struggle to regulate national wealth in the public interest had been the contest over the conservation and use of national resources. As the significance of the electrical industry for general welfare dawned in national consciousness, a sharp contest opened over the way in which water power on the national domain and along navigable rivers should be put to use. The old style had been to turn such sites over to private concerns for perpetual ownership and allow private companies to produce and sell power without federal interference.

This policy outstanding progressives had attacked early in the century. They insisted that all water power should be publicly owned, that public power plants should be built, and that electricity should be distributed by public lines and sold at the lowest possible rates. Modifications of these propositions in the form of compromises, such as short-term leases of sites to companies, combined with strict regulation of rates and services, were also submitted to the country.

Before the World War had come to an end, the question of "federal power" was brought to the front in Congress. In 1920 a comprehensive federal water power act was passed and signed. The measure provided for the establishment of a water power commission and made a beginning at strict control over private utilities using federal power sites.

Not long afterward a project for building a great power plant in the Boulder Canyon of the Colorado River came up for review. Again a compromise was reached: ownership of the power site was retained in the hands of the government. The Secretary of the Interior was authorized to construct and operate a dam and other works on the site, and to allot the water for irrigation, domestic purposes, and the generation of electrical energy. The electrical power so produced he was permitted to sell, at rates sufficient to cover the cost, to states, municipalities, and private corporations for distribution. In selling this power, however, he was compelled to give priority to states and municipalities. In the end only a small portion of it went to private companies. Consequently Congress, under Republican leadership, moved nearer to the production and sale of power by means of public agencies, without the intervention of private enterprise.

When, early in Coolidge's administration, rumors circulated to the effect that during the administration of his predecessor, President Harding, great oil reserves had been corruptly turned over to private concerns, the Senate ordered an investigation. Scandals were uncovered, and prosecutions were begun against offenders. Day by day revelations of bribery and fraud broke into the front pages of the newspapers, giving the people lurid pictures of the way in which unscrupulous men had got hold of and exploited the natural resources of the nation. Private promoters, the testimony revealed, had contributed money to Republican campaign funds and to politicians, in return for leases to tremendous oil reserves from which to enrich themselves.

Under stinging rebukes from members of Congress, the Coolidge administration started lawsuits in the courts against parties charged with fraud, and after the cases were heard the oil lands surreptitiously obtained were restored to the United States Government. No longer was it possible, as it had been fifty years earlier, for private persons or corporations to enter into secret connivance with government officials and gain titles to huge sections of the public domain without risk of exposure or retribution. The public resolve to keep all that remained of the national heritage of resources had been effectively demonstrated.

Another dispute over the disposal of natural resources arose in connection with a great power plant which the government had begun to build at Muscle Shoals, in the Tennessee Valley, for the production of chemicals to be used in munitions during the World War. When peace came, Republicans and Democrats who clung to nineteenth-century traditions of free enterprise in such matters demanded that the plant be sold or leased to a private concern at a low or even nominal figure. With this view Harding, Coolidge, and Hoover agreed in principle if not as to details.

But progressives in Congress, led by Senator George W. Norris, of Nebraska, had other plans—plans for socialization—and fought for them tenaciously. After a seven-year battle they pushed through Congress a resolution providing for government ownership and operation of the Muscle Shoals plant, for the construction of new plants, and for priority to states and municipalities in the sale of power.

President Coolidge killed it with a pocket veto. Again, and still under the leadership of Senator Norris, Congress passed a similar bill in 1931. President Hoover vetoed it, saying that it would help to destroy the "initiative and enterprise" of the American people. Though defeated temporarily in their efforts, congressional advocates of "public power" were able to prevent the adoption of recommendations from Coolidge and Hoover for otherwise disposing of Muscle Shoals, and to keep the plant in the hands of the government.

While conservatives of both parties labored unsuccessfully to turn the power resources of the Tennessee Valley over to private enterprise on easy terms, in the postwar period, few among them proposed repeal of the laws enacted in aid of agriculture during President Wilson's administration. If they had desired to do this, the plight of agriculture would scarcely have permitted the undertaking. After 1921, with the disappearance of the war demand for food products, agriculture started on a course of steep and ruinous decline. The prices of farm produce fell swiftly. Farmers by the tens of thousands went into bankruptcy. Farm mortgages were foreclosed and freehold farmers driven into tenancy or off the land. To make things worse, under the Republican tariff law of 1921 the prices of manufactured commodities which farmers had to buy remained fixed at high levels or in many cases rose still higher. Once more the country resounded with agrarian laments. Even politicians well entrenched in urban centers could hardly fail to note the discontent.

In these circumstances Republicans in control of Congress added to, instead of subtracting from, the Wilson program of agricultural legislation. They kept in force the Farm Loan Act of 1916 extending long-term credits to farmers at low rates of interest and supplemented it by provisions for short-term credits at low rates of interest. The Warehouse Act of 1916, designed to protect farmers against deceptive and fraudulent transactions in the storage of their products, was supplemented by the Packers and Stockyards Act, which gave farmers a similar protection in the shipment and sale of livestock. In 1922 grain growers were safeguarded by legislation against speculators in grains, as cotton growers had been by an act of 1916 against speculators in that commodity. Producers of perishable fruits and vegetables, who had long suffered from cheating and false reports at the hands of middlemen, were afforded more adequate defense by the Perishable Commodities Act of 1930. At the same time federal agencies were established to push the sale of agricultural products abroad in the manner employed to expand the foreign markets for manufactures. Invincibly, government functions were expanding.

But none of these measures did more than touch the fringes of the distress in agriculture. Surpluses of crops continued to pile up. The downward tendency of prices remained unchecked. Ruin spread more widely in farming regions. Farmers were suffering from the kind of calamity that was soon to overtake the middle classes and industrial workers of the cities; and right in the middle of "Republican prosperity" they gave the signal for a new agrarian rebellion. They demanded bigger markets and higher prices for their produce. One of their leaders vented their sentiments in saying: "If we cannot have prosperity too, we will kick the legs out from under the table and all Americans will have to sit on the ground." How to get the markets and higher prices? That was the question.

So deep was the unrest among farmers that Congress was moved to attempt a cure in 1927 by passing a bill to aid in handling the agricultural surpluses. The bill provided for the sale abroad of certain commodities at low prices and for making up the loss by an equalization fee or tax laid on producers in proportion to their sales. This would, its sponsors claimed, dispose of surplus output and raise prices. But whatever the merits of the bill, Coolidge interposed with a veto. The next year Congress passed a similar bill. Again Coolidge applied the veto.

The defeated farm bills represented a positive effort to interfere with the "natural" course of farm production and prices. As such they were generally deemed "unsound" by urban economists. Herbert Hoover was known to be against them. But in the heat of the campaign in 1928 both he and the Democratic candidate, Alfred E. Smith, promised to "do something" about the farm problem.

After his inauguration in 1929, President Hoover proposed and Congress enacted, with modifications, an agricultural marketing bill to control the disposition of various agricultural products. The act was expected to promote the organization of producers on the land into associations and corporations, to discourage overproduction, to foster orderly marketing, and to eliminate "undue" fluctuations and depressions in prices. To administer the law the Farm Board was created and a fund of $500,000,000 put at its command to be used in interfering with the "natural" course of production and prices in agriculture. This experiment, dubious in character, had just been started when the panic of 1929 struck even the cities and knocked "the legs out from under the table" in a wholesale fashion which even farmers had not contemplated in their resentment over their own economic distress.

In respect of labor legislation and social improvement, historic subjects of strife in the United States between and within political parties, the so-called age of reaction and disillusionment was in many respects an age of progress, not of retreat.

The provisions of the Clayton Antitrust Act of 1914 passed by a Democratic Congress, called by Samuel Gompers the "Magna Charta of Labor," had declared that labor was not a commodity and that the activities of organized labor were not to be suppressed under arbitrary injunctions issued by the federal courts. These two provisions, often violated or ignored in fact, were not struck from the statute books by Republicans. They were strengthened instead by a stringent anti-injunction law underwriting the principles of collective bargaining, passed in 1932. The new bill was sponsored by two progressive Republicans, George W. Norris in the Senate and Fiorello H. La Guardia in the House of Representatives, supported by many regular Republicans, championed by Democrats who then had a majority in the lower house, and signed by President Hoover. At no time in the history of the labor movement had its leaders been more powerful in political councils; the Anti-Injunction Act was testimony to the fact.

The La Follette Seamen's Act of 1915 for improving the conditions of sailors on American merchant vessels and assuring them new "human rights" remained on the statute books as another evidence that the influence of organized labor in social legislation was not declining under normalcy. In 1927, Congress gave to longshoremen and harbor workers the benefit of compensation for injuries—a privilege earlier granted to workers on interstate railways. The Railway Labor Mediation Act of 1926 was also in the line of progressive legislation, not a reversal in any respect. If few labor candidates were elected to Congress and setbacks frequently occurred in labor disputes, organized labor was growing in political force and winning sympathy under presidents often dismissed as "reactionary" by radicals.

What was known as the "social movement" was also gaining momentum. A sign of its meliorist advance was the adoption by Congress in 1924, with the approval of President Coolidge, of a resolution amending the Constitution so that federal authorities could regulate or abolish child labor throughout the United States. The amendment was not ratified by enough states to make it law, but some of its aims were later realized in other ways. In the states, almost unobserved by those who kept their eyes only on "national" affairs, laws were being multiplied in the interests of public health, housing, care of dependents, and protection against the hazards of poverty and other misfortunes. By 1930 three fourths of the states had provided pensions for widows and deserted wives with dependent children. By the end of 1931 at least nine states had general old-age pension laws—a main socialist proposal—and the propaganda for national pension legislation was rising throughout the country. In short neither war nor reaction had stifled the American resolve to subdue the evils of poverty in the United States.

CHAPTER XXVII

Economic Crash and New Deal Uprising

IN THE AUTUMN OF 1929, just as the country seemed safe and sound on the "high plateau of permanent prosperity," except for farmers, the business boom attributed to Republican statecraft burst with a resounding crash. The prime stocks of the leading corporations fell nearly forty points on the average in a single day, October 29, when more than 16,000,000 shares were dumped on the market at the New York Stock Exchange. This panic was followed by the explosion of banks, railway companies, and private concerns, by increasing woes among farmers already in straits, by the closing of factories, shops, and offices, and by a steep decline in the opportunities of employment for artists, writers, musicians, architects, engineers, playwrights, and teachers—indeed the whole white-collar class—from New York to California. In the opening months of 1933, it was estimated, 12,000,000 men and women were out of work. Ruin and hunger, if not starvation, haunted not only the shacks of tenants and sharecroppers on the land, not only the back streets inhabited by industrial and professional classes, but also the grand avenues of great cities.

For a moment leaders in business and politics thought that this was "just another panic." President Hoover said: "We have passed through no less than fifteen major depressions in the last century. . . . We have come out of each . . . into a period of prosperity greater than ever before. We shall do so this time." But as the depression dragged through tedious months and into years, belief in "prosperity just around the corner" turned into doubt or despair. As this revulsion of feeling intensified, trust in the "natural" and "normal" processes of "recovery" declined, and leaders in the

economic, intellectual, and moral life of the nation vehemently
declared their unwillingness to endure the crisis with pious resignation as a visitation of God or of natural forces beyond human
control. Long years of research, debate, agitation, and legislative
gains in respect of social improvement had prepared multitudes
of Americans for a different attitude toward poverty, unemployment, and misery in "God's own country."

Outstanding personalities in business and professional circles
such as Owen D. Young and Gerard Swope of the General Electric Company, leaders in the United States Chamber of Commerce,
in the American Federation of Labor, in the Federal Council of
the Churches of Christ in America, and in associations for civic
advancement joined in demanding concerted action against the
depression. They called for deliberate planning and collective
measures to create economic well-being and prevent the return
of such a national misfortune. It was openly asserted in high places
that, if capitalists could not so conduct industrial enterprise as to
avoid periodical depressions of the kind and maintain a steady level
of employment, the government of the United States would have
to assume the responsibility.

In previous panics presidents had said or acted as if they believed
that neither they nor Congress had any constitutional power to
meddle with business activities and relieve the distresses of the millions unemployed. But President Hoover accepted no such de-
featist philosophy while this terrible depression harrowed the nation with bankruptcies, mortgage foreclosures, poverty, hunger,
and degradation. He immediately called upon Congress to make
provision for a large-scale construction of public works to put
labor and capital in action again; and he urged the governors of
states to press for similar remedial measures within their respective
jurisdictions.

As the depression wore on, Hoover acted more energetically
and creatively. He recommended, and Congress adopted, two proposals for interfering in the "natural course" of business enterprise
—from calamity to calamity. The first was the establishment of
the Reconstruction Finance Corporation, which placed federal
credit at the disposal of banks, insurance companies, railways, and
other concerns in financial difficulties. The second was the formation of the Home Owners' Loan Corporation to aid people in peril
of losing their homes under foreclosures of mortgages. He also
approved legislation extending federal credit to states and municipalities struggling with unemployment and poverty. The popular

criticisms launched against President Hoover were not to the effect that he had done nothing, but that he had not done enough or the right things on a scale commensurate with the magnitude of the national catastrophe.

President Hoover was desperately engaged in wrestling with the depression when the time for taking a national referendum on Republican statesmanship—the presidential election of 1932—arrived, as prescribed by the Constitution of the United States. Though the Democrats had won a majority in the House of Representatives in the congressional election of 1930, they had proposed no constructive measures to overcome the depression. Millions of Americans were still unemployed; poverty had become aggravated to menacing proportions; agriculture and industry were in a bad plight. The whole society of the United States was in a state of anxiety and confusion. But Democratic tactics in the House of Representatives were principally confined to obstructing and harassing President Hoover in such undertakings as he ventured to sponsor in trying to cope with the economic disaster.

As far as appearances indicated, the Democratic party, historically committed to the creed of "the less government the better," was even more disinclined than the Republicans to make a frontal drive against the depression by resorting to governmental action. Under Wilson's leadership they had, it is true, interfered with "free enterprise" in significant respects, but they had officially admitted no change in their individualistic creed. Nor in their platform of 1932 did they give any hint that they intended to reverse fundamentally their long role of opposition to federal interference in the "natural course" of national economy.

Neither in their choice of a presidential candidate nor in their campaign did the Democrats give the slightest indication that they intended to embark on a program of wholesale government interference with the processes of industry, agriculture, and labor organization. The man whom they selected to head their ticket, Franklin D. Roosevelt, governor of New York, represented by his sponsors as "progressive," had not in the course of his political career espoused any public policies which could be deemed radical by any stretch of the imagination. In their campaign literature the Democratic managers pictured Mr. Roosevelt as a man who could "perfectly understand the viewpoint of the dirt farmer and the city laborer, the man in the street and the one in high places, . . . quietly, impartially, firmly uphold the rights of each and achieve a fair deal for all."

Whether from sheer unrest or a belief that the Democrats could and would restore prosperity, the voters at the election broke Republican control over the executive and legislative branches of the federal government. They cast 22,800,000 ballots for Roosevelt as against 15,700,000 for President Hoover, the Republican candidate, running to succeed himself. Furthermore they returned huge Democratic majorities to the Senate and the House of Representatives.

What were the Democrats to do with their victory? Some, of course, expected to settle back and enjoy the spoils of office. Others relied on the revered economic philosophy that prosperity would revive in America if enough foreign outlets could some way be found for the products of American factories and farms. Indeed this historic dogma had been reiterated in their platform and in speeches during the campaign. Although their candidate, Mr. Roosevelt, had lent countenance to it, he had endorsed an agrarian program of government intervention for farm relief and promised to adopt several measures of relief for unemployment and poverty.

If the backers of Franklin D. Roosevelt expected a period of Democratic "normalcy," they were disappointed. Between November 1932 and his inauguration in March 1933 another financial panic had hit the country with the force of a cyclone. In every direction banks crashed and closed their doors. On the day of his installation hundreds were in bankruptcy, and practically all the others were shut up under precautionary measures taken by state governments. On March 4, 1933, therefore, circumstances looked black for the enjoyment of political jobs and power in the old style.

As the Democratic organization in Congress had no plans whatever for dealing with the financial disaster, the burden of leadership became President Roosevelt's and he took it upon his own shoulders. Under his direction a multitude of measures known collectively as the New Deal, devised to meet the depression, were quickly adopted and put into effect. These measures were based on the belief that the main business of getting the country out of the depression belonged to the people and the government of the United States, and could not be disposed of by trying to get foreign markets in bankrupt Europe or Asia.

Among Roosevelt's associates in the new Cabinet only one, Cordell Hull, Secretary of State, stuck to the idea of lowering trade barriers as the principal or sufficient mode of escape from the crisis. He admitted that the people at home could do something to help themselves; but putting American economy on a high level of production and prosperity by domestic actions he belittled as an effort to lift oneself by one's bootstraps; so he began to search for new or bigger foreign markets for American goods. While heading the American delegation to the World Economic Conference at London in the spring of 1933, Secretary Hull sought to reach some working agreements with representatives of various foreign governments, also in economic grief, that would enlarge the volume of American exports and imports. He was laboring at this task, though not making much advance, when President Roosevelt practically put an end to the conference by an abrupt message, and turned to the promotion of a domestic program for tackling the depression at home.

Apart from the repeal of the Prohibition Amendment in 1933, the principal domestic measures of the New Deal, adopted during and after 1933, may be summarized in a small compass under six heads: (1) control over banking and currency; (2) federal credit to property owners and corporations in financial difficulties; (3) relief to farmers; (4) regulation and stimulation of business enterprise; (5) systematizing rights of collective bargaining for organized labor; and (6) social security for selected groups of people against the hazards of dependency, unemployment, poverty, and old age. Taken collectively, they represented an effort to establish in the United States a stable economy in place of alternating booms and panics and to protect the people against numerous misfortunes of specific kinds. In the struggle to create the institutions of the New Deal many lines of older social meliorism were brought to a focus.

With the banks shut and the circulation of money palsied on March 4, 1933, the first task undertaken by President Roosevelt was that of opening the banks and managing the currency. Though urged by some of his supporters to nationalize at once all banks of issue and vest in the federal government the sole power of issuing currency, the President chose a less extreme course—one more in accord with the interests of private banking, and yet extending the scope and nature of regulation. All banks were put under closer federal supervision; credit was extended to banks which, it was thought, could be put into sound condition; and banks beyond redemption were liquidated. The gold standard was abandoned. Gold and silver coins and bullion were called in, ordered to be deposited with the government; and the right of citizens to demand gold and silver coins in exchange for paper money was abolished. For a currency based on gold was substituted a currency issued and managed under the authorities of the United States. Thus the power of private banks possessing stores of gold and silver to dominate the issue of currency by the United States was abrogated.

To afford relief to individuals and concerns in peril of bankruptcy or of losing their homes or farms, the policy of granting federal credit and aid was extended and made more effective. The farm loan banks were reorganized and supplemented by other credit institutions. The amount of security farmers were required to give for loans was reduced, and to those who could provide such security money was lent at lower rates of interest, on long terms, with easy methods of repayment in installments. Through new special agencies similar arrangements were made to lend money to people in towns who were in debt, had mortgages on their homes, and were in danger of losing their property. The Reconstruction Finance Corporation, established under President Hoover's administration, was revised; and billions of dollars were lent to banks, railways, insurance companies, industries, and other enterprises whose earnings temporarily fell short of their needs. By these measures the United States Government became the biggest money borrower and lender in the country and assumed heavy responsibilities for the fortunes of property owners in distress.

Rejecting the idea that all the huge surpluses of wheat, corn, cotton, meat, and other prime farm products could be sold abroad, or even "dumped" on foreign countries by any method, sponsors of farm relief adopted another course. By the Agricultural Adjustment Act of 1933 and later amendments, Congress provided for the curtailment of farm production by direct action. Instead of providing for the expansion of the home market, it adopted plans for organizing farmers who raised the leading agricultural staples, for reducing the amount which they produced, and for compensating them for that reduction by subsidies of money proportioned to their respective acreages withdrawn from production. With these measures were coupled other acts designed to restrict farm production, including livestock, to existing markets, stabilize supply in relation to demand, and create what was called by the Secretary of Agriculture, Henry A. Wallace, an "ever-normal granary."

Yet the dream of selling more agricultural produce abroad was not wholly given up. Under a law passed by Congress in 1934, on the insistence of Secretary Hull, the President and Secretary of State were authorized, for a period of three years, later extended, to make reciprocal trade agreements with other countries, free from the necessity of submitting their treaties to the Senate for ratification. In these agreements they could lower, within limits, the tariff rates on manufactures and other commodities in return for pledges on the part of foreign governments to reduce their rates on American imports. By this means, it was argued, outlets for a large amount of cotton, corn, meat, and other farm produce could be found in foreign markets.

But American manufacturing interests were also suffering from surpluses which could not be sold; millions of people, more than ten million at the highest point of unemployment, were out of work. Who was to buy the mountains of manufactured goods piled up in warehouses?

An attack on this problem was made under the National Industrial Recovery Act of 1933. The act authorized the expenditure of billions of dollars for the construction of public works with a view to stimulating building activities and creating purchasing power for the workers. Under it also an immense effort was made to organize business enterprises in the United States for a drive to increase employment, production, and sales in the home market. Enterprises were grouped together according to their nature. Their representatives were given power to adjust supply to demand, to fix prices within limits, and otherwise regulate their operations. For the purpose of preventing excesses in stock-market speculation and in the financing of great supercorporations, the Securities and Exchange Commission was established and given autocratic authority over all such transactions.

In the New Deal program special favors were afforded to organized labor which warmly supported President Roosevelt in elections. The National Industrial Recovery Act made provisions for collective bargaining between employers and employees, but the Supreme Court in 1935 declared unconstitutional nearly all of that act. Then Congress passed the National Labor Relations Act, making collective bargaining generally mandatory on employers and employees. Industrial and other workers were authorized to form or join unions of their own choosing and to elect representatives empowered to bargain for them in matters of hours, wages, and working conditions. To enforce the act the National Labor Relations Board was created. By other legislation Congress tightened the hold of organized labor on the processes of industrial bargaining.

Although a split occurred in the ranks of the American Federation of Labor under William Green and another organization, the Congress of Industrial Organizations, was formed, at first under the leadership of John L. Lewis, head of the United Mine Workers, both national federations flourished. The Congress of Industrial Organizations was highly successful in organizing industrial and white-collar workers, especially outside the old-line crafts. Both branches of national organized labor, with support from the National Labor Relations Board, increased rapidly in membership.

Taking into account millions of workers largely unorganized, Congress added the Wages and Hours Act to the labor program. Under this statute steps were taken to fix standard hours and wages in numerous industries and enterprises—particularly those in which the hours were long and the wages low.

By a series of measures the Roosevelt administration attacked more directly the problems of unemployment, poverty, and misery. Billions of dollars were appropriated for immediate relief to the hungry and homeless, to be spent directly through federal agencies and in co-operation with state and local governments. Later, jobs were provided for millions of the unemployed, including large numbers of the white-collar classes, on numerous projects set up under the Works Progress Administration and other federal agencies.

Various forms of social security were instituted under the Social Security Act of 1935; for example, insurance against unemployment to a limited extent and, for certain classes of workers, insurance against dependence in old age, and grants in aid of persons suffering from poverty, blindness, and other afflictions. Federal grants of money were made to states with a view to encouraging the establishment of a complete scheme of old-age pensions in every state in the Union. Briefly stated, a "floor" of minimum security was placed under millions of people. At the same time new projects for including all persons exempted from such benefits were proposed and brought under debate by sponsors of the New Deal.

Despite criticisms brought against it, frequently outrageous, and its many undoubted shortcomings and extravagances, the New Deal did so much for discouraged and desperate people that it won great popular support. In the circumstances relatively few persons with political aspirations proposed to abolish it completely and entrust the welfare of the people entirely to competitive enterprise.

While indulging in many denunciations of the New Deal in general, the Republicans, in their platform of 1936, endorsed the chief relief principles of the New Deal and pledged themselves to apply those principles more efficiently and at less cost. The Republican candidate, Alfred M. Landon, who had been associated with progressive politics in the West, stood by the planks of the Republican platform during the campaign of that year and in one respect he outbid the New Deal—by offering larger aids to agriculture.

Nevertheless, the Democrats won the election. Renominated by acclamation, President Roosevelt promised to uphold and expand the Democratic program. Reviewing with praise the New Deal activities since 1933 and declaring that he had just begun his fight in the interest of general welfare, he so captivated the public that he received 27,500,000 votes as against 16,700,000 cast for Landon. Whatever their deficiencies, New Deal endeavors to overcome the depression and relieve misery, mainly by domestic measures, seemed to be anchored in the affections of an enormous majority of the voters, so many of whom had personal reasons for being grateful.

Yet in fact the depression was by no means mastered when President Roosevelt took the oath of office for a second term on January 20, 1937—the date as fixed by the Twentieth Amendment, which moved closer to the election the installation of the President, senators, and representatives. At least 6,000,000 Americans were still unemployed. Business was still far below the peak of 1928. And in the year 1937, notwithstanding domestic pump-priming, another crisis struck the stock market, and prices of stocks went down even more rapidly than in the crash of 1929.

Financial analysts for the *American Year Book* of 1937 reported: "A new depression overtook the country in September. Unemployment increased with almost unprecedented swiftness. Relief rolls expanded. . . . The number of commercial failures was increasing. . . . New financing continued during 1937 in a state of comparative stagnation. . . . The decline in [stock] prices during September, October, and November was not only drastic. In fact there are few instances on record where a larger percentage decline has occurred in so short a period of time." Meanwhile the national debt mounted and yet no end of borrowing was in sight. On the contrary New Deal "experts" were now advocating the adoption of borrowing and spending as a permanent fiscal policy for fostering and directing industrial and agricultural production.

☆

During the early stages of the concentration on domestic problems and on measures designed to lift the nation out of the depression, the mood of the country seemed to become more and more concerned with the character of society in the United States, with its grave difficulties, its extraordinary opportunities, its values and potentialities. To this mood the term "isolationism" was often applied. The term was new. It had been coined as a term of reproach for opponents of President Wilson's type of internationalism. Now it was often employed against New Dealers by Americans who believed that general prosperity could only be recovered by lowering trade barriers and entering into some form of collective security with the other nations of the earth. Although President Roosevelt proposed that the United States join the World Court, created under the League of Nations, the Senate rejected the recommendation and he declined to press the issue.

The spirit of disgust with war and Europe was intensified by reports from an investigation of the munitions traffic, pursued by a special committee of the Senate, which unfolded a seamy story of international intrigues, sinuous diplomacy, and profiteering devoid of patriotism, running through the years of the "war for democracy" and the planning for "permanent world peace." Sworn testimony, covering hundreds of pages in the volumes issued by the Senate committee, demonstrated that many men who had applauded Wilson's idealism had in fact made huge sums of money out of the war. Widely publicized, the Senate committee's revelations deepened the dillusionment over the nature and results of that "great crusade." Even President Roosevelt was accused of isolationism and in his reply he lent verisimilitude to the criticism by saying: "We are not isolationists except in so far as we seek to isolate ourselves completely from war."

Out of the uproar over the munitions inquiry and the refusal of Great Britain, France, Italy, and other associates in the World War to pay the debts they owed to the government of the United States came two acts of Congress designed to keep the country out of the next European war, already visible on the horizon. The first was the Johnson Act of 1934, forbidding the flotation of any more loans in the United States for foreign governments that had in effect repudiated the aforesaid debts. The second act was the Neutrality Resolution of 1935. It prohibited the sale of "arms, munitions, and implements of war" to foreign belligerents in time of war and provided that Americans who insisted on traveling aboard the ships of belligerents in wartime must do so at their own risk.

The two acts, in the intentions of the authors, were to prevent a repetition of events which had facilitated the involvement of the United States in the recent European war. When the Neutrality Resolution expired in 1936 it was renewed and made more stringent. Supported by overwhelming majorities in the Democratic Congress, neutrality legislation appeared to represent a reasoned desire on the part of the American people to avoid being entangled in another European war.

By words and actions President Roosevelt indicated that he was in full accord with this desire to keep out of Europe's next war, should another one break. In 1933 he virtually closed the World Economic Conference in London, where the representatives of great Powers had assembled to consider ways and means of overcoming the terrible economic depression through agreements on international trade and currencies. He refused to bring special pressure on the Senate to secure the approval of American participation in the World Court project. He adopted a "good neighbor" policy in Latin America, substituting conferences and cordiality for the straight imperialist coercions of former years.

He induced Congress to free Cuba from the protectorate imposed upon her by the so-called Platt Amendment of 1901. He signed with commendation an act of the Democratic Congress under which the imperialist experiment in the Philippine Islands was to be liquidated by granting them independence, to become effective in 1946.

In his campaign for re-election in 1936, President Roosevelt encouraged the people to fortify their resolve against taking part in another foreign war. He said in his address at Chautauqua, for example: "The Congress of the United States has given me certain authority to provide safeguards of American neutrality in case of war. . . . We can keep out of war if those who watch and decide have a sufficiently detailed understanding of international affairs to make certain that the small decisions of each day do not lead toward war and if, at the same time, they possess the courage to say 'no' to those who selfishly or unwisely would let us go to war."

CHAPTER XXVIII

Global War and Home Front

WHILE Americans were entrapped in the wreckage of the depression, casting about fitfully for methods of full "recovery," and in a mood of revulsion against participation in any more foreign wars, the economy of Europe was falling into chaos and the democracy for which the world was to have been made safe, according to President Wilson's formula, began to collapse in those parts of Europe where it had existed. The depressed state of the Old World now damped plans for maintaining or starting booms in the United States by lending American money to foreigners so that they could buy the "surpluses" of American goods. As a matter of fact, all over central and eastern Europe the march of events for years had been away from the solution of any nation's domestic problems by the mere promotion of freer trade. The march had been in the direction of dictatorships, controlled economy, and revived imperialism.

From its establishment in 1917 by revolution, under V. I. Lenin's strategy, the government of Soviet Russia was frankly an unlimited dictatorship, described as communist and headed by men who, without equivocation, avowed their contempt for democracy, constitutional government, and civil liberties. In 1922 parliamentary government was overthrown in Italy by Fascist bands under the leadership of Benito Mussolini who derided democracy and civil liberty as "stinking corpses," but who went beyond the Russian revolutionists by glorifying war and brute force as good in themselves. One after another smaller states—Yugoslavia, Greece, Spain, and Poland—repudiated popular government in favor of strong-arm government.

Germany's experiment with a republic and a democracy under a constitution adopted at Weimar in 1919 was brief. In 1933, Adolf Hitler, commanding a private army of banditti, called National Socialists, achieved political supremacy in Germany, destroyed the republic, suppressed civil liberty, and started a more than savage persecution of Jews, Social Democrats, Communists, and Liberals. Years before 1933, Hitler had announced his ambitions and intentions in his book *Mein Kampf* (*My Battle*). As there exhibited they embraced a merciless battle at home against all his opponents and a war, east or west or in both directions, against the neighbors of Germany.

To gain time for his operations, however, Hitler spoke publicly of peaceful intentions. In fact he immediately began to rearm Germany and train soldiers for a career of conquest. Many European and American writers warned mankind that Hitler and Mussolini were planning assaults far and wide, but conservative heads of governments in Great Britain, France, and elsewhere—the neighbors against whom they had warlike designs—refused to heed the warnings. Rejoicing in the fascist suppression of communists in Italy and hoping later to turn the full force of Nazi Germany against Russia and communism, they gave comfort and aid to Mussolini and Hitler, even after these dictators became allies in a Rome-Berlin Axis and were joined by Japanese warlords; even after these three aggressors began open wars on their neighbors.

Although popular sympathies in the United States during the years of fascist aggression in Europe and Asia were undoubtedly on the side of the victims of Italy, Germany, and Japan, the American resolve to stay out of the next war, as expressed in the successive neutrality acts, seemed to remain unshaken. But after his second overwhelming triumph at the polls in 1936, President Roosevelt turned upon what his critics called his "isolationism." In an address at Chicago in October 1937, to the amazement of the country, he indicated a change in his position. He denounced, without naming them, Germany, Italy, and Japan, for bringing on "the present reign of terror and international lawlessness." He denied that the United States could keep out of war if it came: "Let no one imagine that America will escape, that it may expect mercy, that this Western Hemisphere will not be attacked." Then he declared that the peace-loving nations must make concerted efforts to restrain the three dangerous Powers—and to lower trade barriers.

When popular protests greeted his Chicago speech and Presi-

Paintings by Eastman Johnson and W. A. Walker. Brown Brothers photos.

With the disappearance of free land and the transfer of natural resources to private persons and corporations, a plutocracy, or money aristocracy, was created and Eastern merchants and lawyers were enriched by Western business. As slum areas spread and tenant farming increased, the mirage of universal prosperity vanished and the revolt against plutocracy grew. War was declared on vested "rights" and many groups and organizations were aligned in a struggle for general welfare which transcended personal desires for wealth, prestige and power.

The rise of national democracy opened the era of monster parades, torchlight processions, popular campaign songs, and huge barbecues attended by thousands of men, women, and youths who swarmed to "camp grounds" in wagons, buggies, and carts to see and hear the candidates. All across the land men and women talked politics, even while they "traded" at little village stores.

As Americans from farming regions and immigrants from abroad turned increasingly to industries and commerce for employment, the growth of urbanism destroyed the almost undisputed supremacy of the rural regions that had characterized the American past. By 1890 about one third of the people lived in towns of 4,000 inhabitants or more, and the growth of great cities was even more remarkable.

Painting by Arthur Crisp. Juley photo.

With the expansion of farm production in the West numerous shipping centers arose on the Great Lakes. Chicago, a petty village when Cook County, Illinois, was organized in 1831, soon became a focal point for the handling of farm produce and Eastern manufactures. After the establishment of the McCormick reaper works in 1849, Chicago developed into the leading city for the manufacture of farm machinery.

Painting by Joseph Boggs Beale. Modern Enterprises, Phila., Pa.

In the growth of manufacturing cities, immigrants of the Old World became factors of increasing importance. Steamship companies and employers of labor seeking a plentiful supply to keep wages low, stimulated this inflow of labor forces, and the promotion of immigration became a highly profitable money-making enterprise. By 1840 immigration had become so extensive that loud objections were raised against it, but it was not until organized labor began a national struggle to improve standards of living that effective pressure for restrictions appeared in Congress.

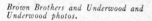

The foreign policy of the United
States, as formulated by Washington, Jefferson, and Monroe, rested
on the proposition that the fundamental interest of the American
people was the advancement of
their own civilization and abstention from European wars. But
about 1890 politicians began seriously to plan the transformation of
the United States into an imperialist "world power." Theodore
Roosevelt, a colonel in the Spanish-
American war of 1898, was a
vigorous champion of the new
policy coupled with a program of
social reform at home.

Paintings by Charles Allen Winter. Keystone View Co. photos.

American cities, with few exceptions, had grown up rapidly and in a haphazard fashion under the stimulus of free enterprise. With their growth the functions of city government became more complex. Matters of crime, fire, and traffic, education, recreation, water supply, sanitation, and public welfare presented only a few of the problems for solution and continuous functioning. In response to a growing interest in municipal affairs, a city planning movement came into being and in 1909 the National City Planning Association was founded.

By building bigger navies, raising bigger armies, seizing territories in Asia, Africa, and islands of the seas, and forming secret alliances, European Powers prepared for the climax—the World War starting in 1914. As neutrals, Americans had commercial rights under international law that were violated in this war. After trying to make Germany quit destroying American lives and property, the United States entered the conflict. In 1919 President Wilson took part in the conference at Paris which framed the treaty of peace.

Paintings by John Singer Sargent and William Orpen. Ewing Galloway photos.

Paintings by Wm. Cropper and David Stone Martin.
Courtesy Section of Fine Arts, Public Buildings Administration.

A phase of the struggle to regulate natural resources was a contest over water power. In 1920 a federal power commission was established to control the use of federal power sites. Afterward Congress authorized the construction and operation of a power plant in the Boulder Canyon of the Colorado River to provide water for irrigation, household, and commercial purposes, and the generation of electricity. Another program of dam building, power production, and flood control was undertaken by the Government in 1933 under the Tennessee Valley Authority.

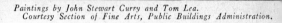

Paintings by John Stewart Curry and Tom Lea.
Courtesy Section of Fine Arts, Public Buildings Administration.

Cities shot up overnight and farms quickly spread to the horizons following the wild dash made on April 13, 1889 by settlers to file claims on Oklahoma land purchased from the Indians by the United States government. An aftermath of prodigal farming in regions of the great West subject to drought was the "dust bowl." To counter the evils of impoverished natural resources and people, conservation was expanded to include the planting of trees and hardy grasses, contour ploughing, irrigation, and flood control.

Painting by Peter Helck. Courtesy Pennsylvania Railroad.

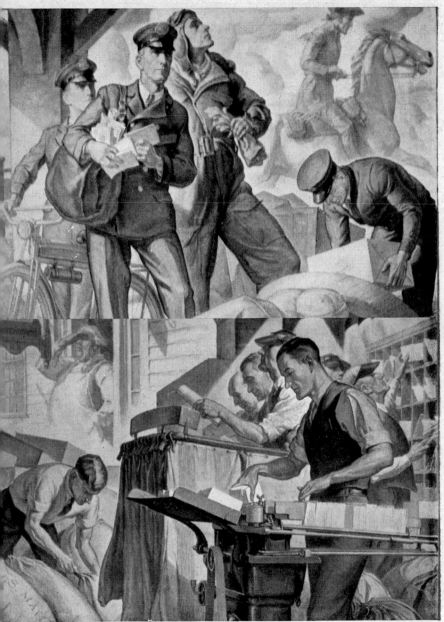

Paintings by Robert Lambdin. Courtesy Section of Fine Arts, Public Buildings Administration.

Benjamin Franklin was made the first Postmaster-General, in 1775, under the Continental Congress. The Constitution of 1789 provided for a Postmaster-General but he was not made a member of the President's Cabinet until 1829. In time the pony express and mail coach were superseded by rail service and airplane for the delivery of mail and the business of handling it grew into a major industry.

Painting by Geoffrey Biggs.
Courtesy Pennsylvania Railroad.

Painting by Stevan Dohanos. Courtesy Section of Fine Arts, Public Buildings Administration.

In the expansion of capitalist enterprise immense new coal beds were exploited in Pennsylvania, Illinois, West Virginia, Alabama, and other parts of the continent. Enormous deposits of iron ore were unearthed and the processes of iron production were revolutionized.

HE WHO TOILS HERE
HATH SET HIS MARK

Painting by Arthur Covey. Courtesy Kohler of Kohler.
Painting by Glen Shaw. Courtesy Section of Fine Arts, Public Buildings Administration.

It was upon the minerals available for gigantic industries that the Carnegie and Morgan interests were built. To the mines and mills workers of many nationalities flocked in search of employment. Powerful trade unions appeared in the coal and steel industries and constant strife marked the relations of capital and labor.

Painting by John Clymer. Courtesy Pennsylvania Railroad.

Under the Lend-Lease Act of March 11, 1941, the President was given power to furnish munitions of war and other supplies to the countries at war with the Axis governments. In December of that year the United States became involved in war. Soon the Global War affected every aspect of civil and military government, and the various relations of men, women, and children. Millions of men were enrolled in the armed forces for combat. Women served as auxiliaries at home and abroad.

Paintings by Dean Cornwell. Courtesy Pennsylvania Railroad.

Every branch of economy—agriculture, industry, and labor—was affected by the impact of total war. Before the close of 1943 approximately 8,700,000 men had been withdrawn from farms, industries, shops, mines, offices, college halls, and from all the professions. Millions of women were recruited, voluntarily, for war production industries to release more men for the armed forces. To supply war materials in greater quantities billions of dollars were pumped into the construction of gigantic new plants.

The development of mammoth airplanes for combat purposes and for carrying cargoes swiftly to the most distant places offered a menace to the steamship which had long before driven the slow sailing vessel from the seas. Fabulous dreams of a vast world trade now gave rise to constant talk in the United States about capturing larger foreign markets. Would any amount of foreign trade which could be won for this country really solve the problems of farm "surpluses," industrial "overproduction," and unemployment that loomed over the war horizon?

dent Roosevelt was asked to amplify his argument, he lapsed into silence. But early the following year, 1938, he called upon Congress for an extra appropriation for the Navy and expressed his opinion that dangers of war were drawing closer to the United States. Meanwhile he supported the government of Britain in its professed "non-intervention" policy in Spain where, aided by the armed might of Hitler and Mussolini, fascist rebels were demolishing the Spanish Republic, to whose assistance Russia alone had come, and by so doing he aided, if unwittingly, in the triumph of fascism there.

After Germany launched a war on Poland in the autumn of 1939 and Great Britain and France retaliated by declaring war on Germany, President Roosevelt called upon Congress to repeal the embargo provision of the neutrality legislation or modify it in such fashion as to permit Americans to sell munitions to the British and French governments. In his message to Congress, however, he assured Congress that the repeal which he demanded was in the interest of American abstention from the war—in the interest of "American neutrality, American security, and above all, American peace." Apparently accepting the President's explanation, Congress made changes in the Neutrality Act in the direction which he indicated; but tightened it in other respects. In vain opponents of repeal or alteration insisted that the changes were steps toward entry into another war along the very road Woodrow Wilson had traveled from 1915 to 1917.

On September 3, 1940, President Roosevelt informed Congress that he had, by executive act, acquired lease rights to naval and air bases in Newfoundland, in the British West Indies, and in British Guiana; and that in exchange for certain of these bases he had given Great Britain fifty of our "over-age destroyers."

Objectors charged that, besides being an arbitrary action which the President had no lawful right to take, it was a plain act of war as defined by international law—the transfer of war vessels by a presumptive neutral to a government at war with another power. But the President simply replied that his Attorney General, Robert H. Jackson, had pronounced the destroyer deal lawful. To members of his party in Congress inclined to interpret it as a war measure he gave some reassurance by declaring: "This is not inconsistent in any sense with our status of peace."

☆

It was amid the thrumming of war alarms that the presidential campaign of 1940 opened. Brushing aside the third-term tradition established by Jefferson, the Democrats nominated President Roosevelt for a third term; and on his insistence chose Henry A. Wallace, a member of his Cabinet, for Vice-President. Passing over party regulars, the Republicans selected as their candidate for the presidency Wendell Willkie, a former Democrat, utility lawyer, and public relations agent, who had long opposed President Roosevelt's domestic policies.

Whatever party managers had in view, peace was an issue uppermost in the minds of the people. On this issue both candidates seemed to be reassuring. "The American people," declared Wendell Willkie, "do not want war. . . . They are determined to keep America at peace. In that determination I stand with them. I am for keeping out of war." To Willkie's challenge President Roosevelt responded in the closing days of the campaign. France had fallen. Mussolini had stabbed her in the back. But speaking at Boston at that hour of European stress and strain, on October 30, 1940, Roosevelt gave a solemn pledge to his country: "And while I am talking to you mothers and fathers, I give you one more assurance. I have said this before, but I shall say it again and again and again. Your boys are not going to be sent into any foreign wars. They are going into training to form a force so strong that, by its very existence, it will keep the threat of war away from our shores. The purpose of our own defense is defense."

Franklin D. Roosevelt was granted a third term by a vote of 27,000,000 in round numbers against the 22,000,000 polled by Willkie. In his annual message of January 6, 1941, to Congress, he announced his intention to have the United States send to the nations at war with Hitler and Mussolini "in ever-increasing numbers, ships, planes, tanks, guns." This action, he realized, might lead to war and yet he said: "Such aid is not an act of war, even if a dictator should unilaterally proclaim it so to be."

Then he had drawn up and introduced into Congress, in January, a measure "to promote the defense of the United States," known as the Lend-Lease bill. After extensive hearings and a long debate, this bill, modified by amendments, became a law on March 11, 1941. The Lend-Lease Act authorized the President to sell, transfer, exchange, lend, lease, or otherwise dispose of ships, aircraft, implements of war, and other commodities to the "government of any country whose defense the President deems vital to the defense of the United States." In effect, it empowered the

President to sell or give, to any and all governments actually or nominally at war with the Axis Powers, war implements and supplies in immense quantities.

Under international law as hitherto recognized, this law was an act of war. Opponents of the bill so characterized the gift of military supplies to China in her conflict with Japan and similar aid to Great Britain and her Allies in their war on Germany and Italy. But it was entitled a bill to promote the defense of the United States; and its sponsors in Congress assured the country that it was intended to keep the country out of war.

On July 7, 1941, about two weeks after Hitler's armies invaded Russia, President Roosevelt notified Congress that the armed forces of the United States had occupied Iceland, jointly with British forces for the time being; and that he had ordered the American Navy to defend the sea lanes between the United States and that island.

In August the President and the British Premier, Winston Churchill, met "somewhere in the Atlantic," and agreed upon measures to be taken in providing for the safety of their respective countries against Germany and the governments associated with her. They also drew up at their conference a declaration of principles, soon called the Atlantic Charter, for the conduct of affairs, not only during the war but also after the destruction of Nazi tyranny.

On October 27, 1941, President Roosevelt informed the country that Germany had started war on the United States. "Hitler," said the President, "has attacked shipping in areas close to the Americas. . . . Many American-owned ships have been sunk on the high seas. One American destroyer was attacked on September 4. Another destroyer was attacked and hit on October 17. Eleven brave and loyal men of our Navy were killed by the Nazis. We have wished to avoid shooting. But shooting has started. . . . America has been attacked."

☆

Although the attention of the American people was now directed especially to the war in Europe, trouble was brewing in another foreign quarter. The government of Japan, taken over by ruthless militarists, had for years been seizing territory in China and waging war on that country. Under the slogan of "Asia for the Asiatics," Japanese imperialists nourished projects for conquering and ruling immense areas of the mainland and islands in the Far East. This region they called Japan's "sphere of influence."

Japan's aggression, of course, ran counter to American foreign policy in the Orient and to the letter and spirit of treaties signed by the Japanese government and other Powers, including the United States. In upholding that policy President Roosevelt took the position that Japan was violating treaties and international law, destroying the independence of China, and transgressing American rights in the Orient.

In response to such complaints the Japanese government, by this time allied with Germany and Italy as the third party to the Axis, offered some concessions, but in the main adhered to its own imperialistic line. It insisted that the United States was violating Japan's rights as a belligerent by giving financial aid to the government of China and by sending munitions to that government at Chungking, by way of the Burma Road. For months, as indeed for years in the past, the State Department at Washington refused to surrender any part of its Far Eastern policy. Diplomatic exchange between the governments of the United States and Japan continued without softening the asperity of their differences.

Eager to avoid the awful perils of a two-front war, Great Britain tried conciliation with Japan. For a long time the two countries had been formal allies united by treaty. Though, on the insistence of the United States, their alliance had been severed in 1922, they had managed to keep on workable terms. Yielding to protests from the Japanese government, Great Britain in 1940 closed the Burma Road to shipments of munitions and supplies bound for Chungking, still in the hope of warding off a war with Japan.

But the British closure of the Burma Road brought objections from the United States. When he heard rumors of the proposal Secretary of State Cordell Hull declared that the United States had a "legitimate interest in the keeping open of the arteries of commerce in every part of the world," and that shutting the road would "constitute unwarranted interposition of obstacles to world trade." When her agreement with Japan expired at the end of six months, Britain complied with American desires and opened the road again to the transport of munitions to Chungking.

By November 1941 the tension between the government of the United States and the government of Japan approached a climax, as Japanese armed forces moving southward into French Indo-China increased in number. Late in that month, according to the statement of Wilfred Fleisher, long a resident in Tokyo and a careful student of Japanese affairs, in his *Our Enemy Japan,* a kind of truce with Japan was reached in Washington, with the approval of the British and Australians and reluctantly of the Dutch. But Hu Shih, the Chinese ambassador, protested to President Roosevelt against the proposed truce; and the plan for avoiding an immediate conflict with Japan was dropped. Subsequent efforts to reach an agreement failed.

As early as January 27, 1941, the American ambassador to Tokyo, Joseph Grew, had reported to the State Department that Japanese military forces were planning a surprise attack on Pearl Harbor in case of trouble with the United States. On November 25 and November 28, 1941, Secretary Hull told "high officials" of the United States Government that relations with Japan were critical and that Japan might launch sudden attacks at various points. While negotiations were still going on with Japan, on December 7, a surprise attack did occur. By bombing planes and submarines Japanese forces, without warning, fell upon Pearl Harbor in the Hawaiian Islands and decimated American naval, land, and air forces in that American outpost.

One of two things had happened. Either President Roosevelt, as Commander in Chief, or Frank Knox, Secretary of the Navy, or Henry L. Stimson, Secretary of War, had not duly and sternly put the American officers in charge at Pearl Harbor on their guard for defense; or those officers had been inexcusably negligent in the performance of duty. Wherever the responsibility lay, the United States had been assaulted by Japan and was severely crippled for quick counterblows by the disaster at Pearl Harbor. At the same time the Japanese had attacked American and British imperial outposts in the Far East.

On December 8, 1941, the day after the attack on Pearl Harbor, the United States declared war on Japan, and so did Great Britain. Three days later Germany and Italy proclaimed war on the United States and agreed with Japan, their Axis colleague, not to make a separate peace. In a little while nearly all the world was engulfed in war. The conflict of 1914–18 had been comparatively limited—mainly to Europe and the Atlantic Ocean. Now all the continents and seas became scenes of armed combats. Only minor Powers, such as Switzerland, Sweden, Turkey, and Argentina, remained outside the circle of fighting or belligerency.

At first the combat activities of the United States, apart from the war on submarines in the Atlantic, were confined to the Pacific

THE THEATERS OF AMERICAN
The black and shaded areas show the

470

ACTION IN THE GLOBAL WAR
extreme limits of Axis conquests.

area. Handicapped by the destruction of American resources at Pearl Harbor, the United States was powerless to check the southward sweep of Japan's ships, planes, and armies for many months. Manila soon succumbed under Japanese assaults. British and Dutch forces quickly yielded to the invaders—at Hong Kong and Singapore and in the Dutch East Indies. After displaying extraordinary courage in defense, Americans had to give up all the Philippines.

Before the end of 1942, Japanese forces had spread out in a great arc covering all the islands southward and were close to the shores of Australia. There Americans and Australians stopped the advancing horde and opened an offensive war for recovering ground and wearing down Japanese strength. While Australia was being saved and the Japanese tide turned slowly backward, British and American troops landed in the French colonies of North Africa, in November 1942, and established a front there against Italians and Germans. After some initial setbacks, they began a conquering advance.

Before a year passed they had crushed the Italians and Germans in Africa, invaded and occupied Sicily, brought about the overthrow of Mussolini and his Fascist government, invaded the Italian mainland, forced the Italian government out of the war, and were driving the Germans slowly but steadily northward by incessant hammering and bombing. Meanwhile American air forces, in co-operation with the British, intensified the systematic destruction of German industrial cities, as Russian armies drove the Germans backward to the Dnieper River and beyond.

Hard fighting remained ahead in the opening weeks of 1944 but the powerful and terrifying Axis had been disrupted. The Italian people, formerly an Axis partner, was struggling on its own soil for survival. Hitler was on the defensive, retreating before the Russian onslaughts and weakening under the relentless blows of Allied forces. The Japanese, without prospect of aid from any quarter, were losing one island stronghold after another under American and Australian attacks by air, land, and sea. At this point the political complications of the Global War began to unfold in their fullness, even for American novices.

☆

In respect of its regimenting and disruptive effects in American society, the Global War was so revolutionary that it made the World War look like an episode. Every branch of economy—agriculture, industry, and labor—all the relations of men, women, and children, every phase of education, every medium of expression and communication, all processes of government, all aspects of civil and military government, were affected by the impacts of the total war and presented far-reaching reactions. Many of the reactions—perhaps all of them—were of incalculable significance for destiny and opportunity in the United States.

Under Selective Service Acts of 1940, 1941, and 1942, provisions were made for armed forces numbering two or three times the 4,000,000 men raised for the war of 1917–18. Before the close of 1943 approximately 8,700,000 men had been enlisted—withdrawn from farms, industries, shops, mines, offices, college halls, and from all the professions—deranging the course of economy and social practices. Doctors were taken from medical practice, often leaving hospitals and whole communities without adequate medical services. Teachers by the thousands went to war or left their school-rooms to engage in war production; and all over the land, in town and country, no substitutes could be found to carry on the work of primary and secondary education as before. Small business enterprises not "essential" to war production were denuded of manpower and, hard pressed, were often shut up or driven into bankruptcy.

To release more men for the fighting fronts and to aid in the military and naval administration, tens of thousands of women were recruited as volunteers from homes, schools, colleges, and business positions, organized in auxiliary corps, put into uniforms, given disciplinary instruction and war indoctrination such as the armed forces were receiving, granted military ranking and titles, with economic benefits akin to those accorded to men in the services. Thousands were sent overseas to the battle fronts to render various services under military orders. Women nurses and doctors were also drawn into the tasks associated with war.

To supply war materials in greater quantities and varieties than ever before nearly every manufacturing plant adaptable to war production was wholly or in part shifted from the manufacture of civilian goods to the manufacture of war goods; and billions of dollars were pumped into the construction of gigantic new plants, to make the United States the "arsenal of the democracies," as President Roosevelt phrased it. Millions of men were transferred from all kinds of occupations to war industries or other work deemed essential to war efforts; and finally all men, within broad age limits, were warned that unless they were in essential work they were liable to be inducted into the armed forces.

Millions of women were also recruited, voluntarily, from civilian employments for war production industries to release more men for the armed forces. Among them were throngs of women who had never been gainfully employed. As the war proceeded, demanding constantly more womanpower, greater and greater calls were made upon women still outside war work.

This disruption of civilian economy, this transformation of old manufacturing plants into war plants and the construction of new plants often in districts purely rural, induced an enormous migration of men and women, boys and girls, singly and in families, from one end of the country to the other. Old towns and cities thus became terribly congested while, in the new centers of war production, the provision of adequate facilities for housing and sanitation lagged far behind the industrial expansion. Despite efforts of the governments, federal and local, to contend with the situation, menaces to health, education, welfare, and every other human value reached frightening proportions.

In these circumstances, especially with so many mothers employed for long hours, by day or by night, outside the home, family life was not only shattered but hordes of young children were turned into the streets to fend for themselves. Older children left school in droves to work in factories for fabulous wages and, refusing to return to schools, took their lives into their own keeping. With children unguided by teachers or parents, juvenile delinquency and crimes increased to an extent that threatened the moral basis of American society. In August 1943, J. Edgar Hoover, head of the federal police force, exclaimed: "The tragedy revealed by our latest survey is found in the fact that the arrests of boys and girls seventeen years of age increased 17.7% [last year]. In reviewing the further trends for the past six months we find an 89% increase in the arrests of girls for offenses against common decency."

While various women's organizations were rejoicing in the equalities of opportunity, honors, and monetary rewards offered to women by the war and were pushing the recruiting of women for war work of all kinds, individual women, and to some extent organized women, began to appreciate the social peril of juvenile delinquency and also the problems of caring for the babies of mothers engaged in war work. Amid the pressures for complete concentration on war, therefore, women interested in social welfare urged that responsibility for looking after the children be mainly assumed by governments, federal, state, and local.

There was no doubt that families were undergoing disintegration; for men were being drafted for war, women drawn into the auxiliary armed forces, war production, and civilian defense, children of school age crowding into war industries, adolescents left to roam the streets for excitement, and the energies of parents distracted from the care of homes and children. The fact was indisputable and its social import was recognized by leaders in public affairs. It was discussed in newspapers, in meetings of organizations concerned with public welfare, in journals devoted to surveys of social and economic conditions, and in popular magazines. It was emphasized during debates in Congress over a proposal to defer pre-Pearl Harbor fathers.

Yet no generally accepted and workable plans were devised for successfully countering disruptive effects of war activities and war regimentation on the homes and family life of the nation. New houses for war workers were built under the national housing authorities; nurseries were installed in factories; and more nurseries were established in urban and rural communities. But none of these undertakings was on a scale commensurate with the problem. And indeed they were at best inadequate substitutes for the provisions of orderly home living.

The war necessities, demanding men and women by the millions for the armed forces and war production, also broke into education, that adjunct of family life in the care and rearing of the young generations. Every branch of it, from the primary schools to colleges and universities, was deeply affected by the same intrusive tendencies. Old programs of instruction designed to prepare youth for civilian life and employment were either thrown away or recast in the interest of preparation for combat service or activities connected with it. The war sciences crowded aside the old liberal arts and civilian sciences, with their emphasis on humane letters and living.

As one leader in this educational upheaval put it: "What is probably the greatest mass-educational system the world has ever known is quietly teaching thousands of American men the science and skills of modern technical warfare." Not only that. A regimentation of education and educational thought in this direction gathered momentum from Maine to California, under the auspices of the military arm of the government. So serious was civilian alarm over this tendency, savoring of militarism, that one of the great foundations made a grant of money to a learned association for the purpose of examining anew the nature and utility of "liberal education" at every level of the American school system.

Authority over life and property far greater in its extent than that conferred upon President Wilson in the World War was granted to President Roosevelt—power almost without limit over industry, agriculture, wages, prices, use of plant facilities, the erection of new plants, and rationing of supplies for civilians. The enforcement of social legislation providing for safety in industries, for sanitary standards of housing, and for safeguarding the health and welfare of the people was relaxed or openly disregarded amid the rush of war mobilization. Industrial plants were commandeered entirely or compelled to divert a percentage of their production to war purposes. Men and women in numerous vital industries were "frozen" in their jobs—compelled to remain where they were employed instead of being free to seek and accept more attractive positions. New plants of staggering dimensions were built from coast to coast, often at the expense of the government. Through public financing of industries, the rationing of commodities, the fixing of prices, and the multiplication of federal officials to administer the new laws, the tentacles of the government reached wider and wider, and deeper and deeper, into the life, liberty, and property of the people as well as into old practices known as "free enterprise."

Strenuous efforts were made to hold down wages and strikes; and in 1943, by the Smith-Connally Act, Congress imposed heavy penalties on labor leaders who fomented strikes, and forbade organized labor to contribute money to the campaign funds of political parties. In many respects, of course, trade unions had gained advantages out of war industries; more millions were employed; and under the policies of the New Deal many of these millions were, in effect, compelled to join unions and pay dues in order to get war production jobs. On the whole, labor loyally cooperated in war activities, the Communists giving enthusiastic support, as the extraordinary output of munitions, armaments, and other goods demonstrated.

There had been "rackets" in the labor world, corrupt and disgraceful rackets, but responsible labor leaders deprecated these blots on the labor movement and sought to maintain equable relations with industry and the government. Finding themselves caught in the pinch of rising prices and government control, however, they began to draw together more closely in efforts to deal with their new situation. John L. Lewis, of the United Mine Workers, having left the Congress of Industrial Organizations, offered to take his organization back into the American Federation of Labor. Moves were made to consolidate the Federation and the Congress, with a combined membership of more than 10,000,000, or at least to effect working agreements on a common program for meeting the strains of war regimentation on trade-union policies and standards.

In the domain of opinion, as well as in other phases of national life, government controls expanded. The press, the radio, and the moving picture were put under the scrutiny or censorship of official agencies. Government films were produced and film industries were largely diverted to meet the purposes and demands of war propaganda. The Espionage Act of 1917 was kept alive and applied by the courts. And to this measure for the control of opinion and expression was added what was in effect a new sedition act—Title I of the Alien Registration Act of 1940—which introduced into American law, for the first time, a principle of the European state-police system: namely, that anyone may be arrested and punished, not for what he says or does, but because he is a member of an association whose avowed purposes are revolutionary. Universities, colleges, and schools all over the country were turned into institutions for military training, and their programs and methods of education were subjected to the approval, supervision, or direct dominance of military authorities.

In financial terms the war outstripped all human experience. On June 30, 1914, the net debt of the United States stood at $1,000,000,000 in round numbers. In 1930 the Treasury Department estimated that the cost of the first World War up to that time was in excess of $37,000,000,000; and it was reckoned that, counting pensions to soldiers and additional charges, its total cost would run to $100,000,000,000. These figures were staggering for Americans who had once boasted that their nation was not like the debt-burdened nations of the Old World. But before a year of the Global War had passed, Congress authorized an expenditure amounting to $240,000,000,000.

While the debt mounted, taxes grew in weight. Under the income-tax law of 1942 every single person with more than $600 a year and every married couple with more than $1200 a year, subject to certain deductions, had to pay an income tax rising steeply with the amount of the income. Tens of millions of Americans who had never paid a direct tax for the support of the federal government were compelled to make out returns and pay. In addition they were subjected to stamp taxes and other forms of indirect taxation, profuse in variety. Taxes on the earnings and excess profits of corporations reached heights that approached confiscation in the upper levels.

Under the impulse of war imperatives the industrial facilities of the United States for productive purposes were expanded with astounding swiftness. In 1939 the manufacturing plants of the country represented an investment of about $50,000,000,000—the accumulation of all the previous years. Within three years new plants, involving an additional investment of $22,000,000,000, were either built or under construction, many of them wholly or partly owned by the federal government. In terms of annual output in dollar values the production of wealth, which had fallen below $50,000,000,000 in the midst of the great depression following the panic of 1929, was lifted by 1943 to the neighborhood of $150,-000,000, revealing in this astronomic figure the titanic productive powers of capitalists, managers, and workers, equipped with the agencies of modern science and technology.

By seeming necessity the expansion of heavy industries for the production of steel, guns, ships, tanks, trucks, planes, and other implements of war expedited the long-time trend toward the concentration of capitalist activities and interests. For more than a hundred years, especially since the enactment of the Sherman Anti-Trust Act of 1890, farmers, owners of small industries, shopkeepers, and other heads of little economic units had inveighed against this tendency. Statesmen had called for a reversal of the process. Agitators had stirred up excitement about it. Political revolts had been raised against it. But nothing had forced a return to the system of village smithies, corner stores, horses, and buggies. Concentration had been accelerated by the World War under the leadership of President Wilson who, in his campaigns, had denounced the "masters of big business" and promised to emancipate the people from their dominion.

Now the Global War, fought in support of foreign policies world-wide in purpose and range, made heavy and unprecedented demands upon mass production industries directed by masters of big business. To get quickly and in fabulous amounts the quantities and kinds of implements absolutely needed for such a war, it was necessary for the government to turn immediately to industries already monstrous in size and force their immediate conversion from peacetime production into war production. As the demand for war goods rose higher and higher and plants covering ten, twenty, eighty, or more acres of ground had to be built, it was to the experienced managers of gigantic industries that the government had to resort for swift and efficient construction of new buildings.

Special efforts were made to favor little business concerns, but by the close of 1943 seventy per cent of the war business had gone to the hundred biggest business establishments. The building of at least one hundred plant extensions was assigned to the General Motors Company alone. In response to this stimulus great business leaders sprang to their duties and, with the co-operation of labor, turned out war goods in quantities that astounded the world. Ardent sponsors of the war execrated the tendency to concentration. Vice-President Wallace lashed out at the "monopolists" in wrathful language. New Deal members of Congress spread denunciation over pages of the *Congressional Record*, while on the insistence of the War and Navy departments the prosecution of trusts and combinations was relaxed by the Department of Justice. Businessmen claimed that they could not keep their industries going at full tempo and also spend days and weeks in courtrooms defending themselves against civil and criminal charges as monopolists. So the process of centralization went on under the "economic royalists" anathematized by President Roosevelt and the New Dealers. In these circumstances was raised anew, and in a novel form, Henry Adams' question of 1895: Are we in the midst of the last great centralization, with its overtones and undertones, with all its implications as a pattern of culture enclosing politics, education, ethics, and esthetics?

☆

Permeating all the discussions about the immediate problems thrust upward by war mobilization, regimentation, and the disruption of family and national life were debates over two fundamental questions looking to the future. First: What kind of international settlement is to be made or can be made at the close of the armed combat? Second: What will American society look like when the war comes to an end, and what is to be done, or can be done, about the new problems and tasks arising on every hand?

As to the first of these questions, Americans were practically unanimous on the proposition that a peace more enduring than the truce patched up at Paris in 1919 must be made, if possible, if within the grasp of American statesmen and the people of the United States. But how was this end to be gained? There was the rub.

To the public were offered from various sources innumerable

plans for a pacific postwar world. The range was wide. It embraced a revived League of Nations, new types of world federations, the establishment of a world police force to hold down aggressors, the education of all nations in American principles of democracy, and economic schemes for bringing peace, prosperity, and fraternity to everybody, everywhere. Perhaps simplest of all, on its face, was a project for an open alliance between the United States, Great Britain, Russia, and China, committed to the maintenance of peace and the suppression by force of any and all nations attempting to defy their authority by arms. Yet none of these plans received an official blessing from President Roosevelt.

In the course of the World War, President Wilson had set forth his war aims in the form of definite points as a foreign policy for the United States—largely vain in respect of peace, as events proved. Before and during the Global War, President Roosevelt merely expounded his views on war aims as American foreign policy in the most general language.

In his annual message to Congress in January 1941, Roosevelt said: "In future days, which we seek to make secure, we look forward to a world founded upon four essential human freedoms.

"The first is freedom of speech and expression—everywhere in the world.

"The second is freedom of every person to worship God in his own way—everywhere in the world.

"The third is freedom from want—which, translated into world terms, means economic understandings which will secure to every nation a healthy peacetime life for its inhabitants—everywhere in the world.

"The fourth is freedom from fear—which, translated into world terms, means a world-wide reduction of armaments to such a point and in such a thorough fashion that no nation will be in a position to commit an act of physical aggression against any neighbor—anywhere in the world."

In the Atlantic Charter of August 1941 President Roosevelt and Premier Churchill announced principles of policy on which they agreed: "Their countries seek no aggrandizement, territorial or other; . . . they desire to see no territorial changes that do not accord with the freely expressed wishes of the peoples concerned; . . . they respect the right of all peoples to choose the form of government under which they will live." To these principles they added hopes for other changes, such as freer trade, co-operation among nations in the economic field; a peace which will "afford assurance that all the men in all the lands may live out their lives in freedom from fear and want"; freedom of the seas; the abandonment of force in the world; and general disarmament, "pending the establishment of a wider and permanent system of general security."

An indefinite kind of agreement on war aims and purposes was reached among countries at war with two or more Axis Powers, on January 2, 1942, when the agents of twenty-six governments signed at Washington a joint declaration and formed a loose organization known as the United Nations. Some of the official signers represented only governments in exile from countries overrun by Hitler, but they all "subscribed" to the principles of the Atlantic Charter and pledged their countries to employ all their military and economic resources in waging war on those Axis Powers with which they were then actually at war, to co-operate in waging the war, and to make no separate peace.

The signers of the United Nations Declaration were the President of the United States, the Prime Minister of Great Britain, the Soviet ambassador, the Chinese foreign minister, and officials from Australia, Belgium, Canada, Costa Rica, Cuba, Czechoslovakia, the Dominican Republic, El Salvador, Greece, Guatemala, Haiti, Honduras, India, Luxembourg, the Netherlands, New Zealand, Nicaragua, Norway, Panama, Poland, South Africa, and Yugoslavia. Later other governments joined the United Nations. Although this was not an alliance binding the United States by treaty, President Roosevelt expressed the hope that the union so formed would co-operate not only during the war but also in making the settlement at the end of the war.

Many complications lay in the way of reducing the broad principles of the Atlantic Charter to specific plans of action likely to guarantee their realization, especially in view of the fact that no one could foresee the exact state of things at the end of the war. Many Americans believed and publicly declared during the war that the idea of giving everybody, everywhere in the world, freedom of speech and expression, freedom of religious worship, freedom from want, and freedom from fear was a chimera; that these are freedoms which cannot be given gratuitously or imposed by force. The number of Americans who thought that some kind of alliance or world association should be formed to keep the peace was very large, according to every indication. But no simple or intricate plan that was set forth commanded wholesale approval.

In the discussion of plans for reordering the world, even Americans who had been champions of the League of Nations or some other form of permanent world organization, and who still were fervently international in their outlook, displayed strong diversities of opinion over specific proposals for achieving a world order. The plight of world affairs was in fact far more confused by 1943 than it had been at the conclusion of the World War. Russia signed the United Nations Declaration but its head, Joseph Stalin, let the other nations know that his government did not intend to restore to independence and self-government certain small countries on the western borders of the Soviet Republic. British authorities officially announced that the British Empire was not to be liquidated and that outside interference with the government of its dominions and dependencies would not be tolerated. As France was prostrate before Hitler's armies of occupation, there was only a self-constituted committee of Frenchmen to speak for her interests, but it cast about for allies and claimed a place for France in the postwar world. At a London conference attended by representatives of governments in exile, in September 1943, protest was made against the rumor that their affairs were to be controlled by any Anglo-American system of power, with or without the aid of Russia. Above all, it was recognized that Russia, owing to her tremendous victories over German forces and the terrifying strength of her armies, might well be the most powerful nation in the determination of the final settlement, and might oppose Pan-Slavism to Pan-Latinism, Pan-Arabianism, and Pan-Anglo-Saxonism, notwithstanding the declaration at Moscow signed by representatives of Russia, Great Britain, the United States, and China and announced on November 1, 1943.

That the debates over foreign and domestic problems would continue to be tempestuous and more and more penetrating was foreshadowed by the outcome of the congressional elections of 1942, nearly a year after the outbreak of the war. In the campaign, supporters of the Roosevelt administration demanded a wholesale repudiation of citizens who had formerly opposed getting into the war. Of the total vote cast at the polls, Republicans received 50.6%; the Democrats 47.4; and independents 2%. A large proportion of the candidates who had been against intervention prior to Pearl Harbor were successful at the polls. Although the Democrats managed to hold a majority in the House of Representatives and in the Senate, their sway was materially weakened in both houses. About 80% of the members in the House of Representatives who had voted against the Lend-Lease bill in 1941 were returned to their seats—a percentage larger than that of the members who had voted for it.

All members of the new Congress were fully committed to the vigorous prosecution of the war, but many of them soon began to show a virulent opposition to President Roosevelt's policies and administration. Again and again, in both chambers, combinations of Republicans and Democrats overrode his plans, proposals, and desires. They abolished his National Resources Planning Board, the domestic branch of the Office of War Information, and the National Youth Administration. They investigated and criticized the Lend-Lease Administration and demanded to know how the $60,000,000,000 appropriated to aid other nations enlisted in the war on the Axis Powers was being distributed and spent. They attacked in long debates the President's aides and advisers, demanded a reduction in the enormous bureaucracy of more than 3,000,000 federal civilian employees, and in some instances attempted to oust officials by cutting off their salaries.

Only on two fundamentals was there anything like universal agreement in Congress. The first was that the war must be supported by appropriations of money so large that they appalled the senators and representatives as they voted them. The second was that efforts to establish an enduring peace must be made. Evidences of the former appeared in the war appropriations by Congress equaling in amount more than the appropriations of all the Allied governments combined. Evidences of the latter were made manifest in two resolutions on the peace settlement—one by the House of Representatives and the other by the Senate.

The House of Representatives resolution, bearing the name of its author, J. W. Fulbright, of Arkansas, came up for final debate in September 1943 and was passed by an overwhelming majority. It read: "Resolved by the House of Representatives [the Senate concurring], That the Congress hereby expresses itself as favoring the creation of appropriate international machinery with power adequate to establish and to maintain a just and lasting peace, among the nations of the world, and as favoring participation by the United States therein through its constitutional processes."

The Senate, however, refused to concur with the House on the Fulbright resolution. For this proposal it substituted one of its own, cast in more circumspect terms. The Senate resolution, bearing the name of Tom Connally, chairman of the Foreign Relations Committee, gave a pledge that the United States would co-operate with its comrades in arms in securing a "just and honorable peace" and that the United States, "acting through its constitutional processes," would join with "free and sovereign nations" in the establishment and maintenance of international authority with power to prevent aggression and preserve the peace of the world.

While the Connally resolution was being debated in the Senate, with much deference to the constitutional right of that body to pass upon treaties negotiated by the Chief Executive, the proceedings were made somewhat academic by the announcement, on November 1, that President Roosevelt, on his own motion, had committed the United States to "united action" with Russia, Great Britain, and China to be "continued [after the war] for the organization and maintenance of peace and security." These four Powers pledged themselves to "consult with one another and as occasion requires with other members of the United Nations with a view to joint action on behalf of the community of nations." They also bound themselves not to employ their military forces, after the war, within the territories of other states "except for purposes envisaged in this declaration and after joint consultation." As the declaration, agreed to in Moscow, was not given the form of a treaty, the President did not submit it to the Senate for ratification before proclaiming it.

After the Moscow declaration was made public the Senate modified and adopted by an overwhelming majority the Connally resolution. It incorporated in the original proposal a section from that declaration and added a proviso that any commitment to a world organization must be made in the form of a treaty duly approved by the Senate, two thirds of the Senators concurring.

Other efforts to draw the great Powers together were made at two conferences held late in November 1943. At the first, in Cairo, President Roosevelt, Premier Churchill, and Generalissimo Chiang Kai-shek confirmed their unity and agreed that Japan was to be stripped of all the territories won by aggression against her neighbors. At the second conference, at Teheran in Iran, President Roosevelt, Premier Churchill, and Premier Stalin pledged themselves to solidarity in war and expressed a determination that the United States, Great Britain, and Russia would work together in the peace to follow victory. They also referred generally to the co-operation of all nations dedicated to liberty but refrained from giving any details as to a world organization at the end of the war.

☆

Formulating verbal declarations as to what the United States might or should do in conducting foreign relations after the war was easy in comparison with answering fundamental questions looking to the future on the home front after the war. These involved the demobilization of the armed forces unless used for world policing or another war, dismantling the regimenting machinery of the war administration, the provision of employment for the millions to be released from war activities—indeed all the issues of civilization in the United States. And by the people and their representatives in Congress home-front problems received a consideration more extensive, more searching, and more anxious than ever before displayed in the history of the Republic, even during the Revolution and the Civil War. Everybody presumably knew that the war boom, like the New Deal spending before it, had not permanently solved the problem of depressions and poverty, and that no kind of peace settlement with other nations would materially relieve the high tensions in domestic affairs.

In connection with the war and foreign policy, it is true, many advocates of internationalism revived and brought to the center of discussion the theory that only by joining other nations in promoting foreign trade and lowering or abolishing trade barriers could the United States find outlets for the surpluses of goods and enjoy steady prosperity. But this theory was not universally accepted. Moreover there was little assurance that all or even most, if any, of the nations associated with the United States in the war were willing to co-operate in such an undertaking. Along the shadowy shorelines of the foreign trade dominion other Americans also rekindled the false lights of imperialism.

Judging by debates in Congress, composed of a new House elected by the voters in 1942 and a Senate one third of which was renewed at the same election, another view was the most widely held. According to this outlook, whatever happened after the war in the way of international arrangements, the domestic problems of the United States would be greater, not smaller; more difficult, not less difficult, at the close of the global conflict. Equally prominent in the debates of Congress and popular discussions was the voicing of another conviction: the main burden of coping with these problems will fall upon the American people; it will be inescapable; and in discharging this responsibility Americans will be compelled to resort mainly to actions on the home front. In any event it was generally realized in Congress that, whatever the outcome of the Global War, the old conflicts of interests over problems of social welfare would continue; and that the social and economic conditions of the country, even in the midst of the war spending boom, were such as to evoke anxiety for the future.

As if forcibly to remind the nation of these conditions, Arthur J. Altmeyer, chairman of the Social Security Board, statistically and summarily described them in an address on March 13, 1943—an address reprinted in the *Congressional Record* of March 17 at the request of Senator Robert F. Wagner, a loyal supporter of the New Deal and President Roosevelt's foreign policies. A single paragraph in Mr. Altmeyer's address was an index to problems that would confront the nation, no matter what world settlement was made at the peace table: "I need only remind you that at one time, not so long ago, there were 28,000,000 people who were dependent upon their Government for the necessities of life. Not so very long ago, there were 12,000,000 workers unemployed through no fault of their own. Even today there are over 5,000,000 people who are still dependent upon their Government to supply them with the necessities of life and there are still approximately 1,500,000 workers unemployed through no fault of their own. On this very day, we know that there are 7,000,000 people who are unable to work because of sickness or physical disability of some sort and that 3,500,000 of these are permanently totally disabled. We know that 45% of the persons examined under the Selective Training and Service Act have physical defects which caused their rejection for general military service and which must affect their earning capacity in private life. Whether or not we establish a social security system, as a civilized and progressive Nation, we shall still have these problems and their economic consequences to solve and we will undertake to solve them."

Confirmation of the view that through the coming years the domestic conflict would persist, indeed increase rather than diminish in intensity, came from other official sources. The release of news by men in President Roosevelt's official family to the effect that he would be nominated and elected for a fourth term in order to carry forward his work at home and abroad indicated that the making of the peace would not bring to a close the struggle on the home front.

In a speech at Detroit on July 25, Vice-President Henry A. Wallace attacked President Roosevelt's opponents, whom he classified as "isolationists," "reactionaries," and "American Fascists." Having called the tune in this language, Wallace, while expressing his belief in "our democratic capitalistic system," proceeded to outline a sweeping program for world peace, the enlightenment of all peoples, "full production and full employment," and the establishment of world prosperity which, if attempted, would put a greater strain on historic capitalism in America than any important representative of the New Deal had ever yet proposed. To this address Alfred M. Landon shortly afterward replied by presenting his version of Republican policies and asserting that Vice-President Wallace had declared a "civil war."

No colorful vision of a warless and forever joyful world, such as that with which President Wilson had inflamed the imaginations of the people in his time, obscured for a moment the clashes of opinion in the grand coalition of United Nations or the persistent diversities of the "one world." Something superexcellent, beyond the defeat of the Axis Powers, might, it was conceded, arise from the Global War; but the contours of that superexcellence were not so plainly obtrusive on any horizon as to resolve all doubt.

While in war production, in family sacrifices, in blood and treasure, Americans bowed their backs to duty and necessity, they were poignantly aware of the overhanging portents—of conflicts already converging on the home front, of approaching tasks on this continent greater than the Republic had yet endured in its long history. And in their minds shadowy plans for a world order and for enforcing the four freedoms throughout the world in the "century of the common man" sank in the scale of weight as compared with concerns crucial to life in America and to the survival of constitutional government.

How far in the scale? History would give an indisputable answer, sometime. But a poll of the people in the forty-eight states reported by the American Institute of Public Opinion on October 2, 1943, furnished clues to the answer. Citizens from Maine to California were asked by the poll takers what they thought would be the "greatest problem facing this country" from 1944–48. Fifty-eight per cent of them named "jobs or the economic readjustment of the country as the most vital long-range issue ahead for the next few years." And only thirteen per cent named as the most vital issue the "problem of drawing up a lasting peace."

☆

Could Americans really effect this readjustment—this wise and efficient ordering of their national life? Could full employment be provided for all the millions who had to have it for their very

livelihood? The New Deal had failed to solve the problem of unemployment between 1933 and 1939, that is, before the war boom
started; for there were still five or six million men and women
without steady employment in 1938. And there was nothing in
experience to indicate that the New Deal could solve the still
greater problem of unemployment looming on the horizon of the
coming peace. Nor did the fact that the most devastating panic in
the nation's history had occurred under Republican auspices indicate that a return to the days of freer, if not free, enterprise, still
yearned for in nostalgic circles, offered any better prospects, even
if it was feasible.

It was here that two theories alien to the democratic processes
of constitutional government entered into the discussion of destiny and opportunity ahead in the United States. One was communism in its new form of Russian despotic statism; the other,
fascism; both were in a large measure outcomes of the frustrations
and revolutions that followed the World War of 1914–18. Communism was supported in the United States by a political organization, the Communist party—which grew out of the labor unrest in
America following the Russian Revolution of 1917. Though its
membership was small, it was active in propaganda and tortuous in
operations, on the Moscow line, in and through labor unions and
old party machines, even to the point of considering its own
ostensible dissolution in 1944. Fascism was represented by no
openly organized party but believers in it carried on propaganda,
aboveground and underground, and had their key members in
places of influence.

Although true-blue defenders of communism and fascism differed in their professed objectives relative to human welfare, the
systems were alike in two essential respects: in the suppression
of civil liberties, representative government, and intellectual freedom; and in the regimentation of the people under a despotic
leader untrammeled by popular elections, legislative bodies, and
a free press. This was generally recognized in the United States.
But it was said for both creeds that, in times of great social disloca-
tions, depression, and unemployment, communist and fascist
dictators had established order, given work to the idle, and organized industrial production, if mainly for war purposes; and that
some such methods might be attempted or actually employed in
the United States in case the postwar depression was far more
calamitous than the breakdown of 1929–38.

That such a turn in American affairs would be disastrous to civil liberties and the democratic process of constitutional government was admitted by all citizens loyal to the American heritage. The very thought of it inspired leaders in business, industry, organized labor, and organized agriculture to great and concerted efforts in studying postwar problems and in planning measures for grappling with them by associational and co-operative undertakings, private and public, designed to maintain full production, furnish adequate employment, raise the standards of life throughout the nation, and sustain the American spirit.

Selected Documents from American History

1. THE ROYAL CHARTER FOR THE VIRGINIA CORPORATION (1606).

I. *JAMES*, by the Grace of God, King of *England, Scotland, France,* and *Ireland*, Defender of the Faith, &C . . . do . . . for Us, our Heirs, and Successors, GRANT and agree, that the said Sir *Thomas Gates*, Sir *George Somers, Richard Hackluit,* and *Edward-Maria Wingfield*, Adventurers of and for our City of *London*, and all such others, as are, or shall be, joined unto them of that Colony, shall be called the *first Colony*; And they shall and may begin their said first Plantation and Habitation, at any place upon the said Coast of *Virginia* or *America*, where they shall think fit and convenient, between the said four and thirty and one and forty Degrees of the said Latitude; And that they shall have all the Lands, Woods, Soil, Grounds, Havens, Ports, Rivers, Mines, Minerals, Marshes, Waters, Fishings, Commodities, and Hereditaments, whatsoever. . . . And shall and may inhabit and remain there; and shall and may also build and fortify within the same, for their better Safeguard and Defence. . . .

And we do also ordain . . . that each of the said Colonies shall have a Council, which shall govern and order all Matters and Causes, which shall arise, grow, or happen, to or within the same several Colonies, according to such Laws, Ordinances, and Instructions, as shall be, in that behalf, given and signed with Our Hand or Sign Manual, and pass under the Privy Seal of our Realm of *England*; Each of which Councils shall consist of thirteen Persons, to be ordained, made, and removed, from time to time, according as shall be directed and comprised in the same instructions; And shall have a several Seal, for all Matters that shall pass or concern the same several Councils. . . .

And that also there shall be a Council established here in *England*, which shall, in like Manner, consist of thirteen Persons, to be, for that Purpose, appointed by Us . . . , which shall be called our *Council of Virginia*; And shall, from time to time, have the superior Managing and Direction, only of and for all Matters, that shall or may concern the Government, as well as of the said several Colonies. . . .

And moreover, we do Grant . . . that the said several Councils, of and for the said several Colonies, shall and lawfully may . . . give and take Order, to dig, mine, and search for all Manner of Mines of Gold, Silver, and Copper, as well within any part of their said several Colonies, as for the said main Lands on the Backside of the same Colonies . . . the fifth Part only of all the same Gold and Silver, and the fifteenth part of all the same Copper, . . . without any other Manner of Profit or Account, to be given or yielded to Us. . . .

And that they shall, or lawfully may, establish and cause to be made a Coin, to pass current there between the People of those several Colonies, for the more Ease of Traffick and Bargaining between and amongst them and the Natives there. . . .

And we do likewise . . . give full Power and Authority to the said Sir *Thomas Gates* [and others] . . . and to the said several Companies, Plantations, and Colonies, that they . . . shall have, take, and lead . . . towards the said several Plantations and Colonies . . . such and so many of our Subjects, as shall willingly accompany them . . . ; with sufficient Shipping, and Furniture of Armour, Weapons, Ordinance, Powder, Victual, and all other things, necessary for the said Plantations. . . . PROVIDED always, that none of the said Persons be such, as shall hereafter be specially restrained by Us. . . .

ALSO we do . . . DECLARE . . . that all and every the Persons, being our Subjects, which shall dwell and inhabit within every or any of the said several Colonies and Plantations, and every of their children, which shall happen to be born within any . . . of the said several Colonies and Plantations, shall HAVE and enjoy all Liberties, Franchises, and Immunities, within any of our other Dominions, to all Intents and Purposes, as if they had been abiding and born, within this our Realm of *England*, or any other of our said Dominions. . . .

2. THE "MAYFLOWER" COMPACT PRESAGES SELF-GOVERNMENT IN AMERICA.

In the name of God, Amen. We whose names are underwriten, the loyall subjects of our dread soveraigne Lord, King James, by the grace of God, of Great Britaine, Franc, & Ireland king, defender of the faith, &c., haveing undertaken, for the glorie of God, and advancemente of the Christian faith, and honour of our king & countrie, a voyage to plant the first colonie in the Northerne parts of Virginia, doe by these presents solemnly & mutualy in the presence of God, and one of another, covenant & combine our selves togeather into a civill body politick, for our better ordering & preservation & furtherance of the ends aforesaid; and by vertue hearof to enacte, constitute, and frame such just & equall lawes, ordinances, acts, constitutions, & offices, from time to time, as shall be thought most meete & convenient for the generall good of the Colonie, unto which we promise all due submission and obedience. In witnes wherof we have hereunder subscribed our names at Cap-Codd the 11. of November, in the year of the raigne of our soveraigne lord, King James, of England, France, & Ireland the eighteenth, and of Scotland the fiftie fourth. Anno: Dom. 1620.

3. DECLARATION OF INDEPENDENCE.

In Congress, July 4, 1776,

THE UNANIMOUS DECLARATION OF THE THIRTEEN UNITED STATES OF AMERICA,

When in the Course of human events, it becomes necessary for one people to dissolve the political bands which have connected them with another, and to assume among the Powers of the earth, the separate and equal station to which the Laws of Nature and of Nature's God entitle them, a decent respect to the opinions of mankind requires that they should declare the causes which impel them to the separation.

We hold these truths to be self-evident, that all men are created equal, that they are endowed by their Creator with certain unalienable Rights, that among these are Life, Liberty and the pursuit of Happiness. That to secure these rights, Governments are instituted among Men, deriving their just powers from the consent of the governed, That whenever any Form of Government becomes destructive of these ends, it is the Right of the People to alter or to abolish it, and to institute new Government, laying its foundation on such principles and organizing its powers in such form, as to them shall seem most likely to effect their Safety and Happiness. Prudence, indeed, will dictate that Governments long established should not be changed for light and transient causes; and accordingly all experience hath shown, that mankind are more disposed to suffer, while evils are sufferable, than to right themselves by abolishing the forms to which they are accustomed. But when a long train of abuses and usurpations, pursuing invariably the same Object evinces a design to reduce them under absolute Despotism, it is their right, it is their duty, to throw off such Government, and to provide new Guards for their future security.—Such has been the patient sufferance of these Colonies; and such is now the necessity which constrains them to alter their former Systems of Government. The history of the present King of Great Britain is a history of repeated injuries and usurpations, all having in direct object the establishment of an absolute Tyranny over these States. To prove this, let Facts be submitted to a candid world.

He has refused his Assent to Laws, the most wholesome and necessary for the public good.

He has forbidden his Governors to pass Laws of immediate and pressing importance, unless suspended in their operation till his Assent should be obtained; and when so suspended, he has utterly neglected to attend to them.

He has refused to pass other Laws for the accommodation of large districts of people, unless those people would relinquish the right of Representation in the Legislature, a right inestimable to them and formidable to tyrants only.

He has called together legislative bodies at places unusual, uncomfortable, and distant from the depository of their Public Records, for the sole purpose of fatiguing them into compliance with his measures.

He has dissolved Representative Houses repeatedly, for opposing with manly firmness his invasions on the rights of the people.

He has refused for a long time, after such dissolutions, to cause others to be elected; whereby the Legislative Powers, incapable of Annihilation, have returned to the People at large for their exercise; the State remaining in the mean time exposed to all the dangers of invasion from without, and convulsions within.

He has endeavoured to prevent the population of these States; for that purpose obstructing the Laws for Naturalization of Foreigners; refusing to pass others to encourage their migration hither, and raising the conditions of new Appropriations of Lands.

He has obstructed the Administration of Justice, by refusing his Assent to Laws for establishing Judiciary Powers.

He has made Judges dependent on his Will alone, for the tenure of their offices, and the amount and payment of their salaries.

He has erected a multitude of New Offices, and sent hither swarms of Officers to harass our People, and eat out their substance.

He has kept among us, in times of peace, Standing Armies without the Consent of our legislature.

He has affected to render the Military independent of and superior to the Civil Power.

He has combined with others to subject us to a jurisdiction foreign to our constitution, and unacknowledged by our laws; giving his Assent to their acts of pretended legislation:

For quartering large bodies of armed troops among us:

For protecting them, by a mock Trial, from Punishment for any Murders which they should commit on the Inhabitants of these States:

For cutting off our Trade with all parts of the world:

For imposing taxes on us without our Consent:

For depriving us in many cases, of the benefits of Trial by Jury:

For transporting us beyond Seas to be tried for pretended offences:

For abolishing the free System of English Laws in a neighbouring Province, establishing therein an Arbitrary government, and enlarging its Boundaries so as to render it at once an example and fit instrument for introducing the same absolute rule into these Colonies:

For taking away our Charters, abolishing our most valuable Laws, and altering fundamentally the Forms of our Governments:

For suspending our own Legislature, and declaring themselves invested with Power to legislate for us in all cases whatsoever.

He has abdicated Government here, by declaring us out of his Protection and waging War against us.

He has plundered our seas, ravaged our Coasts, burnt our towns, and destroyed the lives of our people.

He is at this time transporting large armies of foreign mercenaries to compleat the works of death, desolation and tyranny, already begun with circumstances of Cruelty & perfidy scarcely paralleled in the most barbarous ages, and totally unworthy the Head of a civilized nation.

He has constrained our fellow Citizens taken Captive on the high Seas to bear Arms against their Country, to become the executioners of their friends and Brethren, or to fall themselves by their Hands.

He has excited domestic insurrections amongst us, and has endeavoured to bring on the inhabitants of our frontiers, the merciless Indian Savages, whose known rule of warfare, is an undistinguished destruction of all ages, sexes and conditions.

In every stage of these Oppressions We have Petitioned for Redress in the most humble terms: Our repeated Petitions have been answered only by repeated injury. A Prince, whose character is thus marked by every act which may define a Tyrant, is unfit to be the ruler of a free People.

Nor have We been wanting in attention to our British brethren. We have warned them from time to time of attempts by their legislature to extend an unwarrantable jurisdiction over us. We have reminded them of the circumstances of our emigration and settlement here. We have appealed to their native justice and magnanimity, and we have conjured them by the ties of our common kindred to disavow these usurpations, which, would inevitably interrupt our connections and correspondence. They too have been deaf to the voice of justice and of consanguinity. We must, therefore, acquiesce in the necessity, which denounces our Separation, and hold them, as we hold the rest of mankind, Enemies in War, in Peace Friends.

We, therefore, the Representatives of the united States of America, in General Congress, Assembled, appealing to the Supreme Judge of the world for the rectitude of our intentions, do, in the Name, and by Authority of the good People of these Colonies, solemnly publish and declare, That these United Colonies are, and of Right ought to be Free and Independent States; that they are Absolved from all Allegiance to the British Crown, and that all political connection between them and the State of Great Britain, is and ought to be totally dissolved; and that as Free and Independent States, they have full Power to levy War, conclude Peace, contract Alliances, establish Commerce, and to do all other Acts and Things which Independent States may of right do. And for the support of this Declaration, with a firm reliance on the Protection of Divine Providence, we mutually pledge to each other our Lives, our Fortunes and our sacred Honor.

SIGNERS OF THE DECLARATION OF INDEPENDENCE

Arranged by states, not in the order in which they appeared in the original copy of the document.

NEW HAMPSHIRE

Josiah Bartlett
Wm. Whipple
Matthew Thornton

MASSACHUSETTS

John Hancock
Saml. Adams
John Adams
Robt. Treat Paine
Elbridge Gerry

RHODE ISLAND

Step. Hopkins
William Ellery

CONNECTICUT

Roger Sherman
Sam'el Huntington
Wm. Williams
Oliver Wolcott

NEW YORK

Wm. Floyd
Phil. Livingston
Frans. Lewis
Lewis Morris

NEW JERSEY

Richd. Stockton
Jno. Witherspoon

Fras. Hopkinson
John Hart
Abra. Clark

PENNSYLVANIA

Robt. Morris
Benjamin Rush
Benja. Franklin
John Morton
Geo. Clymer
Jas. Smith
Geo. Taylor
James Wilson
Geo. Ross

DELAWARE

Cæsar Rodney
Geo. Read
Tho. M'Kean

MARYLAND

Samuel Chase
Wm. Paca
Thos. Stone
Charles Carroll of Carrollton

VIRGINIA

George Wythe
Richard Henry Lee
Th. Jefferson
Benja. Harrison
Thos. Nelson, jr.
Francis Lightfoot Lee
Carter Braxton

NORTH CAROLINA

Wm. Hooper
Joseph Hewes
John Penn

SOUTH CAROLINA

Edward Rutledge
Thos. Heyward, Junr.
Thomas Lynch, Junr.
Arthur Middleton

GEORGIA

Button Gwinnett
Lyman Hall
Geo. Walton

4. CONSTITUTION OF THE UNITED STATES

PREAMBLE

We, the People of the United States, in Order to form a more perfect Union, establish Justice, insure domestic Tranquility, provide for the common defence, promote the general Welfare, and secure the Blessings of Liberty to ourselves and our Posterity, do ordain and establish this Constitution for the United States of America.

ARTICLE I.

Section 1. All legislative Powers herein granted shall be vested in a Congress of the United States, which shall consist of a Senate and House of Representatives.

Section 2. The House of Representatives shall be composed of Members chosen every second Year by the People of the several States, and the Electors in each State shall have the Qualifications requisite for Electors of the most numerous Branch of the State Legislature.

No Person shall be a Representative who shall not have attained to the Age of twenty-five Years, and been seven Years a Citizen of the United States, and who shall not, when elected, be an Inhabitant of that State in which he shall be chosen.

Representatives and direct Taxes shall be apportioned among the several States which may be included within this Union, according to their respective Numbers, which shall be determined by adding to the whole Number of free Persons, including those bound to Service for a Term of Years, and excluding Indians not taxed, three-fifths of all other Persons. The actual Enumeration shall be made within three Years after the first Meeting of the Congress of the United States, and within every subsequent Term of ten Years, in such Manner as they shall by Law direct. The Number of Representatives shall not exceed one for every thirty Thousand, but each State shall have at Least one Representative; and until such enumeration shall be made, the State of New Hampshire shall be entitled to choose three, Massachusetts eight, Rhode-Island and Providence Plantations one, Connecticut five, New-York six, New Jersey four, Pennsylvania eight, Delaware one, Maryland six, Virginia ten, North Carolina five, South Carolina five, and Georgia three.

When vacancies happen in the Representation from any State, the Executive Authority thereof shall issue Writs of Election to fill such Vacancies.

The House of Representatives shall choose their Speaker and other Officers; and shall have the sole Power of Impeachment.

Section 3. The Senate of the United States shall be composed of two Senators from each State, chosen by the Legislature thereof, for six Years; and each Senator shall have one Vote.

Immediately after they shall be assembled in Consequence of the first Election, they shall be divided as equally as may be into three Classes. The Seats of the Senators of the first Class shall be vacated at the Expiration of the second Year, of the second Class at the Expiration of the fourth Year, and of the third Class at the Expiration of the sixth Year, so that one-third may be chosen every second Year; and if Vacancies happen by Resignation, or otherwise, during the Recess of the Legislature of any State, the Executive thereof may make temporary Appointment until the next Meeting of the Legislature, which shall then fill such Vacancies.

No Person shall be a Senator who shall not have attained to the Age of thirty Years, and been nine Years a Citizen of the United States, and who shall not, when elected, be an Inhabitant of that State for which he shall be chosen.

The Vice-President of the United States shall be President of the Senate, but shall have no Vote, unless they be equally divided.

The Senate shall choose their other Officers, and also a President pro tempore, in the Absence of the Vice-President, or when he shall exercise the Office of President of the United States.

The Senate shall have the sole Power to try all Impeachments. When sitting for that Purpose, they shall be on Oath or Affirmation. When the President of the United States is tried, the Chief Justice shall preside: And no Person shall be convicted without the Concurrence of two-thirds of the Members present.

Judgment of Cases of Impeachment shall not extend further than to removal from Office, and disqualification to hold and enjoy any Office of honor, Trust or Profit under the United States: but the Party convicted shall nevertheless be liable and subject to Indictment, Trial, Judgment and Punishment, according to Law.

Section 4. The Times, Places and Manner of holding Elections for Senators and Representatives, shall be prescribed in each State by the Legislature thereof; but the Congress may at any time by Law make or alter such Regulations, except as to the Places of choosing Senators.

The Congress shall assemble at least once in every Year, and such Meeting shall be on the first Monday in December, unless they shall by Law appoint a different Day.

Section 5. Each House shall be the Judge of the Elections, Returns and Qualifications of its own Members, and a Majority of each shall constitute a Quorum to do Business; but a smaller Number may adjourn from day to day, and may be authorized to compel the Attendance of absent Members, in such Manner, and under such Penalties as each House may provide.

Each House may determine the Rules of its Proceedings, punish its Members for disorderly Behaviour, and, with the Concurrence of two-thirds, expel a Member.

Each House shall keep a Journal of its Proceedings, and from time to time publish the same, excepting such Parts as may in their Judgment require Secrecy; and the Yeas and Nays of the Members of either House on any question shall, at the Desire of one-fifth of those Present, be entered on the Journal.

Neither House, during the Session of Congress, shall, without the Consent of the other, adjourn for more than three days, nor to any other Place than that in which the two Houses shall be sitting.

Section 6. The Senators and Representatives shall receive a Compensation for their Services, to be ascertained by Law, and paid out of the Treasury of the United States. They shall in all Cases, except Treason, Felony and Breach of the Peace, be privileged from Arrest during their Attendance at the Session of their respective Houses, and in going to and returning from the same; and for any Speech or Debate in either House, they shall not be questioned in any other Place.

No Senator or Representative shall, during the Time for which he was elected, be appointed to any civil Office under the Authority of the United States, which shall have been created, or the Emoluments whereof shall have been increased during such time; and no Person holding any Office under the United States, shall be a Member of either House during his Continuance in Office.

Section 7. All Bills for raising Revenue shall originate in the House of Representatives; but the Senate may propose or concur with Amendments as on other Bills.

Every Bill which shall have passed the House of Representatives and the Senate shall, before it becomes a Law, be presented to the President of the United States; If he approve, he shall sign it, but if not, he shall return it, with his Objections, to that House in which it shall have originated, who shall enter the Objections at large on their Journal, and proceed to reconsider it. If after such Reconsideration two-thirds of the House shall agree to pass the Bill, it shall be sent, together with the Objections, to the other House, by which it shall likewise be reconsidered, and if approved by two-thirds of that House, it shall become a Law. But in all such Cases the Votes of both Houses shall be determined by Yeas and Nays, and the Names of the Persons voting for and against the Bill shall be entered on the Journal of each House respectively. If any Bill shall not be returned by the President within ten Days (Sundays excepted) after it shall have been presented to him, the Same shall be a Law, in like Manner as if he had signed it, unless the Congress by their Adjournment prevent its Return, in which Case it shall not be a Law.

Every Order, Resolution, or Vote to which the Concurrence of the Senate and House of Representatives may be necessary (except on a question of Adjournment) shall be presented to the President of the United States; and before the Same shall take Effect, shall be approved by him, or being disapproved by him, shall be repassed by two-thirds of the Senate and House of Representatives, according to the Rules and Limitations prescribed in the Case of a Bill.

Section 8. The Congress shall have Power: To lay and collect Taxes, Duties, Imposts and Excises, to pay the Debts and provide for the common Defence and general Welfare of the United States; but all Duties, Imposts and Excises shall be uniform throughout the United States;

To borrow Money on the credit of the United States;

To regulate Commerce with foreign Nations, and among the several States, and with the Indian Tribes;

To establish an uniform Rule of Naturalization, and uniform Laws on the subject of Bankruptcies throughout the United States;

To coin Money, regulate the Value thereof, and of foreign Coin, and fix the Standard of Weights and Measures;

To provide for the Punishment of counterfeiting the Securities and current Coin of the United States;

To establish Post Offices and post Roads;

To promote the Progress of Science and useful Arts, by securing for limited Times to Authors and Inventors the exclusive Right to their respective Writings and Discoveries;

To constitute Tribunals inferior to the supreme Court;

To define and punish Piracies and Felonies committed on the high Seas, and Offences against the Law of Nations;

To declare War, grant Letters of Marque and Reprisal, and make Rules concerning captures on Land and Water;

To raise and support Armies, but no Appropriation of Money to that Use shall be for a longer Term than two Years;

To provide and maintain a Navy;

To make Rules for the Government and Regulation of the land and naval Forces;

To provide for calling forth the Militia to execute the Laws of the Union, suppress Insurrections and repel Invasions;

To provide for organizing, arming, and disciplining the Militia, and for governing such Part of them as may be employed in the Service of the United States, reserving to the States respectively, the Appointment of the Officers, and the Authority of training the Militia according to the discipline prescribed by Congress;

To exercise exclusive Legislation in all Cases whatsoever, over such District (not exceeding ten Miles square) as may, by Cession of particular States, and the Acceptance of Congress, become the Seat of Government of the United States, and to exercise like Authority over all Places purchased by the Consent of the Legislature of the State in which the Same shall be, for the Erection of Forts, Magazines, Arsenals, dock-Yards, and other needful Buildings;—And

To make all Laws which shall be necessary and proper for carrying into Execution the foregoing Powers, and all other Powers vested by this Constitution in the Government of the United States, or in any Department or Officer thereof.

Section 9. The Migration or Importation of such Persons as any of the States now existing shall think proper to admit, shall not be prohibited by the Congress prior to the Year one thousand eight hundred and eight, but a Tax or duty may be imposed on such Importation, not exceeding ten dollars for each Person.

The Privilege of the Writ of Habeas Corpus shall not be suspended, unless when in Cases of Rebellion or Invasion the public Safety may require it.

No Bill of Attainder or ex post facto Law shall be passed.

No Capitation, or other direct, Tax shall be laid, unless in Proportion to the Census or Enumeration herein before directed to be taken.

No Tax or Duty shall be laid on Articles exported from any State.

No Preference shall be given by any Regulation of Commerce or Revenue to the Ports of one State over those of another: nor shall Vessels bound to, or from, one State, be obliged to enter, clear, or pay Duties in another.

No Money shall be drawn from the Treasury, but in Consequence of Appropriations made by Law; and a regular Statement and Account of the Receipts and Expenditures of all public Money shall be published from time to time.

No Title of Nobility shall be granted by the United States; And no Person holding any Office of Profit or Trust under them, shall, without the Consent of the Congress, accept of any present, Emolument, Office, or Title, of any kind whatever, from any King, Prince, or foreign State.

Section 10. No State shall enter into any Treaty, Alliance, or Confederation; grant Letters of Marque and Reprisal; coin Money; emit Bills of Credit; make any Thing but gold and silver Coin a Tender in Payment of Debts; pass any Bill of Attainder, ex post facto Law, or Law impairing the Obligation of Contracts, or grant any Title of Nobility.

No State shall, without the Consent of the Congress, lay any Imposts or Duties on Imports or Exports, except what may be absolutely necessary for executing it's inspection Laws: and the net Produce of all Duties and Imposts, laid by any State on Imports or Exports, shall be for the Use of the Treasury of the United States; and all such Laws shall be subject to the Revision and Control of the Congress.

No State shall, without the Consent of Congress, lay any Duty of Tonnage, keep Troops, or Ships of War in time of Peace, enter into any Agreement or Compact with another State, or with a foreign Power, or engage in War, unless actually invaded, or in such imminent Danger as will not admit of delay.

ARTICLE II.

Section 1. The executive Power shall be vested in a President of the United States of America. He shall hold his Office during the Term of four Years, and, together with the Vice-President, chosen for the same Term, be elected, as follows:

Each State shall appoint, in such Manner as the Legislature thereof may direct, a Number of Electors, equal to the whole Number of Senators and Representatives to which the State may be entitled in the Congress: but no Senator or Representative, or Person holding an Office of Trust or Profit under the United States, shall be appointed an Elector.

The Electors shall meet in their respective States, and vote by Ballot for two Persons, of whom one at least shall not be an Inhabitant of the same State with themselves. And they shall make a List of all the Persons voted for, and of the Number of Votes for each; which List they shall sign and certify, and transmit sealed to the Seat of the Government of the United States, directed to the President of the Senate. The President of the Senate shall, in the Presence of the Senate and House of Representatives, open all the Certificates, and the Votes shall then be counted. The Person having the greatest Number of Votes shall be the President, if such Number be a Majority of the whole Number of Electors appointed; and if there be more than one who have such Majority, and have an equal Number of Votes, then the House of Representatives shall immediately choose by Ballot one of them for President; and if no Person have a majority, then from the five highest on the List the said House shall in like Manner choose the President. But in choosing the President, the Votes shall be taken by States, the Representation from each State having one Vote. A quorum for this Purpose shall consist of a Member or Members from two-thirds of the States, and a Majority of all the States shall be necessary to a Choice. In every Case, after the Choice of the President, the Person having the greatest Number of Votes of the Electors shall be the Vice-President. But if there should remain two or more who have equal Votes, the Senate shall choose from them by Ballot the Vice-President.

The Congress may determine the Time of choosing the Electors, and the Day on which they shall give their Votes; which Day shall be the same throughout the United States.

No Person except a natural born Citizen, or a Citizen of the United States, at the time of the Adoption of this Constitution, shall be eligible to the Office of President; neither shall any Person be eligible to that Office who shall not have attained to the Age of thirty-five Years, and been fourteen Years a Resident within the United States.

In Case of the Removal of the President from Office, or of his Death, Resignation, or Inability to discharge the Powers and Duties of the said Office, the Same shall devolve on the Vice-President, and the Congress may by Law provide for the Case of Removal, Death, Resignation or Inability, both of the President and Vice-President, declaring what Officer shall then act as President, and such Officer shall act accordingly, until the Disability be removed, or a President shall be elected.

The President shall, at stated Times, receive for his Services, a Compensation, which shall neither be increased nor diminished during the Period for which he shall have been elected, and he shall not receive within that Period any other Emolument from the United States, or any of them.

Before he enter on the Execution of his Office, he shall take the following Oath or Affirmation:—"I do solemnly swear (or affirm) that I will faithfully execute the office of President of the United States, and will, to the best of my Ability, preserve, protect and defend the Constitution of the United States."

Section 2. The President shall be Commander-in-Chief of the Army and Navy of the United States, and of the Militia of the several States, when called into the actual Service of the United States; he may require the Opinion, in writing, of the principal Officer in each of the executive Departments, upon any Subject relating to the Duties of their respective Offices, and he shall have Power to grant Reprieves and Pardons for all Offences against the United States, except in Cases of Impeachment.

He shall have Power, by and with the Advice and Consent of the Senate, to make Treaties, provided two-thirds of the Senators present concur; and he shall nominate, and by and with the Advice and Consent of the Senate, shall appoint Ambassadors, other public Ministers and Consuls, Judges of the Supreme Court, and all other Officers of the United States, whose Appointments are not herein otherwise provided for, and which shall be established by Law: but the Congress may by Law vest the Appointment of such inferior Officers, as they think proper, in the President alone, in the Courts of Law, or in the Heads of Departments.

The President shall have Power to fill up all Vacancies that may happen during the Recess of the Senate, by granting Commissions which shall expire at the End of their next Session.

Section 3. He shall from time to time give to the Congress Information of the State of the Union, and recommend to their Consideration such Measures as he shall judge necessary and expedient; he may, on extraordinary Occasions, convene both Houses, or either of them, and in Case of Disagreement between them, with Respect to the Time of Adjournment, he may adjourn them to such Time as he shall think proper; he shall receive Ambassadors and other public Ministers; he shall take Care that the Laws be faithfully executed, and shall Commission all the Officers of the United States.

Section 4. The President, Vice-President and all civil Officers of the United States, shall be removed from Office on Impeachment for, and Conviction of, Treason, Bribery, or other high Crimes and Misdemeanors.

Article III.

Section 1. The judicial Power of the United States shall be vested in one Supreme Court, and in such inferior Courts as the Congress may from time to time ordain and establish. The Judges, both of the Supreme and inferior Courts, shall hold their Offices during good Behaviour, and shall, at stated Times, receive for their Services, a Compensation, which shall not be diminished during their Continuance in Office.

Section 2. The judicial Power shall extend to all Cases, in Law and Equity, arising under this Constitution, the Laws of the United States, and Treaties made, or which shall be made, under their Authority;—to all Cases affecting Ambassadors, other public Ministers and Consuls;—to all Cases of admiralty and maritime Jurisdiction;—to Controversies to which the United States shall be a Party;—to Controversies between two or more States;—between a State and Citizens of another State;—between Citizens of different States;—between Citizens of the same State claiming Lands under Grants of different States, and between a State, or the Citizens thereof, and foreign States, Citizens or Subjects.

In all Cases affecting Ambassadors, other public Ministers and Consuls, and those in which a State shall be Party, the Supreme Court shall have original Jurisdiction. In all the other Cases before mentioned, the Supreme Court shall have appellate Jurisdiction, both as to Law and Fact, with such Exceptions, and under such Regulations as the Congress shall make.

The Trial of all Crimes, except in Cases of Impeachment, shall be by Jury; and such Trial shall be held in the State where the said Crimes shall have been committed; but when not committed within any State, the Trial shall be at such Place or Places as the Congress may by Law have directed.

Section 3. Treason against the United States, shall consist only in levying War against them, or in adhering to their Enemies, giving them Aid and Comfort. No Person shall be convicted of Treason unless on the Testimony of two Witnesses to the same overt Act, or on Confession in open Court.

The Congress shall have Power to declare the Punishment of Treason, but no Attainder of Treason shall work Corruption of Blood, or Forfeiture except during the Life of the Person attainted.

Article IV.

Section 1. Full Faith and Credit shall be given in each State to the public Acts, Records and judicial Proceedings of every other State. And the Congress may by general Laws prescribe the Manner in which such Acts, Records and Proceedings shall be proved, and the Effect thereof.

Section 2. The Citizens of each State shall be entitled to all Privileges and Immunities of Citizens in the several States.

A Person charged in any State with Treason, Felony, or other Crime, who shall flee from Justice, and be found in another State, shall on Demand of the executive Authority of the State from which he fled, be delivered up, to be removed to the State having Jurisdiction of the Crime.

No Person held to Service or Labour in one State, under the Laws thereof, escaping into another, shall, in Consequence of any Law or Regulation therein, be discharged from such Service or Labour, but shall be delivered up on Claim of the Party to whom such Service or Labour may be due.

Section 3. New States may be admitted by the Congress into this Union; but no new State shall be formed or erected within the Jurisdiction of any other State; nor any State be formed by the Junction of two or more States, or Parts of States, without the Consent of the Legislatures of the States concerned as well as of the Congress.

The Congress shall have Power to dispose of and make all needful Rules and Regulations respecting the Territory or other Property belonging to the United States; and nothing in this Constitution shall be so construed as to Prejudice any Claims of the United States, or of any particular State.

Section 4. The United States shall guarantee to every State in this Union a Republican Form of Government, and shall protect each of them against Invasion; and on Application of the Legislature, or of the Executive (when the Legislature cannot be convened) against domestic Violence.

Article V.

The Congress, whenever two-thirds of both Houses shall deem it necessary, shall propose Amendments to this Constitution, or, on the Application of the Legislatures of two-thirds of the several States, shall call a Convention for proposing Amendments, which, in either Case, shall be valid to all Intents and Purposes, as Part of this Constitution, when ratified by the Legislatures of three-fourths of the several States, or by Conventions in three-fourths thereof, as the one or the other Mode of Ratification may be proposed by the Congress; Provided that no Amendment which may be made prior to the Year One thousand eight hundred and eight shall in any Manner affect the first and fourth Clauses in the Ninth Section of the first Article; and that no State, without its Consent, shall be deprived of its equal Suffrage in the Senate.

ARTICLE VI.

All Debts contracted and Engagements entered into, before the Adoption of this Constitution, shall be as valid against the United States under this Constitution, as under the Confederation.

This Constitution, and the Laws of the United States which shall be made in Pursuance thereof and all Treaties made, or which shall be made, under the Authority of the United States, shall be the supreme Law of the Land; and the Judges in every State shall be bound thereby, any Thing in the Constitution or Laws of any State to the Contrary notwithstanding.

The Senators and Representatives before mentioned, and the Members of the several State Legislatures, and all executive and judicial Officers, both of the United States and of the several States, shall be bound by Oath or Affirmation, to support this Constitution; but no religious Test shall ever be required as a Qualification to any Office or public Trust under the United States.

ARTICLE VII.

The Ratification of the Conventions of nine States, shall be sufficient for the Establishment of this Constitution between the States so ratifying the Same.

Done in Convention by the Unanimous Consent of the States present the Seventeenth Day of September in the Year of our Lord one thousand seven hundred and Eighty-seven, and of the Independence of the United States of America the Twelfth. In witness whereof We have hereunto subscribed our Names, Attest

William Jackson
    Secretary

                Go: Washington—
                Presidt. and deputy from Virginia

NEW HAMPSHIRE

John Langdon
Nicholas Gilman

MASSACHUSETTS

Nathaniel Gorham
Rufus King

CONNECTICUT

Wm. Saml. Johnson
Roger Sherman

NEW YORK

Alexander Hamilton

NEW JERSEY

Wil: Livingston
David Brearley

Wm. Paterson
Jona: Dayton

PENNSYLVANIA

B. Franklin
Thomas Mifflin
Robt. Morris
Geo. Clymer
Thos. Fitzsimons
Jared Ingersoll
James Wilson
Gouv Morris

DELAWARE

Geo: Read
Gunning Bedford Jun
John Dickinson
Richard Bassett
Jaco: Broom

MARYLAND	Richd. Dobbs Spaight

MARYLAND

James McHenry
Dan of St. Thos Jenifer
Danl. Carroll

VIRGINIA

John Blair—
James Madison Jr.

NORTH CAROLINA

Wm. Blount

Richd. Dobbs Spaight
Hu Williamson

SOUTH CAROLINA

J. Rutledge
Charles Cotesworth Pinckney
Charles Pinckney
Pierce Butler

GEORGIA

William Few
Abr Baldwin

AMENDMENTS.

ARTICLES in addition to and Amendment of the Constitution of the United States of America.

ARTICLE I.

Congress shall make no law respecting an establishment of religion, or prohibiting the free exercise thereof; or abridging the freedom of speech, or of the press; or the right of the people peaceably to assemble, and to petition the Government for a redress of grievances.

ARTICLE II.

A well-regulated Militia, being necessary to the security of a free State, the right of the people to keep and bear Arms, shall not be infringed.

ARTICLE III.

No Soldier shall, in time of peace be quartered in any house, without the consent of the Owner, nor in time of war, but in a manner to be prescribed by law.

ARTICLE IV.

The right of the people to be secure in their persons, houses, papers, and effects, against unreasonable searches and seizures, shall not be violated, and no Warrants shall issue, but upon probable cause, supported by Oath or affirmation, and particularly describing the place to be searched, and the persons or things to be seized.

ARTICLE V.

No person shall be held to answer for a capital, or other infamous crime, unless on a presentment or indictment of a Grand Jury, except in cases arising in the land or naval forces, or in the Militia, when in actual service in time of War or public danger; nor shall any person be subject for the same offence to be twice put in jeopardy of life or limb; nor shall be compelled in any criminal case to be a witness against himself, nor be deprived of life, liberty, or property, without due process of law; nor shall private property be taken for public use, without just compensation.

Article VI.

In all criminal prosecutions, the accused shall enjoy the right to a speedy and public trial, by an impartial jury of the State and district wherein the crime shall have been committed, which district shall have been previously ascertained by law, and to be informed of the nature and cause of the accusation; to be confronted with the witnesses against him; to have compulsory process for obtaining witnesses in his favor, and to have the Assistance of Counsel for his defence.

Article VII.

In Suits at common law, where the value in controversy shall exceed twenty dollars, the right of trial by jury shall be preserved, and no fact tried by a jury, shall be otherwise re-examined in any Court of the United States, than according to the rules of the common law.

Article VIII.

Excessive bail shall not be required, nor excessive fines imposed, nor cruel and unusual punishments inflicted.

Article IX.

The enumeration in the Constitution, of certain rights, shall not be construed to deny or disparage others retained by the people.

Article X.

The powers not delegated to the United States by the Constitution, nor prohibited by it to the States, are reserved to the States respectively, or to the people. [First ten Amendments adopted in 1791]

Article XI.

The Judicial power of the United States shall not be construed to extend to any suit in law or equity, commenced or prosecuted against one of the United States by Citizens of another State, or by Citizens or Subjects of any Foreign State. [1798]

Article XII.

The Electors shall meet in their respective states, and vote by ballot for President and Vice-President, one of whom, at least, shall not be an inhabitant of the same state with themselves; they shall name in their ballots the person voted for as President, and in distinct ballots the person voted for as Vice-President, and they shall make distinct lists of all persons voted for as President, and of all persons voted for as Vice-President, and of the number of votes for each, which lists they shall sign and certify, and transmit sealed to the seat of the government of the United States, directed to the President of the Senate;—The President of the Senate shall, in the presence of the Senate and House of Representatives, open all the certificates and the votes shall then be counted;—The person having the greatest number of votes for President, shall be the President, if such number be a majority of the whole number of Electors appointed; and if no person have such majority, then from the persons having the highest numbers not exceeding three on the list of those voted for as President, the House of Representatives shall choose immediately, by ballot, the President. But in choosing the President, the votes shall be taken by states, the representation from each state having one vote; a quorum for this purpose shall consist of a member or members from two-thirds of the states, and a majority of all the states shall be necessary to a choice. And if the House of Representatives shall not choose a President whenever the right of choice shall devolve upon them, before the fourth day of March next following, then the Vice-President shall act as President, as in the case of the death or other constitutional disability of the President. —The person having the greatest number of votes as Vice-President, shall be the Vice-President, if such number be a majority of the whole number of Electors appointed, and if no person have a majority, then from the two highest numbers on the list, the Senate shall choose the Vice-President; a quorum for the purpose shall consist of two-thirds of the whole number of Senators, and a majority of the whole number shall be necessary to a choice. But no person constitutionally ineligible to the office of President shall be eligible to that of Vice-President of the United States. [1804]

Article XIII.

Section 1. Neither slavery nor involuntary servitude, except as a punishment for crime whereof the party shall have been duly convicted, shall exist within the United States, or any place subject to their jurisdiction.

Section 2. Congress shall have power to enforce this article by appropriate legislation. [1865]

Article XIV.

Section 1. All persons born or naturalized in the United States, and subject to the jurisdiction thereof, are citizens of the United States and of the State wherein they reside. No State shall make or enforce any law which shall abridge the privileges or immunities of citizens of the United States; nor shall any State deprive any person of life, liberty, or property, without due process of law; nor deny to any person within its jurisdiction the equal protection of the laws.

Section 2. Representatives shall be apportioned among the several States according to their respective numbers, counting the whole number of persons in each State, excluding Indians not taxed. But when the right to vote at any election for the choice of electors for President and Vice-President of the United States, Representatives in Congress, the Executive and Judicial officers of a State, or the members of the Legislature thereof, is denied to any of the male members of such State, being twenty-one years of age, and citizens of the United States, or in any way abridged, except for participation in rebellion, or other crime, the basis of representation therein shall be reduced in the proportion which the number of such male citizens shall bear to the whole number of male citizens twenty-one years of age in such State.

Section 3. No person shall be a Senator or Representative in Congress, or elector of President and Vice-President, or hold any office, civil or military, under the United States, or under any State, who, having previously taken an oath, as a member of Congress, or as an officer of the United States, or as a member of any State legislature, or as an executive or judicial officer of any State, to support the Constitution of the United States, shall have engaged in insurrection or rebellion against the same, or given aid and comfort to the enemies thereof. But Congress may by a vote of two-thirds of each House, remove such disability.

Section 4. The validity of the public debt of the United States, authorized by law, including debts incurred for payment of pensions and bounties for services in suppressing insurrection and rebellion, shall not be questioned. But neither the United States nor any State shall assume or pay any debt or obligation incurred in aid of insurrection or rebellion against the United States, or any claim for the loss or emancipation of any slave; but all such debts, obligations and claims shall be held illegal and void.

Section 5. The Congress shall have power to enforce, by appropriate legislation, the provisions of this article. [1868]

ARTICLE XV.

Section 1. The right of the citizens of the United States to vote shall not be denied or abridged by the United States or by any State on account of race, color, or previous condition of servitude.

Section 2. The Congress shall have power to enforce the provisions of this article by appropriate legislation. [1870]

ARTICLE XVI.

The Congress shall have power to lay and collect taxes on incomes, from whatever sources derived, without apportionment among the several States, and without regard to any census or enumeration. [1913]

ARTICLE XVII.

The Senate of the United States shall be composed of two Senators from each State, elected by the people thereof, for six years; and each Senator shall have one vote. The electors in each State shall have the qualifications requisite for electors of the most numerous branch of the State legislature.

When vacancies happen in the representation of any State in the Senate, the executive authority of such State shall issue writs of election to fill such vacancies: *Provided,* That the legislature of any State may empower the executive thereof to make temporary appointment until the people fill the vacancies by election as the legislature may direct.

This amendment shall not be so construed as to affect the election or term of any Senator chosen before it becomes valid as part of the Constitution. [1913]

ARTICLE XVIII.

Section 1. After one year from the ratification of this article the manufacture, sale, or transportation of intoxicating liquors within, the importation thereof into, or the exportation thereof from the United States and all territory subject to the jurisdiction thereof for beverage purposes is hereby prohibited.

Section 2. The Congress and the several States shall have concurrent power to enforce this article by appropriate legislation.

Section 3. This article shall be inoperative unless it shall have been ratified as an amendment to the Constitution by the legislatures of the several States, as provided in the Constitution, within seven years from the date of the submission hereof to the States by the Congress. [1919]

Article XIX.

The right of citizens of the United States to vote shall not be denied or abridged by the United States or by any State on account of sex.

Congress shall have power to enforce this article by appropriate legislation. [1920]

Article XX.

Section 1. The terms of the President and Vice-President shall end at noon on the 20th day of January, and the terms of Senators and Representatives at noon on the 3d day of January, of the years in which such terms would have ended if this article had not been ratified; and the terms of their successors shall then begin.

Section 2. The Congress shall assemble at least once in every year, and such meeting shall begin at noon on the 3d day of January, unless they shall by law appoint a different day.

Section 3. If, at the time fixed for the beginning of the term of the President, the President elect shall have died, the Vice-President elect shall become President. If a President shall not have been chosen before the time fixed for the beginning of his term, or if the President elect shall have failed to qualify, then the Vice-President elect shall act as President until a President shall have qualified; and the Congress may by law provide for the case wherein neither a President elect nor a Vice-President elect shall have qualified, declaring who shall then act as President, or the manner in which one who is to act shall be selected, and such person shall act accordingly until a President or Vice-President shall have qualified.

Section 4. The Congress may by law provide for the case of the death of any of the persons from whom the House of Representatives may choose a President whenever the right of choice shall have devolved upon them, and for the case of the death of any of the persons from whom the Senate may choose a Vice-President whenever the right of choice shall have devolved upon them.

Section 5. Sections 1 and 2 shall take effect on the 15th day of October following the ratification of this article.

Section 6. This article shall be inoperative unless it shall have been ratified as an amendment to the Constitution by the legislatures of three-fourths of the several States within seven years from the date of its submission. [1933]

Article XXI.

Section 1. The eighteenth article of amendment to the Constitution of the United States is hereby repealed.

Section 2. The transportation or importation into any State, Territory, or Possession of the United States for delivery or use therein of intoxicating liquors, in violation of the laws thereof, is hereby prohibited.

Section 3. This article shall be inoperative unless it shall have been ratified as an amendment to the Constitution by conventions in the several States, as provided in the Constitution, within seven years from the date of the submission hereof to the States by the Congress. [1933]

5. PRESIDENT GEORGE WASHINGTON, IN HIS FAREWELL ADDRESS, WARNS THE PEOPLE AGAINST DOMESTIC AND FOREIGN CONFLICTS (September 17, 1796).

Friends and fellow citizens: The period for a new election of a citizen to administer the executive Government of the United States being not far distant, and the time actually arrived when your thoughts must be employed in designating the person who is to be clothed with that important trust, it appears to me proper, especially as it may conduce to a more distinct expression of the public voice, that I should now apprize you of the resolution I have formed to decline being considered among the number of those out of whom a choice is to be made. . . .

Here, perhaps, I ought to stop. But a solicitude for your welfare which cannot end but with my life, and the apprehension of danger natural to that solicitude, urge me on an occasion like the present to offer to your solemn contemplation and to recommend to your frequent review some sentiments which are the result of much reflection, of no inconsiderable observation, and which appear to me all-important to the permanency of your felicity as a people. . . .

The unity of government which constitutes you one people is also now dear to you. . . . This Government, the offspring of our own choice, uninfluenced and unawed, adopted upon full investigation and mature deliberation, completely free in its principles, in the distribution of its powers, uniting security with energy, and containing within itself a provision for its own amendment, has a just claim to your confidence and your support. Respect for its authority, compliance with its laws, acquiescence in its measures, are duties enjoined by the fundamental maxims of true liberty. The basis of our political systems is the right of the people to make and to alter their constitutions of government. But the constitution which at any time exists till changed by an explicit and authentic act of the whole people is sacredly obligatory upon all. The very idea of the power and the right of the people to establish government presupposes the duty of every individual to obey the established government. . . .

It is important, likewise, that the habits of thinking in a free country should inspire caution in those intrusted with its administration to confine themselves within their respective constitutional spheres, avoiding in the exercise of the powers of one department to encroach upon another. The spirit of encroachment tends to consolidate the powers of all the departments in one, and thus to create, whatever the form of government, a real despotism. . . .

It is substantially true that virtue or morality is a necessary spring of popular government. The rule indeed extends with more or less force to every species of free government. Who that is a sincere friend to it can look with indifference upon attempts to shake the foundation of the fabric? Promote, then, as an object of primary importance, institutions for the general diffusion of knowledge. In proportion as the structure of a government gives force to public opinion, it is essential that public opinion should be enlightened. . . .

Observe good faith and justice toward all nations. Cultivate peace and harmony with all. . . .

The great rule of conduct for us in regard to foreign nations is, in extending our commercial relations, to have with them as little *political* connection
as possible. So far as we have already formed engagements let them be
fulfilled with perfect good faith. Here let us stop.

Europe has a set of primary interests which to us have none or a very
remote relation. Hence she must be engaged in frequent controversies, the
causes of which are essentially foreign to our concerns. Hence, therefore, it
must be unwise in us to implicate ourselves by artificial ties in the ordinary
vicissitudes of her politics or the ordinary combinations and collisions of
her friendships or enmities.

Our detached and distant situation invites and enables us to pursue a
different course. If we remain one people, under an efficient government, the
period is not far off when we may defy material injury from external annoy-
ance; when we may take such an attitude as will cause the neutrality we may
at any time resolve upon to be scrupulously respected; when belligerent
nations, under the impossibility of making acquisitions upon us, will not
lightly hazard the giving us provocation; when we may choose peace or
war, as our interest, guided by justice, shall counsel.

Why forego the advantages of so peculiar a situation? Why quit our
own to stand upon foreign ground? Why, by interweaving our destiny with
that of any part of Europe, entangle our peace and prosperity in the toils
of European ambition, rivalship, interest, humor, or caprice?

6. PRESIDENT THOMAS JEFFERSON PLEADS FOR REPUBLICAN UNITY IN HIS FIRST INAUGURAL ADDRESS (1801).

Called upon to undertake the duties of the first executive office of our
country, I avail myself of the presence of that portion of my fellow citizens
which is here assembled to express my grateful thanks for the favor with
which they have been pleased to look toward me, to declare a sincere
consciousness that the task is above my talents, and that I approach it with
those anxious and awful presentiments which the greatness of the charge
and the weakness of my powers so justly inspire. A rising nation, spread
over a wide and fruitful land, traversing all the seas with the rich produc-
tions of their industry, engaged in commerce with nations who feel power
and forget right, advancing rapidly to destinies beyond the reach of mortal
eye—when I contemplate these transcendent objects, and see the honor, the
happiness, and the hopes of this beloved country committed to the issue
and the auspices of this day, I shrink from the contemplation, and humble
myself before the magnitude of the undertaking. . . .

During the contest of opinion through which we have passed the anima-
tion of discussions and of exertions has sometimes worn an aspect which
might impose on strangers unused to think freely and to speak and to write
what they think; but this being now decided by the voice of the nation,
announced according to the rules of the Constitution, all will, of course,
arrange themselves under the will of the law, and unite in common efforts
for the common good. All, too, will bear in mind the sacred principle, that
though the will of the majority is in all cases to prevail, that will to be rightful must be reasonable; that the minority possess their equal rights, which
equal law must protect, and to violate would be oppression. Let us, then,

fellow citizens, unite with one heart and one mind. Let us restore to social intercourse that harmony and affection without which liberty and even life itself are but dreary things. And let us reflect that, having banished from our land that religious intolerance under which mankind so long bled and suffered, we have yet gained little if we countenance a political intolerance as despotic, as wicked, and capable of as bitter and bloody persecutions. During the throes and convulsions of the ancient world, during the agonizing spasms of infuriated man, seeking through blood and slaughter his long-lost liberty, it was not wonderful that the agitation of the billows should reach even this distant and peaceful shore; that this should be more felt and feared by some and less by others, and should divide opinions as to measures of safety. But every difference of opinion is not a difference of principle. We have called by different names brethren of the same principle. We are all Republicans, we are all Federalists. If there be any among us who would wish to dissolve this Union or to change its republican form, let them stand undisturbed as monuments of the safety with which error of opinion may be tolerated where reason is left free to combat it. I know, indeed, that some honest men fear that a republican government cannot be strong, that this Government is not strong enough; but would the honest patriot, in the full tide of successful experiment, abandon a government which has so far kept us free and firm on the theoretic and visionary fear that this Government, the world's best hope, may by possibility want energy to preserve itself? I trust not. I believe this, on the contrary, the strongest Government on earth. I believe it the only one where every man, at the call of the law, would fly to the standard of the law, and would meet invasions of the public order as his own personal concern. Sometimes it is said that man cannot be trusted with the government of himself. Can he, then, be trusted with the government of others? Or have we found angels in the forms of kings to govern him? Let history answer this question.

Let us, then, with courage and confidence pursue our own Federal and Republican principles, our attachment to union and representative government. Kindly separated by nature and a wide ocean from the exterminating havoc of one quarter of the globe; too high-minded to endure the degradations of the others; possessing a chosen country, with room enough for our descendants to the thousandth and thousandth generation; entertaining a due sense of our equal right to the use of our own faculties, to the acquisitions of our own industry, to honor and confidence from our fellow citizens, resulting not from birth, but from our actions and their sense of them; enlightened by a benign religion, professed, indeed, and practised in various forms, yet all of them inculcating honesty, truth, temperance, gratitude, and the love of man; acknowledging and adoring an overruling Providence, which by all its dispensations proves that it delights in the happiness of man here and his greater happiness hereafter—with all these blessings, what more is necessary to make us a happy and a prosperous people? Still one thing more, fellow citizens—a wise and frugal Government, which shall restrain men from injuring one another, shall leave them otherwise free to regulate their own pursuits of industry and improvement, and shall not take from the mouth of labor the bread it has earned. This is the sum of good government, and this is necessary to close the circle of our felicities. . . .

7. PRESIDENT JAMES MONROE PRESENTS TO CONGRESS HIS DOCTRINE FOR THE WESTERN HEMISPHERE (1823).

... In the discussions to which this interest [claim of Russia on the northwest coast] has given rise, and in the arrangements by which they may terminate, the occasion has been judged proper for asserting, as a principle in which the rights and interests of the United States are involved, that the American continents, by the free and independent condition which they have assumed and maintain, are henceforth not to be considered as subjects for future colonization by any European powers. ...

It was stated at the commencement of the last session, that a great effort was then making in Spain and Portugal, to improve the condition of the people of those countries, and that it appeared to be conducted with extraordinary moderation. It need scarcely be remarked, that the result has been, so far, very different from what was then anticipated. Of events in that quarter of the globe, with which we have so much intercourse, and from which we derive our origin, we have always been anxious and interested spectators. The citizens of the United States cherish sentiments the most friendly, in favor of the liberty and happiness of their fellow men on that side of the Atlantic. In the wars of the European powers, in matters relating to themselves, we have never taken any part, nor does it comport with our policy so to do. It is only when our rights are invaded, or seriously menaced, that we resent injuries, or make preparation for our defence. With the movements in this hemisphere, we are, of necessity, more immediately connected, and by causes which must be obvious to all enlightened and impartial observers. The political system of the allied powers is essentially different, in this respect, from that of America. This difference proceeds from that which exists in their respective governments. And to the defence of our own, which has been achieved by the loss of so much blood and treasure, and matured by the wisdom of their most enlightened citizens, and under which we have enjoyed unexampled felicity, this whole nation is devoted. We owe it, therefore, to candor, and to the amicable relations existing between the United States and those powers, to declare, that we should consider any attempt on their part to extend their system to any portion of this hemisphere, as dangerous to our peace and safety. With the existing colonies or dependencies of any European power, we have not interfered, and shall not interfere. But with the governments who have declared their independence, and maintained it, and whose independence we have, on great consideration, and on just principles, acknowledged, we could not view any interposition for the purpose of oppressing them, or controlling, in any other manner, their destiny, by any European power, in any other light than as the manifestation of an unfriendly disposition towards the United States. In the war between those governments and Spain, we declared our neutrality at the time of their recognition, and to this we have adhered, and shall continue to adhere, provided no change shall occur, which, in the judgment of the competent authorities of this government, shall make a corresponding change, on the part of the United States, indispensable to their security.

The late events in Spain and Portugal, shew that Europe is still unsettled. Of this important fact, no stronger proof can be adduced than that the allied powers should have thought it proper, on any principle satisfactory to themselves, to have interposed, by force, in the internal concerns of Spain. To what extent such interposition may be carried, on the same principle, is a question, in which all independent powers, whose governments differ from theirs, are interested; even those most remote, and surely none more so than the United States. Our policy, in regard to Europe, which was adopted at an early stage of the wars which have so long agitated that quarter of the globe, nevertheless remains the same, which is, not to interfere in the internal concerns of any of its powers; to consider the government *de facto* as the legitimate government for us; to cultivate friendly relations with it, and to preserve those relations by a frank, firm, and manly policy; meeting, in all instances, the just claims of every power; submitting to injuries from none. But, in regard to those continents, circumstances are eminently and conspicuously different. It is impossible that the allied powers should extend their political system to any portion of either continent, without endangering our peace and happiness; nor can any one believe that our southern brethren, if left to themselves, would adopt it of their own accord. It is equally impossible, therefore, that we should behold such interposition, in any form, with indifference. If we look to the comparative strength and resources of Spain and those new governments, and their distance from each other, it must be obvious that she can never subdue them. It is still the true policy of the United States to leave the parties to themselves, in the hope that other powers will pursue the same course.

8. PRESIDENT ANDREW JACKSON ATTACKS BANKING MONOPOLY IN A MESSAGE TO THE SENATE (1832).

To the Senate:

. . . A bank of the United States is in many respects convenient for the Government and useful to the people. Entertaining this opinion, and deeply impressed with the belief that some of the powers and privileges possessed by the existing bank are unauthorized by the Constitution, subversive of the rights of the States, and dangerous to the liberties of the people, I felt it my duty at an early period of my Administration to call the attention of Congress to the practicability of organizing an institution combining all its advantages and obviating these objections. I sincerely regret that in the act before me I can perceive none of those modifications of the bank charter which are necessary, in my opinion, to make it compatible with justice, with sound policy, or with the Constitution of our country.

The present corporate body, denominated the president, directors, and company of the Bank of the United States, will have existed at the time this act is intended to take effect twenty years. It enjoys an exclusive privilege of banking under the authority of the General Government, and a monopoly of its favor and support, and, as a necessary consequence, almost a monopoly of the foreign and domestic exchange. The powers, privileges, and favors bestowed upon it in the original charter, by increasing the value of the stock far above its par value, operated as a gratuity of many millions to the stockholders.

An apology may be found for the failure to guard against this result in the consideration that the effect of the original act of incorporation could not be certainly foreseen at the time of its passage. The act before me proposes another gratuity to the holders of the same stock, and in many cases to the same men, of at least seven millions more. This donation finds no apology in any uncertainty as to the effect of the act. On all hands it is conceded that its passage will increase at least 20 or 30 per cent more the market price of the stock, subject to the payment of the annuity of $200,000 per year secured by the act, thus adding in a moment one-fourth to its par value. It is not our own citizens only who are to receive the bounty of our Government. More than eight millions of the stock of this bank are held by foreigners. By this act the American Republic proposes virtually to make them a present of some millions of dollars. For these gratuities to foreigners, and to some of our own opulent citizens the act secures no equivalent whatever. They are the certain gains of the present stockholders under the operation of this act, after making full allowance for the payment of the bonus.

Every monopoly and all exclusive privileges are granted at the expense of the public, which ought to receive a fair equivalent. The many millions which this act proposes to bestow on the stockholders of the existing bank must come directly or indirectly out of the earnings of the American people. It is due to them, therefore, if their Government sell monopolies and exclusive privileges, that they should at least exact for them as much as they are worth in open market. The value of the monopoly in this case may be correctly ascertained. The twenty-eight millions of stock would probably be at an advance of 50 per cent, and command in market at least $42,000,-000, subject to the payment of the present bonus. The present value of the monopoly, therefore, is $17,000,000, and this the act proposes to sell for three millions, payable in fifteen annual installments of $200,000 each.

9. DOROTHEA DIX SPEAKS TO THE MASSACHUSETTS LEGISLATURE IN BEHALF OF THE HELPLESS (1843).

Gentlemen: I come to present the strong claims of suffering humanity. I come to place before the Legislature of Massachusetts the condition of the miserable, the desolate, the outcast. I come as the advocate of helpless, forgotten, insane, and idiotic men and women; of beings sunk to a condition from which the most unconcerned would start with real horror; of beings wretched in our prisons, and more wretched in our almshouses.

I must confine myself to a few examples, but am ready to furnish other and more complete details, if required.

I proceed, gentlemen, briefly to call your attention to the *present* state of insane persons confined within this Commonwealth, in *cages, closets, cellars, stalls, pens! Chained, naked, beaten with rods,* and *lashed* into obedience.

I offer the following extracts from my notebook and journal.

Springfield: In the jail, one lunatic woman, furiously mad, a state pauper, improperly situated, both in regard to the prisoners, the keepers, and herself.

It is a case of extreme self-forgetfulness and oblivion to all the decencies of life, to describe which would be to repeat only the grossest scenes. In the almshouse of the same town is a woman apparently only needing judicious care and some well-chosen employment to make it unnecessary to confine her in solitude in a dreary unfurnished room. Her appeals for employment and companionship are most touching, but the mistress replied "she had no time to attend to her."

Lincoln: A woman in a cage. *Medford:* One idiotic subject chained, and one in a close stall for seventeen years. *Pepperell:* One often doubly chained, hand and foot; another violent; several peaceable now. *Brookfield:* One man caged, comfortable. *Granville:* One often closely confined, now losing the use of his limbs from want of exercise. *Charlemont:* One man caged. *Savoy:* One man caged. *Lenox:* Two in the jail, against whose unfit condition there the jailer protests.

Dedham: The insane disadvantageously placed in the jail. In the almshouse, two females in stalls, situated in the main building, lie in wooden bunks filled with straw; always shut up. One of these subjects is supposed curable. The overseers of the poor have declined giving her a trial at the hospital, as I was informed, on account of expense.

Besides the above, I have seen many who, part of the year, are chained or caged. The use of cages is all but universal. Hardly a town but can refer to some not distant period of using them; chains are less common; negligences frequent; wilful abuse less frequent than sufferings proceeding from ignorance, or want of consideration. I encountered during the last three months many poor creatures wandering reckless and unprotected through the country. . . . But I cannot particularize. In traversing the state, I have found hundreds of insane persons in every variety of circumstance and condition, many whose situation could not and need not be improved; a less number, but that very large, whose lives are the saddest pictures of human suffering and degradation description fades before reality.

Men of Massachusetts, I beg, I implore, I demand pity and protection for these of my suffering, outraged sex. Become the benefactors of your race, the just guardians of the solemn rights you hold in trust. Raise up the fallen, succor the desolate, restore the outcast, defend the helpless, and for your eternal and great reward receive the benediction, "Well done, good and faithful servants, become rulers over many things!"

Injustice is also done to the *convicts*: it is certainly very wrong that they should be doomed day after day and night after night to listen to the ravings of madmen and madwomen. This is a kind of punishment that is not recognized by our statutes, and is what the criminal ought not to be called upon to undergo. The confinement of the criminal and of the insane in the same building is subversive of that good order and discipline which should be observed in every well-regulated prison. I do most sincerely hope that more permanent provision will be made for the pauper insane by the state, either to restore Worcester Insane Asylum to what it was originally designed to be or else to make some just appropriation for the benefit of this very unfortunate class of our fellow beings.

Gentlemen, I commit to you this sacred cause. Your action upon this subject will affect the present and future condition of hundreds and of thousands. In this legislation, as in all things, may you exercise that "wisdom which is the breath of the power of God."

10. THE WOMEN'S DECLARATION OF SENTIMENTS AT SENECA FALLS (1848).

When, in the course of human events, it becomes necessary for one portion of the family of man to assume among the people of the earth a position different from that which they have hitherto occupied, but one to which the laws of nature and of nature's God entitle them, a decent respect to the opinions of mankind requires that they should declare the causes that impel them to such a course.

We hold these truths to be self-evident: that all men and women are created equal; that they are endowed by their creator with certain inalienable rights; that among these are life, liberty and the pursuit of happiness; that to secure these rights governments are instituted, deriving their just powers from the consent of the governed. Whenever any form of government becomes destructive of these ends, it is the right of those who suffer from it to refuse allegiance to it, and to insist upon the institution of a new government laying its foundation on such principles, and organizing its powers in such form, as to them shall seem most likely to affect their safety and happiness. Prudence indeed will dictate that governments long established should not be changed for light and transient causes; and accordingly all experience hath shown that mankind are more disposed to suffer, while evils are sufferable, than to right themselves by abolishing the forms to which they were accustomed. But when a long train of abuses and usurpations pursuing invariably the same object evinces a design to reduce them under absolute despotism, it is their duty to throw off such government and to provide new guards for their future security. Such has been the patient sufferance of the women under this government, and such is now the necessity which constrains them to demand the equal station to which they are entitled.

The history of mankind is the history of repeated injuries and usurpations on the part of man toward woman, having in direct object the establishment of an absolute tyranny over her. To prove this, let facts be submitted to a candid world:

He has never permitted her to exercise her inalienable right to the elective franchise.

He has compelled her to submit to laws, in the formation of which she had no voice.

He has withheld from her rights which are given to the most ignorant and degraded men—both natives and foreigners.

Having deprived her of this first right of a citizen, the elective franchise, thereby leaving her without representation in the halls of legislation, he has oppressed her on all sides.

He has made her, if married, in the eyes of the law, civilly dead.

He has taken from her all right in property, even to the wages she earns.

He has made her, morally, an irresponsible being, as she can commit many crimes with impunity, provided they be done in the presence of her husband. In the covenant of marriage, she is compelled to promise obedience to her husband, he becoming to all intents and purposes, her master—the law giving him power to deprive her of her liberty and to administer chastisement.

He has so framed the laws of divorce, as to what shall be the proper causes, and in case of separation, to whom the guardianship of the children shall be given, as to be wholly regardless of the happiness of the woman—the law, in all cases, going upon a false supposition of the supremacy of man, and giving all power into his hands.

After depriving her of all rights as a married woman, if single, and the owner of property, he has taxed her to support a government which recognizes her only when her property can be made profitable to it.

He has monopolized nearly all the profitable employments, and from those she is permitted to follow, she receives but a scanty remuneration. He closes against her all the avenues to wealth and distinction which he considers most honorable to himself. As a teacher of theology, medicine, or law, she is not known.

He has denied her the facilities for obtaining a thorough education, all colleges being closed against her.

He allows her in Church, as well as State, but a subordinate position, claiming Apostolic authority for her exclusion from the ministry and, with some exceptions, from any public participation in the affairs of the Church.

He has created a false public sentiment by giving to the world a different code of morals for men and women, by which moral delinquencies which exclude women from society, are not only tolerated, but deemed of little account in man.

He has usurped the prerogative of Jehovah himself, claiming it as his right to assign for her a sphere of action, when that belongs to her conscience and to her God.

He has endeavored, in every way that he could, to destroy her confidence in her own powers, to lessen her self-respect, and to make her willing to lead a dependent and abject life.

Now, in view of this entire disfranchisement of one-half the people of this country, their social and religious degradation—in view of the unjust laws above mentioned and because women do feel themselves aggrieved, oppressed, and fraudulently deprived of their most sacred rights, we insist that they have immediate admission to all the rights and privileges which belong to them as citizens of the United States.

In entering upon the great work before us, we anticipate no small amount of misconception, misrepresentation, and ridicule; but we shall use every instrumentality within our power to effect our object. We shall employ agents, circulate tracts, petition the State and National legislatures, and endeavor to enlist the pulpit and the press in our behalf. We hope this Convention will be followed by a series of Conventions embracing every part of the country.

11. JOHN C. CALHOUN, MARCH 4, 1850, WARNS THE NORTH AGAINST AGITATION OF THE SLAVERY ISSUE.

I have, Senators, believed from the first that the agitation of the subject of slavery would, if not prevented by some timely and effective measure, end in disunion. Entertaining this opinion, I have, on all proper occasions, endeavored to call the attention of both the two great parties which divide the country to adopt some measure to prevent so great a disaster, but without success. The agitation has been permitted to proceed . . . the Union is in danger. . . . How can the Union be preserved? . . .

What is it that has endangered the Union? To this question there can be but one answer,—that the immediate cause is the almost universal discontent which pervades all the States composing the Southern section of the Union. . . . It commenced with the agitation of the slavery question. . . . The next question, going one step further back, is—What has caused this widely diffused and almost universal discontent? . . . It will be found in the belief of the people of the Southern States, as prevalent as the discontent itself, that they cannot remain, as things now are, consistently with honor and safety, in the Union. . . .

To place this subject distinctly before you, I have, Senators, prepared a brief statistical statement, showing the relative weight of the two sections in the Government under the first census of 1790 and the last census of 1840. . . . To sum up the whole, the United States, since they declared their independence, have acquired 2,373,046 square miles of territory, from which the North will have excluded the South, if she should succeed in monopolizing the newly acquired territories, about three-fourths of the whole, leaving to the South but about one-fourth. . . .

But if there was no question of vital importance to the South, in reference to which there was a diversity of views between the two sections, this state of things might be endured, without the hazard of destruction to the South. But . . . there is a question of vital importance to the Southern section, in reference to which the views and feelings of the two sections are as opposite and hostile as they can possibly be. I refer to the relation between the two races in the Southern section, which constitutes a vital portion of her social organization . . . the Southern section regards the relation as one which cannot be destroyed without subjecting the two races to the greatest calamity, and the section to poverty, desolation, and wretchedness; and accordingly they feel bound, by every consideration of interest and safety, to defend it.

12. EMANCIPATION PROCLAMATION (JANUARY 1, 1863).

Whereas, on [September 22, 1862], a proclamation was issued by the President of the United States, containing, among other things, the following, to wit:

"That on [January 1, 1863], all persons held as slaves within any state or designated part of a state, the people whereof shall then be in rebellion against the United States, shall be then, thenceforward, and forever, free; and the Executive Government of the United States, including the military and naval authority thereof, will recognize and maintain the freedom of such persons, and will do no act or acts to repress such persons, or any of them, in any efforts they may make for their actual freedom.

"That the Executive will, on the first day of January aforesaid, by proclamation, designate the states and parts of states, if any, in which the people thereof, respectively, shall then be in rebellion against the United States; and the fact that any state, or the people thereof, shall on that day be in good faith represented in the Congress of the United States, by members chosen thereto at elections wherein a majority of the qualified voters of such states shall have participated, shall, in the absence of strong countervailing testimony, be deemed conclusive evidence that such state, and the people thereof, are not then in rebellion against the United States."

Now, therefore, I, ABRAHAM LINCOLN, President of the United States, by virtue of the power in me vested as commander-in-chief of the army and navy of the United States, in time of actual armed rebellion against the authority and Government of the United States, and as a fit and necessary war measure for suppressing said rebellion, do, on this first day of January, . . . [1863] . . . , and in accordance with my purpose so to do, publicly proclaimed for the full period of one hundred days from the day first above mentioned, order and designate as the states and parts of states wherein the people thereof, respectively, are this day in rebellion against the United States, the following, to wit:

Arkansas, Texas, Louisiana, (except the parishes of St. Bernard, Plaquemines, Jefferson, St. John, St. Charles, St. James, Ascension, Assumption, Terre Bonne, Lafourche, St. Mary, St. Martin, and Orleans, including the city of New Orleans,) Mississippi, Alabama, Florida, Georgia, South Carolina, North Carolina, and Virginia, (except the forty-eight counties designated as West Virginia, and also the counties of Berkeley, Accomac, Northampton, Elizabeth City, York, Princess Ann, and Norfolk, including the cities of Norfolk and Portsmouth,) and which excepted parts are for the present left precisely as if this proclamation were not issued.

And by virtue of the power and for the purpose aforesaid, I do order and declare that all persons held as slaves within said designated states and parts of states are, and henceforward shall be, free; and that the Executive Government of the United States, including the military and naval authorities thereof, will recognize and maintain the freedom of said persons.

And I hereby enjoin upon the people so declared to be free to abstain from all violence, unless in necessary self-defence; and I recommend to them that, in all cases when allowed, they labor faithfully for reasonable wages.

And I further declare and make known that such persons, of suitable condition, will be received into the armed service of the United States to garrison forts, positions, stations, and other places, and to man vessels of all sorts in said service.

And upon this act, sincerely believed to be an act of justice, warranted by the Constitution upon military necessity, I invoke the considerate judgment of mankind and the gracious favor of Almighty God. . . .

13. LINCOLN'S ADDRESS AT GETTYSBURG (1863).

Fourscore and seven years ago our fathers brought forth on this continent a new nation, conceived in liberty, and dedicated to the proposition that all men are created equal.

Now we are engaged in a great civil war, testing whether that nation, or any nation so conceived and so dedicated, can long endure. We are met on a great battle-field of that war. We have come to dedicate a portion of that field as a final resting-place for those who here gave their lives that that nation might live. It is altogether fitting and proper that we should do this.

But, in a larger sense, we cannot dedicate—we cannot consecrate—we cannot hallow—this ground. The brave men, living and dead, who struggled here, have consecrated it far above our poor power to add or detract. The world will little note, nor long remember, what we say here, but it can never forget what they did here. It is for us, the living, rather, to be dedicated here to the unfinished work which they who fought here have thus far so nobly advanced. It is rather for us to be here dedicated to the great task remaining before us;—that from these honored dead, we take increased devotion to that cause for which they gave the last full measure of devotion;—that we here highly resolve that these dead shall not have died in vain, that this nation, under God, shall have a new birth of freedom, and that government of the people, by the people, for the people, shall not perish from the earth.

14. PRESIDENT ULYSSES S. GRANT INSTRUCTS CONGRESS ON WAYS OUT OF THE GREAT DEPRESSION (1874).

Since the convening of Congress one year ago the nation has undergone a prostration in business and industries such as has not been witnessed with us for many years. Speculation as to the causes for this prostration might be indulged in without profit, because as many theories would be advanced as there would be independent writers—those who expressed their own views without borrowing—upon the subject. Without indulging in theories as to the cause of this prostration, therefore, I will call your attention only to the fact, and to some plain questions as to which it would seem there should be no disagreement.

During this prostration two essential elements of prosperity have been most abundant—labor and capital. Both have been largely unemployed. Where security has been undoubted, capital has been attainable at very moderate rates. Where labor has been wanted, it has been found in abundance, at cheap rates compared with what—of necessaries and comforts of life—could be purchased with the wages demanded. Two great elements of prosperity, therefore, have not been denied us. A third might be added: Our soil and climate are unequaled, within the limits of any contiguous territory under one nationality, for its variety of products to feed and clothe a people and in the amount of surplus to spare to feed less favored peoples. Therefore, with these facts in view, it seems to me that wise statesmanship, at this session of Congress, would dictate legislation ignoring the past; directing in proper channels these great elements of prosperity to any people. Debt, debt abroad, is the only element that can, with always a sound currency, enter into our affairs to cause any continued depression in the industries and prosperity of our people. . . .

Our commerce should be encouraged; American shipbuilding and carrying capacity increased; foreign markets sought for products of the soil and manufactories, to the end that we may be able to pay these debts [owed abroad]. Where a new market can be created for the sale of our products, either of the soil, the mine, or the manufactory, a new means is discovered of utilizing our idle capital and labor to the advantage of the whole people. But, in my judgment, the first step toward accomplishing this object is to secure a currency of fixed, stable value; a currency good wherever civilization reigns. . . . Gold and silver are now the recognized medium of exchange the civilized world over, and to this we should return with the least practicable delay.

15. PRESIDENT GROVER CLEVELAND MAKES TARIFF REDUCTION THE MAIN ISSUE IN A MESSAGE TO CONGRESS (1887).

Our present tariff laws, the vicious, inequitable, and illogical source of unnecessary taxation, ought to be at once revised and amended. These laws, as their primary and plain effect, raise the price to consumers of all articles imported and subject to duty by precisely the sum paid for such duties. Thus the amount of the duty measures the tax paid by those who purchase for use these imported articles. . . .

It is not proposed to entirely relieve the country of this taxation. It must be extensively continued as the source of the Government's income; and in a readjustment of our tariff the interests of American labor engaged in manufacture should be carefully considered, as well as the preservation of our manufacturers. It may be called protection or by any other name, but relief from the hardships and dangers of our present tariff laws should be devised with especial precaution against imperiling the existence of our manufacturing interests. . . .

The reduction of taxation demanded should be so measured as not to necessitate or justify either the loss of employment by the working man or the lessening of his wages; and the profits still remaining to the manufacturer after a necessary readjustment should furnish no excuse for the sacrifice of the interests of his employees, either in their opportunity to work or in the diminution of their compensation.

16. RADICAL PLANKS IN THE DEMOCRATIC PLATFORM OF 1896.

Recognizing that the money question is paramount to all others at this time, we invite attention to the fact that the federal Constitution names silver and gold together as the money metals of the United States, and that the first coinage law passed by Congress under the Constitution made the silver dollar the money unit, and admitted gold to free coinage at a ratio based upon the silver dollar unit.

We declare that the act of 1873 demonetizing silver without the knowledge or approval of the American people has resulted in the appreciation of gold and a corresponding fall in the prices of commodities produced by the people; . . . the enrichment of the money-lending class at home and abroad; the prostration of industry and impoverishment of the people. . . .

We demand the free and unlimited coinage of both silver and gold at the present legal ratio of sixteen to one without waiting for the aid or consent of any other nation. . . .

We demand that all paper which is made a legal tender for public and private debts . . . shall be issued by the government of the United States and shall be redeemable in coin. . . .

Until the money question is settled we are opposed to any agitation for further changes in our tariff laws, except such as are necessary to meet the deficit in revenue caused by the adverse decision of the Supreme Court on the income tax. . . . We declare that it is the duty of Congress to use all the constitutional power which remains after that decision, or which may come from its reversal by the court as it may hereafter be constituted, so that the burden of taxation may be equally and impartially laid, to the end that wealth may bear its due proportion of the expenses of the government.

We hold that the most efficient way of protecting American labor is to prevent the importation of foreign pauper labor to compete with it in the home market, and that the value of the home market to our American farmers and artisans is greatly reduced by a vicious monetary system which depresses the prices of their products below the cost of production, and thus deprives them of the means of purchasing the products of our home manufactories; and, as labor creates the wealth of the country, we demand the passage of such laws as may be necessary to protect it in all its rights. . . .

We denounce arbitrary interference by federal authorities in local affairs as a violation of the Constitution of the United States and a crime against free institutions, and we especially object to government by injunction as a new and highly dangerous form of oppression by which federal judges, in contempt of the laws of the States and rights of citizens, become at once legislators, judges, and executioners. . . .

17. PRESIDENT THEODORE ROOSEVELT OPENS THE TWENTIETH CENTURY IN MESSAGES TO CONGRESS.

The tremendous and highly complex industrial development which went on with ever accelerated rapidity during the latter half of the nineteenth century brings us face to face, at the beginning of the twentieth, with very serious social problems. The old laws, and the old customs which had almost the binding force of law, were once quite sufficient to regulate the accumulation and distribution of wealth. Since the industrial changes which have so enormously increased the productive power of mankind, they are no longer sufficient.

The growth of cities has gone on beyond comparison faster than the growth of the country, and the upbuilding of the great industrial centers has meant a startling increase, not merely in the aggregate of wealth, but in the number of very large individual, and especially of very large corporate, fortunes. The creation of these great corporate fortunes has not been due to the tariff nor to any other governmental action, but to natural causes in the business world, operating in other countries as they operate in our own. . . .

In the interest of the whole people, the Nation should, without interfering with the power of the States in the matter itself, also assume power of supervision and regulation over all corporations doing an interstate business. . . .

The most vital problem with which this country, and for that matter the whole civilized world, has to deal, is the problem which has for one side the betterment of social conditions, moral and physical, in large cities, and for another side the effort to deal with that tangle of far-reaching questions which we group together when we speak of "labor." . . .

When all is said and done, the rule of brotherhood remains as the indispensable prerequisite to success in the kind of national life for which we strive. . . . (1901)

When our tax laws are revised the question of an income tax and an inheritance tax should receive the careful attention of our legislators. . . .

Our aim is to recognize what Lincoln pointed out: The fact that there are some respects in which men are obviously not equal; but also to insist that there should be . . . an equality of rights before the law, and at least an approximate equality in the conditions under which each man obtains the chance to show the stuff that is in him when compared to his fellows. . . . (1907)

We wish to see the farmer own his own land; we do not wish to see the farms so large that they become the property of absentee landlords who farm them by tenants; nor yet so small that the farmer becomes like a European peasant. . . .

There should no longer be any paltering with the question of taking care of the wage-workers who, under our present industrial system, become killed, crippled, or worn out as a part of the regular incidents of a given business. (1908)

18. THE PROGRESSIVE PLATFORM EXALTS NATIONAL WELFARE (1912).

The conscience of the people in a time of grave national problems has called into being a new party, born of the nation's awakened sense of justice. . . .

We hold, with Thomas Jefferson and Abraham Lincoln, that the people are the masters of their Constitution, to fulfill its purposes and to safeguard it from those who, by perversion of its intent, would convert it into an instrument of injustice. In accordance with the needs of each generation the people must use their sovereign powers to establish and maintain equal opportunity and industrial justice, to secure which this government was founded and without which no republic can endure.

This country belongs to the people who inhabit it. Its resources, its business, its institutions, and its laws should be utilized, maintained, or altered in whatever manner will best promote the general interest. It is time to set the public welfare in the first place . . . to build a new and nobler commonwealth. . . .

The Progressive party, believing that no people can justly claim to be a true democracy which denies political right on account of sex, pledges itself to the task of securing equal suffrage to men and women alike. . . .

19. THE SOCIALIST PLATFORM DENOUNCES THE CAPITALIST SYSTEM (1912).

The representatives of the Socialist party in national convention at Indianapolis, declare that the capitalist system has outgrown its historical function, and has become utterly incapable of meeting the problems now confronting society. We denounce this outgrown system as incompetent and corrupt and the source of unspeakable misery and suffering to the whole working class.

Under this system the industrial equipment of the Nation has passed into the absolute control of a plutocracy which exacts an annual tribute of millions of dollars from the producers. . . .

Multitudes of unemployed walk the streets of our cities. . . .

The farmers in every State are plundered. . . .

Capitalist concentration is mercilessly crushing the class of small business men. . . .

It is this capitalist system that is responsible for the increasing burden of armaments, the poverty, slums, child labor, most of the insanity, crime and prostitution, and much of the disease that afflicts mankind. . . .

20. PRESIDENT WOODROW WILSON'S FOURTEEN POINTS ON INTERNATIONAL RELATIONS (1918).

I.—Open covenants of peace, openly arrived at, after which there shall be no private international understandings of any kind but diplomacy shall proceed always frankly and in the public view.

II.—Absolute freedom of navigation upon the seas, outside territorial waters, alike in peace and in war, except as the seas may be closed in whole or in part by international action for the enforcement of international covenants.

III.—The removal, so far as possible, of all economic barriers and the establishment of an equality of trade conditions among all the nations consenting to the peace and associating themselves for its maintenance.

IV.—Adequate guarantees given and taken that national armaments will be reduced to the lowest point consistent with domestic safety.

V.—Free, open-minded, and absolutely impartial adjustment of all colonial claims, based upon a strict observance of the principle that in determining all such questions of sovereignty the interests of the population concerned must have equal weight with the equitable claims of the Government whose title is to be determined.

VI.—The evacuation of all Russian territory and such a settlement of all questions affecting Russia as will secure the best and freest cooperation of the other nations of the world in obtaining for her an unhampered and unembarrassed opportunity for the independent determination of her own political development and national policy, and assure her of a sincere welcome into the society of free nations under institutions of her own choosing; and, more than a welcome, assistance also of every kind that she may need and may herself desire. The treatment accorded Russia by her sister nations in the months to come will be the acid test of their goodwill, of their comprehension of her needs as distinguished from their own interests.

VII.—Belgium, the whole world will agree, must be evacuated and restored, without any attempt to limit the sovereignty which she enjoys in common with all other free nations. No other single act will serve as this will serve to restore confidence among the nations in the laws which they have themselves set and determined for the government of their relations with one another. Without this healing act the whole structure and validity of international law is forever impaired.

VIII.—All French territory should be freed and the invaded portions restored, and the wrong done to France by Prussia in 1871 in the matter of Alsace-Lorraine, which has unsettled the peace of the world for nearly fifty years, should be righted, in order that peace may once more be made secure in the interest of all.

IX.—A readjustment of the frontiers of Italy should be effected along clearly recognizable lines of nationality.

X.—The peoples of Austria-Hungary, whose place among the nations we wish to see safeguarded and assured, should be accorded the freest opportunity of autonomous development.

XI.—Rumania, Serbia, and Montenegro should be evacuated; occupied territories restored; Serbia accorded free and secure access to the sea; and the relations of the several Balkan States to one another determined by friendly counsel along historically established lines of allegiance and nationality; and international guarantees of the political and economic independence and territorial integrity of the several Balkan States should be entered into.

XII.—The Turkish portions of the present Ottoman Empire should be assured a secure sovereignty, but the other nationalities which are now under Turkish rule should be assured an undoubted security of life and an absolutely unmolested opportunity of autonomous development, and the Dardanelles should be permanently opened as a free passage to the ships and commerce of all nations under international guarantees.

XIII.—An independent Polish State should be erected which should include the territories inhabited by indisputably Polish populations, which should be assured a free and secure access to the sea, and whose political and economic independence and territorial integrity should be guaranteed by international covenant.

XIV.—A general association of nations must be formed under specific covenants for the purpose of affording mutual guarantees of political independence and territorial integrity to great and small States alike.

21. JUSTICE OLIVER WENDELL HOLMES UPHOLDS "FREE TRADE IN IDEAS."

Persecution for the expression of opinions seems to me perfectly logical. If you have no doubt of your premises or your power and want a certain result with all your heart you naturally express your wishes in law and sweep away all opposition. To allow opposition by speech seems to indicate that you think the speech impotent, as when a man says that he has squared the circle, or that you do not care wholeheartedly for the result, or that you doubt either your power or your premises. But when men have realized that time has upset many fighting faiths, they may come to believe even more than they believe the very foundations of their own conduct that the ultimate good desired is better reached by free trade in ideas—that the best test of truth is the power of the thought to get itself accepted in the competition of the market, and that truth is the only ground upon which their wishes safely can be carried out. That at any rate is the theory of our Constitution. It is an experiment, as all life is an experiment. Every year if not every day we have to wager our salvation upon some prophecy based upon imperfect knowledge. While that experiment is part of our system I think that we should be eternally vigilant against attempts to check the expression of opinions that we loathe and believe to be fraught with death, unless they so imminently threaten immediate interference with the lawful and pressing purposes of the law that an immediate check is required to save the country. [Dissenting Opinion, Abrams *v.* United States, 1919.]

22. PRESIDENT HERBERT HOOVER ON SOCIAL AND ECONOMIC PHILOSOPHY (1922).

Five or six great social philosophies are at struggle in the world for ascendancy. There is the Individualism of America. There is the Individualism of the more democratic states of Europe with its careful reservations of castes and classes. There are Communism, Socialism, Syndicalism, Capitalism, and finally there is Autocracy—whether by birth, by possessions, militarism, or divine right of kings. . . .

It is not the individualism of other countries for which I would speak, but the individualism of America. . . . In our individualism we have long since abandoned the *laissez faire* of the eighteenth century—the notion that it is "every man for himself and the devil take the hindmost." We abandoned that when we adopted the ideal of equality of opportunity—the fair chance of Abraham Lincoln. We have confirmed its abandonment in terms of legislation, of social and economic justice,—in part because we have learned that it is the hindmost who throws the bricks at our social edifice, in part because we have learned that the foremost are not always the best nor the hindmost the worst—and in part because we have learned that social injustice is the destruction of justice itself. We have learned that the impulse to production can only be maintained at a high pitch if there is a fair division of the product. We have also learned that fair division can only be obtained by certain restrictions on the strong and the dominant. . . .

The social force in which I am interested is far higher and far more precious a thing than all these [assumptions of some group dominating somebody else]. It springs from something infinitely more enduring; it springs from the one source of human progress—that each individual shall be given the chance and stimulation for development of the best with which he has been endowed in heart and mind; it is the sole source of progress; it is American individualism.

The rightfulness of our individualism can rest either on philosophic, political, economic, or spiritual grounds. It can rest on the ground of being the only safe avenue to further human progress. . . .

To curb the forces in business which would destroy equality of opportunity and yet to maintain the initiative and creative faculties of our people are the twin objects we must attain. . . . This the deadline between our system and socialism.

23. PRESIDENT HERBERT HOOVER'S ECONOMIC PHILOSOPHY APPLIED TO HIS VETO OF THE MUSCLE SHOALS BILL (1931).

I am firmly opposed to the government entering into any business the major purpose of which is competition with our citizens. There are national emergencies which require that the government should temporarily enter the field of business, but they must be emergency actions and in matters where the cost of the project is secondary to much higher considerations. . . . But for the Federal Government deliberately to go out to build up and expand such an occasion to the major purpose of a power and manufacturing business is to break down the initiative and enterprise of the American people; it is destruction of equality of opportunity amongst our people; it is the negation of the ideals upon which our civilization has been based.

This bill raises one of the important issues confronting our people. That is squarely the issue of Federal Government ownership and operation of power and manufacturing business not as a minor by-product but as a major purpose. Involved in this question is the agitation against the conduct of the power industry. The power problem is not to be solved by the Federal Government going into the power business, nor is it to be solved by the project in this bill. The remedy for abuses in the conduct of that industry lies in regulation. . . . I have recommended to the Congress on various occasions that action should be taken to establish Federal regulation of interstate power in co-operation with state authorities. This bill would launch the Federal Government upon a policy of ownership and operation of power utilities upon a basis of competition instead of by the proper government function of regulation for the protection of all the people. I hesitate to contemplate the future of our institutions, of our government, and of our country if the preoccupation of its officials is to be no longer the promotion of justice and equal opportunity but is to be devoted to barter in the markets. That is not liberalism, it is degeneration.

24. PRESIDENT FRANKLIN D. ROOSEVELT FACES THE CALAMITY OF 1933.

This is a day of national consecration. I am certain that on this day my fellow Americans expect that on my induction into the Presidency I will address them with a candor and a decision which the present situation of our nation impels. . . .

So first of all let me assert my firm belief that the only thing we have to fear is fear itself—nameless, unreasoning, unjustified terror which paralyzes needed efforts to convert retreat into advance. . . .

Values have shrunken to fantastic levels; taxes have risen; our ability to pay has fallen; government of all kinds is faced by serious curtailment of income; the means of exchange are frozen in the currents of trade; the withered leaves of industrial enterprise lie on every side; farmers find no markets for their produce; the savings of many years in thousands of families are gone.

More important, a host of unemployed citizens face the grim problem of existence, and an equally great number toil with little return. Only a foolish optimist can deny the dark realities of the moment. . . .

I am prepared under my constitutional duty to recommend the measures that a stricken nation in the midst of a stricken world may require. . . .

But in the event that the Congress shall fail to take one of these two courses, and in the event that the national emergency is still critical, I shall not evade the clear course of duty that will then confront me.

I shall ask the Congress for the one remaining instrument to meet the crisis—broad executive power to wage a war against the emergency as great as the power that would be given to me if we were in fact invaded by a foreign foe. . . . [First Inaugural Address.]

25. PRESIDENT FRANKLIN D. ROOSEVELT CALLS ATTENTION TO A THIRD OF THE NATION IN HIS SECOND INAUGURAL ADDRESS (1937).

Let us ask again: Have we reached the goal of our vision of that fourth day of March, 1933? Have we found our happy valley?

I see a great nation, upon a great continent, blessed with a great wealth of natural resources. Its hundred and thirty million people are at peace among themselves; they are making their country a good neighbor among the nations. I see a United States which can demonstrate that, under democratic methods of government, national wealth can be translated into a spreading volume of human comforts hitherto unknown, and the lowest standard of living can be raised far above the level of mere subsistence.

But here is the challenge to our democracy: In this nation I see tens of millions of its citizens—a substantial part of its whole population—who at this very moment are denied the greater part of what the very lowest standards of today call the necessities of life.

I see millions of families trying to live on incomes so meager that the pall of family disaster hangs over them day by day.

I see millions whose daily lives in city and on farm continue under conditions labeled indecent by a so-called polite society half a century ago.

I see millions denied education, recreation, and the opportunity to better their lot and the lot of their children.

I see millions lacking the means to buy the products of farm and factory and by their poverty denying work and productiveness to many other millions.

I see one-third of a nation ill-housed, ill-clad, ill-nourished.

It is not in despair that I paint you that picture. I paint it for you in hope —because the Nation, seeing and understanding the injustice in it, proposes to paint it out. . . .

In taking again the oath of office as President of the United States, I assume the solemn obligation of leading the American people forward along the road over which they have chosen to advance.

26. THE ATLANTIC CHARTER.

. . . The President of the United States of America and the Prime Minister, Mr. Churchill, representing His Majesty's Government in the United Kingdom, being met together, deem it right to make known certain common principles in the national policies of their respective countries on which they base their hopes for a better future for the world.

FIRST, their countries seek no aggrandizement, territorial or other;

SECOND, they desire to see no territorial changes that do not accord with the freely expressed wishes of the peoples concerned;

THIRD, they respect the right of all peoples to choose the form of government under which they will live; and they wish to see sovereign rights and self-government restored to those who have been forcibly deprived of them;

FOURTH, they will endeavor, with due respect for their existing obligations, to further the enjoyment by all States, great or small, victor or vanquished, of access, on equal terms, to the trade and to the raw materials of the world which are needed for their economic prosperity;

FIFTH, they desire to bring about the fullest collaboration between all nations in the economic field with the object of securing, for all, improved labor standards, economic advancement, and social security;

SIXTH, after the final destruction of the Nazi tyranny, they hope to see established a peace which will afford to all nations the means of dwelling in safety within their own boundaries, and which will afford assurance that all the men in all the lands may live out their lives in freedom from fear and want;

SEVENTH, such a peace should enable all men to traverse the high seas and oceans without hindrance;

EIGHTH, they believe that all of the nations of the world, for realistic as well as spiritual reasons, must come to the abandonment of the use of force. Since no future peace can be maintained if land, sea or air armaments continue to be employed by nations which threaten, or may threaten, aggression outside of their frontiers, they believe, pending the establishment of a wider and permanent system of general security, that the disarmament of such nations is essential. They will likewise aid and encourage all other practicable measures which will lighten for peace-loving peoples the crushing burden of armaments.

FRANKLIN D. ROOSEVELT
WINSTON S. CHURCHILL

Dated August 14, 1941.

27. THE MAIN THREE-POWER DECLARATION AT TEHERAN.

We, the President of the United States of America, the Prime Minister of Great Britain, and the Premier of the Soviet Union, have met in these four days past in this the capital of our ally, Teheran, and have shaped and confirmed our common policy.

We express our determination that our nations shall work together in the war and in the peace that will follow.

As to the war, our military staffs have joined in our round-table discussions and we have concerted our plans for the destruction of the German forces. We have reached complete agreement as to the scope and timing of operations which will be undertaken from the east, west and south. The common understanding which we have here reached guarantees that victory will be ours.

And as to the peace, we are sure that our concord will make it an enduring peace. We recognize fully the supreme responsibility resting upon us and all the nations to make a peace which will command good will from the overwhelming masses of the peoples of the world and banish the scourge and terror of war for many generations.

With our diplomatic advisers we have surveyed the problems of the future. We shall seek the co-operation and active participation of all nations, large and small, whose peoples in heart and in mind are dedicated, as are our own peoples, to the elimination of tyranny and slavery, oppression and intolerance. We will welcome them as they may choose to come into the world family of democratic nations.

No power on earth can prevent our destroying the German armies by land, their U-boats by sea, and their war plants from the air. Our attacks will be relentless and increasing.

Emerging from these friendly conferences we look with confidence to the day when all the peoples of the world may live free lives untouched by tyranny and according to their varying desires and their own consciences.

We came here with hope and determination. We leave here friends in fact, in spirit, and in purpose.

Signed at Teheran, Dec. 1, 1943.

ROOSEVELT, STALIN, CHURCHILL.

28. PLANKS ON DOMESTIC AND FOREIGN AFFAIRS FROM THE
PROGRAM OF THE POSTWAR PLANNING COMMITTEE
OF THE AMERICAN FEDERATION OF LABOR (April, 1944).

We want a regime of economic freedom, but our enterprise system must demonstrate that it can function so as to husband and utilize, not to waste and dissipate our natural resources. We want free enterprise, but our productive system must be committed to the progressive raising of the national income and the maintenance of full employment. Such a system is necessarily opposed to all tendencies toward monopolistic restriction. We want free enterprise, but we also want an economy which will provide ample support for the health, educational, recreational, and similar public services so essential to the welfare of the working people in our industrial society. Finally, we want a program of economic enterprise which will not be repressive, but will support the free exercise of civil and political liberties. . . .

The right to work and the right to quit work are among the basic rights of free men. . . .

Free and independent organizations of the people are an indispensable means of checking concentration of economic and governmental power. . . .

All will suffer disaster, if the powerful organizations of finance, business, farmers, and labor seek merely to advance their own interests without regard for the consequences on the community as a whole. . . .

There has been, there is, and there can be no lasting conflict between a movement created by the working people and democratic purposes and processes. . . .

[As to foreign relations] It is imperative that the United States do its full part to help develop a general system of mutual security. . . . [but not a world government].

29. THE PRESIDENT OF THE UNITED STATES CHAMBER OF
COMMERCE, ERIC JOHNSTON, EXPRESSES HIS
VIEWS ON THE HOME FRONT.[1]

I believe—I may say we believe—that the individual man and woman is the pivotal element in a desirable society. The individual safety, freedom, and happiness come first and last. The state in any of its forms, for us, has no standing or authority per se as an end in itself, but only as the tool and servant of the individual. A rich and powerful state would be meaningless to Americans, if it rested on weak and poor individuals.

We deny that America faces a choice between a congealed old order and some experimental new order. On the contrary, we feel that those who narrow down the choice between such repugnant extremes are dangerously confusing the issue.

We believe in the middle way: the way of realistic adjustment between old-style laissez-faire capitalism and socialized economy.

I have an abiding faith in the common sense of the American people. I believe that our instincts are right, not because we are better or more intelli-

[1] A compilation of public expressions by Eric Johnston, prepared with the permission and approval of the U.S. Chamber of Commerce.

gent than other peoples, but because we have been conditioned by a hundred and fifty years of freedom. Relying on themselves, rather than on state or fate, has become second nature to people who faced and conquered a continent with their bare hands and their indomitable will.

A great duel is under way in the world today.

I refer to the fateful duel between two conceptions of human existence, two ways of life, that may be summed up in the over-simplified formula: individualism versus statism.

The contest cannot be identified in terms of party labels or regions, because it cuts across political and geographical boundaries.

I believe capitalism has no need of apologetics. Capitalism is neither "good" nor "bad." It is a process, and all that we need to judge is how it works. I see three main capitalisms in the world.

There is the capitalism of the bureaucrats. I am against it in its extreme forms in the totalitarian countries. I am against it in its seedling growths in our own country.

Second, there is the capitalism of private monopoly and special privilege. I am against it wherever it seeks to control and to dominate.

Finally, there is what I venture to call a people's capitalism. I come from it. I want to see it survive for every boy and girl in America after me.

We Americans have been able to make the magnificent contribution of our industrial genius toward winning the war precisely because we were rich, industrious, immensely productive, and economically free.

The upsurge of energy, inventiveness, productivity evoked by an external enemy can and must be maintained for war against internal enemies such as poverty, low living standards, chronic unemployment. These are challenges as real as the Axis and can be met in the same spirit.

Americans must not become slaves of any ideology—not even the ideology of free capitalism. The techniques of capitalism are tools to be used, not fetishes to be worshipped.

I believe there should be special tax concessions for new enterprises for a limited number of years—the period of dangerous infant mortality in business—and special tax treatment for capital invested in plant expansion and other job-making efforts.

An amicable management-labor picture is not a secondary matter to be dealt with in spare time. It is a central challenge. Nothing less than the life or death of our free economy is at stake.

In recent travels I have been less impressed with the "oneness" of the world than with its dizzy multiplicity. Space has been telescoped by the airplane, but the differences between nations and peoples are as formidable as ever.

The devastation that has swept the world in our time is not alone physical. We may survive physically, but we shall be moral casualties if in the process of winning the war we lose any portion of our hatred for its brutalities and its sufferings. In the preoccupation with slogans, propaganda, postwar planning, let us never lose the tragic sense that war is hell and that no price is too big to stave it off.

Chronology of Events

1673 Marquette and Joliet discover the northern Mississippi
1681 Pennsylvania chartered to Penn
1682 La Salle claims Louisiana
     William Penn founds Philadelphia
1689 King William's War (to 1697)
1692 College of William and Mary founded
     New charter for Massachusetts
1699 First French colony, at Biloxi
1701 Yale College founded; later at New Haven
1702 Queen Anne's War (to 1713)
1719 Carolina made a royal province
1729 Division of Carolina
1733 Georgia settled at Savannah
1735 Freedom of the press (Zenger trial)
1744 King George's War (to 1748)
1754 French and Indian War (to 1763)
     Albany Plan of Union
     King's (Columbia) College founded
1755 Braddock's defeat in Pennsylvania
1759 Surrender of Quebec
1761 Writs of assistance, Massachusetts
1762 France cedes Louisiana to Spain
1763 Spain cedes Florida to England
1765 Stamp Act
     Stamp Act Congress protests
1770 The Boston Massacre
1773 The Boston Tea Party
1774 Continental Congress, Philadelphia
1775 Battles of Lexington and Concord
     Second Continental Congress
     Battle of Bunker Hill
1776 Declaration of Independence signed
     British occupy New York
1777 Howe occupies Philadelphia
     Burgoyne surrenders at Saratoga
     Articles of Confederation adopted by Congress
     Washington at Valley Forge
1778 British evacuate Philadelphia
1781 Cornwallis surrenders at Yorktown
1783 Treaty of Peace with England
     England cedes Florida to Spain
1786 Shays' Rebellion in Massachusetts
     Annapolis (pre-federal) Convention
1787 Philadelphia convention; Constitution
     Northwest Ordinance adopted
1788 The Constitution adopted
1789 First Congress meets, New York
     Supreme Court established
1790 Philadelphia as capital (10 years)
     First census taken

1791 United States Bank chartered (to 1811)
      First ten Amendments (Bill of Rights) ratified
1793 Whitney invents the cotton gin
1794 Whisky Rebellion in Pennsylvania
1798 Eleventh amendment ratified
      Alien and Sedition laws passed
1800 Spain cedes Louisiana to France
      Washington becomes the capital
1801 War with Tripoli (to 1805)
1803 The Louisiana Purchase
1804 Lewis and Clark Expedition
      Twelfth amendment ratified
1807 Fulton's passenger steamer *Clermont*
      The Embargo Act passed
1808 Slave importations prohibited
1812 War of 1812 (to 1814)
1814 Hartford (tri-state) Convention
1815 Battle of New Orleans
1816 Second United States Bank (to 1836)
1819 Annexation of east Florida
1820 Missouri Compromise
1823 Monroe Doctrine declared
1825 Erie Canal opened
1829 Delaware and Hudson Company imports first railway locomotive
1831 Garrison's *Liberator* (to 1865)
1832 Nullification Ordinance (S. C.)
      Morse invents magnetic telegraph
1837 Financial panic
1845 Texas annexed (28th state)
1846 War with Mexico (to 1848)
      Howe invents the sewing machine
      Anesthetics used in Boston
      Oregon boundary dispute settled
      Smithsonian Institution founded
1848 Mexico cedes the Southwest
1849 California gold rush begins
1850 Second Fugitive Slave Law
1853 Gadsden Purchase (Mexican border)
1854 Kansas-Nebraska squatter sovereignty
1857 Dred Scott decision
1859 John Brown at Harper's Ferry
1860 South Carolina secedes
1861 Confederate States of America
      Civil War (to 1865)
1862 Battle of the *Monitor* and *Merrimac*
      Farragut takes New Orleans
      Homestead (free land) Act
1863 Emancipation Proclamation
      Battle of Gettysburg
      Vicksburg surrenders to Grant

1864 Campaign of the Wilderness
     Sherman takes Atlanta and Savannah
1865 Grant takes Richmond
     Surrender of Lee
     Assassination of Lincoln
     Thirteenth amendment
1866 Field lays the Atlantic cable
1867 Reconstruction Act passed
     Purchase of Alaska
1868 Fourteenth amendment ratified
1869 First railroad to the Pacific opened
1870 Fifteenth amendment ratified
1873 Financial panic (to 1878)
1876 Philadelphia Centennial
     Bell's speaking telephone first shown
1877 Edison's talking machine
1878 Edison's incandescent electric light
1882 Chinese immigration suspended
1883 Civil Service Commission created
1884 Mergenthaler invents the linotype
1886 American Federation of Labor formed
1887 Interstate Commerce Commission
1889 First Pan-American Conference
1890 Sherman Anti-Trust Act
1892 Homestead steel and other strikes
     Duryea's first American automobile
1893 Financial panic and depression
     Edison's motion-picture machine
1894 Pullman strike
1898 Spanish-American War
     Annexation of Hawaii
     Spain cedes Puerto Rico, Guam, and the Philippines
1899 Open-Door Policy in China
1904 Panama Canal strip acquired
     Wrights' first airplane flights
1906 De Forest invents vacuum radio tube
1907 Financial panic and depression
1908 Japanese immigration restricted
1911 Nicaragua protectorate (ratified 1916)
1913 Sixteenth amendment ratified
     Seventeenth amendment ratified
     Federal Reserve System created
1914 Marines occupy Vera Cruz; mediation
     Panama Canal officially opened
1916 Protectorate over Haiti ratified
     Intervention in Santo Domingo
1917 War declared on Germany; first World War
1918 Armistice signed, November 11
1919 Eighteenth amendment ratified
     Peace conference; Versailles Treaty
1920 Nineteenth amendment

1921 Immigration Act establishes quotas
Washington Conference (naval arms limitation)
1922 Railway shopmen's and coal strikes
1927 Disarmament Conference, Geneva
1928 First talking picture demonstrated
1929 Stock market collapse; long depression
1932 Reconstruction Finance Corporation
1933 Twentieth amendment ratified
Prohibition amendment repealed
New Deal begins
Agricultural Adjustment Agency
Federal Emergency Relief Administration
National Industrial Recovery Act
1934 Act authorizing the Philippines to prepare for independence
Securities and Exchange Commission
1935 National Labor Relations Act
Social Security Act
Committee for Industrial Organization formed
1937 United States Housing Authority
1938 Fair Labor Standards Act
1939 Federal Administrative Reorganization Act
Neutrality proclaimed
1941 Lend-Lease Act
The Atlantic Charter
"Shooting war" starts in the Atlantic
Japan attacks Pearl Harbor; Global War
1942 United States forces in North Africa
1943 Invasion of Italy
Casablanca, Quebec, Moscow, Cairo, and Teheran conferences
1944 Invasion of Europe

PRESENTS AND VICE-PRESIDENTS

President	Born in	Party
1. George Washington	Virginia, 1732	No party
2. John Adams	Massachusetts, 1735	Federalists
3. Thomas Jefferson	Virginia, 1743	Republicans
4. James Madison	Virginia, 1751	Republicans
5. James Monroe	Virginia, 1758	Republicans
6. John Quincy Adams	Massachusetts, 1767	Republicans
7. Andrew Jackson	North Carolina, 1767	Republicans
8. Martin Van Buren	New York, 1782	Republicans
9. William Henry Harrison	Virginia, 1773	Whigs
10. John Tyler	Virginia, 1790	Whigs
11. James K. Polk	North Carolina, 1795	Democrats
12. Zachary Taylor	Virginia, 1784	Whigs
13. Millard Fillmore	New York, 1800	Whigs
14. Franklin Pierce	New Hampshire, 1804	Democrats
15. James Buchanan	Pennsylvania, 1791	Democrats
16. Abraham Lincoln	Kentucky, 1809	Republicans
17. Andrew Johnson	North Carolina, 1808	Republicans
18. Ulysses S. Grant	Ohio, 1822	Republicans
19. Rutherford B. Hayes	Ohio, 1822	Republicans
20. James A. Garfield	Ohio, 1831	Republicans
21. Chester A. Arthur	Vermont, 1830	Republicans
22. Grover Cleveland	New Jersey, 1837	Democrats
23. Benjamin Harrison	Ohio, 1833	Republicans
24. Grover Cleveland		Democrats
25. William McKinley	Ohio, 1843	Republicans
26. Theodore Roosevelt	New York, 1858	Republicans
27. William H. Taft	Ohio, 1857	Republicans
28. Woodrow Wilson	Virginia, 1856	Democrats
29. Warren G. Harding	Ohio, 1865	Republicans
30. Calvin Coolidge	Vermont, 1872	Republicans
31. Herbert Hoover	Iowa, 1874	Republicans
32. Franklin D. Roosevelt	New York, 1882	Democrats

OF THE UNITED STATES

Elected from	Years of Service	Died	Vice-President
1. Virginia	1789–1797	1799	John Adams
2. Massachusetts ...	1797–1801	1826	Thomas Jefferson
3. Virginia	1801–1809	1826	{ Aaron Burr, 1st term { George Clinton, 2nd term
4. Virginia	1809–1817	1836	{ George Clinton, 1st term { Elbridge Gerry, 2nd term
5. Virginia	1817–1825	1831	Daniel D. Tompkins
6. Massachusetts ...	1825–1829	1848	John C. Calhoun
7. Tennessee	1829–1837	1845	{ John C. Calhoun, 1st term { Martin Van Buren, 2nd term
8. New York	1837–1841	1862	Richard M. Johnson
9. Ohio	1841 (one month)	1841	John Tyler
10. Virginia	1841–1845	1862	
11. Tennessee	1845–1849	1849	George M. Dallas
12. Louisiana	1849–1850	1850	Millard Fillmore
13. New York	1850–1853	1874	
14. New Hampshire .	1853–1857	1869	William R. King
15. Pennsylvania	1857–1861	1868	John C. Breckenridge
16. Illinois	1861–1865	1865	{ Hannibal Hamlin, 1st term { Andrew Johnson, 2nd term
17. Tennessee	1865–1869	1875	
18. Illinois	1869–1877	1885	{ Schuyler Colfax, 1st term { Henry Wilson, 2nd term
19. Ohio	1877–1881	1893	William A. Wheeler
20. Ohio	1881 (6mos.)	1881	Chester A. Arthur
21. New York	1881–1885	1886	
22. New York	1885–1889	1908	Thomas A. Hendricks
23. Indiana	1889–1893	1901	Levi P. Morton
24. New York	1893–1897		Adlai E. Stevenson
25. Ohio	1897–1901	1901	{ Garret A. Hobart, 1st term { Theodore Roosevelt, 2nd term
26. New York	1901–1909	1919	Charles W. Fairbanks, 2nd term
27. Ohio	1909–1913	1930	James S. Sherman
28. New Jersey	1913–1921	1924	Thomas R. Marshall
29. Ohio	1921–1923	1923	Calvin Coolidge
30. Massachusetts ...	1925–1929	1933	Charles G. Dawes
31. California	1929–1933		Charles Curtis
32. New York	1933–		{ John N. Garner, 1st, 2nd term { H. A. Wallace, 3rd term

TERRITORIAL GROWTH OF THE UNITED STATES, 1783–1912

Territorial Division	Year Acquired	Area added. Square miles	Purchase price	Ceded by
Louisiana Purchase	1803	827,987	$15,000,000	France
Florida	1819	72,101	6,489,768[1]	Spain
Texas	1845	389,166	Annexed	....
Oregon Territory	1846	286,541	.........[2]	Great Britain
Mexican Cession	1848	529,189	18,250,000[3]	Mexico
Purchase from Texas	1850	......[4]	10,000,000	Texas
Gadsden Purchase	1853	29,671	10,000,000	Mexico
Alaska	1867	590,884	7,200,000	Russia
Hawaii	1898	6,449	Annexed	....
Porto Rico	1899	3,435	....	Spain
Guam	1899	210	....	Spain
Philippines	1899	115,026	20,000,000	Spain
Tutuila Group, Samoa	1899	77	....	(rights settled)
Panama Canal Zone (lease)	1904	436	10,000,000	Panama
Total		2,851,172	$96,939,768	

[1] Interest payments included.
[2] Date of settlement with Great Britain.
[3] Includes payments to American citizens for claims against Mexico.
[4] 123,784 square miles which had become a part of the United States territory with the annexation of Texas in 1846.

READING LIST

GENERAL

BEARD, CHARLES A., and MARY R., *The Rise of American Civilization:* Vol. I, *The Agricultural Age;* Vol. II, *The Industrial Era;* Vol. III, *America in Midpassage* (1929–38); Vol. IV, *The American Spirit: A Study of the Idea of Civilization in the United States.*

BEARD, CHARLES A. (editor), *A Century of Progress—1833–1933;* (a symposium by specialists on invention, industry, transportation, agriculture, labor, banking, government and law, social progress, the position of women, natural science, medicine, education, the arts, and literature).

COLONIAL FOUNDATIONS AND POPULATION

NETTELS, CURTIS P., *The Roots of American Civilization* (the colonial age in general).

BRIDENBAUGH, CARL, *Cities in the Wilderness* (rise and growth of the leading colonial towns).

WERTENBAKER, T. J., *The Old South* (study of Southern culture and civilization).

CLARKE, M. P., *Parliamentary Privileges in the American Colonies* (establishing the rights of self-government).

HANSEN, M. L., *The Immigrant in American History.*

DU BOIS, W. E. B., *Black Folk: Then and Now* (the struggle of Negroes to win a place in American society).

GARIS, R. L., *Immigration Restriction* (historical).

ESSENTIALLY POLITICAL

SCHLESINGER, A. M., and HOCKETT, H. C., *Political and Social History of the United States* (Vols. I, II).

MORISON, S., and COMMAGER, H. S., *Growth of the American Republic* (Vols. I, II).

ECONOMIC

FAULKNER, H. U., *Economic History of the United States.*
BINING, A. C., *The Rise of American Economic Life.*
HACKER, L., *The Triumph of American Capitalism* (historical).

INVENTIONS

KAEMPFFERT, W., *A Popular History of American Invention* (Vols. I, II).

AMERICAN POLITICAL THEORIES

MERRIAM, C. E., *A History of American Political Theories* (to about 1900).
LEWIS, E. R., *A History of American Political Thought* (from the Civil War to the World War).
COKER, F. W., *Democracy, Liberty, and Property* (extracts from great writings on American political and social ideals from colonial times to 1941).
SMITH, B., *The Democratic Spirit* (extracts from great writings on the spirit of political, social, and economic reforms).

LITERATURE IN RELATION TO AMERICAN SOCIAL AND ECONOMIC LIFE

CURTI, M., *The Growth of American Thought* (general, with comprehensive bibliographies).
PARRINGTON, V. L., *Main Currents in American Thought* (Vols. I–III, from colonial times to about 1930).
KAZIN, A., *On Native Grounds* (from about 1875 to 1942).

INDEX

543

Charlotte Brontë: The Self Conceived

HELENE MOGLEN, *1936 –*

Charlotte Brontë *, 1816–1855*
The Self Conceived

W · W · NORTON & COMPANY · INC ·

NEW YORK

FIRST EDITION

The text of this book was set in photocomposition Times Roman on the Variable Input Typesetter. Composition, printing, and binding are by the Vail-Ballou Press.

Library of Congress Cataloging in Publication Data
Moglen, Helene, 1936–
    Charlotte Brontë: the self conceived.
    Bibliography: p.
    Includes index.
    1. Brontë, Charlotte, 1816–1855.
PR4168.M575   823'.8 [B]   76–16010

ISBN 0 393 07505 2

1 2 3 4 5 6 7 8 9 0

To Sig

who

when we were children
helped me to conceive myself
and as we grew to maturity
helped me to realize that self
we had conceived

Contents

Illustrations

Acknowledgments

*T*HE PRECIOUS gift of time was bestowed upon me by the American Council of Learned Societies in the form of a fellowship for the academic year 1973–74. It relieved me of teaching and administrative duties and took me to England: to the British Museum in London, to the Brontë Parsonage Museum at Haworth and, perhaps most importantly, to the Yorkshire moors. At the Parsonage Museum, Mr. Norman Raistrick, the custodian, guided me through the Brontë Society's collection of books and papers and has been of continuing help in sending me necessary material and information.

From the beginning, I have associated my project with the special pleasures and activities that have been part of establishing a new college. To my colleagues at Purchase, who put aside their own work to read and discuss mine, I am affectionately grateful. Interchanging ideas with Evelyn Keller, Marcia Cavell, Bell Chevigny, Geoffrey Field, Myra Jehlen, and Michael O'Loughlin was an interdisciplinary treat and a perpetual reaffirmation of friendship. Carl Resek exerted his deaconal powers to find me extra pockets of time, and then insisted that I protect myself against his own forays into them. The students who labored in my two Charlotte Brontë seminars amazed me with their capacity for hard work, delighted me with their enthusiasm, educated me with the freshness of their insights, and confirmed my belief that the book was one worth writing. Isabel Murray refused to be simply an expert typist: she read the novels, checked my sources, stuffed me with candy, and never allowed me to feel discouraged. Lauren Wood, who typed the last draft, met my insanity with good humor and got the job done with patience and intelligence.

I am indebted also to Barbara Gelpi, who read the completed manuscript with extraordinary care and thoroughness and made a number of valuable suggestions. To George Brockway of Norton, I offer the respect due someone who accomplishes what he does with such easy competence.

My sons, Eben, Damon, and Seth, tramped the Yorkshire moors day after rainy day, sharing my curiosity and delight, and remained—in the years since—philosophically tolerant of my "incessant scribbling."

Finally, there are those acts of love which can be recorded but never repaid. Sig, my husband, came home on innumerable evenings, weary of editing other people's books, and surrendered his own thoughts to edit mine: finding the patterns of meaning which hid inside the maze of words; cajoling, reasoning, explaining, teasing—until my best had been done. His dedication was to the utmost clarification of my vision and, as always, to the integrity of thought itself.

Preface

LITERARY BIOGRAPHIES interest me least when they set out to tell exhaustively and "objectively" the history of an individual, tallying dates, genealogies and events, friends and lovers, geographical locations, and the titles of books written and read. Such studies leave one freshly awed by the miracle of the creative process. Art seems to be self-generating, not parented by personality. Often, after reading such a work—tirelessly researched, masterfully organized, representing a martyrdom of sources pursued and handwriting deciphered—one is left with the suspicion that fiction is more satisfying than fact: more competent to capture the mystery and power of a life.

These diligent books are usually compiled by those who believe biography valuable to an understanding of literature but reject the notion that the analysis of an author's work is essential to an understanding of his or her experience. Although their perspective seems opposed to that of the "new critics," who insist that each work of poetry or fiction establishes its own guidelines for study, the two views jointly theorize that biographical and critical explorations are desirably exclusive. Many of us employ this compatibility to nod knowingly in the direction of biography while continuing on our way to the serious business of literary analysis.

There are lives, however, which won't leave one alone: which compel by the psychological problems they raise, which fascinate by their tragic configurations. They promise to reveal the barely submerged secrets of the relationship between art and personality. They whisper confessions of their bondage to social and historical influences. Such lives tempt even the most sceptical to view themselves provisionally as biographers in search of a new form.

For me—Charlotte Brontë's was such a life. It seemed extraordinary, not only in its dramatic power, but in its accessibility. From her childhood, Brontë's fantasies organized themselves into stories which revealed both the shape of a personality struggling for definition and the nature of those forces which conspired to thwart and even to destroy it. Here in the domestic tragedy and the prodigies of juvenile creativity are laid bare the ores from which the profound later works would be refined. An almost unique opportunity for the perception of psychological and artistic formation was afforded.

I saw that there were two dimensions of her too brief self-expression—the life Brontë lived and the life she transmuted into fiction. I perceived the growth of that interaction and knew that its flowering would suggest fresh readings of the novels. It became plain to me that the interaction itself was the critical element. The events of the life could no longer be melodramatically recounted, as they have so often been. The novels could not simply be examined as quirky stages in a developing genre. The centrality of the romantic impulse—the psychosexual and social meaning of the Byronic influence—had to be defined and credited. What emerged was an interpretive critical biography that takes for granted earlier, exhaustive studies, that places chronology at the service of causality, that risks partiality in the interest of emphasis.

Because the nineteenth-century world in which Charlotte Brontë lived is the world which we have ourselves inherited, I discovered that to diagram the process of Brontë's growth was also to explore explicitly formations of the modern female psyche. It was to indicate the nature of the feminist struggle through which men and women today define themselves—both in support and opposition. In our families, in our society, in our political and sexual lives, we are still the victims of the patriarchal forces which protect our economic structures. We continue to reenact our roles in the romantic mythology which embodies and validates that pervasive power. And as we too strive for autonomous definition, we see ourselves reflected in different aspects of Brontë's struggle.

It was for these reasons that I came to write this "life."

But, seeking ostensibly for the "truth," attempting to create a new version of an old literary form, I find that I have done what so many of us always seem to do. I have pursued my own shadow through the beckoning recesses of another's mind, hoping to discover its substance at the journey's end.

But, seeking ostensibly for the "truth," attempting to create a new version of an old literary form, I find that I have done what so many of us always seem to do. I have pursued my own shadow through the beckoning recesses of another's mind, hoping to discover its substance at the journey's end.

Charlotte Brontë: The Self Conceived

CHAPTER ONE

Survival

Lonely as I am—how should I be if Providence had never given me courage to adopt a career—perseverance to plead through two long, weary years with publishers till they admitted me? How should I be with youth past—sisters lost—a resident in a moorland parish where there is not a single educated family? In that case I should have no world at all: the raven, weary of surveying the deluge and without an ark to return to, would be my type. As it is, something like a hope and motive sustains me still. I wish all your daughters—I wish every woman in England had also a hope and motive: Alas, there are many old maids who have neither.[1]

*C*HARLOTTE BRONTË wrote these words at the age of thirty-three at Haworth Parsonage. The same house still sits atop the Yorkshire hills like a ship amidst huge storm-tossed waves. The family with whom she had voyaged—her mother, her brother, her four sisters, had perished. The bodies of all but one lay in the churchyard beyond. No wonder then that she should summon an image of deluge; of herself a raven-survivor. In six years time, like the wearied raven forced to descend, she too would drown.

The Brontë story is mythic in its power, a dramatization of personal needs and historical forces purged of the prosaic. The children—Maria, Elizabeth, Charlotte, Branwell, Emily, and Anne—are proper tragic figures, products of their society, yet

---

1. Charlotte Brontë to W. S. Williams, July 3, 1849. *The Brontës, Their Lives, Friendships and Correspondence in Four Volumes*, ed. Thomas J. Wise and J. Alexander Symington (New York: Oxford University Press, 1933), III, 6. All subsequent references will be given as "Wise and Symington."

strangers to it. The moors of Yorkshire, with their desolate expanse of heath and sky, are their milieu: the wild beauty well-earned by that company of children who could endure the harsh, intemperate seasons.

A woman of twenty-five, Charlotte Brontë wrote:

> My home is humble and unattractive to strangers, but to me it contains what I shall find nowhere else in the world—the profound, the intense affection which brothers and sisters feel for each other when their minds are cast in the same mold, their ideas drawn from the same source—when they have clung to each other from childhood, and when disputes have never sprung up to divide them. . . .[2]

The parsonage and the moors were the only haven that the young Brontës were to know. In the rest of the world, even in Haworth—the town in which they were set apart as the minister's children—they were insecure and alien. Their fierce devotion to one another and to their home grew out of their isolation and confirmed it. Virtually from infancy, they looked to one another for nurturance and support. Their inability to confess to—perhaps even to allow themselves to feel—the common hostilities of sibling rivalry, locked them into painful dependencies on one another which imprisoned even as they solaced.

Their mother, little more than a shadowy presence in their lives, was a crucial force in death. She bore six children in seven years and in the year and a half which followed Anne's birth, she was bedridden. As Elizabeth Gaskell, Charlotte's biographer, was told by a family servant:

> She was not very anxious to see much of her children, probably because the sight of them, knowing how soon they were to be left motherless, would have agitated her too much. So the little things clung quietly together, for their father was busy in his study and in his parish, or with their mother, and they took their meals alone; sat reading, or whispering low, in the "children's study" or wandered out on the hillside, hand in hand.[3]

One can only imagine how traumatic an effect Mrs. Brontë's long painful illness must have had upon them. And the mystery sur-

2. To Henry Nussey, May 9, 1841. Wise and Symington, I, 232.

3. Elizabeth Gaskell, *The Life of Charlotte Brontë* (New York: Dutton, 1971), p. 30. First published 1857.

rounding it, the connection which they might have drawn linking their mother's severe abdominal pains, her childbearing, and her death[4] would have created severe and lasting anxieties of which Charlotte's own lifelong fear of childbearing is but a single example. The actual effect which their mother's death had upon the children's lives—the way in which it touched their minds—is nowhere recorded. But one feels the naiveté of the critics and biographers who have brushed those effects aside, observing that the children were too young and had known their mother too little to have been much moved by the event. The fact that Charlotte speaks only once of Mrs. Brontë in her copious correspondence and journals[5] does not confirm the idea that the memory of her death and dying was so trivial that it could be easily dismissed, but rather suggests that it was so painful that it had to be repressed.

The greater ordeal was still to come. It was the oldest child, Maria, who took their mother's place. She was the "best" of these "good, quiet children": intellectually gifted, humane, and kind; a saint in the judgment of her brother and sisters, adored by her father, enshrined by Charlotte in the portrait of Helen Burns in *Jane Eyre,* a recurrent figure in Branwell's poetry. Her death at the age of twelve (Elizabeth died just a few weeks later) meant to the others the loss of a second mother, better known than the first, perhaps more familiarly—more consciously—loved: a shining ideal, forever fixed, perfect and unattainable.

4. This connection is supported by a recent essay written by Philip Rhodes, an English gynecologist. In "A Medical Appraisal of the Brontës" (*Brontë Society Transactions,* 16, 2 [1971], 102), Dr. Rhodes questions the diagnosis of stomach cancer which was reported by Mrs. Gaskell and accepted ever since. He suggests that it was more likely that Mrs. Brontë died as a result of some chronic disorder consequent upon her rapid childbearing, probably chronic pelvic sepsis together with increasing anemia.

5. When she was thirty-four, Charlotte wrote to her closest friend, Ellen Nussey (February 16, 1850. Wise and Symington, III, 18.)

A few days since, a little incident happened which curiously touched me. Papa put into my hands a little packet of letters, telling me that they were Mamma's, and that I might read them. I did read them, in a frame of mind I cannot describe. The papers were yellow with time, all having been written before I was born. It was strange now to peruse, for the first time, the records of a mind whence my own sprang; and most strange and at once sad and sweet, to find that mind of a truly fine, pure, and elevated order. They were written to Papa before they were married. There is a rectitude, a refinement, a constancy, a modesty, a sense of gentleness about them indescribable. I wish she had lived, and that I had known her.

Again, one imagines. The experience would have been most painfully endured by Charlotte. She and Emily had been sent with the two older girls to the Clergy Daughters' School at Cowan's Bridge. She had watched with full comprehension (the proof is in *Jane Eyre*) Maria's stoical suffering under the harsh regimen there. She had seen her sister's health decline until even the neglectful authorities could no longer ignore the signs of danger. Maria was sent home in the last stages of tuberculosis and died in May. Charlotte was spared the anguished end of the ordeal which Branwell had to bear, but by the time the news of Maria's death had reached Cowan's Bridge, a typhoid epidemic had broken out and Charlotte saw Elizabeth stricken. Now Elizabeth too was sent home, only to die weeks later.

Surrounded by scores of desperately ill children, many of them dying; having to come to terms alone with the fact of Maria's death, the probability of Elizabeth's, the possibility of her own, Charlotte was thrust into a nightmare world of searing, ambivalent feeling. Impotence before circumstances which she could in no way control. Responsibility as the oldest surviving child. And then the guilt and shame which are always the companions of mourners who have been the voyeurs of disaster. Guilt and shame experienced toward the dead whom one has not helped, whom one has allowed to die, whom one has betrayed by remaining alive.[6] The special guilt that Charlotte must have felt at her own pleasure when the epidemic brought to the well children—to her—an alleviation of the usual dreadful routine: a chance to play all day out of doors (as Jane Eyre does) while others inside are dying.

It was an extraordinary burden to carry: this guilt of a child who, having wished for the death of a parent (as most children at some time do) mistakes the wish for the cause. That guilt compounded by the death of a sibling—an older, much admired, always successful sibling who has first competed for nurturance and then herself becomes a nurturing figure, a surrogate mother.

6. See Robert J. Lifton, *History and Human Survival* (New York: Random House, 1970), p. 128. Lifton explains: "For the survivor can never inwardly simply conclude that it was logical and right for him, and not others, to survive. Rather . . . he is bound by an unconscious perception of organic social balance which makes him feel that his survival was made possible by others' deaths: if they had not died, he would have had to, and if he had not survived, someone else would have."

This second death confirming the sense of unworthiness initially aroused by the symbolic rejection of the first. That sense of unworthiness never to be erased.

Guilt, shame, unworthiness, anxiety, insecurity: all were projected onto the hallucinatory visitations from the dead which Charlotte endured throughout her life and recorded in her juvenile fiction, in her journals, and in the novels of her maturity. They are reflected in the recurrent "survivor's dream" which she described as a child to her close friend, Mary Taylor, and which Mary Taylor described, after Brontë's death, to Elizabeth Gaskell.

> She used to speak of her two elder sisters, Maria and Elizabeth, who died at Cowan Bridge. I used to believe them to have been wonders of talent and kindness. She told me, early one morning, that she had just been dreaming: she had been told that she was wanted in the drawing room, and it was Maria and Elizabeth. I was eager for her to go on, and when she said there was no more, I said, "But go on! *make it out*. I know you can." She said she would not; she wished she had not dreamed, for it did not go on nicely; they were changed; they had forgotten what they used to care for. They were very fashionably dressed, and began criticising the room, etc.[7]

While anxiety and fear found expression in dream and transmutation in the games and imaginings of childhood, the events which had given them form remained too threatening to be directly faced.

Reunited at Haworth after their sisters' deaths, the four children began their long journey of escape. Experience had taught them to expect the worst of an alien and hostile world. Never after would they be able to meet strangers with anything less than suspicion. Agonizingly shy and withdrawn, they clung together, drawing a circle round themselves. Inside its limits they allowed their minds to stretch, their imaginations to grow. Here they revealed themselves to one another in a fantasy language which they alone could understand.

The boundaries of that world were inviolable. Even those who shared their home were excluded. There was an aunt, a strict Calvinist, who came to live with them. Possessed of a rigid and

---

7. Wise and Symington, I, 91.

unyielding nature, she attempted to take charge of their souls but succeeded primarily in looking after their bodies. Of their emotional conflicts, of their intellectual and creative achievements, she seems to have remained largely ignorant. In their servant, Tabby, they found an affectionate but necessarily distanced presence. Only their father touched them in an important way—and only he had a formative influence upon their secret world and its development.

Like many another Victorian patriarch, Patrick Brontë bound his children to him by the strength of a fiercely dominating personality balanced by an undeniable capacity for love. His wit amused them, his intelligence stimulated them, his reading and writing shaped their aspirations and formed their tastes. An Irishman by birth, the eldest of ten children, Patrick had been carried to Cambridge by ambition and curiosity; to the Anglican ministry by ambition and self-discipline. He was suited to his profession by unwavering principles and a moral fiber which was durable. Of more importance to his children, there was in him as well the shadow of a failed writer. In the nine years of his marriage, he had published a volume of religious poetry and two didactic and sentimental novels intended for the "common reader." The writer's need and aspiration had to some degree been his. The imaginative territory which his son and daughters explored was terrain over which he himself had wandered.

In matters of education, Patrick Brontë had apparently been influenced by the theories of Rousseau. He believed in the importance of freedom and the advantages of an active out-of-door life. While he served as the children's tutor, he left them largely to their own devices—attending to his ministerial duties, taking his meals by himself.[8] He shared with them, to an unusual extent, his views, his journals, and his library. Although he was a committed Tory, he nevertheless reserved the right to follow his own conscience and reach his own conclusions. To be informed of both sides of every issue he subscribed to Tory and Whig newspapers. His own love of independence and his sympathy with the working classes had liberalized his political views.[9] He was more

8. Throughout his life, Patrick Brontë ate his meals alone, apparently because of a persistent and probably nervous stomach disorder.

9. It is interesting to note that Brontë supported the first reform bill of 1832. His position was too liberal for his children—they opposed it—but that

flexible too in sexual matters than was common for his time and spoke up vigorously against the unjust treatment of women. He went so far on one occasion as to advise an ill-used wife to leave her husband.[10]

From conversations with their father, the children acquired a love of debate and argument. From him they derived a sense of the centrality of politics in human affairs, the appeal of the military, the lure of power. In his library they first discovered those works which helped form their adolescent interests and fantasies: Homer and Virgil in the original (although only Branwell, the son, was educated in the classics), Milton's works, Johnson's *Lives of the Poets,* Thompson's *Seasons,* Goldsmith's *History of Rome,* Hume's *History of England,* Scott's *Life of Napoleon Bonaparte,* and the works of Cowper, Southey, and—most importantly—of Byron.[11] It was their father also who catalyzed their creative energies, presenting a set of wooden soldiers to Branwell in June 1826, just one year after the deaths of Maria and Elizabeth. The soldiers comprised the dramatis personae for the games, plays, and ultimately the "Glass-Town" literature which first preoccupied and then obsessed the Brontës into adulthood.

Fannie Ratchford has provided an invaluable chronicle of the development of the Brontë juvenilia from the little plays and magazines produced by the four children in collaboration with one another to the sophisticated collections of stories and poems which belonged to two different kingdoms separately conceived: Angria, invented by Charlotte and Branwell, and Gondal, created by Emily and Anne.[12] (The two collaborations determined the configuration of division and companionship which extended to adulthood. Charlotte stood outside of her sisters' secret lives as they were excluded from hers and Branwell's.) The children's fantasies were focused here. Their needs and deprivations found

---

they were influenced by his open-mindedness is suggested in their later writings, most notably in *Shirley.*

10. Annette Hopkins, *The Father of the Brontës* (Baltimore: Johns Hopkins Press, 1958), p. 63. Hopkins also points out that in the baptismal records Patrick Brontë inserted the full parentage of each child instead of indicating just the father's name, as was the custom.

11. Winifred Gerin, *Charlotte Brontë, The Evolution of Genius* (New York: Oxford University Press, 1967), p. 24.

12. Fannie Ratchford, *The Brontë's Web of Childhood* (New York: Russell and Russell, 1964).

form in wishes and dreams which could be shared and structured into art. Mary Taylor, writing of Charlotte's preference for imaginative activity over all other forms of play, explained the process to Gaskell:

> The habit of "making out" interests for themselves, that most children get who have none in actual life was very strong in her. The whole family used to "make out" histories, and invent characters and events. I told her sometimes they were like growing potatoes in a cellar. She said, sadly, "Yes! I know we are!"[13]

Angria had as its hero no lesser a man than Arthur Wellesley, the first duke of Wellington. He was adored by all the children and had long occupied a central position in Charlotte's imagination. She admired him profoundly for his self-control and strong sense of duty, qualities she wished that she could herself possess. But Byron, the second hero who dominated the imaginative lives at Haworth, expressed deeper aspirations; the repressed needs and feared passions of her "other" self. The two men established the polar possibilities of definition both for her and for the heroines of her novels, serving functions not unlike those served by Rochester and St. John Rivers for Jane Eyre.

II

The children's first memorable contact with Byron has been traced back to August, 1825, when, in a *Blackwood's* review of Parry's *Last Days of Lord Byron,* they first learned the circumstances of the poet's death and began fitting his legend into the pattern of the Napoleonic wars which had already kindled their imaginations. From this time "Byron's name was synonomous with everything that was forbidden and daring."[14]

By the time she was thirteen, Charlotte was fully acquainted with Byron's work. In 1829, after reading Branwell's copy of "Childe Harold," she modeled Arthur Wellesley (also known as the Marquis of Douro and the Duke of Zamorna), the duke of Wellington's eldest son, after her understanding of Byron's character. By her fifteenth year, when she was well into her adoles-

13. Gaskell, p. 68.
14. Winifred Gerin, "Byron's Influence on the Brontës," *Keats-Shelley Memorial Bulletin,* 17 (1966), 2.

cence, Zamorna had completely replaced his father as the hero of Angria. This description of him, written several years later, leaves no question about Zamorna's ancestry:

> His figure was toweringly, overbearingly lofty, molded in statue-like perfection, and invested with something I cannot describe—something superb, impetuous, resistless. His hair was intensely black, curled luxuriantly, but the forehead underneath . . . looked white and smooth as ivory. His eyebrows were black and broad, but his long eye-lashes and large clear eyes were deep sepia brown. . . . The upper lip was very short—Grecian—and had a haughty curl. . . . At the first glance I discerned him to be a military man.[15]

As the description suggests, it was Zamorna's sexual magnetism rather than his military exploits that most interested Charlotte, even if the latter were Branwell's primary concern.

In fact, the collaboration between brother and sister had taken an interesting turn during their adolescent years. Branwell continued to take the lead, as he had always done, outlining elaborately complicated plots which Charlotte was able to validate through her growing mastery of characterization. Both were preoccupied with power. But while Branwell's fantasies were still concerned with martial accomplishments, political intrigue, and the building of empires, Charlotte fantasized about social and psychological interaction in a world of wits and beautiful women; about courtships and, increasingly, about seduction and adultery. As Branwell was enraptured by the possibilities of political power, so Charlotte became obsessed with the implications of sexual domination. If Branwell saw that Zamorna's courage and treacherous cunning made it inevitable that he could conquer kingdoms, Charlotte perceived that his capacity for feeling would make it impossible for women to resist him. In creating their characters they were responding to the Byronic vision which represented the Zeitgeist of their time. To understand the effect that Byron had upon them, one must understand this larger cultural phenomenon.

The Byronic hero and Lord Byron the poet—the vision and the man—were inseparable in the public mind. From the time of

---

15. "My Angria and the Angrians," October 1834, Brontë Parsonage Museum.

Childe Harold's publication in 1812, Byron was—first in England and then throughout Europe—the embodiment of the Romantic movement. In his life and in his work he was its spokesman and its symbol. He represented the possibility of escaping from or rebelling against the pressures exerted by a society in the process of radical change: an increasingly industrialized society which decreasingly valued the individual. It was a society which—as major twentieth-century psychohistorians have pointed out—thwarted the satisfaction of those needs most fundamental to personal happiness: the pleasure principle placed at the service of the performance principle.[16] It was a society which purchased the souls of its members with the metallic coinage of materialism. More spiritual ideals of self-realization would yield to a narrower standard of physical self-interest. The Victorians experienced the full effects of industrialization. The Romantics simply felt the first waves of instability and reacted to them by attempting to assert the ascendancy of the individual and the primacy of feeling. Byron was the supreme embodiment of this effort, standing not only against a dehumanized system of labor but also against traditionally repressive religious, social, and familial institutions. He spoke not only to members of the aristocracy and upper-middle class who shared his educational background and condoned his sexual habits. He spoke also to members of the burgeoning lower-middle class—the small capitalists, tradesmen, and clerks—to all who felt themselves alienated, wasted, and unfulfilled.

Club-footed from birth, morose in public, temperamental and mercurial, Byron seemed to bear the ominous mark of Cain. A descendent of two eccentric and dissolute aristocratic families,

16. See, for example, Sigmund Freud, *Civilization and Its Discontents,* trans. and ed. James Strachey (New York: W. W. Norton, 1961); Herbert Marcuse, *Eros and Civilization* (New York: Vintage Books, 1955); Norman O. Brown, *Life Against Death* (New York: Vintage Books, 1959). Marcuse explains, ". . . the necessity of repression, and of the suffering derived from it, varies with the maturity of civilization, with the extent of the achieved rational mastery of nature and of society. Objectively, the need for instinctual inhibition and restraint depends on the need for toil and delayed satisfaction. . . . (In) the system of institutional authority characteristic of mature civilization, domination becomes increasingly impersonal, objective, universal, and also increasingly rational, effective, productive. At the end, under the rule of the fully developed performance principle, subordination appears as implemented through the social division of labour itself. . . . Society emerges as a lasting and expanding system of useful performances . . ." (pp. 80–81)

living a profligate life while identifying himself with liberal causes (the Nottingham weavers during the Luddite uprisings, Catholic emancipation; lastly, Greek independence) Byron appeared to be divorced from class and even national affiliation. Pursued by women everywhere he went, dropping mistresses like pocket-handkerchiefs, he dared finally to commit the one moral crime which his society fantasized about but would not forgive. He maintained an incestuous relationship with his half-sister, Augusta Leigh, and flaunted it before his wife and friends. Divorced and ostracized, forced to leave England, Byron spent the last eight years of his life living promiscuously and writing in Switzerland and Italy, dying finally in Greece, where he had gone to join the rebellion against the Turks.

Byron's hero was modeled upon the role which the poet himself had chosen to play. Misanthropic and adventurous, he also defined himself as rebel. He not only rejected the ugliness of the new world he saw coming to birth, but also the old repressions of the world from which it had descended. Central to his rebellion was the assertion of a self freed from external limitations and control. Without religion, he proclaimed himself his own God, master of his own fate. Living as an outlaw, he rejected society's claims and rewards, even its punishments. Emerging from a mysterious past, he was without apparent familial ties, most notably, perhaps, without a father. Promethean, he was courageous, proud and ambitious, and asserted as his primary power his ability to shape his own destiny, even if that destiny was death.

Although the Byronic hero is a radical and rebel, he cannot be a revolutionary. Having rejected his culture he exists in isolation. All of his efforts refer essentially to himself: to his own feelings, his own sensations, his own capacities. Because his isolation is unbearable, he undertakes the romantic quest: to resolve aesthetically or erotically the subject-object conflict—obliterating the division between the "I" and the "not-I" by fusing the two in a redemptive state of feeling. To those who were part of Byron's cult, the drive for integration was focused in eroticism. The search by the self for "the other" was intended to culminate in physical and spiritual union. But the effort did not advance beyond narcissism. The result was quite different from the ideal. Instead of the oceanic feeling which allows the self to negate and transcend its own limits, union is realized through a pattern of

domination in which the ego masters and absorbs "the other."
Metaphysical striving acquires a political form. Questions concerning the structure of reality and modes of knowing are resolved into far more concrete problems of dominance and submission. That such relationships will be sadomasochistic to
varying degrees seems inevitable since they are defined by subjugation and the exercise of power.[17] It is in this nexus that the
work of Brontë and Byron is joined. The myth of romantic love
articulated—as Byron himself acted out and as Brontë's life and
works archetypically captured—the sexual fantasies shared by
middle- and upper-class men and women. Once scrutinized, the
myth discloses those economic and social forces which determine
the nature of psychosexual interaction.

The advent of industrialization and the growth of the middle
class was accompanied by a more diffuse yet more virulent form
of patriarchy than any that had existed before. As men became
uniquely responsible for the support of the family, women became "possessions," identified with their "masters' " wealth.
The status of the male owner derived from the extent of his
woman's leisure time and the degree of her emotional and physical dependence upon him. Sexual relationships followed a similar
pattern of dominance and submission. Male power was affirmed
through an egoistic, aggressive, even violent sexuality. Female
sexuality was passive and self-denying. The woman, by wilfully
defining herself as "the exploited," as "victim"; by seeing herself as she was reflected in the male's perception of her, achieved
the only kind of control available to her. Mutuality was extraordinarily difficult, if not impossible, to achieve.[18]

17. Gregory Zilborg observes: "I might suggest that future researches into
the psychology and origin of the economic factors of human culture might very
well prove that property originated in the sadistic act of overcoming the free
mother—women may be considered chronologically the first piece of property,
in the true sense of the word, in that sense which Ward defined with unique simplicity and brilliance: Property is possession beyond one's immediate needs. It
was the possession beyond his immediate, purely sexual needs that man established over women." "Masculine and Feminine: Some Biological and Cultural Aspects," in *Psychoanalysis and Women,* ed. Jean Baker Miller, M.D.
(Baltimore: Penguin, 1973), p. 119.

18. The conflicts involved in this extremely complex sadomasochistic
relationship are brilliantly, if only half-consciously, revealed in Samul Rich-
ardson's mid–eighteenth-century novel, *Clarissa.* Written when the forces of
capitalism were only beginning to exert pressure upon religious, sexual, social,
and familial values, *Clarissa* contains, significantly enough, the first of the

So the reasons for Byron's symbolic importance begin to emerge. The ideal by which Byron attempted to define his life expressed not only personal but collective longings for psychic and social liberation. But the reality of his circumstances betrayed the potency of the forces which obstructed freedom and thwarted realization. In his own relationships with women, and in the relationships which he created for his heroes, the poet expressed the complex destructive and self-destructive attitudes which define romantic love. In him the desire to obliterate the boundaries between the "I" and the "not-I," between the self and "the other," is channeled by a culturally formed and supported sexism. For all his rebelliousness, he was the product of his society—prey to its patriarchal neuroticism. He was open in his disdain of women. He not only avowed his dislike of them, he acted out that dislike in sadistic behavior that ranged from the subtle to the absurd.[19] If he did not himself pursue women, he did rely on their pursuit of him. His vanity was fed by their admiration, but the more they admired, the more he despised them for the weakness they betrayed. The eroticism they offered was not desired because it yielded knowledge of "the other," thereby expanding the limits of the self, but because, in the stimulation of his own sensibilities, he was better able to feel himself feeling. Certainly he preferred the company of men. Here were his intellectual and spiritual equals. And if rumors of homosexuality surrounded him, that reality would have been more appropriate than ironic. If love as mutuality was in fact at all possible it was most likely to be realized with others of his own sex. If love of himself were primary, homosexuality was one expression of that narcissism.

In all likelihood, then, Byron's incestuous love of his sister represented more than a simple act of rebellion: a form of the

---

proto-Byronic heroes—Lovelace. This emphasizes the fact that Byron himself served to focus forces which had been actively at work in the culture for a substantial period of time.

19. Speaking of Byron's attitudes toward women at the time of the publication of *Childe Harold,* Leslie Marchand observes: ". . . he had always been most successful with girls below his intellectual level, with those who had flattered his ego and looked up with awe at his title, and he had come to have a kind of oriental scorn of women as creatures in no way capable of sharing a man's thoughts or feelings." (*Byron: A Biography* [New York: Alfred A. Knopf, 1957], I, 330.)

romantic commitment to the forbidden. It was a perfect compromise, expressive of the romantic impulse, linking implied ideals of narcissism with those of heterosexual love. In his union with Augusta Leigh, Byron was in fact striving to achieve union with himself: attempting to become purely self-dependent by possessing his past in his present, affirming a more complete identity by enveloping and containing his other, complementary self. But to incorporate "the other" is also after all to negate it. No space remains for the female. She can either allow herself to be devoured or she can retreat into isolation.

A form of love which is inseparable from annihilation must threaten the lover as well as the beloved. Byron betrays his fear of his own destructive power when he writes of one of his mistresses:

> . . . the Guiccioli is going into a consumption. Thus it is with everything and everybody for whom I feel anything like a real attachment . . . I never even could keep alive a dog that I liked or liked me.[20]

The romantic rebellion which has as its urge the desire to reorder reality in a transcendent unity has as its effect sadism or solipsism. Erotic love, ideally the neutralizer of power, proves instead to be power's most lethal weapon.

The road that points to freedom is paved in fantasy. At its end lies disullusionment. The rebel builds the guillotine for his own beheading. Byron, the symbol of romanticism, was ironically a neoclassicist. His affinity was with the eighteenth century. Theoretically searching for an antiauthoritarian system of values, Byron's great giftedness was as a satirist. In assuming this essentially conservative stance, he wedded himself to his society—criticizing but never denying it altogether. It is not surprising that his life was characterized by frustration, cynicism, and remorse, that his death was a gesture toward liberty and a veiled suicide. He mounted the revolution and betrayed it, reenacting the plight of most revolutionaries who are defeated by their identification with the power they strive to overthrow.[21]

20. Quoted in Peter Quennell, *Byron in Italy* (London: Collins, 1951), p. 156.

21. "In every revolution, there seems to have been a historical moment when the struggle against domination might have been victorious—but the moment passed. An element of *self-defeat* seems to be involved in this dynamic

As children, Charlotte and Branwell participated in Byron's mass romantic dream-wish. Identifying with the striving, they were unaware of the contradictions. They adored the hero and never tried to analyze the man. For them, the heroic fantasy of romantic love concretized in their writing was particularly powerful. They were not able to recognize its dangers because they had minimal contact with a reality that could offer a corrective perspective. To disengage themselves from delusion, they would have had to understand and control in their own lives the social and psychosexual forces which were acting through them. For Branwell, this was impossible. His identification with the romantic hero was immediate, total, and ultimately fatal. His self-destruction of course assumed a parodic form: he was a pitiable Manfred. But although his conflict was domesticated, its outlines were familiar and its end predictable. He was trapped in the mythological mode as Byron had been himself. Charlotte's problem was more complex. Because she was female, her identification with their beloved, Byronic Zamorna was equivocal. She could not, after all, *be* the fantasized hero. She was, in fact, "the other." The dream by which she was fascinated could not contain her. The need for psychic expression propelled her from the paralysis of myth into the surging reality of history and the complexities of society. For her, the creation of Angria initiated a long and painful process of self-investigation which did finally yield to discovery and knowledge: to a true if tragic freedom.

III

Branwell was a victim of the romantic illusion as it was molded by the mythologies of Victorian life—for the Brontë family, with all its eccentricities, was quintessentially Victorian in its

---

(regardless of the validity of such reasons as the prematurity and inequality of forces). In this sense, every revolution had also been a betrayed revolution.

Freud's hypothesis on the origin and the perpetuation of guilt feelings elucidates, in psychological terms, this sociological dynamic: It explains the 'identification' of those who revolt with the power against which they revolt." (Marcuse, pp. 82–83.)

Fred Weinstein and Gerald Platt, in *The Wish to Be Free* (Berkeley: University of California Press, 1969), concern themselves with the insecurities that naturally accompany an attack on a contemporary system of values and the anxieties which are part of an attempt to build a system of values from within.

structures and patterns of interaction. He was the gifted only son of a powerful, domineering father: the adored only brother of three adoring sisters:

> If Branwell Brontë was born with an extravagant sense of the high destiny he could achieve, he was not alone in holding it; it was fostered and fanned by all those who stood nearest to him and who, from the beginning, made a distinction in his treatment from that of his sisters. In this, it should hastily be added, his sisters themselves wholeheartedly shared, neither questioning nor seeking to undermine the position accorded their only brother. The little girls might receive the petting of servants, the confidence and attention of their father, but it was Branwell who was the main purpose, the fond hope and pride of that bereaved father's heart.[22]

As in most Victorian families, the girls did not share in the freedom and absence of discipline which characterized their brother's childhood and adolescence. Theirs was the awareness and habitual practice of duties and obligations thought to be appropriate to the lives of women.

> . . . any one passing by the kitchen door, might have seen (Emily) studying German out of an open book, propped up before her, as she kneaded the dough; but no study, however interesting, interfered with the goodness of the bread, which was always light and excellent. Books were, indeed, a very common sight in that kitchen; the girls were taught by their father—theoretically and by their aunt practically, that to take part in the household work was, in their position, women's simple duty; but in their careful employment of time, they found many an odd five minutes for reading while watching the cakes, and managed the union of two kinds of employment better than King Alfred.[23]

What they could only do in their spare time and what they could only fantasize about, Branwell—the male, the son, the brother—could become. He could be their effective agent in the world, well worth the sacrifice of personal achievement.

From his family and his admiring friends in the little village of Haworth, Branwell derived a sense of his own position which

22. Winifred Gerin, *Branwell Brontë* (London: Thomas Nelson and Sons, 1961), p. 2.
23. Gaskell, p. 91.

was as inflated as the self-image which he synthesized from his reading and writing. Neither was tested externally. Although he, as the Brontë male, was always intended to represent the others in the active competitive world beyond the parsonage, he was the least fitted to venture outside the threshold of his imagination. While his sisters had been forced—first at Cowan Bridge, later at Miss Wooler's school at Roe Head—to measure their illusions against reality, Mr. Brontë would not trust Branwell's education to any direction but his own. The course of study he followed emphasized the heroic example and the military ideal. The father's reverence for the real and fictitious heroes of history and literature was echoed in the son's admiration of Napolean and Wellington. That Branwell's reading provided his private and literary fantasies is suggested by the titles of his first two "books": "My Battell Book," written when he was nine, and "History of the Rebellion in my Army," a product of his eleventh year. The themes of these early attempts reemerged in more complex and intricate forms in his adolescent fiction, but they never really changed. In a similar way, his heroes remained much the same throughout his literary career, although his identification with them became more intimate as his worldly ambitions were thwarted.

One is forced to ask how this isolated, protected boy—stunted in size, ignorant of the sophisticated world—could formulate in personal terms the heroic ideal which was fundamental to his concept of masculine effectiveness. The compromise he reached with the help of his family might seem at first to have been eminently sensible. He focused his hopes on his giftedness as an artist. Like his sisters, he aspired to being a painter. Unlike them, his aspirations were taken seriously—more seriously than his talent warranted. The admiration of his family had weakened him for the task of testing himself against the formidable model which had been defined by them and by his own illusions. To match this model he would have had to expand himself tenfold. The fragile threads with which we are all bound together frayed through as Branwell first rubbed against the abrasive world outside.

To sacrifice for his success was, of course, part of the responsibility of the women. His aunt drew from her small store of savings an amount which would be adequate to subsidize his journey to London and his education there at the schools of the Royal Academy of Arts. It was also part of Charlotte's professed obligation to take upon herself the hateful task of governess-teacher at Roe Head, so that she could contribute to Branwell's support.

But others' sacrifices could not substitute for personal self-confidence. How unheroic and sad a tale it is: this history of Branwell's brief stay in London, his inability to present for judgment the best of his work which he had brought with him: his inability to do anything, apparently, but drink away his money, miserably aware of his own failure and cowardice.[24] How unlike his revered heroes he must have felt when he returned to the security of his home—to his father, his sisters, the friends in his tiny village—telling vague tales about robbers who had set upon him and stolen everything he had. At nineteen he was overwhelmed by the world of possibilities which lay beyond Haworth. He had received a blow from which he would never recover. Failure followed failure. Branwell turned from painting to sculpture. The unsuccessful sculptor became a careless and lazy tutor. The tutor gave way to a debauched railway clerk, ultimately dismissed for a default in his accounts. His last tutoring job culminated in an adulterous affair with his student's mother, raging dismissal by the deceived husband, a horrible decline and miserable death. Through it all Branwell never surrendered his romantic aspirations, although the forms into which they were translated became increasingly parodic: bizarre actualizations of nightmare.

In his obsession with boxing, Branwell continued to express the need to prove himself physically, to find a substitute for heroic exploits and military trials. Gambling provided his only excitement. Alcohol and eventually opium were his primary means of escape. As he became increasingly absorbed in his fantasy-worlds, even his ties to his family were gnawed. His guilt and sense of inadequacy, as well as their disapproval, alienated him. He had lost his childhood and could not find his place as a man:

> Yes—now at last I've reached my native home,
> And all who love me joy to see me come . . .
> I have seen my Father full of honoured days,

24. See Gerin's account of this stage of Branwell's life, in *Branwell Brontë*, pp. 95–110.

> Whom last I saw adorned with manhood's grace . . .
>   . . . I have seen her too
> The first I loved on earth—the first I knew—
> She who was wont above that very bed
> To bend with blessing o'er my helpless head,
> I have seen my sister—I have seen them all—
> All but myself. They have lost me past recall,
> As I have them. And vainly have I come
> Three thousand leagues—my Home is not my Home.[25]

Feeling himself inadequate to the roles defined for him as only son and brother and unable to translate his fantasy-self into reality, Branwell increasingly identified with his fictive hero, the rebellious Northangerland—Zamorna's rival, a more mature version of the "Rogue" of his childhood. He could not confront real people or real feelings. Mary Taylor, Charlotte's extraordinary girlhood friend, a feminist and radical, terrified him into flight by falling in love with him. Charlotte writes of the events to Ellen Nussey:

> Did I not once tell you of an instance of a Relative of mine who cared for a young lady till he began to suspect that she cared more for him and then instantly conceived a sort of contempt for her? You know to what I allude—never as you value your ears mention the circumstance—But I have two studies—*you* are my study for the success of a quiet, tranquil character. Mary is my study—for the contempt, the remorse—the misconstruction which followed the development of feelings in themselves noble, warm—generous—devoted and profound— but which being too freely revealed—too frankly bestowed— are not estimated at their real value—God bless her—I never hope to see in this world a character more truly noble—she would *die* willingly for one she loved—her intellect and her attainments are of the very highest standard yet I doubt whether Mary will ever marry.[26]

Mary's love did indeed represent the ultimate threat to the instability of romantic subjectivity: a threat of equality. From her there would have been insupportable expectations and demands.

25. From Branwell's poem, "The Wanderer," later retitled "Sir Henry Tunstall," published in Mrs. Oliphant's *Annals of a Publishing House* (1897) and in the *DeQuincey Memorials* in 1891.
26. November 20, 1840. Wise and Symington, I, 221–22.

It was preferable to him to play at being his own hero, Northangerland; to indulge, as Byron had, in adulterous games which never had to be won: to court a woman who—married— was unattainable, although she held out the promise of ideal union. And so he "fell in love" with Lydia Robinson, the mother of the boy he tutored. It was an outrageous business, but he fiercely seized the opportunity which had been offered him to give everything to love and, finding it inadequate, to die. The fact that Mrs. Robinson was apparently incapable of feeling, that when her husband died she rejected Branwell completely—and dishonestly—in order to marry an "eligible" old man; this all demonstrated the self-destructive nature of his delusions and his behavior.

In the three years that followed his separation from Lydia Robinson and preceded his death, Branwell was finally able to bring to fruition in himself a demonic if perversely domestic version of the Byronic hero. Although he plays the part of rebel in the Brontë myth, his situation was marked by agonizing depen- dence. He was dependent upon alcohol and opium, the primary causes of his death. He was dependent upon his sisters who nursed him, paid his debts, and provided an audience for his melodrama of disintegration—representing in their horror and disapproval, the "society" of which he saw himself as victim. But most of all he was dependent upon his father. Of all the emo- tional dependencies which he had not been able to outgrow, this was the most profound:

> I know only that it is time for me to be something when I am nothing. That my Father cannot have long to live, and that when he dies, my evening, which is already twilight, will become night—That I shall then have a constitution so strong that it will keep me years in torture and despair when I should every hour pray that I might die.[27]

He played at the oedipal battle as he had played at love. There was never any contest, although there were absurd charades of vi- olent rebellion:

> For some time before his death he had attacks of delirium tremens of the most frightful character; he slept in his father's

27. To J. B. Leyland, January 24, 1847. Wise and Symington, II, 124.

room, and he would sometimes declare that either he or his father should be dead before morning. The trembling sisters,
sick with fright, would implore their father not to expose himself to this danger; but Mr. Brontë is no timid man, and perhaps he felt that he could possibly influence his son to some
self-restraint, more by showing trust in him than by showing
fear. The sisters often listened for the report of a pistol in the
dead of night, till watchful eye and hearkening ear grew heavy
and dull with the perpetual strain upon their nerves. In the
mornings young Brontë would saunter out, saying with a
drunkard's incontinence of speech, "The poor old man and I
have had a terrible night of it; he does his best—the poor old
man: but it's all over with me . . ."[28]

The urge to self-destruction was supreme. He died in his father's
arms.

IV

The course which Branwell's life followed profoundly affected Charlotte's personal and artistic development. Initially,
she defined herself almost exclusively in terms of their sym-
biosis. In its way, their relationship was as incestuous as was
Byron's with Augusta Leigh. Theirs was not an incest of body
but of mind: an incest of the imagination. In the intense privacy
of shared fantasy, their identities were fused. Eventually, in order
to free herself, Charlotte would find it necessary to initiate a violent separation which helped to destroy the pattern of Branwell's
self-image and rend the fabric of his life. It seemed that nothing
less than this could release her from the bonds woven by the concentration of their familial situation. In the course of their relationship, Charlotte's art offered her the means of exploring and
expressing aspects of her feeling for Branwell which she could
not consciously accept. Their collaborative efforts were tunneled
by dark passageways through which Charlotte burrowed in search
of hidden sources of illumination which could irradiate her consciousness.

Ellen Nussey, reminiscing about the nature of Charlotte's attachment to Branwell when she and Charlotte were adolescents at
the Roe Head School, recalls:

28. Gaskell, pp. 197–98.

> . . . he was *then* a very dear brother, as dear to Charlotte as
> her own soul; they were in perfect accord of taste and feeling,
> and it was mutual delight to be together. . . . Happy, indeed,
> she then was, in Himself, for she, with her own enthusiasms,
> looked forward to what her brother's great promise and talent
> might effect.[29]

To accept unquestioningly the reality of such complete harmony, such complacent idolatry, is impossible, although one can accept the appearance of its existence on a conscious level. The complementary ambivalence which we suspect is indeed found in Charlotte's writing, rather than in her friendly confidences or overt behavior.

Her initial criticisms are humorous and tolerant. At the age of thirteen Charlotte had produced a volume entitled "Characters of the Great Men of the Present Time," authored by "Captain Tree," one of the many male personae she adopted in her juvenile writings. In the characters of Captain Bud and Young Salt the Rhymer, she drew the first two of a series of satirical portraits of Branwell, exaggerating those faults with which she was all too familiar: his tendency to bombast, his poetic effusions, his "tiresome gravity," his nervous disposition, and inflamed imagination.[30]

By this time Charlotte had taken the first crucial steps toward independence, but the early recognitions which she made and the minimal criticism which she allowed herself had little actual effect upon her relationship with Branwell or upon her sense of herself within that relationship. Rational analysis is generally inadequate to psychic defense. Branwell could, after all, be forgiven his flaws. Flaws—even vices—were central to the romantic concept of masculinity, It was part of the female's role to understand and overlook. Patience, understanding, tolerance, duty—these were aspects of the self-abnegating personality which complemented the idolatrous needs of the masculine posture.[31] Much

29. "Reminiscences of Charlotte Brontë by 'E,' " *Scribner's Monthly,* II (1871), quoted in Wise and Symington, I, 106.

30. Ratchford, pp. 28–29.

31. I have no desire to further the debate about the nature and sources of female masochism. My intention is not to discuss pathological states but to indicate, in a nonclinical way, general patterns of psychosexual interaction. I accept the point of view of many contemporary psychoanalysts—some of them quite traditional—who describe masochism as part of an adaptational apparatus

stronger than rational analysis were the social forces which inhibited even normal levels of female aggression and stunted women's intellectual and psychic growth; forces which defined marriage as women's only appropriate occupation and nurturance as their only mode of relation.[32]

Already plagued by the survivor's sense of inadequacy and guilt, Charlotte must easily have fallen prey to masochistic submission. She would have embraced the domination of her father and brother, accepted the social pressures as interpreted by her aunt. She would have recognized the wisdom of purchasing love with self-denial. Then, feeling exploited, she would have turned the anger back upon herself transmuting it to self-doubt, finding that preferable to being alienated from those upon whom she was so painfully dependent.[33]

Both Mary Taylor and Ellen Nussey remembered most vividly their friend's extraordinary "sense of duty"—that quality she so admired in the duke of Wellington. Both recalled how conscientiously she studied at Roe Head, never playing with the other children, avoiding competitive activity, ever mindful of the expense of her education, intent on becoming a governess—a job

---

rather than an instinctual drive. See, for example: Irving Bieber, M.D., "The Meaning of Masochism," *American Journal of Psychotherapy,* 7 (1953), 443–48; Marcia Cavell, "Since 1924: Toward a New Psychopathology of Women," *Woman and Analysis,* ed. Jean Strouse (New York: Grossman, 1974); Helene Deutsch, *The Psychology of Women,* I (New York: Bantam, 1973).

32. John Stuart Mill wrote in 1869 in *The Subjugation of Women:* "All the moralities tell women that it is their duty and all the current sentimentalities that it is their nature to live for others; to make complete abnegation of themselves, and to have no life but in their affections." Women's psychological plight was intensified by their economic dependence and many social Darwinians (Freudians came later) rationalized the belief in women's biological and intellectual inferiority.

33. "Masochism is not an instinct; it is an adaptational device. The pain, or its equivalents, is never sought or self-inflicted for the pleasure in the pain, per se . . . the apparent pleasure is both a facade to cover up the intense underlying hostile responses consequent to the masochistic act, and an attempt at self-conviction that the sustained injury is not painful but even pleasurable, to prevent the expression of this hostility. Hostility always accompanies the masochistic act and is directed toward the feared person from whom the injury is expected and for whom the defensive masochistic act is being performed. Since this hostility frequently cannot be openly expressed, it feeds back by being turned inwards and increases his masochism." (Bieber, p. 447.) See also Karen Horney, "The Problem of Female Masochism," *Psychoanalysis and Women,* ed. Jean Baker Miller, M.D. (Baltimore: Penguin Books, 1973).

she dreaded except for the fact that it would allow her to maintain herself and help the others, particularly Branwell. Ellen Nussey's account of Charlotte's single attempt at self-assertion, her single public expression of a desire *not* to be "good," is profoundly moving:

> The last day Charlotte was at school she seemed to realize what a sedate, hard-working season it had been to her. She said, "I should for once like to feel *out and out* a school-girl; I wish something would happen. Let us run round the fruit-garden (running was what she never did); perhaps we shall meet some one, or we may have a fine for trespass." She evidently was longing for some never-to-be forgotten incident. Nothing, however, arose from her little enterprise. She had to leave school as calmly and quietly as she had there lived.[34]

Similar fears inform a dream of her early adolescence. It was recorded in one of her "little books," and is described by Lucile Dooley, an early biographer:

> (She speaks) of finding herself in a cave under the ocean, of feeling the terror of the walls heaving and cracking, of the floods about to overwhelm her. Then the scene changed to a desert and a roaring lion rushed toward her while she remained rooted to the spot.[35]

Both the dream and the thwarted schoolgirl experience suggest the extraordinary repression which characterized Charlotte's inner life and colored her behavior—the flimsiness of her defense against the attacks of the external world. The point would seem to be that in these adolescent years Charlotte, overwhelmed by her sense of inadequacy, denied her needs, repressed her anger, and withdrew into a womblike world of fantasy. There in Angria the raging lion of sexuality could be controlled in the same process of sublimation which made all of her desires and anxieties, her guilt and her fear, manageable.

The dream image is compelling. This secret fantasy world became her second Eden and she protected the repressed self which dwelt within it from any contact with a threatening reality. Her

34. Wise and Symington, I, 100.

35. Lucile Dooley, "Psychoanalysis of Charlotte Brontë as a Type of the Woman of Genius," *The American Journal of Psychology*, 31 (July 1920), 243.

tiny, cramped handwriting, virtually unreadable, is the most direct clue to Charlotte's relation to her work. She kept her stories secret from her friends. Only Mary was told of the "magazines" the children wrote and she was never shown any of them.[36] It was Branwell alone who shared this interior space: her vital self. Towards him, free of care and responsibility, beloved, so full of promise in these years, her feelings must have been increasingly ambivalent: resentment tinging, then suffusing, dependence. It was not simply that Branwell, although younger, was, as a male, the one sibling with whom she could not compete. It was not simply that he was the "other," better self who sealed her failure because she could bind herself to him only by denying her own ego. It was also that he further appropriated her identity as her collaborator and became an integral part of the guilt which she experienced in response to the repressed fantasy life of which her writing was an expression.

The important adolescent crisis of feeling occurred when Charlotte returned to the Roe Head School in 1835 at age nineteen, now as a teacher-governess. Emily accompanied her as a student paid for by Charlotte's services. When Emily's homesickness became intense, Charlotte sent her back to Haworth and arranged for Anne to take her place. Despairing as she was herself, sympathetic as she felt to her sister's needs, she was driven still by the same compulsions that had driven her in childhood. As she confessed to Ellen: "I am sad—very sad—at the thoughts of leaving home; but duty—necessity—these are stern mistresses, who will not be disobeyed."[37] But the psychic effort began to have its physical effect. Although Gaskell reports that "Charlotte's life at Miss Wooler's was a very happy one, until her health failed,"[38] the fragments of a journal which Charlotte kept during these years suggested that her profound unhappiness was the cause and not the effect of her failing health.

Mary Taylor, describing Charlotte at this time, says, "She seemed to have no interest or pleasure beyond the feeling of duty, and when she could get, used to sit alone, and "make out.""[39] Ostensibly the conflict was as Winifred Gerin describes it: "be-

36. Gaskell, p. 66.
37. July 6, 1835. Quoted in Gaskell, p. 89.
38. Gaskell, p. 91.
39. Gaskell, p. 97.

tween two fiercely striving forces within her soul; the urge to create and the determination to do her duty.''[40] In fact, there was a deeper conflict which derived from Charlotte's intense preoccupation with her fantasy life, with her feelings of guilt at the nature of her creation and, perhaps, with her growing consciousness of her ambivalence toward Branwell.

As always before, Branwell's function was to establish the outlines of their plots, but now Charlotte—isolated, homesick, thwarted—had to wait for occasional letters or infrequent visits to discover how Branwell had disposed of their characters; how he had, on some level, disposed of *her*. In 1836, for example, he writes to tell Charlotte that he has decided to kill Mary Percy, Zamorna's wife. It is the only act of aggression that Zamorna imagines as effective against his treacherous father-in-law, Northangerland. He will, in the gallant Byronic style, reject Mary (whom, he does, of course, love) so that she will die slowly, agonizingly, of a broken heart, while her father helplessly looks on.

It is an ingenious plan, but it overlooks one thing: Charlotte's great devotion to Mary, with whom she closely identifies. Charlotte, writing in her journal of this event, betrays no anger (she never, at this point in their lives, speaks angrily of Branwell). Her tones are those of great sorrow and impotence:

> I wonder if Branwell has really killed the Duchess. Is she dead? Is she buried? Is she alone in the cold earth on this dreary night with the ponderous coffin plate on her breast under the black pavement of a church in a vault closed up with lime and mortar. Nobody where she lies—she who was watched through months of suffering—as she lay on her bed of state. Now quite forsaken because her eyes are closed, her lips sealed and her limbs cold and rigid . . . a set of wretched thoughts are rising in my mind. I hope she's alive still partly because I can't abide to think how hopelessly and cheerlessly she must have died. . . .[41]

Certainly her awareness of the inequality of their collaboration must have intensified her suffering during this period of isolation: a period of three years' separation from the sources of herself.

40. Gerin, *Charlotte Brontë*, p. 100.
41. Roe Head Journal, unpublished. Bonnell Collection: Brontë Parsonage Museum.

I'm just going to write because I cannot help it. . . . There is a
voice, there is an impulse that wakens up that dormant power
which smites torpidity I sometimes think dead. That wind
pouring in impetuous currents through the air, sounding
wildly, unremittingly from hour to hour, deepening its tone as
the night advances, coming not in gusts, but with a rapid, gathering, stormy swell, that wind I know is heard at this moment
far away on the moors at Haworth. Branwell and Emily hear it
and as it sweeps over our house down the church-yard and
round the old church, they think perhaps of me and Anne—
glorious! that blast was mighty. It reminded me of Northangerland, there was something so merciless in the heavier rush, that
made the very house groan as if it could scarce bear this accel-
eration of impetus. O it has wakened a feeling that I cannot satisfy—a thousand wishes rose at its call which must die with
me for they will never be fulfilled. Now I should be agonized if
I had not the dream to repose on—its existence, its forms, its
scenes do fill a little of the craving vacancy.

The reality of the school overwhelms her with its alien nature:

Stupidity the atmosphere, schoolbooks the employment, asses
the society: What in all this is there to remind me of the divine,
silent, unseen land of thought, dim now, and indefinite as the
dream of a dream, the shadow of a shade?

Here at last she can express her anger at the necessity of "doing
her duty," even her "rage," directed overtly at the students, but
derived from her sense of fragmentation:

The Thought came over me: Am I to spend all the best part of
my life in this wretched bondage, forcibly suppressing my rage
at the idleness, the apathy and the hyperbolical and most asi-
nine stupidity of these fat-headed oafs, and on compulsion assuming an air of kindness, patience and assiduity? Must I from
day to day sit chained to this chair, prisoned within these four
bare walls, while these glorious summer suns are burning in
heaven and the year is revolving in its richest glow, and declaring at the close of every summer day, the time I am losing will
never come again.

But the demands of her job are not adequate to explain her inability to write freely. Her physical distance from Haworth is not adequate to explain the psychological distance she experiences.

> And now once more on a dull Saturday afternoon, I sit down to
> try to summon around me the dim shadows, not of coming
> events but of incidents long departed, of feelings, of pleasures,
> whose exquisite relish I sometimes fear it will never be my lot
> again to taste. How few would believe that from sources purely
> imaginary such happiness could be derived! Pen cannot portray
> the deep interest of the scenes, of the continued train of events
> I have witnessed in that little room with the narrow bed and
> bare white-washed walls twenty miles away. What a treasure is
> thought! What a privilege is reverie! I am thankful I have the
> power of solacing myself with the dream of creations whose
> reality I shall never behold. May I never lose that power, may I
> never feel it grow weaker.

Her desire now is to escape: to live in that cave under the ocean—
cherishing the kernel of herself that is the poet-dreamer. She
would share her sanctuary with those "creations," her other
selves, tempting in their unreality. But: "I cannot write of them
except in total solitude I scarce think of them." There is a
forbidden quality about this world that derives from its immoral
and sexual nature: from the adulterous adventures of Northangerland and Zamorna; the passionate desires of her heroines. She can
only allow herself to explore it freely when she is hidden from
public scrutiny—at Haworth, where she doesn't feel the pressure
of the ocean beating against the walls of her cavern.

The letters written to Ellen Nussey from Roe Head during this
period, suggest the extent to which Charlotte was subject to extremes of shame and guilt:

> Don't deceive yourself by imagining I have a bit of real
> goodness about me—my darling. If I were like you, I should
> have my face Zion-ward, though prejudice and error might oc-
> casionally fling a mist over the glorious vision before me—*but
> I am not like you.* If you knew my thoughts, the dreams that
> absorb me, and the fiery imagination that at times eats me up,
> and makes me feel society, as it is, wretchedly insipid, you
> would pity and I dare say despise me.[42]

Later in the same year she writes more specifically of the self-en-
forced repression and its cost:

> . . . I have some qualities that make me very miserable,
> some feelings that you can have no participation in—that few,

42. May 10, 1836. Wise and Symington, I, 139.

very few, people in the world can at all understand. I don't
pride myself on these peculiarities. I strive to conceal and
suppress them as much as I can; but they burst out sometimes,
and then those who see the explosion despise me, and I hate
myself for days afterwards. . . .[43]

The crisis of conscience briefly sought religious expression.

I *do* wish to be better than I am. I pray fervently sometimes to
be made so. I have stings of conscience, visitings of remorse,
glimpses of holy, of inexpressible things, which formerly I
used to be a stranger to: it may all die away, and I may be in
utter midnight, but I implore a merciful Redeemer, that, if this
be the dawn of the Gospel, it may still brighten to a perfect
day. . . . I am in that state of horrid, gloomy uncertainty that,
at this moment, I would submit to be old, grey-haired, to have
passed all my youthful days of enjoyment, and to be settling on
the verge of the grave, if I could only therefore ensure the prospect of reconciliation to God, and redemption through His
Son's merit.[44]

But Charlotte could return only briefly to the harsh religion of her
aunt. The conventional form of sublimation embraced by Ellen
was inappropriate to her needs. Surely some relief derived from
the journal entries and the agonized letters, all filled with veiled
allusions and confessions, guilt, renunciation, and a burning
sense of unworthiness: ". . . it seems as if some fatality stood
between you and me. I am not good enough for you, and you
must be kept from the contamination of too intimate society."[45]
But it was only in Angria that the real confrontation could occur.
That confrontation's form is reflected in the remarkable change
that took place in the fiction during this same time.

Between 1836 and 1839, at Haworth for holidays or brief
respites from teaching and governess duties, Brontë wrote her
last five Angrian stories, the last of her juvenilia. "Passing
Events," "Julia," "Mina Laury," "Henry Hastings," and
"Caroline Vernon" were all produced independently. They were
completely her own. The tales are crucial to an understanding of
Brontë's personal and artistic development, bridging as they do
the fantasies of the child-woman and the conscious, self-explor-
ing art of the adult. All are responses to the increased pressure

43. Roe Head, 1836. Wise and Symington, I, 141.
44. Roe Head, 1836. Wise and Symington, I, 140.
45. To Ellen Nussey, December 29, 1837. Quoted in Gaskell, p. 108.

she felt to free herself from her paralyzing relationship with Branwell and to overcome the deeply disturbing effects of her sexual
fantasies. All are exercises in confrontation, keyed at different
levels, employing varieties of technique. They suggest a new, if
painfully achieved, mastery.

To a limited extent, Charlotte explored the confusion of her
own feelings about Branwell by developing further, in these
stories, Zamorna's relationship with Northangerland, the persona
and alter ego which Branwell had adopted in earlier tales. Attempting to out-Byron his Byronic hero, Branwell seems to have
projected onto the outrageously immoral Northangerland—
Zamorna's father-in-law and treacherous minister—his own guilt
at his betrayal of his family's hopes as well as some complex elements of his oedipal conflict. Charlotte emphasizes the tensions
of the Zamorna-Northangerland relationship, bending them to her
own purpose. She underlines the attraction and repulsion which
bind the two men in a reciprocal erosion. She explores the way in
which the desire of each for power is thwarted—particularly in
Zamorna's case—by a desire for the approval and love of the
other. She suggests—most movingly in "Caroline Vernon"—
the persistent and troubling effect which loving bonds of the past
have upon a deteriorating relationship. The emotional ties and
crucial rivalries that so complicate the feelings of parent and child
reflect the sibling conflicts she knows so well. Brontë's ability to
define these conflicts along with her inability to resolve them,
suggest the depth both of her knowledge and her doubt.

In her choice of narrative voice, Brontë attempts a more direct
confrontation. In four of the five stories ("Mina Laury" is the
only exception) Brontë continues to develop for herself the persona of Zamorna's younger brother, Charles Towneshend: disen-
franchized, powerless, a cynical victim of the circumstances of
his birth and of Zamorna's heedless cruelty. His introduction
dates back to 1833, to a book entitled "Arthuriana," which deals
with Charles's critical view of Zamorna. Fannie Ratchford comments on the interest of this work:

> The increasing antagonism between the two reflects a growing
> conflict within Charlottte herself, as her conscience condemns
> while her romantic imagination rejoices in the moral lapses of
> her hero. To satisfy conscience she shaped Lord Charles into a

yet more precise instrument of censure through which she
roundly denounces the sin that made her hero glorious.[46]

In these late tales, the earlier tendency intensifies. Charles is alternately repelled and attracted by his tyrannical older brother.
The ironic, witty tone which he sometimes adopts in describing
Zamorna's exploits, successfully transports the hero from the
amorality of the Byronic world to a more recognizable universe
of values. The problem is that Brontë cannot maintain this aspect
of Charles's tone consistently. An explanation can be found in
the nature of her projection. Charles is a part of herself, the
superego cast as a man (a woman in this mythology would be
merely the shadow of powerlessness). Zamorna is identified with
her own deepest desires while also representing Branwell. Her
bondage and her unsuccessful attempt at liberation are, in this
way, simultaneously expressed. While the chronological relation
to Branwell is inverted, the affective relationship is maintained,
i.e., although cast as a male, she is—as the *younger* brother—
completely vulnerable. Conscience is as inadequate to the economy of her personality as she herself is impotent before Branwell.

At the same time that Brontë is testing the strengths and inadequacies of this most crucial of all her relationships, she is
beginning to confront more directly and more analytically the
sexual fantasies which have dominated her private life. Writing
independently during this period, Brontë for the first time thrusts
both Zamorna and Northangerland into a series of explicit and
adulterous love affairs.

As always before, fantasies reveal frustrations and yearnings
rather than realities. Brontë's circumstances and absence of self-
esteem have made her despair of the possibility that she could
herself ever in fact be loved. But at the same time that she writes
to Ellen Nussey that she will never marry, she is projecting in her
stories the illusion of the "great love," the sexuality that overwhelms and solves all of life's problems. The configuration of
this illusion is typically masochistic.

> In the constellation of pathological dependency, the individual
> or individuals depended on are generally perceived by the pa-
> tient to be supermen or superwomen. The need to endow these

46. Ratchford, p. 71.

individuals with magical power arises in part from the patient's belief that no ordinary mortal like himself can solve his problems or do the things that he is so thoroughly unable to do. Another basis for such endowment is the attempt to recreate a mother or father figure in order to act out or work out problems originally related to these figures.[47]

The pathology which Irving Bieber describes would commonly be found in women raised in patriarchal families, subject to the values of patriarchal societies. Certainly it seems predictable of Brontë—the guilty "survivor," the submissive daughter, the adoring sister—and predictable also of those surrogate selves: her heroines.

The concept of romantic love which informs these late stories is traditionally Byronic. The relationships described are conventionally sadomasochistic. The male is possessive, tyrannical, capable of casual, defensive cruelty. The woman is submissive, adoring, disinterested: deriving pleasure from the pain of an unequal attachment. This passage from "Julia," written in 1837, suggests the dominat elements of the mythology:

> . . . Fury was the feeling at his heart, he desired something that he could not have . . . he imagined the bliss but could not attain it. . . . Recollection showed him her image as he had seen it a hundred times—young, pallid, seldom smiling, waiting his approach in a salon of gorgeous state. . . . The Duke thought he at that hour looked down on her fair cheek resting on his shoulder, met the adoration of her eyes, felt the beating of her heart against his circling arm, saw the pulse flutter on her heaving breast, beheld the folds of satin disclosing her exquisite form. With his whole enthusiastic soul he loved her. . . . It had been to him the delight of his life at times to satisfy and soothe her intense idolatry—he was in the mood for that benevolent office now . . .[48]

Brontë still identifies with her heroine's "intense idolatry" and is appealed to by the selfish domination of the male. But she has begun to struggle against the force of that appeal. She has started to question the desirability of that identification. The mild irony

47. Bieber, p. 444. Horney makes a similar observation in "The Problem of Female Masochism," p. 32.
48. "Julia," *Five Novelettes,* ed. Winifred Gerin (London: The Folio Press, 1971), p. 113.

of the final observation ("It had been to him the delight of his life at times to satisfy and soothe her intense idolatry—he was in the mood for that benevolent office now") undercuts the serious romantic tone of the section which precedes it. Psychological analysis has begun to accompany mute sympathy and, although the two attitudes are still maintained in conjunction with one another, the first suggests the direction which will dominate the next three novelettes of this period (1837–39): "Mina Laury," "Caroline Vernon," and "Henry Hastings." These are marked by a maturing consciousness which attempts to bring chaotic emotionality under moral and psychological control.[49]

Although Brontë's sympathies remain confused and ambiguous in these tales, the focus of her interest changes. For example, while she can no longer invest Zamorna and Northangerland with the old romantic idealism, she is still appealed to—as she was in "Julia"—by their masculine selfishness, their cynicism and gratuitous cruelty. But this becomes less important because it is no longer the heroes who occupy her attention. It is the appeal itself. Unable now to embrace wholeheartedly the concept of romantic love, she is still not willing to apply the scorn of Victorian sensibility to her own psychosexual insights. She attempts instead to understand the nature of infatuation. She attempts, in fact, to penetrate the complexities of the masochistic personality, groping for the meaning of her own femininity and sexuality. It is the birth of a consciousness which will stunningly dominate the process of the mature novels.

The unhappiness of Brontë's heroines permeates these stories. They suffer, all of them, because their lovers are unfaithful and capricious. They suffer because they are deserted. But they suffer most of all in their dependence upon Zamorna, a male who, himself profoundly flawed, must define and affirm them. Rejection fulfills their expectations, confirms their doubts. Deprived of sense of self, they cannot accept responsibility: moral choice is impossible (in "Caroline Vernon," for example, we are told that "conscience was feeble"). Love for them cannot be completion. It is a means of self-abnegation, a rationalization of self-denial. Her women are defined by their noble capacity for love; but they never love or esteem themselves. They depend

49. Winifred Gerin cites this change of emphasis in her article, "Byron's Influence on the Brontës," p. 9.

upon their dependency. For them, the greatest horror is not the physical loss of their lovers—but the psychological loss: to have autonomy thrust upon them—to be forced back into the void of the self. Alone, they barely exist. This complex of attitudes is the female version—the obverse side—of the male romantic experience: the compulsion to see everything through the lens of the self until all reality disappears in the mysterious terrain of one's own personality.

In the novelettes, Zamorna distributes his wife and mistresses about the countryside, placing them in castles where they sit like so many enchanted princesses before their mirrors, carefully preserving their lover's image of them, until he chooses to return and bring them back to life. He describes Caroline Vernon's feelings about her incarceration ("I placed her where she is safe and happy") with the same painful accuracy that he uses to describe his wife's devotion:

> When did I ever tyrannize over Mary? Ask herself, ask her at this moment, when she is as much exasperated against me as she ever was in her life. Tell her to leave me. She will not speak to me or look at me, but see what her answer would be to that.[50]

Mary Percy, Mina Laury, and Caroline Vernon are not simply Zamorna's victims. They victimize themselves since they alone can unlock their castle doors to enter a world of mature responsibility. Charlotte perceives their dilemma but she does not yet know where they can find the requisite keys.

The ambiguities and conflicts of the female predicament are more fully explored in "Mina Laury." In fascinating ways, Mina combines spiritual strength with emotional weakness: independence of mind with psychic submission. Having played an idealized Claire Claremont of Zamorna's Byron, she accompanied her lover into exile, cared for his child, became part of the political intrigues that surrounded him—a confidante and agent of those most highly placed: "So clever and earnest was she in all she said and did that the haughty Aristocrats did not hesitate to communicate to her often on matters of first rate importanee."[51] But despite the fact that Mina achieves a position of her own, she

50. "Caroline Vernon," *Five Novelettes,* p. 310.
51. "Passing Events," ibid., pp. 43–44.

does not experience herself as an independent entity. She accepts the role she plays as a duty: "Had her life been different, she would not have interfered in such matters. She did not interfere now—she only served."[52] She has known only one lover in her life and to him, to Zamorna, she is completely faithful. She describes the effect upon her of the infatuation which overwhelmed her from the beginning:

> I lost the power of properly appreciating the value of the world's opinion, of discerning the difference between right and wrong.[53]

She defines herself as Zamorna's property. She sees herself as his object. She exists only as she exists for him: denying her own capacities, her potential, her integrity:

> Strong-minded beyond her sex—active, energetic, accomplished in all other points of view—here she was as weak as a child—she lost her identity—her very way of life was swallowed up in that of another.[54]

She accepts, even embraces, humiliation: "Shame and reproach have no effect on me. I do not care for being called a camp follower."[55] It is enough for her to feel "the condescending touch" of Zamorna's hand, to accept his embrace "as a slave ought to take the caress of a Sultan." [56] She lives in a state of thralldom: a woman obsessed.[57]

> She had but one idea—Zamorna, Zamorna—! It had grown up with her—become part of her nature—absence—coldness—to-

52. "Mina Laury," ibid., p. 142.
53. "Mina Laury," p. 147.
54. Ibid., p. 165.
55. "Passing Events," p. 44.
56. Ibid., p. 46.
57. An observation of Freud's is interesting in this context: "The maiden whose desire for love has for so long and with such difficulty been held in check, in whom the influences of environment and education have formed resistances, will take the man who gratifies her longing, and thereby overcomes her resistances, into a close and lasting relationship which will never be available to any other man. The experience brings about a state of thralldom in the woman that assures the man lasting and undisturbed possession of her and makes her able to withstand new impressions and temptations from without." "The Taboo of Virginity," *Collected Papers,* trans. Joan Riviere (New York: Basic Books, 1959), 4, 217. Freud traces this condition of thralldom to the loss of virginity in women and the overcoming of impotence in men (p. 218).

> tal neglect—for long periods together—went for nothing—she
> could no more feel alienation from him than she could from
> herself—[58]

In fact, it is because she is alienated from herself that she so
dreads alienation from him. It is because she experiences herself
as incomplete and unworthy that she looks to him to fill her emptiness. She is a completely male-identified woman—''female acquaintance she never sought''—and only to Zamorna, who rejects her autonomy (not to Lord Hartford, for example, who
would offer her marriage and adoration) can she ascribe the magical power that will affirm her being.

Brontë uncompromisingly emphasizes the irrationality of
Mina's infatuation by presenting its object as a comic figure. In
the late story, Zamorna has passed his prime and has become the
''great blithering king of Angria.'' His heroic dimensions have
gotten out of hand. He is a ''man mountain'' whose political adventures have been replaced by mealtime quibbling. His once
treacherous prime minister father-in-law is reduced to parental
nagging: ''I wish you would masticate your food better.''[59] But if
Brontë can place the hero in a new, essentially antiromantic perspective, she is still unable to suggest what can be done to prevent or overcome the heroine's infatuation. She does not yet see
how the intensity of need and feeling might be constructively
channeled. Still, she deals with these problems more fruitfully in
''Henry Hastings,'' the most developed of the last short novels.
The success here derives from her emphasis upon the functioning
of the masochistic female personality in a context which is real
and immediate to her: the relationship of sister to brother.

The ''dissipated and drunken mushroom,'' Henry Hastings,
had been created by Branwell after he returned from his disastrous stay in London in 1837. Through this new persona, Branwell expressed his growing guilt and impotence as well as his
alienation from his family.

> Besides, conscience with withering sting was constantly strik-
> ing into my heart—king, country and cause forsaken, old asso-
> ciations severed, friendships torn away—and had I not re-
> ceived a letter from my father coldly saying he and all at home

58. ''Mina Laury,'' p. 143.
59. Ibid., p. 128.

had cut me for ever and ever, all which matters, like hot sweet-meats, the more and more incited me to drink.[60]

In "Julia," Brontë merely appropriates Branwell's character, portraying him as a shiftless, vain, and unstable alcoholic. In "Henry Hastings" she develops the hero further, rejecting Branwell's early definition of him as simply a debased traitor and murderer. She provides him with a motive, explaining how the extraordinary rise in his fortunes—a function of his giftedness and heroism—had negatively affected his character and initiated his ruin. But Hastings is not at the center of the story. That position is occupied by his sister, Elizabeth, who, fully recognizing her brother's flaws and degradation, risks everything she values to save his life:

> It was very odd that his sister did not think a pin the worse of him for all his dishonor: it is private moments not public infamy that degrade a man in the opinion of his relations. Miss Hastings had heard him cursed by every mouth, saw him denounced in every newspaper, still he was the same brother to her he had always been—still she beheld his actions through a medium peculiar to herself. She saw him go away with a triumphant Hope—that his future actions would nobly blot out the calumny of his enemies. Yet after all she knew he was an unredeemed villain—human nature is full of inconsistencies—natural affection is a thing never rooted out where it has once existed.[61]

The heroine is defined, as the other heroines had been, by her self-sacrifice. In Elizabeth's case, however, self-sacrifice seems to be a function of choice and a source of strength rather than the sterile result of blind idolatry as it was with Mina Laury.

This is the first of her stories in which Brontë models her heroine upon herself. In this respect, "Henry Hastings" is the forerunner of the mature novels. Elizabeth is—like Brontë, like Jane Eyre, like Lucy Snowe—"plain and undersized."

> Young indeed she was—but not handsome—she had a fair, rather wan complexion, dark hair smoothly combed in two plain folds from her forehead—features capable of much

60. Fragment, dated July 12, 1837. Brontë Parsonage Museum.
61. "Henry Hastings," *Five Novelettes*, p. 242.

varied expression and a quick wandering eye of singular and
by no means common-place significance.[62]

She is possessed of that odd mixture of qualities which makes
Jane Eyre so appealing a heroine. Serious and thoughtful, she is
also humorous. Shy, she is fiercely proud. Retiring, she can be
moved easily to passion:

> . . . still the exclusive proud being thought she had not met
> with a single individual equal to herself in mind, and therefore
> not one whom she could love . . . , she was one who scorned
> respect . . . she was always burning for warmer, closer at-
> tachment.[63]

In her presentation of Elizabeth's situation, Brontë places fantasy
at the service of analysis, beginning to transmute the dream into
art. For example, one level of the story seems to draw upon her
sense of her own and Branwell's rivalry for their father's love.
Hastings's transgressions place Elizabeth in a situation of open
competition in which she can, for the first time, be victorious as
the "good" albeit female child. But Brontë recognizes that the
urge to punish the father may be stronger, and more real, than the
urge to claim the love of which he has deprived her—love, therefore, that may not exist. After Henry has been painfully disowned
by his father because of his treasonous activities, Elizabeth
chooses to come to his defense and is therefore cast out as well.
Not able to reject her brother openly, she joins him in the rebellion against the paternal authority. This too is a kind of victory.
She is superior to father *and* brother. In her fidelity she proves
that it is *her* love for Henry which is most enduring. Tested, she
claims the prize. The sister's sacrifice totally vindicates her own
character and exposes her brother's, without creating an incredible reconciliation with the father which would be unacceptable to
the psyche. The family romance, we find, has many levels.[64]

Given these terms, Elizabeth's commitment to her brother is
not an enslavement. Rather it frees her as a rebel from the traditional role within the family. It frees her from the rivalry for
parental approval. It frees her even from the problems accom-

62. "Henry Hastings," p. 181.

63. Ibid., pp. 243–44.

64. As we shall see, Charlotte did—for her own reasons—accept the role
of the "good child," and became Branwell's most vehement judge. Still, like
Elizabeth, she was freed by her brother's deterioration.

panying the brother-sister relationship, for, between them, no
relationship at all is now possible. Henry's weakness of character
is proof against her fidelity. Always spoiled and self-centered, he
has become soured by guilt.

It is in this way that Elizabeth has independence thrust upon
her. Without conventional supports she must discover her own
values and role. She has to test herself in areas which define her,
quite terrifyingly, as a person rather than as a woman. She becomes a successful teacher and schoolmistress. The sense of self
which is actualized by her dedication to Henry gives her enough
self-confidence to transform her in the eyes of others. Her intelligence and capacity for feeling illuminate her from within.

Sir William Percy is one of those who fall in love with her
but, because of his position and his pride, he can offer her only
the small satisfactions and large humiliations of an illicit relationship. Although she longs for love and is attracted to him
"with an intensity of romantic feeling that very few people in this
world can form the remotest conception of,"[65] Elizabeth rejects
him, as Jane will later reject Rochester. It is a courageous act, for
she has no more hope than do Brontë's later heroines, than
Brontë does herself, that she can derive important alternate satisfactions from the teaching that makes her financially independent:

> She spent her mornings in her drawing-room surrounded by
> her class and not wearily toiling to impart the dry rudiments of
> knowledge to yawning, obstinate children—a thing she hated
> and for which her sharp, irritable temper rendered her wholly
> unfit.[66]

It is finally by her integrity, her disillusionment, and her extraordinary loneliness that she is defined.

> Sometimes, when she was alone of an evening, walking
> through her handsome drawing room by twilight, she would
> think of home—long for home, till she cried passionately at the
> conviction that she would see it no more. So wild was her
> longing that where she looked out on the dusky sky, between
> the curtains of her bay-window . . . fancy seemed to trace on
> the horizon, the blue outlines of the moors.[67]

65. "Henry Hastings," p. 294.
66. Ibid., p. 243.
67. Ibid., p. 244.

Here, in the development of Elizabeth Hastings, Brontë begins the painful work of her maturity.

Biographers have been quick to comment on the irony which emerges from a comparison of Elizabeth's fidelity to Henry and Charlotte's later rejection of Branwell. But they have been blind to the central albeit disguised point of "Henry Hastings": that Branwell's disintegration was essential to Charlotte's discovery of herself; that his failure was necessary if she was to succeed; that her separation from him, begun at this point in her life, expressed at this stage of her work, allowed her to begin to reject as well the universe of mythic values which had locked her into the artistic and personal infantilism by which Branwell had been trapped. Charlotte, with her heroine, cannot avoid looking back but, with Elizabeth, she realizes that she cannot return. Her "Farewell to Angria" (written at the end of 1839, when she was twenty-two) is profoundly moving. It suggests that self-knowledge can only be sought within a historical reality that denies escape into fantasy but encourages the discovery of the truth buried in the dream.

> I have now written a great many books and for a long time have dwelt on the same characters and scenes and subjects. I have shown my landscapes in every variety of shade and light which morning, noon, and evening—the rising, the meridian, and the setting sun can bestow upon them. Sometimes I have filled the air with the whitened tempest of winter: snow has embossed the dark arms of the beech and oak and filled with drifts the parks of the lowlands or the mountain-pass of wilder districts. Again, the same mansion with its woods, the same moor with its glens, has been softly colored with the tints of moonlight in summer, and in the warmest June night the trees have clustered their full-plumed heads over glades flushed with flowers. So it is with persons. My readers have been habituated to one set of features, which they have seen now in profile, now in full face, now in outline, and again in finished painting,—varied but by the thought or feeling or temper or age; lit with love, flushed with passion, shaded with grief, kindled with ecstasy; in meditation and mirth, in sorrow and scorn and rapture; with the round outline of childhood, the beauty and fulness of youth, the strength of manhood, and the furrows of thoughtful decline;—but we must change, for the eye is tired of the picture so oft recurring and now so familiar.

Yet do not urge me too fast, reader: it is not easy to dismiss from my imagination the images which have filled it so long; they were my friends and my intimate acquaintances, and I could with little labour describe to you the faces, the voices, the actions, of those who peopled my thoughts by day, and not seldom stole strangely even into my dreams by night. When I depart from these I feel almost as if I stood on the threshold of a home and were bidding farewell to its inmates. When I try to conjure up new inmates I feel as if I had got into a distant country where every face was unknown and the character of all the population an enigma which it would take much study to comprehend and much talent to expound. Still, I long to quit for awhile that burning clime where we have sojourned too long—its skies flame—the glow of sunset is always upon it—the mind would cease from excitement and turn now to a cooler region where the dawn breaks grey and sober, and the coming day for a time at least is subdued by clouds.[68]

IV

Although Brontë's descent from the "burning clime" of her fantastic imaginings to the "cooler region" of mature self-knowledge and artistic control began in the emotional crisis of 1839, it was several years before she understood its implications and its cost. What she had divined in the experience of her heroines, she had to comprehend in her own life. She had to emerge from the swaddling of societal mythology and the richly projective fantasy self. To penetrate that constricting wrap she had to find in herself the sources of the mysterious romantic conspiracy, suffer the agony of disillusionment, and struggle toward the freedom implicit in uninsulated reality. Ultimately, the initial trauma passed, she had to examine the scars of confrontation on her own masochistic personality, replacing rationalization with reason. This was to be her personal and artistic goal. It provided the motivating force and the form of her fictions.

The duties which she felt it necessary to assume did not augur well for her undertaking. In 1839, while she was creating Elizabeth Hastings and bidding farewell to Angria, she was beginning a series of trials which might well have sent her scurrying back to

68. *Legends of Angria,* compiled by Fannie Ratchford and William De-Vane (New Haven: Yale University Press, 1933), p. 316.

the security of her fantasies. For three months she was a governess in the family of a Mr. and Mrs. Sedgewick of Yorkshire. She had virtually no relationship with Mr. Sedgewick but, writing to Ellen of her situation, she reveals herself to be drawn to her new "master"—astonishingly attracted to the role of submissive woman when it is played opposite that of a domineering man:

> One of the pleasantest afternoons I have spend here—indeed, the only one at all pleasant—was when Mr. _____ walked out with his children, and I had orders to follow a little behind. As he strolled on through his fields, with his magnificent Newfoundland dog at his side, he looked very like what a frank, wealthy Conservative gentleman ought to be.[69]

But while she still accepted domination within the context of male-female interaction, she was withered by her powerlessness in the broader circumstances of her life. The fear of inadequacy which had marked her childhood was validated now. Occupying, as all governesses did, an undefined area between the domestic servants and the members of the family, she had neither friends nor rights. Even her relationship to the children for whom she cared was ambiguous and demeaning. The pain of her situation, the humiliation which she felt as a result of her servitude and, above all, the anger and resentment which she could not overtly express and which she therefore turned against herself—all of this is suggested in a letter which she wrote to Ellen a couple of years later when she was again a governess, now to the children of Mr. and Mrs. John White:

> But no one but myself can tell how hard a governess's work is to me—for no one but myself is aware how utterly averse my whole mind and nature are to the employment. Do not think that I fail to blame myself for this, or that I leave any means unemployed to conquer this feeling. Some of my greatest difficulties lie in things that would appear to you comparatively trivial. I find it so hard to repel the rude familiarity of children. I find it so difficult to ask either servants or mistress for anything I want, however much I want it. It is less pain to me to endure the greatest inconvenience than to request its removal.[70]

69. June 8, 1839. Quoted in Gaskell, p. 115.
70. March 3, 1841. Wise and Symington, I, 226.

There were few enough alternatives for a young woman who had to be self-supporting. The obvious one was marriage. But in 1839 Charlotte still shared her heroines' romantic dreams of love and was unwilling to compromise. In writing to Ellen of her second proposal of marriage (her first had been made by Ellen's brother, Henry, in the same year) she explained:

> I had a kindly leaning towards him, because he is an amiable and well-disposed man. Yet I had not, and could not have, that intense attachment which would make me willing to die for him; and if ever I marry, it must be in that light of adoration that I will regard my husband. Ten to one I shall never have the chance again; but n'importe.[71]

If her sentiments remained the same during the following year, her tone changed compellingly;

> Do not be over-persuaded to marry a man you can never respect—I do not say *love;* because, I think, if you can respect a person before marriage, moderate love at least will come after; and as to intense *passion,* I am convinced that is no desirable feeling. In the first place, it seldom or never meets with a requittal; and in the second place, if it did, the feeling would be only temporary: it would last the honeymoon, and then, perhaps, give place to disgust, or indifference worse, perhaps, than disgust. Certainly, this would be the case on the man's part; and on the woman's—God help her, if she is left to love passionately and alone.
>
> I am tolerably well-convinced that I shall never marry at all. Reason tells me so, and I am not so utterly the slave of feeling but that I can *occasionally hear* her voice.[72]

The intensity of her idealism provided the measure of her frustration and disappointment. The depth of her need, her absence of self-confidence, her growing despair: all determined the degree of her scepticism. The fate of her childhood heroines, with whom she had identified so closely, had been confirmed in her own limited experience by Branwell's treatment of Mary Taylor. The strains combined to produce a stance of surprising militancy.

> No young lady should fall in love till the offer has been made, accepted—the marriage ceremony performed and the first half-

71. March 12, 1839. Wise and Symington, I, 174.
72. May 15, 1840. Wise and Symington, I, 206–7.

year of wedded life has passed away—a woman may then
begin to love, but with great precaution—very coolly—very
rationally—If she ever loves so much that a harsh word or a
cold look from her husband cuts her to the heart—she is a
fool—if she ever loves so much that her husband's will is her
law—and that she has got into a habit of watching his looks in
order that she may anticipate his wishes she will soon be a neglected fool—Did I not tell you of an instance of a relative of
mine who cared for a young lady till he began to suspect that
she cared more for him and then instantly conceived a sort of
contempt for her?[73]

But, as events were to prove, Charlotte was in fact neither sceptic
nor militant. Experience found her to be as susceptible to infatuation and as vulnerable to rejection, as were Mary Percy or Mina
Laury. Brussels replaced Angria as the scene of her ordeal. It was
here—to the Pensionnat Heger—that she and Emily came to prepare themselves to open, with Anne, a school of their own. It was
a venture which could free them in time from the bondage of the
governess role.

Now twenty-six years old, Charlotte had undeniably tired of
the constricted life she led. Intellectually, emotionally, psychologically, and sexually she longed for an opportunity to grow, to
learn, to experience. A few months before she left for Brussels,
she had written to Ellen:

. . . Mary's letter spoke of some of the pictures and Cathe-
drals she had seen—pictures the most exquisite—and cathe-
drals the most venerable—I hardly know what swelled to my
throat as I read her letter—such a vehement impatience of restraint and steady work. . . . Such a strong wish for wings—
wings such as wealth can furnish—such an urgent thirst to
see—to know—to learn—something seemed to expand boldly
for a minute—I was tantalized with the consciousness of faculties unexercised—then all collapsed and I despaired.[74]

Her feeling for M. Heger, headmaster of the school in Brussels,
offered her those wings, and in the nine months of her first stay
there, she began to understand what it meant to fly.

It would seem at first that M. Heger had little in common with
the Byronic heroes of Brontë's adolescent fantasies but the simi-

73. November 20, 1840. Wise and Symington, I, 221.
74. August 7, 1841. Wise and Symington, I, 218.

larities are actually striking. The schoolmaster might indeed have been Zamorna, transplanted to a domestic setting. The death of his young first wife and child in a cholera epidemic had left him not only with a haunting past, but also with a rather morose and gloomy presence. A domineering man, possessed of a quick temper, he used his position and his personality as weapons: substitutes for reason, excuses for petty tyrannies. But he was also a man who could inspire devotion by virtue of his warmth and patience.[75] Not least of all, he was a gifted teacher: knowledgeable and insightful, appreciative of his serious students, responsive to their intellectual and emotional requirements. He exploited the teacher-student relationship, with its undisputed hierarchy of power, its always latent sexuality, its allowance for dependence—even idolatry—without humiliation. All of this provided a channeling of psychosexual forces acceptable within the Victorian culture. The friendship with Heger provided Brontë with a viable transition between her relationships with her father and brother and the more mature heterosexual interaction of which she was becoming capable. Revealingly, Brontë writes to Ellen, after she has had time to accustom herself to the regimen of the Hegers:

> I was twenty-six years old a week or two since; and at this ripe time of life I am a school-girl, and, on the whole, very happy in that capacity. It felt very strange at first to submit to authority instead of exercising it—to obey orders instead of giving them: but I like that state of things. I returned to it with the same avidity that a cow, that has long been kept on dry hay, returns to fresh grass. Don't laugh at my simile. It is natural to me to submit and very unnatural to command.[76]

Recognizing Charlotte and Emily's giftedness, Heger devised a new technique for teaching them French by emphasizing the spirit and rhythm of the text rather than simple grammatical rules. The technique must have made Charlotte more aware of her own literary style.[77] Then too, Heger's comments on her composi-

---

75. See Gerin, *Charlotte Brontë*, p. 194.

76. May, 1842. Wise and Symington, I, 260.

77. ". . . he proposed to read to them some of the master-pieces of the most celebrated French authors . . . and having thus impressed the complete effect of the whole, to analyze the parts with them, pointing out in what such or such an author excell'd and where were the blemishes . . . he hoped thereby to help them catch 'the echo of a style.' " (Gaskell, pp. 151–52).

tions represented the first objective criticism of her writing that she had ever received. Beside this informed interest and intellectual stimulation, Charlotte's feelings of alienation from the other students, her dislike of Catholics, even her persistent self-consciousness seemed trivial indeed. She was questioning herself; stretching and growing in a world which no longer seemed to demand abnegation.

When Charlotte and Emily were called home in November of 1842 because of their aunt's death, it was unthinkable to Charlotte that she would remain at Haworth. Their status at the school had already changed. In return for their board and studies in French and German, Emily was teaching music, Charlotte English. Now, in addition, M. Heger offered them a salary if they would return.[78] Never happy away from Haworth, never charmed as Charlotte was, by Heger, Emily welcomed the opportunity to take her aunt's place at home. But Charlotte sped back to Brussels, compelled by feelings which had little to do with M. Heger's generous terms of employment. Almost three years later, Brontë wrote of this compulsion to Ellen:

> I returned to Brussels after aunt's death against my conscience, prompted by what then seemed an irresistible impulse. I was punished for my selfish folly by a total withdrawal for more than two years of happiness and peace of mind . . .[79]

The words could have been spoken by Mina Laury of her involvement with Zamorna. But if the words seem similar, the nature of the involvement was not. In fact, it was the necessity of the difference which made Charlotte's involvement possible at all. The relationship between Charlotte and Heger, *could* exist only in some shadowy world that blurred fantasy and reality. The attraction and the protection from the attraction were simultaneously present. The sources of conflict were submerged, but its power became increasingly more difficult to deny.

When she returned to the Pensionnat, Brontë came to know Heger better than she had before. Teaching him and his brother-in-law English, she established herself in a position of greater equality with him. Heger spoke to her more openly, loaned her

78. See Gerin, *Charlotte Brontë,* pp. 180–215 for a complete account of these months in Brussels.

79. October 14, 1846. Wise and Symington, II, 115.

books, showed her the more elusive—and attractive—aspects of his personality as well as the admirable qualities of his mind. But to know him better was to want to know him intimately; to feel closer to him was to understand the great gulf which separated them. The letters written during the spring of her return suggest both her increasing sense of isolation and her increasing confusion.

> As I told you before, M. and Madame Heger are the only two persons in the house for whom I really experience regard and esteem, and, of course, I cannot always be with them, nor even often. They told me, when I first returned, that I was to consider their sitting-room my sitting-room also, and to go there whenever I was not engaged in the schoolroom. This, however, I cannot do. In the daytime it is a public room, where music masters and mistresses are constantly passing in and out; and in the evening I will not and ought not to intrude on M. and Madame Heger and their children. Thus I am a good deal by myself out of school hours; but that does not signify.[80]

Hotly denying rumors that she has been drawn back to Brussels by a love affair, she adds—with a degree of ambiguity and defensiveness that is characteristic of her at this time:

> . . . if these charitable people knew the total seclusion of the life I lead—that I never exchange a word with any other man than Monsieur Heger and seldom indeed with him—they would perhaps cease to suppose that any such chimerical and groundless notion influenced my proceedings . . . not that it is a crime to marry—or a crime to wish to be married—but it is an imbecility which I reject with contempt—for women who have neither fortune nor beauty—to make marriage the principal object of their wishes and hopes and the aim of all their actions—not to be able to convince themselves that they are unattractive—and that they had better be quiet and think of other things than wedlock . . .

To Branwell, she admits—albeit unconsciously—that the world around her has become as affectless as has her relationship with Heger: an image of her psychic state:

> I perceive that I grow exceedingly misanthropic and sour . . . nobody ever gets into a passion here. Such a thing is not

80. To Ellen Nussey, March 6, 1843. Wise and Symington, I, 293.

known. The phlegm that thickens their blood is too gluey to boil. They are very false in their relations with each other, but they rarely quarrel, and friendship is a folly they are unacquainted with. The black swan, M. Heger, is the only sole veritable exception to this rule (for Madame always cool and always reasoning, is not quite an exception). But I rarely speak to Monsieur now, for not being a pupil I have little or nothing to do with him. From time to time he shows his kindheartedness by loading me with books, so that I am still indebted to him for all the pleasure or amusement I have.[81]

Her pride can barely protect her from recognition. But she, like the heroines of her adolescence, finds solace in her own capacity for patience, for understanding, for constancy.

There seems to be little doubt that Brontë's schoolgirl attachment to M. Heger was perceived by his wife, who deftly but surely saw to it that Brontë would not be misled about the degree or nature of her husband's interest. For them, withdrawal must have seemed a matter of necessity. The reputation of the school was at stake. It was a kindness to encourage her to develop new friendships. But of course Brontë experienced withdrawal as rejection. The martyrdom of her isolation provided her with the only comfort possible. Here was her castle and she had imprisoned herself within it.

Of late days, M. and Mme. Heger rarely speak to me, and I really don't pretend to care a fig for anybody else in the establishment. You are not to suppose by that expression that I am under the influence of *warm* affection for Mme. Heger. I am convinced that she does not like me—why, I can't tell, nor do I think she herself has any definite reason for the aversion; but for one thing, she cannot comprehend why I do not make intimate friends of Mesdames Blanches, Sophie and Hausse. M. Heger is wondrously influenced by Madame, and I should not wonder if he disapproves very much of my unamiable want of sociability. He has already given me a brief lecture on universal *bienveillance*, and, perceiving that I don't improve in consequence, I fancy he has taken me as a person to be let alone—left to the error of her ways: and consequently he has in a great measure withdrawn the light of his countenance, and I get on from day to day in a Robinson-Crusoe-like condition—

81. May 1, 1843. Wise and Symington, I, 296–97.

very lonely . . . except the loss of M. Heger's good will (if I
have lost it) I care for none of 'em.[82]

The agonies of the next six months made the denial mechanism
increasingly ineffective so that, in a letter written to Ellen in
November, she betrays—although she does not entirely give
away—her awareness of Madame Heger's motivation: "I fancy I
begin to perceive the reason of this mighty distance and reserve:
it sometimes makes me laugh, and at other times nearly cry.
When I am sure of it I will tell it you."[83] It is impossible to deny
the romantic and fundamentally sexual nature of Brontë's interest, although her biographers have politely averted their heads in
order to avoid the recognition.[84] It is also difficult to ignore the
similarity of Brontë's attachment to Heger and those idolatrous
attachments which had entrapped her heroines. It is perhaps sentimentality—more likely, prudery—that leads Winifred Gerin to
assert that Charlotte's love was "innocent," that "what tortured
her was a love that could neither be expressed, returned, or understood by any living soul."[85] In reality, her love *was* understood quite well by Madame Heger. It was this which Brontë
could not forgive. Truly, hers was not an adulterous wish denied,
but rather one which was repressed and never fully confronted.
All of her longings for love, for release, for fulfillment, for
growth, were focused on Heger. This was not a tragic trick of fate
but a psychological necessity. One cites with some confidence,
the phenomena of Victorian repression and sexual fear. But one
also speculates that the impossibility of reciprocation in fact
provided an appropriate outlet for Brontë's masochistic tendencies. How else can one explain the extraordinary passivity which
allowed her to remain for months in a humiliating situation, not
simply unable to fight her dependence upon her "maitre" but
consistently constructing circumstances that would support and
intensify that dependence? Why else couldn't she force herself to
leave Brussels, suffering as she was from severe depressions and

82. To Emily Brontë, May 29, 1843. Wise and Symington, I, 299.
83. November 15, 1843. Wise and Symington, I, 309.
84. This was easier to do before the publication of Charlotte's letters to
Heger in 1913, but even such distinguished biographers as Fannie Ratchford
and, to a lesser extent, Winifred Gerin, who wrote well after the material was
available, did not confront the issue.
85. Gerin, *Charlotte Brontë*, p. 24.

general malaise?[86] Made desperate at last, she turned her anger upon the students, the teachers, Madame Heger, herself—but she never turned it against "the professor." To him she would not allow herself to show the rage of disappointment. This she would probably not even have allowed herself to feel.

> I suffered much before I left Brussels. I think, however long I live, I shall not forget what the parting with M. Heger cost me; it grieved me so much to grieve him, who has been so true, so kind, and disinterested a friend.[87]

How self-deluded was she? How could she have believed her "dear master" to have been so grieved if he had, in fact, rejected her with such consistent coldness? Was it only a last spurt of friendliness on his part, emanating from relief, that made Brontë believe, when she left Brussels in January of 1844, that she and Heger were still good friends, that he would send one of his daughters to the school which she hoped now to open; that he would write to her, that there was still the possibility of communication, that she could look to him for continued support?

In fact, we know that there was some correspondence between them after Brontë returned to Haworth, that Heger sent her advice—as he told Elizabeth Gaskell—"about her character, studies, mode of life."[88] These letters have not survived, but letters written to others of his students have been preserved. They suggest—as does the passage from a letter to a student quoted below—another perspective which must be added to those habitually applied to "Charlotte's infatuation":

> At the end of your nice letter, which is in front of me, you say, "I remain your *little* friend ——" Allow me to disapprove of a phrase too humble to be sincere; you are not little in my eyes, neither in size, nor age nor reason; nor by the affection you have inspired in me and in my family. We feel this as strongly as ever though you are far from us. "If that is true," you will say to me, "why have you been so slow in answering

86. Gerin suggests that Brontë ultimately decided to leave Brussels only after she had received a strong letter from Mary Taylor urging her to do so. (*Charlotte Brontë,* p. 252). Appealing as this theory is, it can remain only conjecture since Mary Taylor destroyed all of Brontë's correspondence.

87. To Ellen Nussey, January 23, 1844. Wise and Symington, II, 3.

88. Elizabeth Gaskell to Ellen Nussey, July 9, 1856. Wise and Symington, IV, 201–3.

me?'' Why? It will be easy for me to show that although it is
true that I have not written, I have nevertheless answered you
frequently and at length, and this is how. Letters and the post
are not, luckily, the only means of communication, or the best,
between people who are really fond of one another: I am referring to the telephone, which allows one to speak, to have conversations, from a distance. I have something better than that. I
only have to think of you to see you. I often give myself the
pleasure when my duties are over, when the light fades. I post-
pone lighting the gas lamp in my library, I sit down, smoking
my cigar, and with a hearty will I evoke your image—and you
come (without wishing to, I dare say) but I see you, I talk with
you—you, with that little air, affectionate undoubtedly, but independent and resolute, firmly determined not to allow any
opinion without being previously convinced, demanding to be
convinced before allowing yourself to submit—in fact, just as I
knew you, my dear M—— —and as I have esteemed and
loved you.

In thinking it over you will have no difficulty in admitting
that you yourself have experienced a hundred times that which
I tell you about communication between two distant hearts, in-
stantaneous, without paper, without pen, or words, or messenger, etc., a hundred times without noticing it, without its having attracted your attention, without anything extraordinary.[89]

Winifred Gerin, thinking of the letters preserved by many of
Heger's students, muses on the qualities of those which he might
have written, indeed probably did write, to Charlotte herself:
''How delightful they could have been, had no fear of Charlotte's
misunderstanding their kindness existed in the writer's mind
. . .''[90] How delightful indeed! And there can be little question
of ''poor Charlotte's'' susceptibility. Heger's theory of spiritual
or magnetic communication (he must have shared it with other
favored students) appears in a somewhat startling, implicitly sexual, but still recognizable form in *Jane Eyre,* when the heroine
hears Rochester's voice calling to her. But then one asks—particularly in an age more aware of the sexual power games played

89. Translation of original letter from M. Heger to Meta Mossman, November 21, 1887, by courtesy of Walter Cunliffe, Esq. Quoted in Winifred
Gerin, *Charlotte Brontë,* pp. 262–63. Gerin explains, in a note, that ''Meta
adored him,'' but she does not draw any parallels between Meta's feelings and
Charlotte's.

90. Gerin, *Charlotte Brontë,* p. 261.

by male professors with female students—"How many of
Heger's little 'friends' would not have been susceptible to letters
such as this one?" "How many would not have woven fantasies
around the affectionate references, the playful, complimentary
tone, the masculine manipulation?" And if this is the role that
Heger played in his correspondence, what role did he play—unconsciously, of course—in the classroom? How many students,
more or less masochistic than Charlotte, but subject still to similar social and psychosexual pressures, might have created fantasies equally disturbing if less consuming and not so naively
tested? In short, how unique was Brontë's response? To what extent was her infatuation, accepted for so long at face value,
simply another manifestation of the sexual politics pervasive in
Victorian society: more insidious because it was socially validated?

Of course, there was a difference. The circumstances of her
life and—most of all—the peculiarity of her art, made it impossible for her to lightly play the games that many other women of
her time were used to playing. Her imagination had already
begun to carry her to deeper levels of consciousness. Once physically separated from Heger, she was freer to return to these. The
distinction between fantasy and reality blurred. The letters she
wrote to him contained the romantic language and tone she had
perfected in the Angrian tales. The degree of intensity was not
one which Heger could allow. It was certainly not one he could
share. It blasted the surface of "conventional interaction." It
grasped implication by the throat. He discontinued the correspondence. The letters which she writes then, in an attempt to
penetrate his silence, are heartbreaking in the degree of vulnerability they reveal; in their need and, ultimately, in their despair.

In the first of the letters which greets his silence, she mentions
that she must abandon altogether her aspirations as a writer: aspirations which he had not apparently encouraged.

> . . . now my sight is too weak to write. —Were I to write
> much I should become blind. This weakness of sight is a terri-
> ble hindrance to me. Otherwise, do you know what I should do
> Monsieur? —I should write a book, and I should dedicate it to
> my literature master—to the only master I ever had—to you
> Monsieur.[91]

91. July 24, 1844. Wise and Symington, II, 13.

The passage is oddly compelling. In no other letter written at this time does Charlotte mention her "failing sight" as a serious problem.[92] Indeed, one is tempted to dismiss the reference as a transparent plea for sympathy or to accept it as one of the many hysterical symptoms which accompanied the depressions of Brontë's mature years. Certainly, the cataract condition which threatened to deprive her father of his vision must have preoccupied her. It might well have created fears linked to the guilt which accompanied her repressed love for Heger. Blindness was, after all, the punishment she later meted out to Rochester, the adulterer.

The connection that Charlotte makes between her "failing sight" and the difficulty she finds in writing, seems to support this line of interpretation. At this crucial point in her life Charlotte truly does not want to "see" clearly the situation which obsesses her. If she could not confront it, she could not write about it, and her obsession prevented her writing about anything else. Furthermore, how could the adoring student write a book which would be worthy of dedication to her "master"? The relationship is predicated upon a presumption of inequality. How could she risk a judgment which would involve not only her work but her "self"?

In October, a brief note to him reveals that, in her agony of frustrated watching and waiting, she has decided that her letters might not have reached him. It is convenient for her to believe that "Madame" has intercepted his mail, but, when she sends another letter to him by personal messenger and still receives no reply, she can deceive herself no longer. Then she betrays the depth of her suffering and dependence:

> Day and night I find neither rest nor peace. If I sleep I am disturbed by tormenting dreams in which I see you, always severe, always grave, always incensed against me.
>   Forgive me then, Monsieur, if I adopt the course of writ-

92. Gaskell acknowledges that it is probable that even her sisters and most intimate friends didn't know of her ultimate dread of blindness, but the biographer tries to rationalize the fears expressed to Heger: "Long-continued ill-health, a deranged condition of the liver, her close application to minute drawing and writing in her younger days, her now habitual sleeplessness at nights, the many bitter noiseless tears she shed over Branwell's mysterious and distressing conduct—all these causes were telling on her poor eyes . . ." (Gaskell, p. 191).

ing to you again. How can I endure life if I make no effort to ease its sufferings? . . .

All I know is that I cannot, that I will not, resign myself to lose wholly the friendship of my master. I would rather suffer the greatest physical pain than always have my heart lacerated by smarting regrets. . . .

I shall not reread this letter. I send it as I have written it. Nevertheless, I have a hidden Consciousness that some people, cold and commonsense, in reading it would say—"She is talking nonsense." I would avenge myself on such persons in no other way than by wishing them one single day of the torments which I have suffered for eight months. We should then see if they would not talk nonsense too.[93]

Three months later, in a letter to Ellen Nussey, she would reveal the bitterness which this attachment had created:

Ten years ago, I should have laughed at your account of the blunder you made in mistaking the bachelor doctor for a married man. I should have certainly thought you scrupulous over-much—and wondered how you could possibly regret being civil to a decent individual merely because he happened to be single instead of double. Now, however, I can perceive that your scruples are founded on common-sense. I know that if women wish to escape the stigma of husband-seeking, they must act and look like marble or clay—cold—expressionless, bloodless—for every appearance of feeling of joy—sorrow, friendliness, antipathy, admiration—disgust, are alike construed by the world into an attempt to hook a husband.[94]

Her knowledge did not change her behavior. The bitterness could not effect the power of the attachment. It only made the agony of her deprivation greater. Still, the last of the existing letters to Heger does reveal some change: resignation perhaps; perhaps weary self-knowledge.

I tell you frankly that I have tried meanwhile to forget you, for the remembrance of a person whom one thinks never to see again, and whom, nevertheless, one greatly esteems, frets too much the mind: and when one has suffered that kind of anxiety for a year or two, one is ready to do anything to find peace once more. I have done everything; I have sought occupations:

93. January 8, 1845. Wise and Symington, II, 23.
94. April 2, 1845. Wise and Symington, II, 30.

I have denied myself absolutely the pleasure of speaking about
you—even to Emily: but I have been able to conquer neither
my regrets nor my impatience. That, indeed, is humiliating—
to be unable to control one's own thoughts, to be the slave of a
regret, of a memory, the slave of a fixed and dominant idea
which lords it over the mind. Why cannot I have just as much
friendship for you, as you for me—neither more nor less? Then
should I be so tranquil, so free—I could keep silence then for
ten years without an effort.[95]

Brontë had come again to question the motives of infatuation.
She had explored them six years earlier in Mina Laury, Mary
Percy, and Caroline Vernon. The problem now is pressingly her
own. Her situation is humiliating. She is powerless: enslaved not
by Heger but by herself: by her obsession, her need. She is one of
her own imprisoned princesses. Always dependent upon others to
confirm her value—to confirm her very identity—she had found
in Heger the possibilities not only of recognition but of growth.
That promise veiled the degradation of her dependence and made
her thralldom seem quite different from that of her heroines. But
by the time she wrote this last letter she must have known it to
have been the same:

To forbid me to write to you, to refuse to answer me, would be
to tear from me my only joy on earth, to deprive me of my last
privilege—a privilege I never shall consent willingly to surrender.[96]

His undeniable rejection of her destroyed whatever shred of self-
confidence might have been left to her by her father, by Branwell, by the masters and mistresses for whom she had worked as
a governess and teacher. Gradually, all around her, the props
upon which her life had been built—however tenuously—were
being removed. Branwell's illness was paralleled by the mental
collapse of Ellen Nussey's brother, George. Her father's impending blindness made the primary authority figure in her life vulnerable and dependent. Heger's apparent inhumanity was the harsh-
est but by no means the only blast at the foundation of the
patriarchal structure which had protected and fostered her weakness. To her old teacher, employer, and friend, Miss Wooler, she
wrote:

95. November 18, 1845. Wise and Symington, II, 69–70.
96. Wise and Symington, II, 70.

> You ask me if I do not think men are strange beings—I do in-
> deed. I have often thought so—and I think too that the mode of
> bringing them up is strange, they are not half-sufficiently
> guarded from temptation—girls are protected as if they were
> something very frail and silly indeed while boys are turned
> loose on the world as if they—of all beings in existence, were
> the wisest and least liable to be led astray.[97]

Her growing cynicism phrased her questions. It could not invent
answers. Where should she turn? Mary Taylor had decided to
emigrate to New Zealand. She alone of all the women Brontë
knew could provide a model of independent thought and be a
goad to action. But their lives had prepared them to follow different routes. Mary had been raised to rebel. Charlotte had
merely survived.

After she had returned from Brussels, Brontë had written to
Ellen Nussey:

> I do not know whether you feel as I do, but there are times now
> when it appears to me as if all my ideas and feelings, except a
> few friendships and affections, are changed from what they
> used to be; something in me which used to be enthusiasm is
> tamed down and broken. I have few illusions; what I wish for
> now is active exertion—a stake in life.[98]

During the next year, her fevered letters to Heger and her misery
at his withdrawal demonstrated that she had kept more illusions
than she had imagined. But finally rejection left her too unsure to
define herself through her own efforts. Broken and weak as she
was, she had to withdraw into the old caverns of her childhood:
obligation, duty, self-sacrifice. Suffering was her lot—perhaps
her punishment. But it was also, in its familiarity, her security;
for the waters again threatened to break down the walls and
sweep her away. The toll taken by that dreadful year is described
in a letter by Mary Taylor to Elizabeth Gaskell:

> When I last saw Charlotte [January 1845], she told me she had
> quite decided to stay at home. She owned she did not like it.
> Her health was weak; She said she should like any change at
> first, as she had liked Brussels at first, and she thought that
> there must be some possibility for some people of having a life

97. January 30, 1846. Wise and Symington, II, 77.
98. January 23, 1844. Wise and Symington, II, 3.

of more variety and more communion with human kind, but
she saw none for her. I told her very warmly that she ought not
to stay at home in solitude, and weak health would ruin her,
that she would never recover it. Such a dark shadow came over
her face when I said, "Think of what you'll be five years
hence," that I stopped and said, "Don't cry Charlotte." She
did not cry, but went on walking up and down the room, and
said in a little while, "But I intend to stay, Polly."[99]

Brontë did remain at Haworth. But her fate was not the one which
Mary Taylor saw written on her face. She once again survived
and ultimately she was, in a sense, reborn. The process of her salvation was inevitable. It had been shadowed with the accuracy of
psychological insight and self-knowledge in the story of Elizabeth Hastings. A feminist Victorian creation myth had been subconsciously conceived and was now realized. The sister-mother
was fed by the wasted skeleton of the brother-child. As Elizabeth
had found her strength in Henry's weakness, this phoenix also
rose from the ashes of dissolution: Charlotte's renewal was made
possible by Branwell's disintegration. Her own obsession, her
guilt, her humiliation were given concrete form in Branwell's illicit affair with Lydia Robinson. Heger's rejection was acted out
in Lydia's denial. And in Branwell's long and terrible decline,
there was the punishment which she would never have to accept.

Brontë's biographers have noted with some surprise and not a
little displeasure her inability to sympathize with Branwell's
pain. They have observed, with Winifred Gerin, that "it was
Branwell's crowning misfortune that his own calamity should coincide with Charlotte's."[100] None have seen that if it was Branwell's misfortune it was Charlotte's salvation. Emily and Anne—
close comrades from their childhood—could afford to hope for
their brother's regeneration. Patrick Brontë could weep for his
lost son. They could all see his situation with some objectivity
and, therefore, they could pity him. But once again Branwell had
shown himself to Charlotte as her "other self." Now he had
realized what she had known only in fantasy. She had worshiped,
as Branwell had, and in shame she had hidden herself away at
Haworth:

99. Gaskell, p. 190.
100. Gerin, *Branwell Brontë,* p. 245.

> Idolater I kneeled to an idol cut in rock!
> I might have slashed my flesh and drawn my
>   heart's best blood:
> The Granite God had felt no tenderness, no shock;
> My Baal had not seen nor heard nor understood.
> In dark remorse I rose; I rose in darker shame;
> Self-condemned I withdrew to an exile from
>   my kind;
> A solitude I sought where mortal never came
> Hoping in its wilds forgetfulness to find.[101]

But there was an important difference between them. Branwell had given in to temptation. Charlotte had not:

> Have I not fled that I may conquer?
> Crost the dark sea in firmest faith
> That I at last might plant my anchor
> Where love cannot prevail to death?[102]

Charlotte chose to forget (if her choice was unconscious, it was also essential) that Branwell had been given the opportunity which she had been denied. Rejecting Branwell, she could reject her own humiliation and guilt. It was not his degradation that appalled her. It was the fact that he had acted out her most secret and forbidden desires. How else can one account for the priggish, self-righteous tone of the letters of this period:

> Branwell still remains at home, and while *he* is here, *you* shall not come. I am more confirmed in that resolution the more I see of him. I wish that I could say one word to you in his favour, but I cannot, therefore I will hold my tongue.[103]

> You say well in speaking of Branwell that no sufferings are so awful as those brought on by dissipation—Alas! I see the truth of this observation daily proved—Ann and Mercy must have a weary and burdensome life of it—in waiting upon their unhappy brother—it seems grievous indeed that those who have not sinned should suffer so largely.[104]

101. From "He saw my heart's woe," undated, in *The Poems of Charlotte and Patrick Branwell Brontë*, ed. Wise and Symington (New York: Oxford University Press, 1934), p. 241.
102. "Reason," undated, ibid., p. 241.
103. To Ellen Nussey, November 4, 1845. Wise and Symington, II, 66.
104. To Ellen Nussey, December 31, 1845. Wise and Symington, II, 74.

Branwell offers no prospect of hope—he professes to be too ill to think of seeking for employment—he makes comfort scant at home.[105]

You ask about Branwell; he never thinks of seeking employment and I begin to fear he has rendered himself incapable of filling any respectable station in life, besides, if money were at his disposal he would use it only to his own injury—the faculty of self-government is, I fear, almost destroyed in him . . .[106]

The death of Mr. Robinson, which took place about three weeks or a month ago, served Branwell for a pretext to throw all about him into hubbub and confusion with his emotions, etc., etc.[107]

And, finally, after his death: this ambiguous letter to Williams:

The removal of our only brother must necessarily be regarded by us rather in the light of a mercy than a chastisement. Branwell was his father's and his sisters' pride and hope in boyhood, but since manhood, the case has been otherwise. It has been our lot to see him take a wrong bent; to hope, expect, wait his return to the right path; to know the sickness of hope deferred, the dismay of prayer baffled; to experience despair at last—and now to behold the sudden early obscure close of what might have been a noble career.

I do not weep from a sense of bereavement—there is no prop withdrawn, no consolation torn away, no dear companion lost—but for the wreck of talent, the ruin of promise, the untimely dreary extinction of what might have been a burning and shining light. My brother was a year my junior. I had aspirations and ambitions for him once, long ago—they have perished mournfully. Nothing remains of him but a memory of errors and sufferings. There is such a bitterness of pity for his life and death, such a yearning for the emptiness of his whole existence as I cannot describe. I trust time will allay these feelings.[108]

Branwell's life had become for Charlotte the external form of her fantasy-wish. In her rejection of him, her transcendence was

105. To Ellen Nussey, January 23, 1846. Wise and Symington, II, 75.
106. To Miss Wooler, January 30, 1846. Wise and Symington, II, 77.
107. To Ellen Nussey, June 17, 1846. Wise and Symington, II, 96.
108. To W. S. Williams, October 2, 1895. Wise and Symington, II, 261.

made possible. Upon his hopelessness, Charlotte was at last able to build her future and despite the fact that the effective cause of her growing self-confidence was, in part, the neurotic projection of her own guilt, it moved her in the direction of separation and health. With Elizabeth Hastings she could become independent and directed. She could begin to assume responsibility.

Branwell's crisis developed as the cataracts which darkened Patrick Brontë's vision thickened. Her father's growing blindness loosened the bonds of the other symbiotic relationship which had been so destructive in Charlotte's life. The situation of dependence had radically altered, as she suggests in a letter written to M. Heger in 1845:

> My father is well but his sight is almost gone. He can neither read nor write. . . . My father allows me to read to him. I write for him; he shows me, too, more confidence than he has ever shown before, and that is a great consolation.[109]

It is not inappropriate that this woman, whose masochistic dependence and passivity had evolved within the strictures of a patriarchal Victorian family, should find the sources of freedom in the moral and physical disintegration of her brother and in the growing blindness of her father.[110] Only thus could her ego survive at all. But freedom had also to be developed from within. A female child, a survivor, she had turned from the overwhelming terrors of reality to the imagined world of Angria. Rejecting those fantasies, she had reluctantly reached out to life. But the forces which shaped her fantasies made of her life a prison from which she could only escape—once partially freed—by returning again to art: an art which, as it became increasingly mature, became increasingly self-conscious and analytical. Here the haunting, regressive fantasies could be laid to rest. The key to the enchanted castle could be cast.

109. November 18, 1845. Wise and Symington, II, 70.
110. Although the surgical removal of Mr. Brontë's cataracts in August, 1846, successfully restored his vision, Charlotte remained aware for the rest of her life, of her father's increasing physical and emotional dependence upon her and used this dependence as a reason, or an excuse, for remaining at Haworth.

The Professor: *Androgyny and the Search for Self*

I gave, at first attention close;
  Then interest warm ensued;
From interest, as improvement rose
  Succeeded gratitude.

Obedience was no effort soon,
  And Labour was no pain;
If tired, a word, a glance alone
  Would give me strength again

From others of the studious band,
  Ere long he singled me;
But only by more close demand
  And sterner urgency.

The task he from another took,
  From me he did reject;
He would no slight omission brook,
  And suffer no defect.

If my companions went astray,
  He scarce their wanderings blamed;
If I but falter'd in the way,
  His anger fiercely flam'd.

When sickness stay'd awhile my course,
  He seemed impatient still,
Because his pupil's flagging force
  Could not obey his will.

One day when summoned to the bed
  Where pain and I did strive,

I heard him, as he bent his head,
    Say, God, she *must* revive!

I felt his hand, with gentle stress,
    A moment laid on mine,
And wished to mark my consciousness
    By some responsive sign.

But pow'rless then to speak or move,
    I only felt, within,
The sense of Hope, the strength of Love,
    Their healing work begin.

And as he from the room withdrew,
    My heart his steps pursued;
I long'd to prove, by efforts new,
    My speechless gratitude.

When once again I took my place
    Long vacant, in the class,
Th'unfrequent smile across his face
    Did for one moment pass.

The lessons done: the signal made
    Of glad release and play
He, as he passed, an instant stay'd,
    One kindly word to say.

"Jane, till to-morrow you are free
    From tedious task and rule;
This afternoon I must not see
    That yet pale face in school.

Seek in the garden-shades a seat,
    Far from the play-ground din;
The sun is warm, the air is sweet:
    Stay till I call you in."

A long and pleasant afternoon
    I passed in those green bowers;
All silent, tranquil, and alone
    With birds, and bees, and flowers.

Yet, when my master's voice I heard
    Call, from the window, "Jane!"
I entered, joyful, at the word,
    The busy house again.

He, in the hall, paced up and down;
    He paused as I passed by;
His forehead stern relaxed its frown:
    He raised his deep-set eye.

"Not quite so pale," he murmered low.
    "Now, Jane, go rest awhile."
And as I smiled, his smoothened brow
    Returned as glad a smile.

My perfect health restored, he took
    His mien austere again;
And, as before, he would not brook
    The slightest fault from Jane.

The longest task, the hardest theme
    Fell to my share as erst,
And still I toiled to place my name
    In every study first.

He yet begrudged and stinted praise,
    But I had learnt to read
The secret meaning of his face,
    And that was my best meed.

Even when his hasty temper spoke
    In tones that sorrow stirred,
My grief was lulled as soon as woke
    By some relenting word.

And when he lent some precious book,
    Or gave some fragrant flower,
I did not quail to Envy's look,
    Upheld by Pleasure's power.

At last our school ranks took their ground;
    The hard-fought field I won;
The prize, a laurel wreath, was bound
    My throbbing forehead on.

Low at my master's knee I bent,
    The offered crown to meet;
Its green leaves through my temples sent
    A thrill as wild as sweet.

The strong pulse of Ambition struck
    In every vein I owned;

At the same instant, bleeding broke
A secret, inward would.

The hour of triumph was to me
The hour of sorrow sore;
A day hence I must cross the sea,
Ne'er to recross it more.

An hour hence, in my master's room,
I with him sat alone,
And told him what a dreary gloom
O'er joy had parting thrown.

He little said; the time was brief,
The ship was soon to sail,
And while I sobbed in bitter grief,
My master but looked pale.

They called in haste; he bade me go,
Then snatched me back again;
He held me fast and murmered low,
"Why will they part us, Jane?

"Were you not happy in my care?
Did I not faithful prove?
Will others to my darling bear
As true, as deep a love?

"O God, watch o'er my foster child!
O guard her gentle head!
When winds are high and tempests wild
Protection round her spread!

"They call again; leave then my breast;
Quit thy true shelter, Jane;
But when deceived, repulsed, opprest,
Come home to me again!"

*T*HIS POEM, which appears near the conclusion of Charlotte Brontë's first novel, *The Professor,* is not laudable for its literary qualities.[1] Its importance lies rather in the clarity of its presentation of Brontë's fantasy relationship with Heger. While the formal and thematic elements of the poem are naive,

1. The "Jane" poem was apparently written in 1845; a year before Brontë wrote *The Professor* and the last year of her abortive correspondence with Heger.

extraordinary tension is unconsciously created between the surface reality and the sexuality which underlies it. The interaction of master and pupil is ambiguous. Jane's desire for sexual submission is expressed in humble "obedience" and "gratitude," while the teacher's demanding discipline masks a dominating and frustrated passion. He is both father and lover: she is mistress and daughter. Jane's critical illness elicits a longed-for and ambiguously loving response. The moment of recognition heralds separation instead of the impossible consummation. Finally, their parting is effected by an unnamed enemy (Madame Heger, society, conscience) and is made bearable by the contradictory promise of reconciliation at the end.

This fantasy, variously imaged and developed, recurs in all four of Brontë's novels. Her compulsive reworking of the same themes demonstrates the degree of difficulty she experienced in resolving the conflict with Heger. It also suggests the extent to which that conflict was associated implicitly with attitudes toward her own sexuality, her father, Branwell, and her work. In *The Professor* the fantasy provides the novel's motivating impulses, but not its substance. The form of the fantasy is presented but its energy is suppressed. The distance between the crafted fiction and the emotional energy which informs it, measure the gulf between Brontë's obsession and her capacity for self-analysis.

The "Jane" poem reveals as it veils, functioning on the level of dream as had Brontë's juvenile writing. The novel, on the other hand, intentionally represses and obscures the free play of imagination. Its structure is that of the *Bildungsroman,* conventional in form and subject. Ostensibly it carries the hero, William Crimsworth, from innocence to experience, tracing his development from orphaned outsider (the friendless younger brother bereft of status, wealth, and professional competence) to respectable schoolmaster and "paterfamilias." His initiation involves him in a troubling personal relationship with two elder men— Hunsden, the wealthy mill owner, and Pellet, the successful Belgian school director, both of whom are foils intended to help him in his self-definition. He has one abortive "romantic" relationship with Zoraïde Reuter, a Belgian schoolmistress modeled on Mme. Heger. Her failings instruct him in the genuine value of Frances Henri, the poor young student whom he eventually marries. The hero's progress is praiseworthy and archetypic in form, but there is only formal pattern, deprived of genuinely depicted struggle or conflict.

It is interesting, therefore, that Crimsworth should observe, when he discovers the "Jane" poem among Frances's papers:

> [The lines were] not the writer's own experience, but a com-
> position by portions of that experience suggested. Thus while
> egotism was avoided, the fancy was expressed and, of course,
> satisfied.[2]

Crimsworth's comment is, in fact, more appropriate to the process which has produced the story in which he figures than it is to the poem which he describes. The struggle between willed feeling and felt truth has taken place well beneath the surface of this novel and the characters emerge from it curiously flattened and dispassionate: shadow versions of their poetic counterparts.

A comparison of the themes in the novel with those of the poem is instructive. In the novel, Crimsworth is the peremptory master, bestowing criticism more easily than praise upon his adoring pupil. He shows his regard for Frances by the stringency of the demands he makes upon her: a game which disguises and prefigures their psychosexual interaction. They are separated, as are the Jane of the poem and her "master," by an "enemy," the jealous Mlle. Reuter. Finally, their moment of reconciliation takes place when Frances is in the throes of deepest despair and loneliness after the death of her last living relative.

The outlines of the recurrent fantasy can be discerned but reading the story one finds that the images are not suggestive—simply blurred. Emotion, where it exists at all, is stifled or disjointed. In a perverse way, Brontë has managed to withhold her characters in order to withhold herself, all the while pursuing a well-defined aesthetic plan which she carefully explains to the reader:

> Novelists should never allow themselves to weary of the study
> of real life. If they observed this duty conscientiously, they
> would give us fewer pictures checkered with vivid contrasts of
> light and shade; they would seldom elevate their heroes and
> heroines to the height of rapture—still seldomer sink them to

2. Charlotte Brontë, *The Professor* (New York: Oxford University Press, 1967), p. 208. All subsequent references are to this edition and will be given in the text.

the depths of despair; for if we rarely taste the fullness of joy in this life, we yet more rarely savour the acrid bitterness of hopeless anguish . . . (p. 150)

In writing her first novel, Brontë found security in following these guidelines conscientiously. First in her "Farewell to Angria" and later in the "Preface" she wrote for *The Professor*,[3] she made it clear that she had rejected the mythic dimensions of the romantic world:

I had not indeed published anything before I commenced *The Professor*, but in many a crude effort, destroyed almost as soon as composed, I have got over any such taste as I might once have had for ornamented and redundant composition, and come to prefer what was plain and homely. (p. v)

Unfortunately, she did not understand the options available to her as a "realistic" writer. She did not recognize the potential richness of the psychological insights which had distinguished her early writings from Branwell's: the range and subtlety which a mastery of the psychological perspective would contribute to the "plain and homely" order of life which she had seized upon as her appropriate subject. She did not yet know how crucial some of the old techniques could be in helping her to order psychic chaos while transforming obsession into art. Mistakenly, she purges her fiction of the most compelling tensions of the juvenilia. What remains are unresolved personal and artistic conflicts —an uneasy and, at times, disastrous attempt to wed old and new characters and situations. What is most interesting in this novel, therefore, are its flaws: the subterranean eruption of materials which will become the foci of Brontë's later work.

Although the plot seems to follow the traditional formula of the education of the hero, Crimsworth's growth is not organic. He achieves complacency rather than wisdom. Life seems to happen to him. He has only been moved through time and space. His orphaned childhood is briefly mentioned, never discussed. Reference is made to his quarrel with the aristocratic uncles who have, not ungrudgingly, subsidized his education. His past remains largely an unexplored mystery. We watch his catastrophic ap-

3. The "Preface" was first printed with the permission of Arthur Bell Nicholls, Charlotte's husband, in a posthumous edition of the novel published by Smith, Elder in 1857.

prenticeship to his mill-owner brother, Edward, and are curiously unmoved by it. One is a passive victim: the other a villain without motive. Their underlying resentments are reminiscent of the hostility between Zamorna and Charles, even Zamorna and Northangerland, but while the causes are equally ambiguous, all the passion is gone. Rejecting or, rather, rejected by business as a way of life, Crimsworth happens upon the position of teacher, first in a boys' school in Brussels and later in the girls' school which adjoins it. He is briefly tempted by Mlle. Reuter, the head-mistress, but proof of her emotional unreliability immediately precedes his discovery of Frances, the Anglo-Swiss pupil-mistress who ultimately resolves all of his conflicts: sexual, pro-fessional, even national. His economic difficulties are swept away by good fortune and it remains for him only to marry the still adoring young student with whom he lives happily ever after. The story is neither engaging nor convincing.

Unsatisfactory as a hero, Crimsworth is equally disappointing as the narrator. Standing at the narrative center of the novel, he represents its most crucial problem. Never realized as a fully dimensioned character, Crimsworth is unable to develop a clear narrative voice. Never conscious of his own experience on any but the most immediate level, he is unable to bring to the events he describes a vital complexity of vision.[4] Crimsworth explains, presents, and describes his experience, but his words seem undis-turbed by the pressures of life. In *Villette,* the same narrative dis-tance will be perceived as the functioning of a neurotic personal-ity. But here, because the elements of character are never integrated, distance is felt as a lapse of art in much the same way that Brontë's inability to establish a consistent stance for Crims-worth in relation to the reader[5] is interpreted as a sign of novelis-tic inexperience.

4. It seems hardly necessary to mention Brontë's misjudgment in beginn-ing the novel with Crimsworth's letter to his old friend Charles. Charles, along with the epistolary device, disappears from sight after the first chapter. The rela-tionship, so briefly outlined, seems to look back to the friendship between William Percy and Charles Towneshend and prefigures Crimsworth's am-bivalent relationship with Yorke Hunsden.

5. He withholds information, unexpectedly inserting material relevant to the past, but not mentioned at an appropriate time. He also includes material which seems to add bulk but not substance to the story.

II

Generally, the crudities of plot development reflect the inadequate concept of character which results from Brontë's personal insecurity. She cannot create a persona with whom she identifies her own point of view nor can she adopt an ironic stance without knowing who she is or what she wishes to represent. She is caught in a bind: unable to analyze the facts of her situation while urgently wishing to explore its implications for her as a woman, a sister, a daughter, a lover, a writer. In her need to find ways of expressing her anger and frustration and in her desire to create alternative modes of action, she rummages among bits and scraps of the past and tries to synthesize an image of her potential self. The fascinating, unresolved—barely conscious—conflicts that existed among the Angrians are fused with the superficial events that cloak the trauma of Brussels. Searching for focus Brontë projects herself into her story and becomes a force for fragmentation rather than synthesis. In effect, she divides herself among the three central figures—Crimsworth, Frances, and Hunsden—who are alternate versions of one another, all problematical because they are all incomplete; all unconscious of their own motivations and dependent upon one another for definition. The technique Brontë employs foreshadows the allegorical process of inquiry she will use so effectively in *Jane Eyre*. If she had clearly conceived the central protagonist, she would have been able to project his growth onto other well-articulated characters who could have been fully developed themselves while articulating aspects of ther hero's internal struggle. (Jane Eyre's relationship to Rochester and St. John Rivers offers an obvious example.) But because Brontë had not fully grasped the nature of her hero nor the purpose of his quest, because she had not conceived him as a fully separable and distinct character, she is led to suspend the three in uneasy balance, truncating their progress and leaving them incomplete.

The superficial similarities of Crimsworth, Frances, and Hunsden have been noted as well as their similarities to the novelist herself. All are physically plain, energetic, independent, high-minded. All are argumentative, priggish, embarassingly honest.[6] All are extremely vulnerable and their vulnerability is protected by postures which are variously sarcastic, ironic and, in Hunsden's case, cynical. They are not people who, in the best of circumstances, would communicate easily with others. They are locked within their own suspicions and fears. Given the odd blurring of identity boundaries, the failure of their interaction is assured. Dialogue therefore approximates monologue and discussions are dramatized interior debates in which one aspect of Brontë's personality seeks ascendancy over the others.

We assume that Brontë chose to use a male narrator for reasons similar to those which had dictated the same decision for her in the past: that she is still bound to the ambivalent attitudes of adolescence and accepts automatically the male point of view as the "official" perspective. Never having encountered a "heroine" in her personal, cultural, or political experience—or, for that matter, in literature—it was difficult for her to conceive of any woman as the focus of a work of fiction. Even in those late stories, Mina Laury, Elizabeth Hastings, and Caroline Vernon are seen through the eyes of either Charles Towneshend or an omniscient sexless narrator. Not one of them speaks for herself. Furthermore, although these heroines' conflicts are analyzed with unusual insight and subtlety, their lives are justified and their personalities validated, by the man they love: the "hero." In order to use a woman as the locus of consciousness, Brontë had to reexamine her deepest assumptions. Therefore the inconsistency of her characterizations, and particularly the ambiguous treatment of Crimsworth, must not simply be accepted as indications of artistic incompetence but are rather indications that the reexamination had already, rather uncertainly, begun.

William Crimsworth is her transitional hero: a bridge between her identification with a male persona and her commitment to a female "voice." He is, at times, feminized: almost androgynous. One notices at once his propensity for "feeling," his close identification with his mother and his extreme sensitivity: all met with cynicism by the other male characters—Hunsden, Pellet, and Edward. Of more importance is his initial position of powerlessness which makes him seem most "feminine" to the reader and to himself. An orphaned outsider, without money, deprived

6. See Charles Burkhart, *Charlotte Brontë, A Psychosexual Study of Her Novels* (London: Gollancz, 1973), pp. 50–51.

of social status, he describes himself as "a single lean cormorant, standing mateless and shelterless on poverty's bleak cliff" (p. 189). The image is reminiscent of Brontë's description of herself as "a solitary raven surveying the deluge." Standing lonely at a dance given by his elder brother and master, Edward, Crimsworth betrays his confusion of sexual identity when he observes, "I looked weary, solitary, kept down like some desolate tutor or governess" (p. 18). The confusion persists during his early experience in Brussels, and is revealed by the language and imagery he uses to describe Mlle. Reuter's pursuit of him:

> Still she persevered, and at last, I am bound to confess it, her finger, essaying, proving every atom of the casket, touched its secret spring, and for a moment the lid sprung open; she laid her hand on the jewel within, whether she stole and broke it, or whether the lid shut again with a snap on her fingers, read on, and you shall know. (p. 97)

She is the seductor. He is her passive victim: virginal. For Brontë, gender seems quite astonishingly—if only half-consciously—to be a semantic symbol denoting power in much the same way as "blackness" is, in Jean Genet's play, *The Blacks*, a matter of relative position rather than a color.[7] The perception of sexual role as status will be emphasized more in the writing of *Jane Eyre* and *Shirley*. Still, the terms are established here, in the sense which emerges from Crimsworth's attitude toward his social position and in his relationship with Edward, his older brother.

Although it is difficult to take Edward seriously as a character (he is a cardboard, melodramatic villain) he is important as a representative of a developing class which is antithetical to personal humane values: a product and prophet of industrialization. Crimsworth, looking down from the hills upon his brother's mill, must remind himself to

> Look at the sooty smoke in that hollow, and know that there is your post! There you cannot dream, you cannot speculate and theorize—there you shall out and work. (p. 11)

7. In his introduction to *The Blacks,* Genet asks, "What exactly is a black? First of all, what's his color?" (*The Blacks: A Clown Show*, trans. Bernard Frechtman [New York: Grove Press, 1960]). In the play within his play, the black man who achieves ascendancy is no longer "black" but "white" and his victim, his subordinate, is "black" whatever his "real," apparent color.

In the mill, William's education, his intelligence, his sensitivity count for nothing. They may be experienced as threatening to others, but they are not considered useful. They relegate William to a lower class in a society which is becoming increasingly stratified, a society in which the master-owner has crucial power over his economic inferiors.

Edward's attitude toward his wife is typical of his materialistic orientation. She is his possession, a sign of his status, valueless in herself, part of his "image"—the object of his benevolence when he is successful, the object of his sadistic rage when his position is threatened. And she allows herself to be so defined. Her virtues are "social," synthesized to please. She is deprived of intellect and will. Crimsworth recognizes that she is only a plaything, not an appropriate mate. His choice must be of a different sort, he thinks, for he knows that in a man's life there must be "November seasons of disaster, when a man's hearth and home would be cold indeed, without the clear, cheering gleam of intellect" (p. 9). Crimsworth's woman will still have to satisfy the needs of her dominating male but Crimsworth considers his own needs to be of a higher order of value than his brother's.

In this, as in other ways, Crimsworth would regard himself as an intellectual, not standing in opposition to the class society which rejects him, but placing himself outside it altogether. However, his position must be supported psychologically since it cannot be supported socially. The capacity to define himself through love and meaningful work are necessary conditions of his self-confidence. Significantly, Crimsworth can realize himself in these ways only by leaving England. Crimsworth knows that the social system is too inflexible to accomodate him and he feels that he must put his brother behind him, for Edward cannot help but triumph in his own milieu, despite momentary failures and temporary setbacks.

With magical power characteristic of fairy tale and repression (but not conducive to plot credibility) Crimsworth does, in fact, erase his older brother from his mind and, as a foreign professor in Brussels, achieves a privileged status which places him above the middle-class businessman, his students, and—of course—women. When he does finally return to England, it will be to establish, with Frances, a school of his own: a fulfillment of an ambition which dominated Brontë's own life. The school's success allows him to be accepted, because of his intellectual achievements, by members of the upper class and thus to be placed in a position superior to that of the bourgeoisie.[8] In this way Crimsworth becomes the hero of a fantasy shared, with appropriate variations, by intellectuals and artists who found themselves increasingly deprived of social status in the nineteenth century. The compromised nature of this novel's resolution must have had its source in Brontë's own social insecurity, revealed recurrently in the writer's life and work.

Crimsworth's psychological development from alienated younger brother to successful "maitre" establishes a pattern which is faithfully followed by the heroines of the next three novels: most faithfully by Lucy Snowe. Initially, Crimsworth is virtually immobilized by the "cold disdain" of his guardians' attitude toward him. In fact, having known neither joy nor liberty in his life, Crimsworth accepts disdain as his due. Hunsden accurately describes the effect of this sense of inferiority:

> You see beauty always turning its back on you; you are mortified and then you sneer. I verily believe that all that is desirable on earth—wealth, reputation, love—will forever to you be the ripe grapes of the high trellis: you'll look up at them; they will tantalize in you the lust of the eye; but they are out of reach: you have not the address to fetch a ladder, and you'll go away calling them sour. (p. 195)

To deal with his extreme vulnerability, Crimsworth has become passive. It is his passivity which allows him to stay at the mill, tolerating Edward's sadism, defining his situation as a conflict between duty and the need for freedom; giving in, as Brontë does herself, to the "fetish of perseverance" (p. 24). Only after Edward initiates a violent argument with him, can he justify his departure, reassuring himself that "I had not forced circumstances; circumstances had freed me" (p. 39).

Although other characters refer to Crimsworth's sensitivity, it is not his sensitivity to which the reader responds. It is his coldness and defensiveness. That Brontë cannot make the reader aware of his sensitivity and defensiveness simultaneously—as

8. This point is made by Tom Winnifrith, *The Brontës, and Their Background: Romance and Reality* (New York: Macmillan, 1973), p. 156.

she will in *Villette* with Lucy Snowe—is a failure of her art. Nevertheless, she does demonstrate persuasively the way in which Crimsworth, by withholding himself, makes of his vulnerability a weapon.

When Crimsworth first arrives at Edward's house, seeking a livelihood from a brother whom he has not seen for many years, he wonders whether he should "feel free to show something of my real nature" (p. 7) to Edward and his wife. He is anxious to establish a relationship with them, yet he is fearful of the rejection his past has taught him to expect. Fortunately, as he comes to feel when he learns the cruelty of his brother's nature, he does not betray to them his deeper, more authentic self. But the tendency to withdraw that protects him from Edward, makes him unexpectedly attractive to others. It piques Hunsden's curiosity and makes the older man his patron. It stimulates Mlle. Reuter's interest and makes of her his seductress. It manipulates Frances's love and earns him her half-fearful adoration. In short, his reticence ironically brings him into a world of relationships in which he finds that he must attempt to face himself. Most urgently, he must confront the fears surrounding his own sexuality. To define these, Brontë—caught up in the subconscious complexities of her androgynous vision—must have used as a model the more familiar female fear of penetration to conceive the male fear of castration. They are two aspects of the horror of the loss of the self to the "other." The connection to the ambivalence of the Byronic hero is evident—and fascinating.

At the beginning of the novel, we are told that, despite his uncles' urgings, he would not marry "the large and well-modeled statue, Sarah" (p. 2), who seems to be a precursor of Rochester's Berthe. For Crimsworth, sexually desirable women are small and delicate: completely unthreatening. Because he is repelled by an active sensuality which demands response, his feelings about Zoraïde Reuter are ambivalent. Extremely attracted to her, he tries to deny his attraction by imagining the aftereffects of a marriage based upon sensuality:

> . . . when passion cooled, how dreadful to find a lump of wax and wood layed in my bosom, a half idiot clasped in my arms, and to remember that I had made of this my equal—nay, my idol—to know that I must pass the rest of my dreary life with a creature incapable of understanding what I said, of ap-

preciating what I thought, or of sympathizing with what I felt.
(p. 100)

To the reader, who might well admire the schoolmistress's intelligence and spirit, Crimsworth's judgment might seem harsh
(its egotism does not bear mentioning). The very excessiveness
of his language seems to suggest that he fears Zoraïde's sexuality. His problem is resolved when he discovers (unconvincingly)
that she has been flirting with him while maintaining an engage-
ment to Pellet. Condemning her duplicity, he can rationalize his
rejection of her sexual aggressiveness. But her subservient response to his rejection teaches him a lesson which relieves his
sexual anxieties more effectively and teaches him the path to confident masculinity.

> Servility creates despotism. This slavish homage, instead of
> softening my heart, only pampered whatever was stern and ex-
> acting in its mood. The very circumstances of her hovering
> around me like a fascinated bird, seemed to transform me into
> a rigid pillar of stone. (p. 120)

Again, the image is compelling. His "manhood" is aroused at
last and it is inevitably identified with power:

> I had ever hated a tyrant; and, behold, the possession of a
> slave, self-given, went near to transform me into what I ab-
> horred! There was at once a sort of low gratification in receiv-
> ing this luscious incense from an attractive and still young
> worshiper; and an irritating sense of degradation in the very ex-
> perience of the pleasure. When she stole about me with the soft
> step of a slave, I felt at once barbarous and sensual as a pasha.
> (p. 175)

This aspect of their relationship awakens in him the self-confidence essential to his assertion of the masculine "virtues." He
tells us that Zoraïde's interest in him "had proved that I *could*
impress" (p. 196) and, although the credibility of the plot suffers
from the easy transference of his affections from Mlle. Reuter to
Frances, there is a logic in the presentation which, if it does not
reflect *well* upon him does, in fact, reflect truthfully.

Crimsworth's aggressive masculinity is supported by the role
he is encouraged to play in the schoolroom. Here is a new world
with a hierarchical structure that can accomodate his intellectual
achievements as Edward's world did not. He appropriates the au-

thority and power inherent in his position with extraordinary avidity. The primary satisfaction which he derives from teaching is the display of his own intellectual superiority. (The immaturity he betrays in his attitude towards his students is not censured by Brontë. On the contrary, it seems rather to express the bitterness she herself experienced as a privileged, Protestant student and teacher at the Pensionnat Heger.) All the Belgians with whom Crimsworth comes into contact are dull and stubborn: their intellectual facilities are weak; their animal propensities strong. His male students have "short memories, dense intelligences, feeble reflective powers" (p. 60). He finds bullying to be the only viable approach he can adopt toward them: "I offered them but one alternative—submission and acknowledgment of error, or ignominious expulsion" (p. 61). The girls whom he teaches are flirtatious, sensual, dishonest, and equally stupid. Those possessed of any intelligence have had their minds and souls warped by their religion. Thus, although his adversaries emerge as astonishingly unworthy, his sense of his own superiority is marvelously strengthened.

Frances offers him an appealing opportunity to show off his late-blossoming, newly male ego. She is worthy of him although, or perhaps because, she is still his inferior:

> The toil worn, fagged, probably irritable tutor, blind almost to beauty, insensible to airs and graces, glories chiefly in certain mental qualities: application, love of knowledge, natural capacity, docility, truthfulness, gratefulness, are the charms that attract his notice and win his regard. (p. 112)

In his relationship with Frances there is a nod to a principle of mutual respect which distinguishes the intellectual basis of *their* feeling from the materialism of Edward's marriage. With *her,* Crimsworth's need for power is refined: rationalized and controlled. A subtly expressed domination replaces both the raw arrogance of the classroom pose and the sadism of his approach to Zoraïde. The romantic myth is placed within the context of teacher-student interaction.

> The reproofs suited her best of all: while I scolded she would chip away with her pen-knife and a pencil or a pen; fidgeting a little, pouting a little, defending herself by monosyllables; and when I deprived her of the pen or pencil, fearing it would be all cut away, and while I interdicted even the monosyllabic de-

fence for the purpose of working up a subdued excitement a little higher, she would at last raise her eyes and give me a certain glance, sweetened with gaiety, and pointed with defiance, which, to speak truth, thrilled me as nothing had ever done, and made me in a fashion (though happily she did not know it), her subject, if not her slave. (pp. 168–69).

Crimsworth can "risk" himself emotionally, because Frances does not threaten him sexually. She is a dependent child, waiting to be aroused. Idealizing her, he completely denies her sexual nature. The richly metaphoric language he uses to describe his attachment suggests again the motivating force of sublimation:

> [She is] my ideal of the shrine in which to seal my stores of love; personification of discretion and forethought, of diligence and perseverance, of self-denial and self-control—those guardians, those trusty keepers of the gift I long to confer on her—the gift of all my affections. . . . (p. 160)

Crimsworth's analysis of the attraction is also revealing. (It is most revealing, perhaps, of Brontë's inability to separate herself from her narrator. Her representation of Rochester's sexual fears will be far more sophisticated.)

> It is true Frances' mental points had been the first to interest me, and they still retained the strongest hold on my preference; but I liked the graces of her person, too. I derived a pleasure, purely material, from contemplating the clearness of her brown eyes, the fairness of her fine skin, the purity of her well-set teeth, the proportion of her delicate form; and that pleasure I could ill have dispensed with. It appeared then, that I too was a sensualist in my temperate and fastidious way. (p. 217)

That temperance and fastidiousness are not adequate to calm Crimsworth's fear of sexuality is revealed in the severe attack of depression which immediately follows his declaration of love and proposal of marriage.[9]

9. Experiences such as this one which is attributed to Crimsworth were familiar to Brontë and recurred throughout her life as they recur in her novels. She described one of these painful interludes in a letter to Miss Wooler (undated fragment, circa November 1846; Wise and Symington, II, 117), in which she recalls her experiences as a teacher at Roe Head. It's interesting that she should use imprisonment in a subterranean dungeon—the image from her adolescent dream—as a central image in her description:

> I pity Mr. Thomas from my heart. For ten years—he has now, I think, been a sufferer from nervous complaints—for ten years he has felt the tyranny of

Crimsworth naively attributes the resurgence of "hypochondria" (earlier experiences are associated with his lonely orphaned childhood) to a lack of food and rest. It is clear, however, that the cause must be sought elsewhere: in his fear of sexual initiation; his fear of a commitment which will make him vulnerable, in his fear of impotence which will belie the fantasy-self which emerged from his relationship with Zoraïde, in his fear of failure which will negate the professional good fortune of his professorial appointment. The veneer which is his aggressive Byronic masculinity is easily shattered. Hypochondria appears before him as a woman, of course: tempting him into a "grey darkness"; luring him to death. It is the insecurity of his childhood reborn in the challenges of maturity. She is the mother who died, the woman he would marry, the female component of his being. She tempts him with passivity, withdrawal, negation. However complex and obscure the route followed by Brontë in defining the implications of Crimsworth's psychosexual anxieties, by whatever process the fear of penetration was extended to suggest the fear of castration, it seems that this marked the beginning of a new level of comprehension of the Byronic hero.

The illness which lasts for two weeks is similar to the ordeals later endured by Jane Eyre, Carolyn Helstone, and Lucy Snowe. For all, recovery marks a psychic rebirth: an entry into a new life. Crimsworth emerges from the darkness of hypochondria into a sunny and elevated "place" in society. He exchanges the helplessness of the orphaned child for the secure power of the patriarch: husband, father, "maître." Ultimately, as the director of an English school (no longer an alienated foreigner) he will stand be-

---

Hypochondria—a most dreadful doom, far worse than that of a man with healthy nerves buried for the same length of time in a subterranean dungeon—I endured it but a year—and assuredly I can never forget the concentrated anguish of certain insufferable moments and the heavy gloom of many living hours—besides the preternatural horror which seemed to clothe existence and Nature—and which made life a continual waking Nightmare—under such circumstances the morbid nerves can know neither peace nor enjoyment—whatever touches—pierces them—sensation for them is all suffering. A weary, burdened, nervous patience consequently become to those about them—they know this and it infuses a new gall corrosive in its extreme attitude into their bitter cup—when I was at Dewsbury Moor—I could have been no better company for you than a stalking ghost—

tween the upper and middle classes, with access to the first and superior to the second.

Although orderly, the resolution remains unconvincing. While Crimsworth's identity crisis has theoretically yielded maturity, while his achieved status has defined him unalterably as male—still, Brontë's art has not made him human. The reader who is informed of his development is aware of external change rather than organic process. He moves but never flowers. The *idea* of Crimsworth's progress is fascinating because of Brontë's unconscious revelations. But to the extent that the artistic, psychological, and social perspectives are conscious, they can only be described as naive.

Frances cannot be realized as a fictive character if Crimsworth is not. She is the other side of his experience: conditioned by his definition of her and the victim, as is he, of Brontë's ambiguous and even contradictory vision. Her relationship with her "maître" does force upon her a condition of fragmentation which is potentially valid: the fragmentation of a woman who seeks for independence in life and feels dependent in love. On one hand, she reveals herself, in her immediate responses to Crimsworth's marriage proposal, to be childish and immature:

> You have always made me happy; I like to hear you speak; I like to see you; I like to be near you; I believe you are very good, and very superior; I know you are stern to those who are careless and idle, but you are kind, very kind to the attentive and industrious, even if they are not clever. Monsieur, I should be *glad* to live with you always— . . . (p. 214)

But she demonstrates, at the same time, a commanding desire for freedom and an adult understanding of the needs of her own personality.

> Think of my marrying you to be kept by you, Monsieur! I could not do it; and how dull my days would be! You would be away teaching in close, noisy school-rooms from morning till evening, and I should be lingering at home, unemployed and solitary; I should get depressed and sullen, and you would soon tire of me. (p. 216)

The fragmentation is never realized on the novel's surface as part of the character's psychological conflict. Brontë—apparently trapped in the depths of her own ambivalence—neither allows the conflict to penetrate Frances's consciousness nor to affect her life. By maintaining a larger perspective which is male-oriented, Brontë offers a superficial and unconvincing solution. Frances does not have to *earn* her independence. It is not necessary for her to discover its source within herself. Instead, her freedom is given to her and sustained by Crimsworth, who magnanimously explains:

> I put no obstacle in her way; raised no objection; I knew she was not one who could live quiescent and inactive, or even comparatively inactive. Duties she must have to fullfil, and important duties; work to do—and exciting, absorbing, profitable work; strong faculties stirred in her frame, and they demanded full nourishment, free exercise: mine was not the hand ever to starve or cramp them; no, I delighted in offering them sustenance and in clearing wide a space for action. (p. 237)

That freedom awarded rather than claimed is simply another form of imprisonment, that the price of Frances's professional liberation is personal servitude, becomes clear to the reader although it is not perceived by Frances, since it is not perceived in these terms by Brontë herself. As Madame, the directress, Frances is "a stately and elegant woman," dignified, vigilant, rather cool, worthy of respect. But at six o'clock "the lady-directress vanished before my eyes, and Frances Henri, my own little lace-mender was magically restored to my arms" (p. 241). Frances plays (with astonishing equanimity) two roles which cannot be integrated. In this way, she remains a child, testing her limits, but never able to make a full commitment to herself. Her relationship with Crimsworth can never mature since both of them are forced into static, ultimately paralyzing postures.

It would seem that Brontë could not yet confront her own confusion about the dependence created by "romantic love," nor could she accept as viable any alternative for women to marriage:

> Look at the rigid and formal race of old maids—the race whom all despise; they have fed themselves, from youth upwards, on maxims of resignations and endurance. Many of them get ossified with the dry diet; self-control is so continually their thought, so perpetually their object, that at last it absorbs the softer and more agreeable qualities of their nature; and they die mere models of austerity . . . (p. 207

The conflict is still the one of her childhood—between self-control and passion, reason and feeling, Wellington and Byron. Her experience with Heger had confirmed her fear that the two were never to be, for her, easily compatible: yet she could not help but feel that, for a woman particularly, a life without love was more frightening than a life given up as a victim to love's service. As in her childhood, the sexual power of Byron was more compelling than the sober virtues of Wellington. It was not until *Jane Eyre,* her next novel, that she would begin to explore the ways in which the conflicting demands of passion and personal integrity could be recognized and answered.

Only in their relationships with Yorke Hunsden do Frances and William seem to overcome at all the bifurcations of their personalities. Interacting with him, they allow the unresolved, more genuine aspects of themselves to emerge. Hunsden evokes their anger and hostility. Opposing their views, he makes them assert themselves. Asserting themselves, they cannot hide their confusions behind their customary complacency. In their interplay with Hunsden, they betray the possibilities that exist beyond the roles which they play with one another.

Hunsden himself is gifted with no particular insight. In fact, if he is more interesting than the other two, it is because he is even less completely defined, more mysterious. He is similar to them in ways that all three are similar to Brontë, but single aspects of his character are never assimilated into a personality "system." Still, it is his inconsistencies which suggest the more complex potential of personality: the deeper levels of Crimsworth's and Frances's motivation, as well as Brontë's own psychological probing moving beneath the story's surface, disturbing its calm but never affecting its form.

Although Hunsden is more aggressive than Crimsworth, more assured of his position, he is also insecure—as William recognizes:

> . . . his general bearing intimated complete, sovereign satisfaction with himself; yet at times, an indescribable shade passed like an eclipse over his countenance and seemed to me like the sign of a sudden and strong inward doubt of himself, his words and actions—an energetic discontent at his life or his social position, his future prospects or his mental attainment— I know not which . . . (p. 23)

As with Crimsworth, insecurity is linked to effeminacy. In Hunsden's case, it shows itself in his handwriting "small and rather
neat: neither masculine or exactly feminine" (p. 183), and, more
importantly, in his features:

> Character had set a stamp upon each; expression recast them at
> her pleasure, and strange metamorphoses she wrought, giving
> him now the mien of a morose bull and anon that of an arch
> and mischievious girl; more frequently, the two semblances
> were blent, and a queer composite countenance they made.
> (p. 29)

The sexual division is neither developed nor resolved in Hunsden, perhaps because he serves more as a foil for William and
Frances than as a character in his own right. Still, to the extent
that he is androgynous he is vulnerable. Because he is vulnerable,
he is defensive, although in *him* defensiveness does not take the
form of withdrawal as it does in William.

Brontë draws upon the relationship between Zamorna and
Percy in her conception of the ambiguous interaction between
Hunsden and Crimsworth. Feelings fluctuate—often with incredible suddenness—between love and hate. From one perspective,
the relationship can be characterized as a struggle for power involving two loving antagonists, imprisoned in mutual fascination. But in its progress can also be traced the romantic quest for
the "other": the brother-friend, who is necessary to complete the
self, but who, because of the element of opposition he represents,
is extremely threatening. The two patterns of behavior are not
mutually exclusive. The first implies the second. Together they
represent the ambivalent interaction of siblings, lovers, parents,
and children. The contradictory needs for union and separation
are commandingly expressed in Crimsworth's and Hunsden's interdependence and compulsive assertions of pride, in their fierce
protection of their vulnerable egos, in their readiness to experience themselves as threatened and in the capacity of each to cruelly attack and manipulate the other. Because the two men do not
share a socially defined relationship, the reactions of the moment
define the nature of the role which each will adopt. The flexibility
afforded by the ability of each to occupy surrogate positions of
crucial importance to the other is both anxiety-producing and
liberating. Each stimulated by the other seems capable of growth
and change.

Because Hunsden is Crimsworth's senior by several years and his superior in social and economic status, he naturally assumes the roles of father and elder brother. As the first he nurtures and punishes. He and William speak for the first time—the circumstance is noteworthy—as they are standing before the portrait of William's mother. Hunsden clearly admires her face, but criticizes it for being "too sensitive" (p. 19). This is a quality which he faults Crimsworth for sharing. Much later in the novel, he demonstrates his sympathy with William's needs and feelings, by purchasing and sending him this same portrait. The note which accompanies it is astonishing in its cruelty as it is in its self-revelation:

> There is a sort of stupid pleasure in giving a child sweets, a fool his bells, a dog a bone. You are repaid by seeing the child besmear his face with sugar; by witnessing how the fool's ecstasy makes a greater fool of him than ever; by watching the dog's nature come out over his bone. In giving William Crimsworth his mother's picture, I give him sweets, bells, and bone all in one; what grieves me is, that I cannot behold the result . . . (p. 200)

He sets himself up as patriarchal father in contradistinction to Crimsworth's mother. He denies in himself those "female qualities" of empathy and sensitivity which caused him to purchase the portrait in the first place, and through his sadistic rejection of the validity of William's feelings he asserts his power and superiority over the younger man. He acts out the same pattern repeatedly: finding ways of being kind to Crimsworth, demonstrating his concern, but always expecting and finally demanding those words of gratitude which will secure their relative positions.

> I, by the sovereign efficacy of my recommendation, got you the place where you are now living in clover, and yet not a word of gratitude, or even acknowledgment, have you ever offered in return . . . (p. 183)

It is just to avoid concretizing their positions, to avoid accepting a lesser status, that Crimsworth responds to Hunsden's "tone of despotism" with "gentleman-like irony" (p. 31). He cannot accept his dependence, but neither can he confront and overcome it.

Crimsworth recognizes that Hunsden, like a sibling rival, can afford to be generous only when his superior position is assured.

Thinking it likely that Crimsworth is about to make a disastrous match, Hunsden is all concerned restraint but, as William points out:

> I am morally certain that if he had found me installed in a handsome parlour, lounging on a soft couch, with a pretty, wealthy wife at my side, he would have hated me— . . .
> (p. 192)

And when Hunsden does finally meet Frances and recognizes how happy Crimsworth is likely to be with her—the dimension which Crimsworth's life will have which his own will lack—his response is a marvelous, wordless expression of joy and jealousy: anger and sympathy:

> . . . he swayed me to and fro; so I grappled him round the waist. It was dark; the street lonely and lampless. We had then a tug for it; and after we had both rolled on the pavement, and with difficulty picked ourselves up, we agreed to walk on more soberly. (p. 228)

Their "tug" is neither violent nor affectionate. It underscores their ambivalence and their inability to communicate with one another. Hunsden finally claims the advantage: "Your lace-mender is too good for you, but not good enough for me; neither physically nor morally does she come up to my ideal of a woman" (p. 233). His statement is not persuasive. His ideal woman is only a shadow beside the reality of Crimsworth's wife. Still, now as always, Hunsden reserves the right to question and judge and his judgment alone stands between Crimsworth and total complacency; between growth and paralysis. While Crimsworth is finally able to leave behind the hypochondria connected with childhood, deprivation, and insecurity, and while he has successfully rejected both uncles and brother, he must continue to struggle with the pressures of those lost and repressed relationships as they are presented in his "friendship" with Hunsden. It is here also that his femininity remains potential.

The opinionated mill owner serves a similar catalytic function for Frances. In her interchanges with him she is sparked to growth—not making a game of opposition, as she does with Crimsworth; taking her disagreements seriously, defending them passionately. With Hunsden she can afford to speak for herself, to become angry and hostile. She can be more of a person, as can

Crimsworth, because there is nothing at risk. She can—by asserting her intelligence, her self-confidence, her emotional independence, become "masculine." Through Hunsden, she finds the
path to her androgynous self and she is neither threatened nor
made to feel guilty. Of course, her relationship with Hunsden
does not thrive as a result of the space it allows her in which to
test her personality. In fact, she can claim this space only because
there is an absence of "relationship" between them; an absence,
therefore, of the familiar dependence and the necessity of playing
sexually defined roles. For Frances and Crimsworth, Hundsen is
a gadfly. He tantalizes them with momentary visions of their own
possibility. He annoys them and upsets them, but they are dependent upon him—as he is upon them. Each imposes upon the other
those questions which should emerge from the self if the self is
aware, integrated, troubled enough to ask them. Not one of them,
however, is ready to undertake such questioning independently.
Only Brontë has begun to probe in this way and the partiality of
her understanding is reflected in the fragmentation of her three
central personae.

Appropriately, Hunsden hovers above the next generation,
represented by Victor Crimsworth, with the same appealing, yet
frustrating power, encouraging the child's "spirit," supporting
his desire for a degree of freedom and independence which his
parents perceive as antisocial and dangerous. His effect upon the
boy is treated with predictable ambiguity. But it is clear that
where Frances and Crimsworth would repress Victor's strong
urge to self-assertion, would make of him a model of loving
obedience, Hunsden would push him to experimentation and
deny him the easy conventional solutions which he has also denied the boy's parents.

Brontë does seem to support Frances's and Crimsworth's suspicion and resentment of Hunsden's influence upon the child, as
well as their bemused wonder at the persistence of the friendship's importance in their own lives. Again the writer is unsuccessful in detaching herself from her fiction, and the reader is
able to perceive one of the reasons for the unresolved ambivalence. It is that the Hunsden within herself has pushed Brontë
to begin, in *The Professor,* a radical line of investigation which
must give her future work a new focus. One cannot miss the erup-
tions in the strange, unreal surface of this novel any more than

one can overlook the flaws which mar the absurdly bright patina of Frances's and Crimsworth's relationship. Brontë has begun to reject, perhaps only half-consciously, an exclusively biological definition of femininity. To some extent, she begins to see femininity as an existential condition, determined by psychological and social forces. To be powerless, without social, economic, or legal status; to be unconfident, dependent, insecure, and vulnerable—is to be female. So much is clear. But the implications of this perception are too far-reaching to be adequately confronted by her at this critical point in her development. Her vision as she writes *The Professor* is enlarged but still limited. Insofar as Crimsworth and Hunsden demonstrate qualities and inhabit positions that feminize them, they are perceived as weak, incompetent, worthy of pity. Hunsden, in his apparent inability to marry or openly commit himself, remains a vulnerable and somewhat androgynous figure. Crimsworth becomes a "man" when he becomes successful, when he achieves power and status; when his sympathy and sensitivity are transformed into the means of *binding* Frances to him. Our occasional awareness of Frances's "masculine" qualities awakens our curiosity, concern, and approbation but, in Charlotte Brontë's world, there is yet no way that these can be assimilated or made primary in her heroine's life.

As an artist and as a woman Brontë was caught in a painful bind. She was not, like Emily, a mystic who saw the world in transcendent androgynous terms. She did not, like Emily, function on a mythic level of perception any more than she placed herself with Branwell in a mythic universe of values. She demanded of herself a greater political and social awareness. She could not yet be a feminist because she could not imagine how the destructive social and psychological roles common to the middle-class mythology of romantic love could be changed. But neither could she simply accept. The awareness which so flaws *The Professor*—an awareness which is incomplete and confused—marks the stirrings of a feminist consciousness and with it a new sense of the possibilities of fiction.

CHAPTER THREE

Jane Eyre: *The Creation of a Feminist Myth*

*I*N *The Professor,* Charlotte Brontë asks the question, "What is female?" Her answer is, "powerlessness." Probing further, she discovers that the male alone may rid himself of "effeminacy" by achieving social status. The woman is caught in a double bind. Her femininity and therefore her powerlessness are largely inescapable. She can, in the manner of Frances Henri, develop her intellectual and personal capacities. Still, her potential "as a woman" will be realized only within the strictures of a conventional marriage which maintains her in a position of infantile dependence and subordination. Androgyny, therefore, is presented as a developmental stage. Males, like Hunsden, who do not fully resolve their gender ambiguity in order to achieve a clear sexual identification, are experienced, in the context of the novel, as regressive. On the other hand, "masculine" qualities while attractive, even liberating, in the female become unseemly and threatening when they are dominant (e.g., Mlle. Reuter). The alternative, paradoxically presented as desirable, is the fragmented personality which functions without continuity in its public and private roles.

To the sequential question: "Who is female?" Charlotte Brontë, accepting women's inferior status as inevitable, would have answered: "Sometimes men, but always women." The answer could not have satisfied her. She must have recognized the partiality of the vision in the flawed nature of her first novel: in the discontinuity of its characterizations. She must have known that she had only begun to understand the complexities of the social and psychological problems she was attempting to treat.

Brontë undertook the writing of *Jane Eyre* in August, 1846, immediately after she completed *The Professor*. Her approach to the new work suggests how great a distance she traveled rapidly. This was, of course, a critical period in her life. Her last letter to Heger had been sent. Branwell had left Thorpe Green in disgrace and was living at home in a state of shock and dissipation. Charlotte was with her father in a boarding house in Manchester, nursing him back to health after his cataract surgery. These events, the surrounding circumstances, the very process of writing her first novel, had all prepared her for the creation of a second work which would not only mark a significant change in her own career but would be a milestone in the development of English fiction.

The critical decision involved her commitment to a new kind of heroine, one who would be neither more nor less than herself:

> She once told her sisters that they were wrong—even morally wrong—in making their heroines beautiful as a matter of course. They replied that it was impossible to make a heroine interesting on any other terms. Her answer was, "I will prove to you that you are wrong; I will show you a heroine as plain and as small as myself, who shall be as interesting as any of yours."[1]

She came of age as a writer, as a feminist and as a human being ready to explore herself when she insisted that it was *morally* desirable to establish her heroine on the same terms as the traditional hero—by virtue of her interiority: her qualities of mind, character, and personality. From this vantage point Brontë could question and pose alternatives to a romantic mythology which exaggerated sex roles defined and supported by social structures. This was the "realism" she had groped for but could not find as she wrote *The Professor*.

Paradoxically, in freeing Jane Eyre from the conventional trappings of femininity and granting her liberty to feel and express her feelings, to think and express her thoughts, in asserting her "humanness," Charlotte Brontë created the first "anti-heroine": one who defied the conventions of both fiction and society. Orphaned, poor, and plain, faced with the pressures of making her own way in a world which measured the likelihood of

1. Gaskell, pp. 215–16.

her success by the degree of her marriageability (her familial connections, her economic status, and, above all, her beauty), Jane
tests the limits of social, moral, and psychological possibility,
discovering the kinds of power which are in fact available to a
woman. Of course, the fantasy elements of the juvenile stories
are not eliminated altogether. Brontë did not write of what was,
but of what could be. She had not surrendered her dreams and aspirations to the uncompromising and bitter facts of her own life,
nor could she undervalue the pressures of her own needs. All of
these she shared with her heroine. But she insisted that the
wish—and the possibility of its realization—be consonant with
the truths of Jane's own situation and personality: that the integrity of that personality be maintained. The old mythology was inadequate to this new task. The self could not abandon its search
for a fulfillment capable of delivering it from the anxieties of reality while retaining that reality's essential qualities.[2] It is this interweaving of wish and fact that gives *Jane Eyre* its aura of
romance. Psychological realism is responsible for its depth and
resonance.

The novel is a perfect fusion of experience and invention. The
trauma of Cowan Bridge is there, the dreary years spent as a governess, the thwarted passion for M. Heger. And there are more
subtle truths: the ambivalence of Charlotte's relationship with
Branwell and with her father, her sense of isolation and alienation, the intensity of her imaginative functioning and yearning
sexuality; a religious aspiration that transcended traditional belief. All are expressed in a fictive form which, like the metaphors
and symbols of dream, make reality luminous. All are filtered
through Jane's consciousness and described in her voice. And the
consciousness and the voice, like Jane Eyre herself, are valid if
elevated representations of their author.

> The essential difference between novel and romance lies in the
> conception of characterization. The romancer does not attempt
> to create "real people" so much as stylized figures which ex-
> pand into psychological archetypes. It is in the romance that
> we find Jung's Libido, Anima, and Shadow reflected in a hero,
> heroine and villain respectively. That is why the romance so
> often radiates a glow of subjective intensity that the novel

2. This is the focus of the "quest-romance" as Northrop Frye defines it in
the *Anatomy of Criticism* (Princeton: Princeton University Press, 1957), p. 193.

lacks, and why a suggestion of allegory is constantly creeping in around its fringes.[3]

The form and structure of *Jane Eyre* approximate the form and structure of romance which Northrop Frye describes. There can be little question that Jane is herself portrayed by Brontë as a "real person," but the novel is so much the story of the heroine's psychological development that people and situations seem often to be generated as alternative value systems that she must explore as aspects of her growth. This allegorical quality is underlined by the novel's repetitive structure. As in fairy tale or the quest-romance, characters, situations, and symbols must be rehearsed again and again, the heroine experiencing with each new revolution an increment of pressure and intensity, until the ultimate resolution of conflict is achieved.

We are all familiar with tales of the "dispossessed princess" which focus the conflicts and aspirations of the prepubescent and adolescent female. In these stories (e.g., *Cinderella*), ambivalent attitudes towards members of the family are distanced. Those feelings of rejection, anger, hostility, and thwarted love which are too painful to confront directly, are typically projected onto the wicked stepmother and her cruel children. Guilt translates the blood relationship into one which is necessarily unnatural. The father-protector (the good king) who cannot, in the scenario of the family romance, act in his daughter's behalf, in opposition to the mother, is conveniently absent or dead. The princess must pass through a number of trials—choose among alternative possibilities—which test and prove her moral worth. Ultimately her lover—the "other self" essential to her completion—recognizes the royalty hidden beneath the dust of poverty. He acknowledges their kinship and, through marriage, bestows upon her the family, wealth, and status which are the external signs and guarantees of her true value.

This common fairy tale provides a benign alternative to the Byronic myth. It is responsive to the female dream; not simply an expression of narcissistic male fantasy. Charlotte Brontë adopts the dream form, following the basic pattern of the tale. But she finds that the resolution is not consonant with *her* dream, which is more feminist in impulse.

3. Frye, p. 304.

At the beginning of the novel Jane does indeed appear in the guise of the "dispossessed princess": orphaned (her uncle-protector dead), living in a condition of alienation and dependence with Mrs. Reed and her three children, none of whom accept the responsibilities of familial relationship. It is the Brontë family seen through the distorting lens of sibling rivalry, projected in fantasy. It is an image of Charlotte's jealousy of the companionship of Emily and Anne; her deep ambivalence toward Branwell. And, not least of all, there is her resentment of the parent who has never loved her enough: the mother who died; the father who withdrew. Jane's class and sex define her as victim and she experiences herself as unworthy. She is "humbled by the consciousness of . . . physical inferiority to Eliza, John and Georgiana Reed."[4] Her habitual mood is one of "humiliation, self-doubt, forlorn depression" (p. 14). She has been made unsocial by the status of "outsider" thrust upon her and she is, in turn, punished for her absence of sociability. She learns from the servants that to be plain is to be unloved and rejected even by those who do not occupy a social position superior to her own:

> Bessie . . . sighed and said, "Poor Miss Jane is to be pitied, too, Abbot." "Yes," responded Abbot, "if she were a nice, pretty child, one might compassionate her forlornness; but one really cannot care for such a little toad as that." (p. 26)

But it is from John Reed, the violent, spoiled, bullying son that she learns most painfully what it means to be poor and dependent in a world which respects wealth and position. It is from John that she learns the meaning of powerlessness, the meaning of being a female in a patriarchal society.

His superiority is assumed by his mother, his sisters, the servants, himself. He is incapable of love or affection, concerned only with the appropriation and wielding of power. Because Jane is defenseless, he uses her to inflate his ego. Because she is terrified and "habitually obedient," he preys upon her weakness. His physical presence is loathsome, his appearance "disgusting and ugly." His is the outer form of sadism and excess:

4. *Jane Eyre,* ed. Jane Jack and Margaret Smith (Oxford: The Clarendon Press, 1969), p. 3. All subsequent references are to this edition and will be given within the text.

> [He was] large and stout for his age, with a dingy and un-
> wholesome skin: thick lineaments in a spacious visage, heavy
> limbs and large extremities. He gorged himself habitually at
> table, which made him bilious, and gave him a dim and
> bleared eye and flabby cheeks. (p. 6)

Jane can only escape from him and the other miseries of her
life by withdrawing into fantasy and illusion. She is entranced by
Bessie's tales of love and adventure, by the ballads she sings.
But, like Charlotte Brontë "making out," she enjoys most of all
creating her own stories as she looks at Bewick's *History of British Birds*. She finds in the romantic images of nature, projections
of her own emotional life, seeming symbols of herself.

> . . . the rock standing up alone in a sea of billow and spray
> . . . the broken boat stranded on a desolate coast . . . the
> cold and ghastly moon glancing through bars of cloud at a
> wreck just sinking . . . the quite solitary church-yard with its
> inscribed headstone; its gate, its two trees, its low horizon,
> girdled by a broken wall, and its newly-risen crescent, attest-
> ing the the hour of even-tide . . . (p. 5)

They are images of isolation and despair, of death and infinity.
They are images of the sublime and suggest the kinship of human
feeling with a larger mysterious world that exists beyond the self,
accessible and yet threatening because it cannot be ordered or
contained. This universe of imaginative possibility enthralls Jane
because it offers her a landscape of the mind rather than a canvas
of social interaction. She learns its dangers as well as its potential
for liberation, however, when she surrenders for the first time to
the unconditioned demands of the ego. It is a lesson which haunts
her into maturity.

The incident, which reverberates through the novel, origi-
nates in Jane's unexpected defense against John Reed's casually
cruel physical attack upon her. Her justifiable anger, her pure assertion of self, is interpreted as unjustifiable passion. *His* unjustifiable cruelty is thought to be an appropriate assertion of his role
of "master." Her punishment for allowing herself to be released
into passion is imprisonment in the "red-room" where the principle of irrationality is given concrete form. The cold magnificence
of the bedchamber, its profound silence, the "sense of dreary
consecration" that marks its association with her uncle's death,

the muffled windows, the great looking glass, the "vacant majesty" everywhere, the crimson draperies, hangings, carpets, and coverings; the pinkish walls—all the color of blood, of fire, of passion—contribute to the fearsome sublimity of the scene. It is a terrifying womb-world from which she is born into a new state of being. Within it she is overwhelmed by the feelings and fantasies of the spirit-self. Catching sight of herself in the mirror she does, in fact, think that she has become an inhabitant of that other universe. She feels herself to be totally alienated from the living, thrust alone into a world of the dead and the supernatural.[5] She loses her sense of the boundaries of her identity. She feels the terror of total self-abandonment:

> My heart beat thick, my head grew hot; a sound filled my ears, which I deemed the rushing of wings: something seemed near me; I was oppressed, suffocated: endurance broke down—I uttered a wild, involuntary cry—I rushed to the door and shook the lock in desperate effort.[6] (p. 15)

Forced to remain, she is overwhelmed by feelings of impotence. Her fainting fit marks the end of the submission of her childhood and the beginning of a new stage of growth.

Jane awakens to the knowledge that she must test the strength of her private self against the constraints of the social world. Her ordeal has aroused in her a burning sense of injustice and the realization that although she is badly treated, she is not necessarily guilty: to be a victim is not necessarily to be unworthy:

> "Unjust!—unjust!" said my reason, forced by the agonizing stimulus into precocious though transitory power, and Resolve, equally wrought up, instigated some strange expedient to achieve escape from insupportable oppression—. . .
> (p. 13)

5. Lucile Dooley points out that the moving, gleaming light which Jane sees and interprets as a portent of some supernatural vision, is a typical symptom of adolescent hysteria: "taken literally from an experience of her own at Roe Head School and it is said that her health failed from the time of that shock, and she was finally compelled to go home" (Dooley, p. 242).

6. It is important to note that, in her letters to Ellen Nussey, Charlotte uses the word "imagination" as a euphemism for sexual fantasy. This suggests a connection between the imaginative frenzy of the red-room scene and later experiences of fantasized sexual violation. The sexual implications of "wings" and flight throughout the writing further corroborate the association.

Her new capacity for moral judgment and her nascent sense of self are supported, when she recovers, by the compassion shown to her by Bessie and the apothecary. From Bessie's nurturing she forms a positive image of maternity and it is this which, while fragile, allows her to condemn the bad mother, Mrs. Reed.

Each act of liberation, each assertion of self, brings with it an awareness of possibility. She understands the nature of John's cowardice and sees that her aunt's guilt makes her vulnerable. And while the angry reproach she offers Mrs. Reed is followed by "the pangs of remorse and the chill of reaction" (p. 40), she is, in fact, largely freed from her blind fear of authority. She knows now that a display of powerlessness invites scorn and she learns, therefore, that she too holds the secret of power: that its exercise is within her intellectual and psychological control.

Jane's knowledge that the responsible creation of an authority *within* makes it possible to judge the claims of the authority *without* prepares her to meet the difficulties of the next trial. Like Christian in *The Pilgrim's Progress,* she finds that a temptation overcome is not overcome forever. A capacity achieved must be tested against more formidable obstacles. It is the obsessive movement of dream: the spiraling cycle of allegory. Having vanquished John Reed and demonstrated her superiority to his petty tyrannies, Jane must confront a more substantial representative of the patriarchal system in the Rev. Mr. Brocklehurst.

She first meets the head of Lowood School in Mrs. Reed's breakfast room:

> I looked up at—a black pillar!—such, at least, appeared to me, at first sight, the straight, narrow, sable-clad shape standing erect on the rug: the grim face at the top was like a carved mask, placed above the shaft by way of capital. (p. 33)

The extraordinary phallic imagery makes of Brocklehurst a symbol of male sexuality and associates that sexuality with sadism and death. The association is appropriate. John Reed's crude snobbishness and bullying become, through Brocklehurst's misuse of power, institutionalized oppression motivated by class and sexual bias. The girls at Lowood School cannot and will never be able to assume functions traditionally thought suitable for middle- and upper-class women. They are not marketable commodities, valuable possessions, symbols (like Brocklehurst's wife and daughters) of their owner's wealth and status, themselves adornments and decorations. They are not proper heroines of romance. Poverty deprives them of their sexuality, their individuality, and hence of their humanity. Brocklehurst is an effective agent of this deprivation, insisting that their hair be cut off ("we are not to conform to nature" [p. 73]) and that they all be clothed in the same dreary, childish attire.

Because Brocklehurst is a more threatening expression of male authority than John Reed, because he is sophisticated in the wielding of power, he cannot—like the boy—employ that sadism in its own guise. Instead, he cloaks his greed, selfishness, and vanity in the hypocritical vestments of religious principles, disguising fear and guilt with love of God. And his ultimate crime, murder by neglect, is automatically justified by his claim that the desirable destiny of the charity students must be the same as that which would be appropriate to saints and martyrs.

From the time that Jane first meets him, it is clear that she has not discovered the power of her will only to surrender it to join, through self-sacrifice, the hypocritically defined ranks of the Presbyterian "elect." In some ways it is easier for her to defend herself against his authority, despite the social, sexual, and religious sanctions he brings with him, than it was for her to oppose her cousin. In the allegorical mode, interior conflict is acted out in successive scenes of struggle which yield victories symbolizing psychic growth. At the Reeds, Jane was isolated. Now, because all the students are victims, all are her companions and allies. Because she has achieved power over herself, she has earned the supplemental power she needs to triumph over a more sophisticated threat to her ego. Typically, the earlier victory (John Reed) determines the nature of the succeeding trial (Brocklehurst) and is the best preparation for it.

When Jane arrives at Lowood she is emotionally starved; spiritually and intellectually hungry. Her life has been one of extreme deprivation and her only reinforcement has come from the mercurial Bessie. Living predominantly in the world of her imagination, she has barely begun her social development. Childlike, withdrawn, she responds with most immediacy to the frustration of her physical needs. She is pressingly aware of the cold, the inadequate clothing, and, most of all, the skimpy and spoiled food: the burned porridge, rancid fat, rusty meat. But after Miss Tem-

ple has cleared her of the charges made against her by Brocklehurst, has given her the chance to construct a new identity, her
focus changes. She can apply herself to her work, define herself
as a student, aspire instead of grieve:

> That night, on going to bed, I forgot to prepare in imagination
> the Barmecide supper of hot roast potatoes, or white bread and
> new milk, with which I was wont to amuse my inward crav-
> ings: I feasted instead on the spectacle of ideal drawings . . .
> all the work of my own hands . . . I examined too, in thought,
> the possibility of my ever being able to translate currently a
> certain little French story book which Madam Pierrot had that
> day shown me. (p. 87)

Whereas she had previously accepted the Reeds' values ("I was
not heroic enough to purchase liberty at the price of caste" [p.
24]), and therefore their evaluation of her, she can now observe
happily:

> Well has Solomon said: —"'Better is a dinner of herbs where
> love is, than a stalled ox and hatred therewith.''

> I would not now have exchanged Lowood with all its priva-
> tions, for Gateshead and its daily luxuries. (p. 87)

Indeed, Lowood does, paradoxically, provide Jane with a supportive environment.[7] It is important for her development that the
school is exclusively female and that the students share her social
and economic background. She is no longer an outsider, necessarily inferior. Miss Temple and Helen Burns provide her with
role models, friendship, a new universe of values and the opportunity to excel. Maria Temple (her name suggests the importance
of her position, the degree of her idealization) not only stands between Brocklehurst and Jane, deflecting his power thrusts. But as
the superintendent of the school, she offers an alternative view of
authority. Appropriately, it is from her that Jane receives the first
bit of food that is more than the most minimal nutriment: a seed

7. The original of Lowood School was, of course, the Clergy Daughters
School at Cowan Bridge opened in January 1824, and founded by the Rev.
William Carus Wilson, the model for Mr. Brocklehurst. Charlotte Brontë was at
the school for a year at most, when she was eight years old. It was during this
period that she saw her two sisters, Maria (the model for Helen Burns) and Elizabeth, sicken and die. Her own experience there was profoundly unhappy. She
never forgot it and assured W. S. Williams in 1849 that "the Lowood part . . .
is true" (Wise and Symington, II, 313).

cake. Just, calm, and humane, Miss Temple is a maternal figure, an intelligent guide, a warm companion. She stimulates independence and respect for learning, pride in identity: a corrective to the oppression of male dominance. She also inspires love.

For Jane, this is the most crucial gift of all. Living at the Reeds, Jane had recognized the depth of her own need to love, but her doll had been the only possible recipient of her feelings. At Lowood she learns the depth of her need to *be* loved. When Helen Burns observes:

> If all the world hated you, and believed you wicked, while your own conscience approved you, and absolved you from guilt, you would not be without friends.

Jane replies:

> No; I know I should think well of myself; but that is not enough: if others don't love me, I would rather die than live—I cannot bear to be solitary and hated, Helen. Look here; to gain some real affection from you, or Miss Temple, or any other whom I truly love, I would willingly submit to have the bone of my arm broken, or to let a bull toss me, or to stand behind a kicking horse, and let it dash its hoof at my chest. (p. 80)

Her deprivation of love has been too great and has lasted too long. Jane, like Charlotte Brontë herself, must *be* loved in order to know herself lovable and she cannot accept love without imagining its cost, without expecting, even embracing, the necessity of sacrifice. She cannot perceive the world in moral terms as Helen does. She feels it, knows it, through her emotions. Sensitivity, vulnerability, and disappointment have tinged that knowledge with masochism and dependence.

Oddly enough, although Helen seems to stand at the furthest possible pole from Jane, they have both simply chosen opposite ways of achieving the same goal. Helen accepts the lesson of *Rasselas* (which she is reading when Jane first meets her): that the practice of virtue, rather than happiness, is the desired end of life. Helen makes a strength of humility. She accepts the Calvinist language of morality and religion—Brocklehurst's language—and with it she builds the prison of her life. It is the reverse side of the "red-room" experience. Helen's alternatives are only enslavement through self-denial or enslavement in abandonment. To be devoured in the fire of passion or to "burn" on the altar of

abnegation and repression. Helen is the "good girl" who identifies herself completely with authority. Masochistically oppressed, she participates in the power of the oppressor by accepting
his punishment and assuming his blame.

Jane does not share Helen's temperament and experiences
"impotent anger" on her friend's behalf.[8] But Jane's absence of
comprehension does not make her admire Helen less. She accepts
her friend's moral superiority as she accepts her intellectual superiority. She sees her as a martyr, noble and inspiring, and a martyr indeed she is for she is one of those whose death marks a
period of regeneration at Lowood.

Still, despite Jane's admiration and love—despite the fact that
she learns from Helen lessons of patience, fidelity, serenity, and
the importance of self-discipline—there is also the recognition
that Helen has compromised. Jane sees that her friend has ideals
which release her from the conflict which would accompany confrontation. In Helen's utterances there is "an alloy of inexpressible sadness" (p. 81) and in the words she speaks before she dies,
she reveals the degree to which she undervalues herself because
she is without an adequate sense that she is loved: because she
has been rejected by the one person who ought to cherish her the
most:

> I am very happy, Jane; and when you hear that I am dead you
> must be sure and not grieve. . . . We all must die one day,
> and the illness which is removing me is not painful; it is gentle
> and gradual: my mind is at rest. I leave no one to regret me
> much: I have only a father; and he is lately married, and will
> not miss me. By dying young I shall escape great sufferings. I
> had not qualities or talents to make my way very well in the
> world: I should have been continually at fault. (p. 96)

Helen's reasons for accepting death so easily—perhaps for embracing, even welcoming it—prove justified. She is not mourned
by her family: "Her grave . . . in Brocklebridge churchyard
. . . for fifteen years after death . . . was only covered by a
grassy mound" (p. 97). It is then, after fifteen years, that Jane

8. Elizabeth Gaskell in discussing Charlotte's feelings about the teacher at
Cowan Bridge School who provided the model for Miss Scatcherd, says: "Her
heart, to the latest day on which we met, still beat with unavailing indignation at
the worrying and the cruelty to which her gentle, patient, dying sister had been
subjected by this woman" (Gaskell, p. 44).

places there a marble tablet "inscribed with her name—and the word 'Resurgam' " (p. 97). Thus Jane "bears witness" (as Brontë has done in telling Maria's story). It is the fragile relief of the survivor.[9]

From Miss Temple and Helen Burns, Jane learns to value duty and self-control and by the time she is ready to leave Lowood, she can say, "I appeared a disciplined and subdued character" (p. 99). The word "appeared" is crucial. The childhood trauma of Gateshead had plunged Jane into the awesome depths of passionate response. The fear of irrational experience remains although it is tempered by the ordered life at Lowood. Jane has confronted her commanding need for love and respect and she accepts with some trepidation her consequent condition of dependence: the potential power of passion. She can only attempt to guard herself against extremes of behavior which must result in the loss of selfhood.

This phase of her development is ended and her ties with Lowood severed by Maria Temple's marriage and departure. It is then that Jane begins to long for a new experience. Like Charlotte, who wrote to Ellen of her "wish for wings" there is a nameless need: an unacknowledged yearning for sexual fulfillment. It is this which qualifies and makes more poignant the constructive and realistic compromise which Jane reaches with herself:

> I desired liberty; for liberty I gasped; for liberty I uttered a prayer; it seemed scattered on the wind then faintly blowing. I abandoned it, and framed a humbler supplication; for change, stimulus: that petition, too, seemed swept off into vague space; "Then," I cried, half desperate, "Grant me at least a new servitude!" (p. 101)

She consciously rejects the perspective of romance, but her impassioned language belies the common sense of her plea.

Jane's arrival at Thornfield initiates the next stage of the allegorical journey of development. Although her new environment is pleasant enough (she is warmly treated as Adele Varen's governess and Mrs. Fairfax's companion) Jane is lonely and becalmed. She withdraws again into the world of the imagination in

9. This might well be an expression—indirect, perhaps even unconscious—of Charlotte's feeling that Patrick Brontë was, by his negligence, responsible for the death of Maria.

which fears, aspiration and conflict find form. From the moment of his appearance, Rochester seems to be part of this interior world: an object of need; a cause of anxiety. He comes in response to Jane's restlessness which disappears with his presence. He is linked to the childhood world of "fancies bright and dark," to distant memories of nursery stories. Both the great dog who heralds his coming and the horse he rides out of the stillness of evening against the muted colors of the darkening sunset, seem masks of the "Gytrash," the ill-omened spectral beast who, in Bessie's tales, haunted solitary ways and accosted belated travelers.

Rochester, in turn, associates Jane immediately with an imaginative and romantic world:

> No wonder you have rather the look of another world. I marvelled where you had got that sort of face. When you came on me in Hay Lane last night, I thought unaccountably of fairy tales, and had half a mind to demand whether you had bewitched my horse: I am not sure yet. (p. 149)

He enjoys this sense of her, insists upon it: repeatedly describing her as "elfin," a "nonnette," "a fairy," "his good genii," "a dream or shade," a "strange . . . almost unearthly thing." The fact that she is without family or friends, without social ties, makes her an appropriate dweller within the remote "fairy tale castle" which is his home.

Rochester also lives as an "outsider." Circumstances have made him one and like other Byronic heroes—like Charlotte's beloved Zamorna—he embraces this definition of himself. He knows that "Nature meant to me to be, on the whole, a good man" (p. 166), but he was wronged by fate, weakened—like Branwell—by his education ("suppose you were no longer a girl well-reared and disciplined, but a wild boy, indulged from childhood upwards" [p. 273]). First made desperate and then degenerate by the misery of his enforced marriage, orphaned, the last of his family, he is isolated. Surviving his father and older brother, but still suffering the effects of their cruel and selfish treatment, he rejects external authority, defying the world's judgment and man's opinion, claiming his right to establish for himself the moral laws by which he will live, echoing Milton's Satan in his claim that he has the right to pleasure since he cannot find happiness.

Rochester's economic position, class, and sexual status allow him to act as if he were not, in fact, responsible to society. His imagination defines for him a rebel's role. Energy and will enable him to inhabit it. Jane, on the other hand, seems able to function without society's consideration because she is beneath society's notice. Her education at Lowood was appropriate to an intelligent and moral human being who could bring nothing to the marriage market and did not need, therefore, to be trained as a lady. Her aspirations and her perspective are therefore more human, less sex-typed, than those conventionally held.

> Women are supposed to be very calm generally: but women feel just as men feel; they need exercise for their faculties, and a field for their efforts as much as their brothers do; they suffer from too rigid a restraint, too absolute a stagnation, precisely as men would suffer; and it is narrow-minded in their more privileged fellow-creatures to say that they ought to confine themselves to making puddings and knitting stockings, to playing on the piano and embroidering bags. It is thoughtless to condemn them, or laugh at them, if they seek to do more or learn more than custom has pronounced necessary for their sex. (p. 133)

Having little to lose, she can afford to be spontaneous and open. In her interaction with Rochester, both are liberated from the superficial gestures and restraining, repressive behavior associated with traditional sex roles. Jane feels herself to be freed by Rochester's rude openness: his disregard for "civilities." They communicate on a new level, revealing themselves emotionally and intellectually. They share a profound sympathy of mind and spirit. It is in part from this that their sexual passion derives and passion it is—portrayed with a vividness not found before in the English novel. It is an emotion that pleads for physical expression; the obverse of character revealed through physical features. Rochester's massive head, his "granite-hewn features," jetty eyebrows, "great, dark eyes," his abundant hair: these attract Jane. It is his will, his superb self-confidence, his power and authority and the mysterious promise of emotional intensity by which she is compelled. It is his "masculinity" which arouses her "femininity."

Jane has escaped some forms of social conditioning and can identify and condemn the more obvious forms of social inequality. Still, the circumstances of her life have created in her a psychological need for the kind of symbiotic relationship which is essential to the stability of middle-class patriarchy, and is supported and justified by the romantic myth. Once she is aware that Rochester's urge to dominate her does not rest on class snobbery, her guard is lowered:

> What, you are my paid subordinate, are you? Oh, yes, I had forgotten the salary! Well, then, on that mercenary ground, will you agree to let me hector a little?

> No, sir, not on that ground: but on the ground that you did forget it, and that you care whether or not a dependent is comfortable in his dependency, I agree heartily. (p. 164)

Her pride will not allow her to be humbled by her economic and social situation. Here her history has made her sensitive. But she is not aware of the dangers—potentially more destructive—of psychosexual dependence.

Her vulnerability leads her into the romantic trap. She bows before the strength of Rochester's personality. It has always been her tendency. Rochester has told her, "I am old enough to be your father," and he does, indeed, become the loving father whom she has never known. She treasures this paternal aspect of his feelings and when she is separated from him, she mourns the loss of *that* most deeply.

> I shall never more know the sweet homage given to beauty, youth and grace—for never to anyone else shall I seem to possess these charms. He was fond and proud of me—it is what no man besides will ever be. (p. 459)

She is "mastered" by his "energy, decision and will"; stimulated by his experience of life. Infatuated, she desires to live through him, to give herself to the exploration of his mysterious, tortured personality. She wishes to "look into the abyss at her leisure, explore its secrets and analyze its nature" (p. 235). She wants to save him from himself, from the fate he fears:

> To live, for me Jane, is to stand on a crater-crust which may crack and spue fire any day. (p. 271)

And she:

> I cannot deny that I grieved for his grief, whatever that was, and would have given much to assuage it. (p. 181)

She retains the belief she had shared with Helen Burns that love must be merged with self-sacrifice. She is grateful for his love and tells him: "I'd give my life to save you" (p. 255).

Like Christian, who beholds from a distant shore the outlines of the Eternal City, Jane feels herself to be at the verge of happiness but, like Christian, she has not yet understood the nature of her quest: has not resolved those internal conflicts which block fulfillment. Anxiety is submerged in the bright hopefulness of day. Ambivalence is repressed. But both are released in the psychic images of night.

> Till morning dawned I was tossed on a buoyant but unquiet sea, where billows of trouble rolled under surges of joy. I thought sometimes I saw beyond its wild waters a shore, sweet as the hills of Beulah; and now and then a freshening gale, wakened by hope, bore my spirit triumphantly towards the bourne: but I could not reach it, even in fancy,—a counter-acting breeze blew off land, and continually drove me back. Sense would resist delirium: judgment would warn passion. (p. 188)

Jane is not aware of the extent to which her autonomy is threatened by her love for Rochester. She understands that social differences might separate them. But despite the fact that she calls him "master" and accepts obedience as his due, she believes that they meet as equals. Fortunately her self-confidence is strengthened before she is enlightened. The crucial opportunity for growth is offered when she receives a summons to her Aunt Reed's death-bed. She leaves Rochester, aware both of his love for her and his apparent intention to marry Blanche Ingram. What might seem to be an awkward digression, useful only in creating further suspense, has in fact all of the artistic symmetry and psychological validity of earlier struggles.

In the Ingrams—the overbearing mother, the proud, unfeeling Blanche, the insipid younger daughter and effete son, Jane has confronted another version of the Reed family (the technique of fairy tale need hardly be mentioned again). That she can meet their snobbish rejection with cool self-confidence is, perhaps, an indication of repression, but it is also a measure of her maturity. The depth of that maturity is tested by her return to the substance of which the Ingrams are but the shadow: to that trauma which is buried nine years in her past.

> The same hostile roof now again rose before me: my prospects
> were doubtful yet; and I had yet an aching heart. I still felt as a
> wanderer on the face of the earth: but I experienced firmer trust
> in myself and my own powers, and less withering dread of
> oppression. The gaping wound of my wrongs, too, was now
> quite healed; and the flame of resentment extinguished.
> (p. 285)

Like the fairy tale princess and with the simplicity of wish fulfillment fantasy, Jane has been completely vindicated. By a process
of inversion, rivalries are resolved. The family which had excluded her—the family which she had resented—has itself disin-
tegrated—morally and economically. Her prime oppressor, John
Reed, first "sunk and degraded," is now dead. Georgiana and
Eliza are both frustrated and miserable, imprisoned in mutual
suspicion and dislike. Georgiana, with all of her vanity and para-
sitic selfishness, demonstates the emptiness of upper-class values. Eliza, about to enter a religious order, reveals the meaning-
lessness of discipline practiced for its own sake; the sterility of
religion based upon hatred instead of love.[10] Jane quickly wins
the admiration and trust of her two cousins, proving her superiority to them. She graciously forgives her aunt who proves her own
unadulterated wickedness by dying unrepentant. Jane returns to
Thornfield convinced of the validity of her own values, confirmed in her faith and love, bound to her recognition that personal integrity is crucial to the integrity of her personality. She is
ready for her ordeal. At Thornfield Jane responds to Rochester's
devious game-playing with a degree of courage and depth of feeling which is completely ennobling and feminist in impulse.

> Do you think, because I am poor, obscure, plain, and little, I
> am soulless and heartless?—You think wrong!—I have as
> much soul as you,—and full as much heart! And if God had
> gifted me with some beauty and much wealth, I should have
> made it as hard for you to leave me, as it is now for me to leave
> you. I am not talking to you now through the medium of cus-
> tom, conventionalities, nor even of mortal flesh:—it is my
> spirit that addresses your spirit; just as if both had passed
> through the grave, and we stood at God's feet equal,—as we
> are! (p. 318)

10. She invites comparison with Helen Burns and St. John Rivers, and is
found to occupy a curious middle ground between them.

Rochester replies, "My bride is here . . . because my equal is here, and my likeness" (p. 319), but after their betrothal, his behavior suggests that his bride can be neither his equal nor his likeness. All that drew him to Jane has become irrelevant. She is now his object, his possession, an extension of himself: a demonstration of his taste, a badge of his position, proof of his masculinity. He wants to clothe her in rich silks and magnificent satins: to cover her with jewels. He finds nobility stamped on her brow and "will make the world acknowledge you a beauty, too" (p. 326). Jane is degraded by his changed tone ("You are dreaming, Sir—or you are sneering. For God's sake, don't be ironical" [p. 326]). To be transformed by his snobbery—placed on a pedestal by his insecurity—is to be denied her selfhood and it is for herself that she wishes to be loved.[11]

Rochester would use her to erase his past. Taking her to Europe, he will "revist it healed and cleansed, with a very angel as my comforter" (P. 326). Appropriating her innocence, he believes he can avoid confronting the implications of his own experience. And as Jane feels her independence sifting away, her identity being negated, she tries to regain control. She wants to be his friend and companion, she insists that rudeness is preferable to flattery, she asks to earn her keep by maintaining herself as Adele's governess. She has begun to understand the meaning of economic dependence, the connotations of class inferiority and the subtle implications that both have for sexual relationships.

> He smiled; and I thought his smile was such as a Sultan might, in a blissful and fond moment, bestow on a slave his gold and gems had enriched: I crushed his hand, which was ever hunting mine, vigorously, and thrust it back to him red with the passionate pressure . . ." (p. 339)[12]

As Rochester's sexuality becomes more open, Jane begins to withdraw, alternately "vexing and teasing," keeping him at a distance. It is her only defense against self-abandonment. Her

---

11. The implications of Rochester's treatment of Jane parallel in an interesting way Byron's destructive treatment of Caroline Lamb: "It was Byron's misfortune that he felt impelled to despoil his mistress of those very qualities which had in his romantic imagination made her attractive—the freshness and naiveté of her personality" (Marchand, I, 341).

12. Here we are reminded of Crimsworth's sense of himself as a sultan—a feeling of power inspired in him by the seductive Mlle. Reuter.

fear of sexuality is not the effect of repulsion. Quite the contrary. It is part of her recognition of the depth of her passion: of her capacity for surrender and submergence. She wants to keep both herself and Rochester from "the edge of the gulf" (p. 344) which they have both glimpsed with horror in Rochester's mad wife, Berthe, who stands in the novel at the nexus of romance and allegory.[13] Crucial to the plot as the focus of Gothic horror and suspense, she is the secret of Rochester's destroyed youth, responsible for his bitter disillusionment, the cause of his separation from Jane and, ultimately, the agent of Rochester's physical destruction. But her fascination and power derive from still deeper sources. She is the monstrous embodiment of psychosexual conflicts which are intrinsic to the romantic predicament—paralleled and unconscious in both Jane and Rochester.

Although Berthe is specifically identified with Rochester's past, imprisoned on the third floor of Thornfield Hall, itself "a shrine of memory" (p. 128), she emerges for the reader through enlarging stages of Jane's perception. She comes initially in answer to Jane's same vague sexual longings for freedom and expression which later seem to summon Rochester. Descending from the attic where she delights in the vast prospect of the countryside, Jane hears Berthe's laugh for the first time: "distinct, formal, mirthless." "Tragic" and "preternatural" the laugh is strangely joyless: a sound that denotes neither feeling nor personality. It is heard often when Jane retreats to the attic window

13. Adrienne Rich moves in a somewhat similar interpretive direction in her provocative essay, *"Jane Eyre:* The Temptations of a Motherless Woman," *Ms,* II (October 1973).

It is interesting to note that despite Berthe's symbolic status in the novel, the events surrounding Rochester's first marriage were apparently suggested to Charlotte Brontë while she was teaching at the Roe Head School:

> It was about this time that an event happened in the neighborhood of Leeds, which excited a good deal of interest. A young lady, who held a situation of governess in a very respectable family, had been wooed and married by a gentleman, holding some subordinate position in a commercial firm to which the young lady's employer belonged. A year after her marriage, during which time she had given birth to a child, it was discovered that he whom she called husband had another wife. The report now says, that this first wife was deranged, and that he had made this an excuse to himself for his subsequent marriage. But, at any rate the condition of the wife who was no wife—of the innocent mother of the illegitimate child—excited the deepest commiseration; and the case was spoken of far and wide and at Roe Head among other places. (Gaskell p. 91)

wishing for active involvement, for "a stake in life," for a constructive use of her energies.

As Jane is drawn closer to Rochester, focusing upon him the desires and aspirations which before were undefined yearnings, she has a concrete sense of Berthe's presence—and the danger it represents. The night on which she first admits to herself the centrality of Rochester to her own happiness ("Suppose he should be absent, spring, summer and autumn: how joyless sunshine and fine days will seem!" [p. 182]) is the same night that Berthe sets Rochester's bed aflame. On the evening that Jane vows to her "master" that she will be faithful to him, despite society's opinion, Berthe violently attacks her brother, Richard Mason, who ultimately prevents Rochester and Jane's marriage. Considered together, the events suggest that Berthe expresses a repressed but clearly negative component of Jane's attitude towards her own sexuality and toward her lover as well. This is further borne out by the fact that, as Jane sits in the chamber nursing the bleeding Mason, imprisoned there, in a sense, by her vow of fidelity, the association emerges in her mind between Berthe, the "mystery that broke out, now in fire and now in blood, at the deadest hours of the night" (p. 264) and the dread images of the red-room—reverberating with death, passion, hidden fears of the loss of self. Similar anxieties reveal themselves when Jane and Berthe meet just prior to Jane's wedding day. Then Jane awakens suddenly from a recurrent nightmare in which she sees herself carrying a child:[14]

> I dreamt that Thornfield Hall was a dreary ruin . . . wrapped up in a shawl, I still carried the unknown little child: I might not lay it down anywhere, however tired were my arms— however much its weight impeded my progress, I must retain it. I heard the gallop of a horse at a distance on the road: I was sure it was you; and you were departing for many years, and for a distant country. I climbed the thin wall with frantic perilous haste, eager to catch one glimpse of you from the top: the stones rolled from under my feet, the ivy branches I grasped gave way, the child clung round my neck in terror, and almost strangled me: at last I gained the summit. I saw you like a

14. This was similar to a recurrent dream of Charlotte's own: one in which she carries a weeping, suffering child who will not be comforted (Dooley, p. 242).

speck on a white track, lessening every moment. The blast blew so strong I could not stand. I sat down on the narrow ledge; I hushed the scared infant in my lap: you turned an angle of the road; I bent forward to take a last look; the wall crumbled; I was shaken; the child rolled from my knee; I lost my balance, fell and woke. (pp. 356–67)

But the scene to which she wakens is more terrifying than the one imagined in her dreams. She sees "a woman, tall and large, with thick and dark hair hanging long down her back." The woman places Jane's wedding veil upon her head and looks at herself in the mirror.

It was a discolored face—it was a savage face . . . the lips were swelled and dark; the brow furrowed; the black eyebrows wildly raised over the bloodshot eyes. (p. 358)

Berthe tears the wedding veil in two then leans over Jane's bed in an attitude that suggests a fantasy of sexual violation.

Just at my bedside, the figure stopped: the fiery eye glared upon me—she thrust up her candle close to my face, and extinguished it under my eyes. I was aware that her lurid visage flamed over mine, and I lost consciousness: for the second time in my life—only the second time—I became insensible from terror. (pp. 358–59)

Loss of consciousness was experienced once before: in the redroom. The causes were the same then as they are now: impotence and terror rising from the blurring of the boundaries of the self, an intense fear of submergence—negation. Here the association with the vampire figure makes the sexual implication explicit.

Berthe has from the beginning functioned as a warning against the consequences of Jane's desire for emotional release, her longing to cast aside conventional restraints. In the horror of her presence, Berthe expresses Jane's fear of marriage as violation, her sense of "Mrs. Rochester" as alien, "a being not yet born" (p. 349). She is the menacing form of Jane's resistance to male authority, her fear of that sexual surrender which will seal her complete dependence in passion. Berthe's joyless laugh is a metaphor for sensuality without mind, feeling without control. She is a jealous, vengeful mother who prohibits marriage to the beloved father. An androgynous figure, she is also the violent lover who destroys the integrity of the self; who offers the corruption of sexual knowledge and power—essentially male in its opposition to purity and innocence.

The dream which precedes the apparition expresses Jane's fear of dependence, sexual initiation, and the maturity associated with childbearing. In it, Jane is presented simultaneously as child and mother. She is the child who, dependent upon Rochester, will be betrayed. She is the woman who wishes for independence and maturity, but fears the infant whose conception and birth imply the loss of a part of herself.[15]

As Berthe's importance as an alter ego for Jane is central in the novel, her importance in Rochester's psychosexual development is crucial as well. It must be remembered that from the beginning of their relationship Rochester insists that Jane is elfin, other-worldly, childlike: a "little sunny-faced girl with . . . dimpled cheeks and rosy lips" (p. 325). Appropriately, he makes their love story into an imaginative tale for Adele. Her governess, he says, is a fairy who will bestow upon him the power of flight allowing them both to leave the earth behind and take up their blissful if somewhat fey inhabitance on the moon (p. 337). Thus he denies to Jane her sexuality, her humanness, her social and moral nature. He betrays the fact that he wants to find in her the very opposite of that aggressive sexuality, that uncontrollable passionate will that has its form in Berthe: bestial, athletic, monstrously and paradoxically virile.

If their expression is striking, Rochester's sexual anxieties themselves are not atypical. The fear of the female is common, among civilied as well as primitive men.[16] Since it is a crucial

15. Gregory Zilboorg comments on the common female fear of intercourse: a fear that "contents of her body will be destroyed, stolen or sucked out" and he adds that these "fears . . . are in some way deeply connected with her physical fear of man and of child bearing" (p. 106). The vampire figure appropriately embodies this fear.

16. Freud observes:

Perhaps this fear is founded on the difference of woman from man, on her eternally inexplicable, mysterious and strange nature, which thus seems hostile. Man fears that his strength will be taken from him by woman, dreads becoming infected with her femininity and then proving himself a weakling. The effect of coitus in discharging tensions and inducing flaccidity may be a prototype of what these fears represent; and realization of the influence gained by the woman over a man as a result of sexual relations, and the favours she extorts by this means may all conduce to justify the growth of the fears. (Freud, "The Taboo of Virginity," trans. J. Riviere, pp. 223–24.)

product and cause of Victorian repression, we are not surprised that Berthe is a vampire: one of those who haunted the Victorian imagination. Jane identifies her in this way in describing the nighttime visitation and Berthe does, in fact, suck Mason's blood ("She sucked the blood: she said she'd drain my heart" [p. 267].) as she tries to suck her husband's. She would deprive him, Rochester knows, of his energy, his vitality, his manhood.[17]

Always intrinsically connected to man's insecurity concerning his own sexuality, the fear of women is particularly pronounced in the psychology of the Byronic hero whose need to prove his masculinity by sexual conquest drives him to extremes of behavior. He fears impotence and he loathes the aggression he must summon in himself as a defense against the sexual threat he imagines. In short, he fears with unusual acuteness both powerlessness and power. The hostility, therefore, born of his anxiety, is projected onto the "love object." It is not enough, therefore, for Rochester to reject Berthe. He must protect himself as well against everything in Jane that suggests an affinity with his first wife. He must deny that aspect of her sexuality which is perceived as aggressive and "masculine." He must bifurcate her personality. But because he fears as well the power of his own virility, he incorporates into himself that aspect of feminity which is unthreatening: the capacity for intense and absolute love. In this way Jane is not only divided. She is negated: denied function and space. She becomes quite simply an extension of him. His narcissism is the romantic resolution of sexual conflict. In this, he is truly the Byronic hero.

The discovery of the existence of Rochester's first wife at the very moment that the marriage vows are being exchanged has an extraordinary psychological validity. It is an expression of the ambivalence which Jane and Rochester both experience. In preparing for his wedding, Rochester has revealed a need to dominate strong enough to effectively negate the identity of the woman he loves and therefore fears. And Jane, who feels increasingly that her marriage will not be a union of equals but a submersion of self in the ego of another, is as apprehensive of her wedding ("There was no putting off the day that advanced—the

17. In Rochester's relation to Berthe we have a more striking and psychologically convincing version of the sexual ambivalence expressed in Crimsworth's hypochondria.

bridal day'' [p. 347]), as she is apprehensive of her husband to be: ''the dread, but adored, type of my unknown future day'' (p. 361).

It is appropriate that Richard Mason, acting in behalf of Jane's uncle should be the one to stop the wedding ceremony. When Jane had first recognized the role which Rochester would impose upon her as his wife, she had written to her uncle to identify herself and to inquire about her legacy. Economic and social status seem after all to be minimal conditions of sexual equality. These would at least lend support to the sense of self which makes love possible in a patriarchal world.

From this point of view, Jane's decision to leave Rochester, her decision not to live with him as his mistress, is not simply a moral decision. She does not leave him because she finds him guilty or distasteful. In fact, she forgives him rather easily because she sees in him ''deep remorse'', ''true pity,'' ''manly energy,'' and, not least of all, ''unchanged love'' (p. 381). She will not live with him as his mistress because he will think of her then as he thinks now of the others with whom he has had brief, disillusioning affairs:

> It was a groveling fashion of existence: I should never wish to return to it. Hiring a mistress is the next worse thing to buying a slave: both are often by nature, and always by position, inferior; and to live familiarly with inferiors is degrading. I now hate the recollection of the time I passed with Celine, Giacinta and Clara. (p. 398)

To become one of these women now seems to be her only alternative. In fact, this has always been potentially her situation. With the threat that Berthe represents subconsciously present, Rochester must have attempted, despite his love, to turn Jane into a plaything, a sexual object, a dependent, a slave—as soon as she agreed to marry him. It was her absence of status, her powerlessness, which allowed Rochester to see Jane initially as an appropriate bride, completely vulnerable to him. It is this which she now, on some level, begins to understand. The depth of her love, the profundity of her need, is the measure of her obligation to leave him.

> Not a human being that ever lived could wish to be loved better than I was loved; and him who thus loved me I absolutely

worshipped: and I must renounce love and idol. One drear
word comprised my intolerable duty—"Depart!" (pp.
402–13)

Brontë had written to Ellen Nussey from Roe Head in 1837:

Why are we to be divided? Surely it must be because we are in
danger of loving each other too well—of losing sight of the
creator in idolatry of the *creature*.[18]

Jane Eyre had learned that in idolatry one must also lose sight of
the self and it was to herself that she owed her "intolerable
duty"—to depart. This is the point at which the old romance
failed and the stasis of the old mythology was denied. This is
where a new resolution had to be discovered. Here morality and
psychology meet for the first time in a feminist context.[19]

III

In deciding to leave Rochester, Jane takes the first crucial step
toward independence. She has discovered that there is, after all,
something more important to her than pleasing those whom she
loves, or giving satisfaction to those who love her. Despite the
pain of her conflict, she has acted decisively to preserve her own
integrity. At the moment of her decision, Jane returns to the critical scene of her childhood. She is alone in her room as she was
alone then—powerless before external circumstances and internal
pressures. The limits of the rational world are lost in the boundless universe of imagination:

That night I never thought to sleep: but a slumber fell on me as
soon as I lay down in bed. I was transported in thought to the
scenes of childhood: I dreamt I lay in the red-room at Gates-

18. Quoted in Gaskell, p. 100.
19. Winifred Gerin attributes this departure from the romantic formula to
Charlotte Brontë's own moral victory in her relationship with Heger: "Not until
Charlotte had herself fallen in love, suffered temptation, sought and found the
courage to resist it, endured the heartbreak of fleeing from it, was the Byronic
image superseded in her heart, the Byronic morality outdistanced by a pattern of
conduct whose disciplines she set herself to follow to the end" (*Charlotte
Brontë*, p. 19). But Ms. Gerin does not take into account the fact that Charlotte's love was not, after all, returned: that she had to suffer the humiliation of
her emotional dependence and had to find within herself the strength to overcome her sense of inadequacy.

head; that the night was dark, and my mind impressed with strange fears. The light that long ago had struck me into syncope, recalled in this vision, seemed glidingly to mount the wall, and tremblingly to pause in the centre of the obscured ceiling. I lifted up my head to look: the roof resolved to clouds, high and dim; the gleam was such as the moon imparts to vapours she is about to sever. I watched her come—watched with the strangest anticipation; as though some word of doom were to be written on her disk. She broke forth as never moon yet burst from cloud: a hand first penetrated the sable folds and waved them away; then, not a moon, but a white human form shown in the azure, inclining a glorious brow earthward. It gazed and gazed on me. It spoke, to my spirit: immeasureably distant was the tone, yet so near, it whispered in my heart—

"My daughter, flee temptation!"

"Mother, I will." (p. 407)

The terrifying supernatural experience of the red-room is confronted and resolved at last. The strange powers of the nonhuman world seem now but sympathetic extensions of the compelling, equally mysterious forces of the personality. The authority which Jane has sought is female: the moon, maternal nature, the mother within herself—a cosmic and personal principle of order and control.

The trauma at Gateshead had first been neutralized in the experience at Lowood and now, as part of the more profound conflict of Thornfield, is finally resolved. But the antithetical claims which emerged from Jane's relationship with Rochester have still to be reconciled: the needs of the self and the demands of the "other": passion and discipline, egotism and denial. The dialectic proceeds. The first antithesis to Jane's emotionality had been represented by Helen Burns. The second is offered in the more developed and sophisticated form of St. John Rivers. The allegorical movement of self-discovery, present throughout the novel, is intensified here and its Christian structure is emphasized as Jane moves once again into a level of experience that is social and moral rather than personally and sexually defined.

At Lowood Jane was drawn out of the private fantasy world into which she had been thrust by deprivation. Now, after rejecting the romantic idolatry which parallels her childhood experience on another level, she must consciously relocate herself in a complex hierarchy of values: redefining her relationship to God, to nature, to a heterogeneous society previously unknown. She must create a personality independent enough to be separate within the unity of love, secure enough sexually to temper the passion that cloaks self-abnegation. Hers is a radical trial and is expressed through Christian parable.

Fleeing temptation, Jane is set down at Whitcross which "is no town, nor even a hamlet; it is but a stone pillar set up where four roads meet" (p. 412). She is at a beginning and must discover her own way. Like Bunyan's pilgrim, Christian, she is bereft of friends and family: homeless and penniless. She must be purged of all human vanity, enduring the humiliation of body and spirit. At first she finds comfort in the maternal nature which had always before offered her solace:

> Nature seemed to me benign and good: I thought she loved me, outcast that I was; and I, who from man could anticipate only mistrust, rejection, insult, clung to her with filial fondness. To-night, at least, I would be her guest—as I was her child: my mother would lodge me without money and without price. (p. 413)

But although she, like all men and women, is related to the natural world, she is not truly a part of it:

> What a golden desert this spreading moor! Everywhere sunshine. I wished I could live in it and on it. I saw a lizard run over the crag; I saw a bee busy among the sweet bilberries. I would fain at the moment have become bee or lizard, that I might have found fitting nutriment, permanent shelter here. But I was a human being, and had a human being's wants: I must not linger where there was nothing to supply them. (p. 415)

God, the Father, had given and secured her life. The only mother she can look to in her present trouble is the mother within. She had discovered her presence on the evening of the departure from Thornfield. Now she must test her power:

> Life, however, was yet in my possession; with all its requirements, and pains, and responsibilities. The burden must be carried; the want provided for; the suffering endured: the responsibility fulfilled. I set out. (p. 415)

At Lowood, hunger seemed in part to be experienced as a need for love. Now the mature Jane confronts similar but more pressing deprivations—starvation and death from exposure. Both are spiritual as well as physical trials. She must again discover and assert the self that can endure. Despite privation (reduced to eating pig's food, brought to a state of beggary) Jane is able to retain a degree of pride appropriate to a character strengthened by the resolve of independent choice and action. And that pride is also softened by new sympathy for those who must, as she, endure the humbling miseries of existence.

Finally, at the point of death, Jane follows a light which leads her to Marsh End, a sanctuary of civilization poised at the edge of the wild, open moors. Looking through the window into the scrupulously clean and pleasant kitchen, she sees an elderly female servant and "two young, graceful women—ladies in every point" (p. 424), one with a dog's head resting on her knee, one with a kitten curled in her lap.[20] Busily involved in their translation of German, they are indeed images of "delicacy and cultivation." First denied entrance by the servant, Hannah, Jane is finally admitted by St. John Rivers, the brother of Diana and Mary. Her ordeal is ended. She sleeps for three days and three nights, waking only to eat and drink of the food and water of life. Her sleep renews her spirit as it restores her body and is reminiscent of the crisis that followed her ordeal in the red-room. Her first act after awakening is her forgiveness of Hannah for denying her shelter. She cautions this impotent surrogate for the wicked parent that "Some of the best people that ever lived have been as destitute as I am; and if you are a Christian, you ought not to consider poverty a crime" (p. 437). Her clasping of Hannah's hand marks her entrance into the Christian community and her acceptance of social interrelatedness.

Jane had before found comfort and definition in the female environment at Lowood. Now, after completely identifying with Rochester, it is crucial for her to discover herself anew in the images of women. Through her friendship with Diana and Mary Rivers, she becomes stronger, more confident, more focused. In them, free as they are of dependence upon men, strong in their devotion to one another, she finds the form of a new promise of fulfillment. She shares with them their love of nature. She admires and respects their superior learning, their fine minds. She listens to them talk as she had once listened to Maria Temple and

20. Marsh End seems to be an idealized version of Haworth: Diana Rivers modeled on Emily Brontë; Mary on Anne; their servant, Hannah, on Tabby.

Helen Burns, as Charlotte had listened to Emily and Anne. She responds to the authority in Diana—with her it is natural to be passive, "feminine," "to bend where my conscience and self-respect permitted, to an active will" (p. 439). But there is still equality among them. No longer functioning within the authoritarian context of the master-student relationship she had with Rochester, she finds instead that there can be intellectual reciprocity: a sharing of knowledge and gifts, delight in the interaction of personalities. The strength and confidence which she derives from their friendship allows her to accept the job which St. John offers her as teacher in the village school. Assuming this role, she begins to overcome her feelings of social humiliation:

> I felt desolate to a degree. I felt—yes, idiot that I am—I felt degraded. I doubted I had taken a step which sank instead of raising me in the scale of social existence. I was weakly dismayed at the ignorance, the poverty, the coarseness of all I heard and saw round me. But let me not hate and despise myself too much for these feelings: I know them to be wrong— that is a great step gained; I shall strive to overcome them.
> (p. 459)

And she does largely overcome them (although Jane Eyre, as Charlotte Brontë herself, could not be accused of excessive egalitarian tendencies). She discovers in many of her poor and unlearned students a degree of "natural politeness" and "innate self-respect" which wins her good will and admiration. She takes pride in her accomplishment, in her ability to teach and befriend her students, to be self-sufficient and useful. And her success earns her a position in the little community so that it is enjoyable for her "to live amidst general regard, though it be but the regard of working-people" (p. 468).

The tone of *noblesse oblige* which informs these words provides us with some understanding of the direction which Charlotte Brontë's myth must take. Feminist it might well be, but it is not a feminism which can preach or envision radical social change. Jane, in leaving Rochester, must, it is true, discover her own capacities and strengths. She must learn the pleasures of independence and self-sufficiency. But only economic independence and social position will give her the status essential to the recognition which is the better part of equality.

When St. John informs her of her sizable inheritance and of the fact that he and his sisters are her real cousins, Jane realizes immediately the way in which her life will now be changed. "It was a grand boon doubtless; and independence would be glorious—yes, I felt that—*that* thought swelled my heart" (p. 488). She recognizes also that by sharing her wealth with Diana and Mary she can free them as she herself is now freed, from the dreary servitude of work. She will have with them "a home and connections" and she will be liberated from the necessity of marrying where there is no love.

Discovering her kinship with the Riverses, Jane does, of course follow in the tradition of the heroes and heroines of quest-romance. Social recognition validates internal worth. The implication is that class membership is its very condition. A "lady" is born, not made, even though the secret of her birth might remain hidden. The Riverses are the last of the series of families to which Jane has found herself intimately or distantly connected. In structure they resemble the Reeds and the Ingrams.[21] All have two daughters (Jane stands outside as a stepsister) and a son. The fathers are dead, the mothers living (Hannah is a kindly, unthreatening, surrogate-mother for the Rivers children as Tabby was for the Brontës). But all the earlier families are "bad" or "false." As indications of the incompleteness of Jane's development, they have signaled successive stages of her "trial": a continuing inability to confront a self that has been "earned." It is with her "real" family that Jane shares her birthright, joyously seizing "the delicious pleasure of which I have caught a glimpse—that of repaying, in part, a mighty obligation, and winning to myself lifelong friends" (p. 494). Here is the multi-layered magic of fairy tale. Jane is transformed from stepsister to benefactress. This is the role which Charlotte was to play with her sisters; which she would have wished to play with Branwell, had be been less threatening.

Significantly, it is St. John who pushes her to further recognition of possibility; to further discoveries of herself. He must be the agent of her liberation. If Rochester represents one aspect of Jane's personality, St. John represents the other. On one level, it is the conflict between Byron and the duke of Wellington artic-

21. The Brocklehurst family can be included here as well. The only difference is that both the Rev. Brocklehurst and his wife are still alive.

ulated with psychological subtlety. St. John Rivers is an older and, more importantly, a masculine version of Helen Burns. Without innocence, or naiveté, he is purposeful, directed, threatening. In both of them the spiritual impulse is carried to an extreme: a form of sublimation which can be liberating and creative, but can also destroy.

St. John's Grecian appearance identifies him with the classical virtues of reason and control so admired in *Rasselas*. He is fair and pale, his light is repressed and "burns" as Helen's did, within. While the fire of the red-room and the fire of the wild, impassioned Berthe threaten destruction to others, St. John's fire is, as Jane sees, self-consuming.

> . . . that heart is already laid on a sacred altar: the fire is arranged round it. It will soon be no more than a sacrifice consumed. (p. 469)

In him, Charlotte Brontë has drawn a stunning portrait of the martyr—unsoftened by the childish idealism or female vulnerability which made Helen sympathetic. Defining self-denial as its own virtue, St. John wishes to sacrifice his life to others although he is, by his own admission, a "cold, hard man."

He subscribes, as Helen did, to a Calvinism that is bitter and stern, full of the promise of guilt and punishment. But he identifies himself with the punishing authority of that religion, casting himself as avenging angel rather than as victim. He has found in the missionary's calling a way of channeling his ambitions as soldier, statesman, orator: "a lover of renown, a luster after power" (p. 462), and he brings to his "profession" the hardness and despotism that befit a man of the world. His sadistic arrogance is the male version of Helen's masochism.

Charlotte Brontë describes St. John as "a cold, cumbrous, column" (p. 502). She had used a similar image for Brocklehurst who was "a black pillar . . . a straight, narrow, sable-clad shape."[22] The identification of male sexuality and power on one hand and that same sexuality with rigidity—even death—on the other, is hardly accidental.[23] The extent to which St. John pur-

22. It might be recalled that in *The Professor*, Crimsworth is transformed by Mlle. Reuter's servility, into a "rigid pillar of stone."

23. It would seem that Brontë was ambivalent about many of the parallels which she suggests between St. John and Brocklehurst. Despite strongly negative aspects of St. John's characterization, Brontë chooses to praise him as a martyr whose way, while flawed and not Jane's own, is still worthy of respect.

chases his religious calling at the cost of sexual passion is illustrated in his abortive relationship with Rosamond Oliver, the charming girl whom he rejects precisely because he is attracted to her. And the extent to which his religious fervor is the result of sexual fear and repression is revealed in his more subtle and complex relationship with Jane.

He is attracted to Jane initially because of her courage in adversity. Knowing her past, he is familiar with the strength of her moral fiber. In her attention to her students he sees that she is diligent, orderly, and energetic as well as intelligent. He recognizes in her desire to share her inheritance, a gift for sacrifice, and he feels in her response to him an appropriate recognition of his power. For these reasons, he concludes that she would make him a useful helpmate. But there is an enormous contradiction in his attitude toward her. He does not want to see her as a woman. He would, in fact, have her deny her sexual nature, her feelings, her body—subordinate that which is most vital in her self to his own spiritual quest. Her passivity and masochism respond to him:

> As for me, I daily wished more to please him: but to do so, I felt daily more and more that I must disown half my nature, stifle my faculties, wrest my tastes from their original bent, force myself to the adoption of pursuits for which I had no natural vocation. He wanted to train me to an elevation I could never reach: it racked me hourly to aspire to the standard he uplifted. (p. 509)

The great problem arises from his insistence that she must join him in his missionary labors, not as a friend, not as a "sister," but as a wife: "A sister might any day be taken from me. I want a wife: a soul helpmeet I can influence efficiently in life and retain absolutely till death" (p. 518). He wants to control her completely. For Jane the temptation is strong. Commitment to the work, even to the death which she sees as the inevitable outcome of her existence: this would focus her life and obscure her love for Rochester by employing her physical and intellectual energies. She is willing to defy society and sacrifice her life to participate in that larger mission in which she can only partially believe. It is possible to compromise worldy interests and spiritual doubts, but she cannot sacrifice her sexuality. And there is no question that her sexuality is at issue.

St. John's manipulative power, the loftiness of his aspirations, the largeness of his will—all evoke a response based upon her habitual tendency to submit to a dominating spirit, her need for approval and respect.

> By degrees he acquired a certain influence over me that took away my liberty of mind: his praise and notice were more restraining than his indifference. (p. 508)

The attraction Jane feels is not unrelated to the idolatry of her love for Rochester. It is that aspect of sexuality which is power-oriented, potentially sadomasochistic:

> . . . Though I have only sisterly affection for him now, yet, if forced to be his wife, I can imagine the possibility of conceiving an inevitable, strange, torturing kind of love for him: because he is so talented; and there is often a certain heroic grandeur in his look, manner and conversation. (p. 531)

Jane recognizes that St. John would buy her body with the coin of spirituality, hypocritically posing as God's agent. "Do you think God will be satisfied with half an oblation?" he asks her. "Will he accept a mutilated sacrifice? It is the cause of God I advocate: it is under His standard I enlist you" (p. 519). St. John must make a religious duty of sexual need. He explicitly denies his own and therefore her sexuality, fearing the passion which would make him mortal and vulnerable. As she comes to understand St. John, Jane is so distressed by his twisted, sadistic (albeit unconscious) misrepresentation of his own feeling and by his misunderstanding of hers that she angrily and openly opposes him. When he says: "Undoubtedly enough of love would follow upon marriage to render the union right even in your eyes," she replies: "I scorn your idea of love . . . I scorn the counterfeit sentiment you offer: yes, St. John, and I scorn you when you offer it" (p. 522). It is the extraordinary contempt of a virginal young woman for the Victorian concept of sex as duty, for the Victorian denial of the dignity of human passion. But there still remains in Jane the other side of that Victorian repression: the overwhelming desire to submit to a power that will envelope her, possess her, negate her.

> I was tempted to cease struggling with him—to rush down the torrent of his will into the gulf of his existence, and there lose my own. (p. 534)

Well might she say, "I was almost as hard beset by him now as I had been once before, in a different way, by another" (p. 534).

In the final scene between Jane and St. John, the language of spiritual transfiguration is interlaced with the language and imagery of sexuality. The images of the red-room are recalled as well as the dreams that preceded Jane's decision at Thornfield:

> I stood motionless under my hierophant's touch. My refusals were forgotten—my fears overcome—my wrestlings paralyzed. The Impossible—i.e. my marriage with St. John—was fast becoming the Possible. All was changing utterly, with a sudden sweep. Religion called—Angels beckoned—God commanded—life rolled together like a scroll—death's gates opening, shewed eternity beyond: it seemed, that for safety and bliss there, all here might be sacrificed in a second. The dim room was full of visions.
>
> The one candle was dying out: the room was full of moonlight. My heart beat fast and thick: I heard its throb. Suddenly it stood still to an inexpressible feeling that thrilled it through, and passed at once to my head and extremities. The feeling was not like an electric shock; but it was quite as sharp, as strange, as startling: it acted on my senses as if their utmost activity hitherto had been but torpor; from which they were now summoned, and forced to wake. (pp. 534–35)

Two other profound psychic experiences had occasioned the fear of loss and violation sufficiently terrifying to induce unconsciousness. This third time, much strengthened, Jane is impelled to self-assertive action. Now she is released by orgasmic convulsion into spiritual resolution and sexual redefinition. The response is summoned by the sexual component of St. John's power, but it yields awareness and self-discovery instead of dread annihilation. Much of the dangerous appeal of Rochester's sexuality had derived from a similar charisma of power (a charisma not completely lacking, as masculine force, even in Brocklehurst and John Reed). That appeal is experienced here fully—and finally, absolutely rejected. (Not least of all, the brother-lover is implicitly rejected, literally "sacrificed," as we later learn, in favor of the lover-husband.) Now Jane is free to explore the potential that remains. When she hears Rochester's voice calling to her, she responds as surely to the need it expresses as she responds to the need in herself which she must acknowledge. Rather than accepting the sublimation of desire in a patriarchal religious value system, she finds spiritual meaning in human experience. She rejects sexual passion that derives its force from masochistic self-denial and insists that duty and obligation must be placed within the context of a generous and reciprocal human love.

In rejecting St. John, Jane comes to terms with her need for an external authority. She completes the move toward independence begun in the red-room and continued in her departure from Thornfield. In rejecting St. John's repressive sexuality she rejects the perverse sadomasochism it implies, and she attempts to distinguish the sexuality of love from the sexuality of power: the love born of equality from the love subject to idolatry.

This is the last of the symbolic "separations." At every previous point of parting (from Bessie, Helen, Maria Temple, Rochester) Jane's "self," apparently severed and divided, has become stronger and more integrated than before. The separation from St. John marks the ultimate resolution of her spiritual and sexual being, but the transformation of the Edward Rochester to whom she returns is the crucial condition of the actualization of that being and therefore of the viability of the new romantic myth which the novel has articulated.

In her return to Thornfield, Jane is as little motivated by moral considerations as she had been before in her departure. She is driven by premonition and passion rather than principle or judgment.

> Could I but see him! Surely, in that case, I should not be so mad as to run to him? I cannot tell—I am not certain. And if I did—what then? God bless him! What then? Who would be hurt by my once more tasting the life his glance can give me?
> (pp. 541–42)

She finds Thornfield in ruins: destroyed by the mystery of fire and blood which had been secreted within it for so long: set aflame by Berthe, who was killed while attempting to escape from her husband. The house is the very image of its former master who, Samson-like, maddened by loneliness, desperate and trapped within the futility of his rebellion, had pulled his home down about himself, blinded and crippled his body, deprived himself of that which he had most valued and most feared: the power and pride of his "masculinity." The ambivalence of the Byronic hero towards his own sexuality is nowhere better expressed than in Rochester's attempted rescue of his mad wife, described to Jane by one of the townspeople:

> I witnessed, and several more witnessed Mr. Rochester ascend
> through the skylight to the roof; we heard him call "Berthe!"
> We saw him approach her; and then, ma'am, she yelled, and
> gave a spring, and the next minute she lay smashed on the
> pavement. (p. 548)

The saviour appears to the victim as avenger and rescue itself
becomes a kind of murder. Rochester's heroism, not unlike
Byron's own, is realized in self-destruction.

Jane seeking Rochester at Ferndean reminds us paradoxically—yet justly—of the Prince who comes to awaken the sleeping Beauty with a kiss. Their roles are now reversed. All is dark
and overgrown, the decaying house buried in the gloomy, tangled
forest as Rochester's spirit is hidden in his broken body. Watching him emerge, Jane thinks "of some wronged and fettered
wild-beast or bird, dangerous to approach in his sullen woe . . .
the caged eagle, whose gold-ringed eyes cruelty has extinguished" (p. 552). That she had in past times reminded him of a
small, helpless bird trapped in a nest metaphorizes our sense of
their role reversal.

Brontë has afflicted her hero with the Christian punishment
appropriate to one who has "committed adultery in his heart"
and "put aside his wife."[24] It is the punishment prophesied earlier by Jane in the first agony of her discovery of Rochester's
wife.

> You shall, yourself, pluck out your right eye; yourself cut off
> your right hand: your heart shall be the victim; and you, the
> priest, to transfix it. (p. 379)[25]

And the punishment is appropriate in far more subtle ways as
well: in ways which speak to the social, psychological, and sexual disease of which "romantic love" is a symptom. In the cost
to Rochester of the resolution of Jane's conflict, the severity of
social and psychological pressures are most painfully demonstrated. Just as Henry Hastings's disintegration was essential to
Elizabeth's discovery of her own abilities and as Charlotte's personal and artistic growth were predicated upon both Branwell's

24. One recalls the apparently guilty fantasy of blindness which Brontë reported to Heger in one of her letters.
25. (See Matt. 5:27–32.) Rochester's left eye remains blind. We are told
on p. 552 that he loses his left hand, but on p. 557, Jane contradicts herself and
says it was his right hand that was destroyed.

moral and physical collapse and Patrick Brontë's increasing dependence,[26] so too can Jane's development be maintained only at
the cost of Rochester's romantic self-image. Rochester's mutilation is, in the terms of this nascent feminist myth, the necessary
counterpart of Jane's independence: the terrible condition of a
relationship of equality.[27]

But what, in fact, is the nature of this "equality?" Jane's
flight from the orgasmic knowledge of St. John's sexual power
and Rochester's last catastrophic struggle with his vampire-bride
are not the bases of a mature sexuality which is an extension of
social liberation. They are rather preludes to the desexualization
which is the unhappy compromise necessary when psychosexual
need is unsupported by social reality or political self-consciousness. The mystery of fire and blood is not solved. It is simply
eradicated. Jane's sense of Rochester, as she looks at him on the
morning after her return, is crucial:

> His countenance reminded one of a lamp quenched, waiting to
> be relit—and alas! it was not himself that could kindle the
> lustre of animated expression: he was dependent on another for
> that office. (p. 562)

26. Charlotte's description of Jane's reading and writing for Rochester
recalls her description in a letter to Heger of her own execution of similar services for her father.

27. Carolyn Heilbrun notes that "Jane Eyre's demand for autonomy or
some measure of freedom echoes politically in the cries of all powerless individuals whether the victims of industrialization, racial discrimination or political
disenfranchisement. So we today begin to see that Rochester undergoes, not
sexual mutilation as the Freudians claim, but the inevitable sufferings necessary
when those in power are forced to release some of their power to those who
previously had none." (*Toward A Recognition of Androgyny* [New York:
Alfred A. Knopf, 1973], p. 59.)

Heilbrun's perspective would be acceptable if Brontë had, in fact, been
able to place the problem of her heroine within a political framework. It is just
her inability to do this which creates the ambiguities of the novel's concluding
section.

Most notable among those critics who have applied a Freudian perspective
to the novel and have insisted upon Rochester's symbolic emasculation are: Armour Craig, "The Unpoetic Compromise: On the Relation Between Private
Vision and Social Order in Nineteenth Century English Fiction," in *English In-
stitute Essays* (New York: Columbia University Press, 1965); Earl Knies, *The
Art of Charlotte Brontë* (Athens: Ohio University Press, 1969); Richard Chase,
"The Brontës: A Centennial Observance," *Kenyon Review,* 9 (Autumn 1947),
pp. 486–506; M. H. Scargill, "All Passion Spent: A Reevaluation of *Jane
Eyre,*" *University of Toronto Quarterly,* 9 (1949); Morton S. Day, "Central
Concepts of *Jane Eyre,*" *Personalist,* 40, 1.

He is devitalized; the fire of his passion burnt to ash; the quick of his nature paralyzed. He is not the bereaved lover, expectantly awaiting his mitress's return. His is a comatose soul, unable to cry out for rebirth. It is not a lover he requires, but a mother who can offer him again the gift of life. And it is this function which Jane will gratefully assume.

> I love you better now, when I can really be useful to you, than
> I did in your state of proud independence, when you disdained
> every part but that of the giver and protector. (p. 570)

Brontë, dividing her time between the writing of her novel and the nursing of her weak and sightless father, could well have spoken these words with Jane. They belong to the virginal daughter who has been magically transformed—without the mediation of sexual contact—into the noble figure of the nurturing mother. Once the magical transformation has taken place, the dependence defined, the partial restoration of Rochester's vision cannot reverse the pattern of relationship any more easily than the removal of Patrick Brontë's cataracts could completely reestablish the old patriarchal order.

Jane's money and social status, even her confidence and self-knowledge, would not have offered her sufficient protection against the psychosexual power of Rochester, her "master"; would not have defended her against the arrogance and pride supported by society through its laws, its structures, its attitudes, its mythology. Nor would her new position, her developed self, have protected Rochester from the fears and actual dangers associated with the "masculine" role assigned to him. So strong are these external forces that the reduction of Rochester's virility and the removal of them both from contact with society are necessary to maintain the integrity of the emergent female self. Rochester is brought into the "female" word of love and morality, out of the "masculine" universe of power: out of society, into Jane's sphere of psychic functioning. His transformation heralds the death of the Byronic hero whose many charms were the imaginative instruments of a sexually repressive and oppressive society. But the society into which his maimed Victorian spirit is reborn, is still more repressive and more closed. Brontë's myth reflects those social limitations even as it attempts to define a new feminist freedom. Rochester is, in this sense, a pivotal figure;

marking the transition from the romantic to the modern hero, heralding the paralyzing alienation which will be chronicled by Dickens, by Thackeray, by George Eliot, and Lawrence: by Melville, by Mann, by Kafka, and Dostoevsky. His mangled body projects his psychic scars. His absence of vitality derives from a psychic illness which will become, in many of his successors, spiritual death.

Rochester is the representative and victim of forces over which Jane has triumphed in order to redefine herself. But the self which emerges from the sequential struggles it endures cannot be tested again by former adversaries. The allegorical quest follows a necessary and irreversible path. In its victories, the ego absorbs those components of reality which it has successfully confronted, negating their existence as objective form. The aggressive, even sadistic "masculinity" of John Reed, and Brocklehurst, of St. John and the younger Rochester are all contained within the humbled and broken hero whom Jane ultimately nourishes and sustains. This is, of course, the fantasy element of Brontë's feminist myth. It would not be for almost fifty years that social change and aroused political consciousness would make it possible to test an awareness and achievement like Jane Eyre's against realistic pressures. In England it would not be until the twentieth century and the fiction of D. H. Lawrence that the descendents of the maimed Rochester and the liberated Jane would be able to face each other in the full complexity of their social, sexual, and psychological conflicts.[28] In our own time we struggle still to break through the irrational identification of phallic potency with political, social, and economic domination.

There is, in the naive resolution of *Jane Eyre,* an idealization of Jane and Rochester's life together which is part of the logic of the psychosexual romance. The last chapter begins with an extraordinary statement that places Jane at the center of the relationship. "Reader, I married him," she says and continues:

> I have now been married ten years. I know what it is to live entirely for and with what I love best on earth. I hold myself supremely blest—blest beyond what language can express; be-

28. One thinks, for example, of Gerald and Gudrun in *Women in Love,* of Ursula and Skrebensky in *The Rainbow,* and Clifford and Constance in *Lady Chatterley's Lover.* It ought to be noted that Lawrence's perspective was hardly feminist.

cause I am my husband's life as fully as he is mine. No woman was ever nearer to her mate than I am: absolutely more bone of his bone, and flesh of his flesh. I know no weariness of my Edward's society: he knows none of mine, any more than we do of the pulsation of the heart that beats in our separate bosoms; consequently, we are ever together. To be together is for us to be at once as free as in solitude, as gay as in company. We talk, I believe, all day long: to talk to each other is but an animated and audible thinking. All my confidence is bestowed on him; all his confidence is devoted to me: we are precisely suited in character; perfect concord is the result. (p. 576)

But the truth of this relationship is an interior truth, as remote from social reality as are Gateshead, Lowood, Thornfield, Marsh End, and Ferndean—themselves all landscapes of psychological development. It is the truth of Charlotte Brontë's dream that we have here: the truth of her fantasy. To the extent that it dramatizes the conflict of larger social and psychological forces, it offers also the larger truth of myth. But what is extraordinary is that this novel, born of repression and frustration, of limited experience and less hope, should have offered an insight into psychosexual relationships that was visionary in its own time and remains active in ours.

Branwell Brontë's portrait of his sisters, c. 1825. *From left:* Anne, Emily, and Charlotte. The painted-out space in the center of the painting is thought to have once contained a self-portrait of Branwell / *National Portrait Gallery, London*

A Fragment August the y 1829

One Cold dreary ~~winter~~ night in the month of December
the Marquis ~~Marchioness~~ of Wellesly ~~& all her~~ their children ~~who were~~ who were
all grown up were sitting ~~now~~ in the private parlour round a
~~blazing~~ cheerful fire they appeared quite comfortable in all
outward things & yet they kept sighing & fidgeting & yawning
as if some great trouble oppressed at last Lady Wellesly
rose up from her seat and going to the window she drew
aside the splendid curtain & looked out into the dark
stormy night & after gazing for some time she returned
to the fire saying in a despairing tone "when will little
Authur come". I wonder what he is like now exclaimed
Lord Wellesly "O Authur Authur do come" said the
Honourable & Reverend ~~&~~ Docter Wellesly I dont
know what I shall do if he does not come soon returned
Lord Cowley "its quite miserable without him answered
Lord Maryborough "when we last saw him he was a
pretty little baby said the Marquis of Wellesly sweet
little creature ejaculated the Marchioness just at
this moment the door opened & a tall handsome
young man appeared they all started up joyfuly ex-
claiming thats Authur & runing towards ~~him~~ him
almost smothered him with kisses & caresses while he
in return did the same ~~thing~~ to them after the exuberance
of their joy had a little subsided they ~~all~~ gathered round
the fire once more but now perfectly happy as little
Authur was there ~~————————~~ after a short time the Marquis
of Wellesly said now my dear son tell us all that you have
done & suffered since I placed you in the arms of
your orderly man to be conveyed on board the ship which
was to take you to Eaton college yes do Authur exclaimed the rest Arthur consented & began as follows

C Brontë August the 8 1829

George Smith, the director of Smith, Elder, and Company, Charlotte Brontë's publisher and the model for Graham Bretton in *Villette*
By permission of the Brontë Society

Arthur Bell Nicholls, Charlotte's husband, c. 1854
The Mansell Collection

CHAPTER FOUR

Shirley: *Feminism and Power*

F OR REASONS which I will shortly sketch, Charlotte Brontë turned away from the quasi-allegorical mode of *Jane Eyre* and attempted to write what she conceived as a social and political novel. She would, of course, not abandon the psychological conundrums she had explored in that violent and radical new myth of heterosexual relationship, but she would now emphasize the pressures of the workaday world. She would discipline herself, as she had announced she would try to do in *The Professor,* to the dictates of "realism."

> Something real, cool and solid lies before you; something unromantic as Monday morning, when all who have work wake with the consciousness that they must ride and betake themselves thereto.[1]

Several factors contributed to the change of perspective. Although *Jane Eyre* had received enthusiastic reviews, its unknown author had been accused by many of impropriety and "coarseness."[2] The attacks on the novel's open sexuality and expression of "unseemly" feeling, might well have caused Brontë to regret her self-revelation and sent her scurrying for the comfort of authorial distance. Her respect for the ironic and omniscient posture of Thackeray, whom she considered to be the greatest of all

---

1. Charlotte Brontë, *Shirley, A Tale* (London: Oxford University Press, 1969), p. 1. All subsequent references are to this edition and will be included within the text.
2. For a thorough summation of the critical reception accorded the Brontës' novels, see Winnifreth, Chapter 7.

living writers, would have further reinforced this impulse. She also took seriously the sobering advice of George Henry Lewes who had qualified his praise of *Jane Eyre* with concern about its melodramatic nature. He referred her to Jane Austen. She abjured the model:

> I had not seen *Pride and Prejudice* till I read that sentence of yours, and then I got the book. And what did I find? An accurate daguerreotyped portrait of a commonplace face . . . with neat borders and delicate flowers; but no glance of a bright, vivid physiognomy, . . . no fresh air, no blue hill, no bonny beck. I should hardly like to live with her ladies and gentlemen, in their elegant but confined houses.[3]

But her response to Lewes suggests that she did not weigh his judgment lightly:

> I mean to observe your warning about being careful how I undertake new works; my stock of materials is not abundant, but very slender; and besides, neither my experience, my acquirements, nor my powers are sufficiently varied to justify my ever becoming a frequent writer . . .
>
> If I ever *do* write another book, I think I will have nothing of what you call "melodrama;" I *think* so, but I am not sure. I *think,* too, I will endeavour to follow the counsel which shines out of Miss Austen's "mild eyes," "to finish more and be more subdued;" but neither am I sure of that. When authors write best, or, at least, when they write most fluently, an influence seems to waken in them, which becomes their master—which will have its own way—putting out of view all behests but its own, dictating certain words, and insisting on their being used, whether vehement or measured in their nature; new-moulding characters, giving unthought-of turns to incidents, rejecting carefully elaborated old ideas, and suddenly creating and adopting new ones.[4]

Her awareness of the conflict which might exist between a desired goal and the demands of her genius suggests a new depth of self-knowledge and a more conscious definition of purpose. Reading her correspondence—particularly her letters to her editor and friend, W. S. Williams—one feels the growing intellectual confidence which allows her to advance ideas without timidity or

3. January 12, 1848. Wise and Symington, II, 179–80.
4. Ibid.

apology. She had been vastly successful as a writer. There was the sense of doors opening to welcome her into a world which had previously been inaccessible. Her position at Haworth was central—literary agent for her less successful sisters, nurse to her father, Branwell's righteous judge. All contributed to feelings of worth and responsibility. But there remained, after all, the parochial nature of her experience, the intense and even morbid self-involvement that characterized her psychological life. She must have been thinking of these when she courageously wrote to Lewes of her "slender stock of materials" and of the commanding urgency of her particular genius. She must have had in mind the conflict between the personal demands of her reticent nature and the wrenching disquiet of her growing social awakening when she observed in *Shirley:*

> It is good for women, especially, to be endowed with a soft blindness: to have mild, dim eyes, that never penetrate below the surface of things—that take all for what it seems. Thousands, knowing this, keep their eye-lids drooped, on system; but the most downcast glance has its loophole, through which it can, on occasion, take its sentinel-survey of life. (p. 271)

Like many women whose vulnerability and dependence spawn an exquisite sensitivity to the responses and attitudes of others, Brontë had been "accustomed to silent soul-reading." Professional and intellectual self-confidence gave her a voice—allowed her to abstract and judge. But persistent feelings of personal inadequacy (the habitual stance of a lifetime) made it difficult for her to translate criticism into concepts of antiauthoritarian action relevant to her characters. This clash between intellect and emotion was at least partially responsible for the eccentric nature of her novel: as ambitious as any written during the Victorian period; fascinating in its flaws, frustrating in its inability to offer resolutions, thrilling in its capacity for posing the most meaningful kinds of problems.

There is always present in *Shirley*'s probing analysis of society a haunting cry of personal alienation. One feels that *this* is the cry that marked the novel's birth, that the fiction was conceived out of Brontë's sense, probably quite vague at first, that her misery was part of a larger, complex pain; that the meshes in which she felt herself to be imprisoned represented only a tiny segment of an enormous web in which innumerable others were trapped. At the heart of her view was profound pessimism.

> There are hundreds of human beings who trample on acts of kindness and mock at words of affection. I know this, though I have seen but little of the world. I suppose I have something harsher in my nature than you have, something which every now and then tells me dreary secrets about my race, and I cannot believe the voice of the Optimist, charm he never so wisely.[5]

She had agonizingly experienced personal rebuffs and rejections, bitter disillusionments; but it was not these alone which fostered negative thoughts. The political concerns of her childhood, still primary in her father's life, must have held a place in her own awareness. Her publishers at Smith, Elder kept her supplied with much of the reading material which occupied intellectual London. Her friendship with Mary Taylor had long stimulated her feminist consciousness. The writings of her two new friends, Elizabeth Gaskell and Harriet Martineau, gave that consciousness a more objective focus. The 1840s were years of intellectual and social ferment and Brontë could not have been unaffected by the new free-trade liberalism of the middle class or by the revolutionary socialism which was becoming the faith of increasing numbers of workers. By 1846, with the repeal of the Corn Laws and the beginning of the railway mania, there is all the horror of the modern industrial age. Amelioration would come later.[6]

Her response to these public and private pressures, was to write what was, for her, a different kind of novel. It is set in Yorkshire during the Napoleonic wars. The rebellion of weavers against textile manufacturers (the Luddite uprisings) provided the background. There are two heroines. Caroline Helstone, abandoned as a small child by her mother, has been grudgingly raised by her minister uncle, the brother of her dead father. Caroline is hopelessly in love with Robert Moore, her Belgian cousin who, as a beleaguered mill owner, cannot afford the fripperies of romance. The second heroine, Shirley Keeldar, does not appear until a third of the way through the novel, but occupies a position

5. To W. S. Williams, October 18, 1848. Wise and Symington, II, 267.
6. See Barbara Ward, "Charlotte Brontë and The World of 1846," *Brontë Society Transactions*, XI, 56 (1951), 3–13. The essay is illuminating but underestimates Brontë's grasp of dominant social issues.

of special importance. She is the "lady" of the parish manor house, a wealthy orphaned heiress, secretly in love with Robert Moore's brother, Louis, her impoverished former tutor. In the process of conducting her heroines through their romantic trials, Brontë introduces her readers to various aspects of life in this transitional society. She examines the state of the church, England's political struggles, the position of women, attitudes of owners and workers.

When the novel was published in 1849, Lewes wrote in the *Edinburgh Review* that *Shirley* was "a portfolio of sketches" lacking in unity. Critics and readers have agreed ever since, persistently confusing the novel's fragmented and unresolved conclusions with its fundamental unity of concept. Having underestimated the power of Brontë's social vision, critics have not been able to see the way in which the breadth of that vision is unsupported by an adequate political consciousness. Blind to the subtlety of the novel's design, they have justified their claim of its absence by a sympathetic depiction of her tragic milieu. It is typical of the undermining sentimentality that has typified Brontë biography and criticism.[7]

For the most part, then, even those who have attempted to approach the novel seriously have been unable to connect the author's ironic treatment of the clergy, her use of the Luddite riots, references to the Napoleonic wars, the jaundiced presentation of marriage, the sympathetic, even agonized analyses of spinster life, and the impassioned pleas for useful work for women. They have not reconciled the strongly antiromantic strain of the novel

7. Among more recent critics who have dismissed or underestimated the novel because of its absence of unity are: Lord David Cecil, *Early Victorian Novelists* (Indianapolis: Bobbs-Merrill, 1935), pp. 117–54; Ivy Holgate, "The Structure of *Shirley*," *Brontë Society Transactions*, 14 (1962), 27–35; Fanny Ratchford, *The Brontës' Web of Childhood;* J. M. S. Tompkins, "Caroline Helstone's Eyes," *Brontë Society Transactions*, 14 (1961), 18–28; Janet Spens, "Charlotte Brontë," in *Essays and Studies by Members of the English Association*, 14 (1929), 54–70; Asa Briggs, "Private and Social Themes in *Shirley*," *Brontë Society Transactions*, 13 (1958), 203–14.

In recent years only Jacob Korg, "The Problem of Unity in *Shirley*," *Nineteenth Century Fiction*, 12 (September 1957); Arnold Shapiro, "Public Themes and Private Lives: Social Criticism in *Shirley*," *Papers on Language and Literature*, 4 (Winter 1968); and most persuasively, Carol Ohman, "Charlotte Brontë: The Limits of her Feminism," in *Female Studies*. 6, The Feminist Press (Old Westbury, N.Y.) 1972, 152–64 have argued for coherent principles of unity within the novel.

and its conventionally "happy ending." They have sought to place the novel's focus, wondering why Brontë chose to use two heroines instead of one. They have rejected as extraneous the Yorke family—modeled on Mary Taylor's "people"—interesting in themselves, apparently irrelevant to the work as a whole.

Masking this misreading, clumsy criticism has then advanced the needless apology of tragic circumstance. At this time, the novelist had herself confessed to James Taylor, another of her publishers:

> I took great pains with *Shirley*. I did not hurry; I tried to do my best, and my own impression was that it was not inferior to the former work; indeed, I had bestowed on it more time, thought and anxiety: but a great part of it was written under the shadow of impending calamity and the last volume, I cannot deny, was composed in the eager, restless endeavor to combat mental sufferings that were scarcely tolerable.[8]

Three deaths in nine months. Three times the writing had been interrupted—three times resumed in an increasing mood of hopelessness and despair: "Too often I feel like once crossing an abyss on a narrow plank—a glance round might quite unnerve. . . ."[9] How small the pretense of art must have seemed to Brontë in comparison with the realities of her situation. Caroline Helstone could be miraculously revived in the chapter, "Valley of the Shadow of Death," but Anne, the youngest of them all, had just been placed in her coffin. Emily and Branwell had been buried several months before. The tone of the novel would naturally have been affected by Brontë's grief and it is altogether likely that she might have modified her heroines' characters, as displayed in the earlier chapters, after the deaths of her sisters.[10]

8. Wise and Symington, III, 154.

9. To W. S. Williams, January 18, 1849. Wise and Symington, II, 301.

10. Winifred Gerin suggests that "as Emily's life ebbed away (Shirley) became increasingly endowed with the characteristics of her sister. Finally there was a change in Caroline's character. Even the color of her eyes and hair came to resemble Anne's in the end" (pp. 389–90).

According to Gaskell, Shirley Keeldar was "what Emily Brontë would have been had she been placed in health and prosperity" (p. 277). Ivy Holgate ("The Structure of *Shirley*") suggests that Shirley began as a portrait of Mary Taylor but that, after Emily's death, Charlotte felt free to incorporate into that portrait elements of her sister's personality:

> Thus in Shirley Keeldar we find the noblest traces that were to be found in Emily Brontë. We also find in the heroine the commercially-minded Mary,

Still, the modifications involved are relatively minor. Ruthlessly shunting the tragedies aside, we are able to find the principle of unity which reconciles what for so long have been seen as disparate themes, dissonant chords.

By the time Brontë sat down to write *Shirley* she had so matured psychologically, artistically, and intellectually that she could place the psychosexual problems which had long concerned her within a larger social context. We have seen how, in both *The Professor* and *Jane Eyre,* she drew parallels between women and statusless men. In *The Professor* she had described as effeminized, men deprived of social or economic power. But their effeminacy was often transitional. Her impotent female, on the other hand, could not be released from the double bind of both her gender and her social situation. In *Jane Eyre,* working with the same recognitions, she resolved the dilemma of her heroine by awarding her social and economic status at the same time that she drastically redefined the role and identity of the male. She could do this only by isolating Jane and Rochester within an asocial, mythic universe.

The time had come for her to confront more directly the nature of female oppression and to consider as analytically as possible the way in which this form of oppression was related to others: to find the connections which could be drawn between women and the poor and socially dispossessed, between women and unemployed laborers, between women and children. She had reached a level of consciousness which allowed her to ask what characteristics "women" shared with other groups of powerless "victims": in what ways the nature of women's interaction with men and with other women was determined by the complexity of their impotent situation. The theme of her new book would be nothing less then the misuse of power within a patriarchal society, and "women," rather than a particular woman, would stand for her as the appropriate and central symbol of powerlessness. She realized that in the female subculture values have been developed in relative isolation. Because they are different from those of the "official" society, they offer a critical perspective of accepted structures and attitudes.

---

the feminist, the pioneering woman. But Charlotte was at this time by no means at her best; she derived a kind of stimulus of mind from her obsession, but the grafting has not been skillfully done. (pp. 27–35)

It is an extraordinary subject for Charlotte Brontë to have conceived: not less impressive when one remembers that Engels had just published *The Condition of the Working Class in England in 1844*. The differences between their analyses derive from the fact that Engels's political consciousness—infinitely more powerful, of course, than Brontë's own—was formed in response to his sophisticated social awareness. The result was a vision of radical social change completely absent from *Shirley*. Still, Brontë was asking, in her novel, questions as acute as any which were then being asked in England.

II

In the first chapter of *Shirley*, Brontë demonstrates her resoluteness of purpose by launching immediately into an attack on the Church—the church of which Patrick Brontë was minister. By 1812, the year in which her story begins, the Anglican Church—respected arbiter of value, source of divine inspiration and support—has become increasingly indifferent to its people. Its spine broken, the organism must collapse. In the rotted moral fiber of those who should intercede between God and man, the extent and nature of society's disease can be diagnosed.

The symptoms of the disease are found in the false pride, the petty vanities, the egotism of the curates. The trivial concerns of Donne, Malone, and Sweeting imply much: their "love of feasting and drinking," their endless socializing and foolish squabbling; the grudging condescension towards the members of their parishes to whom they are strangers and from whom they are alienated; the preoccupation with females as so many sexual objects with so much dowry value. Significantly, the curates do not number their landladies, upon whom their comforts depend, among the rest of "the fair sex." Because these females have no "human" qualities, they share the same name, always spoken in tones of cruel command. The name is "woman." It designates function: to clean, to cook, in short—to serve.

> "Cut it woman," [said Mr. Malone] and the "woman" cut it accordingly. Had she followed her inclinations, she would have cut the parson also; her Yorkshire soul revolted absolutely from his manner of command. (p. 5)

In two of their rectors—the Reverends Matthew Helstone and Hiram Yorke—the curates' symptoms become more pronounced, made virulent by class and status. The nature of the disease is now identifiable: it is the desire for and the misuse of power. Brontë had suggested, in her portraits of Brocklehurst and St. John Rivers, the ministry's potential for self-delusion and cruelty, for sexual sadism linked to sexual repression. Here she widens her perspective. Yorke and Helstone are not starkly drawn figures of allegory. Their complexity, particularly Yorke's, rejects simplistic summation. They are men, not villains. But neither is appropriately a man of the church. Both are manipulative, arrogant, and worldly. Of Helstone:

> He was not diabolical at all. The evil simply was, he had missed his vocation: he should have been a soldier, and circumstances had made him a priest. For the rest, he was a conscientious, hard-headed, hard-handed, brave, stern, implacable, faithful little man; a man almost without sympathy, ungentle, prejudiced, and rigid; but a man true to principle, honourable, sagacious and sincere. (p. 34)

And of Yorke:

> The want of veneration . . . made him dead at heart to the electric delight of admiring what is admirable; it dried up a thousand pure sources of enjoyment; it withered a thousand vivid pleasures. He was not irreligious, though a member of no sect, but his religion could not be that of one who knows how to venerate. He believed in God and heaven, but his God and heaven were those of a man in whom awe, imagination and tenderness lack.
>
> The weakness of his powers of comparison made him inconsistent; while he professed some excellent general doctrines of mutual toleration and forbearance, he cherished towards certain classes a bigoted antipathy; . . . at heart he was a proud man: very friendly to his workpeople, very good to all who were beneath him, and submitted quietly to be beneath him, but haughty as Beelzebub to whomsoever the world deemed (for he deemed no man) his superior. (p. 44)

There is little place for the human affections in a world characterized on every level by conflict, competition, and aggression. England is at war with France. National interests divide: Jacobin against Loyalist; Tory against Whig. It is a world in which religious sects line up as armies—Dissenters, Methodists, Baptists, Wesleyans, Independents. It is a world in which birth assigns status and material success confirms it. And everywhere, at the head of every faction, leading every battle, filling the ranks of armies, political parties, professional workers, and simple laborers—there are men, only men: each one defining his situation according to his own self-interest: each one attempting to retain whatever bit of social, economic, and sexual power he possesses: each one attempting to garner more.

Thus when the unemployed textile workers rebel against the mill owner, Robert Moore, first smashing the machinery he has purchased to replace them and finally, in desperation, attacking his mill,[11] Helstone who feels no sympathy for them, and Yorke who does, both join against the workers in an expression of class solidarity. Social and economic interests ally them with the Belgian despite their professional responsibilities and national allegiance.

As for Moore himself, he typifies in his attitudes the crass selfishness of the growing middle class:

> All men, taken singly, are more or less selfish, and taken in bodies they are intensely so. The British merchant is no exception to this rule; the mercantile classes illustrate it strikingly. These classes certainly think too exclusively of making money; they are too oblivious of every national consideration but that of extending England's (i.e., their own) commerce. Chivalrous feeling, disinterestedness, pride in honour, is too dead in their hearts. (p. 167)

Robert, too, is guided virtually exclusively by the economic motive softened only slightly by the necessity he feels of paying his father's debts. He sees himself as "a man [who] has been brought up only to make money, and lives to make it, and for nothing else, and scarcely breathes any other air than that of mills and markets" (p. 122). With other mill owners, he is a Whig, "at least as far as opposition to the war-party was concerned, that

11. Asa Briggs suggests that the account of the workers' rebellion against Robert Moore was based upon events which initiated the Luddite movement near Nottingham during the winter of 1811–12. The rebellion represented a protest against machinery and was stimulated by the scarcity of work and the high price of provisions. The model for Robert Moore, according to Briggs, was William Cartwright who bravely defended his mill with four of his workmen and five soldiers. ("Private and Social Scenes in *Shirley*," pp. 208–9.)

being the question which affected his own interest; and only on that question did he profess any British politics at all'' (p. 34). But, with the other mill owners, he also wants stricter government intervention to suppress machine-wrecking and attacks on property. Like Helstone and Yorke, he enjoys the exercise of power, and even welcomes being wronged so that he can avenge himself and demonstrate his courage—his possession of the manly virtues. Emotion is not among them. It is a luxury he can ill afford. He rejects a love-match with Caroline, whose devotion he acknowledges, whose attraction he feels, in favor of a possible union with Shirley, whose fortune would guarantee his future. For the poor he feels no sympathy. "Poverty is necessarily selfish, contracted, groveling, anxious" (p. 60), he observes, with the smug superiority born of class consciousness and separation. When William Farren, one of his unemployed workers, gives voice to his frustration:

> Invention may be all right, but I know it isn't right for poor folks to starve. Them that governs mun find a way to help us: they mun mak' fresh orderations. Ye'll say that's hard to do—so much louder mun we shout out, then, for so much slacker will t'Parliament-men to be set on to a tough job.
> (p. 137)

Moore cannot understand that they share a common problem: "Worry the Parliament-men as much as you please . . . but to worry the mill-owners is absurd; and I, for one, won't stand it" (p. 137). He is neither capable of the kind of social analysis which will demonstrate that he, like Farren, is a victim of the same system: that both are, in fact, powerless; nor does he grasp the fundamental meaning of need and deprivation: that "misery generates hate" (p. 28). His kinship with Farren escapes him. In fact, if he is only slightly less frustrated and miserable than the starving members of the working class, he is not less self-involved. The threat of economic ruin deprives him of humane attitudes. Hungry, all men—Brontë observes—are the same:

> National honour was become a mere empty name, of no value in the eyes of many, because their sight was dim with famine; and for a morsel of meat they would have sold their birthright.
> (p. 27)

It is interesting that Farren, striving to maintain moral principles, should identify himself with Caroline and Shirley:

> Human natur', taking i' th' lump, is nought but selfishness. It is but excessive few, it is but just an exception here and there, now and then, sich as ye two young uns and me, that being in a different sphere, can understand t'one t'other, and be friends wi'out slavishness o'one hand, or pride o' t'other. (p. 325)

In fact, there is both "slavishness" and "pride." They patronize him. He treats them with deference. His class expectations are such that he accepts this as "equality." But still he is right. There are ways in which they are "like." The introduction of machinery has made Farren as extraneous as women to the cash nexus. Cut off from the patriarchal hierarchy he becomes, quite appropriately, a gardener—part of the natural world from which most men are estranged but with which women are still associated. This association gives them their special "intuitive" knowledge, but it is a kind of knowledge which cannot be translated into action or made a meaningful part of history.

To the extent that the laborer remains within the structures of industrialization he becomes economically, socially, and psychologically alienated. He, like women, is made to experience himself as "victim": powerless and oppressed. Increasingly devalued as "things" become more valuable, he is assessed according to his usefulness just as women are desired according to their material wealth and physical attractiveness—their "sexuality." As long as he is enmeshed in a competitive system which rewards him with money, he is alienated from other men, from his work, from the natural world and from himself. So women compete with one another for the status of marriage, seldom realizing that the marriage relationship, based on impersonal considerations, cannot yield "love." The inner quality of the power structure places husband and wife in a situation of conflict which approximates the one that exists between owner and worker. Sexual politics can be defined in terms similar to those of class antagonism. At every point, workers and women are expected to recognize their inferiority and their dependence. Joe Scott speaks for most men when he explains to Caroline and Shirley that "Women is to take their husbands' opinion, both in politics and religion—it's wholesomest for them'' (p. 328). Although he could be speaking also of Robert Moore's expectation of *him,* it is clear that he still sees himself as in a position superior to any woman's, no matter what her class. The androgynous vision of *The Professor* has finally been subject to social and economic analysis.

That Charlotte Brontë perceived her world in much the same way as Engels did[12] (as a power struggle conducted on personal and familial as well as on socioeconomic levels), is repeatedly demonstrated in the male and female attitudes recorded—relationships described—in *Shirley*. Men and women are mysteries to one another: inevitably sealed and separate. Marriage—the most fundamental social relationship—is materially based. The curate, Malone, rejects "marriage in the vulgar, weak sense, as a mere matter of sentiment" although he accepts its value when it offers "an advantageous connection" (p. 20). And when he observes to Moore that "you and I will have no gray mares in our stable when we marry," Moore responds with typical pragmatism, "If the gray mare is handsome and tractible, why not?" (p. 24). So, too, Shirley's uncle, Mr. Sympson, is anxious that she make "a suitable match": "a fine unencumbered estate; real substance; good connections" (p. 465), since, " 'Love' is Preposterous stuff! indecorous! unwomanly!'' (p. 467). Shirley correctly observes to Caroline:

> If men could see us as we really are, they would be a little amazed; but the cleverest, the acutest men are often under an illusion about women: they do not read them in a true light: they misapprehend them, both for good and evil: their good woman is a queer thing, half doll, half angel; their bad woman almost always a fiend. (p. 350)

It is the classic distinction between the Virgin Mary and the Whore of Babylon: man projecting his own bifurcated nature onto women: Rochester divided between the elfin Jane and the vampire Berthe.

Helstone's insecurity, his desire for power, his fear of feeling, all express themselves in his cruel, sexual sadism. His vanity

12. See *The Origin of the Family, Private Property, and the State* (New York: International Publishers, 1942). It is interesting to note that Engels's relationship with the Irish factory girl, Mary Burns—and her sister, Lizzie—hints of the class and sexual chauvinism attacked in *Shirley* as well as in Engels's own work.

prods him to flirtation: "Yet, at heart, he neither respected nor liked the sex, and such of them as circumstances had brought into intimate relation with him had ever feared rather then loved him" (p. 113). He finds it convenient to see women as "a different, probably a very inferior, order of existence" (p. 50).

> He could not abide sense in women: he liked to see them as silly, as light-headed, as vain, as open to ridicule as possible; because they were then in reality what he held them to be, and wished them to be—inferior: toys to play with, to amuse a vacant hour and to be thrown away. (p. 115)

His former wife, Mary Cave, had found physical death preferable to the spiritual death of her marriage. She had also been loved by Hiram Yorke, who thought her "perfect." But, as Yorke admits to Robert Moore: ". . . The odds are, if Mary loved me and not scorned me; if I had been secure of her affection, certain of her constancy . . . the odds are I should have left her" (p. 537). His is a psychology that Shirley understands. She explains it to Caroline, while they watch the attack on Moore's mill. In this moment of crisis it is clear that there cannot be a real place in the serious world of male affairs for an idealized woman. Where there is no heroism there is no room for inspiration: "These are not the days of chivalry: it is not a tilt at a tournament we are going to behold, but a struggle about money, and food, and life" (p. 340). Idealization has little place in the best of courtships. In marriage, it can find no place at all. Although men pursue women, and women can imagine marriage as the only desirable goal of life, few who are or who have been married speak of that state with anything less than either Helstone's practical bitterness: "A yoke-fellow is a fellow sufferer" (p. 99), or Mrs. Pryor's agonized understanding:

> [Love] is said to be strong—strong as death! Most of the cheats of existence are strong. As to their sweetness, nothing is so transitory: its date is a moment—the twinkling of an eye; the sting remains forever. It may perish with the dawn of eternity, but it tortures through time into its deepest night. (p. 378)

Only one "family" appears in the novel: Hiram Yorke and his six children. Most critics have cited the inclusion of the Yorkes—based on the family of Mary Taylor—as the prime example of *Shirley's* absence of unity: a demonstration of Brontë's inability to combine fact and fiction in a satisfactory whole. The inclusion is crucial, however, even if the integration is not wholly successful. Through the Yorkes, Brontë raises a number of sophisticated questions which are central in her consideration of the nature and effects of the patriarchal structure.

On the face of it, the Yorkes are a good, "successful" family; Yorke himself a loving and proud father. He stimulates the minds of his children as he cares for their bodies: appreciating their intelligences, recognizing their gifts, respecting their freedom. He, in turn, earns *their* respect and affection by virtue of his character, his personality, and, not least of all, his position in the community and in his home. The boys share their father's self-possession. Despite personal differences and moments of discord, the three are guaranteed, by virtue of sexual privilege, a strong stake in the future, secure positions and the promise of success.

For Rose and Jessy—as blithe, as imaginative, as strong as their brothers—the future is less certain. Raised in equality by their father, they are not treated with equality by others:

> There are plenty of people . . . who take notice of the boys. All my uncles and aunts seem to think their nephews better than their nieces; and when gentlemen come here to dine, it is always Matthew, and Mark, and Martin that are talked to and never Rose and me. (p. 155)

Although they share their brothers' aspirations and attitudes, their prospects are inferior. Their mother acts, ironically, as society's representative: interpreting for them its sexist will: urging upon them suspicion and repression ("discretion and reserve is a girl's best wisdom" [p. 155]): attempting to restrain their spirits, limit their sense of possibility, reduce them as she has been reduced.

A strong-minded woman, intelligent and able, circumstances have turned her sour and cynical. Since she cannot move happily in the demanding, rigidly defined insularity of her life, she will, at least, move efficiently—making a martyrdom of her domesticity and a model of her martyrdom. Defined only as a wife and mother—all her prodigious energies focused here—she is possessive of her husband ("if she could have had her will, she would not have permitted him to have any friend in the world beside herself" [p. 147]) and dictatorial with her children:

> I would advise all young ladies . . . to study the characters of such children as they chance to meet with before they marry and have any of their own; to consider well how they would like the responsibility of guiding the careless, the labour of persuading the stubborn, the constant burden and task of training the best. (p. 401)

She depresses where she ought to cheer, angers where she ought to comfort, stimulates rebellion instead of love.[13] Powerless in a larger world, she behaves in a way which renders her powerless in her home as well. There too, her husband rules:

> Mrs. Yorke often complained that her children were mutinous. It was strange that with all her strictness, with all her "strong-mindedness"; she could gain no command over them. A look from their father had more influence with them than a lecture from her. (p. 405)

Although she is chiefly bent on forcing her daughters into her own mold (their independence threatens the foundations of her life) her example becomes the primary motive in their rejection of the traditional role defined for them. Rose refuses—as will Jessy—to bury her talents in domestic tasks:

> If my Master had given me ten talents, my duty is to trade with them, and make them ten talents more. Not in the dust of household drawers shall the coin be interred. I will *not* deposit it in a broken-spouted teapot, and shut it up in a china-closet among tea things. I will *not* commit it to your worktable to be smothered in piles of woolen hose. I will *not* prison it in the linen-press to find shrouds among the sheets; and least of all, Mother . . . least of all, will I hide it in a tureen of cold potatoes, to be ranged with bread, butter, pastry and ham on the shelves of the larder. (p. 399)

She is only twelve and will submit to her apprenticeship for four more years, learning those household arts which are useful for all to know. Then she is resolved to travel, to "see the outside of our own round planet at least" (p. 398). She believes that it is "better

13. Winifred Gerin writes: "Mrs. Taylor, née Ann Tickell, seems to have united in her person all the disagreeable qualities of Mrs. Gummidge, Mrs. Wilfer, and Mrs. Vardon; she was cordially disliked by Charlotte and not particularly loved by her daughters, whose life she oppressed with her gloom and tyranny." (*Charlotte Brontë*, p. 71)

to try all things and find all empty than to try nothing and leave your life a blank'' (p. 399).

Brontë's depiction of Jessy's eventual death on a foreign shore, while moving, *is* perhaps extraneous. But her inclusion of the Yorke family and her suggestion of the girls' emigration are not. In the characterization of Mrs. Yorke still another chain of reactions to sexism is revealed. In the functioning of the family— one of the ''best'' in Yorkshire—some of the undermining effects of patriarchy are described. And in Rose and Jessy, who represent the glorious success of enlightened education, who are the most authentic achievements of their father's confused liberalism, the cruel moral of the novel is drawn. For feminism that is wholly committed and uncompromised there can be no place in England. For the woman who, like Rose, has ''a fine, generous soul, a noble intellect profoundly cultivated, a heart as true as steel'' (p. 156), a woman who would use her talents and her mind, who will accept neither dependence nor oppression, who defines herself in terms of freedom and possibility, for a woman refusing alienation, a new home must be built on alien soil.

III

Charlotte Brontë loved and respected Mary Taylor. She was much influenced by her ideas; inspired by her fervor. But Mary's form of feminism was different from her own. Brontë's vision was less whole than Taylor's: less clear, less radical, more troubled—as her personality was less free. Where Mary's childhood had prepared her for rebellion, Charlotte's had made her long for survival. She was bound by her own insecurity. Feelings of inadequacy projected outward became forebodings of doom. If, after her Brussels experience, she could not make herself leave the stultifying security of Haworth, how could she conceive of emigrating to a strange country? For Brontë, the dilemma of women was as inescapable as hunger. Both, as we have seen were related to the larger problem of exploitation, defined politically, economically, socially, culturally, sexually. To such problems Charlotte Brontë, who was not a revolutionary, could offer no large solutions. She could conceive only of compromise. To work out the terms of that compromise, to define the nature and limits of the power which women could claim, she placed two heroines at the center of her story: two women who, by virtue of their personal, social, and economic differences would suggest alternative personal styles and possibilities. Of the two, Caroline Helstone occupies the more conventional position. Left penniless by her father, a cruel, sadistic man who died when she was a child, abandoned by her mother, she is completely dependent upon the benevolence of Matthew Helstone, the uncle with whom she lives. Helstone is not unkind to her. He is simply unconcerned. She is of no greater value to him than is any other woman and because he cannot flirt with her, she is of less interest. She has been educated according to her uncle's standards ("stick to the needle—learn skirt-making, and gown-making, and pie-crust making, and you'll be a clever woman some day" [p. 96]). She has learned to sew a little, draw a little, speak a little French. She reads the books she finds in Helstone's library. In short, she has been prepared for nothing and can do nothing. She must wait passively for "events" to offer her an appropriate occupation, i.e., marriage. Mistreated by her father, rejected by her mother, ignored by her uncle, she is insecure and repressed: "slow to make fresh acquaintance, she was always held back by the idea that people could not want her, that she could not amuse them" (p. 205). Caroline is merely pretty, intelligent, gentle, serious, and good. Only a woman. Without fortune, she is without prospects. She has "fallen in love" with her cousin, Robert Moore, one of the few men who have treated her with kindness. But she doesn't really know him. He will not, as Shirley points out, allow himself to *be* known:

> You can't fix your eyes on him but his presently flash on you.
> He is never off his guard; he won't give you an advantage;
> even when he does not look at you, his thoughts seem to be
> busy amongst your own thoughts, tracing your words . . . at
> his ease. (p. 273)

Caroline looks to Robert as her superior in everything and he obligingly treats her with condescension; patronizing his "little democrat," enjoying the fact that with him, she is like a "happy, docile child" (p. 93).

Despite the fact that the rules of courtship do not allow her to initiate action,[14] Caroline tries, quite movingly, to be open with

---

14. Charlotte Brontë had written to Ellen Nussey:

Ten years ago I should have laughed heartily at your account of the blunder you made in mistaking the bachelor doctor of Burlington for a married

Robert, allowing him to know her feelings for him, risking the rejection which is ultimately his response. When he tells her, with intended kindness, "If I could guide that benignant heart, I believe I should counsel it to exclude one who does not profess to have any higher aim in life than that of patching up his broken fortune" (pp. 122–23), he leaves her without hope. Having nothing to divert her mind, she dwells endlessly on the small details of their relationship, punishing herself for surrendering her pride: remembering, for example, that it was she who first asked *him* for the lock of hair which she now wears upon her heart:

> It was my doing, and one of those silly deeds it distresses the heart and sets the face on fire to think of—one of those small but sharp recollections that return, lacerating your self respect like tiny penknives and forcing from your lips, as you sit alone, sudden, insane-sounding interjections. (p. 227)

Her preoccupation with trivia would be absurd, her dependency pathetic, if her bitterness were less real; if Charlotte Brontë's sense of her as a victim of power were less persuasive: if her position as a woman were not convincingly presented as universal in its implications:

> A lover masculine so disappointed can speak and urge explanation: a lover feminine can say nothing; if she did, the result would be shame and anguish, inward remorse for self-treachery . . . Take the matter as you find it; ask no questions, utter no remonstrances; it is your best wisdom. You expected bread, and you have got a stone; break your teeth on it, and don't shriek because the nerves are martyrized; do not doubt that your mental stomach—if you have such a thing—is strong as an ostrich's: the stone will digest. You held out your hand for an egg, and Fate put into it a scorpion. Show no consterna-

---

man. I should have certainly thought you scrupulous over much—and wondered how you could possibly regret being civil to a decent individual merely because he happened to be single instead of double. Now, however, I can perceive that your scruples are founded on common-sense. I know that if women wish to escape the stigma of husband-seeking, they must act and look like marble or clay—cold—expressionless, bloodless—for every appearance of feeling of joy—sorrow—friendliness, antipathy, admiration—disgust are alike construed by the world into an attempt to hook in a husband—never mind, Nell—well meaning women have their own conscience to comfort them after all. (April 2, 1845. Wise and Symington, II, 30)

tion; close your fingers firmly upon the gift; let it sting through your palm. Never mind; in time, after your hand and arm have swelled and quivered long with torture, the squeezed scorpion will die, and you will have learned the great lesson, how to endure without a sob. For the whole remnant of your life, if you survive the test—some, it is said, die under it—you will be stronger, wiser, less sensitive. (p. 103)

So is the pride of martyrdom born. So is the masochist made: "Robert had done her no wrong; he had told her no lie; it was she that was to blame, if anyone was" (p. 104). To defend oneself against rejection requires self-confidence. A life of self-abnegation and insecurity produces acceptance. One had to face the truth. It was what Charlotte Brontë had done, as she wrote to Ellen Nussey:

> Not that it is a crime to marry—or a crime to wish to be married—but it is an imbecility which I reject with contempt—for women who have neither fortune nor beauty—to make marriage the principle object of their wishes and hopes and the aim of all their actions—not to be able to convince themselves that they are unattractive and that they had better be quiet and think of other things than wedlock—[15]

But of what can one think? For Caroline life becomes an endless expanse of time which must be filled. She tries to adjust to the idea of leading a spinster's life by coming to know Miss Ainley and Miss Mann, by learning what "old maids" do, the way in which they get through every day. She attempts to confront herself, as Brontë had already done:

> It seems that even a "lone woman" can be happy, as well as cherished wives and proud mothers—I am glad of that—I speculate much on the existence of unmarried and never-to-be married women nowadays, and I have already got to the point of considering that there is no more respectable character on this earth than an unmarried woman who makes her own way through life quietly, perseveringly,—without support of husband or brother, and, who, having attained the age of forty-five or upwards—retains in her possession a well-regulated mind—a disposition to enjoy simple pleasures—fortitude to support inevitable pains, sympathy with the sufferings of oth-

15. April 1, 1843. Wise and Symington, I, 296.

ers, and willingness to relieve want as far as her means extend.[16]

But what Caroline perceives is that the generosity of the spinster does not relieve her loneliness, nor does it earn her a genuine place, "a stake," in society. She is used and manipulated as she has always been used and manipulated. The selfish and materialistic people around her calculatedly allow her desperation to be channeled into altruism, and the altruism turns bitter with the recognition of abuse.

Caroline lives a life which is, as Rose Yorke describes it, "a black trance like the toad's buried in marble . . . a long slow death" (p. 398). It is a life such as Brontë herself lived after she returned from Brussels:

> I can hardly tell you how time gets on here at Haworth—There is no event whatever to mark its progress—one day resembles another—and all have heavy lifeless physiognomies—Sunday, baking day and Saturday are the only ones that bear the slightest distinctive mark—meantime life wears away—I shall soon be thirty—and I have done nothing yet—sometimes I get melancholy—at the prospects before and behind me—yet it is wrong and foolish to repine—and undoubtedly my duty directs me to stay at home for the present—There was a time when Haworth was a very pleasant place to me—it is not so now—I feel as if we were all buried here—I long to travel—to work, to live a life of action.[17]

Carloine's voice is indistinguishable from Charlotte's when she cries out:

> Men of England, look at your poor girls, many of them fading around you, dropping off in consumption or decline; or, what is worse, degenerating to sour old maids—envious, backbiting, wretched, because life is a desert to them; or, what is worst of all, reduced to strive, by scarce modest coquetry and debasing artifice, to gain that position and consideration by marriage, which to celibacy is denied. Fathers . . . seek for them an interest and an occupation which shall raise them above the flirt, the manoeuvrer, the mischief-making talebearer. Keep your girls' minds narrow and fettered, they will still be a plague and a care, sometimes a disgrace to you. Cul-

16. To Miss Wooler, January 30, 1846. Wise and Symington, II, 77.
17. To Ellen Nussey, March 24, 1845. Wise and Symington, II, 28.

tivate them—give them some scope and work—they will be your gayest companions in health, your tenderest nurses in sickness, your most faithful prop in age. (p. 392)

For if, as Caroline observes, labor alone cannot bring happiness, "it can give varieties of pain, and prevent us from breaking our hearts with a single tyrant master-torture" (p. 226).

It is the "stagnant state of things," living on frustrated hope and inactivity, which makes young women ill, which makes "their minds and views shrink to wondrous narrowness" (p. 391). It is their distance from the realities of their society, their inability to bind themselves *in fact* to the complexity of human experience, which makes them long for escape and leads them into the airless, endless, dead-end of the romantic myth. By encouraging acceptance, it chains them to the futility of their condition.

Brontë had learned the value of work through the lonely agony of her bereaved life. She knew, as she wrote to Williams, that only her career had given her a hope and motive adequate to sustain her.[18] The passion of Caroline's plea reflects the certainty of Brontë's knowledge. But there were also questions and doubts which arose from the novelist's awareness of the complexity of social problems and the division within women themselves.

> I often wish to say something about the "condition of women" question, but it is one respect in which so much "cant" has been talked that one feels a sort of repugnance to approach it. It is true enough that the present market for female labour is quite overstocked, but where or how could another be opened? Many say that the professions now filled only by men should be opened to women also; but are not their present occupants and candidates more than numerous enough to answer every demand? Is there any room for female lawyers, female doc-

18. Freud wrote in *Civilization and Its Discontents* (p. 27):
It is not possible, within the limits of a short survey, to discuss adequately the significance of work for the economics of the libido. No other technique for the conduct of life attaches the individual so firmly to reality as laying emphasis on work; for his work at least gives him a secure place in a portion of reality, in the human community. The possibility it offers of displacing a large amount of libidinal components, whether narcissistic, aggressive or even erotic, on to professional work and on to the human relations connected with it lends it a value by no means second to what it enjoys as something indispensable to the preservation and justification of existence in society.

tors, female engravers, for more female artists, more author-
esses? One can see where the evil lies, but who can point out
the remedy? When a woman has a little family to rear and educate and a household to conduct, her hands are full, her vocation is evident; when her destiny isolates her, I suppose she
must do what she can, live as she can, complain as little, bear
as much, work as well as possible.[19]

There is in her observation a greater awareness than that of John
Stuart Mill of the dimension of the economic revolution which
would have to take place if women were to be "allowed" to
work. But this is not her major concern. Despite her cynicism
about love and marriage, Brontë still distinguished, as Caroline
does, between women who had to work and those more fortunate
souls who were able to fulfill themselves in domestic duties. Hers
was a moderate feminism which accepted the fact that women's
natures were fundamentally different from men's; that although
women craved social and psychological equality, they would not
wish—except in extraordinary circumstances—to enter those occupational and political bastions traditionally arrogated by men to
themselves. It was just this distinction which drew from Mary
Taylor an angrily outspoken reproach:[20]

I have seen some extracts from *Shirley* in which you talk of
women working. And this first duty, this great necessity you
seem to think that some women may indulge in—if they give
up marriage and don't make themselves too disagreeable to the
other sex. You are a coward and a traitor. A woman who
works is by that alone better than one who does not, and a
woman who does not happen to be rich and who *still* earns no
money and does not wish to do so, is guilty of a great fault—
almost a crime—a dereliction of duty which leads rapidly and
almost certainly to all manner of degradation. It is very wrong
of you to *plead* for toleration of workers on the ground of their
being in peculiar circumstances and few in number or singular

19. To W. S. Williams, May 12, 1848. Wise and Symington, II, 215–16.
20. Years after Charlotte's death, Mary wrote a treatise called *The First
Duty of Women,* a compendium of a series of articles which she had first contributed to the *Victorian Magazine* in the years 1865–70, when she was living at
High Royd. In this work she insisted that it was woman's duty to earn money
and she pitilessly examined such problems as the redundancy of women, female
earnings, idleness, marriage and poverty (Holgate, p. 33).

in disposition. Work or degradation is the lot of all except the
very small number born to wealth.[21]

Female compliance with the sexist structure was denied by
Mary Taylor's radicalism. Charlotte Brontë recognized it as a
social and psychological constant: undesirable perhaps, but apparently inevitable. The fabric of society would not be slashed
more readily by women than by men. The oppressed conspired
willingly with the oppressors. Had she not seen it demonstrated
repeatedly in Ellen Nussey's futile attachments? Had she not
noted it in Mary Taylor's unfortunate attraction to Branwell? Had
she not discovered the reality stamped upon her own heart? She
knew that if women are trapped on one side by the attitudes of a
patriarchal society, they are trapped also by the attitudes which
they have themselves internalized: by their overwhelming need
for recognition and love, by their search and desire for a "master." With few exceptions (Rose and Jessy Yorke typified these),
only those who are rejected and desperate would cry out for
social and political change. The others would bend to the system,
modifying it only in their fantasies.

It was, apparently, in order to explore the validity of this insight that Brontë conceived Shirley Keeldar, her "other"
heroine, whose external circumstances and personal qualities
suggest alternative possibilities for a woman's acquisition and
use of power and thus for her realization of self. A wealthy young
heiress, Shirley adds to the conventional female virtues of
beauty, charm, and intelligence the more useful attributes of
status and education, the altogether desirable condition of freedom. Orphaned, in full control of her money, she is dependent on
no one for the shape of her life. Good health and self-confidence,
optimism, humor, courage, and creativity: all seem to promise
that her future must be extraordinary, a model of possibility. But
she is, after all, a woman—and this qualifies the rest.

Whenever she wishes to be effective in the "real" world—
the world of business, of politics, of "serious" conversation,
Shirley assumes a "role"':

> Business! Really, the word makes me conscious I am indeed
> no longer a girl, but quite a woman and something more. I am

21. Wellington, New Zealand, April 25, 1850. Wise and Symington, III,
104–5.

an esquire! Shirley Keeldar, Esquire, ought to be my style and
title. They gave me a man's name, I hold a man's position; it is
enough to inspire me with a touch of manhood. (p. 202)

The sense of inadequacy is her birthright, given her by her
parents with the name intended for the son whom they wanted but
never had. To express the unique self molded by her rare good
fortune, to have it perceived and responded to, Shirley must
"play" the conventional male: fragmenting her identity, denying
herself. Experience has taught her that gender negates social and
economic position. Therefore, she must try to be "something
more" than a woman. But the redefinition is only a game. "Captain Keeldar" is a collection of postures, gestures, and words: a
child who, at the sufferance of adults, plays at being one of them.
The game might spark mischief, spirit, and glee but it will not
earn respect. In males like Helstone, female political fervor
arouses not anger but patronizing amusement: "We are independent—we think for ourselves! . . . We are a little Jacobin, . . .
a little freethinker, in good earnest" (p. 198).

Shirley sees men too clearly to allow them to feel comfortable
with her. Her queer, significant smile reveals that she is not endowed with the "soft blindness" that is endearing in a woman.
But she knows that if there is a purpose to be achieved, she can
accomplish it only by playing coquette: manipulating the men she
needs so that they think they are manipulating her.

Her position as mistress of the manor house allows her to
tease the curates, to berate the workers, to lecture the villagers, to
ignore anyone who displeases her. But when there is serious business afoot, business involving money and power, "They won't
trust me . . . that is always the way when it comes to the point"
(p. 313). When her mill must be defended against the laborers, it
is the men who secretly plot to defend it, although the power is
really hers to claim. She is a pawn, allowing herself to be used.
And in fact she is not fit to function amid the harsher realities of
the social system which awards her, by virtue of her class and
money, the place of oppressor: which defines her by virtue of her
sex, as victim. Identifying herself (as "Captain Keeldar") with
the values of the system which has blessed her, she cannot begin
to assume the responsibility of acting upon those impulses which
transcend class allegiance, impulses which cause her "to admire

the great, reverence the good, and be joyous with the genial" (p. 220).[22] Her sympathies move her to charity, but her charity is fundamentally pragmatic:

> I must give more, or, I tell you, my brother's blood will some day be crying to Heaven against me. For, after all, if political incendiaries come here to kindle conflagration in the neighbourhood and my property is attacked, I shall defend it like a tigress—I know I shall. Let me listen to Mercy as long as she is near me . . . (p. 264)

"When it comes to the point" Shirley's position does not isolate her less than other women in her relationships with men. Her wealth and status don't make her their equal. They make her more valuable; a prize worth winning: a trophy worth exhibiting. And since men approach her with motives similar to those with which they approach all other women, they naturally attribute to her, motives typical of all courting females. She talks business and politics with Robert Moore, lends him money, shows concern for his welfare. That she is offering friendship never occurs to him. His pragmatic proposal of marriage is the response he deems appropriate to her apparent infatuation. At first she is humiliated and outraged:

> You have made a strange proposal—strange from *you;* and if you knew how strangely you worded it, and looked it, you would be startled at yourself. You spoke like a brigand who demanded my purse, rather than like a lover who asked my heart. (p. 529)

But finally, when Robert, shocked into recognition, asks her to forgive him, she replies, "I could, if there was not myself to forgive, too—but to mislead a sagacious man so far I must have done wrong" (p. 532). The necessity of role-playing is paralyzing. Even the most well-meaning attempt to function spontane-

22. The confusion of social values is one which Brontë seemed to have shared with her heroine. The patronizing tone of this comment of Shirley seemed to be as unconscious on the author's part as it is on her own: "There is nothing the lower orders like better than a little downright good-humored rating. Flattery they scorn very much; honest abuse they enjoy. They call it speaking plainly, and take a sincere delight in being the objects thereof" (p. 354). This does not, of course, undercut the validity of the novel's perspective. It rather accounts for the probing, questioning quality which makes the fiction so convincing.

ously within power-oriented structures results in behavior which must destroy the integrity of the individual.

So despite her gifts of mind and fortune, despite the fact that she is stable and self-sufficient, Shirley is also thrown back upon herself, lonely in many of the same ways as Caroline. And the two young women find in their relationship with one another the possibilities of a kind of friendship which is rare indeed in their society. Between men, who must guard their own power, there can be common causes (e.g., Helstone and Moore) and manipulative interaction. Some men are like Yorke, focused on their families, with "few intimates." Others, like Robert Moore, are isolated in their suspicions, able only to relate to the few who, like Joe Scott, openly acknowledge their own superiority.

Between most women competing relentlessly with one another for husbands, relationships are superficially polite but equally blocked and frustrated. It is, of course, the intelligence and decency of Caroline and Shirley, their mutual awareness and shared concerns, which make their friendship possible. It is also because Shirley's position, inhabited with full confidence, is supported by Caroline's deference, that their friendship can thrive. While both girls feel comfortable occupying the relative positions with which they are familiar, the absence of strain within the acknowledged hierarchy derives from the fact that, on another level, both are as women, outsiders and equals. Caroline experiences enormous relief at the absence of those feelings of inadequacy which always accompany her interactions with men whom she respects:

> If the company of fools irritates, as you say, the society of clever men leaves its own peculiar pain also. Where the goodness or talent of your friend is beyond and above all doubt, your own worthiness to be his associate often becomes a matter of question. (p. 211)

With Shirley she feels none of the pain that accompanies "love": the pain of enforced passivity, of insecurity, of humiliation: the pain of being denied open, unashamed communication, the spontaneous expression of feeling:

> Shirley, I never had a sister—you never had a sister; but it flashes on me at this moment how sisters feel toward each other—affection twined with their life, which no shocks of

feeling can uproot, which little quarrels only trample an instant that it may spring more freshly when the pressure is removed—affection that no passion can ultimately outrival, with which even love itself cannot do no more than compete in force and truth—Love hurts us so, Shirley—it is so tormenting, so racking, and it burns away our strength with its flame; in affection is no pain and no fire, only sustenance and balm. I am supported and soothed when you—that is, *you only*—are near, Shirley. (p. 261)

Shirley and Caroline seek in their friendship the kind of support that Jane had sought and found first with Helen Burns and Maria Temple, later with Diana and Mary Rivers; that Charlotte had found, in her maturity, with Emily and Anne.

Not insignificantly, they can share with one another their puzzlement about men's "otherness," their hardness, their apparent incapacity for love and fidelity. They wonder whether it is "necessary to be new and unfamiliar to them, in order to seem agreeable or estimable in their eyes" (p. 212); whether it is not true that "we each find an exception in the one we love, till we *are* married" (p. 213). Both are painfully aware of male inadequacies, frightened by the psychological dangers posed by marriage. Both recognize that most men have none of their own intuitive love of nature, and might cut them off from a world which is nurturing. And yet, both are trapped by forces within, by their own feelings of inferiority, by their adoption, largely unconscious, of the values of their society and the fantasies which support them. They can be made whole only if they are elevated by the recognition of "the other"; if they are allowed to partake of *his* status and position, if they are in fact "mastered." Shirley must admit that "nothing ever charms me more than when I meet my superior" (p. 215). Caroline continues to pine, secretly, for the love of Robert Moore. Both find the prospect of sacrifice appealing, and Caroline understands that the greatest pain derives from being deprived of the opportunity for self-denial. When Shirley observes—with the touch of masochism that is familiar—"One could have loved Cowper, if it were only for the sake of having the privilege of comforting him" (p. 224), Caroline responds from the depth of her own experience: "You might have sought Cowper with the intention of loving him; and you would have looked at him, pitied him, and left him, forced away by a sense of the impossible, the incongruous . . . ." (p. 224). Ironically, Shirley asks, "Who told you that? Did Moore?" She reveals that she has as little faith as the men she despises, in a woman's capacity for intelligent perception and serious thought. It is because she has inadequate confidence in herself.

Shirley's ambivalence is reflected in her religious attitudes as well. She feels, as did Jane Eyre, the need for a female mythology, a religion which is not the product of the male imagination, not an extension of the patriarchal structure. And, like Jane, Shirley finds her spiritual affinity in nature. She urges Caroline not to worship God in Helstone's church and offers her, instead of the minister's sermon, her own celebration of "my mother Eve," who dwells still in Nature, an "undying, mighty being." She reminds her resistant, somewhat frightened friend that Eve was the mother of Titans, the daughter of Jehovah, equal to Adam, his son: "The first woman was heaven-born. Vast was the heart whence gushed the well-spring of the blood of nations; and grand the undegenerate head where rested the consort-crown of creation" (p. 319). But although Shirley longs for a maternal deity with whom she can identify, by whom she wil be inspired and ennobled, the myth of creation which she had written for her tutor—Louis Moore—Robert's brother, reveals conflicting prejudices and needs. This is the story of the union of Humanity (the second Eve) and Genius, a son of God who, discovering a portion of himself in the beautiful, solitary, orphaned girl, reclaims it "to foster and aid that it shall not perish hopeless" (p. 484). This story belies the equality claimed by Shirley for the first mother and father. It offers, instead, in its vision of subsequent generations, a deeply personal mythology which justifies inequality and female dependence by reestablishing the patriarchal hierarchy. The attitude it reveals has reverberations in many of Shirley's relationships, including the one which she maintains with Caroline.

Despite Charlotte Brontë's attempt, unique in her own time, to discover in the friendship between women an alternative to the alienation and hostilities that existed between the sexes, her probing exploration yielded the image of a relationship which was, while well-intentioned, deeply flawed: truncated and frustrated by personal ambivalence. It is an image of her own relationships: painful enough to recognize; more painful still for her to admit. It is understandable that the insight she offers should not be clearly emphasized. In its incomplete expression, it seems in fact only half conscious. The evidence that supports it is partial, obscure. The girls' thoughts are not wholly presented. The process of their relationship is fragmented. Still, the implication is there: when women are not drawn together by the indissoluble ties which bound Charlotte to Anne and Emily, ties strengthened for Charlotte by her growing ascendancy, sexual competition and social differences prove more divisive than the unifying influence of shared concerns. Jane's idealized friendship with Diana and Mary Rivers, her good "sisters," the romantic dream of friendship as a union of the self with the "other": this could only be realized where conventional social, cultural, economic, and sexual distinctions were abolished: familial responsibilities ignored or made subordinate. Only with a radically new flexibility could there be the kind of redefinition of traditional structures and roles which made it possible for Mary Taylor and her cousin, Ellen, to forge a different type of friendship in New Zealand.

> Our keeping shop astonishes everybody here; I believe they think we do it for fun. Some think we shall make nothing of it, or that we shall get tired; and all laugh at us. Before I left home I used to be afraid of being laughed at, but now it has very little effect upon me.

> Mary and I are settled together now: I can't do without Mary and she couldn't get on by herself. I built the house we live in, and we made the plan ourselves, so it suits us. We take it in turns to serve in the shop, and keep the accounts, and do the housework—I mean, Mary takes the shop for a week, and I the kitchen, and then we change.[23]

> Besides nonsense, we talk over other things that I never could talk about before she came. Some of them had got to look so strange, I used to think some times I had dreamt them. Charlotte's books were of this kind. Politics were another thing where I had all the interest to myself, and a number of opinions of my own I had got so used to keep to myself that at last I thought one side of my head filled with crazy stuff.[24]

In the more conventional friendship of Caroline and Shirley, there could only be moments of escape from the strains of reality.

23. Ellen Taylor, Wellington, New Zealand, August 1850. Wise and Symington, III, 134.

24. Mary Taylor to Ellen Nussey, Wellington, New Zealand, August 15, 1850. Wise and Symington, III, 136.

There could be no support for the confrontation of those strains, no stimulus to change. Brontë had no models she could use to define their relationship differently. Whatever her initial intention, experience guided her hand. The fact that these women do not develop any more than the other characters who people the novel, suggests the extent to which all are trapped in a "system" which some don't know how, and others don't care to fight. Both remain isolated in their vulnerability: protective even with one another of those aspects of their thought and feeling which are most important and therefore most painful to them.

Robert Moore casts the longest shadow over their relationship. Caroline will not speak freely to Shirley of her feelings for him. She takes if for granted that Shirley knows them, but she takes it for granted also (she is an uncompromising realist) that Shirley will accept the inevitable proposal when he offers it. More curiously (and this is probably a failure on Brontë's part) Shirley makes no attempt to share with Caroline the fact that she is not Caroline's competitor. This can be attributed to the secretiveness of her personality: her tendency to be withdrawn and introspective about the matters that most affect her, and this secretiveness is a response to fear.[25]

> I may be communicative, yet know where to stop. In showing my treasure I may withhold a gem or two—a curious, unbought, graven stone, an amulet of whose mystic glitter I rarely permit even myself a glimpse. (p. 447)

Her "treasure," of course, is Louis Moore. To reveal the nature of her concern for Robert might be to reveal the secret of her interest in his brother. But even after that interest becomes clear, after she and Louis have agreed to marry, she does not—as Caroline explains to Robert—"condescend" to openness:

25. This aspect of Shirley's personality does indeed seem to be based upon Emily Brontë's fierce sense of privacy. Emily never shared Charlotte's agony of isolation. In fact, she derived from the solitude of Haworth the nutriment necessary for her existence. In her birthday letter of July 30, 1845, she wrote:

> I am quite contented for myself: not as idle as formerly, altogether as hearty, and having learnt to make the most of the present and long for the future with the fidgetiness that I cannot do all I wish; seldom or never troubled with nothing to do, and merely desiring that everybody could be as comfortable as myself and as undesponding, and then we should have a very tolerable world of it. (Wise and Symington, II, 51.)

There was no confession—no confidence in the matter; to these things she cannot condescend; but I am sure that man's happiness is dear to her as her own life. (p. 601)

"Condescend" is the key word. Shirley's status is the condition of whatever freedom she does in fact have. Without it, she is "just a woman." And so she separates herself in a confusion of prejudice which is also a partial denial of feeling. She and Caroline never discuss Caroline's passionate desire to work: her ambivalent wish to be a governess. Caroline recognizes the "inappropriateness" of the subject—focusing as it would the disparity between their situations. Shirley does nothing to make the subject seem more appropriate nor does she discuss with Caroline her own growing conviction that Mrs. Pryor is, in fact, Caroline's mother. After the secret has been disclosed she does not explore with her friend its extraordinary implications. Typically, Shirley generously offers to whisk Caroline away on a holiday trip but doesn't help her confront the pressing realities of her life. And when Caroline falls ill she neither postpones nor interrupts her own vacation. She cares—but not too much. The result is that they touch one another only superficially. Caroline finds that the respect and fondness she feels for her friend will not make her less "painfully circumstanced." Shirley remains aloof, mistress of herself, victim of her pride.

If the conflict between the rights and privileges of her social position and those of her sex are largely instrumental in short-circuiting her friendship with Caroline, it is almost cataclysmic in undermining her relationship with Louis. The ambiguity of Shirley's situation is centered here, in her choice of a mate. The love relationship is conceived on one level in terms still reminiscent of the "Jane" poem placed by Brontë in *The Professor*. Louis Moore stands for Shirley in the familiarly interconnected roles of father-teacher-lover.[26] Shirley has said that she "will accept no hand which cannot hold me in check" (p. 546). It is a "master" she wants:

One in whose presence I shall feel obliged and disposed to be good. One whose control my impatient temper must acknowledge. A man whose approbation can reward—whose dis-

26. The critical, if unconvincing, threat of hydrophobia takes the place of the catalytic illness and Shirley's uncle assumes the role of the lover's enemy.

pleasure punish me. A man I shall feel it impossible not to love, and very possible to fear. (p. 547)

As a pupil, she had easily accepted Louis's dominance, bowed before the power of his intellect and sensitivity, been reinforced by his praise and encouragement. But the psychosexual component of this relationship is complicated by the fact that Brontë adds to it the unusual circumstance of Shirley's superior social and economic position. The romantic myth is tested once again and now the force of sexism is measured against that of class elitism. The situation is fascinating even if its outcome is disappointing.

The conflicting claims of their relative positions trap both in their pride. Shirley's psychological need for domination stifles the normal spontaneity of her response. Louis, a paper tiger at best, wants to claim the power over her which is common to one of his sex and requisite to his self-image. He cannot do it without seeming to compromise his self-respect: without appearing to be a "fortune-hunter." Their interchanges are patterned alternations of invitation and rejection:

> "Take a wife that has paid you court to save your modesty, and thrust herself upon you to spare your scruples."
> "Only show me where."
> "Any stout widow that has had a few husbands already, and can manage these things."
> "She must not be rich, then. Oh, these riches!"
> "Never would you have gathered the produce of the gold-bearing garden. You have not courage to confront the sleepless dragon! You have not craft to borrow the aid of Atlas!"
> "You look hot and haughty."
> "And you far haughtier. Yours is the monstrous pride which counterfeits humility."
> "I am a dependent: I know my place."
> "I am a woman: I know mine."
> "I am poor: I must be proud."
> "I have received ordinances and own obligations stringent as yours." (p. 614)

The resolution cannot be effected, as in *Jane Eyre*, by a magical transformation. Neither will it be the result of direct confrontation and redefinition. Society remains for Charlotte Brontë an unchangeable condition of personal life. Shirley and Louis can

only regress to an earlier stage of their relationship in order to acknowledge and accept one another's love:

> "My pupil," I said.
> "My master," was the low answer. (p. 618)

The regression determines the form that marks their future development. Louis Moore had, before his betrothal, represented—albeit tentatively—an alternate mode of male behavior. Poor,
though of a "good" family, identified with nature (it is significant, that Louis alone shares with Shirley the devotion of her
great dog, Tartar), an artist and intellectual, Louis stands outside
of the patriarchal structure in an attitude of defiance. But he is no
more able to find an appropriate way to express his defiance than
can Jessy and Rose Yorke. Like them, he plans to emigrate
across the Atlantic to claim Freedom and Liberty—and a docile
Indian maid. He finds it more convenient, however, to remain in
England, sharing with Shirley the "burden" of her money and
property, the duties and obligations of wealth and position:

> Never was wooer of wealthy bride so thoroughly absolved
> from the subaltern part, so inevitably compelled to assume a
> paramount character. (p. 636)

In abdicating her position, Shirley yields to her ambivalent nature, defined in the "system" which she has conceived: "Louis
would never have learned to rule if she had not ceased to govern;
the incapacity of the sovereign had developed the powers of the
premier" (p. 636).

Although Louis is neatly assimilated into the ruling class,
Shirley finds her own adjustment to simple femininity more difficult. If Brontë compromises her heroine with all she represents
far too easily, considering the complexity of the novel's perspective, she does not completely underestimate the cost of the sacrifice. The image of Shirley, awaiting her wedding day is striking,
although it implies a truth which Brontë cannot directly confront.

> Pantheress!—beautiful forest-born—wily, tameless, peerless
> nature! She gnaws her chain; I see the white teeth working at
> the steel! She has dreams of her wild woods, and pinings after
> virgin freedom. (p. 627)

Shirley's longing remains. It has assumed a reality of its own. It
denies the unsuitability of the conventional structure to which

Brontë is committed: a social structure reflected in the conventional literary form.

When Louis complains of his unhappiness at being forced to wait indefinitely for the fulfillment of his hopes, Shirley responds a bit ominously, "O yes, you *are* happy, you don't know how happy you are: any change will be for the worse" (p. 629). Because no resolution seems possible, this attempt at resolution is profoundly unsatisfying. It expresses the author's confusion no less than her heroine's. Shirley's marriage ironically seals the personal fate that Brontë had predicted for her in another context:

> She does not know her dreams are rare—her feelings peculiar: she does not know, has never known, and will die without knowing, the full value of that spring whose bright, fresh bubbling in her heart keeps it green. (p. 387)

In the almost parodic comic ending, Brontë seems to suggest the sad inevitability of female oppression. Since Shirley represented, in the novel, the single medium through which feminist values might be asserted, her marriage marks her as society's ritual victim. The regressive movement, the weary tones of compromise and futile sacrifice are echoed and reechoed on personal, political, and social levels. The novel—so wise in its comprehension and definition of problems—seems to exhaust itself in resignation. There is no political consciousness capable of unifying the diverse elements. Instead, there is withdrawal from conflict: a dispersal of energy, a movement from social vision to private perspective: a descent from artistic vitality to personal confusion and disillusionment.

Caroline's story moves in a direction parallel to Shirley's. The apparent differences of their situations are submerged by the larger similarities of the female condition. Caroline's profound depression—her response to Robert's rejection—can only be relieved by the development of another symbiotic relationship. ("The deep, secret anxious yearning to discover and know her mother strengthened daily [p. 187].") Ultimately, that discovery saves her from death. But Mrs. Pryor, embittered by the misery of her marriage to a sadistic "gentleman," made cynical by the humiliation of her years as a governess, can only offer Caroline the nurturing love necessary to a dependent child. She cannot provide the supportive, imaginative optimism which would move her daughter to independent maturity. Mother and daughter live together in passive domesticity waiting for Robert to reappear and shelter them both within the benevolence of his enlightened paternalism.

Having been humbled by Shirley's rejection, Robert has, in his absence, learned more readily the lessons of poverty contained in the slums of Birmingham and London, which he has visited. He confides to Hiram Yorke upon his return:

> Something there is to look to . . . beyond a man's personal interest, beyond the advancement of well-laid schemes, beyond even the discharge of dishonouring debts. To respect himself a man must believe he renders justice to his fellow-men. Unless I am more considerate to ignorance, more forbearing to suffering, than I have hitherto been, I shall scorn myself as grossly unjust. (p. 538)

Robert is prepared to see with more justice the needs of the workers and to identify with their humanity but it is not clear that he can yet, or will ever be able to identify with their cause, diametrically opposed as it seems to be to his own. He can also be purified by personal suffering. Shot by a religious fanatic, made helpless in his illness, Robert comes to appreciate his home, his work and Caroline's fidelity and love. But because it is a madman who shoots him, he can maintain his opposition to the "ringleaders" who corrupt the people instead of recognizing the more profound corruption of which all are victims, for which all are responsible. Because Shirley lends him more money, because the war is soon ended and the Orders in Council repealed, none of the larger social issues need be confronted.

Through Robert, Brontë seems to suggest that the individual must change before there can be any hope for social progress, but because she does not equate individual with social interest she does not really suggest how social redefinition can result from personal enlightenment.[27] In fact there is little in this fictive

27. Asa Briggs suggests that Charlotte Brontë's vision extended beyond her own time: extended as far as it could, since she was, "able to state the issues as seen both by employer and workers, to measure the social distance between them, and to point to the healing influence of time and experience, the kind of experience that effected Moore" (p. 214–15). Briggs suggests that Brontë anticipated the thesis of Sir William Beverage, who in 1944 published *Full Employment in a Free Society,* in which he says: "To look for individual employers for maintenance of demand and full employment is absurd. These things are not

world that does ultimately change and there is less optimism at
the end of the novel than there was at the beginning. Although the
heroines find husbands, they seem diminished rather than fulfilled by their marriages. Shirley's potential is thwarted. Caroline's questions are silenced. Legal contracts replace communication.[28] The ideal of friendship has been undermined along
with the ideal of equality. Because Shirley and Caroline are unable to act autonomously in relating to their husbands (and Caroline is also dependent in her relationship to Mrs. Pryor), both ultimately are defined and define themselves as daughters.
Authority, once internalized, can be more easily questioned than
it can be overthrown.

In the last chapters of the novel, Shirley and Caroline recede
into the background, deprived of energy and vitality. With them
perish psychological, moral, and imaginative alternatives. Nature
itself is doomed. The final vision is Robert's. He and Louis will
live out the capitalist patriarchal fantasy. They will divide Briar-
field Parish between them. Louis will become a major political as
well as economic influence. The country will be industrialized,
the land despoiled:

> I can double the value of their mill-property; I can line yonder
> barren Hollow with lines of cottages, and rows of cottage-gar-
> dens . . . the copse shall be firewood ere five years elapse; the
> beautiful wild ravine shall be a smooth descent; the green natu-
> ral terrace shall be a paved street; there shall be cottages in the
> dark ravine, and cottages on the lonely slopes; the rough peb-
> bled track shall be an even, firm, broad, black, sooty road,
> bedded with cinders from my mill. (p. 642)

To Caroline the vision is "horrible" and Robert pats her on the
head, promising her sugar plums in the form of a wonderful

---

within the power of employers. They must therefore be undertaken by the State,
under the supervision and pressure of democracy, applied to the Parliament" (p.
215–16). One can agree with Brigg's general presentation of Brontë's position,
but it is clear that she did not anticipate the necessity of government control.

28. Charlotte was, with her editors, somewhat disappointed in her failure
to delineate well the characters of her heroes ("When I write about women I
am sure of my ground—in the other case, I am not so sure." To James Taylor,
Wise and Symington, II, 312.) But it is most likely that given her perspective,
she could not envision heroes worthy of Caroline and Shirley. The Byronic
hero, who was more truly the child of her imagination, could have no appropriate place in this society.

Sunday-school that she can run all by herself a day-school that she and Shirley can manage, and work for all the poor. Of these embellishments we hear no more, but an ironic commentary is offered on the substance of Robert's dream:

> I suppose Robert Moore's prophecies were, partially at least, fulfilled. The other day I passed up the Hollow, which tradition says was once green, and lone, and wild; and there I saw the manufacturer's daydreams embodied in substantial stone and brick and ashes—the cinder-black highway, the cottages and the cottage gardens; there I saw a mighty mill, and a chimney, ambitious as the Tower of Babel. (p. 644)

At the novel's end, the "present" of the story has become the past: a better time, nostalgically recalled by an old woman who knows that there are no ladies now like Shirley who "had een that pierced a body through" (p. 44). The Hollow, once "a lonesome spot and bonnie," is much altered. The last "fairish that ever was seen on this countryside" appeared there fifty years ago. New curates replace the old: they are better, more efficient. Any hope of successful struggle has passed. The momentary glimmering of light is extinguished. It can only be recaptured in tales told by women to children and to one another.

Villette: *The Romantic Experience as Psychoanalysis*

> Men begin to regard the position of woman in another light than they used to do; and a few men, whose sympathies are fine and whose sense of justice is strong, think and speak of it with a candour that commands my admiration. They say, however—and to an extent, truly—that the amelioration of our condition depends on ourselves. Certainly there are evils which our own efforts will best reach; but as certainly there are other evils—deep-rooted in the foundations of the social system—which no efforts of ours can touch; of which we cannot complain; of which it is adviseable not too often to think.[1]

*I*N THE CREATION OF *Shirley*, Brontë had attempted to write a large-scale social novel, detailed with "realism." She had emerged from her scrutiny of the manifestations of power with the pessimism that infuses her letter to Gaskell. She had journeyed a long distance to return once again to herself. Intellectual exploration confirmed the knowledge long since gleaned from experience. She had found neither a solution, an overriding perspective, nor a positive course of action. It could not benefit her now to probe further into those obscure problems "of which we cannot complain; of which it is adviseable not too often to think." Instead, she had to confront directly—and at last—the one irreducible fact of her life: her loneliness. Its specter had haunted her throughout her girlhood. It had become an agonizing reality after she returned from Brussels to wait through two long years for the letters from Heger, which never came. And then,

1. To Elizabeth Gaskell, August 27, 1850. Wise and Symington, III, 150.

with the deaths of Branwell, Emily, and Anne, it seemed to be a
nightmare from which she could not and never would awaken.

Haworth, her once beloved home, was now almost intolerable to her:

> . . . the deficiency of every stimulus is so complete . . . the
> deadly silence, solitude, desolation were awful—the craving
> for companionship—the hopelessness of relief—were what I
> should dread to feel again.[2]

> For my part, I am free to walk on the moors; but when I go out
> there alone everything reminds me of the times when others
> were with me, and then the moors seem a wilderness, feature-
> less, solitary, saddening. My sister Emily had a particular love
> for them, and there is not a knoll of heather, not a branch of
> fern, not a young bilberry leaf, not a fluttering lark or linnet,
> but reminds me of her. The distant prospects were Anne's
> delight, and when I look round she is in the blue tints, the pale
> mists, the waves and shadows of the horizon. In the hill-
> country silence their poetry comes by lines and stanzas into my
> mind; once I loved it; now I dare not read it, and am driven
> often to wish I could taste one draught of oblivion, and forget
> much that, while mind remains, I never shall forget.[3]

Her only comfort was in the memory of the past and that was accompanied by a pain so deep that she could not think of what she
had possessed but only of what she had lost.

> The two human beings who understood me, and whom I un-
> derstood, are gone. I have some that love me yet, and whom I
> love without expecting, or having a right to expect, that they
> shall perfectly understand me.[4]

Charlotte and her father were united by bonds of mutual grief and
dependence. But the satisfaction Brontë derived from the performance of duty was tempered by the ambivalence of sacrifice, by
their fundamental incompatibility, and by her still constant, overwhelming sense of inadequacy ("Papa has now me only—the
weakest, puniest, least promising of his six children."[5]). Friendship with Elizabeth Gaskell and Harriet Martineau confirmed her
confidence as a writer but offered her little of the emotional sup-

2. To Ellen Nussey, October 23, 1850. Wise and Symington, III, 173–74.
3. To James Taylor, May 22, 1850. Wise and Symington, III, 111–12.
4. To W. S. Williams, September 21, 1849. Wise and Symington, III, 24.
5. To W. S. Williams, June 4, 1849. Wise and Symington, II, 338.

port for which her spirit yearned.[6] If any solace was to be offered her, any promise of change held out, it was by three men who occupied central positions at her publishing firm, Smith, Elder, and Co. William Smith Williams, a sensitive critic of literature and the graphic arts had first read and recognized the potential power of *The Professor*. With him Charlotte carried on a continuing personal correspondence which stimulated her mind and provided an emotional outlet during these terrible years of loss. To him she confided her troubled thoughts and anguished feelings, always receiving sympathy and kindness in return. In James Taylor, the firm's manager, and in George Smith, her publisher, she found two erratic suitors whose attentions were bewildering and ultimately disappointing.

James Taylor was astonishingly like Branwell in appearance, small and redheaded, forceful and domineering.

> . . . the resemblance to Branwell struck me forcibly. It is marked. He is not ugly, but very peculiar; the lines in his face show an inflexibility, and I must add, a hardness of character which do not attract.[7]

Charlotte thought him to be "of the Helstone order of men— rigid, despotic and self-willed." She was suspicious of his kindness, but could not help admitting that "he is horribly intelligent, quick, searching, sagacious and with a memory of relentless tenacity."[8] With his physical resemblance to her brother, and the similarity of his personality to the heroes who had moved so commandingly through her girlhood writings, Taylor alternately attracted and repelled her. There was no question about the nature of his interest. Apparently it was his jealous antagonism toward

6. Charlotte Brontë wrote to W. S. Williams (November 24, 1849. Wise and Symington, III, 45.):

> The note you sent yesterday was from Harriet Martineau; its contents were more than gratifying. I ought to be thankful, and I trust I am for such testimonies of sympathy from the first order of minds. When Mrs. Gaskell tells me she shall keep my works as a treasure for her daughters, and when Harriet Martineau testifies affectionate approbation, I feel the sting taken from the strictures of another class of critics. My resolution of seclusion withholds me from communicating further with these ladies at present, but I now know how they are inclined to me—I know how my writings have affected their wise and pure minds. The knowledge is present support and, perhaps, may be future armour.

7. To Ellen Nussey, April 9, 1851. Wise and Symington, III, 220.
8. Wise and Symington, III, 53.

George Smith which made his youthful superior decide to exile him to their Indian agency, where he remained for five years. Before his departure, he came to Haworth, apparently to make an offer of marriage. The response he received—surprising even to Brontë herself—was adequate discouragement.

> . . . each moment he came near me—and that I could see his eyes fastened on me—my veins ran ice. Now that he is away I feel far more gently towards him—it is only close by that I grow rigid—stiffening with a strange mixture of apprehension and anger—which nothing softens but his retreat and a perfect subduing of his manner. I did not want to be proud nor intend to be proud—but I was forced to be so.[9]

He was abashed. The correspondence that followed was fitful and only tended to increase her frustration and ambivalence.

George Smith was another matter. He had befriended her from the beginning and the happiest moments she experienced after Anne's and Emily's deaths were spent in his company. There were visits to London—even a journey to Edinburgh—when she stayed with him and his mother, attending the theatre and concerts, meeting the reigning writers and intellectuals of her time, learning the secrets of the city which never ceased to excite her. That Brontë seriously considered George Smith a prospective suitor there can be little doubt. That his behavior toward her created such a sense of possibility must be true as well. The fact is that he never proposed and that it is not clear whether she would have accepted him if he had. She was older than he, his inferior in fortune, delicate in health. He was, despite his charm and kindness, insensitive in some ways, perhaps in some respects shallow. The only clue to Brontë's own feelings survives in the representation of him in *Villette* as Graham Bretton, a portrait which fascinates in its ambiguity. It was this portrait and that of his mother (as Louisa Bretton) which ultimately confirmed the rift between them and made a reality of the separation which Brontë had apparently already accepted as inevitable.[10]

In *Villette*, Charlotte Brontë sought to confront not only the meaning of her Brussels experience (this aspect of the novel has been generally recognized) but the implications of the life she

9. To Ellen Nussey, April 9, 1851. Wise and Symington, III, 222.

10. For a complete account of Charlotte Brontë's relationship with George Smith see Gerin, *Charlotte Brontë*, pp. 486–512.

was living then—and the quality of the life she had still to endure. As she revealed to Ellen Nussey, a couple of months before *Villette*'s completion:

> I am silent because I have literally nothing to say. I might indeed repeat over and over again that my life is a pale blank and often a very weary burden, and that the future sometimes appals me; but what end could be answered by such repetition except to weary you and ennervate myself?
>
> The evils that now and then wring a groan from my heart, lie in my position, not that I am a *single* woman and likely to remain a *single* woman, but because I am a *lonely* woman and likely to be lonely. But it cannot be helped and therefore *imperatively must be borne,* and borne with as few words about it as may be.[11]

Her experience with Heger, the personal meaning of Emily's and Anne's deaths, her separation from Branwell, the thwarted relationships with Taylor and Smith, all suggested that she had been singled out for a fate which she had always found too painful to assign to her heroines. She had touched upon it in "Henry Hastings"—the distance of the romance made it possible. But after she had begun in earnest to explore her own identity and her situation as a woman she had persistently grasped at some form of optimism, however muted. This was no longer possible. The aborted resolution of *Shirley* betrayed her doubts. Loneliness—bleak and absolute—was her present companion, her future destiny. To learn how she could make it bearable, she had to look within.

To W. S. Williams, Charlotte had written:

> Labour must be the cure, not sympathy—labour is the only radical cure for rooted sorrow— The society of a calm, serenely cheerful companion—such as Ellen—soothes pain like a soft opiate—but I find it does not probe or heal the wound— sharper, more severe means are necessary to make a remedy. Total change might do much—where that cannot be obtained—work is the best substitute.[12]

The "severe means" appropriate to treat her sorrow involved an approach to her work which while prepared for in all her previous writing, was radically new in the degree of courage and commit-

11. August 25, 1852. Wise and Symington, IV, 6.
12. Wise and Symington, II, 349.

ment it demanded. Each of her fictions had been deeply personal. They had become successively more self-analytical and autobiographical. *The Professor,* with its unresolved compromises, between romance and reality, its awkwardly shrouded truths, gave way to the integrated fairy tale of *Jane Eyre,* a psychosexual and social myth expressed through fantasy and dream. *Shirley,* ostensibly social in its choice of subject, had been—in its unabashed dependence upon personal feelings, relationships, and experiences—the most autobiographical of all. Here Brontë had considered the pressures exerted upon the individual by the forces of the culture. Now her consideration moved her from the oppressive society to the repressed individual—to herself. Romantic allegory was no longer an adequate mode of expression. It had liberated her initially but a deeper form of introspection was necessary. The creating consciousness itself had to be analyzed. The functioning of will, the possibility of choice, the action of "fate" had become for her psychological as well as philosophical problems.

In *Villette* the confrontation of the self by the self is as extraordinarily uncompromising as it must have been painful. That Brontë found this novel unusually difficult to write is a matter of record. Her letters are full of references to periods of depression and illness in which work was impossible. "Certainly the past winter has been to me a strange time, had I the prospect before me of living it over again, my prayer must necessarily be, 'Let this cup pass from me.' "[13] That these were also periods of intense psychological conflict it seems reasonable to assume. Modeling her heroine upon herself, dwelling upon the buried knowledge of the past while attempting to deal effectively with the problems of the present, always forced to confront the truth of her own personality, Brontë sought to bring the unconscious into consciousness and tried to unify the fragmented pieces of the self.

Lucy Snowe is a faithful self-portrait. The contradiction contained in the juxtaposition of her two names (cold, on the one hand, the warmth of light on the other) suggests the form of her "malaise."[14] Seemingly impassive, Lucy is in fact abnormally

13. February 6, 1852 to Elizabeth Gaskell. Gaskell, p. 351.

14. Charlotte Brontë wrote to W. S. Williams (November 6, 1852. Wise and Symington, IV, 18.)

    As to the name of the heroine, I can hardly express what subtlety of thought made me decide upon giving her a cold name; but at first I called

sensitive, unusually emotional. Because her needs have been un-
satisfied, her hopes thwarted, she withdraws from society: rejecting relationships because she herself fears rejection. Hostility and
anger are her defenses against the pain of deprivation. A stance of
superiority, postures of righteous judgement, insulate her feelings.[15]

How could Brontë portray most effectively this tortured,
oddly unsympathetic woman for whom, by her own wry admission, she felt significantly little affection? How best to create a
character whom the reader would at first reject as Lucy and Charlotte Brontë herself were always rejected by casual acquaintances? How to make accessible an individual defined by inacces-
sibility? How to win understanding and respect for this fiercely
private personality which refused to show itself—which barely
knew itself? To succeed was as crucial to Brontë personally as it
was important to her as a writer.

The plan was brilliant. It marked the extent of her artistic
progress since *The Professor*. The narrating voice would be
Lucy's own. The central consciousness would belong to her. The
technique was superficially similar to that of *Jane Eyre*, but for
the guilelessness, the straightforward self-awareness, the friendly
openness of Jane would be substituted indirection, neurotic rationalization, and narrative "unreliability."[16] A comparison of the
opening sections of the two novels makes the differences dramat-
ically clear. Jane is discovered as a child at Gateshead, her

---

her Lucy Snowe (spelled with an "e") which Snowe I afterward changed
to "Frost." Subsequently I rather regretted the change and wished it
"Snowe" again. If not too late I should like the alteration to be made now
throughout the MS. A cold name she must have; partly perhaps on the *lucus
a non lucendo* principle—partly on that of the fitness of things for she has
about her an external coldness.

15. An interesting parallel might be drawn between Lucy Snowe and Jane
Austen's Fanny Price in *Mansfield Park*. Fanny assumes a similar posture of
righteous superiority in order to protect herself against her threatening feelings
of inferiority. She too is deprived of economic and social status. Plain, she is
virtually deprived of sexual definition as well. The crucial difference, of course,
lies in authorial attitude. Jane Austen seems largely unconscious of pressures
which create the personality configuration and identifies uncritically with her
heroine. Charlotte Brontë comprehends these pressures fully and, refusing to
make virtues of the mechanisms of defense, identifies them as neurotic.

16. Charlotte Brontë probably learned many of the possibilities of "unreliable narration" from Emily's use of Lockwood and Nelly Dean in *Wuthering
Heights*.

unhappy story is quickly told, the quality of her mind and the intensity of her feelings directly established. The process of "education" is described by a mature narrator who understands its implications at every point and shares them with the reader. Lucy, on the other hand, is a girl of fourteen at the beginning of *Villette*. She is a temporary visitor in the home of her godmother, Louisa Bretton, who takes notice of her "in a quiet way." Her past is darkly obscure. She lives, for the moment, with "kinfolk" who remain unidentified. The future casts a shadow upon her which "imparts unsettled sadness." The story she tells is ostensibly her own, but she is not its subject.

Lucy hints at the reason for this displacement when she says at the outset, "I liked peace so well, and sought stimulus so little, that when the latter came I almost felt it a disturbance, and wished rather it had still held aloof."[17] Lucy, like her creator, is a "survivor." Her identification is more with the dead than the living. She has already been so hurt by her circumtances that she is unable to talk about her past. She is already so afraid of feeling that she would rather not participate in life at all. Psychologically, she has closed herself off.[18] To the extent that she must play a role, she prefers to be a spectator, a "voyeur." And so she begins exploring her life by telling the reader of Pauline Home, who arrived in Bretton during Lucy's own visit there. As Lucy tells Polly's story, revealing the nature of her identification with the child, as we remark upon the things she chooses *not* to tell us, we first divine the traces of Lucy's singularly defended and complex personality.

Paulina is brought to Bretton by her father, whom she adores. Her mother has died ("a giddy, careless woman, who had neglected her child, and disappointed and disheartened her husband") and Mr. Home is about to embark on a journey to France,

17. Charlotte Brontë, *Villette* (Boston: Houghton-Mifflin, 1971), p. 6. All subsequent references are to this edition and will be given in the text.

18. Lifton (p. 163), speaking of the survivor, observes:

Psychic closing-off is thus related to the defense mechanisms of denial and isolation, as well as to the behavioral state of apathy . . . it enables the organism to resist the impact of death—that is, to survive psychologically in the midst of death and dying. It may well represent man's most characteristic response to catastrophe: one which is at times life-enhancing, or even, psychologically speaking, life-saving; but at other times, particularly when prolonged and no longer appropriate to the threat, not without its own dangers.

intended to relieve his depression. It is the way in which the small child deals with her loss, the way in which she expresses and controls the intensity of her feelings, and, finally, the way in which she risks herself, despite her vulnerability, in a new relationship of devoted love that repels, frightens, and fascinates Lucy. At first the reader is surprised, even appalled by Lucy's coldness. The words she uses to characterize Polly ("creature," "doll," "busy-body," "the child") serve to objectify the little girl. Lucy seldom describes any direct form of interaction between them. She rather presents Polly as she—Lucy—thinks about her: from a distance. It gradually becomes clear, however, that Lucy employs this technique of narration for the same reason that she had employed this technique of interaction: not because she is unable to feel, but because she feels too much; not because she cannot identify with Polly but rather because the degree of her identification is extreme.

Her responses to Polly's open emotionality are disproportionate. For Lucy, the expression of feeling cannot be understood as a healthful, restorative release. She sees it instead as a danger which can overwhelm and obliterate the self and she refuses to relive, through identification with the little girl, the circumstances surrounding her own grief. So, when Lucy hears Polly moaning pathetically, "Papa! Papa!," she explains: "I roused myself and started up, to check this scene while it was yet within bounds" (p. 10). Lucy is intent upon controlling Polly as she has learned to control herself and she does it more for her own sake than for the child's. She has learned what price might be demanded for love, if love is lost or denied. She reveals how deeply fearful that lesson has made her when she observes of Polly's suffering after Mr. Home's departure, "She went through, in that brief interval of her infant life, emotions such as some never feel; it was in her constitution: she would have more of such instants if she lived" (p. 19). And although she betrays her belief that emotional and psychological pain can, in their intensity, destroy life itself, she adds in describing the scene: "I, Lucy Snowe, was calm."

This is the illusion which she must maintain in order to keep her own sanity. Repressing feeling—rejecting, therefore, a past too threatening to be confronted—Lucy appeals to "reason" which gives to repression both justification and authority. "How will she get through this world, or battle with this life?'' Lucy asks. "How will she bear the shocks and repulses, the humiliations and desolations, which books, and my own reason tell me are prepared for all flesh?'' (p. 29). From her "books'' (one notes that she does not cite experience) Lucy has gathered a "tolerable stock'' of philosophical maxims which guide her behavior. These she would share with Polly, who endangers herself still further by becoming attached to Graham Bretton, a charming boy, Lucy's contemporary, who enjoys—somewhat erratically—the attentions of the younger child. The principal "maxim'' is "don't fret, and don't expect too much of him, or else he will feel you to be troublesome, and then it is all over'' (p. 28). So Lucy herself behaves toward Graham, whom she grudgingly praises as being "not quite as other boys are'' (p. 24), but whom she obviously admires from a distance. So she behaves toward everyone (as Brontë always behaved to those outside her family circle), never demanding; reticent and withdrawn, yet always watching, priding herself on being an amused observer of character. And as she represses the pain of rejection (Polly has, after all, appropriated Lucy's place in her godmother's house) so also does she repress the anger, allowing it expression only in the coldness of her tone, in her judgmental attitude, in her uneasy air of intellectual superiority.

It is Lucy's ambivalence, then, which accounts for what might be called the tonal distortions of the Bretton section of the novel. Because Lucy is the anesthetized survivor, passion is described dispassionately: a household warmed by love—by Mrs. Bretton's adoration of her son, by Polly's idolatry first of her father and then of Graham, by Graham's easy affectionate nature—this household feels chill and sterile to the reader. Similarly, it is because of Lucy's will to repression—because of her need to tell another's story as a substitute for her own—that the novel's structure is initially disorienting. Chronicling incidents which are representative of her own circumstances, Lucy compromises a reticence morbid in its intensity. But that reticence continues to express itself in her defensiveness, elusiveness, hostility, and inconsistency. The form of *Villette* is the form of Lucy's neurosis: a representation of the novel's subject. The narrative is as difficult and as indirect as is the heroine's attempt to defeat loneliness by learning to accept and even to reinvent herself.

In this first section Lucy grieves for the natural tendencies of Polly's personality:

> This, I perceived, was a one-idea'd nature; betraying that mon-
> omaniac tendency I have ever thought the most unfortunate
> with which man or woman can be cursed. (p. 11)

What she recognizes in Polly, she must recognize in her own self: an overwhelming need and capacity for love. But instead of condemning it as monomaniacal, she must learn to acknowledge it as the foundation stone upon which she can reconstruct her ego to fill the void of abandonment.

Lucy similarly grants to Polly another quality of mind which she is unprepared to recognize as her own:

> I, Lucy Snowe, plead guiltless of that curse, an overheated and
> discursive imagination; but whenever opening a room-door, I
> found her seated in a corner alone, her head in her pigmy hand,
> that room seemed to me not inhabited, but haunted. (p. 11)

Of course, the description which follows the disavowal effectively contradicts it. But the contradiction is unconscious on Lucy's part and it is not until she learns to trust her imagination as she must trust her feelings and intuitions that she can become "reliable" as a narrator; "whole" as a woman. In a remarkably contemporary way, the fiction strives for its form as the heroine searches out her identity. The concept of narration was too sophisticated to be genuinely appreciated or even understood by Brontë's contemporaries. Her publisher and critics thought the apparent shift of focus from Polly to Lucy a serious aesthetic flaw. Readers into the twentieth century continued to concur. Only now do we begin to recognize the nature of the genius that urged Brontë to accept the risk and challenge of her art.

II

It is as difficult for Lucy to speak of the events which follow her stay at Bretton as it was for her to describe the events which preceded it. As she found an acceptable metaphor in Polly's experience for her own early deprivation, so does she find in the indirect allusiveness of language and imagery a way of expressing the pain of the eight years of tragedy which changed her from an adolescent of fourteen to a young woman of twenty-two.

I will permit the reader to picture me, for the next eight years, as a bark slumbering through halcyon weather, in a harbour still as glass . . .

Picture me then idle, basking, plump, and happy, stretched on a cushioned deck, warmed with constant sunshine, rocked by breezes indolently soft. However, it cannot be concealed that, in that case, I must somehow have fallen over-board, or that there must been wreck at last. I too well remember a time—a long time, of cold, of danger, of contention. To this hour, when I have the nightmare, it repeats the rush and saltness of briny waves in my throat, and their icy pressure on my lungs. I even know there was a storm, and that not of one hour nor one day. For many days and nights neither sun nor stars appeared; we cast with our own hands the tackling out of the ship; a heavy tempest lay on us; all hope that we should be saved was taken away. In fine, the ship was lost, the crew perished. (pp. 29–30)

Here is the deluge which Brontë metaphorized in describing to Williams the tragic experience of her life. Sea and storm imagery are used throughout the novel, as they were used in *Jane Eyre,* to suggest the psychological torment which is a response to separation and loss. Most important of all is Lucy's presentation of herself as the sole survivor of a shipwreck in which all whom she loves are destroyed.[19] Although the actual circumstances of her tragedy are never revealed to us, the emotions which accompanied them are always just beneath the surface, waiting to be summoned, exerting their pressure. There is, of course, sorrow— and desperate loneliness. But there is also the guilt, the anxiety, the sense of inadequacy which had been expressed in Charlotte's own childhood dreams of the dead Maria and Elizabeth: the survivor's sense of unworthiness which was as central in Brontë's character as it is dominant in Lucy Snowe's.[20] And there is also

19. Although Brontë is not faithful to her own experience in the chronology and details of Lucy's circumstances, she does suggest the stages of loss which she endured as well as the nature of her response to the tragic events.

20. From Roe Head, Charlotte had written to Ellen Nussey (Gaskell, p. 95.):

You have been very kind to me of late, and have spared me all those little sallies of ridicule which, owing to my miserable and wretched touchiness of character, used formerly to make me wince, as if I had been touched with a hot iron; things that nobody else cares for, enter into my mind and rankle there like venom. I know these feelings are absurd, and therefore I try to hide them, but they only sting the deeper for concealment.

depression, for the misery of the past conditions the expectations of the future. The deluges of life, as Brontë knew, are all too likely to return again. So Elizabeth Gaskell wrote, after her friend's death: "In after-life I was painfully impressed with the fact that Miss Brontë never dared to allow herself to look forward with hope; that she had no confidence in the future,"[21] and Lucy admits:

> Oh, my childhood! I had feelings, passive as I lived, little as I spoke, cold as I looked, when I thought of past days, I *could* feel. About the present, it was better to be stoical; about the future—such a future as mine—to be dead. And in catalepsy and a dead trance, I studiously held the quick of my nature. (p. 93)

The impulse is to resist change, to avoid involvement, to live as if one had also died.

Psychic withdrawal bound Brontë to her home and imprisoned her in the cavern beneath the sea: the tiny space which was the vestige of the surviving self—drowned yet still alive. Psychic withdrawal makes Lucy welcome the undemanding emotional life at Bretton and ultimately it causes her to accept, when it is offered, the position of companion to Miss Marchmont. Here too the dwarfed and stifled ego finds security in the narrow boundaries of claustrophobic space.

> Two hot, close rooms thus became my world; and a crippled old woman, my mistress, my friend, my all. Her service was my duty—her pain, my suffering—her relief, my hope—her anger, my punishment—her regard, my reward. I forgot that there were fields, woods, rivers, seas, an ever-changing sky outside the steam-dimmed lattice of this sick-chamber; I was almost content to forget it. (p. 31)

In forming this attachment, Lucy comes as close as she can to expressing her identification with those who have died while still asserting a minimal commitment to life. But because a bond does form between her and Miss Marchmont, because there is mutual respect and even affection between them—never openly and therefore never threateningly expressed—these two rooms become in fact a new world for Lucy to discover. Here she learns that she can be more than a self-effacing shadow, that she can be a rock upon which another's life can rest: a source of comfort and

21. Gaskell, p. 77.

aid. Here she has confirmed for her the value of stoicism; the importance even of thwarted love. When Miss Marchmont dies in still another storm (first she shares with Lucy her memory of a profound romantic attachment which, while lost in youth, gave her life its meaning) Lucy is once again a survivor, but now—instead of withdrawing further into herself—she begins to enlarge her existence. Although she has been deprived of a surrogate mother, she knows that she had truly earned the place of "daughter": that she had begun to reconstruct for herself the context of a family. From this knowledge she derives her first store of strength.

> I had wanted to compromise with Fate: to escape occasional great agonies by submitting to a whole life of privation and small pains. Fate would not be so pacified; nor would Providence sanction this shrinking sloth and cowardly indolence.
> (p. 32)

Still using the language of passivity ("Fate," "Providence") Lucy does, for the first time, admit the possibility of a determining personality. Thus she can begin her journey from withdrawal to self-discovery. It is not an allegorical journey and the symbols of opposition are not fixed as clearly as they were in *Jane Eyre* (the red-room—Helen Burns; Rochester—St. John Rivers; resolution at Ferndean). The movement does not follow a neatly repetitive dialectical pattern. It is more fluid, with regressions and progressions, a process in which it is more difficult to perceive linear development because the personal past impinges continually on the present: changing, redefining, distorting. A simplistic antagonism between reason and emotion can be identified again as the basic source of conflict, but the meaning of these terms is more complex and more elusive. Their context is more openly psychological than it was in *Jane Eyre*. Reason is identified predominantly with repression and the "feeling" intuitive self is accepted less fearfully as authentic.

As Lucy enters a strange world which will test her into growth, her public self—sensible and controlled—contends with her aspiring, private being. She notes that "there is nothing like taking all you do at a moderate estimate: it keeps mind and body tranquil; whereas grandiloquent notions are apt to hurry both into fever" (p. 38). But she responds to London as Brontë had herself: finding there an alternative to the claustrophobic space to which she was accustomed, by which she had previously been comforted:

> While I looked, my inner self moved; my spirit shook its al-
> ways-fettered wings half loose; I had a sudden feeling as if I,
> who had never yet truly lived, were at last about to taste life.
> (p. 40)

Discovering independence, she lives, in walking London's streets, a "prodigious amount of life." She wanders in an "ec-stacy of freedom and enjoyment": stimulated, vital, excited; hungry for the first time in many years. In her awakening, Lucy decides to leave England for Brussels. Pushing herself into activ-ity which prohibits withdrawal, making herself deeply vulnera-ble, she acts not out of desperation but hope:

> . . . peril, loneliness, an uncertain future, are not oppressive
> evils, so long as the frame is healthy, and the faculties are
> employed; so long, especially, as Liberty lends us her wings,
> and Hope guides us by her star. (p. 48)

Allowing herself to "feel," she can also allow herself the liberty to imagine. The river she rows on to reach the boat which will take her to the continent reminds her of the river Styx. Her soul, awaiting rebirth, quivers in anticipation and she is brought to the admission that, "I must possess something of the artist's faculty of making the most of present pleasure" (p. 51).[22] Her freedom is confirmed in Brussels, as Crimsworth's had been. As a for-eigner, an Englishwoman, a Protestant (without money, position, or beauty) she is without conventional restraints, automatically accepted as eccentric, granted a special status. Still, despite the fact that "my fancy budded fresh and my heart basked in sun-shine," although the present and future seemed rich in possibil-ities never before dreamt of, threats from the past are always po-tentially present:

> . . . the secret but ceaseless consciousness of anxiety lying in
> wait on enjoyment, like a tiger crouched in a jungle. The
> breathing of that beast of prey was in my ear always; his fierce

22. Brontë's return to Brussels is described by Mrs. Gaskell, (p. 159) in much the same terms as Lucy's journey is presented.

heart panted close against mine; he never stirred in his lair but I
felt him: I knew he waited only for sun down to bound raven-
ous from his ambush. (p. 52)

The juxtaposed images of Brontë's childhood dream are echoed
here: the fragile sea-cavern threatened by pounding waves and
the attacking lion in the desert—claustrophobic space and the fear
of negation.

But although she is frightened, Lucy does not surrender to
anxiety. In a new situation, assigned different roles by the
teachers and students at Madam Beck's Pensionnat, Lucy finds
that instead of being deprived of an identity she has protected
with such difficulty, she can define herself in a number of different ways, playing a variety of roles, responding to other people's expectations of her. Ginevra Fanshawe, the beautiful and
flighty young English girl, summons Lucy's independence by
making her strong in her assertion of disapproval. Ginevra's excessive feminity elicits the masculine side of Lucy's personality,
the "crust and rind of my nature" (p. 402). The triviality and pet-
tiness of her values allow Lucy to express with unusual openness,
her impatience, resentment, and jealousy. Ginevra represents a
world of fashion and sexual role-playing, a world of values unearned. Lucy scorns those values and that world but, as an outsider who has herself been scorned, she cannot help feeling envi-
ous of those who "belong." It is, in part, this ambivalence
toward society which draws her to Ginevra and allows her to indulge the girl as she would a child:

> I don't know why I chose to give my bread rather to Ginevra
> than to another: nor why, if two had to share the convenience
> of one drinking-vessel . . . I always contrived that she should
> be my convive, and rather like to let her take the lion's share,
> whether of the white beer, the sweet wine, or the new milk: so
> it was, however, and she knew it; and, therefore, while we
> wrangled daily, we were never alienated. (pp. 200–201)

But there is also another, more simple and appealing reason for
their friendship. Charlotte had said to Ellen Nussey, explaining
her propensity for easy attachments: "If anybody likes me, I
can't help liking them."[23] Lucy might say the same. Because

23. January 4, 1838. Wise and Symington, I, 164.

rejection has been the rule, her need responds to Ginevra's warmth and respect. Acceptance, though it be predicated on mis-understanding, cannot go unanswered.[24]

Madame Beck, the school's headmistress, also elicits hidden aspects of Lucy's personality. Regarding the young woman as one of those "Anglaises," who will dare anything, Madame Beck continually challenges Lucy to assume roles which express her capacity for leadership, which evoke her Protestant "individualism," her fierce integrity, her pride. When Madame Beck asks her to assume charge of a classroom, Lucy recognizes that she has been offered a "challenge of strength." She meets the test: "I suddenly felt all the dishonor of my diffidence—all the pusillanimity of my slackness to aspire" (p. 66). And she does aspire. She finds that she can be aggressive. But the cost is high, comparable to that which Brontë herself had to pay in the coldness of the public self which she formed to protect her vulnerability.[25] Lucy respects Madame Beck's shrewdness, her cold rationality, her open commitment to self-interest. And she recognizes that Madame Beck might beat her at her own game for, if she watches Madame Beck, Madame Beck also watches her. If voyeurism is Lucy's route to power (judging, she feels herself su-

---

24. One is reminded here of Charlotte Brontë's lifelong relationship with Ellen Nussey: a relationship which seems so strange because of the inequality of the partners. Brontë wrote to W. S. Williams about the friendship (January 3, 1830. Wise and Symington, III, 63.):

> When I first saw Ellen I did not care for her—we were schoolfellows—in the course of time we learnt each other's faults and good points—we were contrasts—still we suited—affection was first a germ, then a sapling—then a strong tree: now, no new friend, however lofty or profound in intellect—not even Miss Martineau herself could be to me what Ellen is, yet she is no more than a conscientious, observant, calm, well-bred Yorkshire girl. She is without romance—if she attempts to read poetry—or poetic prose aloud—I am irritated and deprive her of her book—if she talks of it I stop my ears—but she is good—she is true—she is faithful and I love her.

It is not without significance that Brontë kept from Ellen the secret of her authorship until it was general knowledge and that her letters to Elizabeth Gaskell and particularly to W. S. Williams were more intimate in nature as well as more intellectual than those which she wrote in these same years to Ellen.

25. Rosamund Langbridge (p. 94) commented:

> Very few people were ever to understand Charlotte Brontë, for it is seldom that such appealing weakness is leashed to such appalling strength. All that most people saw of her was that aspect of slight mercilessness which was aimed, in reality, at crushing her own weaker self, and not, as they supposed, at their inferiority.

perior) spying is, for Madame Beck, a way of maintaining the power which she already possesses. More to the point, because Lucy is Madame Beck's employee, her subordinate and victim, it is only by becoming Madame Beck's complicitor, by allowing herself to *be* watched, her possessions to be examined, her secrets to be explored, that Lucy can maintain the illusion of control.

Thus, when Lucy discovers Madame Beck looking carefully through her bureau, she watches her "with a secret glee," admiring her care. Lucy knows that the headmistress suspects her of a romantic intrigue and she exults in the little woman's error. "Loverless and inexpectant of love, I was safe from spies in my heart-poverty, as the beggar from thieves in his destitution of purse" (p. 101). And as Lucy flees so that *she* will not be discovered, she laughs:

> Yet as the laugh died, a kind of wrath smote me, and then bitterness followed: it was the rock struck, and Meribah's waters gushing out . . . I never had felt so strange and contradictory an inward tumult as I felt for an hour that evening: soreness and laughter, and fire, and grief, shared my heart between them. I cried hot tears; not because Madame mistrusted me—I did not care twopence for her mistrust—but for other reasons. Complicated, disquieting thoughts broke up the whole repose of my nature. However, that turmoil subsided: next day I was again Lucy Snowe. (p. 102)

But it is no longer possible for her to suppress turmoil completely, to "be Lucy Snowe," veiling insecurity beneath a pretense of power. Lucy is not like her employer who "devoid of sympathy, had a sufficiency of rational benevolence" (p. 63). Because her repressed self has been awakened, because she has become active and feels what it means to have a stake in life, she is forced to admit—as Brontë admitted to Ellen—that self-alienation, the assumption of a role that does not express her own identity, is insupportable.[26] Lucy finds it increasingly difficult to "hold the quick of her nature in a dead trance" (p. 93). The tran-

26. ". . . What dismays and haunts me sometimes is the conviction that I have no natural knack for my vocation—if teaching only were requisite it would be smooth and easy—but it is the living in other people's houses—the estrangement from one's real character—the adoption of a cold, frigid apathetic exterior that is painful." Charlotte wrote this, when she was a governess, to Ellen Nussey, August 17, 1841 (Wise and Symington, I, 241).

scendent world summons her from the musty enclosures of her limited experience. Her buried self awakens when the storms come and she is "roughly roused and obliged to live." Then she rejects the narrow, interior spaces:

> I did long, achingly, then and for four-and-twenty-hours afterwards, for something to fetch me out of my present existence, and lead me upwards and onwards. (p. 93)

The violent imagery used to describe her consequent repression of feeling, the necessary containment of the beast awakened, suggests the cost to Lucy of momentary peace:

> This longing and all of a similar kind, it was necessary to knock on the head; which I did, figuratively, after the manner of Jael to Sisera, driving a nail through their temples. Unlike Sisera, they did not die: they were but transiently stunned, and at intervals would turn on the nail with a rebellious wrench; then did the temples bleed, and the brain thrill to its core. (p. 94)

Growing knowledge and sensitivity make continuing self-denial increasingly difficult. Finally, when she is left alone at the school during summer vacation (as Charlotte had been left by the Hegers in the summer of '43, when they went off with their children to the seashore) Lucy finds her "self" completely undefended. Deprived of her usual tasks, unable to play her accustomed roles, kept from exploring the terrain of her expanding personality, Lucy endures an experience similar to the one which Charlotte had described to Ellen: "I tried to read, I tried to write; but in vain. I then wandered about from room to room, but the sounds and loneliness of all the house weighs one's spirits like lead."[27]

For all the others, students and teachers alike, this is a time of rest and companionship. For most there is love to enjoy. For

---

Two years earlier when she was a governess for the Sidgewick family, she had written to Emily (June 8, 1839. Wise and Symington, I, 178.):

> I said in my last letter that Mrs. Sidgewick did not know me. I now begin to find that she does not intend to know me, that she cares nothing in the world about me except to contrive how the greatest possible quantity of labor may be squeezed out of me . . . I see now more clearly than I have ever done before that a private governess has no existence, is not considered as a living and rational being except as connected with the wearisome duties she has to fulfill.

27. To Ellen Nussey, November 15, 1843. Wise and Symington, I, 309.

some, like Ginevra, adored by Dr. John, there is still greater love to anticipate. But for Lucy there is regression to the suffering of the past. She is a survivor once again. She knows depression and despair. There is the grueling dependence of the barely human "cretin" assigned to her care; their relationship a nightmarish parody of her situation with Miss Marchmont and a bizarre echo of Jane Eyre's ambivalent dream of carrying the fretful, burdensome child to its death. Then there is Lucy's terrible dream of visitation and rejection from eternity: "the well-loved dead, who had loved *me* well in life, met me elsewhere, alienated: galled was my most inmost spirit with an unutterable sense of despair about the future" (p. 137–38).[28] She is forced once more into the position of voyeur. Her profound need for love finds expression in her identification with Ginevra's imagined love for Dr. John. Her fantasy of their sexual connection recalls Jane's orgasmic awareness of Rochester:

> I conceived an electric chord of sympathy between them, a fine chain of mutual understanding, sustaining union through a separation of a hundred leagues—carrying, across mound and hollow, communication by prayer and wish. (p. 137)

The crisis of feeling, previously repressed, must now be acknowledged. Her pain cannot be borne alone. In turning, upon an impulse, to the comfort of the Catholic priest, she acknowledges implicitly the failure of reason, of discipline, of Protestantism itself: the necessity of recognizing a part of herself too long rejected and denied. That expression should take the form of confession seems appropriate, since in Lucy deprivation has caused guilt and anxiety: feelings of unworthiness and shame. For her, self-expression is tantamount to sin.[29] Lucy does find relief in the

28. The parallel with Brontë's dream of her dead sisters is obvious.

29. On September 1, 1843, in a state of mind of which Lucy's is a reflection, Brontë herself confessed to a Roman Catholic priest in the Cathedral of Ste. Gudule. Writing to Emily on the following day, she explained that the priest refused at first to listen to the confession of a Protestant, "but I was determined to confess, and at last he said he would allow me because it might be the first step toward returning to the true church. I actually did confess—a real confession . . . the adventure stops there, and I hope I shall never see the priest again. I think you had better not tell papa of this. He will not understand that it was only a freak, and will perhaps think that I am going to turn Catholic!" (Wise and Symington, I, 304.)

One can imagine that Brontë's own feelings of sexual longing and jealousy were so much greater than those pictured here in Lucy's vague admiration of Dr.

cathartic experience: "The mere pouring out of some portion of long accumulating, long pent-up pain into a vessel whence it could not be again diffused—had done me good. I was already solaced" (p. 140). Although she fears her own vulnerability too much to accede to the priest's invitation to return to him for help, she has been, to a limited extent, freed. Before she collapses on the darkened street, she has rediscovered the courage and strength, and will to live, which had before carried her to Belgium. She expresses the same wish for transcendence—linked before to sexual experience—that had been Brontë's, as it had also been Jane's: "My heart did not fail at all in this conflict; I only wished that I had wings and could ascend the gale, spread and repose my pinions on its strength, career in its course, sweep where it swept" (p. 141).

The further implications of release become clear when Lucy regains consciousness. The fainting fit does not simply mark a transition to a new level of awareness, her readiness for a new stage of experience, as did similar episodes in *Jane Eyre* (the red-room, the recuperative sleep at the Riverses' home). Now—the parallel with psychoanalysis again suggests itself—Lucy can be moved into the future only through the medium of the past. Lucy wakens to the beginning: the only beginning she has been able to record: the house at Bretton. She is carried back ten years by the ornaments and decorations of the room in which she lies. It is now that we learn that she is twenty-four: that she was only fourteen when the first incident of the novel took place. And as she attempts to orient herself, looking at a portrait of Graham Bretton which hangs upon the wall, we discover how deeply she herself had cared for the young boy, to what extent Polly was not only her surrogate, but her competitor as well.

> "Ah! that portrait used to hang in the breakfast-room, over the mantel-piece: somewhat too high, as I thought. I well remember how I used to mount a music-stool for the purpose of unhooking it, holding it in my hand, and searching into those bonny wells of eyes, whose glance under their hazel lashes seemed like a pencilled laugh; and well I liked to note the

John and envy of Ginevra, and her feeling of guilt about her emotional involvement with Heger—only in the early stages of recognition—much more intense. *Her* impulse to seek the comfort of confession is therefore even more readily understandable.

colouring of the cheek, and the expression of the mouth.'' I hardly believed fancy could improve on the curve of that mouth, or of the chin, even *my* ignorance knew that both were beautiful, and pondered perplexed over this doubt: "How it was that what charmed so much, could at the same time so keenly pain?'' (pp. 146–47).

In this brilliantly convoluted plotting, possessed of such psychological validity, Brontë reveals that Lucy had recognized Graham Bretton in Dr. John—Ginevra's suitor and the school's doctor—and had neither shared her secret with him nor with the reader. We accept Brontë's artifice because we are familiar with Lucy's fear of rejection, with her extreme vulnerability, and with her consequent unreliability as a narrator.

Finding herself in the Bretton's home as it has been reestablished in Brussels, cared for by her godmother and treated with affection and kindness by Graham, Lucy can, in fact, continue to build on the possibility for a relationship begun with her "confession"—the first presentation of herself to another. She imagines that "my calm little room seemed somehow like a cave in the sea'':

> When I closed my eyes, I heard a gale, subsiding at last, bearing upon the house-front like a setting swell upon a rock-base. I heard it drawn and withdrawn far, far off, like a tide retiring from a shore of the upper world—a world so high above that the rush of its largest waves, the dash of its fiercest breakers— could sound down in this submarine home, only like murmurs and a lullaby. (pp. 155–56)

The image is again drawn from Brontë's childhood dream and suggests the tenuousness of her security. Lucy realizes that she must call on Reason in her struggle with feeling so that her life will at least *seem* to "be better regulated, more equable, quieter on the surface, and it is on the surface only the common gaze will fall'' (p. 153). But although she resubmits out of pride to Reason, she struggles more honestly for expression, allowing herself to believe more intensely in the integrity of feeling. A welter of psychic experience replaces the analytical dialectic which traced the self-discovery of Jane Eyre. If Reason would crush her, cow her, break her down, if it is as "vindictive as a devil'' and "envenomed as a stepmother,'' imagination is her "divine love,'' "a goddess representing Help and Hope'' (p. 196). Later, in answering Graham's letters, Lucy writes one message to satisfy Reason, which she sends to him, and one which expresses her feeling, which she keeps for herself. It is a recognition of her own needs as well as of society's demands; a compromise with her understanding of Graham which allows her to maintain a personal integrity newly discovered. The self is protected so that it need not be sacrificed. Only when Graham has encountered Polly once again and has fallen in love with her, does Lucy allow Reason to persuade her of what she has always dimly known: that this "true young Englishman," whom nature has made good enough for a prince, could not find in *her* a fit mate. So she seals her letters in a bottle and buries them in a garden. ("People who have undergone bereavement always jealously gather together and lock away mementos: it is not supportable to be stabbed to the heart each moment by sharp revival of regret" (p. 251). She compares the impulse which compels her to this action to that which moved her to visit the confessional. Both are acts of self-preservation. Self-control is healthfully born of self-knowledge.

If Lucy's attraction to Graham persists despite repression ("Was this feeling dead? I do not know, but it was buried." [p. 307]), it persists because of the power of her ambivalence—not unlike Brontë's ambivalence toward George Smith, Graham's model. Ambivalence grows out of Lucy's recognition that if she cannot be a satisfactory mate for Graham, the fault is as much a function of the defects in *his* character as it is a result of her own inadequacy. Because she cannot rid herself of her sense of the second any more than she can deny her knowledge of the first, the conflict remains unresolved.

> Reader, if in the course of this work you find that my opinion of Dr. John undergoes modification, excuse the seeming inconsistency. I give the feeling as at the time I felt it: I describe the view of character as it appeared when discovered. (p. 164)

Lucy knows that she is plain. (The reader believes in that plainness as it was impossible to believe in Jane's.) Her knowledge is corroborated for her many times. Ginevra, for example, is cruelly critical when she insists upon comparing their mirror images, finding her own to be infinitely superior.[30] On a more

---

30. The incident is reminiscent of one which took place when Charlotte Brontë and Mary Taylor were students at the Roe Head School. Mary Taylor described it to Elizabeth Gaskell (Gaskell, p. 66):

important occasion, Lucy is forced "to see herself as others see her," when she comes unexpectedly upon her own reflection as she stands with Mrs. Bretton and Graham. Then she remarks, "It brought a jar of discord, a pang of regret; it was not flattering, yet, after all, I ought to be thankful; it might have been worse" (p. 180). Although her "feeling self" would probably respond in a tone more anguished than this one struck by Reason, Lucy does know that Graham is a man who can't see far beneath the surface, who can't penetrate further than his own hopes and illusions. To him, she is only "quiet Lucy Snowe," a being "inoffensive as a shadow." His public self—generous, benevolent, modest— approves her: to his private self—vain, selfish, full of masculine egotism—she is unacceptable.

> With now welcome force, I realized his entire misapprehension of my character and nature. He wanted always to give me a role not mine. Nature and I opposed him. He did not at all guess what I felt: he did not read my eyes, or face, or gestures; though, I doubt not, all spoke. (p. 270)

Polly, who molds herself to the needs of those for whom she cares, will not betray Graham's illusions. Because she is also rich and beautiful she will not threaten his vanity. Lucy acknowledges that "society must approve—the world must admire what he did, or he counted his measures false and futile" (p. 313), and she can't help wondering if he might have treated her better had her wealth and station been different.

Lucy's ambivalence remains up to their last encounter in the novel—and beyond. When Lucy sees Graham at the "fete" and entreats him with her eyes not to reveal her presence there, they exchange a glance which reawakens those feelings long buried:

> He resumed his seat, nor did he again turn or disturb me by a glance, except indeed for one single instant, when a look, rather solicitous than curious, stole my way—speaking what

---

It was about this time I told her she was very ugly. Some years afterwards, I told her I thought I had been very impertinent. She replied, "You did me a great deal of good, Polly, so don't repent of it."

Gaskell (p. 380) suggests that Brontë never did overcome an agonizing self-consciousness which derived from her feelings of insecurity:

> Much of this nervous dread of encountering strangers I ascribe to the idea of her personal ugliness, which had been strongly impressed upon her imagination early in life, and which she exaggerated to herself in a remarkable manner.

somehow stilled my heart—"like the south-wind quieting the earth." Graham's thoughts of me were not entirely those of a frozen indifference, after all. I believe in that goodly mansion, his heart, he kept one little place under the skylights where Lucy might have entertainment, if she chose to call . . . I kept a room for him, too—a place of which I never took the measure, either by rule or compass: I think it was like the tent of Peri-Banou. All my life long I carried it folded in the hollow of my hand—yet, released from that hold and constriction, I know not but its innate capacity for expanse might have magnified it into a tabernacle for a host. (p. 386)

Graham is her adolescent hero, the romantic love unmasked, but tempting still. The immature longing remains, but it is contained by an ego increasingly capable of assertion and control.

Although Lucy is fond of the matured Polly, seeing in the girl's capacity for feeling, in her quiet pride and self-respect, reflections of her own personality, and while she needs still to identify herself with the privileged and blessed, Lucy openly refuses to allow Polly to share with her confidences about her love for Graham. When Polly asks her: "Do other people see him with my eyes? Do you admire him?", Lucy replies, with wry honesty, "I *never see* him," and she goes on to explain to the reader: "It was best to answer her strongly at once, and to silence for ever the tender, passionate confidences which left her lips, sweet honey, and sometimes dropped in my ear—molten lead" (p. 359). The sentiment is, in its way, harsh but it is honestly self-protective. If Polly, with the "infatuated egotism" common to lovers "must have a witness to (her) happiness, cost that witness what it may" (p. 359), Lucy with a clear understanding of her own needs, knows that it is not in *her* interests to serve that purpose. In rejecting voyeurism, she asserts her right to a life of her own.

III

Having explored the frustrations of her current relationship with George Smith, Brontë went further back—to that more profound and traumatic relationship which had sparked her to growth and to despair. The movement is progressive in psychoanalytic terms, but regressive in its suggestion that the idealized professor in Brussels became again for Brontë the standard by which all

other men had to be judged. It is, of course, through her love affair with Paul Emanuel, the schoolmaster modeled upon M.
Heger, that Lucy ultimately realizes herself. The pattern of their
interaction is similar to that of the "Jane" poem, which had been
repeated in Frances's relationship to Crimsworth, in Jane's relation to Rochester, in Shirley's relation to Louis. Now the psychological process that shaped the pattern is more insightfully
presented and the emotional power that informed Brontë's love
for her "maitre" finds expression.

M. Paul has undeniable connections with the Byronic hero.
He is "a dark little man . . . pungent and austere" (p. 110),
fiery and grasping. He has dark hair, a "broad, sallow brow" and
thin cheek, a "wide and quivering nostril." He utters groans of
scorn and fierce hisses of rage. Lucy, seeing his love of power,
compares him to Napoleon. She comprehends his capacity for
deep and irrational passion, the volatility of his temper, his jealousy. A rebel at heart, he fervently opposes tyranny and resists
whatever is obligatory. But there is another side to his character.
He is benevolent and charitable, given to acts of extraordinary
kindness. If "he was as capricious as women are said to be" (p.
279), he is also as emotional, as sympathetic, as impulsive, and
intuitive.

> [His heart] was not an ossified organ: in its core was a place,
> tender beyond a man's tenderness; a place that humbled him to
> little children, that bound him to girls and women: to whom,
> rebel as he would, he could not disown his affinity, nor quite
> deny that, on the whole, he was better with them than with his
> own sex. (p. 287)

His is an androgynous nature: not confused and blocked as Huns-
worth's was, not insecure as Crimsworth's; but complex and
whole. He is the romantic hero humanized, offering a promise of
equality. Once he trusts Lucy he is not afraid to reveal to her his
vulnerability, to confess that "there is a fund of modesty and diffidence in my nature" (p. 308), to express that about himself
which is tender and nurturing. Finding Lucy asleep at her desk he
covers her with a warm shawl and explains to her, when she
awakens: "You need watching, and watching over, and it is well
for you that I see this and do my best to discharge both duties"
(p. 307). He is not only the "maitre," the father-lover who

haunts all of Brontë's novels. He is also a maternal figure—and, in his stubborn impulsivity and petulance, a child. To Lucy who has had no relationships, he offers all.

Because Monsieur Paul's is such a comprehensive and vital personality, he evokes and even demands a wide range of responses. Although he likes to dominate, his is not an ego which blocks response. His empathetic nature allows him to define himself through interaction. It is revealing that he should feel an affinity with the theatre and choose to direct amateur performances. It is important that he should persuade Lucy to take part in a school production. Her assigned role is one which she despairs at first of playing properly. She is to be a man: Ginevra's suitor, a fop. But she discovers it to be a part that she can not only play well, but can play "with relish." Imagining that Graham is her rival, responding to Ginevra's flirtatiousness, to the girl's clear preference for herself, Lucy becomes instinctively the dandy, deHamal, with whom Ginevra eventually elopes. In the process she learns something about each of them and, most importantly, she learns to explore and release some hidden androgynous aspect of her own personality. The knowledge she gains is frightening. The possibility she feels makes her wish to withdraw again into the more limited spaces of herself. "A keen relish for dramatic expression had revealed itself as part of my nature; to cherish and exercise this new-found faculty might gift me with a world of delight, but it would not do for a mere looker-on at life" (p. 121). Her reaction is composed of the same elements of attraction and repulsion that she experiences when she later goes with Graham to see Vashti, the great actress.[31] In Vashti's per-

---

31. This incident is modeled on Charlotte Brontë's experience with the French tragedienne, Rachel (Elisa Felix), whom she saw in Scribe's *Adrienne Lecouvreur* and Corneille's *Les Trois Horaces* in London, in June 1851. She wrote to James Taylor of her response (November 15, 1851. Wise and Symington, III, 289.):

> Rachel's acting transfixed me with wonder, enchained me with interest, and thrilled me with horror. The tremendous force with which she expresses the very worst passions in their strongest essence forms an exhibition as exciting as the bull-fights of Spain and the gladiatorial combats of old Rome, and (it seemed to me) not one whit more moral than those poisoned stimulants to popular ferocity. It is scarcely human nature that she shows you; it is something wilder and worse; the feelings and fury of a fiend.

formance she finds the very image of passion. She is almost un-
bearably moved by the "marvelous sight: a mighty revelation
. . . a spectacle low, horrible, immoral" (p. 220). Through
Vashti is revealed the range of passions available to the human
spirit. The actress's power is "like a deep, swollen winter river,
thundering in cataract," which plucks Lucy's soul "like a leaf,
on the steep and steely sweep of its descent" (p. 222). And when
the force of Vashti's conflict, the depth of her passion, becomes
in fact too much for Lucy to bear, the theatre bursts into flames,
much like the mystery of fire which flickers through *Jane Eyre*.

Although Lucy deeply fears such a loss of rational control,
she is magnetically drawn by the potential for extension and self-
exploration which the irrational seems to hold out to her. Paul
Emanuel does not present her with a range of possibilities as vast
as those implied by Vashti's performances. These would overwhelm Lucy, as the fire symbolically suggests. He does, however, continue to place her in role-playing situations which prevent her from becoming again "a mere looker-on at life." Lucy
initially makes the mistake of thinking that Paul Emanuel is simply like all of the others who project upon her roles which express
their sense of her and freeze her into false postures;

> Madame Beck esteemed me learned and blue; Miss Fanshawe,
> caustic, ironic and cynical; Mr. Home, a model teacher, the es-
> sence of the sedate and discreet: somewhat conventional per-
> haps, too strict, limited and scrupulous, but still the pink and
> pattern of governess-correctness; . . . (p. 257)

In fact, M. Paul can read Lucy's eyes, her face, her gestures—
and he responds to the spark of her being instead of the shadow of
her seeming. It is a new experience for her, as she observes with
some amazement to herself: "You are well habituated to be
passed by as a shadow in Life's sunshine: it is a new thing to see
one testily lifting his hand to screen his eyes, because you tease
him with an obtrusive ray" (p. 284). Initially, responding to her

---

She also wrote:

> I neither love, esteem, nor hate this strange being, but (if I could bear the
> high mental stimulus so long) I would go every night for three months to
> watch and study its manifestations. (David Isenberg, "Charlotte Brontë
> and the Theatre," in *Brontë Society Transactions,* 15, No. 3 (1968), p.
> 239.)

strength, her "Protestant independence," Paul sees her as a competitor, "one of those beings who must be *kept down*" (p. 133). His urge to dominate, inspires her resistance, "(gives) wings to aspiration" (p. 298). His belief that she is more learned than she in fact is and his fear that she will use her learning as a weapon against him, stimulate her confidence. His excessive emotionality (so like her inner self) releases her into perverse playfulness and his mercurial disposition makes her "placid and harmonious," almost maternal. So too, his jealousy of Graham, which moves him to petulant accusations concerning her "frivolity" and "vanity," amuses her while awakening a sense of the power of her own femininity. Asserting herself in opposition to him, Lucy discovers a range of responses, feelings, opinions, and ideas which will not be confined to the narrow space of a submerged personality. He sparks her to growth—as Hunsden incites Frances, as Rochester stimulates Jane. But he does not—in the manner of his predecessors—frustrate the spirit he arouses.

As M. Paul becomes aware that Lucy's capacity for passion makes her vulnerable as well as strong, he allows himself to substitute sympathy and support for anger. More secure, he can overcome his suspicions and assure her that "we worship the same God, in the same spirit, though by different rites" (p. 323). His avowal is not a simple assertion of religious tolerance. It is, in its admission of equality, a genuine offer of friendship: an advance towards psychic confrontation: the beginning for each of emotional fulfillment. To acknowledge religious kinship Paul and Lucy must accept the manifestations of each other in themselves for their religions define the dominant aspects of their personalities. Reason and imagination, control and expression, must be placed in appropriate relationship.

Lucy fears Catholicism because she equates its apparent excesses of feeling with loss of self. She fears it because it offers her, as an alternative to the familiar agony of alienation, the self-contained world of religious fanaticism. She knows that if she had returned to Père Silas after the night of her impulsive confession, "I might just now, instead of writing this heretic narrative, be counting my beads in the cell of a certain Carmelite convent on the Boulevard of Crecy in Villette" (p. 141). Lucy prefers Art—the rational ordering of intuition and emotion—to the mystical transfiguration which leaves reality behind. But the power of aversion measures the force of attraction. There is that in Catholicism to which she profoundly responds—both in the sublimity of nature and in the mysticism of her own soul; feelings which represent spiritual and erotic transcendence: the dual temptations of the romantic experience.

For Jane, these feelings were focused in a series of fiery images projected first in the red-room of her childhood; later associated with the vampire, Berthe. Lucy's fear is typically one of deprivation rather than anticipation. It finds its object in the ghostly figure of the nun who haunts her at the Pensionnat. But we are aware of its presence earlier in the novel: when Lucy first begins to confront herself after Miss Marchmont's death. It is then that she unexpectedly meets an old school friend:

> . . . What a beautiful and kind-looking woman was the good-natured and comely, but unintellectual girl become! Wifehood and maternity had changed her thus, as I have seen them change others even less promising than she. Me she had forgotten. I was changed, too; though not, I fear, for the better. (p. 37)

The girl's life contrasts sharply with the one Lucy has led as nurse to the invalided old woman. Lucy allows herself to feel regret as she looks at the young mother, believing that this kind of transformation will never be hers; that she, Lucy Snowe, can have no hope of wifehood and maternity. And yet—she cannot live contentedly with the certainty of that impossibility.

Later, at the Pensionnat, as she cares for Madame's children, to whom she is "only a governess," she does often seem (as the billet-doux intended for Ginevra describes her) "revêche comme une religieuse" (p. 95). It is understandable that she would identify with the nun who is said to haunt the house, the ghost of a girl who had been buried alive "for some sin against her vow" (p. 90). Lucy has also been "buried alive," and the specter is the dread shape of the imprisoned, undeserving self of the past: the sterile and isolated self of the future. The chill form of enforced virginity hovers prophetically over Lucy, as Berthe—unleashed sensuality—had menaced Jane. Both are the perverse offspring of sexual desire and the repression which results from guilt and fear. Both represent the wish for union and the horror of negation. In aspect, Berthe is the projection of Jane's expectant sexuality which is passionate though fearful. The figure of the nun expresses Lucy's only nascent sexuality, anticipatory of rejection and sterility.

When Lucy reads Graham's first letter, her intense joy is countered by terror at the depth of her own happiness: a fear of risk, a resurgence of insecurity. It is then that she first sees the nun. Panicked, she asks: "Are there wicked things, not human, which envy human bliss?" (p. 210). And when she decides at last to bury Graham's letters—repressing feelings that can only cause her pain—the apparition offers itself again, apparently validating her belief that "If life be a war, it seemed my destiny to conduct it single-handed" (p. 253).

As Lucy's relationship with Paul begins to flourish, the specter returns as a warning. But now Paul sees it as well and their kinship is expressed in their shared sensitivity, derived from a surprising similarity of personal history. For him, too, the nun has had a special significance. He associates her with Justine Marie, a young woman who had died in the convent in which she had been placed because of him, by relatives who thought him unsuitable as a lover. The power the girl exerts over him in death creates for Paul a life which is as stunted as the one which the nun seems to prophesy for Lucy. Faithful to Justine's memory, trapped in guilt and sentimentality, Paul has sacrificed everything to her family and friends, demonstrating his worthiness repeatedly. To Madame Walravens and Père Silas he has given his energy, his wealth, his hopes for an independent life. He, too, has been a survivor—identifying with the dead. He has lived as a monk, in a space as limited as the one which enclosed Lucy and Miss Marchmont. Now he fears that Justine Marie has come herself, motivated by jealousy of his friendship with Lucy.[32]

The power of the nun is diminished before the secret of her identity is discovered. The Gothic motif is imparted a realism by the psychological validity of Brontë's insight.[33] Because they are functions of human fear, specters respond to assertions of human

32. One must remember that Heger was also a survivor, who witnessed the deaths of his first wife and child. By metaphorically developing this aspect of his experience, Brontë undercuts the importance of his second marriage—and second family.

33. For a useful discussion of Charlotte Brontë's adaptation of Gothic forms and technique to psychological purposes, see Robert B. Heilman, "Charlotte Brontë's New Gothic," in *From Jane Austen to Joseph Conrad*, ed. Robert C. Rathburn and Martin Steinmann, Jr. (Minnesota: University of Minnesota Press, 1958), pp. 118–32.

will. Superstition is dispelled as Lucy and Paul's belief in one another is substantiated. Learning of Paul's past fidelity and magnanimity, experiencing his tenderness and sympathy, Lucy surrenders to the force of her feeling and to the promise of romance. When they exchange their vow of friendship she believes that she might evade her fate after all: "I envied no girl her lover, no bride her bridegroom, no wife her husband" (p. 344). Despite his Catholicism, Paul has become for her a "Christian hero." He is Apollyon, Great Heart, "my Champion."

But although Lucy's happiness seems less threatened by the mysterious forces within, it is threatened still by the jealousy and selfishness of Paul Emanuel's "friends," as well as by Paul's own fanatic self-sacrifice: his apparent inability to assert himself in behalf of his own needs. Succumbing totally to irrational fear, Lucy perceives Père Silas, Madame Walravens, and Madame Beck as the malicious villains of a Gothic tale in which she and Paul are cast as helpless victims. It is in the distorting mirror of Lucy's Protestant prejudices that the reader perceives Père Silas, the bigoted, devious priest and Madame Walravens, who is "Cunegonde, the sorceress! Malevola, the evil fairy" (p. 329). But if the colors Lucy uses to paint their portraits are lurid, the plan she attributes to them is real. With Madame Beck, they do intend to send Paul Emanuel off to the West Indies for three years on a final "errand of mercy." There he will be secured from her heretical influence while looking after their material interests. In Madame Beck's jealous opposition to their love, we hear the outrage of Madame Heger,[34] and in Lucy's wordless desperation as she waits for Paul's last visit, in her sense of impotence before feeling, we feel the passion which Brontë had never before expressed so openly. Because Lucy is secure in Paul's feeling for her as Brontë could never have been in M. Heger's, she is finally able to overcome her passivity, confronting her rival and un-

34. Writing to Ellen of Madame Heger's coldness towards her, Charlotte comes as close as she did in any of her existing letters to sharing her secret infatuation (November 15, 1843. Wise and Symington, II, 309.):

> You will hardly believe that Madame Heger (good and kind as I have described her) never comes near me on the occasions . . . I own, I was astonished the first time I was left alone thus . . . you remember the letter she wrote me when I was in England? How kind and affectionate that was! is it not odd? I fancy I begin to perceive the reason of this mighty distance and reserve; it sometimes makes me laugh and at other times nearly cry. When I am sure of it I will tell you.

masking her ("I saw underneath a being heartless, self-indulgent, and ignoble." [p. 377]).

Madame Beck's attempts to keep Lucy and Paul separated are self-defeating. The drug which she administers to make Lucy sleep sharpens her senses and intensifies her perceptions. It arouses her, moves her to definitive action.[35] Lucy seeks freedom again as she had sought it before, but now she gives herself completely to her quest. It is a holiday evening and everyone she knows has gathered in the spacious park—radiant with moonlight, alive with the promise of celebration. It is a fitting place for her to seek an encounter with Paul, another of the meetings which have taken place in natural settings, in moonlit gardens, in the open air where the limits of the self are expanded: where the soul can aspire and breathe. Once more a solitary voyeur, Lucy is still not lonely. She projects herself into everything around her. She denies nothing, not even, when she sees Graham, that part of her infatuation for him which always remains potentially alive. Now she searches out experience, eagerly pursuing her "fate." She is humorous and ironic, purged of bitterness. Even the reality that undercuts the melodrama of her Gothic vision insists upon recognition:

> Hail, Madame Walravens! I think you looked more witchlike than ever. And presently the good lady proved that she was indeed no corpse or ghost, but a harsh and hardy old woman; for, upon some aggravation in the clamorous petition of De-sirée Beck to her mother, to go to the kiosk and take sweetmeats, the hunchback suddenly fetched her a resounding rap with her gold-knobbed cane.

> There, then, were Madame Walravens, Madame Beck, Père Silas—the whole conjuration, the secret junta. The sight of

35. Elizabeth Gaskell writes (Gaskell, chap. xxvii):
I asked her whether she had ever taken opium, as the description given of its effects in *Villette* was so exactly like what I had experienced,—vivid and exaggerated presence of objects, of which the outlines were indistinct, or lost in golden mist, etc. She replied, that she had never, to her knowledge, taken a grain of it in any shape, but that she had followed the process she always adopted when she had to describe anything which had not fallen within her own experience; she had thought intently on it for many and many a night before falling to sleep,—wondering what it was like, or how it would be,—till at length, sometimes after the progress of her story had been arrested at this one point for weeks, she wakened up in the morning with all clear before her, as if she had in reality gone through the experience, and then could describe it, word for word, as it had happened.

them thus assembled did me good. I cannot say that I felt weak
before them, or abashed, or dismayed. They outnumbered me,
and I was worsted and under their feet; but, as yet, I was not
dead. (p. 388)

The most crucial recognition comes in relation to Paul Emanuel.
When she sees him there with his goddaughter, whom she believes to be his intended bride, she responds with a degree of intensity she would never have allowed herself before: "And
then—something tore me so cruelly under my shawl, something
so dug into my side, a vulture so strong in beak and talon, I must
be alone to grapple with it" (p. 395). Her jealousy teaches her the
depth of her love. When she returns to her room with the pain and
comprehension of that knowledge, she finds once again—the
nun. But the self that has penetrated to truth, and the sexual longing which is at last awakened, both disdain the imagination that
builds illusion:

> Warm from illuminations, and music, and thronging thou-
> sands, thoroughly lashed up by a new scourge, I defied spec-
> tra. In a moment, without exclamation, I had rushed on the
> haunted couch; nothing leaped out, or sprang, or stirred; all the
> movement was mine, so was all the life, the reality, the sub-
> stance, the force; as my instinct felt. (pp. 396–97)

In the absurd reality of the nun (a costume disguise for Ginevra's
suitor) Lucy recognizes the power of the mind to create its own
fears and anxieties; its own guilt, even its own prison. She knows
that now she can "handle the veil and dare the dread glance."
Once the harsh demands of her Protestantism are softened, the
repressive ban lifted, Lucy's faith can be confirmed and the integrity of her personality preserved.

The final trial and the ultimate victory remain. Anticipating a
meeting with Paul before he sails, fearing that it will not, in fact,
take place, Lucy is "pierced deeper than I could endure, made
now to feel what defied suppression." Forced to the center of her
soul, touching the very quick of her nature, Lucy is undefended
at last. When they are reunited she, who has never described herself to the reader (unexpectedly coming upon her reflection in a
mirror she had seen simply "a third person in a pink dress and
black lace mantle" [p. 179]), she, Lucy Snowe, risks herself totally, asking: " 'Ah! I am not pleasant to look at—? I could not
help saying this; the words came unbidden: I never remember the

time when I had not a haunting dread of what might be the degree
of my outward deficiency; this dread pressed me at the moment
with special force.' " It is a validation of her transformed self
that she requires. Paul does not disappoint her:

> A great softness passed upon his countenance; his violet eyes
> grew suffused and glistening under their deep Spanish lashes:
> he started up: "Let us walk on."
>   "Do I displease your eyes much?" I took courage to urge:
> the point had its vital import for me.
>
>   He stopped, and gave me a short, strong answer—an an-
> swer which silenced, subdued, yet profoundly satisfied. Ever
> after that, I knew what I was for *him;* and what I might be for
> the rest of the world, I ceased painfully to care. (p.407)

With Paul she, who has always found it so difficult to speak,
becomes eloquent. She who has hardly dared to tell herself her
thoughts, she who has hoarded every feeling, can say, "I want to
tell you all" and she can tell him freely and unbidden of her anxieties and fears. She can tell him also of her love: "I spoke. All
leaped from my lips. I lacked not words now; fast I narrated;
fluent I told my tale; it streamed on my tongue" (p. 412). Her capacity for love, newly discovered, newly explored, brings with it
self-knowledge and expression.

In his love, Paul has also been able to find the will to self-assertion. He will make this one last journey in Justine Marie's service. Then, returning to marry Lucy, he will commit himself to
life. Meanwhile, he plans to make it possible for Lucy to realize
her freedom. With the home which he has rented for her and the
school which he has established in her name, he offers her the impossible gift of independence. It is the gift which Crimsworth had
bestowed upon Frances. But because Lucy must support herself
in Paul's absence, because the school is nothing until she creates
it, his gift is genuine. Its implications however, are ambiguous.
The role which Paul will play in the school upon his return and
the effect which that role will have upon Lucy's functioning:
these are not defined. But the novel's conclusion is, in part, an attempt to come to terms with the crucial if unexpressed problems.

When they separate, Paul has demonstrated his sensitivity to
Lucy's needs, his generosity in satisfying them. His personality
has been softened—the more aggressive and domineering quali-

ties purged. In Lucy's idealized vision, only those elements remain which sustain and nourish. His fidelity is proven. Still, theirs is not a relationship of equality. Lucy sees him as her king: "royal for me had been that hand's bounty: to offer homage was both a joy and a duty" (p. 410). It is only in his absence that she can and does discover the possibilities of her own strength. Her words are telling: "M. Emanuel was away three years. Reader, they were the three happiest years of my life" (p. 414). The tone is more telling still. It could be the tone of Jane Eyre. The unreliable narrator has been replaced by one who confronts her reader directly. Lucy Snowe has rejected the silences, the claustrophobic spaces, and the labyrinthian ways of anxiety and repression. She achieves with Brontë herself the maturity of her creator's art. She does not share the totality of Brontë's awareness, however; nor is she allowed the disturbance of her author's subconscious doubts.

Although Lucy can finally assert her independence to become the antithesis of a romantic heroine (neither a "little spaniel" like Polly nor a thoughtless doll like Ginevra) she is oblivious to the dangers which would confront her if Paul Emanuel should, in fact return. In this novel, as in her three earlier books, it is Brontë who must try to reconcile the heroine's independent self-realization with her need to be submerged in the powerful, masculine "other." For Brontë it had always been impossible to accommodate these two commanding impulses which psychosexual conditioning and social reality place in extreme conflict.

Harriet Martineau, the redoubtable intellectual and social reformer, mistook Charlotte Brontë for Lucy Snowe. With an obtuseness born of militancy, she overlooked the novel's psychological center and, while noting the resolution of Lucy and Paul Emanuel's relationship, did not mark the significance of the story's ending. In a review which she wrote for the *Daily News,* she evinced the kind of outrage that had typified Mary Taylor's earlier response to *Shirley:*

> All the female characters, in all their thoughts and lives are full of one thing, or are regarded by the reader in the light of one thought—love. It begins with the child of six years old, at the opening—a charming picture—and it closes with it at the last page; and so dominant is this idea—so incessant is the writer's tendency to describe the need of being loved—that the heroine

who tells her own story, leaves the reader at last with the uncomfortable impression of her having either entertained a double love, or allowed one to supersede another without notification of the transition. It is not thus in real life. There are substantial, heartfelt interests for women of all ages and, under ordinary circumstances, quite apart from love; there is an absence of introspection, an unconsciousness, a repose in women's lives—unless under peculiarly unfortunate circumstances—of which we find no admission in this book; and to the absence of it may be attributed some of the criticism which the book will meet with from readers who are no prudes, but whose reason and taste will reject the assumption that events and characters are to be regarded through the medium of one passion only.[36]

Brontë was deeply hurt by the response of this intimidating woman whom she had only just begun to think of as a friend:

I know what *love* is and I understand it; and if man or woman should be ashamed of feeling such love, then there is nothing right, noble, faithful, truthful, unselfish in this earth as I comprehend rectitude, nobleness, fidelity, truth and disinterestedness.[37]

Her words, while naively courageous, suggest her continuing inability to break free entirely of that circle of romantic idealism which had bound her life.

Charlotte Brontë had shared Harriet Martineau's feminist outrage when she had intuitively created Elizabeth Hastings, when she had confusedly defined Francis Henri, when she had constructed the mythology of *Jane Eyre* and tested it—unsuccessfully—against the social vision of *Shirley*. But she had never been able to deny what remained for her the most profound of human truths: that to be able to love and to be loved are essential conditions of a maturely realized life. How to reach that loving state, how to treasure it, while still maintaining independence: here was the difficulty. Brontë could offer no clear resolution—witness her elimination of Paul Emanuel—but she would not deny the possibility of resolution altogether. She could only assert the incontrovertible fact of her own situation, revealing in this way the nature and limits of her feminist consciousness. Her

36. Wise and Symington, IV, 44.
37. To Harriet Martineau, January, 1853. Wise and Symington, 42.

personal history had made it impossible for her to draw upon the kind of strengths that had carried Mary Taylor to New Zealand and had allowed Harriet Martineau to create for herself a life-style and work defined by radical action and social service. Brontë had neither the self-confidence nor the militance to leave behind the conventional patterns of her world. Her freedom was private and subjective, conceived neither in political nor collective terms. Her femininism derived from her persistent attempt to define herself autonomously, resisting predetermined cultural formulations, responding to the powerful demands of her own personality. Knowledge and growth were garnered from the metaphor of Yorkshire nature and the revelations of introspection. And, of course, for her action was the process of writing.

As she struggled with herself to bring her novel to conclusion, Brontë wrote to George Smith:

> If Lucy marries anybody, it must be the Professor—a man in whom there is much to forgive, much to "put up with." But I am not leniently disposed to Miss Frost: from the beginning I never meant to appoint her lines in pleasant places. The conclusion of this third volume is still a matter of some anxiety: I can but do my best, however. It would speedily be finished, could I ward off certain obnoxious head-aches which, whenever I get into the spirit of my work are apt to seize and prostrate me.[38]

The words suggest that Brontë paid to the end the price of personal confrontation. She could not appoint Lucy Snowe's lines in pleasant places because she could not bury again the self which she had so painfully uncovered. Therefore, she could not resolve the conundrum raised by Lucy's situation with the illusions, evasiveness, and facility of the earlier novels.

Paul Emanuel could not return. He could not return because Brontë's fantasy relationship with Heger would not then have been laid to rest. The Belgian's idealization would not have been balanced by his irrevocable loss. The tragic circumstances of her life would have been denied. No matter how great her desire and how firm her wish to believe, no matter how unprepared she was to confront directly the irreducible fact of Heger's indifference, Brontë could not betray the larger reality of her experience.

38. November 3, 1852. Wise and Symington, IV, 16.

Then, too, Paul Emanuel could not return for a reason which Martineau would have found congenial had she been able to perceive it through her rigidly structured feminism. Always intensely personal in her writing—faithful to the truths she had learned and to the confusions which remained—Brontë knew that Lucy had come to her independence through love. She understood that for Lucy to be certain of keeping that independence, she would have to pay the price of solitude. Brontë could not be sure that there was in fact another alternative. She did not know what would happen to that emergent self if it were joined in marriage to "a man in whom there is much to forgive, much to 'put up with' "; if it were joined in marriage, in fact, to any man. Her own marriage might have taught her the answer and the answer might well have provided her with another novel. Now she eschewed the former compromises of myth and fantasy.

Paul Emanuel's death *can* be compared to the symbolic castration of Rochester. It too represents a rejection of patriarchal forces and suggests the personal and imaginative losses which result from social failure. But Paul Emanuel cannot be reborn, as Rochester was, into a new version of psychosexual romance. Romance itself is no longer viable. It belongs to the realm of princes and princesses of Fortune: the Graham Brettons and Pauline Homeses. For Lucy Snowe, the conventions of literary form—the shroud of domesticity and the implied perpetuation of social values—are as inadequate as the social conventions which call them into being.

Lucy speaks often of lives which are blessed, of love which ends in happiness and marriage, but when she does, she refers always to the relationship between Polly and Graham and theirs is not a relationship which she herself could value. This much she had revealed to Polly:

> I shall share no man's or woman's life in this world, as you understand sharing. I think I have one friend of my own, but I am not sure; and till I *am* sure, I live solitary.

To Polly's response, "But solitude is sadness," Lucy adds, "Yes; it is sadness. Life, however, has worse than that. Deeper than melancholy, lies heartbreak" (p. 359). Because Lucy—like Miss Marchmont—has loved and been loved, the harshness of her "fate" has been softened. She need not know heartbreak, only sadness. After Paul's death, she receives at last the inheritance from Miss Marchmont. She is responsible for her school. She is of use. She pursues her talents and maintains relationships. Without hope, she is not happy, but she is strong. Virginal, she has still experienced passion. Childless, her life is full of children and will not be sterile. Alone and lonely, she is not alienated. Surviving, she need not live as a survivor. She does not have to tell the story of another. Now she can tell and understand her own.

Paul Emanuel dies at sea as he journeys home. The storm in which he perishes limns the paradox at the novel's center. It expresses as well the struggle at the heart of the romantic experience and the irony of Brontë's life and death. The expanded self is poised between knowledge and annihilation. The self that is limited and withdrawn neither risks the second nor achieves the first. For Lucy the storm has always had a double meaning. Sometimes it has brought the horror of suffocation. At other times, it has stood for explosive transcendence. Always it has involved a terrible risk. Now Lucy's growth rests—with Brontë's integrity—upon the awful inevitability of Paul's loss. It is an uncompromising vision, but within the context of this novel, which gathers together the threads of all the fictions and the fragments of the life itself, it is undeniable and right.

Birth and Death

*A*FTER COMPLETING *Villette* in the winter of 1852, Charlotte
Brontë found herself in the position of the disappointed
rock-climber who achieves a difficult and heretofore un-
conquered peak only to find a distressingly familiar prospect
before her. The analysis to which she had subjected herself had
yielded a new level of insight, but the reality she had now to
confront remained remarkably unchanged. In creating Lucy
Snowe, Brontë had ruthlessly dissected herself. She had recorded
the effects of survivorship. She had defined the withdrawn and
masochistic personality. She had shown her hostility to be a
defense, and revealed repeatedly the pain of her vulnerability.
But that vulnerability had not been meaningfully diminished. The
insight gained had stripped away layers of repression and confusion, but since her analysis had been self-directed, it had also
been self-enclosed. Perceptions turned back upon themselves,
untested, in the convoluted chambers which had characterized
Lucy Snowe's own inner space. Brontë had journeyed alone,
without a companion to define with her a relationship which
could nourish where others had left her starved. Action did not
follow understanding.

Brontë's technique had been radical and was easily misunder-
stood. The novel was perceived by some to be flawed and disuni-
fied; by others—like Martineau—to be unabashedly sentimental.
Most immediately disturbing was the effect of the story upon
George Smith. By describing Lucy's unrequited love for Graham
Bretton, Brontë had revealed to her publisher, with extraordinary
candor, her own sense of the forces which had been at work in
their relationship. She insisted upon the integrity, however am-

biguous, of her feeling for Smith and the thoughtless superficiality of his attachment to her. She characterized the cloying possessiveness of his mother and claimed her right to use their lives as material for her novel. Smith, who understood the implications of the Bretton sections of the story, responded harshly. He attacked the art of the novel, he underpaid the novelist,[1] and he offered cold civility in the place of the warm relationship they had shared.

The break with Smith initiated a break with Williams as well. Further intimacy between them was difficult. Their correspondence gradually dwindled and died. Friendship with Harriet Martineau was also at an end. The acerbity of Martineau's judgment of the novel had burned a wound so deep that it could not be healed by words or time. Elizabeth Gaskell was the only "literary" friend left to her and she was hardly more than an acquaintance: a dim promise for the future.

Brontë had effectively cut her lifeline with London and the world of letters. It had not proven to be a world in which she could function without great psychological and emotional strain. At the height of her fame and success, she was more alone than she had ever been before.

She could say, with Lucy Snowe, "To see and know the worst is to take from fear her main advantage."[2] The writing of *Villette* had been an act of courage. Undoubtedly, in confronting the terrors of loneliness through Lucy Snowe, Brontë had parried the more fatal thrusts of fear. But what to do with the days of quiet desperation at Haworth? How could she apply her knowledge and her strength to these? She and her father lived side by side, but not together. She dutifully cared for him. He worried endlessly about her health. They shared few concerns and no interests. There were occasional letters written to Ellen Nussey and Margaret Wooler. Occasional letters in turn received. A correspondence still with Mary Taylor. And there was the grinding tedium of the daily routine—unrelieved by the painful emancipation of writing. Brontë had written herself to the

---

1. Brontë, as was the custom, had no contractual agreement with Smith and Elder. But she expected a payment of at least £ 700 for her new novel: a recognition of her status and position. Instead Smith paid her £ 500, the same as he had given her for *Jane Eyre* and *Shirley*.

2. *Villette*, p. 393.

depth and edge of her experience. She was an explorer sitting in a ship becalmed.

A dream saved her; a scrap of illusion, or, perhaps more fairly, the last belief which she allowed herself. "I know what *love* is as I understand it," she had written angrily to Harriet Martineau, "and if man or woman should be ashamed of feeling such love, then is there nothing right, noble, faithful, truthful, unselfish in this earth, as I comprehend rectitude, nobleness, fidelity, truth and disinterestedness."

All her life she had thought and written about love. She had learned to understand the ways in which it could be manipulative and selfish, the ways in which it could destroy, the ways in which it could offer cowardly submission and escape. But private and solitary, inward-turning as she was, she knew it to be the only alternative to solipsistic strangulation. Once love *had* been that to her. Ambiguously she writes, "I know what love is." She still could not have admitted: "I know what it is to love; but I do not know what it means to have been loved." That is the truth she refuses to penetrate—the truth from which she protected Lucy Snowe and herself. In some corner of her mind, Brontë clung still to a dream of possibility. And when that possibility offered itself—in a strange, almost incongruous form—she had become strong enough to respond to her hope, despite her doubts and disappointment. She would dare to separate—as Lucy Snowe had not—commitment from romance.

The man who did in fact love her had been her father's curate for more than seven years. For more than seven years he had barely impinged upon her consciousness. She had damned him with faint praise as Mr. Macarthey in *Shirley:* the man who replaced Malone and was "decent, decorous and consientious . . . sane and rational; diligent and charitable."[3] Elizabeth Gaskell found him to be bigoted and stern. None found him charming or magnetic. He was never mistaken for an intellectual nor was he thought to have a poet's soul. Friends then and readers now shrug and wonder, mostly sighing at poor Charlotte's compromise.

And yet her decision to marry him had a motive which establishes still further the continuity of the life and work. Despite appearances, Arthur Bell Nicholls was of the same stamp as all

3. *Shirley,* p. 632.

the men who had haunted Brontë's fantasies and dominated her experience. Gaskell had insightfully observed of Nicholl's appeal:

> I am sure that Miss Brontë could never have borne not to be well-ruled and ordered. . . . She would never have been happy but with an exacting, rigid, law-giving, passionate man . . .[4]

It is a less romanticized relation of Rochester and Paul Emanuel she describes. It is a strong patriarchal figure she draws: a possible portrait of Maria Branwell's young suitor, an image of the commanding presence who marked indelibly the lives at Haworth parsonage, a reflection of the father-lover whom Charlotte sought in Monsieur Heger. He was Byron distorted, Lord Wellington diluted. He embodied the authority which Brontë needed to sustain her: the authority which a lifetime of socialization had taught her to equate with masculinity. And she recognized that, despite his unyielding presence,

> Mr. Nicholls is one of those who attach themselves to very few, whose sensations are close and deep—like an underground stream, running strong but in a narrow channel.[5]

Nicholls offered her that gift which had never in actuality been offered her before; and he offered it unbidden: continued to offer it even after it had been rejected. He offered it from the depth of his regard and the depth of his need.

It must have been his need which convinced her, for his need balanced the authority which she required but understood well enough to fear. That authority had threatened all of her juvenile heroines. It had threatened Jane and Lucy. It had incapacitated Shirley. It had made her resentful of Branwell, ambivalent toward her father, miserably dependent upon Heger, repelled by James Taylor. Nicholls's need gave her room to be herself. It suggested mutuality and allowed her self-respect.

She watched Nicholls's suffering as he delivered his last sermon. He was to leave Haworth in order to escape the continuing reminder of what he had been denied in her rejection of his first proposal:

4. To John Foster, April 23, 1854. Wise and Symington, IV, 117–18.
5. To Ellen Nussey, January 2, 1853. Wise and Symington, IV, 32.

> He struggled, faltered, then lost command over himself, stood
> before my eyes and in the sight of all the communicants,
> white, shaking, voiceless.[6]

She found in him a capacity for feeling—feeling for *her*—that
she had only imagined in Rochester and Paul Emanuel: that she
had been able to imagine in them because she had experienced it
in herself:

> I found him leaning against the garden door in a paroxysm of
> anguish, sobbing as women never sob. Of course, I went
> straight to him. Very few words were interchanged, those few
> barely articulate. Several things I should have liked to ask him
> were swept entirely from my memory. Poor fellow! But he
> wanted such hope and such encouragement as I *could* not give
> him. Still I trust he must know now that I am not entirely blind
> and indifferent to his constancy and grief.[7]

And so, after finally gaining Patrick Brontë's permission (dissatisfied with Nicholls's replacement, the infirm and habitually selfish old man found it preferable to "settle" for a husband than to
train an intransigent curate), Charlotte agreed to become "what
people call engaged."[8] The phrase suggests the enormous ambivalence she felt. What she had learned of Nicholls "inclined me
to esteem and if not love—at least affection."[9] Her decision was
not based upon that powerful attraction, that promise of transcendence, that is the keystone of romantic love. It was based on her
evaluation of a man capable of altruistic feeling. Her evaluation
rested, in turn, on the pride in self which had been born during
these years of success and had burgeoned as she developed the
character of Lucy Snowe who becomes at last, because of *her* capacity for love, most worthy.

Still, reservation had been written into the very structure of
Shirley. It informed the psychological insights of *Villette* and per-
vaded the author's later life at Haworth. Nicholls seemed to offer
her contradictory hope for the future but she could not help but be
troubled since her optimism rested upon so little that was tangible
and sure. It was not a decision which she could have made before
the writing of *Villette*. Did the fact that she could make it now

6. To Ellen Nussey, May 16, 1853. Wise and Symington, IV, 65.
7. To Ellen Nussey, May 27, 1853. Wise and Symington, IV, 68–69.
8. To Elizabeth Gaskell, April 18, 1854. Wise and Symington, IV, 116.
9. To Ellen Nussey, April 11, 1854. Wise and Symington, IV, 112.

mean that it was "right"? Like Shirley tamed, fearfully awaiting her wedding day, Brontë wrote: "Care and Fear stand so close to Hope, I sometimes scarcely can see her for the shadows they cast."[10] Remembering the specters of Berthe and the nun, we can only guess the causes of her "care and fear." A permanent commitment where there was respect but not love? A surrendering of privacy always essential to her inner life? Risking her success and fame? Giving to another her time, her thoughts—her body, so long virginal? How easily as a girl she had written of passionate, sexual love. How odd a contrast with those romantic fantasies is this oblique and guarded letter, sent to Ellen while she was on her wedding trip:

> Dear Nell—during the last six weeks—the colour of my thought is a good deal changed: I know more of the realities of life than I once did. I think many false ideas are propagated, perhaps unintentionally. I think those married women who indiscriminately urge their acquaintance to marry—much to blame. For my part—I can only say with deeper sincerity and fuller significance—what I always said in theory—Wait God's will. Indeed—indeed Nell—it is a solemn and strange and perilous thing for a woman to become a wife. Man's lot is far—far different.[11]

Where innocence had spoken, experience is still. The new relationship must have been traumatic and disorienting. As a consequence, she returns to a dependency that had been submerged in the confidence of recent years. The pleading tone and childlike diction of this note to Ellen belie the relief she tries to suggest:

> My husband is not a poet or a poetical man—and one of my grand doubts before marriage was about "congenial tastes" and so on. The first morning we went out on to the cliffs and saw the Atlantic coming in all white foam, I did not know whether I should get leave or time to take the matter in my own way. I did not want to talk—but I *did* want to look and be silent. Having hinted a petition, license was not refused—covered with a rug to keep off the spray, I was allowed to sit where I chose—and he only interrupted me when he thought I crept too near the edge of the cliff. So far he is always good in this way—and this protection which does not interfere or pre-

10. To George Smith, April 25, 1854. Wise and Symington, IV, 119.
11. To Ellen Nussey, August 9, 1854. Wise and Symington, IV, 145–46.

tend is I believe a thousand times better than any half sort of pseudo sympathy. I will try with God's help to be as indulgent to him whenever indulgence is needed.[12]

The ambivalence remains when they return to Haworth. The days are busy, filled with activity, adjustments. The letters Brontë writes to Nussey and Wooler are ambiguous, lending themselves to contradictory interpretations. But a new cheerful tone does seem to gain ascendance, and a new tinge of equality appears to establish itself in their relationship.

The problem which she describes as pressing most upon her is one of time. She repeats, in various contexts, in different ways, that her time is not her own:

> Someone wants a good portion of it—and says we must do so and so accordingly, and it generally seems the right thing— Only I sometimes wish that I could have written the letter as well as taken the walk.[13]

But she had written so many letters as substitutes for conversations and had walked so many miles in solitude, that she could not undervalue her husband's company and concern. The "doing" was good for her. It enlarged her interests and occupied her mind without disturbing the continuity of her life.

Haworth had always been her home. Her tragic history— much of which her husband had watched unfold—bound her there. Always before she had been a stranger in the town. Only Branwell had not kept himself apart. The duties she had observed as the minister's daughter, she had now to assume as the minister's wife. Her new status allowed her to enter society with a confidence freshly experienced. There was pleasure to be derived from sharing and participation. She came to feel that "it is not bad for me that his bent should be so wholly towards matters of real life—so little inclined to the literary and contemplative."[14] Because he was neither intellectual nor poet, because he was not her "maitre" or competitor, she was free still to range in that other, private world. Sharing his interests would earn for her that

12. To Catherine Winkworth, Cork, July 27, 1854. Wise and Symington, IV, 137-38.

13. To Margaret Wooler, August 22, 1854. Wise and Symington, IV, 148.

14. To Margaret Wooler, September 14, 1854. Wise and Symington, IV, 153.

stake in life for which she had so longed and although she acknowledged that "If true domestic happiness replace Fame—the exchange will indeed be for the better,"[15] she had begun to write another novel,[16] and had not abandoned her literary aspirations.

Five months after the wedding anticipated with so much doubt, Brontë wrote to Margaret Wooler:

> It is long since I have known such comparative immunity from head-ache, sickness and indigestion, as during the last three months.
>
> My life is different from what it used to be. May God make me thankful for it! I have a good, kind attached husband and every day makes my own attachment to him stronger.[17]

Brontë's pleas, "May God make me thankful for it!" may pose uneasy questions for us—but the difficulty of interpretation is slightly eased by the fact of her physical well-being: an indication more important than any other that Brontë had begun to find the peace that comes with an integrated life, relatively freed from anxiety.

The constant note of sadness which sounded through her earlier letters was replaced by varying tones of humor and tolerance. Her husband's stern seriousness amused her. Increasingly sure of herself and him, she grew less dependent upon the paternal aspects of his personality. Their relationship seemed to grow in mutuality. Finally she was the mistress of her home. Arthur Nicholls was, in many ways, Patrick Brontë's temperamental son and had inherited the mantle of the aging minister. Her husband's presence enabled Charlotte to complete the movement to independence begun ten years earlier when Patrick's vision failed. Now, as she made the transition from daughter to wife, her relation to her father changed. Her feelings seemed largely purged of the bitterness and resentment she had lived with and repressed for many years:

> My dear father was not well when we returned from Ireland—I am however most thankful to say that he is better now—May God preserve him to us yet for some years! The wish for his

15. Ibid.
16. See *Emma,* this novel fragment, printed with an introduction by W. M. Thackeray, "The Last Sketch," *Cornhill Magazine* 1 (April 1850), pp. 485–98.
17. November 15, 1854. Wise and Symington, IV, 160.

> continued life—together with a certain solicitude for his happi-
> ness and health seems—I scarcely know why—stronger in me
> now than before I was married.[18]

The oedipal struggle was at least calmed. The long years of neurotic illness and depression gave way to healthier activity and
perhaps—one hopes, but does not know—to a satisfactory sexuality.

But the elements in Brontë's life which were conducive to
tranquility were inhospitable to other kinds of psychic growth.
Recognitions yielded by the writing of *Villette* had not released
new energies. The analysis begun was not, apparently, continued. Life moved regressively. In marrying Nicholls, Brontë
risked less than she would have risked in most other marriages.
Risking less, she could dare little. Remaining at Haworth, a
daughter still, married to a father substitute, reenacting now the
role of her mother, Brontë took refuge in a version of the past.
Lulled by the deceptions of the familiar patriarchal trap, she
waited there, unarmed, for the crucial trial which was to come.

II

There was another facet to marriage. Not one which middle-
class Victorians spoke of any more openly than they did of sex itself. Not one which Brontë herself discussed, although it might
well have been in her mind when she wrote of the "care and
fear" which obscured the hope of her approaching union. To be a
wife meant also to be a mother. The mysteries and dangers surrounding childbearing made the prospect fearful for most women:
even for those whose lives had best prepared them for maternity.
But for Brontë the problems were particularly difficult: long-
lived, complex.

As children, all desire union with the mother who gives and
sustains life. Later, each girl seeks reconciliation with the mother
after whom she has modeled herself, from whom she strives to
separate herself, whom she even tries to replace. Finally, to
achieve maturity and freedom, every woman must discover—often through her own maternity—the mother that dwells within.

18. To Margaret Wooler, August 22, 1854. Wise and Symington, IV,
149.

This pattern can be traced in Brontës life as she traced it in the lives of her heroines.

Orphaned, all the central figures of the novels and the novelist herself are snatched from the vital source of nurturance. All find temporary surrogates who are more or less effective in providing them support. For Frances there is an aunt; for Jane, there is Maria Temple; for Caroline, Hortense Moore; for Shirley, Mrs. Pryor; for Lucy, Miss Marchmont. For Charlotte Brontë herself there had been her Aunt Branwell; her housekeeper, Tabby; Miss Wooler, her teacher and friend. None had satisfied her. In *Jane Eyre* and *Villette,* Brontë gives her heroines adversaries who are representative of the mother who stands between them and the father-lover. For Jane, Berthe plays such a role; for Lucy, Madame Beck. For Charlotte there was Madame Heger. Seeking the guiding spirit in themselves, all of Brontë's heroines turned to nature as their intermediary—much as Emily, Anne, and Charlotte had found on the moors and in the open skies of Haworth, the irreplaceable sources of spiritual renewal. Caroline, of course, finds her mother *in fact* and, after her discovery, regresses to a position of dependence which her marriage only confirms. Shirley's development is truncated as well. Its correlative is presented in the confused and contradictory mythologies she creates. Only in *Jane Eyre* and *Villette* do the heroines reach the third and final stages of their quests. But in the allegorical formulation of Brontë's second novel and in the rapid conclusion of her fourth, success is assumed and not really demonstrated. Never achieving full integration, Brontë could not herself have satisfactorily explored its meaning.

The years of professional success and growing fame gave her confidence which she had not known before. In the writing of *Villette* she had confronted her public and private selves. But there was still to be borne the effects of a lifetime of failed relationships. The neurotic interaction with a domineering father who had never loved her enough. Her own rejection of Branwell, essential to her growth but profoundly troubling. The tragic loss of her sisters—her feeling complicated by her recognition that she had always stood outside of their charmed circle, an awkward third, as they had stood outside the gates of Angria. And then the rejections of Heger and Smith; her frustrating indecision about James Taylor—his advances and withdrawals. There was only

Nicholls's unquestioning devotion to balance thirty-eight years of humiliation and self-doubt. Indeed, the feelings which that devotion had begun to induce in her were sufficiently optimistic to illumine, however dimly, the dark and menacing psychic recesses that the past had slowly and painfully etched. In the growing tenderness of her relationship with Nicholls, "my dear boy," Brontë had begun to discover and trust the maternal principle in herself. But many doubts remained. Autonomy, defined in agony, was threatened everywhere. Her personal independence had not yet been truly won. Her professional freedom was still in question. In her writing and in her experience she had wrestled with the life-defeating forces of romantic mythology and personal history. She had described them. She had confronted them. But, Antaeus-like, they seemed to reappear—renewed by the social powers by which they had been formed.

Seven years earlier Brontë had given to Jane Eyre a dream which she herself had dreamt recurrently. Jane, we recall, is fleeing from the ruins of Thornfield in pursuit of Rochester. A strange child clings to her neck, almost strangling her in its terror. And as Jane scrambles up the rocks to watch her lover disappear beyond the hills, the baby falls from her arms and she awakens. The dream had been relevant to Jane's experience—to her anxieties and fears—as it had been and remained relevant to her author's. Brontë—like Jane—seems simultaneously to be child and mother. Her anxiety belongs to the helpless waif and the dependent wife. She fears the loss of the protective male, the loss of the child whom she must fail, the loss of herself—unable to assume the responsibilities of mature womanhood.

The dream is prophetic. Perhaps, in time, Nicholls would have been able to help erase the survivor's guilt and shame. Perhaps in learning to be a wife, in gaining assurance as a person, Brontë would have learned also to anticipate maternity. Perhaps in her own growing strength, she would have found the confidence to sustain another. It is more likely, however, that the unresolved ambivalence of her relationship with Nicholls and the regressive circumstances in which she lived, militated against the development which could have freed her psychologically as she had been liberated intellectually. Her fears had, after all, conspired in the construction of this—her final prison. At Haworth still, she would have felt more powerfully the effects of Maria

Branwell's last dreadful illness, associated always in her mind with childbearing. The signs are there in her persistently negative expectations of childhood, in her sense of helplessness before it. Never having resolved the traumas of her own childhood, Brontë continued to find all children strangers, impossible to relate to, certainly difficult to care for.[19] She had to feel the child that was herself mature before she could shelter in her womb another life.

A year and a half after her marriage, Charlotte Brontë conceived a child and fell ill of the conception: sickened, apparently by fear.[20] It was the last of her neurotic illnesses; the last of her masochistic denials. Love had come too late, too briefly, in too ambiguous a form. The past was the deluge which had long threatened—which had been long and courageously resisted. Now it overwhelmed her and she drowned. On March 31, 1855, at thirty-nine years of age, in the early months of pregnancy, Charlotte Brontë died. She could not bring to birth the self she had conceived.

19. Brontë had written to Gaskell of her children (Gaskell, p. 343):

Whenever I see Florence and Julia again, I shall feel like a bashful suitor, who views at a distance the fair personage to whom, in his clownish awe, he dare not risk a near approach. Such is the clearest idea I can give you of my feeling toward children I like, but to whom I am a stranger;—and to what children am I not a stranger? They seem to me little wonders; their talk, their ways are all matter of half-admiring, half puzzled speculation.

20. Gerin comments that "the sickness of early pregnancy was quite disproportionate in Charlotte's case" (*Charlotte Brontë,* p. 562), and Philip Rhodes has added this enlightening explanation ("A Medical Appraisal of the Brontës," p. 107):

The evidence is quite clear that she died of hyperemesis gravidarum . . . an excess of the nausea and sickness which most women suffer in early pregnancy. This morning-sickness, so-called, is probably due to the effects of the hormones from the conceptus affecting the nervous centres in the brain which control vomiting. The disease only seems to become excessive in those who display neuroticism, and they require firm, kind treatment to get them better. But this was not known in 1855. The constant vomiting depletes the body of water and sodium and chlorides, as well as potassium and other electrolytes. The deficiency of sodium chloride leads to increasing apathy, drowsiness and inability to concentrate on anything, and gives a feeling of lassitude. Moreover, the electrolyte loss is probably a cause of stasis of the gastric contents leading to further dilation of the stomach and nausea with vomiting. It is a terrible malady when unchecked and yet it is so easy to nip in the bud when the pathology is understood.

The point is that Brontë's condition, while not unfamiliar in our own time, is responsive to modern medical and psychological treatment.

Selected Bibliography

I Primary Texts

Brontë, Charlotte. *Emma: A Fragment by Currer Bell with "The Last Sketch,"* by William Makepeace Thackeray in *Cornhill Magazine*, 1 (1866), 485–98. Reprinted in *Brontë Society Transactions*, 2 (1899), 84–101.
———. *Five Novelettes.* Transcribed and edited Winifred Gerin. London: The Folio Press, 1971.
———. *Jane Eyre.* Ed. Jane Jack and Margaret Smith. London: Oxford University Press, 1969.
———. *Legends of Angria.* Compiled by Fannie E. Ratchford and William Clyde DeVane. New Haven: Yale University Press, 1933.
———. *Shirley.* London: Oxford University Press, 1969.
———. *The Professor.* London: Oxford University Press, 1967.
———. *Villette.* Ed. Geoffrey Tillotson and Donald Hawes. Boston: Houghton Mifflin, 1971.
Brontë, Charlotte, and Patrick Branwell. *The Miscellaneous and Unpublished Writings of Charlotte and Patrick Branwell Brontë.* 2 vols. Oxford: Shakespeare Head Press, 1934.
———. *The Poems of Charlotte and Patrick Branwell Brontë.* Oxford: Shakespeare Head Press, 1934.
Shorter, Clement. *The Brontës: Life and Letters.* 2 vols. New York: Haskell House, 1969. First published, 1908.
Wise, T. J., and Symington, J. A., eds., *The Brontës: Their Lives, Friendships and Correspondences.* 4 vols. Oxford: Shakespeare Head Press, 1932.

II Secondary Sources

Adler, Alfred. "Sex," *Psychoanalysis and Women.* Ed. Jean Baker Miller, M.D., Baltimore: Penguin, 1973.
Banks, Joseph and Olive. *Feminism and Family Planning in Victorian England.* New York: Schocken Books, 1964.
Beer, Patricia. *Reader, I Married Him.* New York: Barnes and Noble, 1974.
Bentley, Phyllis. *The Brontës.* London: Barker, 1947.
———. *The Brontës and Their World.* New York: Viking Press, 1969.
———. *The Brontë Sisters.* London: Longmans-Green, 1950.

Bieber, Irving, M.D. "The Meaning of Masochism." *American Journal of Psychotherapy*, No. 7 (1953).

Briggs, Asa. "Private and Social Themes in *Shirley*." *Brontë Society Transactions*, 13, No. 3 (1958).

Brown, Norman O. *Life Against Death*. New York: Random House, 1959.

Burkhart, Charles. *Charlotte Brontë: A Psychosexual Study of Her Novels*. London: Victor Gollancz, 1973.

Burns, Wayne. "Critical Relevance of Freudianism" *Western Review*, 20 (1956), 301–14.

Cavell, Marcia. "Since 1924: Toward a New Psychology of Women." *Women and Analysis*. Ed. Jean Strouse. New York: Grossman, 1974.

Cecil, Lord David. *Early Victorian Novelists*. Indianapolis: Bobbs-Merrill, 1935.

Chadwick, Ellis H. "Charlotte Brontë and Thackeray." *Brontë Society Transactions*, 4, No. 21 (1967).

Chase, Richard. "The Brontës: A Centennial Observance." *Kenyon Review*, No. 9 (1947).

Cominos, Peter T. "Innocent Femina Sensualis in Unconscious Conflict." *Suffer and Be Still: Women in the Victorian Age*. Ed. Martha Vicinus. Bloomington, Ind.: Indiana University Press, 1972.

Craig, G. Armour. "The Unpoetic Compromise: On the Relation Between Private Vision and Social Order in Nineteenth Century English Fiction." *Society and Self in the Novel*, English Institute Essays, 1955. New York: Columbia University Press, 1956.

Crandall, Norma. *Emily Brontë, A Psychological Portrait*. New York: Kraus Reprint Co., 1970.

Day, Morton S. "Central Concepts of *Jane Eyre*." *Personalist*, No. 4.

Deutsch, Helene. *The Psychology of Women*. Vols. 1 and 2. New York: Bantam, 1973.

Dooley, Lucile. "Psychoanalysis of Charlotte Brontë, As a Type of the Women of Genius." *The American Journal of Psychology*, July 1920, 31, No. 3.

Dunbar, Janet. *The Early Victorian Woman: Some Aspects of Her Life*. London: 1973.

Engels, Friedrich. *The Origin of the Family, Private Property and the State* (1884). New York: International, 1942.

Erickson, Donald. "Imagery as Structure in *Jane Eyre*." *Victorian Newsletter*, Fall 1966, pp. 18–22.

Ewbank, Inga-Stina. *Their Proper Sphere: A Study of the Brontë Sisters as Early Victorian Female Novelists*. London: Arnold, 1966.

Fletcher, Angus. *Allegory: The Theory of a Symbolic Mode*. New York: Cornell University Press, 1964.

Freud, Sigmund. *Civilization and Its Discontents*. Trans. J. Strachey. New York: W. W. Norton, 1950.

———. *Collected Papers*. Ed. J. Riviere. Vols. 1–4. New York: Basic Books, 1959.

Gaskell, Elizabeth. *The Life of Charlotte Brontë*. London: J. M. Dent, 1960. First published, 1857.

Gerin, Winifred. *Branwell Brontë*. London: Thomas Nelson and Sons, 1961.

———. "Byron's Influence on the Brontës." *Keats-Shelley Memorial Bulletin*, 17 (1966), pp. 1–19.

————. *Charlotte Brontë: The Evolution of Genius.* London: Oxford University Press, 1967.

Greg, W. R. *Why Are Women Redundant?* London, 1869.

Hays, H. R. *The Dangerous Sex: The Myth of Feminine Evil.* New York: Pocket Books, 1965.

Heilbrun, Carolyn G. *Toward a Recognition of Androgyny.* New York: A. A. Knopf, 1973.

Heilman, Robert. "Charlotte Brontë, Reason and the Moon." *Nineteenth Century Fiction,* 14 (March 1960).

Hinkley, Laura J. *The Brontës, Charlotte and Emily.* New York: Hastings House, 1945.

Holgate, Ivy. "The Structure of *Shirley*." *Brontë Society Transactions,* 14, No. 2 (1962), pp. 27–35.

Hopkins, Annette. *The Father of the Brontës.* Baltimore: Johns Hopkins Press, 1958.

Horney, Karen. "The Problem of Feminine Masochism." *Psychoanalysis and Women.* Ed. Jean Baker Miller. Baltimore: Penguin, 1973.

Isenberg, David. "Charlotte Brontë and the Theatre." *Brontë Society Transactions,* 15, No. 3 (1968), pp. 237–41.

Knies, Earl A. *The Art of Charlotte Brontë.* Ohio: Ohio State University Press, 1969.

Korg, Jacob B. "The Problem of Unity in *Shirley*." *Nineteenth Century Fiction,* 12 (Sept. 1957).

Kroeber, Karl. *Styles in Fictional Structure: The Art of Jane Austen, Charlotte Brontë, George Eliot.* Princeton: Princeton University Press. 1971.

Langbridge, Rosamund. *Charlotte Brontë, A Psychological Study.* London: William Heinemann, n.d.

Langford, Thomas. "The Three Pictures in *Jane Eyre*." *Victorian Newsletter,* 31 (Spring 1967), pp. 97–98.

Lewes, George Henry. "Currer Bell's *Shirley*." *Edinburgh Review,* 91 (1850).

Lifton, Robert. *History and Human Survival.* New York: Random House, 1961.

Marchand, Leslie A. *Byron, A Biography.* Vols. 1–4. New York: A. A. Knopf, 1957.

Marcus, Steven. *Engels, Manchester and the Working Class.* New York: Random House, 1944.

Marcuse, Herbert. *Eros and Civilization.* New York: Vintage Books, 1955.

Martin, Hazel T. *Petticoat Rebels: A Study of the Novels of Social Protest of George Eliot, Elizabeth Gaskell, and Charlotte Brontë.* New York: Helios, 1968.

Martin, Robert. *The Accents of Persuasion: Charlotte Brontë's Novels.* London: Faber and Faber, 1966.

Mill, John Stuart. *The Subjection of Women* (1889). Reprinted in *Three Essays by J. S. Mill.* London: Oxford University Press, 1966.

Millett, Kate. *Sexual Politics.* New York: Doubleday, 1970.

Moglen, Helene. "The Double Vision of *Wuthering Heights:* A Clarifying View of Female Development." *The Centennial Review,* XV (Fall 1971), pp. 391–405.

Momberger, Philip. "Self and World in the Works of Charlotte Brontë." *ELH,* 32 (Sept. 1965).

Moser, Laurence. "From Portrait to Person: A Note on the Surrealistic in *Jane*

Eyre." *Nineteenth Century Fiction,* 20 (Dec. 1965), pp. 275–81.

Neff, Wanda. *Victorian Working Women: An Historical and Literary Study of Women in British Industries and Professions, 1832–1850.* London: Cass, 1966.

Ohmann, Carol. *Charlotte Brontë: The Limits of Her Feminism,* Feminine Studies VI. Old Westbury, N.Y.: The Feminist Press, 1972.

Peckham, Morse. *Victorian Revolutionaries, Speculations on Some Heroes of a Culture Crisis.* New York: George Braziller, 1970.

Peters, Margot. *Charlotte Brontë: Style in the Novel.* Wisconsin: University of Wisconsin Press, 1973.

———. *Unquiet Soul: A Biography of Charlotte Brontë.* New York: Doubleday, 1975.

Praz, Mario. *The Romantic Agony.* Trans. Angus Davidson. London: Oxford University Press, 1970.

Quennell, Peter. *Byron in Italy.* London: Collins, 1951.

———. *Byron: The Years of Fame.* London: Collins, 1950.

Rallo, Eino. *The Haunted Castle: A Study of the Elements of English Romanticism.* New York: Humanities Press, 1964.

Ratchford, Fannie Elizabeth. *The Brontës' Web of Childhood.* New York: Russell and Russell, 1964.

Rathburn, R. C., and M. Steinmann, Jr., eds. *From Jane Austen to Joseph Conrad.* Minneapolis: University of Minnesota Press, 1958.

Rhodes, Philip. "A Medical Appraisal of the Brontës." *Brontë Society Transactions,* 16, No. 2 (1972).

Rich, Adrienne. "*Jane Eyre:* The Temptations of a Motherless Woman." *Ms,* II (October 1973).

Rigby, Elizabeth. "*Vanity Fair, Jane Eyre* and the Governesses Benevolent Institution—Report for 1847." *Quarterly Review,* 84 (1848), pp. 153–85.

Scargill, M. H. "All Passion Spent: A Reevaluation of *Jane Eyre.*" *University of Toronto Quarterly,* No. 9 (1949).

Sewell, Mrs. S. A. *Woman and the Times We Live In.* London: Simpkin, Marshall and Co., 1869.

Shapiro, Arnold. "Public Themes and Private Lives: Social Criticism in *Shirley.*" *Papers on Language and Literature,* 4 (Winter 1968).

Sinclair, May. *The Three Brontës.* New York: Kennikat Press, 1967.

Spens, Janet. "Charlotte Brontë." *Essays and Studies by Members of the English Association,* No. 14 (1929).

Thorslev, Peter L. *The Byronic Hero.* Minneapolis: University of Minnesota Press, 1962.

Tillotson, Kathleen. *Novels of the 1840's.* London: Oxford, 1965.

Tompkins, J. M. S. "Caroline Helstone's Eyes." *Brontë Society Transactions,* No. 14 (1961).

Vicinus, Martha, ed. *Suffer and Be Still: Women in the Victorian Age.* Bloomington: Indiana University Press, 1972.

Ward, Barbara. "Charlotte Brontë and the World of 1846." *Brontë Society Transactions,* 11, No. 56 (1951), pp. 3–13.

Weinstein, Fred, and Gerald Platt. *The Wish to Be Free.* Berkeley: University of California Press, 1969.

West, Rebecca. "The Role of Fantasy in the Work of the Brontës." *Brontë Society Transactions,* 12, No. 4 (1954), pp. 255–67.

Winnifreth, Tom. *The Brontës and Their Background: Romance and Reality.* New York: MacMillan, 1973.

Wroot, Herbert. *The Persons and Places of the Brontë Novels.* New York: Burt Franklin, 1970. First published, 1906.

Zilboorg, Gregory. "Masculine and Feminine: Some Biological and Cultural Aspects." *Psychoanalysis and Women.* Ed. Jean Baker Miller, M.D. Baltimore: Penguin, 1973.

Index

(For references to novels and characters, see entry for Brontë, Charlotte)